Radar and ARPA Manual

To Keith

Radar and ARPA Manual

Second Edition

Alan Bole, Extra Master Mariner, FRIN, FNI

Bill Dineley, Extra Master Mariner, MPhil

Alan Wall, PhD, FRIN, MNI, Master Mariner

ELSEVIER
BUTTERWORTH
HEINEMANN

AMSTERDAM • BOSTON • HEIDELBERG • LONDON • NEW YORK • OXFORD
PARIS • SAN DIEGO • SAN FRANCISCO • SINGAPORE • SYDNEY • TOKYO

Butterworth-Heinemann is an imprint of Elsevier
Linacre House, Jordan Hill, Oxford OX2 8DP, UK
30 Corporate Drive, Suite 400, Burlington, MA 01803, USA

First edition 1990
Paperback edition 1992
Reprinted 1997, 1999 (twice), 2000, 2001, 2003
Second edition 2005
Reprinted 2006 (twice), 2007

British Library Cataloguing in Publication Data
A catalogue record for this book is available from the British Library

Library of Congress Cataloging-in-Publication Data
A catalog record for this book is available from the Library of Congress

ISBN: 978-0-7506-6434-9

For information on all Butterworth-Heinemann publications
visit our website at books.elsevier.com

Transferred to Digital Printing in 2009

CONTENTS

Preface to Second Edition

While the principles upon which radar and ARPA are based have not changed, the technological advances in recent years have meant that radar equipment as we knew it for so many years is hardly recognizable on ship's bridges today.

Most of the changes have resulted from being able to manipulate the returning radar signals and, in particular, to digitize them. This permitted the vast power of computers to be applied to radars. Masses of data could be processed and stored, but what has been most significant is the ability to integrate and display the radar images with data from other sensors such as ECDIS, AIS and GPS.

In step with these and other changes has come an expansion of the specifications governing the equipment and also the requirements for the vessels to be equipped. This is covered in an enlarged section in which we have endeavoured to include the majority of the most recent applicable documentation from the IMO and the MCA in the UK. The effect of these new regulations is discussed throughout the book. This includes treatment of the ATA (Auto Tracking Aid) and EPA (Electronic Plotting Aid) that are alternative plotting systems to the original ARPA and also radar equipment for high speed craft.

Although small vessels and many pleasure craft are not specifically required to carry this equipment, many of them do and in their interest, it is hoped that many aspects of the material covered here will prove of value for them.

Nonetheless, the correct use of the equipment is paramount and it is in this area that we have continued to stress the importance of 'good practice' that has been built up over the years.

Some material relating to the development of radar has been retained in order to provide a background to understand where today's equipment is coming from and to underpin the theory upon which present day radars are based.

In the main text of this edition we refer to the current IMO perfomance standards published between 1997 and 2001 for radar and ARPA equipment on new vessels. In Chapter 11, the new perfomance standards published in 2005 for vessels to be built in 2008 have been included and there are appropriate references to those future standards. The rationale behind the changes in standards is explained including a description of the new technology of radar system that these new standards are designed to allow.

A.G.B.
A.D.W.

Preface to First Edition

This manual has been planned not only as a comprehensive practical reference for mariners on board ship and managers ashore, but also to provide all essential information for candidates following ENS, radar observer and professional certificate courses.

Over the past decade there have been considerable developments in ARPA design, but perhaps the more significant changes have been seen in the design of basic radar systems: ARPA features are now almost entirely integrated with the radar display – which means that neither can be treated in isolation. Thus this new manual supersedes our earlier *ARPA Manual*, representing a thorough revision and extension to cover the complete radar/ARPA installation.

The changes in radar displays that are likely to be of greatest significance to the observer are the developments in signal processing and the advent of raster-scan displays: these receive exhaustive treatment. The effects of changes in shipboard operations, such as false echoes from containers, are also dealt with.

Throughout the book the operational significance of the IMO Performance Standards is stressed, as is the role of radar and ARPA in navigation and collision avoidance.

With the completion of the SOLAS updating and fitting schedule in view, it has been possible to bring together a body of practical information on equipment and techniques which, it is hoped, will both serve the observer using traditional equipment and provide reliable guidance to the use of newer equipment for some years to come.

A.G.B.
W.O.D.

Acknowledgements

First edition

The authors wish to express their gratitude to:

The International Maritime Organization for permission to reproduce the various extracts from resolutions adopted by the Assembly;

The Controller of Her Majesty's Stationery Office for permission to reproduce the extracts from M 1158 and Statutory Instrument No. 1203 (1984);

Captain C. E. Nicholls of Liverpool Polytechnic for his major contribution to Chapter 8;

Mr B. Price of Sandown College, Liverpool for his helpful comments based on a reading of Chapter 2;

Mr Andrew O. Dineley for his assistance in producing the computer printout of the manuscript;

Families and friends without whose assistance, support and understanding this undertaking would never have been completed.

Second edition

We again express our thanks to the IMO for permission to reproduce updated extracts from various resolutions adopted by the Assembly.

In this edition we are grateful for the considerable assistance of June Bole and Alison Wall in proofreading the manuscript and for their help, support and encouragement in our completion of this book.

1 Basic radar principles

1.1 Introduction

The word RADAR is an acronym derived from the words *Radio Detection and Ranging*. In the United Kingdom it was initially referred to as *radio direction finding* (RDF) in order to preserve the secrecy of its ranging capability.

The scientist Heinrich Hertz, after whom the basic unit of frequency is named, demonstrated in 1886 that radio waves could be reflected from metallic objects. In 1903 a German engineer obtained a patent in several countries for a radio wave device capable of detecting ships, but it aroused little enthusiasm because of its very limited range. Marconi, delivering a lecture in 1922, drew attention to the work of Hertz and proposed in principle what we know today as marine radar. Although radar was used to determine the height of the ionosphere in the mid-1920s, it was not until 1935 that radar pulses were successfully used to detect and measure the range of an aircraft. In the 1930s there was much simultaneous but independent development of radar techniques in Britain, Germany, France and America. Radar first went to sea in a warship in 1937 and by 1939 considerable improvement in performance had been achieved. By 1944 naval radar had made an appearance on merchant ships and from about the end of the war the growth of civil marine radar began. Progressively it was refined to meet the needs of peacetime navigation and collision avoidance.

While the civil marine radars of today may, in size, appearance and versatility, differ markedly from their ancestors of the 1940s, the basic data that they offer, namely target range and bearing, are determined by exploiting the same fundamental principles unveiled so long ago. An understanding of such principles is an essential starting point in any study of marine radar.

1.2 Principles of range measurement

1.2.1 The echo principle

An object (normally referred to as a target) is detected by the transmission of a pulse of radio energy and the subsequent reception of a fraction of such energy (the echo) which is reflected by the target in the direction of the transmitter. The phenomenon is analogous to the reflection of sound waves from land formations. If a blast is sounded on a ship's whistle, the energy travels outward and some of it may strike, for example, a cliff. The energy which is intercepted will be reflected by the cliff. If the reflected energy returns in the direction of the ship, and is of sufficient strength, it will be heard as an audible echo which, in duration and tone, resembles the original blast. In considering the echo principle the following points can usefully assist in a preliminary understanding of radar detection:

(a) The echo is never as loud as the original blast.
(b) The chance of detecting an echo depends on the loudness and duration of the original blast.
(c) Short blasts are required if echoes from close targets are not to be *drowned* by the original blast.
(d) A sufficiently long interval between blasts is required to allow time for echoes from distant targets to return.

While the sound analogy is extremely useful, it must not be pursued too far as there are a number of ways in which the character and behaviour of radio waves differ from those of sound waves. In particular at this stage it is noteworthy that the speed of radio waves is very much higher than that of sound waves.

1.2.2   Range as a function of time

It is almost self-evident that the time which elapses between the transmission of a pulse and the reception of the corresponding echo depends on the speed of the pulse and the distance which it has travelled in making its two-way journey. Thus, if the speed of the pulse is known and the elapsed time can be measured, the range of the target producing the echo can be calculated.

While it is recognized that the velocity of radio waves is dependent on the nature of the medium through which they travel, for the practical purpose of marine radar ranging the speed may be assumed to have a constant value of 300 000 000 metres per second. Because this number is rather large, it is expedient in practical calculations to use the microsecond as the time unit. One μs represents one millionth part of a second (i.e. 10^{-6} seconds). The speed can thus be written as 300 metres per μs. Using this value it is possible to produce a simple general relationship between target range and the elapsed time which separates the transmission of the pulse and the reception of an echo in any particular case (see Figure 1.1).

Let D = the distance travelled by the pulse (metres)
    R = the range of the target (metres)

T = the elapsed time (μs)
S = the speed of radio waves (metres/μs)

Then $D = S \times T$
and $R = (S \times T)/2$
hence $R = (300 \times T)/2$
thus $R = 150\,T$

The application of this relationship can be illustrated by the following example.

Example 1.1   Calculate the elapsed time for a pulse to travel to and return from a radar target whose range is (a) 40 metres (b) 12 nautical miles.

(a) $R = 150\,T$
thus $40 = 150\,T$
hence $T = 40/150 = 0.27\mu s$

This value is of particular interest because 40 metres represents the minimum detection range that must be achieved to ensure compliance with the IMO Performance Standards for Navigational Radar Equipment (see Section 11.2.1). While this topic will be fully explored in Section 3.2.4, it is useful at this stage to note the extremely short time interval within which transmission and reception must be accomplished.

(b) $R = 150\,T$
Since 1 nautical mile = 1852 metres,
                  $12 \times 1852 = 150\,T$
hence $T = 12 \times 1852/150 = 148.16\mu s$

This result is noteworthy as it represents the elapsed time for a commonly used marine radar range scale. Further reference will be made to this value in the succeeding section.

Figure 1.1   The echo principle

1.2.3 The timebase

It is clear from the values established in the previous section that the elapsed times are of the order of millionths of a second and are thus so short as to be beyond the capability of any conventional time-measuring device. This difficulty is overcome by using an electronic device known as a cathode ray tube (CRT). The electronic principles of this important device are discussed in some detail in Section 2.6.1; it is sufficient at this stage to appreciate that its display feature is a glass screen across which travels a very small spot of light. The speed of this travel can be accurately controlled at values which allow the spot to transit the screen in as little as a few microseconds. At such speeds it moves literally 'faster than the eye can see' and hence appears as a line rather than a spot, but it is important that the concept of a moving light spot is appreciated as it is fundamental to an understanding of radar display principles.

The CRT can be used to perform an electronic stopwatch function by arranging that the time taken for the spot to cross the screen is the same as the time taken for a radar pulse to make the two-way journey to a target at a chosen range. This can be compared with a mechanical stopwatch in which the second hand transits the circumference of a dial in the same time as the earth rotates through approximately 15 seconds of arc. It is useful to illustrate the principle with reference to the method originally employed in the early radars of the 1940s. While this type of display, known as A-scan, is no longer used in civil marine applications (other than in the form of an oscilloscope such as may be used for servicing) it demonstrates the principle clearly and is a suitable point from which to progress to a description of the ways in which the display has been subsequently refined.

1.2.3.1 The A-scan display

In the A-scan display, the spot is used to produce a horizontal line (the trace) which originates close to the left-hand side of the screen of the CRT. The following features are of particular importance:

(a) The trace commences at the instant each radar pulse is transmitted and this event is indicated by an instantaneous vertical deflection of the spot which produces a 'spike', known as the transmission mark.

(b) The speed of the spot (the sweep rate) is adjusted so that it completes the trace in the same time as a radar pulse will take to travel to and from a target located at the maximum range which the scaled line is presently intended to represent. When the spot has completed the trace, the brilliance is automatically reduced to zero and the spot flies back to the origin to await the transmission of the next pulse. At this event it initiates a further trace along the same path as its predecessor.

(c) A returning echo is used to generate an instantaneous vertical deflection of the spot, thus producing a further spike. The amplitude of this spike, within certain limits (see Section 2.5.2.5) is a function of the strength of the echo.

Consideration of these three features and Figure 1.2 will indicate that the horizontal distance between the transmission mark and the echo spike is a measure of

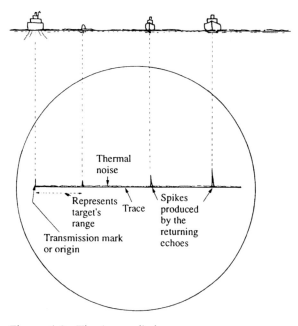

Figure 1.2 The A-scan display

the range of the target. Using the result from Example 1.1(b), it is evident that if the full extent of the trace is to represent a range of 12 miles (the selected range scale) the spot must complete the trace in approximately 148 μs. This quantity is referred to as the *timebase* and it is on this value that the displayed range of all targets is based. If a target lay at a range of 6 miles, its echo would return in half the timebase and would be displayed at half the maximum range of the scale in use. Different range scales are obtained by operating the range scale selector which selects the correct timebase for the chosen range scale. For example, on the 3 mile range scale the spot must travel four times faster than on the 12 mile range scale and hence a timebase of approximately 37 μs would be selected.

A limitation of the A-scan display is its inability to display information from any direction other than that in which the antenna (or aerial) is trained at that moment. This shortcoming led to the development of the plan position indicator (PPI).

In radar terminology the words *antenna, aerial,* and *scanner* are all used to describe the device which beams the transmitted energy into space. Throughout this text these words may be regarded as synonyms.

1.2.3.2   The radial-scan plan position indicator (PPI) display

In a radial-scan PPI display, the spot produces the trace in the form of a radial line whose origin is (normally) placed at the centre of the circular screen (Figure 1.3). An echo return from a target is used to produce an increase in the brilliance of the moving spot. To this end, a competent observer will, in setting up the display, adjust the brilliance of the trace so that it is barely visible (see Section 6.2.3.1), hence maximizing the probability that small increases in brilliance will be detected. Within certain limits (see Section 2.5.2.5) the brightening of the trace by a target return is a function of the strength of the received echo. As with the A-scan display, the origin of the trace coincides with the instant of transmission of the pulse and the duration of the trace is the selected timebase. Thus a target which lies at the maximum range represented by the selected scale will appear at the edge of the screen.

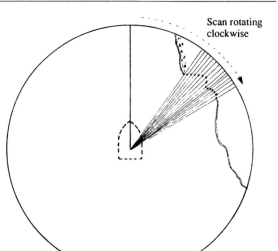

Figure 1.3   The radial-scan PPI display

When the spot has completed the trace, the brilliance is automatically reduced to zero and the spot flies back to the origin to await the incidence of the next transmission. At this event it initiates a further line which, in contrast with the A-scan case, is drawn along a path which is separated from the previous one by a small angle (about one tenth of a degree). In a PPI system the antenna rotates continuously and automatically in a clockwise direction, generating approximately some 3600 lines in one complete rotation. The resultant rotating trace makes it possible to display simultaneously targets in all directions in the correct angular relationship, one to another. Echoes painted by the trace as it passes will glow for a short period due to a property of the screen known as persistence or afterglow. Thus, in general the picture persists until refreshed on the next revolution of the trace (see Section 1.3.3). The PPI display is particularly suited to collision avoidance and navigational applications; the angular build-up of the picture will be described in Section 1.3.3.

1.2.4   Calibration of the timebase

It has been shown that by making the duration of one trace equal to the timebase of the selected range scale, the echo of a target will be displayed at a distance from the origin which is proportional to its range. Thus, when observing the display, it may be possible to estimate the range of a target by mentally dividing the trace into equal sections. However, to measure a range with an acceptable degree of accuracy (see Section 6.9.8), the subdivision must be carried out by electronic methods.

A device known as an oscillator is used to generate a succession of signals which occur at *equal intervals of time*. It is arranged that the first signal of any group coincides with the instant of transmission and that the interval between successive pulses is a sub-multiple of the timebase of the selected range scale. Each signal is used to produce an instantaneous brightening of the spot, and as a result bright marks, sometimes called *calibration pips* or *calibration marks*, will subdivide the trace into equal intervals of time and therefore, by virtue of the timebase value, into equal intervals of range. Hence, on the 12 mile range scale, as illustrated by Figure 1.4, the echo from a target at a range of 6 miles

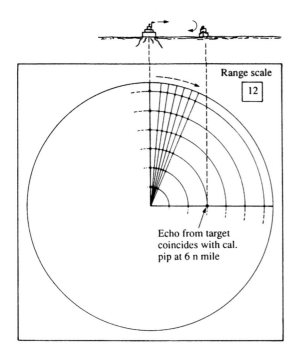

Echo from target coincides with cal. pip at 6 n mile

Figure 1.4 Calibration marks

will arrive after transmission by an elapsed time equal to half the timebase, and therefore will be displayed at the same time, and in the same place, as the 6 mile calibration pip. (Notice that the 6 mile calibration pip is the third from the origin, the mark at the origin counting as zero.) It is evident that the range scale selector must control not only the timebase duration but also the interval between calibration marks. This is illustrated, for some range scales, by the values in Table 1.1.

The timing of the calibration marks can be achieved with an extremely high degree of accuracy which in turn becomes implicit in the accuracy with which the range of a target can be measured provided that its echo coincides with a mark. If the echo lies between two marks, some form of interpolation will be necessary. In some circumstances it may be that this can be done by eye, but in other cases an acceptable degree of accuracy (see Section 6.9.1) will demand electronic assistance.

Interpolation is facilitated by the generation of a single pip, known as a *variable range marker*, which occurs at a selected elapsed time after transmission. The time is selected by the operation of a manual control which is also connected to some form of numerical read-out. The latter will show the number of miles of timebase represented by the selected time. Thus, as illustrated by Figure 1.5, if the observer adjusts the variable range marker to read 3 miles, the single pip will be produced approximately 37 μs after transmission, i.e. after one quarter of the 12 mile timebase.

Table 1.1 Timebase and calibration interval values

Range scale (n miles)	Timebase duration (μs)	Calibration (n miles)	interval (μs)	Remarks
0.75	9.3	0.25	3.1	Normally only 3 rings
1.5	18.5	0.25	3.1	
3	37.0	0.5	6.2	
6	74.1	1.0	12.4	6 rings in each case
12	148.2	2.0	24.7	
24	296.3	4.0	49.4	
48	592.6	8.0	98.8	

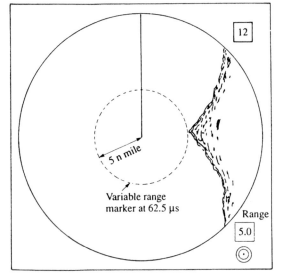

Figure 1.5 The variable range marker

In conclusion, it is clear that the precision with which the calibration marks are produced is fundamental to the accuracy of range measurement. For a detailed treatment of the correct procedure for their use and the accuracy which can be achieved, the reader is referred to Section 6.9.

1.2.5 The synthetic display

The displays produced in the ways so far described have become known as 'real-time' displays. The term describes the fact that the echoes are written on the trace concurrently with their reception, rather in the way in which one might write down a navigation warning, as it is received. It was recognized for many years that if the range data could be stored in such a way that it could be manipulated, considerable benefits might accrue, such as the ability to improve the picture quality and to carry out automatic tracking of targets. Pursuing the analogy of the navigation warning somewhat further, this may be compared with writing down the warning quickly as it is broadcast and subsequently re-writing it slowly and neatly. As with most analogies, care should be exercised in its indefinite pursuit. The term *real-time display* is used

to differentiate between the traditional type of display and the modern, computer controlled 'Synthetic Display'.

The microprocessor, a computer device capable of storing and manipulating data at very high rates, became available from the early 1970s; as the cost of computer memory decreased through the 1980s, a revolution took place in the way in which range (and other) data was handled. As a result, in modern radar systems the range data is stored in a computer memory. The data, once processed, can be used to synthesize a picture for display on a radial-scan PPI. Such a picture is sometimes referred to as a *re-timed display*. In the mid-eighties it became progressively more common to produce the picture on a television screen. This is now universally the case. Such a display is referred to as a *raster-scan* PPI in order to distinguish it from the traditional *radial-scan* PPI. Detailed consideration of raster-scan displays is deferred to Chapter 2 (see Section 2.6.7), as an understanding of basic radar principles is more readily gained from a study of the radial-scan display. However, regardless of whether the synthetic picture is finally produced on a raster-scan or radial-scan PPI, the principle of range measurement is as described below.

For a general introduction to the principle of storage, the computer memory may be likened to a large number of 'two-position' switches each of which can be either on or off. Consider a computer that will sample the received signal 1200 times in the duration of one complete radial trace. The sampling process commences at the instant of transmission and the result of each sampling is registered using, consecutively, each of 1200 memory elements. If a returning echo is present at the time of sampling, the appropriate switch is set to 'on', whereas if no echo is present the switch is left in the 'off' position. Thus the range of each echo will be implicit in the number of the memory element in which its presence is recorded.

In diagrams, it is usual to depict each element of memory as a box in which the number '1' appears if the switch is on and the number '0' appears if the switch is off. This form of representation is particularly suitable because the computer uses a counting system known as *binary* in which there are only two digits,

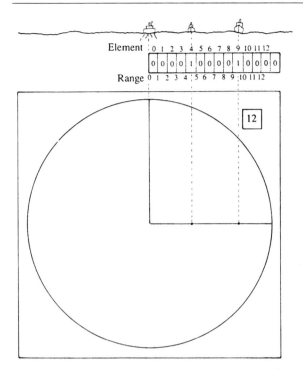

Figure 1.6 Storage of range data

brightening of the trace at a distance from the origin which is proportional to the range of the targets which produced the echoes.

In the example that has been chosen, the range data was written in and read out at the same rate. In a synthetic display this will only be true for one range scale. This is best illustrated by considering what will happen if the 6 mile range scale is selected (Figure 1.7).

When the 6 mile range scale is selected, the data must be written into the memory over the duration of the 6 mile timebase (i.e. approximately 74 μs) because the writing time is determined by the speed of radio waves. The received signal will be sampled twice as often so that, if 12 elements are used to represent 6 miles, each element of memory will represent a range interval of 0.5 miles. (If 1200 elements were used, the range interval would be 0.005 miles.) If the stored range data for 6 miles is read out of memory at half the rate at which it was written in (i.e. at the same rate

namely '1' and '0' (see Section 2.6.6.1). Further, it is practical to show 12 elements, rather than 1200. Subject to these qualifications, Figure 1.6 illustrates the generation of one radial line of a synthetic picture when the 12 mile range scale has been selected. In writing the data into the memory, which will be carried out in the duration of the 12 mile timebase (i.e. approximately 148 μs), the sampling process stores a '1' for each received echo and thereby the range of each target producing a detectable echo is implicit in the place in which it is registered in the memory. For example, a target in element 7 lies within the range limits 7 to 8 nautical miles (using 1200 elements, a target in element 700 would lie within the range limits 7.00 to 7.01 nautical miles).

In reading the range data out of the memory, a standard rectangular pulse is produced for each '1' in the memory. If the data is read out in the duration of the 12 mile timebase (i.e. approximately 148 μs) and the sweep rate produces a trace whose radial duration is the same, each of these pulses will produce a

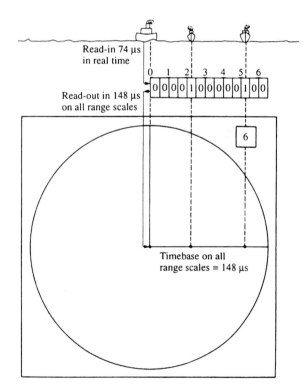

Figure 1.7 Fixed sweep rate display

as it is read out on the 12 mile range scale) *and* the sweep rate is maintained at the value for the 12 mile scale (i.e. giving a timebase of approximately 148 μs), a radial trace representing 6 miles will be produced.

Thus, in general, where computer storage is used to develop a radial PPI display, the range data for each radial line is written into memory during one timebase of the selected range scale but is read out in a fixed time, and displayed at a fixed sweep rate both of which are independent of the range scale selected. The duration of the fixed read-out time will be determined by the individual radar designer. Commonly, but not invariably, it is made equal to the 12 mile timebase. A representative set of values is shown in Table 1.2. Calibration marks and a variable range marker will be available on a synthetic display but it should be borne in mind that the interval between the calibration pips will depend on the fixed sweep rate chosen by the designer. Additionally it may be possible to have the computer read out the range of a target directly from the knowledge of the number of the memory element in which it lies.

The above process is sometimes called digital storage, because the presence or absence of an echo is registered by the binary digits '1' or '0' respectively. It is considerably more complex than the above introduction might suggest and there is great variation in the way in which radar designers have exploited the basic principle. For example, the simple model described produces synthetic echoes all of which are identical in brightness. In some systems this is true but it is by no

means invariably the case. Further, if (as in practice) some 1200 memory elements are used, many targets will register sequentially in more than one element. The topic is discussed in greater detail in Section 2.6.6.

1.3 Principles of bearing measurement

1.3.1 Directional transmission and reception

To examine the principles of bearing measurement it is useful to return to the sound analogy of Section 1.2.1. If the suggested blast was transmitted in low visibility it would not be easy to assess the precise direction from which the sound had returned. The difficulty arises from two principal features:

(a) The whistle If it is well placed it will transmit sound in all directions and thus echoes will return from all directions.
(b) The ear Evolution has designed the human ear to be highly receptive over more than 180 degrees on either side of the head.

These two properties are precisely the reverse of what is required. To determine the bearing of a target, transmission in the horizontal plane must be restricted to one direction at a time, and reception must be restricted to that same direction.

In a marine radar system a single antenna (known as the scanner or aerial) is used for both transmission and reception. It is designed in such a way (see Section 2.4.2) as to focus the transmitted energy in a beam which is very narrow in the horizontal plane. The angle within which the energy is constrained is called the *horizontal beamwidth* (Figure 1.8). It must have a value of not more than 2.5° if it is to comply with IMO Performance Standards for Navigational Radar Equipment (see Section 11.2.1). There is an exception for high speed craft in that the horizontal

Table 1.2 Range data – typical write and read times

Range scale (n miles)	Write time (μs)	Read-out (μs)	Sweep time (μs)
0.75	9.3	148	148
1.5	18.5	148	148
3	37.0	148	148
6	74.1	148	148
12	148.2	148	148
24	296.3	148	148
48	592.6	148	148

Figure 1.8 The horizontal beam

beamwidth can be up to 4° for S-band radar only (see Section 11.2.4). However, horizontal beamwidths of less than 2° are commonplace and shipborne civil marine radars are available with values as low as 0.75°. The reception property of the antenna is such that it will only detect energy which has returned from within the angular limits of the horizontal beamwidth. It follows from the directional characteristic of the antenna that only those targets which lie in the direction of the beam will appear on the trace. Thus a single trace represents the ranges of targets lying along a specific line of bearing.

1.3.2 Synchronization of scanner and trace

An essential feature of the modern marine radar display is that it should provide continous coverage over 360° of azimuth. To achieve this both the scanner and the trace are rotated, at the same rate, clockwise, continuously and automatically. To comply with the current IMO Performance Standards the duration of one revolution must not exceed 5 seconds (1.5 seconds for high speed craft); values of about 2 to 3 seconds are typical for shipborne radar.

The interval between successive transmitted pulses (and hence between the start of successive traces on the PPI) may fall within a range of values (see Section 2.3.1) but for the purposes of illustration an average value of 1/1250s (800 μs) will suffice. If a representative time for one revolution of the scanner is taken to be 3 seconds, one can deduce that some 3600 pulses are transmitted during one revolution and that the scanner rotates through 0.1° between pulses. Thus while the rotation is continuous, it may be found

convenient to imagine that the antenna scans the area around the ship in about 3600 steps of 0.1° and that each step is represented by a separate trace on the screen. The picture is thus 'built up' of approximately 3600 radial lines.

1.3.3 The build-up of the picture

The echo of a detectable target will be 'painted' once per revolution of the scanner. The inside of the CRT screen is coated with a luminous material (see Section 2.6.1.2) so that any area, once painted, will glow for at least 2 to 3 seconds. Thus the afterglow can be made sufficiently long to cause the echo paint to persist until it is painted again on the next revolution. (There are a few marine systems in which the persistence is less than one revolution but they are very much the exception.)

Because the scanner and trace rotate at the same rate, the radar beam and the trace describe equal arcs in equal intervals of time. Thus targets will be displayed in the correct angular relationship, one to another. If two ships subtend an angle of 50° at the observing vessel, the centres of their echoes will be separated on the PPI by a similar angle. As the beam sweeps across a geographical feature, such as a coastline, echoes on successive traces will add together, side by side, to produce a plan representation of that feature (see Figure 1.9).

The calibration marks, which may be switched on or off by the observer, will be painted on each trace and thus when switched on will appear as concentric circles. The variable range marker will similarly appear as a single circle of variable radius.

1.3.4 The heading marker

In general, a bearing is the angle between the direction of a chosen reference and that of an object of interest. On a PPI display the fundamental reference is the instantaneous direction of the observing vessel's head. As the axis of the horizontal beam crosses the ship's fore-and-aft line in the forward direction, a set of contacts is closed, producing a pulse of a few milliseconds duration. This pulse is used to increase the

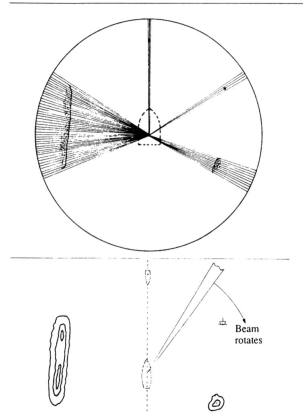

Figure 1.9 The build-up of the picture

brilliance of the spot and hence produce the complete brightening up of several successive traces, resulting in the distinctive 'heading marker' or 'heading indicator' (see also Section 2.4.6). Thus all targets are displayed, not only in the correct angular relationship to one another but also in the correct angular relationship to the observing ship's heading (see Figure 1.9).

The angle between the observed vessel's heading and the direction of the horizontal beam is known as the *aerial angle*. In the case of a synthetic display (see Section 1.2.5) the instantaneous value of the aerial angle will be measured and stored in digital form alongside the corresponding set of range data (see Section 2.6.6).

The IMO Performance Standards (see Section 11.2.1) require that the line be able to be aligned to within 0–1°. The procedure for checking this accuracy

is discussed in Section 6.9.9. Clearly, because both targets and the heading marker are produced by a brightening of the spot, there is a danger that a target may be masked if it lies in the direction of the heading marker. The specification recognizes this danger by requiring that there is a provision for switching the heading marker off. However, the provision must be such that the heading marker cannot be left in the *off* position. Normally this requirement is complied with by the use of a spring-loaded switch which is biased in the *on* position. The danger of the heading marker being left in the *off* position is that, in the absence of the correct reference, an erroneous reference (such as the bearing marker – see Section 6.9.5) might be used inadvertently.

The appearance of the heading marker confirms the orientation of the picture (see Section 1.4) and consequently whether the bearings are relative or true (see Figure 1.10).

1.3.5 Bearing measurement

The picture described above offers a plan view representation of the area surrounding the ship in such a form as to make it possible to measure the range and bearing of any detected target. It is this characteristic that gave rise to the term 'plan position indicator' which distinguished the rotating trace display from the earlier A-scan display. It is also this characteristic which makes the display particularly suitable for use in collision avoidance and navigation.

The IMO Performance Standards (see Section 11.2.1) require that provision be made for quickly obtaining the bearing of any object whose echo appears on the display. Traditionally such provision was fulfilled by a variety of mechanical and electromechanical devices which enable the observer to measure the angle between the heading marker and the object of interest. In general the target is intersected either by an engraved line along the diameter of the rotatable disk of transparent plastic located above the screen of the CRT, or by an electronic line emanating from the origin of the display (see Figure 1.10). The bearing is read off, in the former case from some form of fixed circular scale around the edge of the screen and

Figure 1.10 Measurement of bearing: (a) relative bearing, (b) true bearing

in the latter case from an analogue or digital indicator coupled to the bearing marker control. In a modern synthetic display it is usual to have the computer read out the bearing of a target directly from a knowledge of the radial line on which its echo appears. A variety of bearing measurement facilities and the correct procedure for their use are discussed in Section 6.9.

Facilities should also be provided to compensate for an offset aerial position (see Section 11.2.1).

1.4 Picture orientation

In marine radar literature, there is frequently an understandable descriptive overlap between the concepts of picture 'orientation' and picture 'presentation'. In this text orientation is defined as the choice of directional reference to be represented by the 000° (12 o'clock) graduation on the fixed bearing scale around the CRT (see Figure 1.11). Although the heading marker should always appear at the instant the axis of the beam crosses the fore-and-aft line in the forward direction, it is in theory possible to rotate the whole picture so that the 000° graduation on the fixed bearing scale represents any direction. In practice one of three preferred directions will be chosen, namely:

1 The ship's instantaneous heading, in which case the orientation is said to be *ship's-head-up (unstabilized)*.
2 True north, in which case the orientation is said to be *true-north-up (stabilized)*.
3 The ship's true course, in which case the orientation is said to be *course-up (stabilized)*.

Picture presentation (see Section 1.5) will be used to specify the reference with respect to which echo motion is displayed. In more general terms, the type of presentation indicates to the observer that the movement of the displayed echoes is shown with respect to his own ship, or with respect to the water, or with respect to the ground, i.e. *relative motion or true motion (sea-stabilized)* or *true motion (ground-stabilized)*.

1.4.1 Ship's-head-up orientation (unstabilized)

This orientation is so called, because the observer views the picture with the heading marker (and thus the ship's head) at the 'top' of the screen (see Figure 1.11). When the original PPI displays were introduced, it was the only orientation available. At that time, no provision

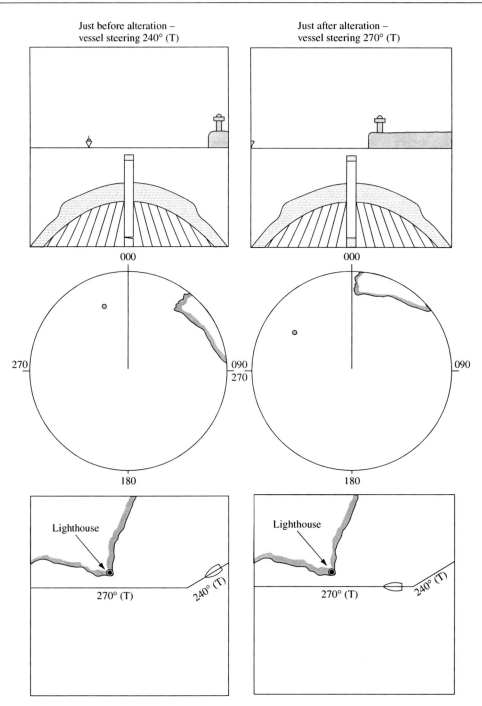

Figure 1.11 Ship's-head-up orientation (unstabilized)

was made for 'azimuth stabilization', by which is meant the input of compass information to the display (see Section 2.6.3). In the absence of such an input it is not possible effectively to maintain either of the other two preferred orientations. In modern marine radar systems, almost invariably the ship's-head-up orientation is unstabilized, i.e. a compass signal is *not* used in the control of the orientation. Historically there have been two designs which did associate the ship's-head-up orientation with azimuth stabilization but they were special cases in that the stabilization was applied twice. With the advent of raster-scan displays, the concept may well be exploited again in the future.

The single attractive feature of the ship's-head-up orientation (unstabilized) is that it corresponds directly with the scene as viewed through the wheelhouse window. A well placed display unit will be sited so that the officer viewing the screen faces forward. (United Kingdom vessels are required to have at least one display sited in this way – see Section 11.4.1.) Thus, irrespective of whether the officer is viewing the radar screen or looking forward through the wheelhouse window, objects on the starboard side of the ship will lie on the right and those on the port side will lie on the left.

A major shortcoming of the unstabilized orientation is that at every change in the direction of the observing vessel's heading, the entire picture (apart from the heading marker), will rotate by an equal but opposite angle (see Figure 1.11). This characteristic limits the usefulness of the orientation in three specific ways:

1 If a large alteration of course is made, any areas of land echoes are smeared across the screen, making it difficult to identify specific features. The afterglow created during the alteration may obscure isolated fixed or floating targets for some time after the vessel is steady on her new course (see Figure 1.11).

2 In ideal conditions the ship's heading would coincide at all times with the chosen course; in practice, due to the effect of wind and sea, the ship will 'yaw' about the correct heading. On a display using an unstabilized orientation, this superimposes an angular wander on the movement of all targets (see Figure 1.12) which limits the ease and speed with which bearings can be measured. It becomes

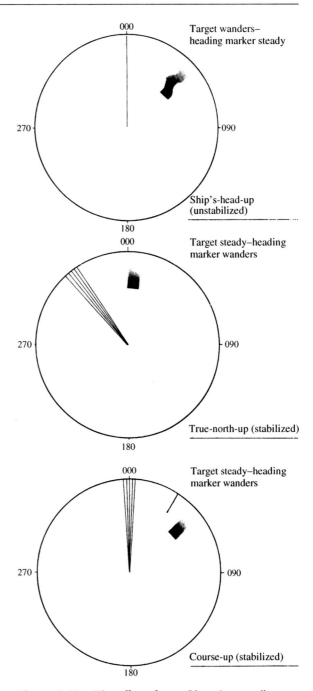

Figure 1.12 The effect of yaw. Observing vessel's course 330° (T), yaw ±4°. Target vessel approaching on steady bearing of 015°(T)

necessary to choose an instant when the target can be intersected with the cursor or electronic bearing line *and* the vessel's instantaneous heading read off simultaneously, or, alternatively, to wait until the vessel is *right on* course. The latter is necessary because the bearings read off from this orientation are measured relative to the ship's head and must be converted to true bearings for use in collision avoidance and navigation. The practical procedure for obtaining bearings from an unstabilized orientation is described in Section 6.9.3.

3   The disruption of the echo movement due to yaw limits the ease and speed with which an observer can plot the movement of targets for collision avoidance purposes, even if a reflection plotter is used (see Section 7.8.7). Further, an unwary or untrained observer may be dangerously misled by such angular movements. For example, a small change of course by the observing vessel may give the impression that the bearing of a target is changing, while in fact the true bearing is remaining constant. The extremely important topic of systematic observation of target movement is discussed at length in Chapter 7.

1.4.2 True–north–up orientation (stabilized)

In true-north-up orientation, the heading marker is aligned with that graduation on the fixed bearing scale which corresponds with the instantaneous value of the ship's heading. As a result, the 000° graduation represents true north. Thus the observer views the picture with north at the 'top' of the screen and it is for this reason that the orientation is so named. Compass stabilization is essential so as to maintain the orientation true-north-up when the observing vessel alters course or yaws about her chosen course (see Figures 1.12 and 1.13). In the absence of stabilization, the picture would rotate by an amount equal and *opposite* to any change in the observing vessel's heading (see Section 1.4.1). The compass stabilization signal is used to produce simultaneously a commensurate rotation of the picture in the *same* direction as the change of heading. As a

result there is no *nett* rotation of the picture, the heading marker rotates to the new value of heading, and true north remains coincident with the 000° graduation on the fixed bearing scale. The stabilization signal can be derived from any transmitting compass but in practice the signal source is almost invariably a gyro compass. The process whereby the signal is used to effect stabilization is described in Section 2.6.3.

The addition of compass stabilization overcomes the serious, inherent limitation of the ship's-head-up (unstabilized) orientation by removing the angular smearing which is associated with any change in heading. Not only does this eliminate the masking of targets by the afterglow generated during an alteration of course, but it allows true bearings to be read off directly and quickly from the fixed bearing scale without the need to check the direction of the ship's head at the same instant. These features are of particular importance in both collision avoidance and navigation applications. Further, there is no angular disruption of the tracks of targets as their echoes move across the screen. This greatly facilitates the systematic observation of targets for collision avoidance purposes and removes a characteristic which, probably more than any other, has demonstrated over many years its potential to mislead the untrained or unwary observer (see Section 7.12.7).

The orientation compares directly with the chart and very many observers find this agreeable or at least acceptable. However, despite the advantages of stabilization, some officers have a subjective preference for the ship's-head-up orientation. They find it awkward or uncomfortable to view a north-up orientation, particularly when the vessel is on southerly courses. This point of view is advanced by some river and estuary pilots who argue that in locks and narrow channels the angular smearing is secondary when compared with the importance of port and starboard through the window corresponding with left and right on the radar screen. It is a view also held by some more senior officers whose initial radar experience was gained before the availability of azimuth stabilization and by some whose prime concern is visual conning of the vessel. Since then there has been a steady increase in the number of observers having a preference for a stabilized orientation.

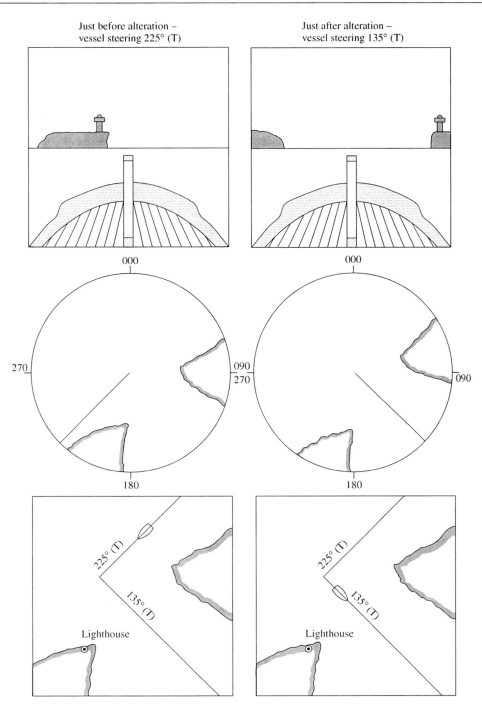

Figure 1.13 True-north-up orientation (stabilized)

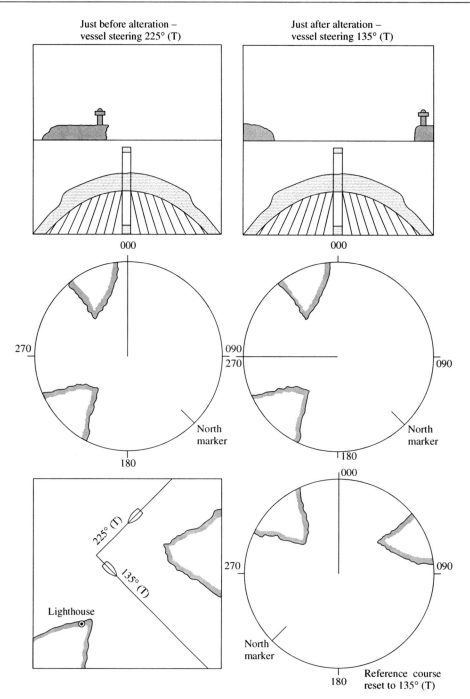

Figure 1.14 Course-up orientation (stabilized) – resetting the reference course

1.4.3 Course-up orientation (stabilized)

In a course-up (stabilized) orientation the heading marker is aligned to the 000° graduation on the fixed bearing scale at an instant at which the vessel is right on the chosen course. By virtue of the azimuth stabilization, changes in the vessel's instantaneous heading are reflected by sympathetic angular movement of the heading marker, thus maintaining the ship's course (referred to as the reference course) in alignment with the zero of the fixed bearing scale. For the same reason, the angular wander of echoes associated with an unstabilized display is eliminated. In some modern systems a north marker is displayed at the edge of the screen (see Figure 1.14).

Provided that the observing vessel does not stray very far from her chosen course, this orientation effectively combines the attractive features of both of the orientations previously described. It eliminates the angular wander of the picture due to yaw, while maintaining the heading marker in a substantially (though not exactly) ship's-head-up position.

Inevitably a major alteration of course will become necessary either due to the requirements of collision avoidance or to those of general navigation. When the vessel is steadied on the new course the orientation, although not meaningless, will have lost its property of being substantially ship's-head-up. The problem is that the orientation is still *previous-course-up* and the picture must be reorientated to align the heading marker with the zero of the fixed bearing scale at an instant when the vessel is right on the new chosen course (see Figure 1.14). In older systems it was necessary to carry out the realignment by rotating a manual control, but in most modern displays it can be achieved simply by pressing a button.

1.4.4 Choice of orientation

The fundamental function of any civil marine radar is to afford a means of measuring the ranges and bearings of echoes and hence to make possible the tracking of target movements for collision avoidance and the determination of the observing vessel's position in order to ensure safe navigation. The ease with which these objectives can be attained is affected by the choice of orientation. Where the various techniques of collision avoidance and navigation are described in this text, appropriate attention will be given to the influence of orientation. The theory of the production of the orientations is described in Section 2.6.3 and the practical

Table 1.3 Picture orientations compared

Feature	Orientation		
	Ship's-head-up, unstabilized	True-north-up, stabilized	Course-up, stabilized
Blurring when observing vessel yaws or alters course	Yes: can produce very serious masking	None	None
Measurement of bearings	Awkward and slow	Straightforward	Straightforward
Angular disruption of target trails when observing vessel yaws or alters course	Yes: can be dangerously misleading	None	None
Correspondence with wheel-house window view	Perfect	Not obvious	Virtually perfect except after large course change
Correspondence with chart	Not obvious	Perfect	Not obvious

setting up procedures in Chapter 6. It is appropriate at this point to summarize the features of the three orientations so far described in the context of the foregoing fundamental requirements (see Table 1.3).

Except in specialized pilotage situations, the ship's-head-up unstabilized orientation has nothing to offer other than its subjective appeal, because by its very nature it regularly disrupts the steady-state condition conducive to measurement of bearing and tracking of echo movement (see Figure 1.12). True-north-up and course-up orientations do not exhibit this angular disruption and hence are equally superior in fulfilling the fundamental requirements. Fortunately they are complementary in that while one is north-up, the other is orientated in such a way as not to alienate the user who has a ship's-head-up preference (see Figure 1.12).

1.5 Picture presentation

As suggested in Section 1.4, there is frequently some overlap between the concepts of picture orientation and picture presentation. In this text, the term 'picture presentation' will be used to indicate if the movement of displayed echoes is shown with respect to (a) the observing vessel, (b) the water, or (c) the ground. In all three presentations, the observing vessel is represented by the electronic origin of the display, i.e. by the centre of rotation of the trace or by the own ship marker on a raster display.

1.5.1 The relative-motion presentation

In the relative-motion presentation the origin of the display is stationary and the movement of all targets is shown with respect to the observing vessel. Commonly the origin is located at the centre of the circular screen (or, in the case of a raster-scan display, at the centre of the display circle) but this need not be the case as off-centred relative-motion presentations are available in many display systems. The essential

feature is that the origin is stationary and as a consequence targets exhibit their motion relative to the observing vessel. This is best illustrated by an example. (The scenario used to illustrate the three cases listed in Section 1.5 is subject to the assumption that the effect of leeway may be neglected.)

For the purpose of illustration it is convenient to consider the case of an observing vessel on a steady heading of 000° (T) at a speed of 10 knots through the water in a tide (which is uniform throughout the area) setting 270° (T) at a rate of 4 knots. The chart (see Figure 1.15(a)) also shows four targets:

(i)   Vessel A which is located 7 miles due north of the observing vessel and is stopped in the water heading 045° (T).

(ii) Vessel B which is located 8 miles due east of vessel A and is on a steady heading of 270° (T) at a speed of 10 knots through the water.

(iii) Vessel C which is located 5 miles due north of vessel A and is on a steady heading of 180° (T) at a speed of 5 knots through the water.

(iv) A large automatic navigational buoy (lanby) L which is anchored and therefore is stationary over the ground. Its position is 7 miles due west of vessel A.

To assist in the understanding of relative motion, Figure 1.15(b) represents the observing vessel's PPI as it would appear at 1000. For comparison, Figure 1.15(c) represents the same PPI showing the positions of the echoes as they would appear at 1030 together with a record of their 1000 positions. It will be noticed that the shape of the echoes gives no indication of the outline of the targets. This fundamental limitation of marine radar will be discussed at length in Section 2.6.5. Consider now the movement of each of the four echoes in turn, commencing with that of the water-stationary target A which offers a simple basis on which an understanding of all relative motion can be built. It is important to remember that it is being assumed that the observing vessel maintains a steady heading. If the vessel were yawing, azimuth stabilization would be essential to achieve the continuity of movement described below.

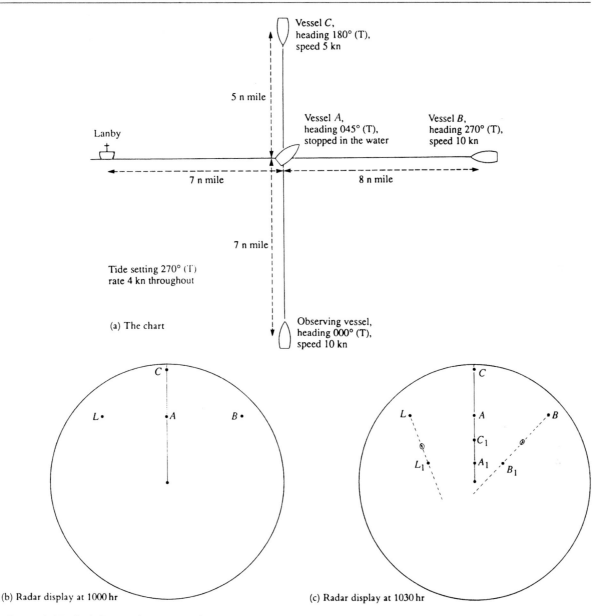

Figure 1.15 Relative-motion presentation

In the period 1000 to 1030 the observing vessel will move north by a distance of 5 miles through the water. Because the origin remains stationary, and the range of target *A* decreases at 10 nautical miles per hour, it follows that the echo of *A* will move down the heading marker by a distance of 5 miles in the 30 minute interval. This reveals the basic property of the relative-motion presentation which is that the echo of a target which is stationary in the water will move across the screen in a direction reciprocal to that of the observing vessel's heading, at a rate equal to the observing vessel's speed through the water.

Consider now the movement of the echo of vessel *B* which at 1000 was 8 miles due east of the stationary vessel *A*. As *B* is heading directly toward *A* at 10 knots, it follows that its 1030 position will be 3 miles due east of *A*. Figure 1.15(c) reveals that the afterglow trail left by the echo of vessel *B* offers an indication of how far off the target will pass if neither vessel manoeuvres. However, the echo has moved across the screen in a direction and at a rate which is quite different from the target's course and speed. An appreciation of this fact is absolutely essential if the presentation is to be interpreted correctly and used in assessing collision avoidance strategy. Further consideration of the figure will show that the relative motion of echo *B* is the resultant of that of a water-stationary target (which is determined by the observing vessel's course and speed through the water) and the true motion of the vessel *B* through the water. The proper use of radar for collision avoidance is based on systematic observation and analysis of both the relative motion and the true motion of the other targets in an encounter (see Chapter 7).

Consider now the movement on the screen of the echo of vessel *C*. At 1000 its position was 5 miles due north of the water-stationary vessel *A* and heading directly towards it at 5 knots. It follows that at 1030 its position will be 2.5 miles north of vessel *A*. As shown in Figure 1.15(c), because the echo of vessel *A* has itself moved across the screen by 5 miles in a direction of south, the aggregate movement of echo *C* is 7.5 miles in the same direction. Thus, as in the case of vessel *B*, the echo has moved across the screen in a way that is different from the movement of the vessel through the water. However it should be noted that, by coincidence, the track across the screen of echo *C* is in the same direction as that of the water-stationary target *A*. This reveals a further feature of the relative-motion presentation, which is that the echoes of targets which are stopped in the water, targets which are on a reciprocal course to the observing vessel and targets which are on the same course as the observing vessel, but slower, will all move

across the screen in the *same* direction (but at different speeds). This feature has the potential to mislead the untrained or unwary observer into confusing, for example, a target that is being overtaken with one that is on a reciprocal course. This further emphasizes the necessity of systematic analysis of the information presented, as opposed to inspired guesswork, when using the radar for collision avoidance (see Chapter 7).

Initially the east/west distance between the lanby and the stationary ship was 7 miles. As the tide is setting the stationary vessel down on to the buoy at 4 knots, it follows that this distance will have reduced to 5 miles by 1030. A study of Figure 1.15(c) will show that the echo of the buoy has moved across the screen in a direction and at a rate which are the resultant of the motion of a water-stationary target and the reciprocal of the tide. Further consideration of this point will reveal that a property of the relative-motion presentation is that a land-stationary target will move across the screen in a direction which is the reciprocal of the observing vessel's ground track at a speed equal to the speed of the observing vessel over the ground. This property is exploited in the use of radar for navigation (as opposed to collision avoidance); the various procedures are set out in Chapter 8.

1.5.2   The true-motion presentation

It has been shown that in a relative-motion presentation the movement of all echoes across the screen is affected by the course and speed of the observing vessel. In a correctly adjusted true-motion presentation, the echo movement of all targets is rendered independent of the motion of the observing vessel. This is achieved by causing the origin of the picture to track across the screen in a direction and at a rate which correspond with the motion of the observing vessel. Immediately one must ask the question, 'Should the observing vessel's course and speed be measured with respect to the water or with respect to the ground?'. The answer will have a fundamental effect on the movement of the displayed echoes. At this juncture, it is important to recognize that either reference can be used: it is appropriate to consider both possibilities and subsequently debate the suitability of each.

If the course and speed through the water are selected, the true-motion presentation is said to be sea-stabilized. It was shown that with azimuth stabilization, the input of ship's heading data is used to maintain true north (or the ship's chosen course) in a fixed direction on the screen. By simultaneously feeding in speed data (measured with respect to the water) it is possible to stabilize the picture so that a water-stationary target is maintained in a fixed position on the screen. This is illustrated by the same scenario as was used in section 1.5.1.

1.5.2.1   *True-motion sea-stabilized presentation*

To produce a true-motion sea-stabilized presentation, the origin of the picture must be made to track across the screen in a direction and at a rate that corresponds with the observing vessel's course and speed through the water. In the example in the illustration (Figure 1.16) the course is 000° (T) and the speed is 10 knots.

Figure 1.16(b) shows the PPI of the observing vessel as it would appear at 1000. The origin of the picture is offset in such a way as to make optimum use of the available screen area (see Section 6.8.2, paragraph 5). Figure 1.16(c) shows the position of the four echoes as they would appear at 1030 together with an indication of their 1000 positions for the purpose of comparison. The movement of each of the four echoes will now be considered in turn, commencing with target *A* which is stopped in the water.

In the interval 1000 to 1030 the origin will move due north by a scale distance of 5 miles, while in the same time target *A* will remain on the heading marker but its range will decrease by 5 nautical miles. It follows that the nett motion of the echo of target *A* will be zero. Consideration of Figure 1.16 reveals the basic property of a correctly set up true-motion sea-stabilized presentation, which is that the echo of a target which is stationary in the water will maintain constant position on the screen.

Figure 1.16 True-motion sea-stabilized presentation

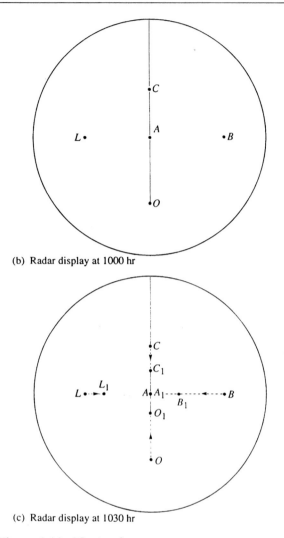

(b) Radar display at 1000 hr

(c) Radar display at 1030 hr

Figure 1.16 (*Continued*)

At 1000 the moving target B was located 8 miles due east of vessel A. As it is heading directly toward A its bearing from A will remain steady but the range will have decreased to 3 miles by 1030. Figure 1.16(c) shows that the echo of target B will move across the screen in a direction and at a rate which corresponds with the target vessel's course and speed through the water. A similar argument will reveal that the echo of vessel C will move across the screen in a direction of 180° (T) at a scale speed of 5 knots. The

presentation thus has the property that the afterglow trails offer an indication of the headings of all moving targets. This feature is complementary to the corresponding property of the relative-motion presentation (see Section 1.5.1). It must be stressed that collision avoidance strategy must be based on systematic analysis of the displayed target movements as detailed in Chapter 7.

As a result of the tide, the water-stationary vessel A will be set directly toward the lanby and by 1030 the east/west distance between the two will have reduced to 5 miles. It has been established that echo A will maintain its position on the screen and thus it follows that in the interval from 1000 to 1030 echo L will move east across the screen by a scale distance of 2 miles. Consideration of Figure 1.16(c) will show that a third property of the true-motion sea-stabilized presentation is that land-stationary targets will move across the screen at a rate equal to the tide but in the opposite direction to the set.

In considering the properties of the true-motion, sea-stabilized presentation it is essential to appreciate that the accuracy with which the displayed target movements are presented is completely dependent on the accuracy with which the direction and rate of the movement of the picture origin represents the observing vessel's course and speed through the water. The true-motion presentation is only as good as the input data.

The mechanics whereby the tracking of the origin is achieved, the practical procedure for setting up the presentation and the effect of errors and inaccuracies are covered in Sections 2.6.4, 6.8 and 7.10 respectively.

Because the scenario used a heading of north for the observing vessel, the question of whether the orientation was north-up or course-up did not arise. It should be noted that either orientation can be used with true motion, irrespective of heading.

1.5.2.2   True-motion, ground-stabilized presentation

To create ground stabilization of a true-motion presentation, the origin of the picture is made to move across the screen in a direction and at a rate which correspond with the observing vessel's track over the ground. To achieve this, the input data must have a component which represents the observing vessel's course and speed through the water plus a further component which represents the set and rate of the tidal stream or current. There are several ways in which the resultant of these components may be deduced and applied as input data. A detailed description of the methods is set out in Section 2.6.4.4. At this stage it is important to appreciate that the accuracy of the presentation depends on the accuracy of both components. In particular it should be remembered that the values of set and drift may have to be based on past positions. For comparison purposes it is convenient to illustrate the presentation with reference to the same scenario as was used in the two preceding examples. Figure 1.17(b) shows the PPI of the observing vessel as it would appear at 1000, while Figure 1.17(c) shows the echoes as they would appear at 1030 together with recorded plots of the 1000 positions. It should be noted that the origin of the picture has moved in a direction which differs from that of the heading marker. The latter represents the direction in which the observing vessel is heading at any instant and is independent of any tidal influence.

In this case it is helpful to start by considering the ground-stationary target *L*. Reference to Figure 1.17(c) shows that in the period 1000 to 1030 the origin of the display will have moved to a position which is a scale distance of 5 miles due north (representing the vessel's movement through the water) and 2 miles due west (representing the set and drift experienced) of its 1000 screen location. In the same interval, the north/south distance between the observing vessel and the lanby will have decreased by 5 nautical miles (the d.lat.) while the east/west distance will have decreased by 2 miles (the departure). It follows from these two statements that the echo of the buoy *L* will exhibit neither north/south movement nor east/west movement across the screen. This reveals the key

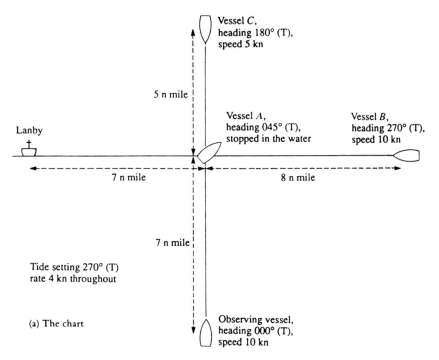

Figure 1.17   True-motion ground-stabilized presentation

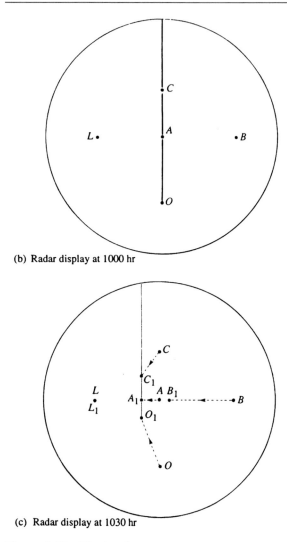

(b) Radar display at 1000 hr

(c) Radar display at 1030 hr

Figure 1.17 (*Continued*)

property of the correctly set up true-motion ground-stabilized presentation, which is that the echo of a land target will remain stationary on the screen.

Consider now vessel *A* which is stopped in the water heading 045° (T). As previously established, it will be set directly toward the buoy by a distance of 2 miles in the period 1000–1030. It follows from this, and the fact that echo *L* is stationary on the screen, that the echo of vessel *A* will move in a direction of

due west by a scale distance of 2 miles in the interval considered. This reveals a second property of the true-motion ground-stabilized presentation, which is that the echo of a target which is stopped in the water will move across the screen in a direction and at a rate that corresponds with the set and rate of the tidal stream.

Having regard to target *C*, it is clear that at 1030 its position will be 2.5 miles north of vessel *A*. A study of Figure 1.17(c) will show that, because the movement of echo *A* represents the tide, the echo of vessel *C* will therefore move across the screen in a direction and at a rate which is the resultant of the set and drift of the tidal stream, and her course and speed through the water. This shows the general property of the correctly set up true-motion ground-stabilized presentation, which is that echoes of vessels that are underway will move across the screen in a direction and at a rate which represents their track over the ground. The example of the vessel *A* which is underway but stopped is a special case of this general rule. The movement of the echo of vessel *B* also illustrates this feature, but perhaps not so dramatically because it is heading in the same direction as the set of the tidal stream.

Consideration of the movements of echoes *A* and *C* in particular will emphasize how an untrained or unwary observer might be misled into *erroneously* concluding that vessel *A* was slow-moving and crossing showing a red sidelight (when in fact it is stopped in the path of the observing vessel) and that vessel *C* was a passing vessel showing a red sidelight (when in fact it is head on).

It is thus essential to appreciate that in this presentation the movement of the echoes of vessels that are underway does *not* represent their headings. Information on headings is essential for the proper use of radar in collision avoidance. It follows that, in principle, this presentation is not appropriate as a basis for planning collision avoidance strategy and can be dangerously misleading if used for this purpose. This extremely important topic is further discussed in Sections 2.6.4.4 and 6.8.3.

As noted in the previous section, it should be appreciated that either north-up or course-up orientation can be used with true motion.

1.5.3 Choice of presentation

The choice of presentation made in any given circumstances will be influenced by a number of factors. The available equipment may not offer the choice of all three presentations described in this chapter. Material to the decision will be the question of whether the radar is being used primarily for collision avoidance or for position fixing and progress monitoring. It may be that the requirements of both must be satisfied with a single presentation. Subjective preferences are likely to make themselves felt. It is appropriate to defer more detailed discussion of the factors affecting such a choice until after further consideration has been given to the operating principles of the radar system, the practical procedures for the setting up and maintaining of the presentations, and the general philosophy of the use of radar for collision avoidance and navigation (see Chapters 6, 7, and 8). However, at this stage it is useful, for comparison purposes, to summarize the major features of each presentation and comment briefly on its suitability for use in collision avoidance and navigation.

In the relative-motion presentation the echo movement of targets which are underway is that of the target relative to the observing vessel. Systematic observation of this movement readily offers a forecast of the distance off at which a target will pass (the closest point of approach or CPA) and the time at which the target will reach its closest point of approach (TCPA). This information is an effective measure of the risk of a close-quarters situation developing. The presentation gives no direct indication of the heading or speed of target vessels. Such information is essential to the choice of avoiding action in encounters with other vessels and has to be obtained by the resolution of a vector triangle. This may be done graphically or with the aid of some semi-automatic plotting device, or automatically by computer. Thus the relative-motion presentation gives direct indictation of some of the information required for collision avoidance but the remainder must be found by deduction (see Chapter 7).

The echoes of land targets on a relative-motion presentation trace out a trail which is the reciprocal of the observing vessel's track made good over the ground. This feature is particularly useful in progress monitoring and position fixing when the radar is being used for navigation as opposed to collision avoidance (see Chapter 8).

The true-motion sea-stabilized presentation makes the headings and speeds of targets available directly but the observer is required to deduce the CPA and TCPA. In respect of the use of radar for collision avoidance it can be seen that the relative motion and the true-motion sea-stabilized presentations are complementary. The true-motion does have the added advantage that it makes it very much easier to identify target manoeuvres and, further, the continuity of target motion is not disrupted when the observing vessel manoeuvres or yaws.

The true-motion ground-stabilized presentation has little to offer other than its ability to maintain land targets in a fixed position on the screen. No apology is made for re-stating the fact that it gives no direct indication of any collision avoidance information and can even result in confusion.

Table 1.4 summarizes the features of the presentation described above.

1.5.3.1 Constant display true-motion

Many manufacturers have introduced another variation on the true-motion display presentation to avoid the need to reset the screen. The variation is now practical because of the processing of radar data before display (see Section 2.5) and use of automatic techniques to stabilize the display (see Section 5.3).

The own-ship position is fixed at a display position, either at the centre or offset according to observer preference, in a similar way to setting up relative motion. The own ship does not move across the screen and reach a position where it is significantly off-centre and showing a lot of coverage astern and very little coverage ahead. Normally in these circumstances a reset of the screen is then required.

Effectively all the display data around the ship is artificially moving in a reciprocal direction to the ship's course and speed, so that although we have

Table 1.4   Presentations – summary of features

Feature	Presentation		
	Relative motion	*True-motion sea-stabilized*	*True-motion ground-stabilized*
Ease of assessing target's CPA/TCPA	Directly available	Resolution required	Resolution required
Ease of assessing target's course, speed and aspect	Resolution required	Directly available	Resolution required – potentially misleading
Need for additional sensor inputs: course and speed	No	Yes	Yes
Need for data on tide set and rate	No	No	Yes
Displayed information relative to:	Observer	The water	The ground
Particular application for collision avoidance/navigation	Partial contribution to collision avoidance data. Ideal for parallel indexing	Partial contribution to collision avoidance data	Difficult to achieve without ARPA but if achieved provides stationary map
Limitations for collision avoidance	Target heading not directly available	CPA not directly available	No collision avoidance data directly available
Limitations for navigation	Movement of land echoes may hinder target identification	Limited movement of land echoes	None if stabilization effective

true-motion, the vessel remains at the same position on the screen. True trails (afterglow) are shown, but close inspection will show that both target and afterglow are not advancing on screen in the direction of the afterglow. This feature is usually termed constant display true-motion (CDTM) or similar and is very convenient.

However, as the own ship no longer moves across the screen, the main danger is that despite the display presentation being indicated in one corner of the screen, the unobservant navigator may think that the display is in relative-motion when in fact all afterglow and target trails will be as if for true-motion and mistakes could result.

2 The radar system – operational principles

2.1 Introduction

In Chapter 1 the fundamental principles of range and bearing measurement which underly the generation of a marine radar picture were discussed and the way in which the target information is displayed for use in navigation and collision avoidance was described in general terms. The operation of marine radar systems is now studied in greater detail in order to provide the reader with that thorough understanding of the relevant engineering and communication principles which are essential for safe and seamanlike application of the practical procedures described in Chapter 6.

An overall appreciation of system operation is readily achieved by reference to a simple block diagram (see Figure 2.1) in which the system is represented by a small number of main functional units. This makes it possible to identify the relationships between the units before proceeding to a more detailed anatomy of each functional block. It must be appreciated that while Figure 2.1 subdivides the system in such a way as to best illustrate operational principles, it may not coincide exactly with the physical subdivision of the units installed on board ship. For example, part of the receiver is commonly situated in the same cabinet as the transmitter, but the remainder may well be located in the display console. Such details of physical distribution may be neglected when considering general principles but are clearly relevant to a full understanding of a shipboard installation. Accordingly

the typical physical subdivision of a system will be discussed in Section 2.7.

2.2 Function of units

This section gives a brief description of the function of each block in the diagram and the interrelationship between the units, to provide a concise overall picture of radar operation. In subsequent sections a detailed exposition of the principles employed in each unit and of the characteristics required will be given. The treatment of these principles is substantially qualitative and should be readily followed by any reader having a rudimentary background of school physics.

2.2.1 The transmitter function (see also Section 2.3)

The function of the transmitter is to generate pulses of electromagnetic energy having the correct repetition frequency, length, shape, power and radio frequency. The pulses normally travel to the aerial by way of hollow copper tubing which has a precisely machined rectangular or circular cross-section and is known as *waveguide*.

It is sometimes considered convenient to visualize the radio energy as flowing, like water, along the inside of the tube and there is no doubt that this is a helpful

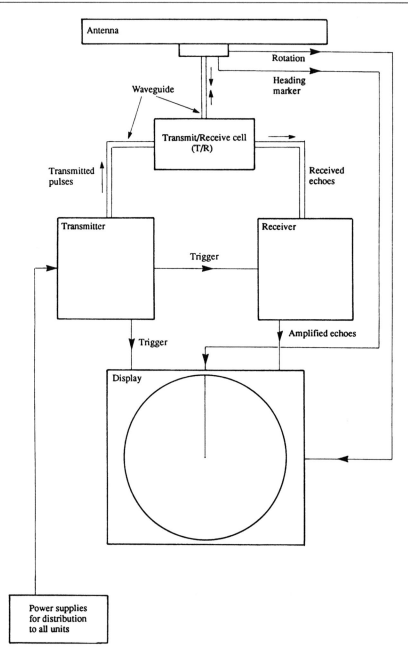

Figure 2.1 Simple block diagram of a radar system

and practical way of illustrating how the waveguide works. Nonetheless, in the interests of veracity it must be stated that the energy actually travels, in the form of electric and magnetic fields, within the conducting walls of the waveguide. However there is no simple qualitative explanation for this mode of transmission. We are left with the choice between accepting the water analogy or pursuing a mathematical treatment which is beyond the scope of this book.

Historically, waveguide was used because of the considerable losses which were encountered in attempting to transmit the extremely short wavelengths associated with radar frequencies along conventional cables of any significant length. While some manufacturers have now developed co-axial cables which will pass radar frequencies, others still consider waveguide to be the more suitable method. (A co-axial cable is one having a central conductor surrounded by insulating material and a screening sheath.)

An essential feature of range measurement is that timing must commence at the instant of transmission (see Section 1.2.3.). This is achieved by using the same pulse to initiate transmission as is used to start the corresponding trace on the CRT display. This pulse is known as the 'synchronizing pulse' or 'trigger' and is shown in the block diagram as travelling along the line connecting the transmitter to the display.

In the block diagram a further line is shown connecting the transmitter to the receiver. This also carries the trigger pulse but in this case the pulse is used to initiate sea clutter suppression. Sea clutter is the name given to the echoes which are returned by the sea waves in the vicinity of the observing vessel (see Section 3.6). A variety of techniques exist for suppressing this unwanted effect. Most depend on the fact that the maximum response occurs at minimum range and hence suppression can conveniently be initiated by the trigger pulse.

2.2.2 The aerial function (see also Section 2.4)

Aerial, scanner and antenna are all names commonly used to describe the device which radiates the radio energy into space and intercepts the returning echoes.

Its construction defines the power distribution of the radar beam in both the horizontal and the vertical planes. In order to achieve the required directional characteristic (see Section 1.3.1) the horizontal limits must be narrow. By contrast, the beam is wide in a vertical sense in order to maintain adequate performance when a vessel is rolling (or pitching) in a seaway. The IMO Performance Standards (see Section 11.2.1) set out certain range performance requirements and these must be achieved when the vessel is rolling or pitching up to $\pm 10°$. While in theory one might contemplate using some form of gyro stabilization to maintain the beam in a horizontal plane, in practice the standard has the effect of defining a minimum vertical beam width of 20°.

To achieve the desired 360° of azimuth coverage (see Sections 1.3.2 and 2.4.4) the scanner is rotated continuously and automatically in a clockwise direction (when viewed from above). A signal representing this rotation, either in analogue or in digital code form, must be relayed to the PPI display in order to drive the trace in sympathetic rotation with the scanner. (In a raster-scan display the signal will update the aerial angle against which the range data is being read in.) The transmission of this signal is represented in Figure 2.1 by one of the two lines connecting the aerial unit to the display. The second line carries the heading marker pulse (see Section 1.3.4) which fully brightens several successive traces as the axis of the main beam crosses the ship's fore-and-aft line in the forward direction.

Where the waveguide extends from the aerial to a *remote* transmitter/receiver, some form of rotating joint is required in the waveguide to allow the energy to pass from the fixed part of the aerial unit to the rotating part. This is achieved by using two short sections of circular waveguide (one fixed and one rotating) and a special co-axial joint.

2.2.3 The receiver function (see also Section 2.5)

The function of the receiver is to amplify the very weak echoes intercepted by the aerial so as to generate pulses whose form and power will produce a visible response on the screen of a cathode ray tube (or provide a suitable input for digital storage).

It will be noticed that because a single aerial is used for transmission and reception, the waveguide is common to both transmitter and receiver. It would thus appear that the powerful pulses generated by the transmitter might be able to pass directly into the receiver. The receiver is protected from this by a device known as a transmit/receive switch (or T/R cell) which is situated in the waveguide immediately before the input to the receiver. The T/R cell blocks the input to the receiver during transmission; it will be discussed further in Section 2.5.

In effect there are thus two inputs to the receiver, the received signals from the aerial and the trigger pulse to initiate sea clutter suppression. The output line from the receiver carries the amplified signals to the display.

2.2.4   The display function (see also Section 2.6)

The prime function of the display is to indicate the presence of detectable objects by generating, on the screen of the cathode ray tube, a visible response whose angular and radial position with respect to the heading line and the origin of the trace are representative of the bearing and range, respectively, at which the corresponding target lies. A less formal way of expressing this is to state that the display generates a radar picture. Four input signals are necessary to produce such a picture (see Figure 2.1). Each of these signals, namely trigger, echo signals, heading marker and aerial rotation, has already been mentioned in this chapter when its source was discussed. However, in consolidating an understanding of the mechanics of producing a radar picture it is helpful to summarize them as follows:

1   *The trigger.* This ensures that each trace commences at the instant of a transmission (see Section 1.2).
2   *The amplified echoes.* Each echo on any given trace produces a brightening of the spot on the cathode ray tube at an elapsed time after the transmission which initiated that trace. The length of the elapsed time is directly proportional to the range of the

target which reflected the echo and hence the distance of the echo from the origin is a measure of its range (see Section 1.2).
3   *The rotation signal.* This signal causes the trace to rotate at the same angular rate as the aerial. Consequently all targets on any given trace will appear in the correct angular relationship to all other targets on the PPI (see Section 1.3).
4   *The heading marker signal.* This generates the brightened radial indicator corresponding with the forward direction of the ship's fore-and-aft line, thus providing a reference from which bearings can be measured (see Section 1.3).

These four fundamental signals that generate the radar picture are shown as inputs to the display in Figure 2.1. It should be borne in mind that the time relationship between the signals is of particular importance. These are illustrated by Figure 2.2 which uses some representative values. Figure 2.2 is drawn in two parts because, although all four signals are repetitive in their nature, the former two recur several thousand times per second whereas the latter two have a period of a few seconds. It is thus not practical to show the time sequence of all four signals on the same time axis.

It will be noticed in Figure 2.2(a) that there is a comparatively long delay between the completion of one trace and the commencement of the next. This is a design feature of all marine radars and is incorporated in an attempt to ensure that echoes from distant targets do not arrive after the transmission of the next pulse. If this does occur, echoes from two different transmissions may appear on the same trace. The late responses, which will display at a range very much shorter than the correct value and may mislead the observer, are known as *second-trace echoes*. They are discussed in detail in Section 3.9.6.

Before leaving the simple block diagram it must be mentioned that the four input signals described above would produce an unstabilized relative-motion picture. The addition of a compass input would be necessary if azimuth stabilization was required, while true-motion would necessitate an input of the ship's speed. Such additional inputs are discussed in Sections 2.6.3 and 2.6.4.

(a)

(b)

Figure 2.2 Typical time sequence of display input signals
(a)   High-frequency signals: PRF = 1250 pps, range scale 12 n mile
(b)   Low-frequency signals: Aerial rotation = 20 rpm

2.3 Transmitter principles

In Section 2.2.1 it was noted that the function of the transmitter was to produce pulses of radar energy having the correct repetition frequency, length, shape, power and radio frequency. In this section a more detailed study of the transmitter shows how these important properties are determined and discusses their relevance to the operation of marine radar.

Figure 2.3 shows the three essential elements of the transmitter:

1   The trigger generator, which controls the repetition frequency of the transmitted pulses.
2   The modulator and associated pulse-forming network, which define the length, shape and power of the transmitted pulses.
3   The magnetron, which determines the radio frequency of the pulse which travels up the waveguide to the aerial.

When a pulse is transmitted, each element operates sequentially and it is thus appropriate to describe the characteristics of the pulses in the order set out above.

2.3.1 The pulse repetition frequency

The trigger generator is a free-running oscillator which generates a continuous succession of low voltage pulses known as *synchronizing pulses*, or *trigger* pulses. Commonly they are referred to simply as *triggers*. Each trigger causes the remainder of the transmission elements to generate a radio frequency pulse which is sent up the waveguide to the antenna. The trigger generator thus controls the number of radar pulses transmitted in one second. The latter quantity is referred to as the *pulse repetition frequency* (PRF) or sometimes the *pulse repetition rate* (PRR). Because the trigger generator controls the PRF, it is sometimes referred to as the PRF generator.

Most PRF generators make available two or three pulse repetition frequencies from which the observer may select the one most appropriate. In practice this may be achieved by designing the oscillator to 'free run' at the highest required frequency and using every second trigger to produce a medium PRF and every fourth trigger to produce a low PRF. Typical values might be 3400, 1700 and 850 pulses per second. In civil marine radars it is unusual to find PRFs outside the range 400 to 4000 pulses per second (pps). It is

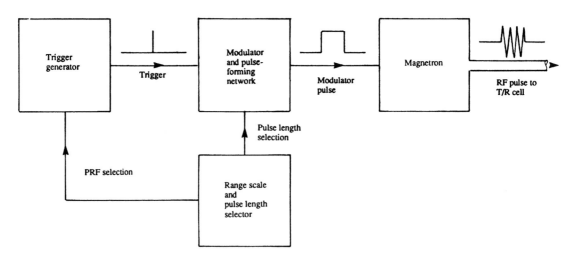

Figure 2.3 The transmitter – a block diagram

common practice to quote the PRF as a number, leaving the units of pulses per second to be understood.

In general there is a requirement for a low PRF when long range scales are selected and a high PRF in the case of short range scales. This is to some extent, but not completely, dependent on the duration of the transmitted pulse (the pulse length). Where more than one PRF is available it will be found that selection of the appropriate value is made automatically according to the range scale *and* pulse length selected by the observer. The relationship between selected range scale and PRF is discussed after the concept of pulse length has been introduced in the next section.

2.3.2 The pulse length, power and shape

The function of the modulator and its associated pulse-forming network is to produce a pulse of the correct length, power and shape on each occasion that it is activated by the trigger. Pulse length and power are of considerable importance in the effective detection of targets, as is pulse shape in the accurate measurement of their range.

2.3.2.1 *The pulse length*

Pulse length is defined as the duration of the transmitted radar pulse and is usually measured in microseconds (μs). In general, if a long pulse is used, the probability of detecting a target (other than one at extremely short range) will be higher than if a short pulse is used under the same circumstances. This important general theoretical principle is implicit in the fact that any given radar receiver can amplify long pulses more effectively than short pulses. This receiver characteristic is discussed in Section 2.5; however, the designer must take this principle into consideration when deciding which pulse lengths to make available to the observer, as must the observer in selecting a pulse length appropriate to the task in hand.

In stating the above general principle a proviso was made concerning the case of a target at extremely close range. This was necessary because in such circumstances the strength of the echo is likely to be so great that the effectiveness of amplification will be of minor importance. The critical factor in such a case is that where the radar uses the same waveguide and aerial for both transmission and reception (see Figure 2.1), it cannot perform both functions at the same time. The T/R cell (see Section 2.2.3) blocks the receiver for the duration of the transmitted pulse. It follows that the shorter the pulse length employed, the smaller the theoretical minimum detection range will become, i.e. closer targets will be detectable (see Section 3.2.4).

In certain special circumstances, such as those where targets are difficult to detect against the background of sea or weather clutter, the use of a short pulse may improve the probability of detection of a wanted target. It is important to appreciate that this does not contradict the above principle but attempts to exploit it by reducing the response from both the clutter and the wanted target in the hope that the clutter can be removed from the screen while the target's echo is retained (see Section 3.6.3).

Two, three or even four pulse lengths may be available, according to the complexity of the system design. In civil marine radar it is unusual to find pulse lengths outside the range of 0.05 to 1.3 μs. It is likely that the pulse length produced by the system in any given circumstance will depend on both the pulse length requested by the observer and the range scale selected.

The philosophy of this semi-automatic selection is that if the radar is being used for general surveillance on the longer range scales, a long pulse is more appropriate because the receiver will have to handle weak signals returning from distant targets. On shorter range scales the returns are likely, in general, to be stronger and the observer is more likely to be concerned with the detail of the picture. The theoretical minimum radial length of any echo as it is eventually displayed on a conventional PPI is determined by the pulse length. Hence the shorter the pulse length the better the detail. The ability of the radar to display separately two targets which are on the same bearing and closely spaced in range is known as range discrimination and this is discussed fully in Section 2.6.5.5. Thus, in general usage, a short pulse is likely to be more appropriate on the shorter range scales. There are fewer occasions on which it may be helpful to use long pulses on the shorter range scales and short pulses on the longer range scales.

Table 2.1 PRF and pulse length – some representative values

| Range scale selected (n mile) | Pulse length selected | | | |
| | Short | | Long | |
	PRF (Hz)	PL (μs)	PRF (Hz)	PL (μs)
0.25	2000	0.05	2000	0.05
0.5	2000	0.05	1000	0.25
0.75	2000	0.05	1000	0.25
1.5	2000	0.05	1000	0.25
3.0	1000	0.25	500	1.0
6.0	1000	0.25	500	1.0
12	1000	0.25	500	1.0
24	500	1.0	500	1.0
48	500	1.0	500	1.0

Where two pulse lengths are offered it is common for a long pulse to be automatically selected on range scales of 12 miles and upwards, and a short pulse on scales below that value. There is likely to be some facility for the observer to override the system selection and choose a long pulse on the shorter scales, though there may be a bar on selecting the long pulse on a very short range scale. In such systems it is less common to find an override facility allowing the short pulse to be used on the longer range scales.

Where more than two pulse lengths are offered, the selection becomes more complex and can take a variety of forms. An example is illustrated in Table 2.1. Notice that although there are three pulse lengths available, only two are available on any given range scale, with the exception of the shortest and two longest scales which will allow only the shortest and longest pulse lengths respectively.

The correct use of pulse length selection requires an understanding of a number of interacting factors which will be discussed at the appropriate points in this text. However at this stage it is useful to summarize the various factors as set out in Table 2.2.

Table 2.2 Short and long pulses – features compared

Feature	Short pulse	Long pulse
Long range target detection	Poor. Use when short range scales are selected	Good. Use when long range scales are selected and for poor response targets at short range
Minimum range	Good. Use when short range scales are selected	Poor. Use when long range scales are selected and minimum range is not a major consideration
Range discrimination	Good	Poor
Effect on echo paint	Short radial paint. Produces a well defined picture when short range scales are selected	Long radial paint when short range scales are selected but the effect is acceptable when long range scales are selected
Effect on sea clutter	Reduces the probability of the masking of targets due to saturation	Increases the probability of the masking of targets due to saturation
Effect in precipitation	Reduces the probability of the masking of targets due to saturation	Increases the probability of the masking of targets due to saturation. However the use of long pulse helps to combat the attenuation caused by precipitation and will increase the probability of detecting targets which lie beyond rain

2.3.2.2   The power of the transmitted pulse

It is almost self-evident that the range at which a target can be detected is dependent on the power of the transmitted pulse. While many other factors can affect the range at which detection may take place, in any given circumstances the *theoretical* maximum radar detection range is limited by the transmitter power. It can be shown (see Section 3.1) that the theoretical maximum detection range varies as the fourth root of the transmitter power.

The power of the radar pulse is a function of its amplitude (see Figure 2.4) which is determined by the pulse-forming network and its associated circuitry (see Section 2.3.2.4). For small craft radar systems a transmitter power of as low as 3 kW may be used, whereas for merchant ships powers in the range 10 to 60 kW may be encountered.

2.3.2.3   The pulse shape

The pulse shape is of particular significance in the accurate determination of range. Ideally the outline (or envelope) of the pulse should be rectangular and, particularly, the leading edge of the pulse should take the form of a vertical rise. The significance of this is illustrated by Figure 2.4 which shows the envelope of an ideal pulse and then compares the range measurement obtained using an ideal pulse shape with that obtained using a pulse shape which is less than ideal.

Because of the great disparity between the strength of the transmitted pulse and that of the returning signals, it is not practical to show their amplitudes to scale. Thus, when considering Figure 2.4, it must be appreciated that the transmitted pulse is of extremely high power whereas the received echo, even after amplification, is comparatively weak and will only be observed where its amplitude rises to the minimum level at which the receiver can detect signals. That level is called the 'minimum detectable signal' and is a receiver characteristic which is described in Section 3.2.3.

It follows that the *elapsed time* on which range measurement is based (see Section 1.2.2) commences at the instant of the trigger and ends when the received signal crosses the threshold of detection. Figure 2.4 shows that the range obtained will be in error by an amount which depends on the time taken by the received signal to reach minimum detection level. The time taken for the pulse amplitude to reach 90 per cent of its maximum value is known as the *rise time* of the pulse and ideally should be zero, as would be the case with a perfectly rectangular pulse. In practice, such an ideal cannot be realized, but the modulator and its associated pulse-forming network are designed in such a way as to produce a pulse having a rise time which is so short as to introduce a negligible ranging error. (Consideration must also be given to rise time in the design of the radar receiver, to ensure that it is capable of responding to the very fast rise times of the pulses produced by the transmitter and thus to avoid further degradation of ranging accuracy. This topic is covered in Section 2.5.2.4.)

While not being such crucial characteristics as rise time, the forms of the upper limit of the envelope and of the trailing edge are also important. The former should be flat in order to produce an echo of uniform brightness, and the trailing edge should be steep in order to give a clean-cut termination of the displayed echo so as to minimize any overlap with a subsequent return (see also *range discrimination* in Section 2.6.5.5). Both of these properties are achieved by the careful design of the pulse-forming network and the characteristics of the receiver.

2.3.2.4   The modulator unit

Having considered the length and form which the envelope of the pulse must take, some attention will now be given to the way in which the envelope is generated. The pulse-forming network (PFN) may be considered to be a reservoir of electrical energy which is charged up comparatively slowly from the power supply in the period between pulses and is discharged very quickly in the duration of the pulse envelope. Consider an example in which typical values such as a PRF of 1000 and a pulse length of 1 μs are used. The interval between pulses, which is referred to as the pulse repetition period (PRP), is

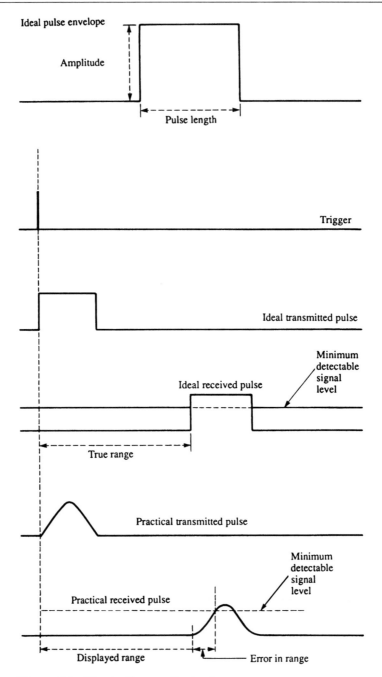

Figure 2.4 The significance of pulse shape

$1000\,\mu s$ and hence the time during which the energy can be stored is $999\,\mu s$. As the energy is released in only $1\,\mu s$ (i.e. very nearly one thousandth of the time in which it was stored), it is apparent that a comparatively low power source can be used to produce a very high power radar pulse, albeit for a very short duration.

The modulator unit includes a very fast-operating switch which allows the discharge of the energy stored in the PFN. A solid state device known as a silicon controlled rectifier (SCR) is suited to this task. (In some literature it is referred to as controlled silicon rectifier (CSR).) The SCR, like a diode, will allow current to pass in one direction (the forward direction) but not in the other direction (the reverse direction). However, in the case of the SCR, forward current will only begin to flow when a trigger pulse is applied to a control electrode. When the trigger pulse is present the opposition to current offered by the device drops instantly to virtually zero, producing a pulse of current having an extremely fast rise time.

The storage property of the PFN is essentially that of electrical capacitance. When energy from a capacitor is discharged through a resistance, the rate of discharge is not constant but shows an exponential decay. This clearly would be unsatisfactory because to produce a rectangular pulse the rate of energy discharge must be constant as long as energy remains in the storage network. Figure 2.5(b) shows that the PFN is a network made up of a number of sections of capacitive and inductive elements and it is the interaction of these elements which produces the constant rate of discharge required. No signal is needed to terminate the pulse, as that event will occur immediately all the energy has been discharged. The duration of the discharge is a function of the total amount of capacitance and inductance. Different pulse lengths (e.g. long, medium and short) are obtained by switching in the appropriate number of network sections. The network of elements giving the special property of constant discharge rate is commonly known as an 'artificial line' because its behaviour resembles that of an extremely long transmission cable. An explanation of the mechanics of the constant discharge would not be appropriate here; the reader who wishes

to pursue the topic is referred to any good radar engineering text.

The pulse of current from the PFN is discharged through the primary winding of a step-up transformer whose secondary voltage is used to fire the magnetron which is the final unit in the transmitter.

2.3.3 The radio frequency of the transmitted pulse

A special type of radio valve called a 'magnetron' is used to produce a burst of radio frequency energy (which will radiate into space), the outline or *envelope* of which matches that generated by the modulator and its associated circuitry (see Figure 2.3). The radar transmission represents a special case of amplitude modulation in which the modulating waveform (the input to the magnetron) switches the carrier (the fixed-amplitude radio waves generated by the magnetron) on and off. Thus we have a signal capable of being radiated into space (because it is a radio frequency oscillation) but which has impressed on it, by virtue of its envelope, the pulse characteristics discussed at length in Section 2.3.2. Looking ahead to the consideration of receiver principles (see Section 2.5) it should be apparent that the receiver must be capable of demodulating the returned signals and hence extracting the envelope of the pulse.

The magnetron has been the only viable technique for producing energy of sufficient voltage and power to operate marine radar. Solid state circuitry can produce signals at the required frequency but not with sufficient power. In Section 3.10 a probable alternative radar technology is covered that needs far less power and it may be that the magnetron will eventually be superseded.

2.3.3.1 *Choice of frequency*

By international agreement two groups of radio frequencies are allocated for use by civil marine radar systems. One group lies in the X-band and includes those frequencies which lie between 9320 and 9500 MHz. These frequencies correspond with a wavelength of

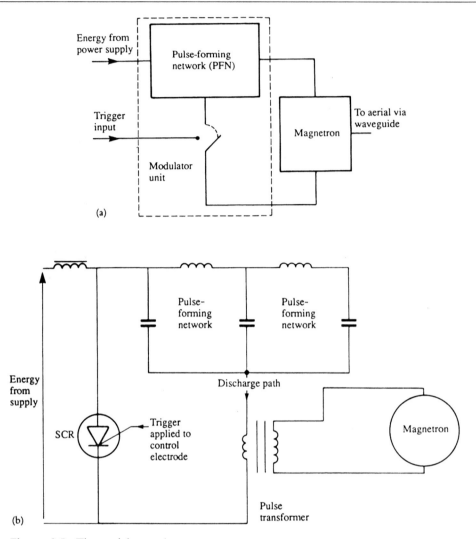

Figure 2.5 The modulator unit
(a) block diagram
(b) circuit diagram

approximately 3 cm. The second group lies in the S-band, and includes the frequencies lying between 2900 and 3100 MHz and corresponds with a wavelength of approximately 10 cm. Because a radar frequency is always a very large number, it is often found more convenient to speak in terms of wavelength.

While the precise frequency allocations made for civil marine radar were a matter of human agreement,

the general area of the allocation was pre-ordained by the laws of physics which demand that the wavelength used be of the order of a few centimetres. A fundamental requirement of marine radar is that of directional transmission and reception, which is achieved by producing a narrow horizontal beam. It will be shown in Section 2.4.2 that, to focus the energy into a narrow beam, either a short wavelength or a large aerial must be used. When it is considered that there is a practical limit to the size of aerial which can be fitted and rotated on board a merchant ship, it is apparent that the general order of the wavelength is similarly limited. Wavelengths lower than about 3 cm are unsuitable because they experience unacceptable attenuation in the gases of the atmosphere and exacerbate the problems of sea and weather clutter (see Table 2.3 and Sections 3.6 and 3.7).

Historically, much civil marine X-band radar development work was done by manufacturers in Great Britain and Europe while in the USA S-band marine radars were more common. There are some circumstances in which X-band performance will be superior to S-band and others in which the reverse will be the case. In the 1950s and 1960s it was uncommon for ships to be fitted with more than one radar and thus the choice of wavelength had to be made at the procurement stage. Now that the fitting of two radars is quite commonplace (see Section 4.1.3), the need to make such a choice is avoided if S-band and X-band systems are fitted. In such a case the observer has the freedom to select the system whose wavelength is best suited to the prevailing circumstances (see also *Interswitching* in Section 2.7.8).

As suggested above, there are many ways in which the characteristics of X-band and S-band transmissions are complementary and a knowledge of these leads to more effective use of the equipment. The various circumstances in which these complementary characteristics can be exploited will be discussed in detail at the appropriate points in this volume; for the moment, it is sufficient to compare their respective characteristics, as set out in Table 2.3.

2.3.3.2 *The magnetron – outline of operation*

The magnetron (or cavity magnetron as it is more correctly named) was invented in Great Britain in 1939 and to this day is considered by civil marine radar manufacturers to be the first choice as a generator of very short pulses of radar energy. When first produced, the magnetron joined the large family of thermionic valves which populated the early radars; now, fifty

Table 2.3 X-band and S-band compared

Feature	Comparison
Target response	For a target of a given size, the response at X-band is greater than at S-band
Bearing discrimination	For a given aerial width the horizontal beamwidth effect in an S-band system will be approximately 3.3 times that of an X-band system
Vertical beam structure	The vertical lobe pattern produced by an S-band aerial is about 3.3 times as coarse as that from an X-band aerial located at the same height
Radar horizon	The radar horizon with S-band is slightly more distant than with X-band
Sea clutter response	The unwanted response from sea waves is less at S-band than at X-band, thus the probability of targets being masked due to saturation is less
Precipitation response	The probability of detection of targets which lie *within* an area of precipitation is higher with S-band transmission than with X-band transmission
Attenuation in precipitation	In any given set of precipitation conditions, S-band transmissions will suffer less attenuation than those at X-band

years on, it is one of the two valves to survive the solid state revolution (the other is the cathode ray tube).

The magnetron is essentially a diode valve in which the anode is a copper cylinder into which are cut cavities (in the form of holes and slots) of very precise dimensions. The cathode is a pillar located along the

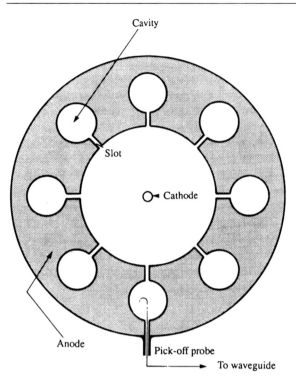

Figure 2.6 The cavity magnetron

central axis of the cylinder. A horseshoe magnet applies an extremely powerful magnetic field which acts along the axis of the cylinder. In the absence of the magnetic field one might expect electrons to flow, in an orderly fashion, radially from the cathode to the anode when a pulse is applied to the cathode. Because the magnetic field created by the permanent magnet is at right angles to the electric field created by the pulse, the electrons are deflected from the path which would take them directly to the anode (an application of the motor principle). Many electrons will eventually reach the anode only after a complex oscillatory journey in which their paths may alternately be directed toward and away from the anode and their speed increased and decreased. The movement of each electron will be further affected by the electromagnetic influence of the millions of other electrons moving in its vicinity. The effect is extremely complex but it can be summarized by saying that if the change of electron velocity

is regular and repetitive then there will be associated with such change a sympathetic fluctuating electromagnetic field. If this is of sufficiently high frequency, it will be capable of radiation into space. There are certain limits of steady electric field (provided by the modulator pulse) and steady magnetic field (provided by the permanent magnet) outside which oscillation will not take place. However, if values are selected which lie within the appropriate limits, the frequency of the oscillations that develop is determined by the physical dimensions of the cavities.

Of the energy supplied to the magnetron, less than half contributes to the maintenance of the oscillations during transmission. Much of the remainder is dissipated as heat in sufficient quantity to require the fitting of cooling fins to the magnetron assembly. It follows that the temperature of the magnetron will increase quite rapidly during the warm-up period (usually considered to be about half an hour) which follows the initial switching on, with a consequent change in the size of the cavities because of expansion of the copper cylinder. The transmitted radio frequency is subject to progressive change during this period. This has important implications when consideration is given to maintaining the receiver in tune (see Sections 2.5.1.3 and 6.2.4.2). Systems which comply with the IMO Performance Standards will have a 'stand-by' condition (see Section 6.7) in which the magnetron is kept warm by means of a conventional valve heater while the magnetron is not being used for transmission. When the system is returned to the transmitting condition, the supplementary heating is reduced or removed as the natural heating returns. During this transition period a similar drift in frequency can be expected.

The output from the magnetron is picked up from one of the cavities by a small probe which couples the radar pulse to the waveguide by means of which it is conducted to the aerial.

2.3.4 Selection of PRF and pulse length and their relationship with range scale

In preceding sections of this chapter it has been suggested that there is a relationship between PRF, pulse length and range scale. A study of Table 2.1, which shows some representative values, will indicate that such an association does exist. Now that both PRF and pulse length have been described, it is appropriate to discuss why the three quantities should be interdependent.

For any given range scale the period between pulses (PRP) must be at least as long as the timebase for that range scale so that the spot has time to write the current radial line and return to the origin of the display before the next line is initiated (or, in the case of digital storage, to allow sufficient time for the range data to be read into the memory in real time). If the pulse repetition period was made equal to the timebase, ambiguity would arise because echoes from a range in excess of the chosen range scale might well arrive during the next timebase (see Section 2.2.4). A time delay, known as the receiver rest time, must thus be inserted between the completion of one timebase and the commencement of the next in an attempt to reduce to a minimum the probability of this happening. The combined length of the timebase and the receiver rest period must be sufficiently long to ensure that, other than in exceptional circumstances (see Section 3.9.6), all echoes that will be returned from any given pulse arrive before the next pulse is transmitted. This defines a minimum pulse repetition period and thus a maximum PRF for any given range scale.

However, to define the minimum acceptable pulse repetition period, an estimate must be made of the maximum range from which it is reasonable to expect echo returns. This range is dependent on, among other factors, the transmitted pulse length (see Sections 2.3.2.1, 2.5.2.4 and 3.2.1), which is one of the variables with which we are presently concerned. Clearly, in estimating the necessary rest period, consideration must be given to the pulse length which is to be employed on the chosen range scale. Longer pulse lengths will increase the maximum range from which returns can be reasonably expected (see Sections 2.5.2.4, 3.2.1 and 3.2.3) and thus necessitate a longer receiver rest period, a longer pulse repetition period and hence a lower PRF. This represents a major reason why each available pulse length is associated with a particular PRF (see Table 2.1).

The pattern which emerges from Table 2.1 is that the long pulses are used on the longer range scales and are associated with the low PRF, while the short pulses are used on the short range scales and are associated with the high PRF.

While the selection of short pulse will reduce the probability of detection of any one return (see Section 2.5.2.4), it should be noted that this will tend to be offset to a limited extent by the fact that the use of a higher PRF will result in more pulses being fired at any given target.

2.4   Aerial principles

The aerial unit is required to focus the transmitted energy into a beam, rotate the beam at an appropriate angular speed, relay rotation and heading marker data to the display and intercept returning signals within the same directional limits as those specified for the transmitted beam. Each of these functions will now be discussed in detail.

2.4.1   Aerial concepts

It has already been established in general terms that the beam should be narrow in the horizontal plane and wide in the vertical plane (see Section 2.2.2). Before these requirements are studied in detail it is helpful to consider some basic aerial concepts.

2.4.1.1   The point radiating source

This is an ideal concept which cannot be realized in practice but offers a useful basis on which to explain radiation from an aerial. The point source is a source of radiation which is assumed to have no dimensions. Clearly any source must have some dimensions but the farther the target lies from the source of radiation the less significant the dimensions become and the more closely any observed effects will approach those which could be expected from a point source.

2.4.1.2   The isotropic source

This is an extension of the concept of the point source and assumes a point source which radiates uniformly in all directions. Again, this cannot be realized in practice because any practical aerial will radiate better in some directions than in others. In fact the essential characteristic of a radar aerial is that it does precisely that, radiating particularly well in one chosen direction. However, a convenient measure of its directional ability can be obtained by comparing the radiation from the practical aerial with that which would be obtained from an isotropic source.

2.4.1.3   Power density

As the power delivered from the transmitter to the aerial moves outward in space it becomes distributed over a continuously increasing area and thus the power available to be reflected by any intervening target decreases progressively. Power density is a measure (W/m^2) of the power per unit area available at any location in the area of influence of an aerial.

To illustrate the concept, consider a *lossless* isotropic radiator to be situated in space. If a pulse is transmitted, the power will travel outward, being uniformly distributed over the inside surface of a sphere of ever increasing radius. If the power delivered by the transmitter to the aerial is W watts then the power density at a distance r metres from the aerial will be given by the power W divided by the surface area of a sphere of radius r. This can be written as

$$\text{power density} = P_r = \frac{W}{4\pi r^2}$$

This relationship forms part of the radar range equation set out in Chapter 3 which shows the theoretical relationship that exists between transmitter power and target detection range.

It can be seen from the above that in the case of an isotropic source the power density is the same in all directions, whereas for a practical aerial it will be greater in some directions than in others. The shape of a directional beam can be illustrated by plotting the power density values for different directions from the aerial and this gives rise to what is known as a *power*

pattern. However, a power pattern is only valid for one particular range.

2.4.1.4   Radiation intensity

For many purposes this is a more convenient measure of the radiation from an aerial because it is independent of the range at which it is measured. Radiation intensity is defined as the power per unit solid angle, i.e. the power incident on that portion of the surface of a sphere which subtends an angle of one radian at the centre of the sphere in both the horizontal and the vertical planes. To illustrate the concept, consider again the case of an isotropic radiator located in space. If the power delivered to the aerial is W watts then as it travels outwards it will be uniformly distributed over the surface area of a sphere of ever expanding radius but which subtends a constant angle of 4π radians at the centre of the sphere. Thus the radiation intensity at any point in the field of an isotropic radiator is given by

$$\text{radiation intensity} = U = \frac{W}{4\pi}$$

In the same way as described for power density, radiation intensity can be plotted for different directions from the aerial and this gives rise to what is known as a *radiation pattern*. It is clearly a three-dimensional figure but in dealing with radar beams it will be unnecessary to attempt to show all three dimensions simultaneously; it is more convenient to use a two-dimensional figure to illustrate either the horizontal beam pattern or the vertical beam pattern as is appropriate to the topic under discussion. Figure 2.7 illustrates the concept, showing the horizontal radiation pattern for an isotropic source and, for comparison purposes, that of a directional aerial.

The radiation in any given direction is represented by the length of a line drawn from the origin, in the chosen direction, which terminates at its intersection with the pattern. The line can be measured in watts per unit solid angle, but as we are principally concerned with representation of shape it is more convenient to use what is known as a 'normalized pattern', in which units are unnecessary. In the normalized pattern the

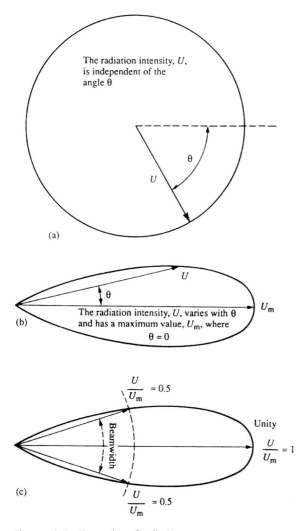

The radiation intensity, U, is independent of the angle θ

(a)

The radiation intensity, U, varies with θ and has a maximum value, U_m, where $\theta = 0$

(b)

$\frac{U}{U_m} = 0.5$

Unity

$\frac{U}{U_m} = 1$

Beamwidth

$\frac{U}{U_m} = 0.5$

(c)

Figure 2.7 Examples of radiation patterns

(a) A radiation pattern for an isotropic source
(b) An absolute pattern for a directional source
(c) A normalized pattern for a directional source

the outset, but it is important to appreciate that while the patterns have the same shape if normalized, the absolute patterns are not measured in the same units. When normalized, the shape produced by both patterns is commonly referred to as an *antenna (or aerial) radiation pattern*.

2.4.1.5 Beamwidth

In considering the shape of the beam we are particularly concerned with its angular width. The beamwidth is defined as the angular limits within which the power does not fall to less than half its maximum value at the same range. This is readily extracted from the normalized radiation pattern as illustrated by Figure 2.7(c).

2.4.1.6 Aerial gain

This is a measure of the effectiveness with which the aerial can radiate the power delivered to it by the transmitter, within specified angular limits of azimuth and elevation. Aerial gain is given the symbol G_0 and is defined as

$$G_0 = \frac{\text{maximum radiation intensity from the chosen aerial}}{\text{maximum radiation intensity from a reference aerial}}$$

The reference aerial is assumed to be a *lossless* isotropic radiator supplied with the same power level.

Clearly the aerial gain is a ratio having no units. Its maximum possible value would occur in the ideal situation in which none of the energy supplied by the transmitter was wasted and all of it was concentrated within the infinitely narrow limits of a straight line. In practice this ideal cannot be achieved because some of the transmitter power will be dissipated in overcoming electrical resistance in the aerial and the energy cannot be concentrated along a single line. However, good design techniques make it possible to reduce the electrical losses in the aerial to very small values, and the special aerials used in marine radar can, where required, concentrate the power within very narrow limits of azimuth.

maximum value is considered to be unity and the other values represent the ratio of the radiation intensity in the chosen direction to that of the maximum radiation intensity. It is of interest that if a power pattern is normalized it will give the same shape as the normalized radiation pattern. This might well have been stated at

An alternative indicator of the measure of concentration achieved by the aerial is called *directive gain* or *directivity*. This is given the symbol D and is defined as

$$D = \frac{\text{maximum radiation intensity}}{\text{average radiation intensity}}$$

This quantity is independent of the aerial losses and is thus a perfect merit figure for describing the ability of the aerial to concentrate the power in a narrow beam.

Both aerial gain and directive gain are of interest to the radar designer, but their numerical values are so close to one another as to render the difference somewhat academic as far as the civil marine radar observer is concerned. However, it would be wrong in principle to use directive gain rather than aerial gain in stating the radar range equation (see Section 3.1) and hence both terms are defined here in the interests of rigour.

2.4.1.7   Receiving characteristic

In the above introduction the antenna has been treated essentially as a transmitting element. It must be remembered that in marine radar the same aerial is used for transmission and reception. By the principle of reciprocity, whatever is said in relation to the directional nature of transmission will apply equally well to reception.

2.4.1.8   Polarization

The energy travelling outward from the aerial is in the form of an electromagnetic wave having electric and magnetic fields which are at right angles to one another and to the direction of propagation. The polarization is defined as the direction of the plane of the electric field. To comply with the IMO Performance Standards (see Section 11.2.1), all marine radars using the X-band must be capable of being operated with horizontal polarization, in order to display radar beacons. Historically, circular polarization (see Section 3.7.4.6) was offered for a time by one civil marine radar manufacturer but at the present time it is unusual to find any aerial which is not solely designed for horizontal polarization.

2.4.2   The horizontal beamwidth

To achieve the directional transmission necessary for the accurate measurement of bearings (see Section 1.3) the horizontal beamwidth must be narrow. This also has the effect of producing very high aerial gain by concentrating all the available power in one direction at a time. Further, such directional transmission is necessary in order to give the system the ability to display separately targets which are at the same range and closely spaced in bearing. This property is known as *bearing discrimination* and will be discussed under 'Display principles' in Section 2.6.5.6.

The wavelengths of the electromagnetic energy contained in radar pulses are much longer than those of visible light but in many ways the radiation exhibits characteristics which are akin to the laws of optics. Until the late 1950s, designers exploited this resemblance by using a parabolic reflector to focus the radar beam, much in the same way as a polished mirror is used in a motorcar headlight or in an Aldis lamp to focus a beam of light. Although in civil marine radar this technique has now been superseded by direct emission from slots cut in one face of a length of waveguide (described as *slotted waveguide*), it is still used in many other surveillance applications. It is worthy of some study as it demonstrates in a relatively simple way how the radiation can be focused into a narrow beam. Further, it provides a platform on which to base some understanding of the modern slotted waveguide aerial which produces a horizontal beam that has an almost identical pattern but which uses a direct emission technique, the mechanics of which are somewhat more difficult to visualize (see Section 2.4.2.2).

2.4.2.1   The parabolic reflector

The significant optical property of the parabolic reflector is that if a point source of light is placed at a particular point, known as the focus, which lies on the axis of symmetry, all the rays of light striking the mirror will be reflected parallel to the axis. Such an ideal situation would produce a perfectly parallel pencil beam of light (Figure 2.8(a)). If radar microwave energy is used instead of light, the results are remarkably similar. However, because in practice the energy cannot be emitted

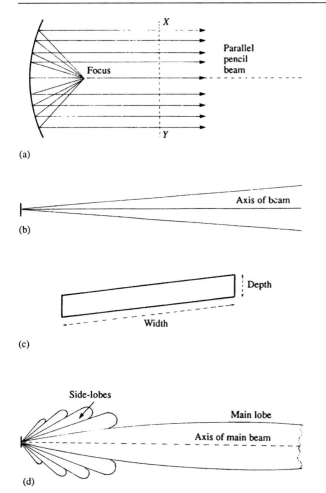

Figure 2.8 Focusing the horizontal beam with a parabolic reflector

(a)   Parabolic reflector
(b)   Fan-shaped beam
(c)   Aperture
(d)   Radiation pattern produced by a practical aerial

necessary for reasons of impedance matching which are beyond the scope of this text. The device was known variously as a flare, a hog horn or simply a horn. The latter term is quite descriptive because, in its effect on microwaves, the behaviour of the device is somewhat analogous to that of an acoustic horn. The result of using a source whose dimensions are not negligible is the production of a horizontal beam which tends to diverge slightly in a fan shape and is illustrated in simple form by Figure 2.8(b).

A further departure from the ideal arises because the wavelengths used in marine radar are not negligible when compared with the size of the reflector, as would be the case with visible light.

The practical radar beam has a more complex form than the simple fan illustrated in Figure 2.8(b). An understanding of why this should be so is assisted by further consideration of Figure 2.8(a). A second geometrical property of the parabola is that if any line such as XY is drawn perpendicular to the axis of symmetry of the parabola, then the distance along any reflective path from the focus to that line will be the same irrespective of the reflective path which is followed. The implication of this is that if all rays of energy were in phase when they left the source (which will be the case) they will be in phase as they cross this line.

The line XY has been drawn some little distance away from the parabola for the sake of clarity. If it were to be moved so that it just touched the ends of the parabola then it would bridge the 'mouth' of the reflector. Thus all the rays will leave the 'mouth' in phase with one another. The aerial thus behaves as if the radiation were emerging from a rectangular surface whose width is equal to that of the length of the line XY and whose depth is the vertical extent of the paraboloid (see Figure 2.8(c)). This area is known as the 'aperture' and its dimensions in relation to the wavelength determine the geometry of the beam. The horizontal beamwidth is determined by the width of the aperture and the vertical beamwidth by its depth. Source and reflector thus behave like a rectangular aperture from which emerges a plane wave with uniform phase-distribution across the aperture.

It can be shown that uniform phase-distribution across a plane aperture will produce a radiation pattern

from a single point, it follows that most of the energy originates from points which are very close to, but not at, the focus. In physical form the source looked like a reversed nozzle (see Figure 2.10) and was produced by flaring out the end of the waveguide so that, while the horizontal dimension was increased slightly, the vertical dimension was increased considerably. The flaring was of the form shown in Figure 2.8(d). It will be noticed that most of the radiation is concentrated in a central main beam or lobe, but that some radiation manifests itself as a series of subsidiary beams, known as side lobes, the maximum radiation intensity of each of which is considerably less than that of the main lobe. The radiation intensity of individual side lobes decreases as their angle from the axis of the main beam increases.

The distribution of the radiation in the lobe pattern which is produced by uniform phase-distribution across a plane aperture can only be fully justified by a mathematical analysis which is beyond the scope of this text. However, by some more simple considerations it can be illustrated that such a pattern is not entirely unexpected.

If one considers a point P (Figure 2.9) which lies on the normal to the aperture, it is reasonable to accept that the distance from P to any point on the aperture is the same provided that P is a distant point. For the purposes of this simple explanation very short ranges will not be considered and hence the distance PY will be of the order of cables if not miles. The

aperture width is likely to be 2–3 metres at the most, and hence the line XYZ can be considered to be a portion of the circumference of a very large circle. It can be concluded that all radiation arriving at P will be of uniform phase and will produce constructive interference, i.e. all the individual signal strengths added together will produce a strong resultant.

By contrast, consider a point Q which lies at an angle to the normal such that the distance XQ exceeds the distance ZQ by one complete wavelength. (At a frequency of 9400 MHz the difference need only be 3.19 cm). The distance XQ will thus exceed the distance YQ by half a wavelength and hence radiation emitted from X will arrive at Q antiphase to that emitted from Y. Each radiating element of the aperture between X and Y can be associated with a corresponding element between Y and Z which, together with it, will produce antiphase signals at point Q. It follows that at point Q, and anywhere along the line YQ produced, destructive interference will result in the nett radiation being zero. Hence the radiation intensity falls from maximum on the normal to the aperture (the axis of the main beam), to zero at some angle defined

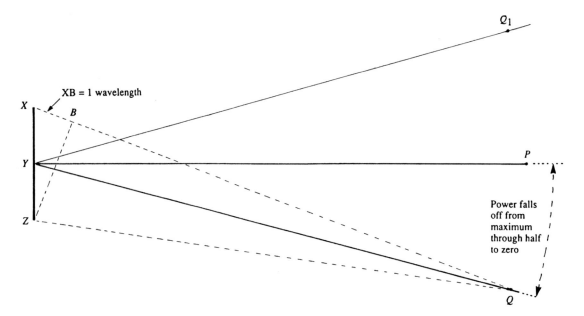

Figure 2.9 Aerial interference pattern

by point Q. Since the figure is symmetrical, a similar reduction in radiation will take place on the other side of the axis to the limit indicated by Q_1. It is self-evident that somewhere between these two angular limits must lie the half power points which by convention define the limits of the horizontal beamwidth. A similar consideration for angles greater than PYQ will reveal the presence of the side lobes.

It can be shown that the horizontal beamwidth is given by the expression

$$\text{HBW (in degrees)} = K \times \frac{\text{transmitted wavelength}}{\text{aperture width}}$$

where K is a constant which has a theoretical value of 51. Authorities differ on the value of this constant that can be achieved in practice. Clearly there are limits to the precision with which any aerial unit, be it parabola or waveguide, can be constructed. However, it is sufficient to say that for practical purposes a value for K of 70 adequately describes the horizontal beam produced by modern civil marine radars using a slotted waveguide aerial.

The important principle is that the horizontal beamwidth is directly proportional to transmitted wavelength and inversely proportional to the effective width of the aerial aperture, i.e. the horizontal beamwidth is a function of the ratio of wavelength to aerial width. The order of the quantities involved is best illustrated by two numerical examples in which a value of $K = 70$ will be assumed.

Example 2.1   Calculate the aerial width necessary to achieve a horizontal beam width of 2° with X-band transmission at 9400 MHz.

$$300 \times 10^6 = \text{frequency} \times \text{wavelength}$$

$$\text{thus wavelength} = \frac{300 \times 10^6}{9400 \times 10^6}$$

i.e. wavelength $= 0.032\,\text{m}$ (3.2 cm)

$$\text{HBW} = K \times \frac{\text{transmitted wavelength}}{\text{aperture width}}$$

$$\text{thus } 2 = \frac{70 \times 0.032}{\text{aperture width}}$$

$$\text{hence aperture width} = \frac{70 \times 0.032}{2}$$

i.e. aperture width $= 1.12\,\text{m}$

Therefore to produce a horizontal beamwidth of 2° with X-band transmission at 9400 MHz, an aerial width of not less than 1.12 m is necessary.

Example 2.2   A marine radar aerial operating in the S-band with a wavelength of 9.87 cm has a width of 3.8 m. Calculate the horizontal beamwidth.

$$\text{HBW} = \frac{K \times \text{tansmitted wavelength}}{\text{aperture width}}$$

thus

$$\text{HBW} = 70 \times \frac{9.87 \times 10^{-2}}{3.8}$$

i.e. $\text{HBW} = 1.82°$

Therefore a marine radar aerial of width 3.8 m, transmitting a wavelength of 9.87 cm, will produce a horizontal beamwidth of 1.82 degrees.

It is clear from the examples why the internationally agreed frequencies (see Section 2.3.3.1) allocated to civil marine radar were bound to be of an order which would give a wavelength of not more than about 10 cm. Longer wavelengths would require an aerial size so large as to preclude practical installation on a merchant ship.

It is evident that for the same horizontal beamwidth an S-band aerial must be three times the width of a corresponding X-band aerial. In general, available S-band aerials are not as large as this and hence X-band systems normally have narrower beamwidths. To comply with the IMO Performance Standards (see Section 11.2.1), a horizontal beamwidth of not more than 2.5° is required. High speed craft are an exception in that S-band radars (only) can be up to 4° (see Section 11.2). Radars designed for use on large merchant ships normally offer horizontal beamwidths somewhere in the range 0.65° to 2° for X-band operation and 1.7° to 2° in the case of S-band.

Figure 2.10   Early parabolic reflectors

(a)   The single cheese aerial
(b)   The tilted parabolic cylinder

Figure 2.10 shows two examples of parabolic reflectors. These are included partly for historical interest and partly because they illustrate much of what has been said in this section.

The single cheese aerial is representative of the early days of marine radar and its 'mouth' clearly illustrates the concept of 'aperture'. Two major problems associated with the cheese aerial were the accumulation of dirt within the cheese and the shadowing along the axis of the main beam caused by the hog horn. These shortcomings were removed by the development of the tilted parabolic cylinder. In this design the reflecting surface was tilted so that the horn could be located below the parabola and therefore out of the path of the reflected energy. The parabolic surface was made circular in a vertical sense in order to produce a wide vertical beam (see Section 2.4.3). It must be appreciated that the aperture in this case is the area of the parabola projected on to a plane surface perpen-

dicular to the axis of the radiated beam and not the total surface area of the reflector.

2.4.2.2   The slotted waveguide aerial

It can be shown that if a narrow slot is cut in an infinite sheet of conducting material, and an alternating signal is applied across the slot at its midlength, it will act as an effective radiator of electromagnetic waves provided that the frequency of the applied signal corresponds with a wavelength which is approximately twice the length of the slot, i.e. if the slot length is approximately half a wavelength. It may be difficult to visualize how such an effect can take place and there is no simple explanation. Those readers who wish to study the effect in more detail are referred to a text dealing with antenna theory. For a practical understanding it will be found sufficient to consider that the slot behaves like a short radio aerial with the exception of the fact that the polarization of the emitted wave is perpendicular to the long side of the slot, i.e. a vertical slot will radiate a horizontally polarized wave.

In the slotted waveguide aerial, the principle of the slot radiator is exploited by cutting a number of slots in one side of a length of waveguide. The slots interrupt the pattern of alternating current flow along the wall of the guide and hence a signal is effectively applied across the centre of each slot. The intact remainder of the waveguide approximates to the infinite conducting sheet. Although the principle assumes an infinite sheet, quite effective results are obtained with comparatively small areas. As the slots measure approximately half a wavelength along their major axis, the conditions for radiation are fulfilled.

The slots are spaced along the length of the guide in such a way as to ensure that all slots are excited in equiphase. The slotted waveguide aerial thus constitutes a large number of radiators having a uniform phase distribution across a plane aperture. This will produce a radiation pattern having the same shape as that illustrated in Figure 2.8(d). Further, the horizontal beamwidth of the pattern can be described by the same relationship between transmitted wavelength and aperture width as was set out in Section 2.4.2.1. However, if the waveguide is fed from one end, as is normally the case in civil marine radars, the pattern will be rotated by a small amount away from the feed end of the guide so that the axis of the main lobe will make a horizontal angle of approximately 3° to 4° with the normal to the aperture. This angle is frequency-dependent and is known as the *angle of squint*. It should present no problem provided that the correct steps are taken to check regularly that the display heading marker occurs at the instant that the axis of the main lobe crosses the fore-and-aft line in the forward direction (see Section 6.9.9). However, it is important to appreciate that the axis of the main beam will therefore not be fore-and-aft when the long axis of the aerial is athwartships.

Figure 2.11(a) shows a detail of the aerial waveguide with a typical pattern of slots. For a horizontally polarized wave one might expect all the slots to be vertical. In practice, the first few slots at the feed end and the last few at the remote end are indeed vertical but between these limits they are inclined to the vertical by a small angle which varies across the face of the guide. Alternate slots are inclined in opposite directions. The need for this refinement of the slot pattern arises from electrical impedance considerations which are beyond the scope of this book. However, it should be noted that despite the angling of the slots, the emitted radiation is horizontally polarized because the horizontally polarized components of radiation from all slots reinforce one another (they are all substantially vertical) while the vertically polarized components of radiation from alternate slots cancel (this is because they are angled in opposite directions).

Figure 2.11(b) shows a full slotted waveguide aerial assembly of a type which has the advantage that all of the parts can be clearly seen. The width of the aperture is determined by the length of the slotted unit. In the vertical plane the aperture is bounded by conducting sheets forming a horn which guides the waves from the narrow vertical dimension of the slotted unit to an aperture of a depth consistent with the correct vertical beamwidth (see Section 2.4.3). A sheet of glass reinforced plastic (GRP – which is often referred to by the proprietary name of fibreglass) protects the aperture from the ingress of water and dirt. GRP is transparent to radar waves (see Section 3.3.3). (The GRP con-

Figure 2.11 The slotted waveguide aerial

(a) Detail of waveguide slots
(b) Slotted waveguide aerial
(c) Enclosed slotted waveguide aerial

struction of the aerial window may include graphite to improve its transparency in addition to a polarizing filter to prevent the entry of stray unwanted vertically polarized waves.) Most paints are not transparent to radar energy and the cover commonly carries the legend 'do not paint'. As illustrated in Figure 2.11(c), a modern practice is to enclose the entire assembly in a GRP envelope.

The slotted waveguide aerial superseded the parabolic reflector for a variety of reasons, important among which was its ability to produce direct emission and to offer higher aerial gain by reducing the power radiated in the side-lobes. Such radiation not only represents a loss of power but can give rise to spurious echoes (see Section 3.9.4).

2.4.3 The vertical beamwidth

It was established in Section 2.2.2 that the minimum vertical beamwidth for compliance with the IMO Performance Standards was 20° because of the need to maintain the required performance when rolling and pitching. A further factor in favour of a wide vertical beam is that it reduces the possibility that a target at close range will escape detection by passing under the lower limit of the beam (see Section 3.2.4). The production of a wide beam presents no problems, but if it is allowed to become too wide the radiation intensity will become unacceptably low. Commercially available aerials normally offer values which lie in the approximate range 20° to 25°, i.e. just a little more than is required to comply with the performance standard, although a value as high as 30° may be encountered.

The aperture is much smaller in the vertical plane than in the horizontal and thus one would expect the vertical radiation pattern to be characterized by a wide main lobe flanked by side-lobes. If the aerial were placed in space this expectation would be fulfilled and, neglecting the side-lobes, the radiation pattern would be of the form shown by Figure 2.12(a). However, as the aerial is placed a relatively short distance above the surface of the sea, the pattern is modified because much of the energy which would form the lower half of the lobe in free space (see Figure 2.12(b)) is reflected from the sea and forms an interference pattern with that energy which has not been reflected.

Figure 2.12(c), which is not to scale, illustrates how the interference pattern is created. Consider two rays of energy which arrive at point P, one having travelled directly and the other having been reflected from the surface of the sea at B. Let us suppose that the reflected path length is one half wavelength longer than the direct path length. It can be assumed that a 180° phase shift takes place on reflection at the sea surface and hence the signals arriving at point P will be in phase. (180° phase shift due to path difference and 180° phase shift due to reflection.) Thus, assuming that there is no loss of energy on reflection, the signal strength at point P will, due to the addition of the reflected signal, be twice what it would have been if the aerial were

located in free space. If the reflected path is produced further it must in due course intersect with a further direct ray at a point at which the path difference is a full wavelength. At that point there will be 180° phase difference (360° due to path difference and 180° due to phase shift on reflection) between the direct and reflected signals and the resultant signal strength will be zero. Clearly this pattern of maxima and minima must repeat itself with height.

Understanding of the form of the pattern can be assisted by noting that the signal conditions at point P, while arising in the way described above, are exactly the same as would be the case if the aerial were located in free space and a second aerial, transmitting in antiphase, were located at A_1 such that $AX = A_1X$. This arrangement (with the exception of the 180° phase shift and the restricted vertical beamwidth) is analogous to the layout of the transmitting stations in hyperbolic position-fixing systems such as Loran, where A and A_1 correspond to the transmitting stations and the distance $A - A_1$ to the baseline. All points having the same path difference will lie along a hyperbola and the pattern of maxima and minima in the vertical plane will take the form of a family of such hyperbolae. This is illustrated by Figure 2.12(d), but it must be appreciated that the analogy should not be pursued very close to the baseline because of the restricted vertical beamwidth.

As a result of the existence of alternate maxima and minima the single main lobe in free space is broken up into a family of lobes of the form shown in Figure 2.12(e). The diagram shows only a few lobes in order to illustrate the pattern of maxima and zeros. In practice, for X-band transmission, there will be approximately 33 lobes per metre of scanner height. Thus the lobes are much more numerous and more closely spaced than could possibly be illustrated in a diagram of reasonable size. For S-band signals the figure is approximately 10 lobes per metre of scanner height. Thus the lobes are much more numerous and more closely spaced than could possibly be illustrated in a diagram of reasonable size. For S-band signals the figure is approximately 10 lobes per metre of scanner height. Thus the S-band vertical pattern has

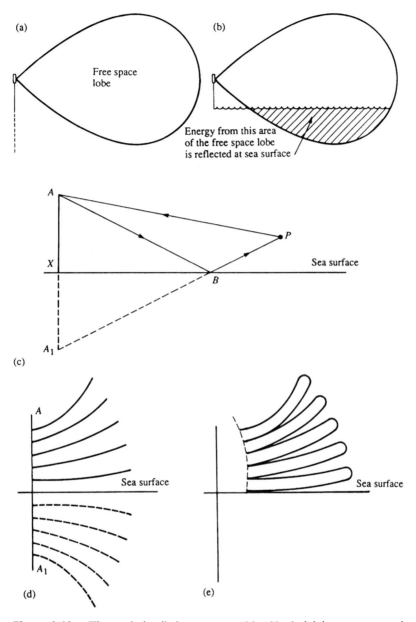

Figure 2.12   The vertical radiation pattern
(a)   Main vertical lobe in free space
(b)   Main vertical lobe close to sea surface
(c)   The interference pattern
(d)   Hyperbolic pattern

(e)   Vertical lobe pattern – only a few lobes are shown. In practice, the number of lobes per metre of scanner height is approximately:
At X-band 33
At S-band 10

Note   The horizontal extent represented in (e) is 2 × that represented in (b) fewer, more widely spaced lobes. The radiation intensity along the axis of a lobe is twice what it would be in free space and an area of zero radiation lies between each pair of lobes. It can be shown that the elevation of the lowest maxima in degrees is approximately 14 times the ratio of wavelength to aerial height. For X-band transmission with an aerial height of 20 metres the lowest maxima will be approximately 8.5 metres above the sea at a range of 12 miles. This gives some idea of the coarseness of the pattern when considered in relationship to many practical targets.

2.4.4 Aerial rotation rate

To comply with the current IMO Performance Standards the scan (i.e. the rotation of the beam) must be clockwise (as seen from above), continuous, and automatic through 360° of azimuth at a rate of not less than 12 rpm. However, for high speed craft a rate of not less than 40 rpm is specified. The equipment is required to operate satisfactorily in relative wind speeds of up to 100 knots. This is achieved by rotating the directional aerial by means of an electric motor driving through a reduction gear train. The speed of rotation of the aerial is a significant factor in the overall performance of a marine radar system.

It will be noted that there is a lower limit to the permitted aerial rotation rate, but no maximum is specified. One can speculate that those who drew up the standards concluded that the cost of manufacturing and maintaining very high speed aerial rotation would create a natural upper limit.

The new IMO standards (see Section 11.2.1) for installations on new vessels built on or after 2008 no longer specify the minimum rotation speed for both conventional and high speed craft. The reason for this is so that new technologies such as static antenna systems (see Section 2.4.7) can be introduced. Such devices need not rotate at a constant speed in order to perform with greatest efficiency. Conventional radar systems will still continue, but the onus is on the manufacturer to select a rotation speed which meets the tracking and detection standards. It is thought that conventional radar antennae will probably continue at current rotation speeds.

If an aerial rotates at 12 rpm, the echo position is updated once every 5 seconds either as a repainting of the echo or as a rewriting of range and bearing data into memory. Clearly a digital memory will retain the echo data until overwritten, but the displayed echo on a PPI will only remain visible on the screen for a period determined by the strength of the echo and the persistence of the screen (see Sections 1.3.3 and 2.6.1.2). Hence if too low an aerial speed is employed, weak echoes, or possibly an entire sector of the picture may fade completely before being refreshed by a further paint on the next scan. While fading due to low scanner speed can be offset by using longer tube persistence, this may bring with it further problems associated with afterglow when range scale or picture presentation is changed. Excessive afterglow is a particular problem when an unstabilized orientation is used (see Section 1.4.1). The choice of aerial rotation rate and tube persistence is made at the design stage and in almost all civil marine radars is such that, except in the case of echoes very close to the threshold of detection, the picture persists for at least the period of one aerial rotation. However, worldwide this is not invariably the case.

An increase in aerial rotation rate will reduce the update period and allow shorter tube persistence. However such an increase cannot be pursued indefinitely because it reduces the time for which the beam actually dwells on any given target. Consider an aerial which is rotated at N rpm and has a horizontal beamwidth of HBW degrees. The time, in seconds, taken for the beam to rotate through HBW degrees is given by

$$t = HBW/6N$$

This also represents the time taken for the beam to sweep across a point target (a target whose dimensions can be regarded as negligible: like a point radiation source (see Section 2.4.1.1), a point target is a theoretical concept which cannot be realized in practice but it is a useful aid to the analysis of some aspects of radar performance). In the time t seconds the radar will transmit a number of pulses given by

$$S = PRF \times t$$

where S represents the theoretical maximum number of pulses which could strike a point target. Thus we have

$$S = PRF \times \frac{HBW}{6N}$$

The greater the number of pulses which are fired at a target, the greater is the probability that one or more of these pulses will be reflected from the target and return a detectable echo. Thus the greater the value of S the higher the probability of detection. It can be seen from the above relationship that an increase in aerial rotation rate will tend to reduce the number of possible strikes per point target. Thus N and PRF are interrelated and a suitable combination must be chosen at the design stage. Clearly a low value of N can be offset by increasing the PRF but the possibility of second trace echoes (see Sections 2.2.4 and 3.9.6) places an upper limit on this option. Such a limit is a function of range scale and pulse length (see Section 2.3.4).

In recognition of the fact that not every strike will necessarily produce a detectable echo, because of the various other factors which can reduce the probability of target detection (see Chapter 3), it is generally believed that the radar design should have a capability of producing not less than 10 strikes per point target. Consider the following numerical example:

Example 2.3 A marine radar system has a PRF of 1000 and a horizontal beamwidth of 2°. Calculate the aerial rotation rate necessary to achieve at least 10 strikes per point target.

$$S = PRF \times \frac{HBW}{6N}$$

thus

$$10 = 1000 \times \frac{2}{6N}$$

hence

$$N = 1000 \times \frac{2}{60}$$

i.e.

$$N = 33.3 \, \text{rpm}$$

Thus an aerial rotation rate of 33.3 rpm or less is necessary to achieve at least 10 strikes per point target with a PRF of 1000 and a horizontal beamwidth of 2°.

In the late 1960s a radar system was produced with the expectionally high aerial rotation rate of 80 rpm. This had the advantage of improving the overall picture brightness because, in the very short update period of three quarters of a second, the brightness of an echo had barely begun to decay before the echo was repainted. The very high rotation rate necessitated a similarly exceptionally high PRF of 6000 on the short range scales.

A further point of interest is that if the rotation speed is progressively increased, a speed will be reached at which the observer ceases to be conscious of the traditional rotating trace and sees merely a steady picture. In theory this will happen when the update period is so short that the decay in echo brightness between paints is not noticeable. What is noticeable is to some extent dependent on expectation. For example, with a very high aerial rotation rate an observer using the picture for navigation and collision avoidance might not be conscious of the rotating trace, whereas someone looking specifically to see if there was a rotating trace might well discern it. This is a fair description of the effect at about 80 rpm.

The above idea does not seem to have found general favour with radar designers and subsequently no civil marine system has offered aerial rotation rates even approaching the value quoted above. Most modern civil marine radar systems use aerial rotation rates in the range 22 to 33 rpm, although high speed craft and some small boats use rates as high as 45 rpm. As the pursuit of the bright steady picture has now taken the road of the digital PPI and raster-scan displays, it seems unlikely that high aerial rates will be seen in the predictable future.

2.4.5 Aerial and display rotation link

A signal which represents the rotation of the aerial must be relayed to the display in order to maintain sympathetic rotation of the trace and/or update the aerial angle data in the digital memory. The signal can be analogue (e.g. a fluctuating voltage) or digital (e.g. a succession of binary numbers) in its form. However, even where a digital signal is required, it is common to find that an analogue signal is transmitted to the display and there converted to digital form. It is therefore appropriate to consider analogue transmission at this stage and subsequently to discuss the conversion to digital form in Section 2.6.6.4, which deals with display principles.

A variety of methods have been and still are used to transmit rotation from aerial to display. Modern methods fall into two broad categories; those which generate a fluctuating signal whose instantaneous value and polarity is a function of aerial angle, and those which generate a pulse train whose repetition rate is a function of instantaneous aerial speed.

2.4.5.1 Synchro system

A synchro system is suitably representative of the first category and will be described in block diagram form (see Figure 2.13).

The aerial element of the system is known as a synchro transmitter and consists of a rotor wound with many turns of wire and mounted so as to be able to rotate within a cylindrical chamber formed by a set of three fixed multi-turn windings having an angular separation of 120° and known as the stator. The rotor winding is energized with an alternating voltage of constant peak amplitude and thus by transformer action induces voltages in the three stator windings. The three values of induced voltage will form a unique combination for any given angular position of the rotor. If the rotor is driven on a 1:1 basis by the aerial, then the combination of voltages will constitute an

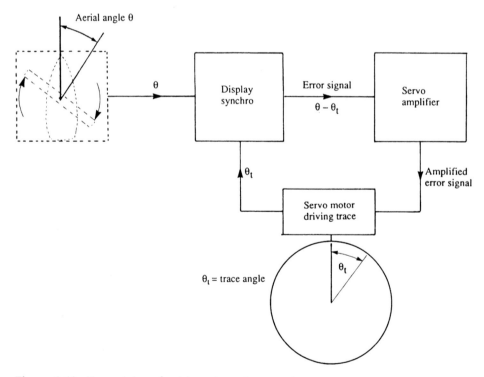

Figure 2.13 Transmission of aerial rotation using a synchro system

analogue representation of aerial angle because it will vary in sympathy with aerial rotation.

The display element of the system is known as a synchro transformer or receiver and is constructed in a similar way to the synchro transmitter. Each stator winding of the display transformer is connected to its partner in the aerial unit and thus the voltages induced in the synchro transmitter are reproduced in the display unit. Hence we have in the display, at any instant, a unique combination of three stator voltages which is a measure of aerial angle. The resultant of these voltages will be induced, by transformer action, in the winding of the synchro transformer rotor. For any given combination of stator voltages, the voltage so induced will, in both polarity and magnitude, depend on the relationship between the angle of the rotor in the aerial and that in the display. The voltage is known as the *error voltage* or *error signal* because it is a measure of the misalignment of the rotors. However, it is important to appreciate that when the misalignment is 90° the voltage induced in the display rotor will be zero. Clearly there are two zero positions. In the synchro case the ambiguity is resolved by the change of polarity which takes place at zero.

Until the late 1970s most (though not all) civil marine radar systems produced a rotating trace by means of a coil assembly which was rotated around the neck of the cathode ray tube (see Section 2.6.1.3) and many are still used at sea today. In such a system the rotor of the synchro transformer in the display is geared to the same motor as controls the rotation of the coil assembly which produces the rotating trace. This motor is driven by an amplified version of the error signal. This arrangement is known as a servo system (see Figure 2.13) and the factor by which the error signal is amplified is known as the gain of the servo amplifier.

To understand the operation of the servo system, consider initially that the synchro rotors are misaligned by 90° (not 270°!). The error signal will be zero. Let the aerial now be moved, in one step, through an angle of exactly 90° clockwise. The error signal will reach its maximum positive value and will cause the motor to drive the trace and the display synchro rotor rapidly clockwise. As the rotor rotates, the error signal

will decrease and, neglecting the effects of angular momentum and friction, the rotor and trace will come to rest when the error voltage is zero and they have both rotated through 90°. Thus the system causes the trace to rotate through the same angle as the aerial.

If the aerial is now rotated at constant angular speed, the trace will similarly rotate but with a small angular lag. The lag arises because the misalignment between the aerial synchro rotor and the display synchro rotor must differ by slightly more than 90° to produce an error signal to drive the servo motor. The magnitude of error signal, and hence the angular lag required to achieve any given constant speed of rotation, is determined by the frictional resistance offered by the servo motor and the associated trace drive mechanism. The angular lag increases with speed of rotation. The presence of the angular lag will not introduce a bearing error as long as it remains constant, because it will generate a constant error signal and a constant servo motor speed. This will produce a steady state condition in which, because the lag is constant, the trace rotation speed will be the same as that of the aerial. This satisfies the basic condition required for bearing measurement as described in Section 1.3.3.

In practice, the aerial will not turn at a perfectly constant rate as it will be subject to angular acceleration and deceleration due to, for example, variations in air resistance as it rotates in the wind. Under these circumstances the angular lag will vary and the design of the system must ensure that this does not introduce unacceptable bearing errors. The IMO Performance Standards (see Section 11.2.1) require that any means provided for obtaining bearings should enable the bearing of a target whose echo appears at the edge of the display to be measured with an accuracy of ±1° or better. Clearly this ±1° must represent the aggregate of the accuracy with which the echo is displayed and the instrument accuracy of the measuring facility. The question of bearing accuracy is discussed in detail in Section 6.9 but it is important at this stage to recognize that any errors introduced by variations in angular lag must be sufficiently small that, when aggregated with other error contributions, they result in an error of not more than 1°.

If the aerial temporarily accelerates by a small amount it will tend to leave the trace behind. However, with the increase in angular lag, the error signal will increase and hence promote an acceleration of the trace rotation. Ideally, in the interests of bearing accuracy this will increase the speed of the trace rotation so that it matches that of the aerial with minimal time delay and negligible increase in angular lag. This can be achieved by using a very high gain servo amplifier and ensuring minimum frictional resistance in the mechanism to be driven. There are limits, however, to how far this ideal can be pursued.

If the servo amplifier gain is made too high, a small increase in angular lag will produce a very large increase in the amplified error signal. This may well impart sufficient angular acceleration to the trace assembly that it is travelling much faster than the aerial when the correct steady state angular lag is reached and it therefore may overtake the aerial direction. If this happens, a negative error signal will reduce the speed of the trace rotation and again, if this is done too violently, overshoot in the other sense will take place. Thus, after an aerial acceleration, if the gain is too high the trace speed will tend to oscillate about the new aerial speed, the amplitude of the oscillation gradually being reduced by the frictional effects in the system. (It has already been argued that for rapid response the latter should be minimized, in which case the tendency to oscillate will be increased.) Conversely, if the gain is too small, the trace speed will be slow to respond to the small changes in aerial speed which are inevitable in practical conditions at sea. Thus at the design stage a compromise value of servo amplifier gain must be selected which will produce the most rapid response possible without generating oscillations. This decision involves quantitative considerations of the mechanical inertia and frictional effects present in the system which are beyond the scope of this text. The reader who wishes to pursue this topic further is referred to any standard text on control engineering.

In many modern PPI systems the rotating trace is produced by a fixed coil assembly energized by voltages controlled by a digital computer. However, it is common to find that the rotation signal is generated in the aerial drive unit by a synchro transmitter (or similar analogue device) and the signals are used as input to a device in the display which converts the aerial angle into a binary code. It is more appropriate to discuss this under the heading of 'Display principles' in Section 2.6.6.4. In a raster-scan system the update of aerial angle may be achieved by analogue transmission to the display and subsequent analogue-to-digital conversion.

2.4.5.2 Aerial rotation pulse generator

Some modern digital systems relay the rotation data to the display by means of a device which transmits a train of pulses, the instantaneous repetition rate of which is dependent on the instantaneous speed of aerial rotation. A common value is 1 pulse per degree of aerial revolution. These pulses are used as input to a digital computer which updates the aerial angle in memory and controls the rotation of the trace. As with synchro-to-digital conversion, this will be discussed further in Section 2.6.6.4.

2.4.6 Heading marker data

The function of the heading marker is to indicate on the display the forward direction of the ship's fore-and-aft line. It forms the fundamental reference from which bearings are measured (see Sections 1.3.4 and 2.2.2). The signal was traditionally initiated by the mechanical closing of a switch located in the aerial drive unit. The closing of the switch activates circuitry in the display unit (see Section 2.6.2) which produces a pulse to fully brighten a number of successive traces. The IMO Performance Standards required that the thickness of the displayed heading line be not more than 0.5°. It follows that the duration of the heading marker pulse must be not more than approximately 1/720th of the period of the aerial rotation. For an aerial rotation speed of 20 rpm the duration would be approximately 4 ms. The number of traces forming the heading marker will also depend on the PRF. With an aerial speed of 20 rpm and a PRF of 1000 the number will be approximately 4. The number of traces for any set of values can be obtained by using the relationship set out in Section 2.4.4 for calculating the number of strikes per point target and substituting the angular width of the heading marker for that of the horizontal beamwidth.

A number of methods have been used to operate the heading marker switch. One such method uses a small cam on a rotating part of the aerial unit to depress the switch as it goes past once during each revolution of the aerial. In all systems it is possible to adjust the point at which contact is made over a range of azimuth of about 5° to 10° so that the instant of heading marker display can be made to coincide with that of the axis of the main beam crossing the ship's fore-and-aft line in the forward direction. It is of critical importance that the setting is made correctly on installation and that the accuracy of the setting is checked by the observer regularly thereafter (see Section 6.9.9). The IMO Performance Standards require that the heading marker can be aligned to an accuracy of 0.1° (see Section 11.2.1).

In some modern systems generation of the heading marker is achieved without mechanical contact by using an electronic sensing device known as a 'Hall effect switch'.

Some systems also offer the facility of a stern marker for the benefit of craft such as short sea ferries which regularly navigate stern-first.

2.4.7 Radar phased array aerial systems

There have not been any major changes in the basic aerial technology in civil marine radar for decades. Radar phased array aerial systems are an alternative technology that could be introduced in the marine commercial and leisure industry in the foreseeable future. The present phased array technology would not work with the large power, high voltage, short pulses required to be transmitted by present day marine radar, but if an alternative new radar pulse technique such as coherent signals (see Section 3.10) is eventually adopted then phased array aerials will become a practical proposition. Phased array aerial systems transmit pulses with longer lengths, lower voltages, and lower powers that are a feature of coherent signals.

The main advantage of the phased aerial systems is that it is a fixed system with no mechanical rotating parts, unlike the traditional aerial. As shown in Figure 2.14 it consists of three or more panels arranged to give 360-degree coverage around a mast. Each panel consists of 60 or more active elements (dipole/transmitter/receiver modules) arranged linearly along the panel. Each active element is controlled individually and emits precise but very low power signals (milliwatts rather than kilowatts). The signals emitted by the active elements in a panel are carefully controlled in amplitude, frequency and phase so that they combine together to produce a beam which can be focused anywhere in the sector to be covered by the panel. The power of the beam will be the sum of powers emitted from the individual active elements.

The advantages of the phased array system are:

2.4.7.1 Flexible and multiple search patterns

Each panel produces its own beam, so there can be three or more beams transmitting simultaneously from each vessel. There is also no requirement for the beams to rotate around the compass at a regular speed. The beams could be 'intelligently' controlled by the radar set and could, for example, dwell on a particular azimuth until the radar has decided whether an echo return is clutter or a genuine target. The new IMO Performance Standards (see Section 11.2.1) no longer specify a minimum rotation rate. This is presumably to allow use of this new aerial technology.

2.4.7.2 Reliability

The lack of moving parts means that there will not be the maintenance and wear and tear associated with a continuously operating mechanical system.

2.4.7.3 Compactness and aerial position

The resulting aerial array is more compact than a mechanical scanner. It will weigh less and need less power to operate. On large vessels the mechanical scanner is ideally fitted to the top of a mast, to avoid shadow sectors (see Section 2.7.1). However, this is not often achieved and any second radar has to be fitted

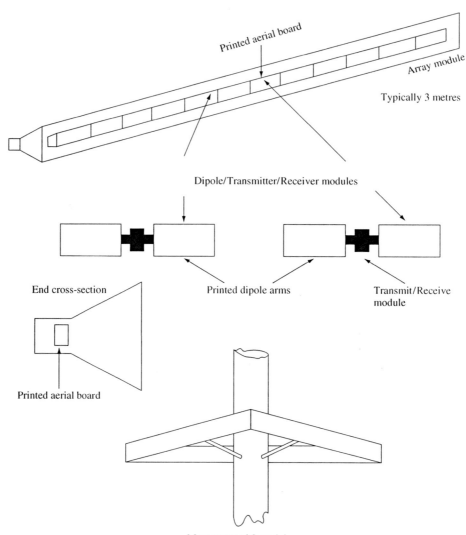

Figure 2.14 Radar phased array systems

lower down the mast. It is common to have shadow sectors with traditional rotating scanners. Phased array systems allow any number of radars to be sited on a single mast without shadow sectors caused by the mast itself. On smaller vessels (especially sailing vessels) the phased array systems would present fewer hazards to rigging and the low power and weight would be particularly attractive. This could lead to larger aerials with the advantage of narrower lower horizontal beamwidths being physically viable for such vessels (see Section 2.4.2).

The disadvantage of the phased array is that they do not work with current marine radar technology; however, in the future this may change (see Section 3.10).

2.5 Receiver principles

The function of the receiver is to amplify the weak returning echoes intercepted by the aerial and hence produce pulses of a strength and form which will generate a visible response on the screen of the display. In older systems the pulses will, in analogue form, produce a brightening of the rotating trace on a PPI. In more modern systems the pulses will be converted into digital form (see Section 2.6.6) and read into memory. After processing they will be read out of memory and used to produce either a radial-scan or a raster-scan PPI. The memory may also produce data for automatic target tracking (see Section 4.3.6.1).

The returning pulses are extremely weak and the receiver must be sufficiently sensitive to detect, at its input, signals having a strength of as little as one millionth of a volt. As explained in Section 2.2.3, the transmitter and receiver share a common section of waveguide. If the extremely powerful transmitter pulse (of the order of kilowatts) was allowed to enter the sensitive receiver, permanent damage would result. This is prevented by the T/R cell. For the purposes of this book the T/R cell may be considered to be an electronic switch which blocks the receiver branch of the waveguide during transmission.

The receiver must amplify the weakest signals by a factor of between 1 and 10 million in order to make them large enough to produce a picture. When the signals arrive at the antenna they are in the form of bursts of radio energy having a frequency lying in the X-band or S-band and an envelope resembling the shape originally imparted to them by the modulator and pulse-forming network (see Section 2.3.2.3). For engineering reasons which are beyond the scope of this treatment it is not practical to produce devices which will amplify signals at frequencies in the bands used for radar transmission and reception (approximately 9300–9500 MHz and 2900–3100 MHz). It is therefore necessary to reduce the frequency of the signal contained within the envelope of the pulse to a value at which such amplification is possible. The device which performs this function is known as the *mixer* and operates in association with another device

known as the *local oscillator* (see Figure 2.15). The value of lower frequency adopted may vary with manufacturer but it is usually in the region of 60 MHz and is referred to as the intermediate frequency (IF).

The signals leaving the mixer are amplified progressively by a series of amplifier stages (probably about 6 to 8 in number) which together constitute the IF amplifier. From the output of the IF amplifier the signals are passed to a device known as a *detector* which extracts the envelope from each burst of IF energy and hence the signals are ideally once more in the form of *rectangular* pulses. They are then referred to as *video pulses* because they are capable, after some amplification in the video amplifier, of producing a picture on a cathode ray tube.

It is evident that the signal path through the receiver can be divided into three convenient sections:

1   The radio frequency section comprising the mixer and local oscillator.
2   The intermediate frequency section comprising the various stages of the IF amplifier.
3   The video section comprising the detector and video amplifier stages.

The sections are particularly convenient as they each represent a stage at which, in setting up and using the radar system, the observer may exercise control over the receiver. The tuning control invariably operates in the radio frequency section. Gain and clutter controls may operate in either the IF or the video section, depending on the receiver design.

2.5.1   The radio frequency section

2.5.1.1   *The mixer principle*

It can be shown that if two sinusoidal signals of differing frequencies are mixed, the resultant complex signal consists of a number of sinusoidal components one of which has a frequency which is equal to the difference between the two frequencies which were mixed and which is known as the beat frequency. (Other components generated include the sum of the mixed frequencies, twice the higher frequency and twice the lower frequency, to name but a few.) The principle is

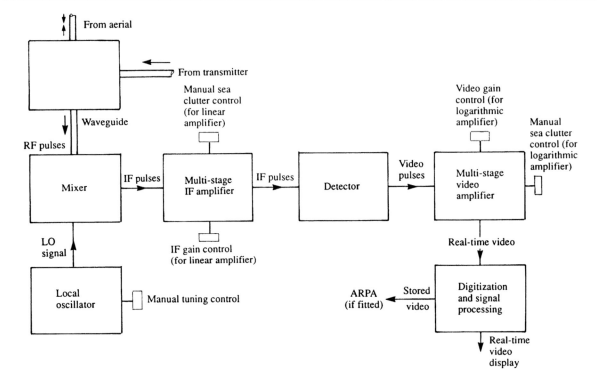

Figure 2.15 The radar receiver – a block diagram

more correctly known as the heterodyne principle and the radar receiver is said to be of the superheterodyne type.

The principle is applied in the radar receiver by mixing the incoming weak echoes, which are bursts of radio signals at magnetron frequency, with a continuous low power radio frequency signal generated by a device known as the local oscillator. The envelope of the pulse produced at the output of the mixer will contain, among others, a component whose frequency is equal to the difference between that of the magnetron and that of the local oscillator. This signal is used as input to the IF amplifier. The IF amplifier is carefully pre-tuned by the manufacturer (to the chosen IF) so that it will respond only to that component of the mixer output which lies at the chosen beat frequency. As a result, all the other frequency components generated by the mixing process are rejected. Thus the IF section deals with pulses whose envelope

resembles the shape originally imparted by the transmitter and which encloses bursts of oscillations at a frequency which is sufficiently low to be amplified using conventional techniques.

2.5.1.2 Tuning principles

Since the IF amplifier is pre-tuned to the chosen IF frequency it follows that the local oscillator must be adjusted so that the frequency which it generates differs from that of the magnetron (and thus the incoming wanted signals) by an amount equal to the chosen intermediate frequency. It is this adjustment which the observer makes when tuning the receiver. The manual tuning control will be located on the display unit so that the observer can view the picture while making the necessary adjustments, but it is important to appreciate that it exercises its influence at the very earliest stage of the receiver.

It is evident from the simple description of the magnetron presented in Section 2.3.3.2 that the generation of microwave frequencies is a complex process. While from an engineering point of view the local oscillator presents fewer problems because there is no requirement for extremely high power or very short pulses, the generation of the oscillations nevertheless depends on some form of resonant cavity. Here, it is sufficient to say that the oscillations are generated in a single cavity (as opposed to the multiple cavities of the magnetron). Coarse control of the generated frequency is obtained by variation of the physical size of the cavity (this is an installation or service adjustment), while fine control is exercised by small variations in the electronic conditions associated with the cavity (this is an operator/observer adjustment). Clearly stability of the local oscillator frequency is of great importance as any drift in its output value will de-tune the receiver and result in the loss of targets.

Because the IF amplifer is pre-tuned to a fixed frequency, the response of the receiver to incoming signals can be as illustrated in Figure 2.16. The response curve can be centred on any chosen frequency within the appropriate band and it will be observed that it has a bell-shaped characteristic which is symmetrical about that frequency. It is not possible to produce circuitry which will respond at a single frequency and exclude all others. The response will be maximum at the tuned frequency and will decay on either side of that value. The range of frequencies over which the response can be considered to be significant is referred to as the *bandwidth* of the receiver.

In most other applications of radio receivers great care is taken to ensure that the bandwidth is as narrow as physically possible. For example, in a broadcast receiver one wishes to obtain maximum response from the desired station and to avoid interference from stations operating on nearby frequencies. In radar systems designed to receive pulsed signals, the bandwidth is deliberately widened. It can be shown that the effect of a very narrow bandwidth is to distort the shape of the pulse to an extent which increases as the pulse length becomes shorter. The increase in bandwidth carries the penalty of loss of response and susceptibility to interference from other radar systems. The value adopted by the designer is thus of necessity a compromise and as it is essentially an IF amplifier characteristic it will be further discussed under that heading (see Section 2.5.2.4).

In most marine radar systems the bandwidth, when long pulse is selected, normally lies in the range 3 to 5 MHz and in the range 15 to 25 MHz in the case of short pulse selection.

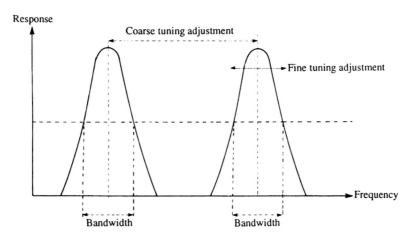

Figure 2.16 The response of the radar receiver

2.5.1.3 Manual tuning control

Most modern marine radar systems have a manual tuning control, situated on the display unit, which enables the observer to carry out fine tuning of the receiver. Coarse tuning should have been carried out by shipboard or shore-based service personnel in such a way as to ensure that the optimum setting of the display control lies close to the centre of its travel. If the optimum setting is found to approach one end of the travel, the coarse tuning should be re-adjusted by a person qualified to service the equipment.

It is crucial to the safe and proper use of marine radar for collision avoidance and navigation that a procedure is adopted which ensures that the manual tuning control is correctly set when the equipment is switched on and that thereafter it is regularly checked and readjusted as may be necessary due to the warming up of the equipment and the passage of time (see Sections 2.3.3.2 and 2.5.1.2). The appropriate procedure is described in detail in Sections 6.2.4.2 and 6.3.4.3.

2.5.1.4 Automatic tuning

It is possible to design circuitry which will seek and find the correct local oscillator frequency when the radar equipment is first switched on and which will maintain the receiver in tune despite changes which may occur due to warm-up or with the passage of time. Such a facility is correctly termed automatic frequency control (AFC) and should not be confused with limited automatic tuning facilities such as *pull-in* or *lock* which are described in Section 2.5.1.5.

In the past, marine radar systems offering fully automatic tuning were not uncommon, but since the 1970s they have tended to become the exception rather than the rule. In systems with full AFC there is usually no facility for the observer to carry out manual tuning at the display position but it will normally be possible for service personnel to switch out the automatic control and adjust the tuning from within the receiver unit.

Even where fully automatic tuning is available, it is essential for the observer to check (with reference to displayed signals) after switching on, and at regular intervals thereafter, that the facility is achieving optimum tuning. This is best done by use of the performance monitor (see Section 6.5).

2.5.1.5 Limited automatic tuning

Such a facility is sometimes referred to as *pull-in* or *lock* and is supplementary to a manual tuning control. Provided that the observer has initially set the manual tuning control at or very close to the correct setting, the pull-in circuitry has the ability to maintain the receiver in tune despite small variations in local oscillator or transmitter frequency during warm-up or with the passage of time.

It is important to appreciate that if the observer does not adjust the manual control to bring the receiver frequency within the limits of pull-in or if for any reason the frequency to which the receiver is tuned subsequently drifts outside these limits, the automatic system will be unable to re-tune the receiver without manual intervention.

Frequently such a limited tuning facility is complemented by a visual indicator (such as a neon light or a magic eye) which is designed to register whether or not the receiver frequency lies within the limits of the automatic tuning. It is important not to confuse such tuning indicators with others which are merely some measure of received signal strength. Tuning indicators are not required under the IMO Performance Standards and it would be unwise to make use of such devices without a clear understanding of the significance, accuracy and limitations of their indication. It should not be necessary to make use of such devices as the criteria set out in Sections 6.2.4.2 and 6.3.4.3 (which are based on the observation of displayed signals) will always provide a more reliable check on the setting of the tuning control. Thus, as with fully automatic tuning, it is essential for the observer to check regularly, by reference to displayed signals, that optimum tuning is being maintained.

2.5.2 The intermediate frequency amplifier

The intermediate frequency (IF) amplifier accepts the echoes produced by the mixer (which are in the form of weak bursts of IF signal within an envelope resembling that produced by the modulator) and boosts them to the level at which it is possible to extract the pulse envelope. As there is a limit to the factor by which any single amplifier stage can increase the strength of a signal, the IF amplifier is assembled in the form of a series of individual stages which progressively amplify the received echoes. It is now necessary to consider some of the characteristics of an amplifier stage and examine how they behave when connected together.

2.5.2.1 Stage gain and saturation

A single amplifier stage may be considered to be a *black box* such that if a signal is applied at the input to the stage an amplified version of the signal will appear at the output. Up to a certain level of input signal (known as the limiting input) the ratio of the strength of the output signal to the strength of the input signal is constant. It is known as the stage gain and is a measure of the magnification of the signal. Thus, below the limiting input, all signals will be amplified by the same factor.

If progressively increasing signals are applied to the input of the amplifier (see Figure 2.17) a situation must eventually arise (at the limiting input) where the output reaches the maximum value which the amplifier can produce. The latter is known as the limiting output. Further increase in the input signal will produce no further increase in the output. The amplifier is then said to be saturated. Thus all input signals which exceed the limiting input will produce the same output. This characteristic is of particular importance in the interpretation of a marine radar picture as it tends to create a substantially monotone picture in which all the strong echoes are displayed with equal brightness. It may allow echoes from the sea waves around the ship, or from areas of rain, to mask the presence of echoes very much stronger than themselves. The importance of this serious limitation of marine radar is dealt with in detail in Sections 3.6 and 3.7.

2.5.2.2 Overall gain

The gain offered by a single stage is a fraction of what is required to amplify the weakest signals received by

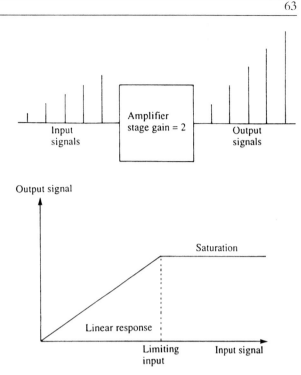

Figure 2.17 A simple amplifier stage

the system. A large overall gain can be achieved by connecting a number of stages in series to form a multi-stage amplifier.

The overall gain of the amplifier is given by the product of the gains of individual stages. Thus, in the example illustrated by Figure 2.18, if all stages have a gain of 10 the overall gain of the amplifier is 10^6, i.e. one million. Where such an amplifier is used in practice it would be normal for the observer to have control of the gain of one of the earlier stages while the gain of the remaining stages would be pre-set.

2.5.2.3 Thermal noise

In any electrical conductor or device at temperatures other than absolute zero there exists random movement of electrons due to thermal agitation and thus there will be random movement of electric charge. This produces an effect known as thermal noise, or sometimes as white noise, because like white light, it is equally distributed across the full frequency spectrum.

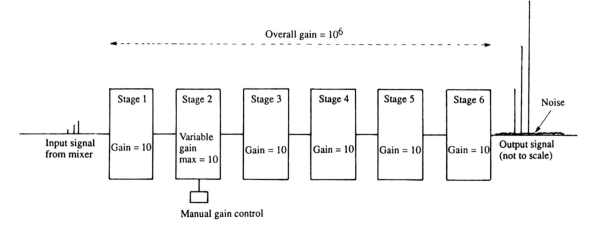

Figure 2.18 A multi-stage amplifier

The movement of the charge manifests itself as a minute random electrical signal which in the case of an amplifier stage will appear at the output of the stage. Although when initially generated the noise signal is of very low level, if it is amplified by a number of stages in a multi-stage amplifier its amplitude may be increased by a factor of as much as a million (see Figure 2.18), rendering it strong enough to produce a detectable signal on the radar display.

The term 'noise' was adopted because, when the phenomenon was first noticed in audio systems, it could be heard as background crackling in earphones and loudspeakers which made it difficult to hear weak signals. In a radar display it appears visually as a close-grained background speckling on the display. As the observer must attempt to discern the echoes of targets against this background, the level of noise generated in the first stage of the amplifier is of fundamental importance in determining the system's ability to display weak echoes. If the returning echo is weaker than the noise produced in this first stage it will not be capable of detection, as successive stages of amplification will merely increase the amount by which the noise exceeds the required signal. However, if initially the signal is stronger than the noise, successive stages of amplification will magnify this difference and improve the probability of detection. Echoes which are close to noise level will always be difficult to detect.

The level of noise displayed on the screen, and hence the probability of detecting weak targets, will depend on how the observer sets the gain control. If the gain is set too low, weak echoes will be lost because they will fail to display. If the gain is set too high, weak echoes will be lost, not because they will not be displayed, but because they will be masked by the background. The correct practical procedure for setting the gain control is discussed in detail in Chapter 6.

2.5.2.4 Bandwidth

The IF amplifier is pre-tuned to a chosen frequency and will respond only to signals at, or within the bandwidth limits of, that frequency. The amplifier is required to handle a sinusoidal signal having a frequency of typically 60 MHz and which is modulated by a rectangular waveform. It can be shown that a rectangular waveform is built up from a large number of sinusoidal waveforms consisting of a fundamental frequency and components known as harmonics at multiples of that fundamental frequency. A proof of this requires a mathematical analysis well beyond the scope of this text. However, Figure 2.19 (a) does show graphically that the assembly of a family of sine waves will tend towards a rectangular waveform.

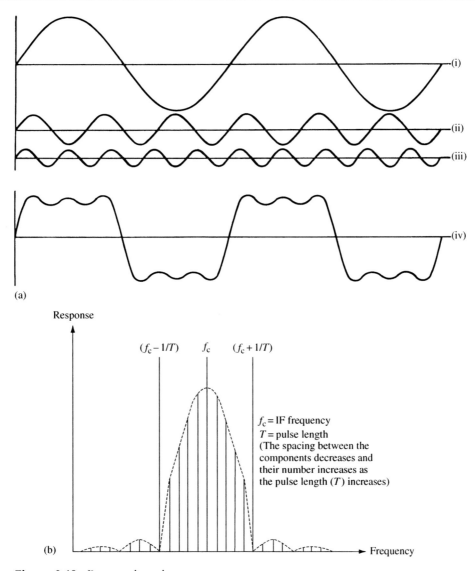

Figure 2.19 Rectangular pulses

(a) Frequency spectrum of a rectangular pulse
   (i)   Sine wave at amplitude A units, frequency f
   (ii) Sine wave at amplitude $A/3$ units, frequency $3f$
   (iii) Sine wave at amplitude $A/5$ units, frequency $5f$
   (iv) Sum of (i)+(ii)+(iii) $\rightarrow$ tends toward a square wave
(b) The frequency components of an IF pulse

The signal to be amplified is a complex waveform each element of which is a burst of sinusoidal signal (referred to as the IF carrier) contained within a rectangular envelope (referred to as the modulating waveform). It can be shown that the fundamental and harmonics of the modulating waveform will combine with the carrier frequency to produce a family of frequency components, known as side frequencies, which lie above and below the intermediate frequency and whose magnitude decreases with separation from the centre frequency (see Figure 2.19(b)). In order to preserve a reasonably rectangular pulse shape the IF amplifier must be able to respond to at least the stronger side frequencies. The shorter the duration of the received pulse, the more important this requirement becomes. It is for this reason that marine radars are designed with a bandwidth which is wider than would be the case in many other radio systems (see also Section 2.5.1.2). The bandwidth is normally considered to extend on either side of the centre frequency to the frequencies at which the response has fallen to half that at the centre frequency.

However, the bandwidth cannot be widened indefinitely (see Figure 2.20) and the value selected by the designer is of necessity a compromise. The curve in Figure 2.20(a) is representative of a sharply tuned amplifier which has high gain at the centre frequency and high selectivity because the bandwidth is very narrow. Clearly the high central response is desirable. However, the narrow bandwidth will reject the side frequencies and distort the shape of the pulse. This will reduce the accuracy of range measurement which is dependent on the echo having a sharp leading edge (see Section 2.3.2.3).

The curve in Figure 2.20(b) is representative of an amplifier having a wide bandwidth. The latter characteristic will ensure that the side frequencies necessary for good pulse shape will not be rejected but this has been bought at the expense of a decrease in central response. Thus the designer must achieve a bandwidth which is sufficiently wide to achieve acceptable pulse shape yet not so wide as to inordinately reduce the amplification provided.

A further factor which the designer must consider is the presence of noise. White noise

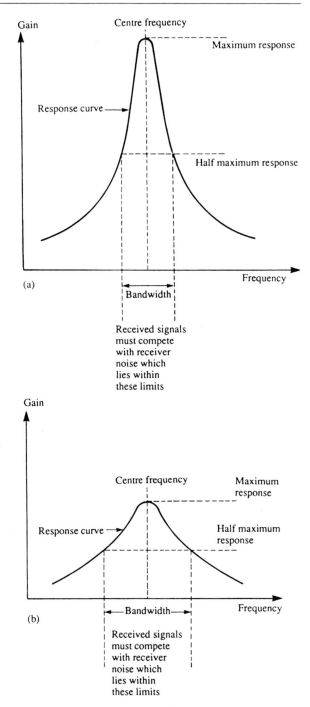

Figure 2.20   (a) Narrow bandwidth and (b) Wide bandwidth

(see Section 2.5.2.3) is generated across the full spectrum of frequencies but only those components which fall within the bandwidth of the receiver will be accepted. Thus increasing the bandwidth allows more noise to be accepted and hence reduces the probability of detection of weak echoes. Again the designer must compromise.

Most civil marine radars designed for large merchant vessels achieve this compromise in part by arranging for the IF amplifier to have two bandwidths which are under the indirect control of the observer by means of the pulse length selector (see Section 2.3.2.1). The narrower bandwidth is switched in if the observer, directly or indirectly, selects long pulse. The logic employed is that if long pulse has been selected, the observer must be concerned with distant targets and detection can be awarded a higher priority than range accuracy. Thus selection of long pulse has the effect of improving the probability of detecting distant echoes.

If the short pulse is selected, the wider bandwidth is used on the basis that the observer will make such a selection when observing targets on the shorter range scales and that as a result some amplification can be traded for an improvement in pulse shape and range accuracy.

2.5.2.5   The linear IF amplifier

Traditionally this was the type of multi-stage amplifier which was employed in all marine radar systems. It has now been superseded by the logarithmic amplifier (see Section 2.5.2.6) in radar systems.

Figure 2.21 shows a representative arrangement of a linear amplifier having six stages connected together in series. For continuity, the first element of the video stage is also shown. This is known as the detector and its function is to extract the envelope from the amplified IF signal (see Section 2.5.3.1).

This type of amplifier is so called because, provided that saturation does not take place at any stage, there is a linear relationship between the output and input signals, i.e. the overall gain is constant. Thus, provided that the input signal is below that value (the limiting input) which will produce saturation of the last stage, all echoes will be amplified by the same *factor*.

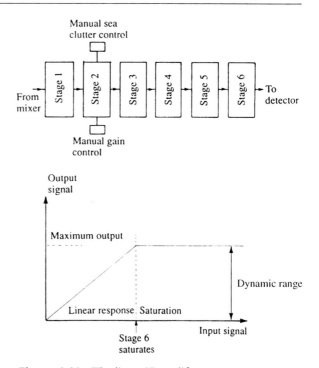

Figure 2.21   The linear IF amplifier

The major shortcoming of the linear amplifier is that it has a limited dynamic range (see Figure 2.21) and a large proportion of received signals will saturate the amplifier under normal conditions. This will allow unwanted responses such as those from the sea and from precipitation to mask even very strong targets (see Sections 3.6 and 3.7). At the root of the problem is the fact that the radar receiver has to handle a very large range of input signal levels. The ratio between the strongest and weakest signals at the input may be of the order of 10 000:1 (for example, a supertanker to a wooden boat). To achieve detection, the weakest signals have to be amplified by a factor of about 1 million which clearly will cause the stronger echoes to saturate the last, and probably a number of earlier stages of the amplifier. Normally all but one or two of the stages will have fixed gain while the observer will have the ability to modify the overall gain by means of the *IF gain control* (usually referred to simply as the gain) and the *sea clutter control*. The latter is a specialized form of gain control which will be discussed in detail in Section 3.6.3.1. These controls may operate in the same or separate stages.

The observer has to seek to offset the shortcomings which the limited dynamic range imposes by judicious adjustment of the overall gain. If the gain is adjusted so that the noise just appears on the display then there will be maximum probability of detecting weak targets, but strong echoes will all appear equally bright and masking will take place. If the gain is adjusted so that masking is eliminated then noise and weaker echoes will be insufficiently amplified to be displayed on the screen. The detailed practical procedures for dealing with this conflict are set out in Section 6.10.

2.5.2.6 The logarithmic amplifier

The logarithmic amplifier is designed to reduce the range of input signals that will saturate the receiver. Some marine radar systems offered logarithmic amplification from the mid-1960s, but it is since the early 1970s that the use of this technique has become commonplace.

The amplifier is so called because at the higher levels of signal input the output signal is proportional to the logarithm of the input. The logarithmic nature of the response is best demonstrated by mathematical analysis which is beyond the scope of this book, but a practical understanding of the operation can be obtained by consideration of Figure 2.22. To facilitate comparison the amplifier is assembled from the same number of stages as the linear amplifier in Figure 2.21.

The essential feature of the logarithmic amplifier is that the gain and limiting output of all stages must be the same, whereas in the case of the linear amplifier this need not necessarily be the case. Further, instead of a single output being taken from the last stage as in the case of the linear type, an output is taken from each individual stage. These contributions are summed to form a composite output. For reasons which are beyond the scope of this work it is expedient to extract the envelope of each contribution before the addition is performed. For this reason the type illustrated is often referred to as a *successive* detection amplifier. Alternatively it is sometimes said that the stages are connected together in *cascade*.

As mentioned previously, it is essential that the gain of each individual stage is fixed and equal to that of all of the others. For this reason the observer has no control of the gain in this unit. Where a logarithmic amplifier is employed, both gain and sea clutter controls operate at a later stage in the video section.

Consider the situation where the input just saturates the last stage. Although the contribution from the last stage will have reached its maximum, further increase in the input signal will nonetheless produce an increase in the total output because of the contributions from the earlier unsaturated stages. It follows that the total output will not saturate until the input signal is sufficiently large to saturate the first stage. Thus, comparing linear and logarithmic amplifiers, it is evident that the former produces a saturated output when the *last* stage saturates whereas the latter will not do so until the input signal has risen to such a level as to saturate the *first* stage. Hence the logarithmic amplifier increases the range of signals which can be handled without saturating the receiver. This increase makes it possible to design a receiver which will not be saturated other than by exceptionally strong echoes. A wide range of echoes may still saturate the screen phosphor (see Section 2.6.1.2) but this is more easily dealt with by the observer than saturation which takes place early in the IF amplifier.

It can be shown that, provided that the last stage does not saturate, the amplifier has a linear characteristic with an overall gain slightly less than a linear amplifier configured from the same stages. At signal levels above this, but below that which will saturate the first stage, the characteristic is logarithmic. Some understanding of the nature of the response can be obtained from the relationships, set out below, between input and output for a six-stage logarithmic amplifier configured as in Figure 2.22.

Input	Output
v_s	$V + v$
$A V_s$	$2V + v$
$A^2 v_s$	$3V + v$
$A^3 v_s$	$4V + v$
$A^4 v_s$	$5V + v$
$A^5 v_s$	$6V$

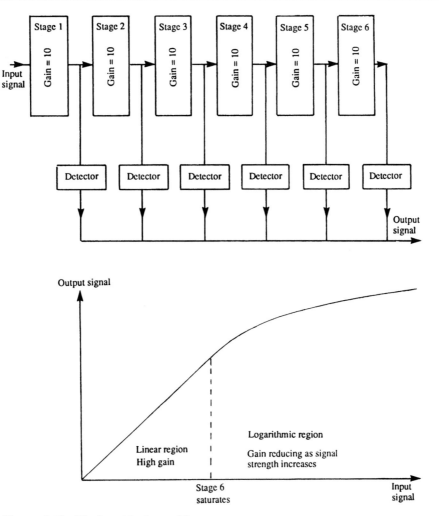

Figure 2.22 The logarithmic amplifier

where ν_s is the input signal which will just saturate stage 6

  A is the gain of each stage
  V is the saturated output of each stage
  ν is the contribution of the unsaturated stages which has a maximum value of $\nu = V|A + V|A^2 + V|A^3 + V|A^4 + V|A^5$.

Before comparing the input and the output columns, it should be noted that ν must always be very

much smaller than V (its largest component cannot exceed $V|A$, where A is the stage gain). Comparing the input and output columns, and for the moment ignoring the effect of ν, we can obtain an appreciation of the response. It should be noticed that at the lower values shown in the table, a tenfold increase in input signal produces a doubling of the output signal. As the input signal level increases, the proportional increase in output produced by a tenfold increase in input progressively decreases until, toward the top end of the values tabulated, a tenfold increase in input merely produces a 20 per cent increase in output signal. Thus the overall gain falls off at high levels along a curve which can be seen to be approximately logarithmic.

A simpler illustration of the logarithmic relationship between input and output is obtained by (i) considering v_s to be unity, (ii) using a stage gain of 10 and (iii) neglecting v which is a small quantity. On this basis the values given above approximate to:

Input	Output
1	V
10	$2V$
100	$3V$
1 000	$4V$
10 000	$5V$
100 000	$6V$

The effect of this logarithmic response is to emphasize the difference between different input echo strengths at the lower end of the range while maintaining a small but finite difference between the output echo strengths at the top end of the range. This considerably reduces the problems created by the masking of targets by sea and precipitation echoes, renders the adjustment of manual clutter controls less critical and provides an IF output which will make possible the use of automatic clutter suppression techniques in the video section (see Sections 3.6, 3.7, and 6.10).

2.5.3   The video section

For the general public the word 'video' has tended to take on a new and popular meaning with the advent of mass produced television tape recorders for use in homes. However, it should be appreciated that for the purposes of this work 'video' means *that signal which, when applied to the CRT, produces the picture.*

The function of the video section is to extract the envelope (i.e. the rectangular outline) of each received pulse and to amplify and condition it so that it can be used as input to computer memory for storage and processing and/or used to produce a visible response on the screen of the cathode ray tube.

2.5.3.1   *The detector*

The function of the detector is to extract the rectangular envelope from the amplified IF signals (see Figure 2.23). In engineering texts it is sometimes referred to as the *second detector*, the mixer being considered to be the first detector. (This arises because the process involved is fundamentally the same.) Alternatively the term *demodulator* may be used. This arises from the general terminology of radio communication in which the term modulation is used to describe the process whereby a signal representing intelligence (e.g. speech, music or data) which cannot be transmitted directly into space, is superimposed on a radio frequency signal (known as a carrier). In the radar case the modulating signal is represented by the rectangular pulse envelope (see Figure 2.4) and the carrier by the radio frequency oscillations produced by the magnetron (see Section 2.3.3.2). Hence, considering the IF oscillations as representative of the original carrier, the function of the demodulator or detector is to recover the modulating signal, i.e. the rectangular envelope (see Figure 2.24).

When it is recalled that the waveform of the envelope is the sum of a fundamental frequency and its harmonics (see Section 2.5.2.4), it will be appreciated that the frequency characteristic of the detector must be such that it will respond to the *relatively* low frequencies of the envelope (usually of the order of a few megahertz) but reject the relatively high intermediate frequency which will normally be in the region of 60 MHz.

2.5.3.2   *The video amplifier*

This unit boosts the pulses which are produced at the output of the detector to a level at which they are suitable for storage in memory or capable of producing a visible response on the screen of the cathode ray tube (see Section 2.6.1). The amplifier may comprise several stages and, like the IF amplifier, each stage must have sufficient bandwidth to pass an adequate range of the harmonics which are present in a rectangular waveform. In most modern marine radar systems the video bandwidth is fixed but there are some systems in which the video bandwidth, rather than the

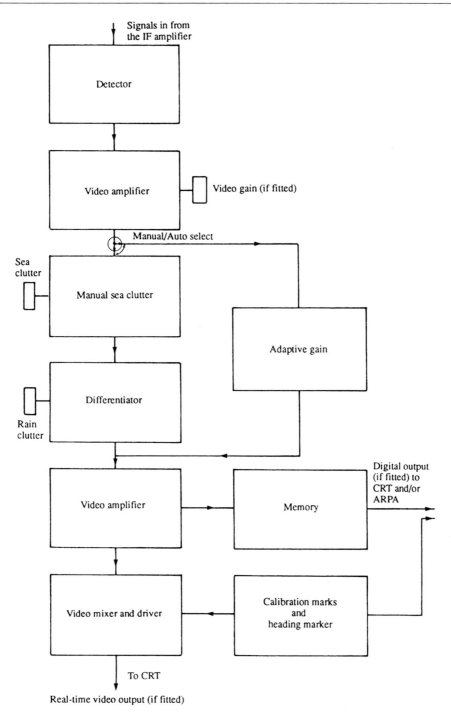

Figure 2.23 The video section

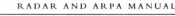

Figure 2.24 Recovering the pulse envelope

IF bandwidth, is switched with pulse length. As the amplitude of the signal is increased through successive stages, its polarity may change from positive to negative with alternate stages. This arises because the operation of many single-stage amplifiers introduces a 180° phase shift between input and output signals. This point need not concern the radar observer but readers who wish to pursue the point are referred to any electrical engineering text dealing with voltage amplifiers.

In older systems, where the video amplifier was preceded by a linear IF amplifier, it was normal to find that the observer exercised control of the gain (by means of gain and sea clutter controls) in the IF stage and that the overall gain of the video section was fixed. However, a few systems did offer a separate video gain control with a view to offering a limited level of independence where the display unit was used as a slave in an interswitched configuration (see 'Interswitching' in Section 2.7.8). In modern systems employing a logarithmic IF amplifier, the gain and sea clutter control is invariably exercised in the video section because operator control of the IF gain would destroy the logarithmic law of the IF section (see Section 2.5.2.6).

Consideration of Figure 2.23 shows that, after the initial section of the video amplifier, the signal path has been split into what can be conveniently called the manual channel and the automatic channel. This configuration will only be found in modern systems in which the video section is preceded by a logarithmic amplifier. In older systems employing a linear amplifier, only the manual channel will be present and it will not normally offer any control of sea clutter as this will have been performed at IF.

2.5.3.3 *The manual channel*

Where both channels are provided, the manual channel allows the observer to carry out manual suppression of sea clutter echoes by means of a special type of gain control, sometimes referred to as swept gain or sensitivity time control (STC). The safe and successful operation of this control requires a sound knowledge of the phenomenon known as sea clutter and a skill which can only be obtained with practice. This topic is dealt with in Sections 3.6 and 6.10.

The second facility offered by this channel is known as *differentiation*. By adjustment of a manual control the observer is able to change the shape of the displayed pulse from that of a rectangle toward that of a spike. This may improve the ability of the display to show separately echoes which are on the same bearing and closely spaced in range, i.e. it may improve range discrimination (see Section 2.6.5.5). This control is often labelled *rain clutter* because it may assist in detecting targets which are masked within echoes from precipitation. Again, the use of this control calls for skill and knowledge; the topic is dealt with in Sections 3.7.4.4 and 6.10.2.

2.5.3.4 *The automatic channel*

The automatic channel provides a facility whereby the signal level is continually sensed and the overall gain is varied automatically in an attempt to remove unwanted signals such as those from sea waves (sea clutter) and precipitation (rain clutter). This automatic technique is known as adaptive gain and can only operate successfully on signals which have been processed initially by a logarithmic amplifier. When the automatic channel is selected, the manual channel is bypassed and thus the manual sea and rain clutter controls are disabled. Adaptive gain is described in detail in Section 3.6.3.3.

2.5.3.5 *Further video amplification*

There may or may not be further video amplification before the signals are fed off to memory and/or mixed with calibration signals before being displayed.

The latter operations are more conveniently described under the heading of display principles below.

2.6   Display principles

The function of the display is to present the radar picture in such a way that, where a detectable response is returned, the observer may reveal the presence of the echo, measure its range and bearing, and track the movement of the target which has produced it.

From the invention of radar to the 1990s the radar picture was presented only on the screen of a cathode ray tube. Since then liquid crystal displays have become increasingly common with the major advantage of being a flat electronic panel (see Section 2.6.7.10).

While the cathode ray tube retained its central position in the radar display over the years, the way in which the picture is presented has undergone three major revolutions over the same period. The first of these was the change from A-scan to PPI (see Section 1.2.3) but as this is of purely historical interest it will not be mentioned further. From the early 1970s

the change from a real-time picture to a synthetic picture (see Sections 1.2.5 and 2.6.6) began, although the radial-scan PPI was retained. From the mid-1980s the first raster-scan displays appeared (see Sections 1.2.5 and 2.6.7) in which the radial scan PPI is replaced by a raster-scan PPI generated on a television-type display which was either a cathode ray tube or liquid crystal display.

In this section consideration will be given to the principles of real-time and synthetic pictures displayed on a radial-scan PPI display and to raster-scan displays. The general treatment of cathode ray tubes is first considered for the radial-scan tube. The tube used in raster-scan radars differs in some respects from the radial-scan tube, and these differences will be highlighted in Section 2.6.7. which deals with this type of display.

The newer display technologies of LCD and plasma screen are considered in Sections 2.6.7.10 to 2.6.7.12 and are only used for raster-scan displays.

2.6.1   The cathode ray tube (CRT)

The CRT (Figure 2.25) is an evacuated narrow glass tube which funnels out at one end to produce a circular screen. Electrons are emitted at the narrow end

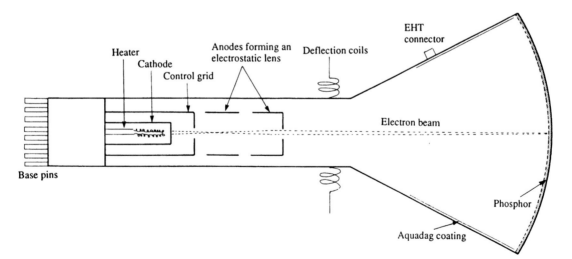

Figure 2.25   The cathode ray tube

of the tube and formed into a very narrow beam which strikes the inside of the screen at the other end and there produces a spot of light whose brightness, size and position may be controlled (see also Section 1.2.3). The generation and control of the spot is best described by considering the CRT to comprise three major elements:

1 The electron gun which emits the electron stream.
2 The coated screen which reacts to produce light when struck by the electrons.
3 The deflection system which controls the location at which the beam strikes the screen.

Each of these elements will now be considered in turn.

2.6.1.1   *The electron gun*

An electron is the fundamental particle which carries unit negative electrical charge. The electron gun is an arrangement of cylindrical metal components which are known as electrodes.

The electrodes are located along the axis of the tube and their function is to liberate, accelerate and concentrate the electrons into a narrow beam which is fired toward the screen.

The electrode which emits the electrons is called the cathode and it is from this that the tube takes its name. The various electrodes which attract the electrons towards the screen are called anodes. These are maintained at very high positive potentials with respect to the cathode in order to accelerate the electrons to speeds of tens of thousands of kilometres per second. The strength of the electron stream is controlled by an electrode known as the control grid, normally referred to merely as the grid.

The cathode is a metal cylinder closed at the end nearer the screen and is coated on the outside with an oxide having an atomic structure such that electrons are emitted from the surface at a relatively low level of heat. The emission is promoted by heating the cathode indirectly as a result of passing electric current through a wire filament, known as the heater, which is located inside the cathode cylinder. The electrons emitted by the cathode form a cloud in its vicinity known as the

space charge. As the cloud builds up, the loss of negative charge to the cloud renders the cathode positive with respect to the cloud; hence some electrons tend to be recaptured. However, at any given temperature a state of dynamic equilibrium will be reached in which as many electrons are leaving the cloud as are joining it and thus a space charge of constant population will surround the end of the cathode. Electrons are drawn from this cloud and accelerated toward the screen to form the electron beam. Returning echoes, after being amplified by the receiver (see Section 2.5), are applied to the cathode as a pulse of negative polarity which will produce an increase in the strength of the beam and hence a brightening of the spot.

The grid is cylindrical in shape with one end closed except for a small hole which constrains electrons travelling along or close to the tube axis to pass through and emerge in the form of a convergent beam. It is located between the cathode and the first anode but closer to the cathode (see Figure 2.25). The grid potential can be adjusted by the observer, using the brilliance control, and will be a few tens of volts negative with respect to the cathode. The effect of the grid potential is to offset the attraction of the anode system to a greater or lesser extent, thus allowing the observer to control the strength of the electron beam and hence the brightness of the spot. Clearly the beam strength could, in theory, be varied by adjusting the anode potentials. However, it is much more practical to exercise control at the grid which is close to the cathode, as this allows small variations in a relatively small voltage to produce an effect which would require large variations in potentials having values of hundreds or thousands of volts at the anode. An automatic signal, known as the *bright-up pulse*, will also be applied to the grid. This ensures that the spot brightness selected by the observer is available when each radial line is being drawn but that it is suppressed when the spot is returning to the origin. Such automatic suppression may also take place when change of range scale or similar operations are performed. (In some systems the video signal has also been applied to the grid instead of the cathode.)

The brilliance control must be correctly set by the observer in the *no signal* condition, i.e. with the input of received signals to the cathode suppressed. This is of fundamental importance as the observer detects echoes by noticing the increase in the *no signal* spot brightness caused by the arrival of an echo (see Section 1.2.3.2). The practical procedure for carrying out this extremely important adjustment is set out in Section 6.2.3.1.

There will normally be two or three anodes in the electron gun and considerable variations in design detail are possible. For example, the cylinders may be of different diameters and lengths. Further, both ends of any one cylinder may be open, or one end may be partially closed to form a small hole, coincident with the axis of the tube. However, a satisfactory understanding of the principles involved can be obtained by considering the simple arrangement of two anodes shown in Figure 2.25. The two anodes are maintained, by a power supply, at a potential which is several hundreds of volts positive with respect to the cathode. Having regard to the interactive force which exists between charged particles (unlike charges attract one another while like charges repel), it is evident that the electrons which are free in the space charge around the cathode will experience a vigorous attraction and will be accelerated toward the positively charged surfaces of the anodes (which are fixed). The electrons will reach the vicinity of the anodes travelling at extremely high speed and those which are close to the axis of the tube will be fired through the small hole in the second anode, thus forming a narrow beam projected at the screen. The electrons then come under the influence of the final anode which takes the form of a conductive coating applied to the inside of the cone-shaped portion of the tube. This is maintained at a potential which is several tens of thousands of volts positive with respect to the cathode and accelerates the electrons towards the screen at an extremely high speed.

It might seem that the incidence of a continuous stream of negatively charged particles would result in an accumulation of free electrons on the screen. This does not occur as the surplus free electrons are drawn off by the final anode and returned through the power supply to the cathode. Thus the CRT forms a continuous electrical circuit in the external portion of which the current flows along wires while within the

vacuum of the tube the current flow is manifest in the form of the electron beam.

Further consideration of Figure 2.25 shows that, although the beam emerging from the grid is initally convergent, the geometry is such that crossover takes place and the beam is divergent when it enters the anode assembly. The interaction between like-charged particles will further contribute to this divergence. Such a beam would produce a large and poorly defined spot on the screen. As the spot is effectively the pencil point with which the picture is drawn on the face of the tube, it is essential that it is small and well defined (see Sections 1.2.3 and 2.6.2). This requires that the electron beam should converge to a point which is coincident with the screen. In modern systems this is achieved by arranging for the second anode to have a potential which is a little more positive than that of the first anode. This has no transverse effect of electrons flowing along the axis of the tube but those whose paths are off the axis experience a force which acts towards the axis. The magnitude of the force experienced by any given electron increases with its distance from the axis. Thus in addition to its perhaps more obvious function of accelerating the electron stream toward the screen, the anodes of the electron gun fulfil a focusing role analogous to that of an optical lens. The anode arrangement forms an electrostatic lens whose focal length is controlled by the difference in potential between the first and second anodes (see Figure 2.26).

A rigorous treatment of the lens operation is beyond the scope of this work but the reader who wishes to study the topic further is referred to any electrical engineering text which deals with electron optics.

The difference in potential between the two anodes is adjusted by means of the focus control. The stability of most modern focusing systems is such that this control should seldom need adjustment and for this reason it is usually located inside the display unit, on the basis that it will be preset on installation and that any subsequent adjustment will be made by competent service personnel. It must be appreciated that although the control is preset, it is not automatic and if for any reason the focus voltage does deviate from the correct value it will not correct itself. In this condition the

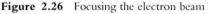

Figure 2.26 Focusing the electron beam
(a)   Mutual repulsion produces divergent beam
(b)   Correct focus: beam converges to point on screen
(c)   Incorrect focus: beam converges to point beyond
       screen
(d)   Incorrect focus: beam converges to point inside screen

beam will converge to a point which lies either inside or outside the tube, producing a spot which is too large and hence a poorly defined picture. It is therefore important that the observer checks that the tube is correctly focused. The appropriate practical procedure for carrying this out is described in Section 6.2.3.2.

2.6.1.2   The screen

The function of the screen is to react with the electron beam to produce a small bright spot of light at the point at which the beam strikes it. This is made possible by coating the inside of the glass with a material known as a phosphor which has the property that when bombarded by electrons it will emit light immediately and for some time thereafter. The instantaneous generation of light by electron bombardment is called fluorescence and for any given phosphor the brightness of the light emitted is a function of the strength of the electron beam. Hence, subject to the limits of saturation of the receiver (see Section 2.5.2.1) and of the phosphor (which will have a maximum light emission capability), stronger targets will produce brighter echoes. With a purely fluorescent coating, light emission will cease immediately the bombardment ceases (as in the case of strip lighting) whereas in the case of a phosphor the light level emitted will decay over a period giving the property known as persistence or afterglow. A wide variety of chemicals are employed in the production of phosphors and the compound selected will depend on the brightness, persistence and colour most suited to the particular application.

In the case of a radial-scan PPI display, the choice of persistence involves some compromise. Long afterglow ensures that strong targets persist for at least one aerial revolution and increases the likelihood of the observer spotting a weak echo. Further, it causes moving targets to leave more obvious afterglow trails. The trails may assist the observer in an early appraisal of encounters with other vessels, but great care must be taken in interpretation (see Section 2.6.7.5 and Chapter 7). However, excessive persistence may produce serious masking when the range scale is changed or where an unstabilized orientation is selected (see Section 1.4.1). Although some radial-scan displays for special applications have used a green phosphor, other civil marine radars employed a phosphor which emitted a pale orange glow.

The phosphor has a limited life because continued excitation of the material progressively destroys the sensitivity of the coating. This is described as CRT burn. Evidence of it can be seen on old CRTs, particularly in the area around the origin and where markers such as range rings are regularly displayed. The effect is inevitable but its serious onset can be delayed by intelligent use of the controls (see in particular Sections 6.9.8 paragraph 7 and 6.10.1.1 paragraph 5). The consequence of the loss of sensitivity is that echoes will not brighten the screen in the burned areas and so may go undetected for a period of time. This can be particularly dangerous when a true-motion presentation is selected if the origin is tracking towards the burn at the centre of the screen.

The dynamic range of signals which can be displayed by the phosphor is limted. As a result, if the receiver noise is just visible, the strongest signals will saturate the screen. This problem is analogous to the saturation which takes place in the receiver (see Section 2.5.2.5) but the adjustments required to cope with screen saturation are much less critical than is the case with saturation which takes place at an early stage in the receiver. Provided that the receiver does not saturate, and the signals are not digitized (see Section 2.6.6), the range of input signals to the tube will be continuous but the range of screen brightness levels which can be discerned by an observer is to some extent subjective and authorities differ on its value. It is unlikely to be less than 8 or more than 15.

The surface of the phosphor remote from the glass is coated with a very fine metallic (normally aluminium) spray. The spray is sufficiently fine to be transparent to the electron bombardment and forms a conducting surface which assists in the return of free electrons to the final anode surface and hence to the power supply. A proportion of these electrons will have originated at the cathode while others will have been dislodged from the screen by the impact of the beam. The aluminized screen also serves to enhance the brightness of the picture by reflecting the light from the phosphor that would otherwise be lost by radiation to the inside of the tube.

The IMO Performance Standards (see Section 11.2.1) specify, according to the gross tonnage of the vessel, the minimum effective diameter of the display which must be available. Three diameters are listed, namely 180 mm, 250 mm and 320 mm. These dimensions correspond to cathode ray tubes in a radial-scan radar having overall diameters of 9, 12, and 16 inches respectively (228 mm, 305 mm and 406 mm).

2.6.1.3 The deflection system

The function of the deflection system is to move the spot across the screen in the correct direction and at the correct rate to produce the rotating trace necessary for the build-up of the picture (see Section 1.3.3). Deflection can be carried out by electrostatic or electromagnetic methods, but the latter technique is invariably employed in civil marine radar applications.

Electromagnetic deflection exploits the motor principle whereby a conductor carrying an electric current in a magnetic field experiences a force which acts at right angles both to the direction of current flow and the direction of the magnetic field. A simplified representative arrangement is illustrated in Figure 2.27.

An explanation of the mechanics of deflection is best commenced by assuming that initially the electron beam, as indicated by the spot, is at the centre of the screen and that the deflection system is not energized. Consider that a voltage is now applied to the scan coil and that accordingly a current flows. This will magnetize the core with the polarity indicated and create the conditions required for the application of the motor principle. In applying the principle it is important to appreciate that, because by convention current flows from positive to negative, the electron beam represents a conventional current flowing from screen to cathode (i.e. in the reverse direction to the electron flow). Thus in Figure 2.27 the current is flowing into the page, the magnetic field lies in the plane of the page and hence the deflection of the spot will be at right angles to both. Should the reader wish to check the validity of the direction of deflection, the application of Fleming's Left-hand Rule will offer the necessary confirmation (an explanation of Fleming's Left-hand Rule should be found in any text dealing with basic electromagnetism).

It is almost self-evident that the extent to which the spot is deflected will depend on the strength of the deflecting magnetic force. Clearly there will be

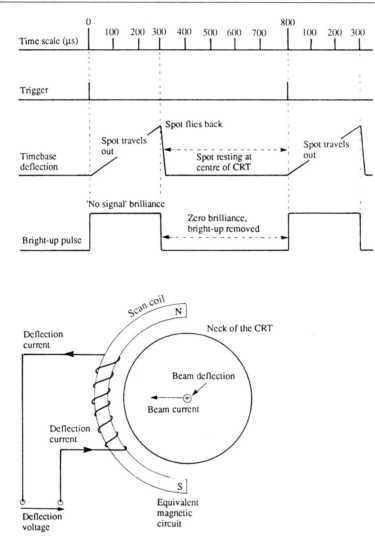

Figure 2.27 Rotating-scan coil deflection: time-sequence diagram for PRF = 1250, range scale 24 n mile

some value, let it be called F_E, which will deflect the spot to the edge of the screen. It will be remembered that, in the case of a real-time display, a single trace is produced by moving the spot from the centre of the screen to the edge of the screen at constant speed in the duration of the timebase appropriate to the selected range scale (see Section 1.2.3). Thus, by the application of a suitable signal to the scan coil, the deflecting force

can be made to increase at a uniform rate from zero to F_E in the duration of one timebase. For example, the duration of the rise will be approximately $150\,\mu s$ when the 12 mile range scale is selected. At the end of the timebase the deflecting force must fall rapidly to zero, allowing the spot to fly back to the centre of the screen. During flyback the spot brilliance will be automatically reduced to zero by the removal of the bright-up signal. The time relationship between the deflecting force, the trigger and the bright-up signal for the 12 mile range scale, assuming a PRF of 1250, is illustrated by Figure 2.27. The deflection signal is sometimes referred to as a *sawtooth* waveform because of its distinctive shape. The circuitry which develops the waveform of the correct duration and slope for the range scale selected by the observer is called the *timebase generator*.

To build up the picture the trace must rotate in sympathy with the aerial (see Section 1.3.3). In the traditional analogue display this is most commonly achieved by physically rotating the scan coil assembly about the neck of the CRT. The motor which drives the assembly forms part of a proportional error servo system whose mode of operation is described under 'Aerial principles' in Section 2.4.5. Such an electromechanical system has been generally superseded by the use of digital techniques and fixed-scan coils (see Section 2.6.6.4).

In order that the picture will be correctly orientated the scan coil assembly must be aligned such that at the instant the heading marker contacts make, the direction of deflection, and hence the displayed heading marker, accurately intersect the correct graduation on the fixed-bearing scale around the outside of the screen. In early systems a manual control was provided to allow the observer to rotate the picture to the correct orientation. In more modern systems, auto-alignment is offered directly by the orientation/presentation selector.

For convenience of explanation it was assumed that, in the absence of the deflection signal, the electron beam would settle along the axis of the tube and hence produce a spot coincident with the centre of the screen. For a variety of reasons it cannot be guaranteed that in practice there will be absolutely zero magnetic field influencing the neck of the tube and hence the spot may settle close to but not exactly at the centre of the screen. The IMO Performance Standards (see Section 11.2.1) require that, after installation and adjustment on board, the specified bearing accuracy must be maintained without further adjustment irrespective of the movement of the vessel in

the Earth's magnetic field. Special screening is sometimes used to isolate the scan coils from ambient magnetic fields. In many circumstances it is of particular importance that the observer should be able to locate the origin of the picture exactly at the centre of the screen (see Section 6.2.3.3). To this end, two fixed coils, set at right angles to one another, and also fitted around the neck of the tube in such a way that one coil allows horizontal adjustment of origin location while the other allows vertical adjustment. The observer is able to locate the origin in the centre of the screen by adjusting two corresponding display controls which are referred to as *shift* controls or *centring* controls. Traditionally the controls will only allow a small amount of movement but in many displays it may be possible to offset the origin by as much as 75 per cent of the radius. Where this facility exists the controls are more correctly called *off-centring controls* and are normally, but not necessarily, associated with a true-motion presentation. This aspect of off-centring is discussed further in Section 2.6.4. The correct practical procedure for checking and adjusting the centring controls is set out in Section 6.2.3.3.

2.6.2   Real-time picture generation

The method of picture generation described in this section is representative of the technique used in the development of the earliest civil marine PPI radars and which, in principle, remained unchanged until the 1970s. The term *real-time display* is used to describe the fact that each radial line of the picture is written during the time taken by each radar pulse to travel the two-way journey to the maximum range of the scale in use. Modern displays employ digital computer techniques to store, process and then reproduce the radar data. The latter development was introduced in Section 1.2.5 and will be considered in detail in Sections 2.6.6 and 2.6.7. The traditional display is sometimes also referred to as an analogue display, or alternatively it is said to produce *analogue video* by which is meant the strength of the displayed echoes is analogous to the strength of the echoes received. More fully, this means that the displayed echoes may lie anywhere in a continuous range between noise level and saturation and that, within these limits, linear amplification will produce display echoes whose brightness is proportional to the strength of the received signals that produced them.

The picture which appears on the screen of the CRT is generated by the combination of a number of signals in a carefully time-related sequence; an outline treatment of this was presented in Section 2.2.4. It is necessary at this stage to recapitulate and consider the relationship between these signals in more detail. Some of these signals originate in the transmitter, receiver and aerial units (see Sections 2.3, 2.4 and 2.5, respectively), while others are generated within the display. An understanding of the relationship between the signals which generate the picture in a real-time display will be assisted by a study of Figures 2.28 and 2.29. Figure 2.28 shows the distribution of the signals within the display. However, it is equally important to appreciate the time relationship which exists between the signals.

It should be remembered that there are four signal inputs to the display, namely rotation, trigger, heading marker and video, which are illustrated in Figure 2.28. The rotation system has been fully described in Sections 2.4.5 and 2.6.1.3.

The trigger originates in the transmitter (see Section 2.3). It may be considered to signify the *time zero* of the radar timing sequence and provides the synchronizing link between transmitter and display. It should be noticed that it initiates both the time base and bright-up signals. This ensures that the spot leaves the origin at the instant of transmission and is visible from that instant. Both timebase and bright-up units are capable of producing waveforms of a duration appropriate to each of the display range scales. At any given instant the value available will be determined by the position of the range scale selector. This ensures that the spot draws each trace in the correct time and that it is only visible on its outward journey.

The trigger is also applied to the calibration unit. From the explanation of the calibration of the timebase presented in Section 1.2.4 it is evident that the time period for both the fixed marks and the variable mark must be initiated at the instant of transmission. The interval between successive calibration marks is a function of the range scale selected and thus the calibration

oscillator must be able to offer the correct frequency of oscillation for each range scale. In older systems this was achieved by employing a separate oscillator for each range scale. A more modern approach is to use a single oscillator whose frequency, usually known as the clock frequency, is that required for the shortest range scale. If the second shortest range scale is twice the range of the shortest, then the correct calibration interval is easily derived by using every second pulse of the clock frequency. Provided that successive range scales increase by the constant factor of two, which is normally the case, the correct calibration interval for each range scale can be obtained by using each alternate calibration mark from the next lower range scale. The precision with which the observer may measure range is dependent on the accuracy with which the calibration marks are generated (see Section 6.9).

The term 'video' has been used above to describe the echo signal which has been processed in the various stages of the receiver as described in Section 2.5. It is this signal which, when applied to the cathode of the tube, will produce an increase in spot brightness for each detected echo. However, it has to be combined with other signals which also produce an increase in spot brightness. These comprise the heading marker signal which is generated in the aerial unit (see Section 2.4.6) and the calibration signals which are generated within the display. The raw heading marker signal from the aerial will normally pass through some preliminary circuitry in the display before being mixed with the other signals. The combination takes place in a unit known as a video buffer (or mixer) and it can be thought of as a device which allows each of the signals access to the output path leading to the cathode but will prevent any one input signal entering the circuit of any of the others.

The combined signal will be referred to as the *composite video* and it takes the form of a sequence of negative-going pulses, each of which will produce a brightening of the spot. As the received echoes are boosted through the several stages of the video amplifier (see Section 2.5.3.2), the polarity of the pulses may change from positive to negative in alternate stages. A similar situation may arise during the development

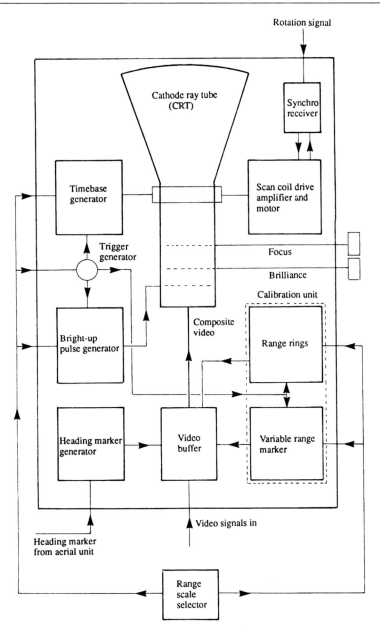

Figure 2.28 Block diagram of real-time radial-scan display

of other waveforms such as trigger, calibration marks and bright-up. For time-sequence considerations polarity is not important and thus for ease of illustration Figure 2.29 uses positive polarity, i.e. signal strength increases toward the top of the page. This convention will be preserved throughout this text in all illustrations related to echo strength, and hence amplitude is indicative of brightness.

Figure 2.29 Radar time-sequence diagram for PRF = 1250, range scale 12 n mile, range ring interval 2 n mile, VRM set to 5.5 n mile

2.6.3 Compass (or azimuth) stabilization

The IMO Performance Standards (see Section 11.2.1) require that means be provided to enable the display to be stabilized in azimuth and states that the accuracy of alignment with the compass transmission should be within 0.5° with a compass rotation rate of 2 rpm.

The time-related combination of signals described by Section 2.6.2 will produce a picture which is inherently unstabilized. This will be adequate for use with the ship's-head-up orientation only (see Section 1.4.1). In Section 2.6.1.3 it was indicated that, on installation, the scan coils would normally be aligned in such a way that at the instant when the axis of the main beam crosses the fore-and-aft line, the spot will be deflected along that radial which lies over the 000° graduation on the fixed-bearing scale. Provided that the heading marker contacts have been correctly set (see Section 6.9.9), such an alignment will ensure

that the heading marker appears in the ship's-head-up position.

If a true-north-up (stabilized) orientation (see Section 1.4.2) is required, an additional signal will be necessary to provide compass stabilization. When switched in, this signal will re-align the scan coils, and subsequently maintain them in the correct angular relationship with the aerial direction so that at the instant when the heading marker contacts make, the spot will be tracing out that radial which respresents, on the fixed-bearing scale, the vessel's instantaneous true heading. As a consequence, at the instant the axis of the main beam sweeps through true north, the spot will draw the trace which passes through the 000° graduation on the same scale. In some older systems, known as manually aligned systems, the observer was required to carry out the initial alignment and thereafter the stabilization signal maintained the correct angular relationship. Most modern systems offer auto-alignment.

To generate the course-up (stabilized) orientation (see Section 1.4.3), a compass stabilization signal is also necessary. However, in this case the initial alignment of the scan coils with respect to the aerial direction is such that at the instant when the axis of the main beam sweeps through the direction of the ship's true course, the spot is tracing out the radial which passes through the 000° graduation on the scale. If, but only if, the vessel is right on her course, the heading marker will also pass through that graduation.

In seeking an understanding of the methods by which compass stabilization is achieved it is helpful first to consider the three angular quantities which are involved. These are illustrated in Figure 2.30(a) which is drawn with particular reference to the true-north-up orientation.

The *aerial bearing* (α), by which is meant the angle of the axis of the main beam, measured clockwise from true north, is indicated on the display by the angular position of the trace as read from the fixed bearing scale. In Figure 2.30(a) it can be seen that, at any instant, the angular position of the trace with respect to the 000° graduation is the sum of two constituent angles. One of these is the *aerial angle* θ through which the axis of the main beam has rotated since the last heading marker. This angle is continuously updated by the aerial/trace servo system (see Sections 2.4.5 and 2.6.1.3). The second angle is the instantaneous value of the ship's heading ϕ and it is this angle which must be supplied when a stabilized orientation is selected and which must be updated with every subsequent change in the vessel's heading.

The process of stabilization is illustrated in block diagram form by Figure 2.30(b). It should be noticed that the figure is similar to Figure 2.13 with the addition of the differential synchro and the compass input. The differential synchro may be considered to be a device which adds the ship's heading to the aerial angle and hence produces an input of aerial bearing (instead of aerial angle) to the scan coil servo mechanism. Applying the principles described in Section 2.4.5.1, the servo system will drive the trace in such a way that its radial direction on the fixed bearing scale maintains alignment with the instantaneous true direction of the axis of the main beam.

The differential synchro has a stator winding similar to that of a synchro receiver. In Section 2.4.5.1 it was explained that such a set of windings would produce a unique signal for any given aerial direction and it is in this form that the aerial angle forms the input to the differential unit. The output stage of the differential synchro is a similar set of windings which can be rotated through 360° with respect to the stator. The output angle differs from the input by an amount equal to the misalignment between the fixed and the free sets of windings. The reader who seeks a more technical description of a differential synchro is referred to any good control engineering text.

The stabilizing signal is derived either from a gyro compass by way of a repeater motor or by an electronic message (see Section 10.4.4). The motor may be one of several different varieties, common among which was the step-by-step type which was produced by a step angular change of shaft position for a fixed fraction (usually $\frac{1}{6}$) of each degree of heading change detected by the master gyro. Through an appropriate ratio gear train the output shaft of the step motor drives the shaft on which is mounted the moving coil assembly of the differential synchro. For a full treatment of the operation of gyro repeater systems the reader is referred to any good text on the gyro compass.

In many older radar systems the two angles were added mechanically by means of a differential gearbox. The electromechanical system described in this section is representative of the method superseded at sea today by the use of microprocessor techniques. This is discussed further under the heading of synthetic displays in Sections 2.6.6 and 2.6.7.

The description of the stabilization process has been presented in terms of a true-north-up orientation but the example of course-up orientation could equally well have been chosen.

2.6.4 The provision of true-motion facilities on a radial CRT display

To generate a true-motion picture it is necessary to arrange for the origin of the display to move across the screen in a direction and at a rate that corresponds with the motion of the observing vessel through the

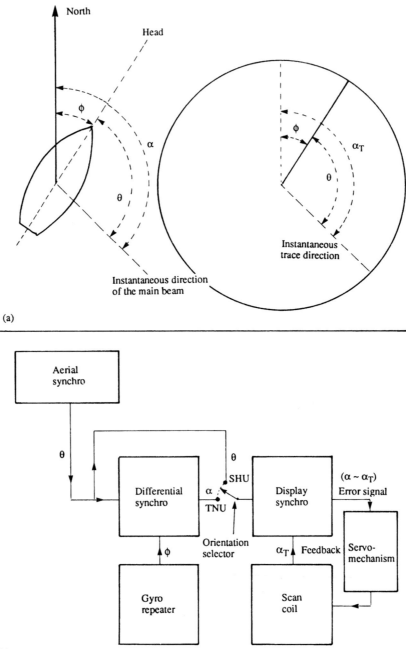

(a)

(b)

Figure 2.30 Compass stabilization

(a)   Angular quantities

(b)   Block diagram

water or over the ground (see Section 1.5.2). This is achieved by energizing two sets of off-centring coils wound on a yoke around the neck of the CRT. The operation of the coils is based on the same electromagnetic principle as that of the shift coils described in Section 2.6.1.3 and the true-motion off-centring may well be produced by the same coils. However, whereas the shift controls normally permit only a small amount of movement to allow the correct setting-up of a centred display, the true-motion off-centring controls (referred to as reset controls) allow the origin to be located anywhere within a playing area which typically extends to some 60–75 per cent of the radius from the centre of the screen. Initially the observer will use the reset controls to locate the origin so as to make the best possible use of the screen area (see Section 6.8.2). Thereafter a unit, usually referred to as the true-motion computer, takes over control of the off-centring coils and continuously updates the screen location of the origin in accordance with input values of direction and speed. As the origin tracks across the screen, sooner or later it will be necessary to reset the origin as the view ahead becomes limited. The observer may at any time temporarily override the computer by using the reset controls. On release of the latter the computer will resume control and the origin will commence tracking from the new location.

2.6.4.1   The analogue true-motion computer

The function of the true-motion computer is to resolve the direction and rate of the observing vessel's true motion into N/S and E/W components and to use these two components to energize the off-centring coils. In the original true-motion units developed in the late 1950s the resolution was carried out solely by mechanical methods using specialized gearboxes. These were in due course superseded by techniques which were electromechanical rather than purely mechanical. The arrangement illustrated by Figure 2.31 is suitably representative of the majority of analogue systems at sea today. It is important to appreciate that the electromechanical arrangements constitute an analogue computer and should not be confused with the microprocessor techniques which

are becoming progressively more common and are associated with synthetic displays (see Sections 2.6.6 and 2.6.7).

The central unit of the true-motion computer is a device known as a resolver. This may be considered to be an electromechanical *traverse table* which converts direction and distance into d.lat. and departure. (Readers who are concerned to understand the technical details of resolvers are advised to consult a good control engineering text under the references of ball resolvers and sin/cos potentiometers.) For sea-stabilization (see Section 1.5.2.1) the inputs to the resolver are the observing vessel's course and speed and the outputs are the signals which must control the N/S and E/W movements of the origin. Where ground-stabilization (see Section 1.5.2.2) is required, additional inputs relating to the tide will be required and these will be discussed separately in Section 2.6.4.4.

There are two outputs from the resolver, one of which is proportional to (ship's speed × cosine heading) while the other is proportional to (ship's speed × sine heading) and these are fed to two parallel channels. In each channel is connected a unit known as a *distance-run integrator* (see Figure 2.31). The integrator is a device which samples the instantaneous resolved speed at short regular intervals and hence develops an output signal which changes progressively with distance run. If the heading is in the first quadrant, the ouput from both integrators will increase with distance run. If it lies in any other quadrant at least one of the outputs will decrease. The signal from each integrator is processed by an amplifier and used to control the current in the shift coil to which it is connected and hence the electromagnetic deflecting force generated by that coil. Thus the location of the origin, which represents the rest position of the electron beam (see Section 2.6.1.3), is determined by the resultant of the mutually perpendicular forces exerted by the shift coils and its movement will be controlled by the progressive changes in these forces.

For any given input speed, the origin must track across the screen at a scale speed which is consistent with the range scale selected by the observer. It is for this reason that a scaling factor signal, controlled by the range selector, is fed to the integrator (see Figure 2.31).

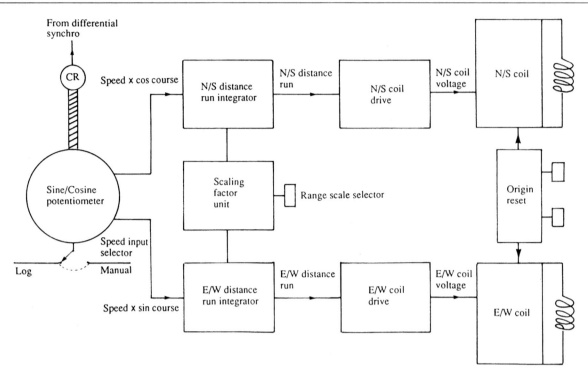

Figure 2.31 The analogue true-motion computer

True-motion facilities are not normally available on the very long or the very short range scales, because in the former case target movements would be so slow as to be barely perceptible, while in the latter case the disruption of tracking caused by the need to reset would arise too frequently to be acceptable.

The IMO Performance Standards (see Section 11.2.1) do not require the fitting of true-motion. However, where it is fitted, they specify that the accuracy and discrimination should be at least equal to that which is otherwise required. A further requirement is that the motion of the origin of the trace should not, except under manual override conditions, continue to a point beyond 75 per cent of the radius of the display. The standards allow the fitting of automatic resetting facilities. Within the limits of the standards, the exact nature of the manual and automatic resetting arrangements made available by different manufacturers vary considerably.

A consequence of the provision of any off-centred presentation is that it requires the display of some targets at ranges in excess of the nominal selected range scale. For example, on the 12-mile range scale with 70 per cent off-centring, the view in one direction will be 1.7 × 12 miles, i.e. 20.4 miles. Thus where true-motion facilities are provided, it is necessary for the timebase to be greater than that which would be required on a centred display for the same range scale. The practical procedures for setting up and maintaining a true-motion presentation, including the use of various reset facilities, are described in Section 6.8.

The preceding description has been presented in terms of a true-north-up orientation. A course-up orientation is also possible but in that case the vessel's speed is resolved into components which are parallel and perpendicular to the reference course (see Section 1.4.3).

2.6.4.2 The compass input

The compass input was almost invariably derived from a gyro repeater motor which, through appropriate gearing, drives the input shaft of the resolver. The repeater will commonly be the same one as is used to provide compass stabilization (see Section 2.6.3).

2.6.4.3 The speed input

The speed input may be derived from a log or it may be fed in manually by the observer. Most true-motion computers are designed to operate with a log which generates a train of constant amplitude voltage pulses, the repetition rate of which is proportional to the indicated speed.

There are a variety of ways in which the pulse train can be used to produce an analogue of the speed. One method is to use a device known as a smoothing circuit.

This accepts a fluctuating input signal and from it produces an output signal whose amplitude is the average value of the input. Since all the log pulses have the same amplitude, the average amplitude will be directly proportional to the frequency at which the pulses are repeated. Thus for any given log speed, the output signal will be a steady voltage whose value is proportional to that speed. This signal can be conditioned if necessary and used as the speed input to the resolver.

An alternative approach is to use an electronic counting circuit which will produce a fixed step of scale distance run for each pulse received from the log. This will give distance travelled which may be used directly or may be differentiated with respect to time to give speed.

Where a manual speed input is used, the observer normally selects the required value by adjusting a control which operates a numerical scale and a unit known as the *artificial log*, both of which are driven by the same shaft. The circuitry of this unit either mimics a log by generating a pulse train at a repetition rate consistent with the speed selected by the observer or may generate an analogue speed voltage directly.

2.6.4.4 Tide inputs

To generate a ground-stabilized presentation, additional inputs representing the effect of the tide will be necessary. While the precise form which the input controls take varies with manufacturer, in principle they all fall into one of two categories according to whether the set and rate are fed in directly or indirectly.

In systems using direct input, the observer feeds the tidal information in terms of set and rate. The set control drives the shaft input of a second resolver, the tide resolver, while the rate control adjusts a manual rate input to the same resolver. The resolver produces two output components which represent the N/S and E/W components of the tide. The operation is exactly analogous to the resolution of the observing vessel's course and speed as described in Section 2.6.4.1. Hence the N/S motion of the ship through the water and the N/S motion of the water over the ground can be summed at the input to the N/S integrator so as to produce an output which is an analogue of the N/S component of the vessel's ground track. A similar addition will be performed in the E/W channel as illustrated by Figure 2.32(a).

The alternative approach adopted in other systems is to feed the tidal data in indirectly by means of a course-made-good correction and a speed-made-good correction. This is illustrated in Figure 2.32(b).

The course-made-good correction is defined as the angle between the course through the water and the direction of the ground track measured in degrees to port or starboard from the course through the water. The correction is made by a control which jointly operates an angular scale and, through appropriate gearing, a shaft which forms one of two inputs to a differential gearbox. The other input is the shaft driven by the compass repeater (see Section 2.6.4.2) while the output shaft of the gearbox drives the resolver of the true-motion computer. Variations in the position of the course-made-good correction control will slew the resolution angle to one side or the other of that indicated by the gyro repeater and hence cause the origin to track crabwise across the screen at an angle to the direction indicated by the heading marker.

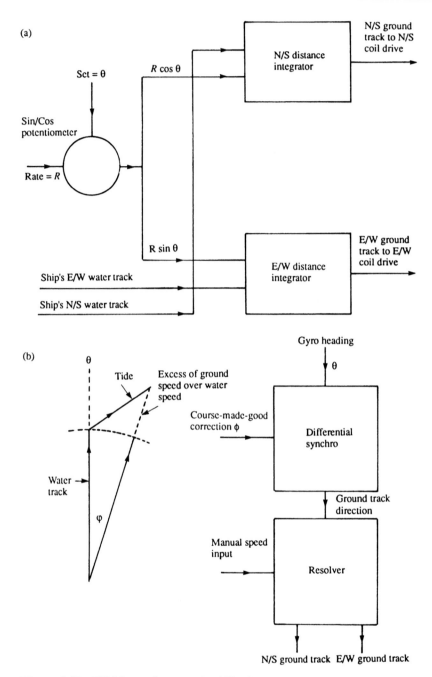

Figure 2.32 Tidal inputs for ground stabilization
(a)   Direct tidal input: set θ, rate R
(b)   Indirect tidal input: course-made-good correction ϕ,
      manual ground speed

The speed-made-good correction is the difference between the speed through the water and the speed over the ground. A separate control is not normally provided, and so the adjustment is made indirectly by selecting manual speed input and setting the manual speed control to the ground speed rather than the water speed.

From the observer's point of view, advantages and disadvantages can be claimed for both approaches and the practical implications of this will be discussed in Section 6.8.3 paragraph 5. In general it should be remembered that any type of ground stabilization generates a picture which is not suited to the normal use of radar for collision avoidance and may seriously mislead the untrained or unwary observer.

2.6.5   Echo paint

'Echo paint' is a term used to describe the size and shape of an echo as it appears on the screen. Except in the case of extremely large or very close targets, the echo paint is almost if not totally dependent on certain characteristics of the radar system and virtually independent of the size and shape of the target. This is an extremely important limitation of civil marine radar and is best explained by considering the echo of a point target. The latter is a theoretical concept which supposes a target that has the ability to reflect radar energy but which has no dimensions. Clearly this cannot be realized in practice, but in due course it will be seen that, because of the dominant effect of the radar characteristics, many practical targets behave in a manner closely resembling that of a point target. Figure 2.33 shows a situation in which a radar beam sweeps across two point targets and illustrates how the echo paint is built up.

The characteristics of the radar system which affect the size and shape of the displayed echo are spot size (CRT), pulse length (transmitter) and horizontal beamwidth (aerial unit). Each of these will be discussed in turn.

2.6.5.1   The effect of spot size

The spot produced on the screen of the CRT may be regarded as the *pencil point* with which the radar picture

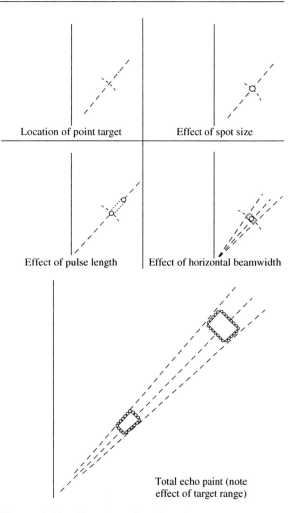

Figure 2.33   The echo paint of a point target

is drawn. While the spot can be focused to a fine point, the mutual repulsion of electrons within the beam (see Section 2.6.1) sets a lower limit to the spot diameter which can be achieved in practice. In civil marine radar applications this minimum is in the region of 0.5 mm (values between 0.2 and 0.6 mm are not uncommon) and represents the smallest mark that can be made on the screen. The distance represented by the spot diameter will vary inversely with screen diameter and will decrease when the shorter range scales are selected. This is illustrated by the following numerical example:

Example 2.4 A certain vessel has two radar displays, having screen diameters of 340 and 250 mm respectively. In both cases the spot diameter is 0.5 mm. Calculate the range represented by one spot diameter on the 12 mile and 1.5 mile range scales.

On the 340 mm screen

The number of spot diameters per screen radius is given by

$$N_{340} = \frac{170}{0.5} = 340$$

When the 12 mile range scale is selected, the range represented by one spot diameter is given by

$$R_s = \frac{\text{range scale in metres}}{\text{spot diameters per radius}}$$
$$= \frac{12 \times 1852}{340}$$
$$= 65.36 \text{ metres}$$

In the case of the 1.5 mile scale,

$$R_s = \frac{1.5 \times 1852}{340}$$
$$= 8.17 \text{ metres}$$

On the 250 mm screen

The number of spot diameters per screen radius is given by

$$N_{250} = \frac{125}{0.5} = 250$$

When the 12 mile range scale is selected, the range represented by one spot diameter is given by

$$R_s = \frac{12 \times 1852}{250}$$
$$= 88.9 \text{ metres}$$

In the case of the 1.5 mile scale,

$$R_s = \frac{1.5 \times 1852}{250}$$
$$= 11.11 \text{ metres}$$

It is important that the observer checks that the spot is correctly focused (see Section 6.2.3.2) otherwise the picture will suffer from loss of definition.

2.6.5.2 The effect of pulse length

A detected echo produces a brightening of the spot and the length of time for which this brightening occurs will depend on the duration of the received echo and hence on the pulse length. Thus each pulse which strikes a point target and is successfully detected will produce a paint on the screen which is one spot diameter wide and which has a radial extent related to pulse length. Consideration of the timebase principle (see Section 1.2.3) indicates that this radial extent is equivalent to half a pulse length. The appearance of the factor of one half may be puzzling at first sight but it can easily be justified by a simple numerical example. Let a radar be switched to the 12 mile range scale. This means that in the time a radar pulse travels 24 miles (i.e. 12 miles out and 12 miles back), the spot traces out a screen distance which represents 12 miles. Let a pulse length of 1 μs be selected. In the interval during which a single pulse is being received, radar waves will travel 300 metres (see Section 1.2.2) but the spot will trace out a screen distance of 150 metres. Thus, in terms of distance, the radial extent of the echo paint of a point target is half the pulse length (see Figure 2.33).

2.6.5.3 The effect of horizontal beamwidth

The IMO Performance Standards (see Section 11.2.1) permit a maximum horizontal beamwidth of 2.5°. As the beam sweeps across the point target, it will be struck at regular intervals (the pulse repetition period) by a number of pulses. Thus the echo paint is built up of a number of the radial elements each of which is one spot diameter wide and of a radial length equivalent to half the pulse length. This is illustrated by Figure 2.33. The angular width of the paint of a point target will depend on the horizontal beamwidth, while the number of radial elements is additionally dependent on the PRF and the aerial rotation rate (see Section 2.4.4).

The angular elongation of the echo paint is sometimes referred to as half-beamwidth distortion because it has the effect of extending the paint by half the beamwidth on either side of the nominal echo position. The angle contained between the limits of the main lobe of the horizontal beam is constant (see Section 2.4.2) but the length of the arc which subtends this angle at the aerial increases in proportion to the range at which the arc is measured. Thus the length which this angular distortion produces increases with the range of the target (see Figure 2.33).

2.6.5.4 Practical considerations

In the case of a point target, the aggregate of the effects described above is a paint whose size and shape depends on the spot size, pulse length, and horizontal beamwidth of the radar system and also on the range of the target. To appreciate the practical significance of these effects it is helpful to consider the following numerical example:

Example 2.5 A marine radar system has a screen of effective diameter 250 mm and spot size 0.5 mm. The horizontal beamwidth is 2°, the pulse length is 1 μs and the display is switched to the 12 n mile range scale. A point target X is detected at a range of 10 miles. Calculate the radial length and the angular width of the echo paint as it appears on the screen, and hence determine the distances, in nautical miles, which these dimensions represent.

Let D = spot diameter, P = radial effect of pulse length and A = angular elongation due to horizontal beamwidth. Let the total dimensions of the echo paint be given by T_R (radial length) and T_A (angular width).

P = screen distance moved by spot in the duration of one pulse

$$= \frac{\text{screen radius}}{\text{timebase duration}} \times \text{duration of pulse}$$

$$= \frac{125}{148.16} \times 1 \, \text{mm}$$

Thus

$$P = 0.84 \, \text{mm}$$

A = radius of screen at which target lies $\times$ HBW in radians

$$= \frac{125 \times 10}{12} \times 2 \times \frac{\pi}{180} \, \text{mm}$$

Thus

$$A = 3.64 \, \text{mm}$$

The radial length of echo paint is given by

$$T_R = \frac{D}{2} + P + \frac{D}{2} = D + P$$

$$= 0.5 + 0.84 \, \text{mm} = 1.34 \, \text{mm}$$

The angular length of the echo paint is given by

$$T_A = \frac{D}{2} + A + \frac{D}{2} = D + A$$

$$= 0.5 + 3.64 \, \text{mm} = 4.14 \, \text{mm}$$

Thus the echo paint has a radial length of 1.34 mm and an angular width of 4.14 mm.

In the example chosen, the radius of the screen (125 mm) represents 12 miles, from which it can be deduced that the natural scale of the PPI is such that 1 mm represents 177.8 m. If this were to be applied to the dimensions of the echo paint this would suggest a target of approximate radial dimension 238 m and approximate angular dimension 736 m. This we know to be absurd. The area which is bounded by these dimensions is referred to as the *resolution cell*. Thus while it is possible to determine the range and bearing of a target with the necessary degree of accuracy by taking the measurement to the centre of the nearer edge of the echo paint (this represents the location of the echoing surface, see Figure 2.33), the size and shape of the paint of all but very large targets bear little or no relationship to the size and shape of the target which produced it. A radar reflector (see Section 3.4) has almost negligible dimensions, but if located at the position of the point target suggested in Example 2.5, would produce an echo paint which covers a screen area equivalent to that of several very large ships. Hence, only when a target has reflecting surfaces which extend beyond the resolution cell does it begin to contribute significantly to the size and shape of the echo.

It is evident that, except at extremely close ranges, a ship will in general produce an echo approaching that of a point target. If the calculation in Example 2.5 is performed for the same radar system, but with the point target located at a range of 2 miles, it will be found that the radial dimension remains unchanged at 1.34 mm (as it is not a function of range) while the angular dimension decreases to 1.23 mm. Thus, if a small target closes from a range of 10 miles to a range of 2 miles, its echo shape will change from one in which the angular width is the greater dimension to one in which the reverse is the case. It is noteworthy that radar characteristics selected in the above examples are representative and do not illustrate the worst possible case. Civil marine radar thus has a very limited ability to display picture detail.

In the use of radar for collision avoidance the principal significance of the above limitation is that the shape of the displayed echo of a ship gives no indication of how the vessel is heading. Heading inference drawn from the shape of the echo is likely to be dangerously misleading. For example, to the unwary or untrained observer, targets toward the edge of the screen may *appear* to be broadside-on (because of the dominance of the angular distortion) whereas targets towards the centre of the screen may *appear* to be head-on. The importance of understanding the specious nature of the impression created by the shape of the echo cannot be overstressed. The techniques for deducing a reliable indication of the heading of other vessels is set out in Chapter 7. The size of the resolution cell also presents limitations when the radar is used for navigation. These will be alluded to briefly in the following two sections and their significance to radar navigation will be discussed in detail in Section 8.2.2.

2.6.5.5 *Range discrimination*

Range discrimination, which may also be referred to as range resolution, describes the ability of the radar system to display separately the echoes of two targets which lie on the same bearing but which are closely spaced in range. The discrimination is normally expressed in terms of the number of metres by which the targets must be separated in order to prevent their echoes overlapping on the screen. In discussing discrimination it must be assumed that both targets are illuminated by the radar beam. If the more distant target is in a blind area caused by the nearer target, no echo will be displayed, irrespective of the ability of the radar to discriminate. The IMO Performance Standards (see Section 11.2.1) set out the requirement for range discrimination in terms of two small targets which lie on the same azimuth and which are separated by 40 metres in range. To comply with the standard, the equipment must, on a range scale of 1.5 miles, be capable of displaying the echoes of two such targets as separate indications when the pair lie at a range of between 50 per cent and 100 per cent of range scale in use.

A study of the factors which limit range discrimination is best commenced by considering two targets lying on the same bearing and investigating the conditions which must be satisfied for two separate echoes to arrive at the aerial. Figure 2.34 shows the limiting case and two other cases for comparison purposes.

A study of the Figure 2.34 will show that if the targets lie on the same bearing, the leading edge of the second echo will just touch the trailing edge of the first echo when the range separation of the targets is half the length of the transmitted pulse. Thus, in theory, the range discrimination can be calculated by expressing half the pulse length in terms of metres. In practice, the radial paint is further elongated by the effect of spot size. For a given screen size and spot diameter, the influence of the spot size on the dimensions of the resolution cell becomes less significant on the shorter range scales. The influence of pulse length is independent of screen size. In theory it is also independent of range scale but in practice shorter range scales are normally associated with shorter pulse

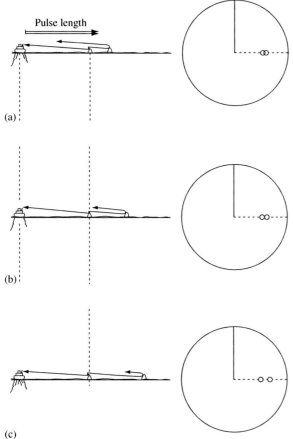

Pulse length

(a)

(b)

(c)

Figure 2.34 Range discrimination

(a)   Targets separated by less than $\frac{1}{2}$ pulse length: echoes merge
(b)   Targets separated by exactly $\frac{1}{2}$ pulse length: echoes just touch
(c)   Targets separated by more than $\frac{1}{2}$ pulse length: echoes display separately

lengths (see Section 2.3.4). The range discrimination is equal to the radial dimension of the resolution cell and this is illustrated by the following numerical example which uses some representative values.

Example 2.6   A radar display has a screen diameter of 250 mm and a spot size of 0.5 mm. On the 12 mile and 1.5 mile range scales the pulse lengths are 1.0 and 0.05 μs respectively. Calculate the range discrimination on each of the given range scales.

On the 12 mile range scale

The range represented by one spot diameter is given by

$$R_S = \frac{\text{range scale in metres}}{\text{spot diameters per radius}}$$

$$= 12 \times \frac{1852}{250} \text{ m} = 88.9 \text{ metres}$$

The range represented by half pulse length is given by

$$R_P = \frac{\text{pulse length in microseconds}}{2} \times 300$$

$$= \frac{1.0}{2} \times 300 \text{ m} = 150 \text{ metres}$$

Range discrimination $= R_S + R_P$

$$= 88.9 + 150 \text{ m} = 238.9 \text{ metres}$$

On the 1.5 mile range scale

$$R_S = 1.5 \times \frac{1852}{250} \text{metres}$$

$$= 11.11 \text{ metres}$$

$$R_P = \frac{0.05}{2} \times 300 \text{ m} = 7.5 \text{ metres}$$

Range discrimination $= 11.11 + 75 \text{ m} = 18.61 \text{ metres}$

It is interesting to note that on the longer range scale the pulse length effect is dominant, whereas on the shorter range scale the reverse is the case.

Best range discrimination can be obtained by selection of the shortest available pulse length and by ensuring optimum focusing. Care must be taken that the latter is not defeated by excessive brilliance, gain or contrast settings (see Sections 6.2.3.1, 6.2.4.1 and 6.3.4.1). In certain circumstances range discrimination may be improved by the use of the differentiator (rain clutter) control (see Section 3.7.4.4).

2.6.5.6 Bearing discrimination

Bearing discrimination, which may also be referred to as bearing resolution, describes the ability of the radar system to display separately the echoes of two targets which lie at the same range but are closely spaced in bearing. The discrimination is normally expressed by the number of metres by which two targets, if they lie at the same range, must be separated in azimuth in order that their echoes will appear separately on the screen. The IMO Performance Standards (see Section 11.2.1) set out the requirement for bearing discrimination in terms of two small similar targets both situated at the same range between 50 per cent and 100 per cent of the 1.5 n mile range scales. To comply with the standard, the equipment must be capable of displaying the echoes separately when the targets are separated by not more than 2.5° in azimuth.

If two targets lie at the same range and are closely spaced in bearing, a minimum requirement for angular discrimination is that the trailing edge of the rotating beam must leave the first target before the leading edge illuminates the second target. This is illustrated by Figure 2.35.

Figure 2.35 shows the limiting case of discrimination and two other cases for comparison purposes. It follows from the illustration that, in theory, the radar can only discriminate between targets which are separated by at least one horizontal beamwidth. In practice, the angular elongation is further increased by the spot size. Thus bearing discrimination is limited by the angular width of the resolution cell.

It is important to appreciate that the distance represented by the horizontal beamwidth increases in direct proportion to the range at which the discrimination is being considered. The influence of spot size will be less on larger screens and on shorter range scales. Some representative values are illustrated by the following numerical example.

Example 2.7   A radar display has a screen of diameter 250 mm and spot size 0.5 mm. If the horizontal beamwidth is 1.5°, calculate the bearing discrimination at a range of 10 miles when the 12 mile range scale is selected and 1 mile when the 1.5 mile range scale is selected.

Targets separated by

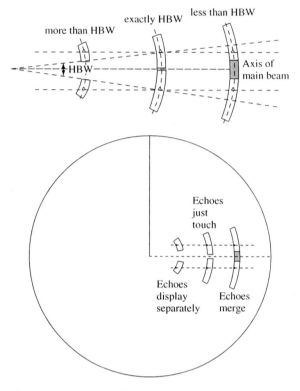

Figure 2.35 Bearing discrimination

At 10 miles

The length of the arc of the horizontal beamwidth at 10 miles is given by

$$A_B = \text{range} \times \text{horizontal beamwidth in radians}$$

$$= (10 \times 1852) \times 1.5 \times \frac{\pi}{180} \text{ metres}$$

$$= 10 \times 1852 \times 1.5 \times \frac{22}{7 \times 180} \text{ metres}$$

$$= 485.05 \text{ metres}$$

The arc represented by one spot diameter is given by

$$A_S = \frac{\text{range scale in metres}}{\text{spot diameters per radius}}$$

$$= 12 \times \frac{1852}{250} \text{m} = 88.9 \text{ metres}$$

Bearing discrimination $= A_B + A_S$

$$= 485.05 + 88.9 \text{ metres}$$

$$= 573.95 \text{ metres}$$

At 1 mile

$$A_B = 1 \times 1852 \times 1.5 \times \frac{22}{7 \times 180} \text{metres}$$

$$= 48.5 \text{ metres}$$

$$A_S = 1.5 \times \frac{1852}{250} \text{m} = 11.11 \text{ metres}$$

Bearing discrimination $= A_B + A_S$

$$= 48.5 + 11.11 \text{ metres}$$

$$= 59.61 \text{ metres}$$

It is noteworthy that, in general, the major influence is that of the horizontal beamwidth. The latter depends on aerial and transmitter characteristics, which for any single installation lie beyond the direct control of the observer (see Section 2.4.2). On older equipment the observer may, however, ensure the best available discrimination by checking that the spot is correctly focused (see Section 6.2.3.2). Care must be taken that this is not defeated by excessive brilliance, gain or contrast settings (see Sections 6.2.3.1, 6.2.4.1 and 6.3.4.1). If the use of an off-centred picture will allow the target to be displayed on a shorter range scale, the influence of spot size can be reduced.

A serious shortcoming of the use of civil marine radar for collision avoidance is its inability to offer direct indication of the heading of other vessels. Beamwidth distortion is a major contributor to this shortcoming. It also limits the usefulness of the radar for navigation by merging coastline details, such as bays and lock entrances which lie within one horizontal beamwidth. The significance of this is discussed in Section 8.2.2.

At least one manufacturer is now using digital signal processing techniques in an attempt to offset the effect of the signals received from the angular limits of the beam (see *beam processing* in section 3.9.5.1).

2.6.6   The radial-scan synthetic display

The progressive availability of low cost microprocessor technology, which began in the 1970s, has made possible the application of computer techniques to civil marine radar systems. This led to the development of what is known as the synthetic display (see Section 1.2.5), at the heart of which is a digital computer. Real-time analogue signals (see Section 2.6.2) are stored in computer memory prior to being processed and used to generate the picture. Synthetic displays designed for large commercial vessels became available from the late 1970s but until about 1985 invariably used what was essentially a radial scan PPI. To the casual observer it might appear that nothing much had changed. However closer and informed inspection would show that there were major changes in the characteristics of the picture (see Section 2.6.6.7).

From the mid-1980s the development of civil marine radar entered a new phase when raster-scan displays that were capable of compliance with the IMO Performance Standards became available. These employ a CRT of a type similar to that of a television set. Its appearance and character differ so markedly from those of a traditional marine radar display that it is described separately in Section 2.6.7.

In terms of the use of radar for collision avoidance and navigation, the processing delays involved in picture generation are infinitely small and can be neglected. However, the effect of the processing which takes place in that short time cannot be neglected. The storage of radar signal data in memory makes it possible to sample, manipulate and analyse the data. From this facility a number of benefits accrue. These include the ability to increase the overall brightness of the picture and to apply certain comparison techniques which assist in the suppression of unwanted responses (see Sections 3.6.3.3, 3.6.3.4 and 3.9.5.1). Storage is also the starting-point for the design of systems which offer automatic tracking of targets and the computation of data related to target motion (see Chapter 4). One can speculate that the pursuit of the latter ability more than of any other led to the birth and growth of the synthetic displays in civil marine radar systems. While benefits do accrue from storage, it is important to appreciate that the processing, in changing the character of the picture as compared with that of a real-time analogue display, also introduces limitations. These will be highlighted as the various types and aspects of processing are described. It is particularly important to note that the response of a synthetic picture to the adjustment of certain controls will differ from that of an analogue display (see Sections 6.3 and 6.4).

2.6.6.1 Digital storage

Radar signals may be stored digitally so that the information, now referred to as data, may be processed and recovered. The adjective *digital* derives from the fact that the data is stored as a pattern of binary digits. Binary is a system of counting in which there are only two digits, namely '0' and '1'. This contrasts with the decimal system which uses ten digits. In the binary system both (i.e. all) digits can be represented simply by a single electronic switch. In the *off* position it represents binary zero and in the *on* position binary one. It may be helpful to think of each element of memory as a mechanical on/off switch, but it must be appreciated that nothing moves and that the 'switch' is an electronic device which has two possible states. The change of state takes place in a time which for all practical purposes is instantaneous.

The comparison between decimal and binary number systems is illustrated by Figure 2.36. Underlying both systems is the concept of *place value*. This means that the significance of any digit is dependent on the column in which it is written. Thus in decimal, the digit 3 can represent 3, or 30 or 3 times any power of 10. In the binary system the digit 1 can represent 1 or 1 times any power of 2.

To understand digital storage as described in this text, the reader will not require the ability to count in binary. However, it is essential to appreciate that any number can be represented by a bank of switches, some of which are on and some of which are off, and that this is the method employed in the memory units of digital computers. It follows that if radar

signals are to be stored in commercially available computer memory they must be represented in this form. The pattern of ones and zeros may represent either a number or some other intelligence such as the presence or absence of echoes on one particular bearing. In such applications the binary pattern is commonly referred to as a *digital word*.

Each element of memory is known as a *bit* which derives from the contraction of the words 'binary digit'. The elements are usually arranged in groups of eight (or binary multiples of eight) which form a *byte*. Total memory capacity used in a radial-scan display may amount to thousands of bits. This may be described in terms of kilobytes each of which represents 1024 bits (the power of 2 nearest to 1000). In raster-scan displays, memory capacity will involve millions of bits and the unit used is the megabyte which represents 1 048 576 bytes. (This is the power of two which is nearest to one million.) The physical entity which forms a block of memory is referred to as a register or switch register. Where the arrangement of ones and zeros represents a number, the digit on the extreme left is referred to as the most significant bit (MSB) while that at the other extreme is the least significant bit (LSB).

2.6.6.2 Threshold detection

The simple principle underlying the storage of echoes is that the presence of an echo is recorded as a binary 1 while the absence of an echo is represented as a zero. To facilitate this, the analogue signal from the video amplifier (see Sections 2.5.3.2 to 2.5.3.5) must be conditioned to produce a two-level signal representing presence and absence of echoes. This operation is carried out by a device known as a threshold detector and is illustrated by Figure 2.37.

A threshold detector may be considered to be a special type of amplifier which has two inputs, one of which is known as the signal input while the other is referred to as the threshold level. The output of the threshold detector can have only two values, one of which is high and the other of which is zero. As shown by Figure 2.37, the video signal is applied to the signal input and the threshold input is preset to a chosen

Decimal

The columns in which the four digits (ONE, FOUR, SIX AND ZERO) are written may be labelled in any of the three ways shown.

Thousands	Hundreds	Tens	Units
1000	100	10	1
10^3	10^2	10^1	10^0
ONE	FOUR	SIX	ZERO

The significance of the arrangement is

ONE	×	1000	=	1000
FOUR	×	100	=	400
SIX	×	10	=	60
ZERO	×	1	=	0
TOTAL				1460

Binary

This requires eleven columns which can be labelled in either of the two ways shown. The binary digits can be indicated in any of the three ways shown.

2^{10}	2^9	2^8	2^7	2^6	2^5	2^4	2^3	2^2	2^1	2^0
1024	512	256	128	64	32	16	8	4	2	1
ONE	ZERO	ONE	ONE	ZERO	ONE	ONE	ZERO	ONE	ZERO	ZERO
ON	OFF	ON	ON	OFF	ON	ON	OFF	ON	OFF	OFF
1	0	1	1	0	1	1	0	1	0	0

The significance of the arrangement is:

ONE	×	1024	=	1024
ZERO	×	512	=	0
ONE	×	256	=	256
ONE	×	128	=	128
ZERO	×	64	=	0
ONE	×	32	=	32
ONE	×	16	=	16
ZERO	×	8	=	0
ONE	×	4	=	4
ZERO	×	2	=	0
ZERO	×	1	=	0
TOTAL				1460

Figure 2.36 Decimal and binary representations of the number 1460

Figure 2.37 Threshold detection

value related to the expected level of received signals. The circuitry within the amplifier is configured in such a way that only if the input signal exceeds the threshold level will the high output be produced. Thus the output from the threshold detector represents the presence or absence of echoes and this data can be read into computer memory as described in the next section.

It should be noticed that in the process of threshold detection, the intelligence relating to echo strength has been lost. This is of particular significance to the radar observer. In some older systems this loss was accepted at the design stage but later systems have introduced multi-threshold storage to retain some of the intelligence relating to echo strength. It is appropriate to describe the general principles of echo storage in terms of single threshold detection and subsequently to discuss its limitations together with developments designed to offset them (see Sections 2.6.6.7 and 2.6.7.4).

In a variation of the arrangement shown in Figure 2.37, the gain of the receiver is preset by its logarithmic characteristic (see Section 2.5.2.6) and the observer exercises control by virtue of the fact that the display gain control operates the threshold level. In principle, both approaches are similar in that an increase in the setting of the gain control moves the baseline of the noise and the threshold level toward one another.

It appears that the threshold detector *decides* whether or not an echo is present. However it is important to appreciate that this *decision* is based on the value of the threshold level (which will normally have been preset

on installation) and on the setting of the gain control selected by the observer. Ideally one would wish that, as illustrated by Figure 2.37, the combination of these settings would produce an output for all echoes and no output for thermal noise (see Section 2.5.2.3). Clearly this is not possible in practice because the noise amplitude is a rapidly fluctuating value. If no noise crosses the threshold, weak echoes close to noise level may not be detected, whereas if noise signals are allowed to cross the threshold they will produce the same output as an echo. The relationship between gain setting, noise amplitude and threshold level is of crucial importance in the detection of targets on a synthetic display. It is discussed in detail in Section 2.6.6.7 and the practical procedure for setting the gain control on a synthetic display is set out in Section 6.3.4.2.

2.6.6.3 *Storage of range*

The concept of range storage was introduced in Section 1.2.5 but now must be examined in more detail. The method used is best understood by studying the storage of the echoes on a single trace and subsequently considering the whole family of radial lines which make up the picture. The video signal is stored by sampling the output from the threshold detector several million times per second and writing (i.e. storing) the result of each sample in individual elements of a type of switch register known as a random access memory (RAM). The device is so called because, under the control of the computer, data can be written into and read (i.e. recalled) from the memory. This distinguishes it from a read only memory (ROM) from which data can be recalled but into which data cannot be written. The latter type of memory is used for storing the programmes necessary for computer control.

The output from the threshold detector is sometimes referred to as a *logic* waveform. This is because it is in a form (i.e. two states only – high or low) which is compatible with a very large family of two-state electronic devices, known as logic elements, which can automatically perform a wide range of logical functions of which sampling and comparison are but two examples. The principle of video sampling is illustrated in Figure 2.38.

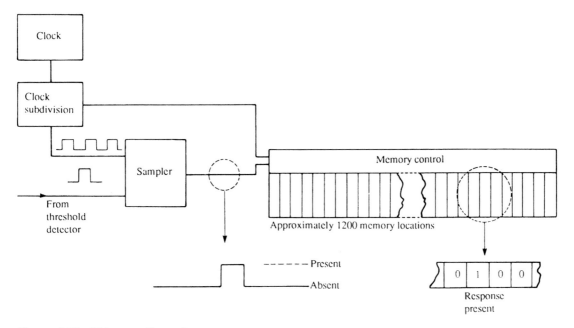

Figure 2.38 Video sampling and storage

The logic element in Figure 2.38 is an *AND* gate, which is a two-state device whose characteristic is such that its output will always be low (corresponding to binary zero) unless both of its two inputs are high. The logic waveform from the threshold detector forms one input while the other derives from an electronic clock. The latter provides a train of extremely short pulses at a very high and constant rate which commence at the instant of transmission. Reference to Figure 2.38 will show that the sampling gate will only produce a high output (corresponding to a binary one) if a radar echo is present at the same instant as a clock pulse. Hence the output of the sampling process indicates the presence or absence of an echo at extremely short, regular time intervals. The result of each sample is written into one of a very large number of separate memory locations or cells which are contained within the RAM. It is important to appreciate that the writing of the data must be done in real-time, e.g. the data for one line of the 12 mile range scale must be written in $148.16\,\mu s$, the duration of the 12 mile timebase (see Example 1.1(b) in Section 1.2.2).

The writing process is supervised by the computer memory control which, through complex logic circuitry, ensures that the data is read in sequentially with range. A binary one is set if the sample indicates the presence of a target, otherwise a zero is written. Thus the range of any detected target is implicit in the number of the cell in which it is recorded. For example if 1200 cells represent the 12 mile time base, a target at 6 miles would register a binary one in cell number 600. The number of memory elements allocated to represent one radius depends on the sampling rate and will vary with manufacturer but is generally in the region of 1000 to 1200. It must be appreciated that larger targets may register in several consecutive range cells.

Commercially available RAMs are produced in blocks which are configured in such a way that the total number of memory locations is a power of two, for example 1024 (1 kilobit). Typically, two blocks of 1 kilobit might be used in series to represent one trace. To allow for the generation of a true-motion picture, provision for about 70 per cent off-centring will usually be made. Thus 2×1024, i.e. 2048 bits will represent 170 per cent of the tube radius. The number of bits per radius is given by $2048 \times 100/170 = 1204$, i.e. approximately 1200.

If the interval between clock pulses is too large, echoes may escape detection or inadequate range accuracy and discrimination may result. The sampling rate, and hence the clock frequency must be sufficiently high to avoid any of these eventualities. This is best illustrated by a numerical example.

Example 2.8 A marine radar system uses its shortest pulse length of $0.05\,\mu s$ on the 1.5 mile range scale. Calculate a suitable sampling rate and quantify its effect on range accuracy and discrimination.

(a) *Pulse length consideration*
In order that no returning echo will be missed, sampling must occur at least once per pulse length.

$$\text{Least sampling rate (LSR)} = 1/\text{pulse length}$$
$$= 1/0.05 \times 10^{-6}$$
$$= 20\,\text{MHz}$$

Thus to sample once per pulse, LSR = 20 MHz. This is illustrated by Figure 2.39 in which consideration of pulse A will show that, regardless of its phase relationship with the clock pulses, it cannot escape sampling.

(b) *Range accuracy consideration*
If one memory location is allocated to each sample, then the number of locations N is given by

$$N = \frac{\text{timebase}}{\text{interval between samples}}$$
$$= \frac{1.5 \times 1852}{150} \times \text{LSR}$$
$$= 18.52 \times 10^{-6} \times 20 \times 10^{6} = 371$$

The range interval (I) represented by each memory location is given by

$$I = \frac{1.5 \times 1852}{371} = 7.5 \text{ metres}$$

It follows that the stored range of any given target will be an integer multiple of 7.5 m. Reference to echo B in Figure 2.39 shows that a target at a range

of almost 48.75 m will have a stored range of 45 m. This represents the maximum error which is half the sample range interval and is within the 30 m accuracy specified by the IMO Performance Standard (see Section 11.2.1) for this range scale. It follows that if the target is moving with respect to the observing vessel its range will appear to change in steps. This is called *range quantizing error* and is of particular significance in automatic tracking (see Section 9.5.3.2).

(c) *Range discrimination consideration*
Reference to echoes C and D in Figure 2.39 will show that the targets producing them are 7.5 m apart (half pulse length) and thus are at the limit of range discrimination. Their stored echoes will just touch because they are in adjacent cells. It should, however, be noted that they will continue to be in adjacent cells until their separation is increased by a further half the sample range interval. The separation is well within the 40 m required by the IMO Performance Standard (see Sections 2.6.5.5 and 11.2.1).

It is evident from the above calculations that a sampling rate of 20 MHz would be adequate to produce one sample per pulse and that the quantizing effect would be a fraction of the ranging error permitted by the IMO Performance Standards. However, in practice, to produce high resolution storage so that automatic tracking can be offered (see Section 9.5.3.2), many radar designers use clock frequencies which are effectively between two and three times higher (i.e. approximately 40–60 MHz) than that suggested in Example 2.8 and consequently allocate a correspondingly larger number of cells to each radius (of the order of 1000–1200). In practice the clock will run at a fixed frequency (the master or basic frequency) equal to that required for the shortest range scale/pulse length. When longer range scales/pulse lengths are selected, submultiples of the master frequency will be obtained by the use of successive *divide by two* devices. These are logic devices which produce an output pulse for every alternate input pulse received. Physical constraints normally limit the master clock frequency to the order of 32 MHz, though it is possible, by using two memory banks in parallel and a technique known as multiplexing, to produce an effective sampling rate of

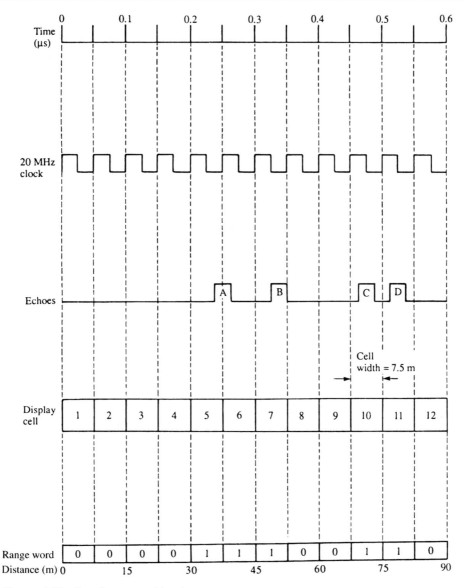

Figure 2.39 Sample rate considerations

twice that frequency. It should be appreciated that if a higher sampling rate is used a point target will be written sequentially in more than one memory location.

Thus far, this section has described the real-time storage of the data on a single trace. The pattern of ones and zeros so obtained is referred to as a *range word*. Clearly, by repeating the procedure the entire picture can be stored by generating a range word for each of the radial lines which make up the picture. This is illustrated by the left-hand side of Figure 2.40. In generating a radial-scan synthetic picture on the screen (see Section 2.6.6.5), each range word is read out of memory almost immediately after it has been read in. Thus a single block of memory having a capacity of one range word can be used to store each line in turn, obviating the need to have a separate block for each individual line. However, where a raster-scan picture is to be produced (see Section 2.6.7), the entire picture must be held in store in the form of the matrix illustrated by Figure 2.40.

2.6.6.4 *Storage of bearing*

This is achieved by converting the analogue signal which represents aerial bearing (see Sections 2.4.5 and 2.6.3) into a digital signal which is called a *bearing word*. The mechanics of the conversion from analogue to digital vary with manufacturer but all systems use the principle that aerial bearing is an angle which increases progressively from 0° to 360° (relative) as

the scanner rotates and can thus be represented by a binary number which increases from zero to some maximum at the same rate and in the same time. Most civil marine systems designed for large vessels use a 12-bit word. A pattern of 12 binary ones represents the decimal number $4095(2^{12} + 2^{11} + \cdots + 2^0)$. If the zero condition is taken into account, there are 4096 binary increments between zero and maximum and hence the 12-bit word can be used to represent 4096 unique angles between 0° and 360°. This means that the angle can be stored in steps of 360°/4096, i.e. just under $\frac{1}{10}$ of a degree. Thus the appropriate incremental bearing word can be read into memory alongside the corresponding range word in the memory matrix as illustrated in Figure 2.40.

A study of the matrix reveals that the range and bearing of any target is defined by the column and row in which its digital sample appears. The range of

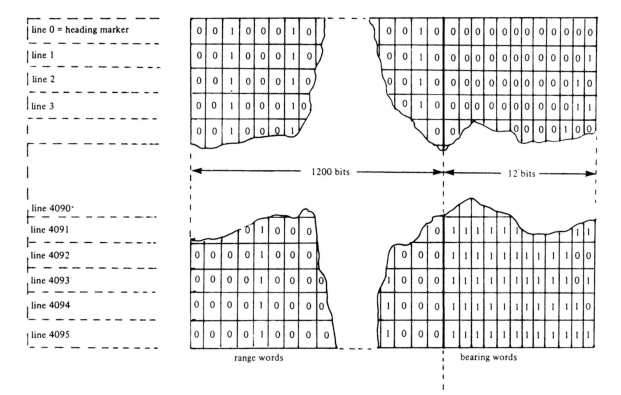

Figure 2.40 Memory matrix

any target is specified by the product of its consecutive range cell number and the range cell interval (see Section 2.6.6.3). Similarly, the bearing is specified by the number of incremental steps which have occurred since binary zero. If a ship's-head-up orientation is selected, the aerial count will be set to zero at the instant that the axis of the main beam is directly ahead and the heading marker contacts close, whereas in the case of true-north-up orientation, zero aerial count will be coincident with true north.

In many systems, the rotation signal is transmitted to the display in synchro or similar analogue form (see Section 2.4.5) and there converted into digital form. For each angular position of the aerial between 0° and 360° the resultant synchro signal available in the display has a value which is unique in magnitude and polarity. A purpose-built solid-state logic device known as a *synchro/digital converter* samples the synchro signal at very short regular intervals and hence calculates the aerial angle which will increment in binary steps

from 0 to 4096 as the aerial rotates. An alternative approach is to employ an aerial-driven pulse generator which will typically produce one pulse per degree of rotation. The pulse train is used as input to a computer circuit which generates 4096 pulses per 360 degrees of rotation. Effectively, the computer circuit fills in the missing pulses between the 360 received from the aerial by sensing the angular speed of the aerial from the interval between successive raw aerial pulses.

A third method employs an electromechanical device known as a *shaft encoder* which is driven 1:1 by the aerial. Although in civil marine applications this technique is much less common than the other two, it is worthy of some study as it provides graphic illustration of analogue-to-digital angle conversion.

Figure 2.41 shows that the moving element of a shaft encoder is a disk formed from a series of concentric rings of equal depth. Each ring is subdivided into an equal number of sectors. The number of sectors per ring increases outward from the centre in

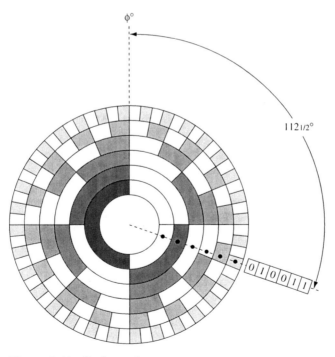

Figure 2.41 Shaft encoder

binary progression, i.e. the nth ring has 2^n sectors. In any given ring, sectors are connected to either a high level or a low level logic signal on an alternate basis, i.e. any sector will be at a logic level different from either of its angular neighbours. A family of sliding contacts (or brushes) lies along a radius with one contact being allocated to each ring. As the disk rotates below the group of fixed contacts, the latter will pick off a pattern of binary ones and zeros which represents the aerial angle and which can be read into memory as a bearing word. It should be noticed that the number of unique words which can be produced by the encoder is equal to the number of segments in the outer ring, i.e. the ring which generates the LSB.

For clarity of illustration, Figure 2.41 shows an encoder having only six rings, i.e. a six-bit encoder. It has $64(2^6)$ segments in the outer ring and thus the digital angle will increase in steps of $360°/64$, i.e. $5.625°$ (one half compass point). Clearly, although this is suitable for purposes of illustration, its steps are much too coarse to be of practical use. In Section 1.3.2 it was established that a real-time picture is built up of approximately 3600 radial lines and that there is one radial line for each transmitted pulse. To emulate this, the aerial angle should be digitized in steps of about $\frac{1}{10}°$ which would require approximately 3600 segments in the outer ring of the shaft encoder. The nearest binary value higher than 3600 is 4096 and thus a 12-bit encoder is appropriate.

Brushes and slip rings provide a convenient illustration of the shaft encoder principle but they are noted for their poor operation, especially in the hostile marine environment. In modern systems, optical techniques are employed.

In general, whatever the type of the transmission device, if it is attached directly to the aerial driveshaft most of the errors resulting from gearing backlash can be eliminated.

The aerial bearing is obtained from the sum of the aerial angle and the vessel's instantaneous heading (see Section 2.6.3). This addition may be performed by adding the analogue signals (e.g. by means of a synchro transformer) or by digitizing both quantities individually and performing the addition thereafter. From the observer's point of view the distinction is academic.

2.6.6.5 Synthetic picture generation

The preceding sections have shown that the analogue video and rotation signals can be digitized and stored in memory in real-time. This section will consider how the range and bearing data are read out from memory and used to generate a radial-scan synthetic picture. The read function is illustrated in block diagram form by Figure 2.42, which also includes the units associated with the write function because the timings of both functions are inextricably linked, as shown by the time sequence diagram of Figure 2.43.

Immediately the last element of range data associated with any given radial line has been stored, the reading out of that line commences. The data which is read out may be processed as described in Section 2.6.6.6 or it may pass directly to circuitry which conditions it and mixes it with the heading line, the calibration marks and other internally generated signals to produce a composite video signal of sufficient power to drive the cathode of the CRT (see Section 2.6.1). In some texts this stage is described as being *analogue*. This is intended to indicate that the circuitry is neither computer memory nor low-voltage logic but is of the conventional type normally used to handle analogue signals. It is, however, somewhat misleading because the signal is clearly digital in character and is no longer analogous to the echoes which produced it, since it is either a single-level signal (see Figure 2.44) or a small number of discrete values (see Figures 2.45 and 2.46). In most, though not all, systems a contrast control is provided. This allows the observer to adjust the brightness level of the synthetic echoes which represent the presence of targets. It is important to appreciate that all targets stored at the same level will have the same brightness. The correct procedure for the adjustment of the contrast control is discussed in Section 6.3.4.1. It should be noted that the function of the contrast control on a radial-scan radar display is somewhat different from the control of the same name found on a domestic television set and on raster-scan displays (see Section 6.4.3.1).

Clearly, it is essential that the data for any radial line is written into memory in real-time, i.e. in the duration of the timebase of the selected range scale, since that is

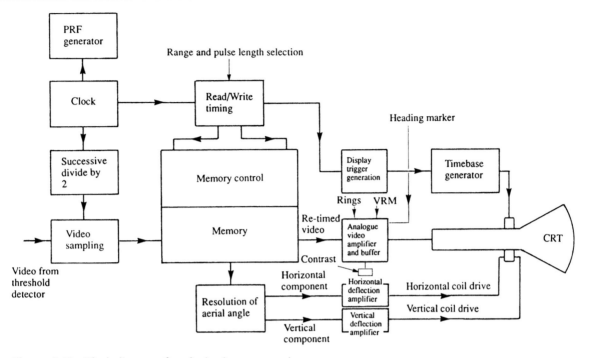

Figure 2.42 Block diagram of synthetic picture generation

the interval in which it is received. Thus the time taken to write the data into memory varies with selected range scale. However, the data can be read out of memory at a constant rate so long as this is done in the same time as it takes for the spot to travel from the centre to the edge of the screen. In a radial-scan synthetic display the read-out and sweep times are the same on all range scales and normally correspond with the timebase of either the 6 or the 12 mile range scale, depending on manufacturer. This means that, on the shorter range scales, the sweep time is slower than it would be in the case of a real-time display. Certain benefits accrue from a slow fixed readout time. From an engineering and production point of view it is advantageous, since it dispenses with the need to provide separate timebase circuitry and associated switching for each range scale. It also avoids the need to produce the very fast sweep times demanded by a real-time picture on the very short range scales. If, for the purposes of discussion, we assume that the read-out time

is $148.16\,\mu\text{s}$ (i.e. the timebase on the 12 mile range scale) then it is evident that, on all range scales less than 12 miles, the time taken for the spot to cross the screen will be a multiple of that which would be required for a real-time display. This slowing down of the spot increases the inherent brightness of the picture.

It has long been recognized that, other than in conditions of darkness, a real-time picture cannot be viewed successfully without the aid of a hood or visor. This is particularly the case on the shorter range scales because the spot travels so fast that it has very limited ability to excite the phosphor (see Section 2.6.1.2). In a radial-scan synthetic display, the effect of the relatively slow sweep rate is to extend the range of ambient light conditions in which it is unnecessary to use a hood. However, the improvement is not sufficient to allow full daylight viewing.

On range scales greater than 12 miles the spot speed will be greater than in the real-time case. This in itself will tend to reduce the inherent brightness

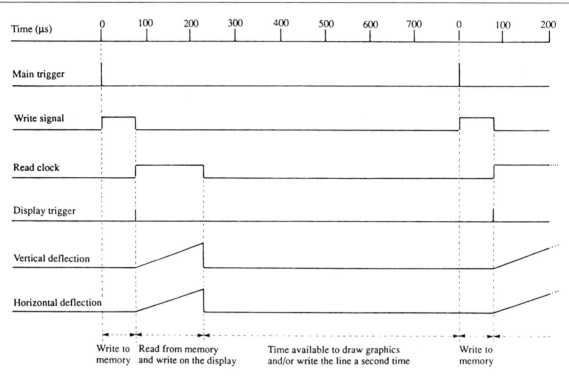

Figure 2.43   Time-sequence diagram for a radial-scan synthetic picture

of the picture, but the effect will be offset by the high synthetic brightness of the displayed echoes and possibly by writing each line more than once (the only theoretical limit to writing each line several times is the need to complete writing before the start of the next time sequence). With regard to echo brightness, the reader is reminded that in a real-time picture the echo brightness of weak targets is a function of signal strength (see Sections 2.5.2.5 and 2.6.1), whereas in a synthetic picture the equal brightness of all displayed echoes is a function of the setting of the contrast control which may be adjusted to suit the ambient light conditions. This is illustrated by Figure 2.44, while the correct practical procedure for the adjustment of the contrast is discussed in Section 6.3.4.1. To improve further the inherent picture brightness on the longer range scales, each line may be written twice (or possibly more often), since on these scales the lowest PRF will be used (see Section 2.3.4), thus offering a

suitably long PRP. The faster timebase on the longer range scales will extend the radial paint of a small target and may assist detection by making it more obvious.

The radial-scan synthetic picture is sometimes referred to as *re-timed video* because it is not read out at the same rate as it was written into memory. There will of course be one range scale on which write and read times are the same. In some earlier synthetic displays a memory bypass was included which allowed the observer to select either a synthetic or a real-time picture, albeit on that one range scale only. To the radar observer this was an extremely attractive feature as it allowed an assessment of the setting of the gain and tuning controls to be made against simple, traditional criteria (see Section 6.2.4), while also ensuring that one range scale would remain available in the event of memory failure.

As each range word is read out of memory, so too is the corresponding bearing word (see Figure 2.40).

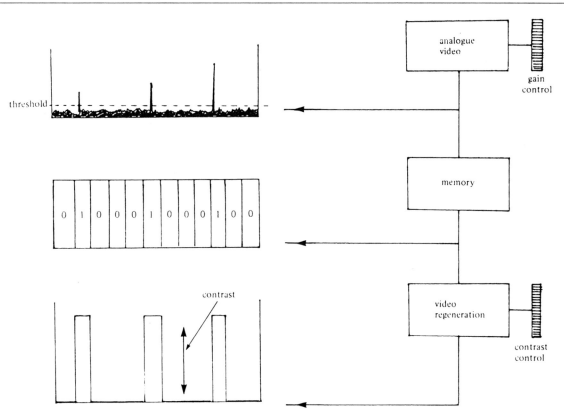

Figure 2.44 Single-level video

The digital computer calculates the sine and the cosine of the instantaneous aerial angle and uses each of these to control the magnitude of two analogue deflection signals which drive two sets of fixed deflection coils that are wound mutually at right angles on a yoke assembly around the neck of the tube. These are named the X coils and the Y coils because they produce deflection parallel to the horizontal and vertical axes respectively (see Figure 2.42). The spot deflection is thus produced by two forces whose directions are at right angles to one another and whose magnitudes vary in sympathy with the sine and cosine of the aerial angle. Hence, although there is no physical rotation of the coils as was described in Section 2.6.1.3, the trace will rotate in sympathy with the aerial angle (see Figure 2.30).

From an engineering point of view there is considerable virtue in using fixed rather than rotating coils.

It dispenses with the progressive wear and continual mechanical noise which are undesirable features of rotating coil assemblies and their associated motors and gearboxes. For technical reasons beyond the scope of this text, at very high sweep rates it is easier to achieve accurate and effective beam deflection by using rotating rather than fixed coils. By making possible a relatively long sweep time on the very short range scales (16 times longer on the $\frac{3}{4}$ mile range scale), the advent of digital storage made the use of fixed coils even more attractive to the radar designer.

True-motion facilities (see also Section 2.6.4) can be provided by digitizing and resolving the analogue course and speed inputs and hence energizing a fixed set (possibly the same set as described above) of off-centring coils.

This section has been concerned with setting out the principles on which the generation of a radial-scan synthetic picture is based and has highlighted the ways in which the techniques differ from those already described for real-time pictures. It must be appreciated that the technical differences between the ways in which the two types of pictures are generated result in the synthetic echoes having characteristics which are radically different from those produced on the traditional real-time display. Failure to appreciate this may result in serious misinterpretation of the picture and maladjustment of the controls. The significance of these differences is discussed in Sections 2.6.6.7, 6.3 and 6.4.

2.6.6.6 Signal processing

While the received signal is stored in memory it can be processed in a variety of ways. In the case of civil marine synthetic radial-scan systems, this provision normally takes the form of interference suppression, noise reduction and echo stretching techniques. Normally these facilities can be selected at will by the observer. Their operation and use are described in Sections 3.9.5.1 and 6.11.1.

Manufacturers now use a variety of signal processing techniques to process the radar signal to distinguish weak solid targets from clutter. They generally now involve the use of computer power and memory to search for targets in the clutter aided by comparison with radar data of previous pulses and scans.

2.6.6.7 Multi-level synthetic video

In the description of single-level threshold detection (see Section 2.6.6.2), attention was drawn to the fact that intelligence relating to echo strength is lost by this process. This can be seen clearly from Figure 2.44 which shows that received echoes of differing strengths produce synthetic echoes all of which have the same brightness. Clearly there is merit in this approach as it has the effect of emphasizing the echoes of very weak targets. Such a target, which may be difficult to detect on an analogue display, will produce an obvious synthetic echo of full brightness even if it barely crosses the threshold. This benefit must be traded against the loss of indication of echo strength and the implications of this loss require serious consideration.

In an analogue receiver, echoes may have any amplitude over a continuous range from receiver noise to amplifier saturation level (see Sections 2.5.2.3 and 2.5.2.1). Although the range of received echoes is continuous, the excitation characteristic of the screen (see Section 2.6.1.2) is such that the stronger signals may saturate the phosphor. Further, there is a limit to the number of discrete brightness levels which the phosphor can display. This is probably not more than eight and is a measure of the intelligence which is lost by single-level storage. However, the usefulness of this intelligence is a matter of some debate. Some mariners do draw conclusions from the strength of the displayed echoes but the validity of these conclusions is very much open to question when it is recognized that a yacht with a radar reflector (see Section 3.4) may return an echo whose strength compares favourably with that from a medium-sized ship. Irrespective of the debate as to the intelligence that can (or cannot) be deduced from a knowledge of echo strength, it is beyond dispute that an understanding of this loss of a continuous range of echo strengths is essential when judging the correct setting of the gain and tuning controls of a synthetic display. The importance of this is discussed further under practical procedures in Sections 6.3.4.3 and 6.4.4.

A major practical problem associated with single-level storage is that any noise which does cross the threshold will be displayed with the same brightness as the echoes from even the strongest targets (see Section 2.6.6.2). This does not compare favourably with an analogue picture in which the brightness of noise echoes is a fraction of that of strong echoes. As radial-scan synthetic displays have developed, designers have attempted to offset this problem by introducing two or more thresholds in order to increase the number of brightness levels which can be allocated to displayed echoes. It is evident that one threshold is necessary for each proposed brightness level. The principle of two-level storage is illustrated by Figure 2.45, which for reasons of clarity shows only 12 range cells per screen radius.

Two thresholds, designated high and low, are used and a separate range word is allocated to each threshold. A target which crosses the high threshold

Figure 2.45 The principle of two-level threshold detection

must also cross the low threshold and will thus be stored as a binary one in both range words. A target which crosses the low-level threshold only will be stored in one range word only and of course a target which fails to cross the low threshold will be stored as a zero in both words. It follows that some intelligence as to signal strength has been preserved and that signals can be classified as *high-level* and *low-level* and thus used to produce one of two brightness levels on the display. (Many systems produce the effect by exciting the phosphor two (or more) times per strong target and thus use the integrating property of the phosphor to obtain the high level brightness.) The relative levels of the thresholds and the ratio of high-level to low-level brilliance are not under the control of the observer and will vary with manufacturer. Figure 2.45 shows a fairly small ratio of high to low level echo brightness which is typical of some earlier systems.

More recent designs have tended to choose a ratio in the region of 10:1 and to place the thresholds fairly close together. The problem of trying to set a single threshold to the correct level was mentioned in Section 2.6.6.2. The general philosophy of twin thresholds is probably best explained in terms of the single-threshold problem. If a single threshold is set too high, weak echoes will not be displayed; if it is set too low, excessive noise will cross the threshold and will make it difficult to detect weak targets because their echoes will have to compete for the observer's attention with a large number of noise pulses, all of which will be of the same brightness as the echoes which are sought. Clearly the perfect setting which would show all echoes and no noise cannot be achieved and in practice, with a single threshold, a compromise must be accepted in which a certain amount of stored noise is tolerated. By employing two thresholds, with one set a little higher than the compromise level, i.e. just clear of the noise peaks, and one a little lower, i.e. just below the peaks of the noise, the problem can be greatly eased. All but the very weak targets will cross the high threshold and produce high-level synthetic echoes which will be obvious against the low-level echo background. The weak echoes which are close to the level of the noise peaks will be detected and, like these peaks, will be displayed as low-level synthetic echoes. The observer thus should have no problem in detecting all but the very weakest echoes as they are the only ones which have to compete with the stored noise. The lower level of video is sometimes referred to as *grey level* and this is illustrated by Figure 2.46.

The positions of the twin thresholds relative to one another are normally preset by the manufacturer but the position of the lower threshold with respect to the noise is adjusted by the observer by means of the gain control. The correct procedure for judging the correct amount of noise, and hence the setting of this control, is described in Section 6.3.4.2.

Many radial-scan synthetic displays offered high-level and grey-level video, but most systems now offer three or more levels. Given the limited dynamic range of the phosphor, one can speculate as to exactly how many threshold levels are necessary fully to mimic an analogue display. One system produced in the mid-1980s pursued this goal by offering sixteen brightness levels. It has to be said that the latter approach is very much the exception rather than the rule.

Note. With two memory planes (as in Figure 2.44) it is actually possible to store a zero level and three different levels of brightness on screen. Thus, the system displayed in Figure 2.44 could have three levels of brightness (not two) with no extra memory required. Adding a third memory plane allows for a zero and seven levels of brightness.

Single-level video will exacerbate the masking effect of sea and rain clutter (see Sections 3.6 and 3.7).

The video produced by threshold detection is sometimes referred to as quantized video. The term *quantized* refers to the fact that the brightness of the displayed echoes can only take one of a number of discrete levels and does not have a continuous range of possible values.

2.6.7   The raster-scan synthetic display

In this type of display the radar picture is produced on a television screen and is built up of a large number

Figure 2.46   Two-level video with grey level

of horizontal lines which form a pattern known as a raster (see Section 2.6.7.1). It is a logical development of the radial-scan synthetic display but is much more complex and requires a much larger amount of memory (Figure 2.40). For both user and designer a number of benefits accrue from the adoption of raster-scan in preference to the more traditional radial-scan techniques, but some deficiencies have also to be accepted. The design factors will be highlighted where appropriate in the following technical description, while Section 6.4 is devoted to the factors which affect the practical setting up and interpretation of the picture. From the observer's point of view, the most obvious advantage of raster-scan is the brightness of the picture which allows it to be viewed, at a distance, by several observers in almost all conditions of ambient light. Most, if not all mariners who have ever used a radial-scan display would agree that its most significant practical limitation is the difficulty of viewing it in daylight. Probably the attractiveness of daylight viewing more than any other benefit has ensured the development of the raster-scan display, despite any disadvantages that may have to be accepted.

2.6.7.1   The monochrome television CRT

In the mid-1980s the introduction of this type of viewing device to civil marine applications represented a major departure from almost fifty years of radar tradition in which the conventional circular screen CRT (see Section 2.6.1) was taken for granted. In the early 1970s one manufacturer did present a marine radar picture on a monochrome television screen, but it was generated from a conventional rotating trace tube which produced a picture on an electronic image-retaining panel. The latter was viewed by a television camera which relayed the picture to the television screen by a closed-circuit television link. Such a system was analogue in its nature and fundamentally different from the modern raster-scan display in which the picture is written into computer memory and read out onto the television screen.

Some systems produce a monochrome picture, while others offer several colours. The following description relates to a monochrome display, i.e. one which can display one colour and black. Colour tubes are described separately in Section 2.6.7.7.

The significant difference between a conventional radar CRT and its television counterpart is that the latter has a rectangular screen. The screen size is specified by the length of the diagonal and the width and height of the screen are traditionally in the approximate ratio 4:3. Starting in the top left-hand corner of the screen, the spot writes the picture by tracing out a pattern of horizontal lines from top to bottom (see Figure 2.47), each individual line running from left to right. While each line is being written the spot brightness is determined by the no-signal setting of the brilliance control as modified by the video signal. Between lines, while the spot flies back from right to left, the brilliance is suppressed. The majority of television tubes are mass-produced for use in domestic television receivers and therefore the number of horizontal lines which form a complete picture (referred to as a frame or field) must conform to an agreed standard. In Europe the agreed line standard is 625 lines per frame, whereas in the USA the value is 525. A lesser number of tubes are produced for special high-resolution applications and are available with a higher line standard such as 1024. Clearly it has been long established that line standards in the region 525–625 produce an acceptable domestic television picture. The question of its suitability for marine radar will be discussed in this section but at this stage it is worth noting that a major advantage of using established line standards is the ready availability of relatively cheap mass-produced components which have been tried and tested in the television industry.

The moving picture viewed on a domestic television is in fact a succession of still pictures (or frames) produced at an extremely high repetition rate in the same way as a movie film is produced from a succession of stills. Provided that the interval between stills is sufficiently small, i.e. the frame repetition rate is sufficiently high, the human eye will fail to notice any flicker between successive stills, and will perceive smooth movement. For a movie film this requires a frame rate of about 25 per second. Unfortunately this is not fast enough for television

Spot writes horizontal line   Spot flies back after line

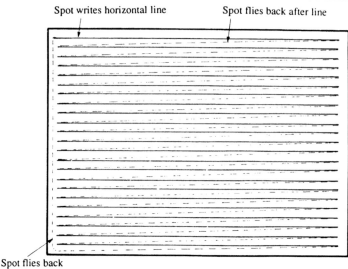

Spot flies back
after frame

Figure 2.47 Television raster

pictures because, whereas in screening a film each still is totally exposed immediately, on a television screen it is exposed progressively from top to bottom. As a result, television requires a frame rate of about 50 per second. This was unattractive to television designers because there are technical difficulties in generating as many as 50 × 625 lines per second.

The necessary compromise was achieved by a technique known as *interlace*. By generating only the odd numbered lines (1,3,5,...,625) in one sequence and the even numbered lines (2,4,6,...,624) in the next sequence it is possible to renew half the picture 50 times per second but the entire picture only 25 times per second. Because the odd and even lines are interlaced, the human eye sees the picture as being renewed 50 times per second and does not perceive any flicker. This allows the designer to halve the rate at which the horizontal lines are generated. In domestic television receivers, for practical reasons, the frame rate is derived from the frequency of the national electricity supply, resulting in frame rates of 50 or 60 per second according to the country in which it is to be used. It is this extremely high refresh rate which gives the raster-scan radar display its daylight viewing potential. In practice, it is not possible to use

all of the horizontal lines for picture presentation, a few being lost at the top and at the bottom. However from the radar observer's point of view this is of academic interest and will not be discussed further.

Unfortunately, interlace, the very technique which is used in domestic television to remove flicker, introduces a flicker effect when a marine radar picture is displayed on a television screen. This arises because a television picture is derived from a television camera which scans a rectangular matrix (i.e. one set out in terms of X and Y) and the picture is read onto the screen at a similar rate and in a similar format; a raster-scan radar display, however, is derived from a relatively slowly updating radial data pattern (i.e. in terms of range and bearing) but read onto the screen as a rectangular matrix (see Section 2.6.7.2) with a high refresh rate. This presents the radar designer with a dilemma. The choice is between selecting mass-produced television technology for its ready and economic availability or opting for more specialized tubes (and associated electronics) and dispensing with interlace to remove the flicker which some observers find tiring and intrusive. Given the limited sea experience which observers have had with raster-scan displays, it is not surprising that some manufacturers elected to use interlace while others decided to refresh the full picture 50–60 times per second.

Nowadays, the use of interlace is much less, as low cost, high refresh rate monitors have become commonly available for the computer industry.

The television CRT has two sets of fixed deflection coils. One set produces horizontal deflection to generate the lines of the raster, while the other produces the vertical deflection necessary to ensure that successive lines are drawn progressively further down the screen from top to bottom. Both the deflection waveforms will have the distinctive *sawtooth* shape illustrated in Figure 2.27 which accompanied the description of rotating coil deflection presented in Section 2.6.1.3, but their repetition rates will differ from the conventional radar case and from one another. The line frequency will be a large multiple of the frame frequency. The precise values will depend on the standard adopted: if one considers the European standard, the frame rate will be 50 per second while, assuming interlace, the line rate will be $50 \times 625/2$ which is 15.625 kHz.

The general properties of phosphors were discussed in Section 2.6.1.2 and it was established that, by the correct choice of chemical constituents, a phosphor having an appropriate colour and persistence can be manufactured. For general monochrome television use the colour is white. This is not ideal for the conditions under which a civil marine radar is viewed. The radar display tends to be viewed from a shorter distance than with television and the observer has to concentrate to a very much greater degree on picture detail for long periods of time. For monochrome raster-scan applications most designers elected to use a green phosphor, probably because this was the colour readily available from CRT types already produced in reasonable numbers for other applications. While there is very limited experience of how observers will react to raster-scan displays, it is believed that a green phosphor provides comfortable viewing and that it is not likely to produce excessive tiredness and stress. Orange is also a suitable colour but the phosphor is not as readily available in television CRTs and has a greater tendency to *burn* (see Section 2.6.1.2). In general, however, television tubes burn less easily and

less quickly than traditional radar CRTs and this represents another benefit of the use of raster-scan. The television tubes are also cheaper, but the complexity of the necessary signal processing for the raster-scan display unit reduces some of the cost advantage.

It was mentioned in Section 2.6.7.1 that in the early 1970s one manufacturer presented a marine radar picture on a monochrome television screen using analogue conversion techniques. The system in question offered two modes of viewing. In the positive mode, light-coloured targets were displayed against a black background, whereas in the negative mode the colours were inverted. This option gave the observer the freedom to select the mode most suited to the ambient light conditions. Some colour raster displays provide day and night viewing modes (see Section 2.6.7.8).

In contrast with a rotating trace tube, the television screen uses a phosphor which has an extremely short persistence. Longer persistence is not only unnecessary, because of the high refresh rate, but would be a positive nuisance when any detail of the picture changed. However, the short persistence does mean that moving targets will not leave the characteristic afterglow trails associated with a conventional radar display. Raster-scan displays use data storage techniques to generate artificial trails; these are described in Section 2.6.7.5.

As in any CRT, the spot diameter (see Section 2.6.5.1) determines the smallest area of light that can be produced on the screen. Thus, along each horizontal line there will be a finite number of picture elements, referred to as *pixels*, the total number of which will be determined by the number of spot diameters per screen width. Assuming a spot diameter of 0.5 mm (values as small as 0.2 mm are available) and the European line standard, a 584 mm (23 inch) tube, which is the theoretical minimum size on which it is possible to produce a 340 mm PPI, will have approximately 940 pixels per line. It follows that the whole screen will be represented by a rectangular matrix of pixels comprising 625 rows and 940 columns. It should also be noted that a 26 inch CRT tube is often used as it allows for text around the display and the loss of about one inch of unusable picture typical of CRT screens.

Thus to produce a synthetic radar picture on a television screen the stored radar data must be read out to the screen in terms of X and Y co-ordinates and not in terms of range and bearing as was the case for a radial-scan display (see Section 2.6.6.5). In a raster-scan display the co-ordinate conversion is carried out by the digital computer within the display and the process is known as digital scan conversion (DSC).

2.6.7.2 Digital scan conversion

Each element of the radar picture may be stored in terms of its range from the origin and bearing from the heading marker, or true north (see Sections 2.6.6.3 and 2.6.6.4). Such storage is said to be in terms of *polar co-ordinates*. Alternatively, each element may be stored in terms of its northings and eastings from the origin, in which case the co-ordinates are said to be *cartesian*. By the very principle of its operation the radar generates the raw data in polar co-ordinates and the function of the digital scan conversion unit is to calculate the corresponding cartesian co-ordinates. The operation is similar to that carried out by the navigator who lays off a range and bearing on the chart to indicate the ship's position and then reads off the latitude and longitude from the scale borders of the chart to record it in lat./long. form in the log book. The technique is illustrated in block diagram and graphic form by Figure 2.48.

For clarity of illustration, Figure 2.48 shows the polar memory to have only twelve elements per radius rather than the representative practical value of 1200 suggested in Sections 2.6.6.3 and 2.6.6.4. To assist in comparison, the cartesian memory is also shown as having 12 elements either side of the origin along both the X and the Y axes. In practice, cartesian memories have less elements per unit radius; the significance of this important point will be discussed in Section 2.6.7.3.

Figure 2.48 shows that the input to the DSC unit is the retimed video and digital angle. For any given polar location specified by a range R and an angle θ, the cartesian co-ordinates will be given by:

$$X = R \times \mathrm{sine}\,\theta \quad \text{and} \quad Y = R \times \mathrm{cosine}\,\theta$$

The arithmetic unit of the digital computer calculates the X and Y values of incoming raw radar data from the polar location R, θ which is then stored (either as a one or a zero) in the cartesian location X, Y.

After one rotation of the aerial, the cartesian memory will contain all the data for one complete radar picture. The digital computer can read out this data and repeatedly generate a picture on the television screen at a rate which is independent of the aerial rotation speed. Thus the raster-scan picture can be refreshed at a rate of about 50–60 times per second, which is about 150–180 times as often as is the case with a radial-scan display which can only be refreshed after each rotation of the aerial (approximately 3 seconds). It is vital to appreciate the significant difference that exists between the refreshing of the picture and the updating of the picture. A real-time radial-scan radar display is updated and refreshed once per revolution of the aerial. A raster-scan display is refreshed once per television frame but only updated once per aerial revolution, since updating can only take place when more recent data has been read into the cartesian memory.

In Figure 2.33 it was shown that the shape of the radar resolution cell was the area of a sector contained between two concentric arcs. The process of scan conversion will tend to degrade this resolution because, if the radar resolution cell even partially overlaps a cartesian memory location, the entire corresponding screen location will be brightened. This is illustrated in Figure 2.48. Any variation of the target return from aerial revolution to revolution will change the pattern of cartesian cells in a way which is more noticeable than is the same effect on a traditional rotating-trace display. This variation of picture content can prove to be distracting and tiring. It may also be found to stress the observer.

2.6.7.3 The raster-scan PPI

The IMO Performance Standards (see Section 11.2.1) require the equipment to produce a plan display with an effective diameter of not less than 180 mm, 250 mm or 320 mm, depending on the size of the vessel. The application of these standards effectively

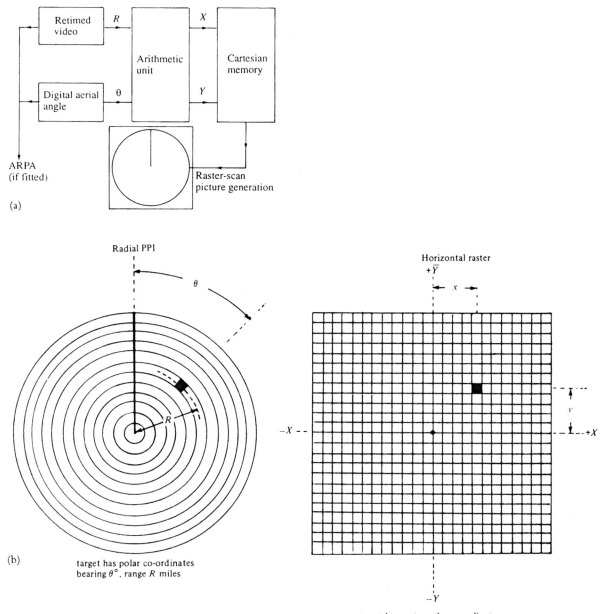

Figure 2.48 Digital scan conversion (DSC)

(a) Block diagram

(b) Memory arrangement

chooses the diameter of a conventional circular screen, whereas, given the shape of the television type screen, the designer has to decide where within the rectangle to have the display computer draw the appropriate size of circle. There is no general consensus on this point; three representative examples are shown by Figure 2.49 and it should be noted that the remaining screen space is used to give a read-out of numerical data or control status. A major advantage of the raster-scan display is the ease with which auxiliary data can be written around or within the picture area (no mechanical dials or scales are necessary).

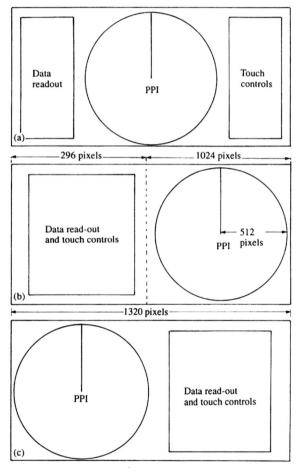

Figure 2.49 The raster-scan PPI: the pixel numbers shown represent high-resolution memory

In some modern systems the television screen has a touch-sensitive characteristic and the observer can operate certain controls simply by touching the appropriate screen location. This is achieved by means of a thin overlay consisting of two layers of plastic between which lies a matrix of a very large number of elemental areas whose conductivity is sensitive to finger pressure. Another modern approach is to exploit the principle of infra-red remote control which is used extensively in the domestic television market.

It is now appropriate to consider the allocation of memory locations, or cells, to represent the picture. To produce a simple illustration of a DSC in Figure 2.48 only twelve memory locations were allocated to represent the radius of the PPI. In Section 2.6.7.1 it was shown that the minimum size of television screen capable of showing a 340 mm PPI would have a matrix of approximately 940 by 625 pixels. Clearly there should be at least one memory cell for each pixel. In practice, designers may arrange that the ratio of memory cells to pixels is a little greater than unity, thus ensuring that the available screen resolution is fully exploited. The arrangement of memory locations is referred to as a *memory plane* and they are in general only produced in a limited number of preferred sizes. Commonly available formats have 512, 768, 1024 or 1360 cells per horizontal or vertical dimension. From these values rectangular matrices having an aspect ratio of approximately 4:3 can be produced. A representative allocation of pixels is shown in Figure 2.49(b).

The memory plane associated with Figure 2.49(b) is suited to a television screen having a frame rate of 1024, as in the vertical dimension the ratio of pixels to lines is unity. Having 1320 cells in the horizontal dimension, the aspect ratio of the memory plane closely approaches the 4:3 ratio of the screen. The diameter of PPI circle which can be drawn is limited by the vertical dimension of the screen; by using the values given in Figure 2.49(b), this results in an allocation of 512 cells per PPI radius.

In Section 2.6.6.3 storage of range was discussed in detail, including the relationship between sampling rate and allocation of memory. Reference to that section, and in particular to Example 2.8, will show that 512 cells per radius exceed the minimum consistent with the least sampling rate and that required to ensure adequate range discrimination and accuracy. However, it is less than the 1000–1200 which was quoted in the same section as being typical of what is used in practice for radial storage. This apparent inconsistency merits some explanation. Values of 1000–1200 cells per radius are normally employed so that the stored data can be used as an input to automatic tracking. Radar systems which provide automatic tracking are referred to as automatic radar plotting aids (ARPA) and are described in detail in Chapters 4, 5 and 9. The storage resolution required for automatic tracking is much higher than that required for synthetic picture generation for reasons which are set out under the heading of range quantization errors in Section 9.5.3.2. Because the radial memory is overwritten line by line as the aerial rotates (see Section 2.6.6.3), the total capacity is a fraction of that required for a cartesian memory. In the case of raster-scan ARPAs it is thus expedient to use the radial memory to feed both the tracking unit *and* the cartesian memory, while the latter is used to refresh the picture.

The raster-scan display does use more memory than is strictly necessary for adequate sampling, accuracy and resolution. A major reason for this is that otherwise the steplike characteristic of the picture would be obtrusive. This is best understood by considering the generation of a circle, for example a range ring. On a radial-scan display this is achieved by illuminating a very large number of resolution cells each of which is a tiny arc. This is completely analogous to the use of a pair of drawing compasses and should result in a perfect circle. On a raster-scan display the circle is produced by illuminating the correct combination of pixels, which are not arcs but rectangles, resulting in steps between adjacent elements of the *circle*. For example, in a vertical sense adjacent pixels forming the circle must be on different lines, and unless these lines are very close together the steps will be obtrusive. A cosmetic technique known as anti-aliasing can be used to camouflage the effect but, in general, designers rely on initially selecting sufficiently high resolution. The steps will also affect the shape of displayed echoes and, if pronounced, could

add to the difficulties of the identification of coastlines and other navigational features (see Section 8.2).

In Figure 2.49 the origin of the display (i.e. the own-ship position) is shown at the centre of the PPI circle. If the memory location corresponding to the origin remains fixed, a relative-motion presentation will result. It is, however, possible to arrange that the targets leave true-motion trails by generating synthetic afterglow (see Section 2.6.7.5). If the origin's co-ordinates in the memory plane are updated in sympathy with the observing vessel's course and speed, the origin will move across the PPI circle and a true-motion presentation will be produced. As with any true-motion presentation, whether produced by moving the origin or by generating synthetic true afterglow, the accuracy of the displayed target motion is crucially dependent on the accuracy of the course and speed inputs (see Sections 1.5.2, 2.6.4 and 2.6.6.5).

2.6.7.4 Multi-plane memories

The memory plane associated with Figure 2.49(b) can register a binary 1 or 0 in any of its memory cells. This limits its ability to merely indicating the presence or absence of a target (or an item of data). Some of the implications of such a restriction were discussed in Section 2.6.6.7. Most raster-scan systems use multi-plane memories, normally having three or four layers. The principle is illustrated for three layers in Figure 2.49.

Figure 2.50 shows that with three memory layers it is possible to store three elements of binary information for each screen location, i.e. the number 1 or 0 may appear in each of the three cells which form a vertical column. This gives rise to eight possible permutations and these can be exploited to produce multi-level video having eight different levels of target brightness. Multi-plane memories also make it possible to generate synthetic afterglow (see Section 2.6.7.5) and to perform a variety of signal processing techniques (see Section 2.6.7.6).

2.6.7.5 Artificial afterglow

Due to the long persistence of the phosphor of a radial-scan radar CRT (see Section 2.6.1.2), echoes

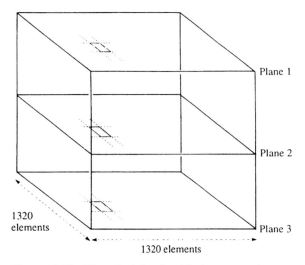

1320
elements

1320 elements

Figure 2.50 The principle of multi-plane memories.
Use of the corresponding element from each plane allows
the following combinations:
Plane 1. 0 0 0 0 1 1 1 1
Plane 2. 0 0 1 1 0 1 0 1
Plane 3. 0 1 0 1 0 0 1 1

which move across the screen leave distinctive afterglow trails. Such trails can be of assistance to the radar observer in making an early appraisal of a developing encounter but care must be taken in their interpretation (a full appraisal of an encounter requires radar plotting or equivalent systematic observation of detected objects, as set out in Chapter 7). Because the very short persistence of the raster-scan display does not allow the trails to build up, most manufacturers make provision for the generation of synthetic afterglow.

Synthetic afterglow is generated by recording the presence of a target not only in the main echo memory plane(s) but also in a further history plane. When a target moves on to a new memory location in the echo plane, its previous location in that plane reverts to the zero condition and in the absence of the history plane that pixel would not be brightened. However, the data in the history plane continues to cause that pixel to be brightened to a progressively lesser extent for some time after the echo has vacated the corresponding cell in the echo plane. Thus the

recent past positions of a moving target will form a trail which fades progressively with time. The mathematical law on which the fading is based is pre-programmed but in some systems the observer can select, from one of two values, the length of time over which the fading takes place (e.g. 3 mins or 6 mins). It is normally possible for the user to switch the afterglow facility on or off. Where a colour display is used (see Section 2.6.7.7) the trails can be generated in a colour which is different from that of the echoes.

Because the trails of all targets are generated over a fixed period of time, their lengths are directly related to the rate at which the target is moving across the screen. This is a significant improvement when compared with real-time afterglow trails. The latter are dependent not only on the rate at which the echo is moving but also on the strength of the echo and the sensitivity of the phosphor in a particular area of the screen. An observer who fails to appreciate this may be seriously misled.

Provided that a suitable course and speed input are available, it is in theory possible for the display computer to deduce either relative-motion trails or true-motion trails irrespective of the picture presentation selected by the observer. A particular application of this is the generation of a true-motion presentation by generating true trails while maintaining the origin in the centre of the PPI circle, or in a suitably off-centred position. Great care should be taken in ascertaining which trails are being generated and it is of paramount importance to remember that the accuracy of true trails, like that of true-motion, is dependent on the accuracy of the input course and speed.

Since they are visible in bright ambient light, the addition of synthetic afterglow may assist with the detection of targets in the background of clutter (see Section 2.6.7.8 and Section 3.6). However, because all displayed echoes are transferred to the history plane there can be a significant build-up in both thermal noise and all forms of clutter. Where the facility is being used, the afterglow should be cleared if the background builds up to a level at which it can impair the detection of genuine echoes. Artificial afterglow trails are normally cleared when the range scale is changed and/or the position of the origin is reset.

2.6.7.6 Signal processing

As suggested in Section 2.6.6, a benefit which accrues from the storage of radar signal data is the ability to sample, manipulate and analyse that data. In radial-scan systems only a fractional sector of the picture is maintained in memory (see Section 2.6.6.3) and this in general limits the processing techniques to those of interference suppression, noise reduction (see Section 3.9.5.1) and echo stretching (see Section 6.11.1). Because in raster-scan systems the data for a complete picture is stored, the number of processing techniques which can be performed is increased. Such techniques are mainly devoted to improving the probability of detection of targets in clutter and it is appropriate to delay consideration of these until after a study of the phenomena of clutter and the corresponding manual techniques of clutter reduction (see Sections 3.6 and 3.7).

2.6.7.7 The colour television CRT

Red, green and blue are known as the three primary colours of light because by mixing them in suitable proportions it is possible to produce most of the colours that the eye can perceive. The phosphor used in a colour television tube has three individual components, one for each of the primary colours, and they are arranged in a rather special way which is illustrated by Figure 2.51.

The colour tube also differs from its monochrome counterpart in that it has three electron guns, designated red, green and blue, each of which activates its own component of the phosphor. As illustrated in Figure 2.51, the phosphor is a mosaic of minute strips of the primary colour phosphor materials arranged in elemental groups of three which are called *triads*. In every such group there is one strip of each primary colour. The shadow mask is a metal sheet in which slots are cut to allow each electron beam to excite the phosphor strips of its own colour and to prevent it falling on the strips of the other two primary colours. This is achieved by very careful attention to the geometry of the positions of the guns, the positions of the phosphors on the tube and of the slots in the mask. The strength of the beam emitted by each gun is controlled individually by the input picture signals and

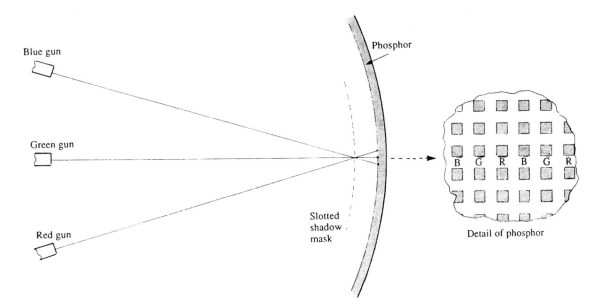

Figure 2.51 The colour television CRT

thus the colour emitted by any given triad depends on the instantaneous balance between the individual beam strengths. The raster is generated by sweeping the three beams across the screen as a group, using the basic principles of beam deflection described in Section 2.6.7.1.

The description given above is a fairly simplified exposition of the principle. Modern colour tubes employ many refinements of the above principles to improve the brightness, focus and colour quality of the picture.

In a single-beam tube the smallest area of light that can be produced on the screen, sometimes referred to as the minimum resolvable picture element, is determined by the spot diameter (see Section 2.6.5.1); the implications of this for a raster-scan radar were discussed in Section 2.6.7.1. In a colour CRT the minimum resolvable element is determined by the spot diameter of each beam and the geometry of the triad. Thus the resolution of a colour tube is inherently poorer than that of a comparable monochrome version. The materials used to produce the coloured phosphors are relatively costly and this, together with other design and manufacturing factors, renders the colour tube the more expensive of the two. The delay in the appearance of colour raster-scan radar displays was due to the excessive costs of tubes with an acceptable screen resolution. The presence of the shadow mask reduces the potential light output of the tube and thus makes it difficult to achieve brightness levels comparable with that of monochrome. However, technology is advancing and low pixel size colour CRT displays are now affordable.

2.6.7.8 The use of colour in radar picture generation

In the early to mid-1980s there was vigorous debate concerning the contribution that colour could make to enhancing the raster-scan picture. As mentioned in the previous section, the use of colour can result in the loss of resolution and brightness in addition to its tendency to be more expensive. However, it can be argued that it does improve the observer's ability to discern picture detail while viewing the display from some distance. There is the temptation to extrapolate the television-based argument that 'colour is better

than black and white'. This argument is specious because, although the advent of colour undoubtedly added the dimension which ensured the future of sports like snooker as television spectacles, there is no direct parallel with the radar picture. In marine radar the use of colour is only productive if it is used to contribute useful and unambiguous information to the observer. If it does this, it makes a positive contribution to the presentation of information albeit one that brings the concomitant penalties of resolution, brightness and cost. Extra cost arises not only from the expense of a colour tube but also from the more complex signal processing which is required. Certain engineering problems relating to magnetic effects, vibration and temperature also have to be overcome.

Some of the earliest colour raster-scan radars used the additional dimension of colour to indicate signal strength. It will be remembered from Figures 2.45 and 2.46 that, by employing digital storage, it is possible to produce a *two-level* picture. It follows that with suitable computer assistance these two levels could be shown as different colours. In early systems three colours, red, amber and green, were used to show high, medium and low signal levels. A wide range of factors affect the strength of signal returned by any given target (see Chapter 3) and there is considerable doubt as to how valuable this information is to the observer (see Section 2.6.6.7). An argument which was sometimes offered was that 'targets show as a different colour against the background of clutter'. A major limitation of marine radar is the ability to detect targets whose signal strength is close to clutter level (see Sections 3.6 and 3.7) and it is almost self-evident that a marginal target would change colour almost continually. This is likely to confuse and mislead the observer and in this regard the use of colour does not make a positive contribution to the information available to the observer.

More recent approaches to the application of colour have tended to support the view that the use of several colours to indicate relative signal strength is counterproductive and they have employed a single colour (for example, yellow or amber) for the present position of all targets, irrespective of signal strength. A second colour (possibly brown) can be used to indicate random responses (such as those from sea clutter) while persistent echoes retain the main echo colour. This facility can be selected at will by the observer but must be used with care and with an understanding of the principle involved. It has to be appreciated, for example, that buoys, boats and similar small floating targets may well return intermittent responses. The technique clearly involves analysis and correlation of signals, the principle and application of which are described in detail under 'Clutter suppression' in Section 3.6.3.4.

An important decision for the designer is the choice of background colour, i.e. that which represents the absence of signal (or data). There is some debate on this issue. One opinion is that for daylight viewing blue is an improvement on the traditional black background. However, its brightness tends to destroy night vision on the bridge and where blue is provided for daylight viewing it is normal for black to be available for selection at night. There is an opposing view that a black background is more suitable for both day and night use. It is probably true to say that many designers have an open mind on the choice of background (and other) colours and their views are likely to be reinforced or modified by the reaction of users as observers gain experience of the use of both monochrome and colour raster-scan radars at sea.

Synthetic afterglow (see Section 2.6.7.5), sometimes referred to as *target tracks* or *trails*, is shown in a colour which contrasts with the background, for example black on blue or blue on black.

Assimilation of picture information is assisted by using a separate colour for the graphics associated with range and bearing measurement, for example range rings, variable range markers, electronic bearing lines, heading markers, bearing scales and data readouts.

The use of red as a warning colour for selected graphics or data suggests itself but set against this is the fact that red does not tend to show up as well as other colours.

Another feature of CRT displays is the need to degauss the screen. The screen acquires magnetism after long periods of operation. This causes small deflections in the electron beams, so that they may not hit the required pixel. It is particularly a problem in colour CRT displays due to the higher pixel density and the first sign of a problem is that the wrong colours are shown on screen. Most CRT displays perform a degaussing procedure to remove the screen magnetism on start-up. Radar colour CRT sets sometimes have a degaussing control, so that the display can be degaussed very quickly, without turning it off.

2.6.7.9 Raster-scan display

The first marine raster-scan radars to appear on the market were designed for the small craft. This arose largely because, although designers recognized, among other benefits, the daylight viewing potential of using a television-style presentation, they were also very much aware of the cost and difficulties of producing the picture on a screen sufficiently large to allow compliance with the IMO Performance Standards (see Section 11.2.1). The latter requires a 320 mm diameter PPI circle for systems on large vessels. However, in due course many of the problems were accepted or overcome and by the mid-1980s a number of manufacturers were offering raster-scan radars which complied with the IMO Performance Standards even for vessels whose gross tonnage exceeded 10 000.

The next change in technology was the introduction of flat panel screens as an alternative to the CRT display. There are two common types: LCD and plasma screens, although other technologies are also under development. The technology behind the LCD screen is covered in Section 2.6.7.10 and plasma screens are covered briefly in Section 2.6.7.11. The three types of display are compared in Section 2.6.7.12.

2.6.7.10 Liquid crystal display (LCD)

LCD screens have proved a popular alternative to the CRT display and may eventually replace the CRT display in the maritime industry, although other screen technologies may get there first. LCD screens are almost universal on small boat radars and compete with larger CRT displays on larger vessels.

Properties of liquid crystals. Liquid crystals are unusual in that they have a state that does not fall into one of three standard matter states of solid, liquid or gas. This extra state is nearer liquid than solid, but the molecules line themselves up in a fixed orientation, which is normally the property of a solid. This is called the nematic phase. Some liquid crystals are called twisted nematics, because in their nematic phase, the orientation of the molecules naturally twists with respect to each other. The amount of the twist can be controlled by applying a voltage across the liquid crystal.

Another property of liquid crystals is that they are transparent substances that allow light to pass through them. In the case of twisted nematics, light penetrating one side of the crystal will be twisted as it goes through the crystal (i.e. the polarization of the light will be rotated, henceforth referred to as twisted in this text. This property is exploited for LCD displays, by putting the liquid crystal (layer 3 in Figure 2.52) and its controlling transparent electrodes (layers 2 and 4), between two pieces of glass (layers 1 and 5) each with a polarizing film coating on one side. Finally a mirror (layer 6) is added to the bottom of the second piece of glass. The polarizing film only allows light to pass through the film that has a certain polarization. Light with incorrect polarization simply does not pass through the film. The top glass layer (layer 1) therefore only allows through external light polarized in one direction. The plane of the polarized light is twisted

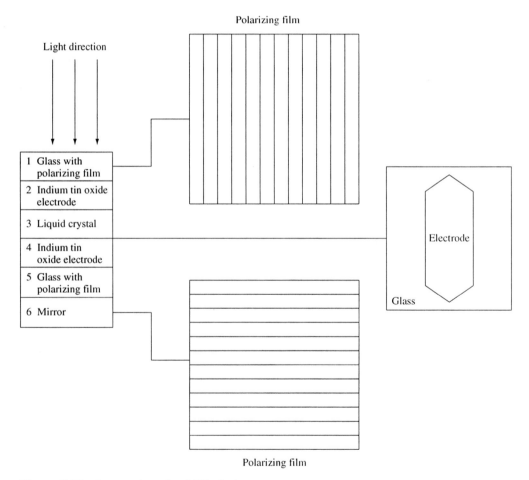

Figure 2.52 Construction of an LCD pixel

by a controlled amount through the liquid crystal, depending on the voltage on the electrodes (layers 2 and 4). In one condition, the twist will be such that the plane of the polarized light will match the polarization of the film on the second piece of glass. The light will therefore pass through and be reflected back through the same path by the mirror. The LCD appears blank to an observer in this case. In the second condition, the amount of twist is adjusted by the voltage across the electrodes so that the plane is polarized at 90 degrees to the polarized film on the second piece of glass and no light gets through. The LCD appears black in this case.

Backlighting. The simple LCD with a mirror background, described in Section 2.6.7.10 above, depends on external light to illuminate it and make it visible. These are sometimes termed reflective LCDs and cannot be seen unaided in the dark.

The alternative system is to provide backlighting. Typically this consists of very thin cold fluorescent strip lights that surround the screen. A white diffusion panel is provided instead of the mirror behind the LCDs, so that the fluorescent light is distributed evenly behind the whole LCD screen. The level of backlighting can usually be adjusted so that power can be conserved during daylight hours and the brightness of the display set to the convenience of the user. One big advantage is that the display can be used in the dark.

Simple LCD. Early LCD elements were quite large and it is still common to find a very simple display of seven LCD elements (each hexagonal in shape) arranged to make a rectangular figure of 8. It is possible to approximate all the alphanumeric characters, by making black the appropriate combination of the seven LCD elements (see Figure 2.53).

However, the interest in this book is the ability to display raster-scans' data, so that each LCD element becomes one of a large number of pixels on a rectangular screen. The LCD pixels are arranged in a rectangular matrix. An early system was the passive matrix system in which the electrodes on one side of the liquid crystal are connected in rows and the electrodes on the other side are connected in columns. Communication of the correct voltage to an individual LCD

Figure 2.53 Seven element alphanumeric display

pixel is achieved by putting the voltage on the row and column for that pixel. All the other pixels on that row and column will only revive the charge on one side, not both, so the voltage they receive will not change their status. This system is noted for its slow response time and the voltage variations to pixels near the one being adjusted can cause the image to appear fuzzy.

TFT LCD. Most modern LCD displays use an active matrix system, which uses a thin film transistor (TFT) to control each LCD pixel. A TFT consists of a switching transistor and a capacitor. The TFT for each pixel is updated by row and column (similar in principle to the passive matrix) and the TFT capacitor holds the correct charge until the TFT pixel is refreshed again. This system is much faster and has the added advantage of being able to more precisely control the voltage applied to the LCD pixel and therefore more precisely control the twist. Up to 256 different amounts (graduations) of twist can be obtained, each graduation letting through a different proportion of light. If a white diffusion panel (see *backlighting* above) is employed behind the LCD the effect is to obtain 256 different shades of grey (greyscale) from pure white to pure black. This provides a good display for monochrome pictures.

The principle behind colour LCD screens is the same as for the CRT display. Each pixel actually consists of three separate sub-pixels fitted with red, green or blue filters respectively. Any colour can theoretically be achieved by mixing the appropriate amount of each of the three primary colours. Assuming the same 256 shades for each sub-pixel, this allows 256^3 or 16 million different colours that can be displayed by each coloured pixel.

2.6.7.11 Plasma screens

Plasma screens enjoy similar advantages to the LCD over CRT. They have not yet been used significantly in the maritime field so will not be covered in detail. In a colour plasma screen each pixel consists of three tiny fluorescent lights coloured red, green and blue. It is similar in operation to the LCD screen in that by applying different voltages to each light, a full range of colours is available.

The LCD has some advantages over plasma screens in that it should last twice as long and it suffers less than CRT and plasma from burn in. Plasma screens are available in larger sizes (up to 80 inch), but the number of pixels is currently similar to a good quality 24-inch display. These larger screens are clearly intended for displaying a reasonable quality picture to a larger audience standing well away from the screen.

2.6.7.12 Comparison of display technologies

LCD and plasma screen technologies are still evolving. Proposals for new systems that would improve the quality, potential size and cost appear frequently.

Dead pixels. One of the current issues is quality control as both LCD and plasma screens can have dead pixels during the manufacturing process as well as appearing after a period of use. These cannot be fixed and, in manufacture, the whole screen must be rejected. The high failure rate has major implications for the manufacturer, as for a given pixel failure rate, a much larger proportion of screens with a high number of pixels will be rejected than a screen with a much lower number of pixels. This has tended to make large screens and/or higher resolution screens containing millions of pixels uneconomic and this is the main

reason why larger and higher resolution LCD and plasma displays have been slow to appear. For instance a good quality 24-inch commercially viable LCD screen that meets IMO standards (see Section 11.2.1) for minimum size of radar display appeared some 10 years after the first appearance of small boat radars with LCD screens about half that size. Larger screen sizes of over 40 inch are available for LCD (80 inch for plasma) but the current position is that the number of pixels does not significantly increase above the mid-size displays of (say) 24-inch. Thus the density of pixels reduces. The larger screens are thus intended for viewing the same quality picture as a 24-inch screen, but perhaps at a longer distance to a bigger audience. This has limited value for most navigational situations.

On the operational front, the appearance of an isolated dead pixel can be very irritating to an observer, but would be unlikely to mask a radar target that would cover several pixels. A larger group of dead pixels would of course represent a hazard. If spares are carried, the current trend on larger vessels of using standard screens developed for the computer markets means that replacement of screens can be a very easy operation, not requiring a skilled technician. The technology of raster-scan CRT displays is very well developed and these displays can endure for very long periods, albeit with a small drop-off in brightness and contrast intensities.

Power, size and weight. One advantage of LCD and plasma screens over CRT is the thickness of the panel, which can be less than one tenth of the depth or thickness of an equivalent CRT. The power requirements and weight are both also significantly less (typically less than 50 per cent). Thus the LCD and plasma displays can be mounted more easily in a variety of arrangements including on vertical bulkheads.

Black level. A CRT display produces a better colour black than both plasma and LCD screens. In both plasma and LCD the colour of black is produced by shutting off the light of all three sub-pixels, so no light is produced. The colour of black therefore depends on the quality of external light and can look dark grey on occasions.

Flat screen and viewing angles. Flat screen CRT displays have also been developed which overcome another advantage of LCD screens. The curved screens of traditional CRTs made them more prone to glare or unwanted reflections from external lighting.

The traditional curved CRT display also allows more people to view the screen at close range. The LCD and plasma screens have a relatively narrow viewing angle.

It should also be noted that about a centimetre strip all round the edge of the CRT screen is not usable due to distortion. The CRT outer casing usually covers this up, so effectively a CRT screen actually displays about one inch less than its stated size. This does not occur on LCD screens so that a 26-inch CRT would be equivalent in size to a 25-inch LCD display.

Image burn-in. If a constant image appears on any screen for a long time the display will suffer from burn-in, i.e. the image becomes fixed 'ghostlike' on the screen. This could be a logo in a corner or a radar control or fairly constant seaclutter at the centre of screen. This is not to be confused with burn-out which frequently occurred at the centre of early radial CRT radars where the phosphor was effectively worn out and nothing would be seen at all (see Section 2.6.1.2). LCD screens are the least prone to this effect, with plasma and CRT screens about equally affected. To reduce burn-in and also prolong display life, many computer systems use a screensaver where the usual picture is replaced by a dim but moving image when the system detects that there has been no keyboard activity by the user. However, for a radar observer whose radar would normally go long periods without requiring adjustment, the regular need to reset the screen could be very irritating.

Focus. The traditional radial CRT screen had a focus control (see Section 2.6.1.1) adjustable by the navigator. Raster-scan CRT displays are not provided with a focus control as it is set by the manufacturer of the display. However, focus can be an issue as the set becomes older. Blurring due to the loss of focus can be a reason for scrapping a CRT display. Focus is not an issue for LCD and plasma screens, which is an advantage.

Summary. The current situation between these displays is shown in Table 2.4. LCD screens currently appear to be a better buy than plasma screens and the LCD is also more useful than the CRT for a small boat display due to its size, weight and power requirements. For a larger ship, where weight, overall size and power requirements are not an issue, the slightly crisper, higher resolution CRT display still just about holds sway for many users, but it is a finely balanced one.

However, one thing that is true is that display technology is going through some very rapid changes and the comparison below will not be valid for long. Not only are the LCD and plasma screen technologies advancing, but display types on other new principles are being developed and will no doubt become available.

2.6.7.13 Display and control layout

The traditional radial CRT display had a large number of analogue and push-button controls surrounding the round screen. Over time the number of features and the corresponding controls/buttons offered on sets generally increased. The first raster-scan displays followed this traditional layout and sets (particularly ARPA/radar sets) with over 80 controls or buttons were becoming common.

This trend has now reversed itself by the use of on-screen menus. This has been encouraged by three interlinked factors:

(a) The increased computer literacy of the general population means that most people are familiar with the concept of pull-down menus.

(b) The increased use of pointing devices (see below) enables a flexible arrangement on screen to operate the pull-down menus.

(c) The adoption of rectangular raster-scan screens means that there are convenient spaces to the side of the circular screen on raster displays to display both information and the drop-down menus (see Figure 2.49).

In the extreme case, the display may only have two buttons and the pointing device. A major advantage is that this considerably reduces the cost and maintenance

Table 2.4   Summary of display type comparison

Criteria	CRT	LCD	Plasma
Resolutions	Best	Mid	Worst
Current maximum screen size	40 inch	40 inch	80 inch
Depth (thickness)	Significant (about same depth as screen size)	Very compact thin panel	Very compact thin panel
Weight	Heavy	Light	Light
Power supplies	Significant	Low	Low
Longevity	Good	Good	About half the duration of others
Relative cost	Cheap, but the flat screen is mid-priced	Mid-priced	Expensive
Flat screen (reduces glare)	Both flat and traditional screens now available, the flat screen being more expensive	Yes	Yes
Focus	Although modern CRTs have automatic focusing arrangements, it can deteriorate with age	No focus required	No focus required
Dead areas	Not a significant problem	Dead pixels can occur	Dead pixels can occur
Image burn-in	Prone	Less prone	Prone
Black level	Best	Acceptable	Acceptable
Viewing angle (relative)	Wide	Narrow	Narrow

of the radar system. Hardware is effectively replaced by software that does not wear out.

The use of drop-down menus enables the manufacturer to provide hundreds of functions without cluttering up the display and radar set. The skill of the manufacturer is arranging the various commands into logical groupings so that an observer can intuitively find the correct information/command through several layers of menus without continual reference to the manual.

Pointing devices. Pointing devices enable the user to control the position of a moving symbol on the display. Two or more 'click' buttons are provided. When pressed they will be programmed to perform an action or display more information.

The most common pointing device ashore is usually referred to as a mouse. Different designs exist but the general principle is that a ball in a casing of the mouse is held in place by three rollers arranged as in Figure 2.54. The rollers record the motion of the ball as the mouse is dragged across a horizontal surface. The first and second rollers measure the X and Y movement (or horizontal and vertical movement) of the mouse and this is used to move the symbol (often an arrow) across the screen. The third wheel

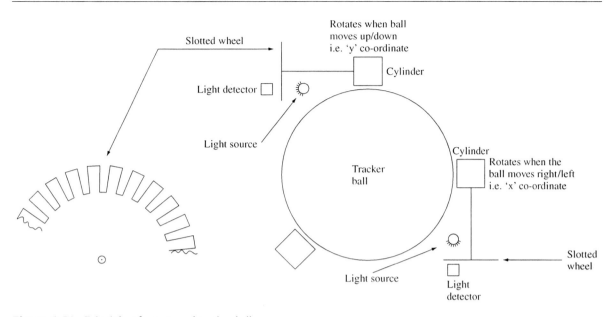

Figure 2.54 Principle of mouse and tracker ball

is simply to hold the ball in place. In one common type of mouse, the rollers are connected to disks with radial slots cut into the disks. There is a light source behind each disk and a light detector on the other side. Movement of the roller results in flashes being detected behind the disk and these are used to move the pointing symbol on the screen. Other technologies to track movement are also employed.

Radar displays on vessels are not usually provided with a mouse, but with a tracker ball (or trackball). A tracker ball is simply an inverted mouse and its components are virtually otherwise identical to the mouse. The user simply spins the ball in the required direction. There are several reasons why a tracker ball is preferable to a mouse for a marine radar display. Firstly, on a rolling ship, the mouse may move of its own volition, the tracker ball is fixed to one place. Secondly, the mouse requires a convenient flat surface to operate and this makes the equipment larger. Thirdly, many users believe that the tracker ball is easier to use from a standing-up position, which is often the case on a ship's bridge.

Display arrangements. Display and data integration has meant that dedicated screens have given way to multifunction screens, which may be used to display data from a variety of sensors, e.g. ARPA or ECDIS as required or integrated from a number of sources, e.g. ARPA, ECDIS, log, gyro and echo sounder etc. One major advantage of the common standardization of display screens across equipment is that in the event of the failure of one screen, the display can be transferred to another. This facility is often referred to as redundancy. A typical radar/ARPA is shown in Figure 2.55.

These advances in shipboard electronics have been very quick to be incorporated into the equipment on smaller vessels where acceptance has in many ways been faster than larger vessels where traditional equipment still existed and there was a certain reluctance to embrace new technology. Smaller multifunction screens display a variety of data, save space, power and weight as well as reduce overall costs and are very popular on small well-equipped craft, such as racing craft. The screens can usually be switched to show standalone data (such as in Figure 2.56(a) and (b)) or the screen can be split (as in Figure 2.56(c)).

Figure 2.55 Example of a raster scan display as might be found on a larger vessel

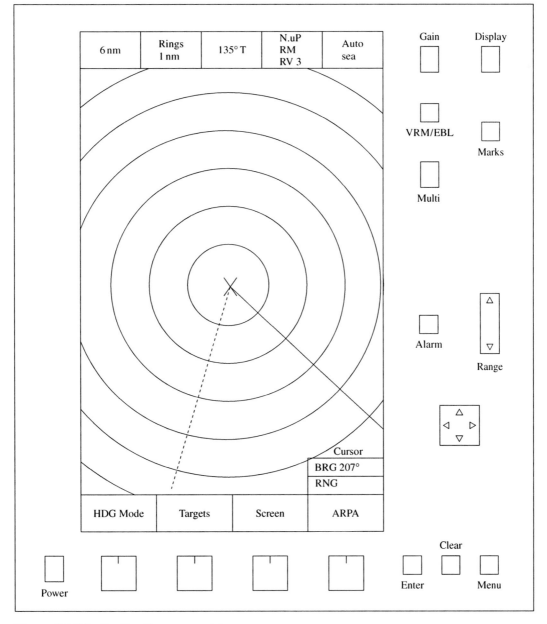

Figure 2.56(a) Small craft raster scan delay

Figure 2.56(b) Small craft ECDIS

Figure 2.56(c) Small craft dual radar and ECDIS display

An additional advantage, as in computers, is that being software driven, advances in technology can more easily be introduced to existing hardware in the form of software updates. This is particularly common for ECDIS data (see Section 10.2) which is available by satellite links; however, it can also apply to software upgrades and updates to all types of equipment.

For many years raster screen displays were fixed in 4:3 ratio, but screens are now available in different ratios, for example, CRT displays of 16:9 are commonly now used for domestic television. In the navigation equipment market, it is particularly noticeable in the smaller screen sizes of the LCD type for small craft that a variety of ratios are used. The screen size ratio is selected by the manufacturer to best show the data required.

2.7   The siting of units on board ship

The preceding treatment of marine radar principles was based on a subdivision of the radar system into four units, namely, transmitter, aerial, receiver and display. This approach is particularly helpful when discussing theoretical principles but the subdivision does not represent the physical units into which the shipboard system is divided. In practice the transmitter and some parts of the receiver are commonly located within the same unit, known as the *transceiver*. The ideal siting of the shipboard units is dictated by a number of navigational criteria but the extent to which such ideals can be realized is limited by certain engineering considerations. In general, the units should be sited so as to avoid failure or undue maintenance difficulties due to heat or fumes and they should be mounted sufficiently rigidly to prevent the performance and reliability of the system being adversely affected by vibration. Particular navigational and engineering aspects of the siting of each of the physical units will be discussed in the following sections and finally an exposition of the concept of interswitching duplicate units will be given.

2.7.1   Aerial siting

It is appropriate to consider the siting of this unit first since a poorly sited aerial can completely offset any benefits that can be gained elsewhere. In the theoretical treatment of aerial principles it was indicated that the aerial unit comprised the scanner, a device to transmit the rotation signal and a heading marker generator (see Sections 2.2.2 and 2.4). This also effectively represents the physical contents of one type of practical aerial unit. A second type of aerial unit also includes some or all of the transmitter and part of the receiver. The implication of the siting of these additional elements within the aerial unit will be discussed in Sections 2.7.2 and 2.7.3. In general, the scanner must be sited on a rigid structure which will not twist and give rise to bearing errors.

The scanner is the eyes and ears of the radar system and its siting is of crucial importance. However, the siting has to take into account a number of conflicting factors and is of necessity a compromise. In most cases radar observers will have had no say in the acceptance of this compromise but it is important that they appreciate the factors which may affect optimum results.

2.7.1.1   *Blind and shadow sectors*

Blind and shadow sectors occur when the radiation from the aerial is intercepted by obstructions (for example, masts, funnel etc.) on board the vessel. The effect is illustrated by Figure 2.57 and it can be seen that it is analogous to that of optical shadows cast when a source of light is obstructed. In the interests of rigour it has to be said that because of the longer wavelength, radar waves experience greater diffraction than light waves. Diffraction is the term used to describe the effect when radiation passes close to a solid object which gives it a slight tendency to bend round the object. In this respect the use of S-band (see Section 2.3.3.1) will tend to reduce the shadow extent when compared with X-band transmissions.

No radiation is incident on the area of a blind sector, whereas a shadow sector represents an area of reduced sensitivity, i.e. an area on which less radiation is incident than would be the case in the absence of

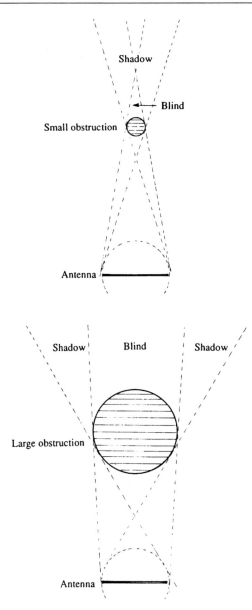

Figure 2.57 Blind and shadow sectors

the obstruction. The size of the antenna, the size of the obstruction and its proximity to the aerial site will determine the angular width of the sector and whether it is 'blind' or 'shadow' in character.

The IMO Performance Standards (see Section 11.2.1) require that the aerial system be installed in such a manner that the efficiency of the display is not impaired by the close proximity of the aerial to other objects.

It might appear at first sight that the best approach is to locate the aerial unit sufficiently high as to be above all obstructions. This may be possible on some ships but there are also disadvantages for excessive aerial height (see Section 2.7.1.3). Although it may not be possible to use the vertical location of the aerial to eliminate blind and shadow sectors, suitable attention to the horizontal siting may reduce the seriousness of their effects. This is illustrated by Figure 2.58.

Figure 2.58(a) shows a fairly traditional siting with impaired sectors ahead and on both bows. Figures 2.58(b) and (c) show how these can be relocated astern or on one side, which could have an advantage in improving detection of targets which are often the 'stand-on' vessels in collision encounters. In considering these solutions it should be remembered that, although in clear weather the collision regulations allocate responsibilities to vessels which relate to the crossing and overtaking situations, when vessels are not in sight of one another the give way/stand on allocation of responsibilities does not apply. Both vessels have a responsibility to take action to avoid a close-quarters situation.

There are practical limits to the physical separation between the aerial unit and the transceiver (see Section 2.7.1.3) and hence if the aerial is sited forward so too must be the transceiver. In bad weather the latter may thus be exposed to vibration and access for maintenance may be a problem. Such siting may also involve very long cable runs to the display. This is a drawback both from the point of view of signal attenuation and because of susceptibility to damage, with the attendant difficulties of locating and repairing such damage should it be sustained.

If the aerial is sited off the vessel's fore-and-aft centreline it is important to remember that the origin of the picture represents the location of the aerial. This factor may be of particular significance in pilotage situations because, as illustrated by Figure 2.58(d), failure to appreciate it could result in the observer

Figure 2.58 Alternative aerial sittings

being seriously misled as to the position of the vessel with respect to mid channel.

All radar observers should be aware of the nature and extent of the shadow sectors on board their vessel. The prudent method of ensuring this is to measure the sectors and illustrate the results on a suitable plan-view diagram posted near the radar display (see Figure 2.59 and Section 11.4.1). In addition, the information should be recorded in the radar log. In some vessels the trim or draught may affect the shadow pattern and if this is believed to be the case it will be necessary to measure the sectors in more than one condition of loading.

The angular extent of the sectors can be measured by observing the response of a weak isolated target such as a buoy which is not fitted with a radar reflector (see Section 3.4) and is located at a range of about one mile. The ship should be swung through 360° and the limits of the sectors determined by measuring the bearings on which the echo disappears and subsequently reappears. It is important that a weak target is chosen to ensure that the areas of reduced sensitivity are effectively revealed. A good target, such as a buoy with a radar reflector, may return an echo

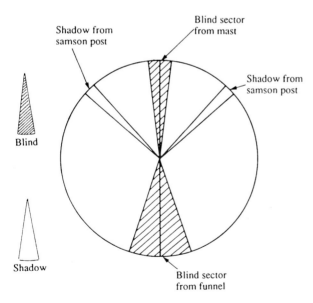

Figure 2.59 Blind and shadow sector record

which is so strong that a response is obtained despite the loss in energy caused by the offending obstruction. The measurement procedure should be carried out in calm conditions so that the echo is not masked by clutter (see Section 3.6) and to avoid an intermittent response due to the rolling motion of the buoy.

An alternative approach is to measure the sectors against the background of the sea clutter pattern (see Section 3.6). For the same reasons given in the preceding paragraph for selecting a weak target, strong clutter conditions should be avoided. The measurements should not be taken when the vessel is in confined waters as the sectors may be obscured by indirect echoes (see Section 3.9.2) due to reflections from the obstructions which produce the shadow sectors.

Having measured the shadow pattern, it is important to appreciate the danger of a target approaching on a steady bearing which lies within one of the sectors. Collisions have resulted from this cause. In poor visibility this danger must be addressed by ensuring that from time to time the vessel is *briefly* swung either side of the course by half the width of the largest sector in an attempt to reveal the presence of any targets within the blind and shadow sectors. In some situations the natural yawing motion of the vessel may adequately fulfil this function.

In ships which frequently navigate astern, for example short sea ferries, the aerial siting must be such as to avoid shadow sectors astern. In many cases such vessels are fitted with a dedicated docking aerial at the stern.

2.7.1.2 Indirect echoes

Obstructions close to the site of the aerial may reflect some of the radar energy on both its outward and return journeys. This gives rise to false echoes known as *indirect* (or *reflected*) echoes. These are discussed in detail in Section 3.9.2.

2.7.1.3 Aerial height

As suggested in Section 2.7.1.1, the location of the aerial above all obstructions is not a simple matter. The height at which the aerial is sited is inevitably a compromise. There are benefits and drawbacks to siting the aerial as high as possible. In respect of shadow sectors, it is worth bearing in mind that if a vessel has crosstrees or similar reflecting areas on the masts, an aerial sited above the level of such an obstruction will cast a shadow on the water, whereas with a lower siting it may cast the shadow in space.

In favour of a high aerial siting is the fact that the distance to the radar horizon, and hence the theoretical maximum detection range of targets, increases with aerial height. This topic is discussed in detail in Section 3.8. The minimum range at which targets can be detected also depends on aerial height. Excessively high and low aerial sitings may increase or decrease this important limit and the implications of this, including the effect on the accuracy with which very short ranges can be measured, are discussed in Section 3.2.4. In general, very short range accuracy is improved with a low aerial. Some vessels have two interswitched aerials (see Section 2.7.8), one high and one low, to obtain the advantages of each.

A serious penalty incurred by the siting of the aerial at a great height is the effect on the amplitude and range of sea clutter response. The amplitude of sea clutter echoes and the maximum range at which they are detectable increases with aerial height. These responses produce a pattern of echoes around the origin which can mask even very strong targets. The danger of targets being lost in sea clutter returns represents one of the most serious limitations of marine radar and is discussed in detail in Section 3.6. Excessive aerial height will exacerbate this fundamental problem and serious consideration must be given to this factor when a shipboard radar installation is planned.

A further problem associated with a high aerial site is the loss of energy which occurs when the transmitted pulse and received signals travel along the necessary lengths of waveguide. These losses place a maximum limit of about 21 m on the separation between transceiver and aerial. In some systems the problem can be overcome by locating part or all of the transceiver within the aerial unit (see Section 2.7.2).

It is evident from this section that choosing an optimum aerial height involves reconciling a number of conflicting factors. The height selected in practice may be limited by the size and type of the vessel,

but experience has shown that a height of between 13 and 20 m above the water level offers the best overall radar performance.

2.7.1.4   Susceptibility to damage

The site of the aerial unit should be well clear of halyards and similar rigging which might be liable to become entangled with the rotating scanner. Alternatively, the aerial can be located in a protective arrangement such as a *radome*. The latter is a spherical moulding made of glass reinforced plastic (GRP) within which the scanner is free to rotate. The surface of the radome must be kept clean because while GRP (more commonly referred to as fibreglass) is transparent to radar energy (see Section 3.3.3), salt, dirt and similar deposits which may accumulate on the surface of the radome are not. In civil marine applications, the use of radomes is in general limited to small craft where the aerial length is less than about one metre.

2.7.1.5   Radiation hazard (see also Section 2.7.2)

It is believed that there is no radiation hazard to shipboard personnel provided that the aerial is rotating. This is based on the premise that the level of radiation outside the turning circle of the aerial is safe. However, *harmful* effects, particularly to the eyes, can be experienced at very short distances from a stationary aerial if energy is being radiated. The distance will depend on the transmitted power, but in civil marine radars designed for merchant ships it is usually in the region of 0.3 to 0.6 m. Many administrations require, and good practice dictates, that manufacturers should make radiation level measurements from which it is possible to determine the safe distance. This distance should form part of a warning contained in the operator's manual and should also be printed on the aerial unit. In the case of slotted waveguide aerials, the safe distance warning is normally written on the GRP envelope or protection panel (see Section 2.4.2.2). If it is necessary for personnel to approach within the safe distance of a stationary aerial, it is important to ensure that the equipment is not transmitting and to take steps to prevent the equipment being switched to the transmit condition. A good practice is to have the person qualified to service the equipment remove the fuses from the transceiver and aerial-turning equipment when this work is being carried out and to place a prominent warning notice on the display.

Service personnel may have to carry out adjustments which require transmission from a stationary aerial, to undertake work on a waveguide while the transmitter is operating and to disconnect the waveguide from the transmitter. All such operations incur a risk of exposure to dangerous levels of radiation. It is essential that such work is only undertaken by fully trained and experienced service personnel. *Permanent damage to the eyes* is likely to result from looking down a waveguide from which radar energy is being radiated. Some appreciation of the possible harmful effects of radiation can be obtained by recognizing that a domestic microwave oven uses radar waves to cook meals in a very short space of time.

It is important to note that some cardiac pacemakers can be affected by radar-frequency radiation.

2.7.1.6 *Effect on radio direction finder (RDF)*

Metal elements close to the direction-finding loop aerial may introduce errors into RDF bearings and this factor may influence the choice of radar aerial site. However, amendments to SOLAS Chapter V in 2001 have resulted in the fairly rapid phasing out of RDF equipment on most vessels (see Section 3.5.7).

2.7.2 The transceiver unit

The transceiver unit is so called because it houses the transmitter (see Section 2.3) and part of the receiver (see Section 2.5). In addition to the mixer, the latter may comprise either the entire IF amplifier (see Section 2.5.2) or a portion of it sometimes referred to as the *pre-IF amplifier.*

Ideally, the transmitter and at least the early stages of the receiver should be located as close to the aerial unit as possible. This reduces the attenuation of the powerful transmitted pulse on its journey up the waveguide to the aerial and, of even greater importance, the attenuation of the weak returning signals as they travel down the waveguide to the receiver. By siting the transceiver close to the aerial unit, it is inevitable that in most cases it will therefore be remote from the display unit. However, by ensuring sufficient receiver gain within the transceiver (see Section 2.5.2.2) the signal can be amplified to an adequate level to make the journey along co-axial cable from the transceiver to the display.

Waveguide is expensive and thus siting the transceiver in close proximity to the aerial also reduces the overall cost of the installation. The cross-section of the waveguide is of critical importance to correct propagation and it must be *plumbed in* with great care, particular attention being given to ensure that bends and twists are formed in such a way as to prevent distortion of the waveguide dimensions. It is usual to have specially preformed sections for bends and twists. In an ideal situation the aerial unit would be mounted vertically above the transceiver so as to allow the use of a straight waveguide run. This is seldom possible in practice. Long waveguide runs are always at risk of accidental damage. The ingress of water or dirt will seriously affect the performance of the guide. Some modern waveguide systems are filled with a suitable gas in an attempt to maintain the guide cavity in a dry condition and, by pressure indication, to serve as an indicator of any accidental puncture in the wall of the guide.

In some systems the transceiver is fitted within the aerial unit (particularly common in small boat systems). This may dispense with the need for a rotating waveguide joint (see Section 2.2.2), eliminates the waveguide run and reduces signal attenuation to a minimum. This approach suffers from the major disadvantage that there may be serious difficulties in servicing the unit in situ, especially in bad weather. The availability of replacement boards or units has reduced the seriousness of this problem.

In general, civil marine radar equipment should not produce undue interference in other radio equipment. However, good practice dictates that radar units in general, and the transmitter in particular, should not be sited close to radio communications equipment.

While modern transceivers are quiet by comparison with older types, the possibility of acoustic noise being a nuisance to personnel on or off watch is a factor which might influence siting of the unit.

The magnetron (see Section 2.3.3.2) is sited within the transceiver and clearly this, together with the associated waveguide, represents a radiation hazard. However, only service personnel should be exposed to such risk and they should have appropriate training to deal with this danger. In some cases there may be risk from X-radiation and if this is the case many administrations require that the transceiver, or other unit should carry a warning notice.

2.7.3   The display unit

The display unit will contain the units necessary to perform the display functions described in Section 2.6. It will also house the video amplifier stages and perhaps some stages of the IF amplifier, the number of which will depend on what proportion of the receiver is located in the transceiver. Provided that there is adequate gain in the transceiver, the display can be located at quite a distance from it. Because the receiver is split between transceiver and display, some service procedures may require transceiver adjustments whose effect is best judged by viewing the display. If the two units are separated by a great distance, a communication link may greatly facilitate such servicing. This need may well be fulfilled by the use of portable VHF or UHF radios.

Where a single display unit is provided it will most likely be located in the wheelhouse because this allows the observer to view the radar and maintain a visual lookout. In the case of dual displays both may be sited in the wheelhouse or, alternatively, the second display may be placed in the chartroom. The advent of raster-scan displays (see Section 2.6.7) makes the provision of multiple displays a simple matter and allows considerable scope for remote control by means of a separate control panel associated with a long cable or by employing a cordless infra-red transmitter.

With the traditional analogue display (see Section 2.6.2), daylight viewing was always a problem and one practical alternative to the use of a viewing hood or visor is to site the display within an area which can be screened by curtains or tinted glass. The advent of the radial-scan synthetic display (see Section 2.6.6) eased this problem to some extent while raster-scan displays should ensure daylight viewing in almost any ambient light condition. A fairly low level of light emanates from the traditional display and this caused few problems at night, though in certain circumstances reflection of the PPI glow and dial lights in the wheelhouse windows could impair night vision. The light level produced by a raster-scan display is considerably higher and this factor has to be considered in choosing a suitable site for the display.

At night it is practical for several observers simultaneously to view the traditional real-time analogue display, but in daytime the viewing hood makes this impossible. A major benefit of the modern raster-scan display is the elimination of this limitation.

It has been established that in general navigators prefer to have the display sited so that it is viewed when facing forward.

2.7.4   Compass safe distances

Many administrations require that all radar units, because of their potential magnetic influence, be tested to establish the safe distance by which they should be separated from the standard magnetic and from the steering magnetic compass. In the United Kingdom the compass safe distance must be indicated on a tally plate attached to the unit concerned. Some radar spares, in particular magnetrons (see Section 2.3.3.2), have very strong magnetic effects. They may be marked with a magnetic safe distance but if not should be stowed at least 7 m from magnetic compasses.

2.7.5   Exposed and protected equipment

Some radar equipment, such as the aerial, must be designed to withstand the elements while others are intended to be protected from the weather. Certain administrations require the class of equipment to be indicated on each unit.

2.7.6 Power supplies

Traditionally, civil marine radar systems were not designed to operate directly from the mains supply. Normally a power supply unit is provided which can be configured to accept a range of power supply inputs and to convert any one of these to the voltage and frequency required. In older systems it was common for such units to be rotary converters which were noisy by virtue of the mechanical nature of their operation. More modern systems used static inverters, but despite the absence of moving parts these too can emit obtrusive acoustic noise. The siting of this unit should be chosen to avoid disturbance to either those involved in watchkeeping or those who are off watch.

Small boat systems are usually designed to run off voltages between 12 and 30 volts. Modern systems can work off mains supply – 110 volts or 220 volts or both. Uninterruptible power supplies are also available, which can provide enough power to keep the radar operational for several hours.

2.7.7 High voltage hazards

Lethal voltages may exist at various points within shipboard radar equipment. The charge held by high voltage capacitors may take some minutes to discharge after the equipment has been switched off. Maintenance adjustments which require the removal of the outside cover of units should only be attempted by fully qualified personnel.

2.7.8 Interswitching

The IMO Performance Standards (see Section 11.2.1) require vessels greater than 3000 tons gross to be fitted with two radar installations. Many vessels below this tonnage limit also carry two radars because the benefits of such a dual installation are recognized. In order to maintain a high degree of reliability and flexibility where a dual installation is fitted, some or all of the units may be made interswitchable and capable of serving either or both displays. This allows unserviceable units to be isolated and also permits the servicing of units requiring maintenance, without affecting the availability of the overall system. The IMO Performance Standards (see Section 11.2.1) require that, where interswitching is fitted, the failure of either radar must not cause the supply of electrical energy to the other radar to be interrupted or adversely affected. A specific limitation of interswitching is that aerial units are only compatible with transceivers designed for the same wavelength, e.g. an X-band aerial cannot be used with an S-band transceiver. A typical fully interswitched system is illustrated in Figure 2.60.

Suitable selection of the characteristics of individual units will extend the capability of the system as

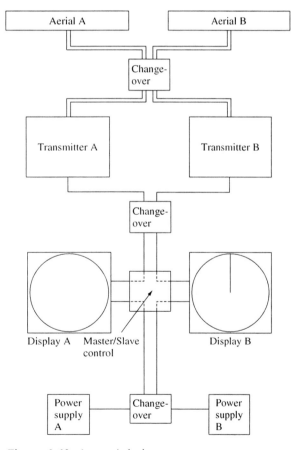

Figure 2.60 Interswitched systems

a whole (see hereafter) to deal with a variety of conditions and circumstances.

2.7.8.1 Choice of frequency

The characteristics of S-band and X-band systems are to some extent complementary (see Section 2.3.3.1) and an interswitched system which offers both options has much to recommend it. It allows the observer to select the frequency which is most appropriate to the particular task in hand. For example, the masking response from sea and rain clutter (see Sections 3.6 and 3.7) is less with S-band whereas, with comparable aerial size (see Section 2.4.2.1, X-band in general offers better bearing discrimination (see Section 2.6.5.6).

2.7.8.2 Choice of picture orientation and presentation

An interswitched system makes possible the simultaneous availability of two different orientations or presentations. In particular, the relative-motion and true-motion presentations are complementary (see Section 1.5.3) and a dual system allows the observer to exploit this.

2.7.8.3 Choice of aerial location

In Section 2.7.1 the question of aerial siting was discussed and it is apparent that in the case of a single aerial the result is a compromise. With an interswitched dual installation, by careful choice of aerial siting it is possible to ensure that each siting gives particular benefits and that these can be exploited by the observer according to the prevailing circumstances. For example, the installation might have one high and one low aerial, one centred and one offset aerial or one forward and one midships aerial. The particular trade in which a vessel is involved might influence the choice of aerial sites.

2.7.8.4 Partial interswitching

A smaller degree of flexibility with lower cost may be achieved by partial interswitching. For example, one aerial and one power unit might serve two transceivers and two displays. Alternatively, a single aerial, transceiver and power supply might be provided with two displays, one as master and one as a slave.

2.7.8.5 Switching protection

Normally the equipment is protected during switching by the *stand-by* condition (see Section 6.7). In some systems this has to be done manually while in others access to the interswitching control is protected by an interlock.

2.7.8.6 Master and slave controls

Where two displays are driven from the same transceiver, one display must be designated as master and the other as slave. This has significance in that it affects the use of the operational controls. The master display will control the receiver tuning (see Sections 2.5.1.2, 6.2.4.2 and 6.3.4.3). If the receiver is of the linear type (see Section 2.5.2.5), the gain and sea clutter functions will be controlled from the master display, whereas with a logarithmic receiver (see Section 2.5.2.6) control can be exercised from each display. Normally the master display will control PRF and pulse length (see Sections 2.3.1 and 2.3.2.1) whereas the selected range scale is controlled by each display. As a result the pulse length and PRF could be inappropriate to the range scale selected at the slave display. To overcome this problem, at least one system has presented, at the slave display, an indication of the range scales that may be selected there. The display will be protected by suitable circuitry from any technical incompatibility but the observer must be aware of any operational limitations, such as minimum range, discrimination and saturation, which may result (see Sections 3.2.4, 2.6.5 and 2.5.2.1). Pure display functions such as brilliance, range rings, range markers, EBL, centring and rain clutter are available at each display (see Chapter 6).

To overcome problems of mutual interference (see Section 3.9.5), a transmission synchronization circuit may be incorporated in the interswitching unit.

2.7.8.7 Combination of radar data from more than one aerial position

The ability to combine the data from more than one aerial position has been used for shore installations for some time. This technology became more practical with the use of raster display systems. It has the advantage of presenting complete radar coverage of an area in one display. The combination can cause some targets to appear twice due to small calibration errors between the overlapping data coverage from two aerials.

Similiar shipboard systems are also available with the major advantage of eliminating blind and shadow sectors (if they exist) due to obstructions on the vessel.

3 Target detection

3.1 Introduction

The ability of the radar system to detect and display a given target depends on a large number of factors some of which are constant and others which may vary in quite a complex manner. The significance of some of these factors may be almost self-evident while that of others may be much less obvious. The *radar range equation* is an expression which attempts to formalize the relationship between the maximum range at which a target can be detected and the parameters on which that range depends. In the form in which the equation is used by radar engineers to predict detection ranges of targets by taking into account all conceivable factors, it is indeed lengthy and complex, containing statistical and empirical components. However, in its simplest form as set out below, it provides at a glance an indication of the significance of many of the factors which are of concern to the radar observer:

$$R_{\max} = \sqrt[4]{\left(\frac{P \times G_0 \times A \times \sigma}{4 \times \pi^2 \times S_{\min}} \right)}$$

where $R_{\max}$ = maximum detection range
P = transmitter power
G_0 = antenna gain
A = antenna aperture area (m^2)
σ = target radar cross-section (m^2)
$S_{\min}$ = minimum detectable signal

All but one of the variables appearing in the equation relate to the characteristics of the radar system and each of these is discussed in turn in Section 3.2. The sole representative of the target is its radar cross-section which is a measure of the size of the target as 'seen' by the radar. Except in the case of certain simple shapes, this is a complex quantity, often having a statistical nature; the implications of this are discussed in Section 3.3. This simple form of the radar equation assumes that the radar and the target are in free space. In practice they are both located on a curved earth having a surface of varying character and surrounded by an atmosphere in which various weather effects may be manifest. The simple equation takes no account of the surface over which, or the medium through which, the radar pulse travels, because many of the effects are extremely difficult to quantify. However, a suitable qualitative treatment of these factors is presented in Sections 3.6, 3.7 and 3.8.

While each of the various factors will be discussed in turn, it is essential to appreciate that in assessing the ability of the radar to detect a target *all* factors will have to be considered and it must be recognized that the relative significance of individual factors will vary with circumstances.

A further result which follows from the equation is that, in general, the signal strength received varies inversely as the *fourth* power of the range of the reflecting surface. (This can be shown by replacing $S_{\min}$ with the more general term S_r representing received signal strength and then making S_r the subject of the equation.) It is thus important to appreciate that, for distant targets, a small increase in range may produce a comparatively large decrease in response. The response from almost all wanted targets follows this law, but some unwanted responses such as those from the sea and from precipitation do not, these will be discussed in Sections 3.6 and 3.7 respectively.

3.2   Radar characteristics

The radar characteristics which appear in the radar range equation as set out above relate directly to the system units described in Sections 2.3, 2.4 and 2.5. One (the power) relates to the transmitter, two (antenna gain and aperture) relate to the aerial and one (S_{min}) relates to the receiver. It is thus appropriate to consider the characteristics under these headings.

3.2.1   Transmitter characteristics

As might be expected, the ability to detect distant targets can be improved by using a more powerful transmitter (see Section 2.3.2.2). In a single radar installation the transmitter power will be a factor which is beyond the control of the observer. However, in dual or interswitched systems (see Section 2.7.8) it may be possible to make a choice between two transmitters of differing powers. The important factor which the radar equation reveals is that the maximum detection range varies as the fourth root of transmitter power. The power of transmitters designed for fitting to large vessels varies with manufacturer, but 10 kW and 50 kW are representative of low and high values. However, it must be noted that a five-fold increase in power only yields an improvement in predicted detection range of approximately 50 per cent. This relationship must also be considered when contemplating the use of a lower power transmitter to reduce unwanted responses (see Sections 6.10.1.1 and 6.10.2.2).

It may seem strange that the pulse length (see Section 2.3.2.1), which is clearly a transmitter characteristic, does not appear in the expression for detection range. Simple observation will show that long range detection is improved by the use of longer pulse lengths. The effect of pulse length is in fact implicit in the quantity S_{min}, the minimum detectable signal, which is a function of pulse length and is discussed in Section 3.2.3.

3.2.2   Antenna characteristics

The radar equation shows that maximum detection range is a function of antenna gain and aperture area.

Clearly these two quantities are related, as a study of Sections 2.4.1.6, 2.4.2.1 and 2.4.3 will reveal. For a given rectangular aperture area, an increase in one dimension at the expense of the other will increase the aerial gain in the plane of the larger dimension. It can be shown that G_0 is directly proportional to A and can thus be replaced in the equation by G_0^2. Hence the predicted maximum detection range varies as the square root of antenna gain. Thus aerial gain has a greater influence than transmitter power on long range performance.

As in the case of transmitter power, where a single radar installation is fitted the observer will have no choice in the matter of aerial gain. In a dual system or interswitched system (see Section 2.7.8.3) the observer may benefit from the ability to select the more suitable aerial. It should be remembered that bearing discrimination will also be improved by selection of the higher gain aerial.

It may seem strange that wavelength does not appear in the equation. It is in fact implicit in the aerial gain and the target radar cross-section, both of which are functions of wavelength (see Sections 2.4.2 and 3.3.5.4).

3.2.3   Receiver characteristics

In the absence of unwanted echoes the criterion for the detection of an echo is that the target response must exceed that of the thermal noise generated at the first stage in the receiver (see Section 2.5.2.3). Thus S_{min}, the minimum detectable signal, is a function of receiver sensitivity. While the theoretical maximum sensitivity is of course limited by the extent to which the radar design can minimize the amplitude of the noise generated in the first receiver stage, it cannot be stressed too strongly that the observer will degrade this sensitivity if the tuning and gain controls are set incorrectly (see Sections 6.2.4, 6.3.4 and 6.4.4).

Whatever the level of noise generated by the first stage of the receiver, the amount of noise which reaches the display depends on the bandwidth of the receiver (see Section 2.5.2.4). This bandwidth must be wider when shorter pulses are selected and hence the receiver sensitivity is inherently poorer in that condition. The receiver sensitivity, and hence the maximum range at which targets can be detected, is thus a function of the pulse length selected by the observer.

Further study of the radar range equation shows that the transmitter power appears as a large quantity on the numerator of the expression while the receiver sensitivity is represented by a small number in the denominator. Radar designers recognize that small improvements in the noise performance are as effective as massive increases in transmitter power; as a result, in recent years efforts have been concentrated on trying to improve receiver performance. This principle is at least as important to the radar observer because it must be borne in mind that minor maladjustments of the tuning or gain controls can have the same effect as a large loss in transmitter power.

Where wanted echoes are present among unwanted signals such as clutter and spurious echoes, it may not be possible to exploit fully the sensitivity of the receiver because the minimum detectable signal level will be determined not by the amplitude of the noise but by the amplitude of unwanted signals. The difficulties posed by such circumstances are discussed in Sections 3.6, 3.7 and 3.9.

It must be appreciated that the available receiver sensitivity can only be fully exploited if the radar display is set up correctly and the controls maintained in correct adjustment to suit changing conditions and requirements. Some adjustments are routine while others, such as searching for targets in clutter (see Sections 6.10.1 and 6.10.2), require considerable skill and practice. In this connection particular attention is drawn to the various practical procedures set out in Chapter 6. There is little doubt that, but for the difficulty of quantifying it, the skill of the radar observer is a factor which would appear in the radar range equation.

3.2.4 Minimum detection range

The radar range equation is specifically concerned with the prediction of maximum detection ranges and in many circumstances the radar observer is concerned with this aspect of target detection. However, there are certain circumstances, for example pilotage situations, in which the minimum detection range is of particular importance. The importance of a small minimum detection range is recognized by the IMO Performance Standards (see Section 11.2.1) which require that specific target types be clearly displayed down to a minimum range of 40 m. The various factors affecting minimum detection range are illustrated by Figure 3.1.

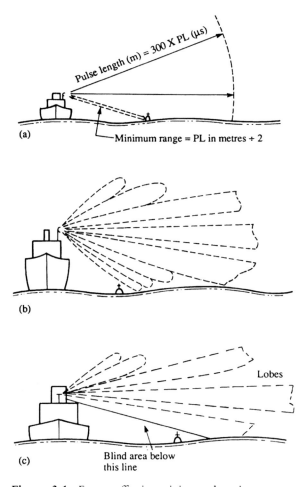

Figure 3.1 Factors affecting minimum detection range
(a)   Pulse length
(b)   Vertical beam structure
(c)   Ship structure shadowing

Clearly the radar cannot receive echoes while the pulse is being transmitted and this limitation determines the *theoretical minimum detection range*. The trailing edge of the transmitted pulse will clear the aerial after the start of the timebase by an elapsed time equal to the duration of one pulse length. This instant will coincide with the arrival of an echo from any reflecting surface which lies at a distance of one-half pulse length from the aerial (see Figure 3.1(a)). The theoretical minimum detection range can thus be determined by calculating the distance travelled by radar energy in one-half the duration of the transmitted pulse.

Example 3.1 Calculate the theoretical minimum detection range for a radar which has three pulse lengths, the durations of which are 1.0, 0.5 and 0.1 μs.

To achieve the minimum detection range the observer should select the shortest available pulse length. Half the duration of the shortest pulse length (PL) is given by

$$\frac{\text{PL}}{2} = \frac{0.1}{2}\ \mu\text{s}$$

The distance travelled by radar energy in this time is given by

$$D_{\min} = \frac{0.1}{2} \times 300\,\text{m (see Section 1.2.2)} = 15\,\text{m}$$

The theoretical minimum detection range $= 15\,\text{m}$

It is evident that the theoretical minimum range illustrated by this example (which uses a typical short pulse length) is considerably less than that required by the IMO Performance Standards. In practice, the theoretical minimum range cannot be achieved for three principal reasons, namely:

1 At close range the target may be below the lower extent of the vertical beam (see Section 3.2.4), though of course it may be illuminated by the vertical sidelobes. Assuming that the beam is not intercepted by the ship's structure (see below), the range at which the lower edge intersects the sea increases with aerial height (see Figure 3.1(b)).

2 At close range the target may be shadowed in the athwartships direction by the ship's side or in the fore-and-aft direction by the ship's bow or stern. The likelihood of this shadowing decreases with aerial height. The question of whether the minimum range is limited by this factor, or by the lower limit of the beam described in item 1, depends on the height at which the aerial is sited, its location with respect to the ship's fore-and-aft line and the dimensions of the vessel (see Figure 3.1(c)).

3 The T/R cell takes a finite time to de-energize.

3.2.5 Detection performance standards

The new IMO Performance Standards (see Section 11.2.1) for new vessels built from 2008 have significantly increased detection standards when compared with current and previous standards.

These new standards represent larger minimum ranges for detection of coastlines and larger ships as well as considerably more detail including standards for detecting buoys and small boats and their radar reflectors. Table 3.1 shows these detection ranges in clutter-free conditions. Another innovation is the separate treatment of X- and S-band frequencies with X-band requiring the higher standards.

The new standards also recognize that performance is much reduced in clutter conditions and the manufacturer is now required to state in the manual the reduction in performance for distinct clutter conditions:

- light rain (4 mm per hour) and heavy rain (16 mm per hour);
- sea state 2 and sea state 5; and
- a combination of these.

This performance should be considered at different radar ranges and for different target speeds.

Table 3.1 Minimum detection ranges in clutter-free conditions (for more detail see Section 11.2.1)

Target description	Target feature	Detection range in nm	
Target description	Height above sea level in metres	X-band nm	S-band nm
Shorelines	Rising to 60	20	20
Shorelines	Rising to 6	8	8
Shorelines	Rising to 3	6	6
SOLAS ships (>5000 gross tonnage)	10	11	11
SOLAS ships (>500 gross tonnage)	5.0	8	8
Small vessel with radar reflector meeting IMO Performance Standards	4.0	5.0	3.7
Navigation buoy with corner reflector	3.5	4.9	3.6
Typical navigation buoy	3.5	4.6	3.0
Small vessel of length 10 m with no radar reflector	2.0	3.4	3.0

3.3 Target characteristics

Energy in the pulse which is intercepted by the target is then available for return towards the antenna and hence to the receiver which is now in a receptive state. The amount of energy which is returned toward the antenna, as opposed to that energy which is absorbed and scattered by the target, is dependent upon the following five prime characteristics of the target.

3.3.1 Aspect

The simplest approach to target response is to consider that the energy suffers 'specular' reflection, i.e. the sort of reflection that occurs when light strikes a plain mirror. Aspect is the angle which the radar rays make with the plane of the mirror and, as can be seen in Figure 3.2, the response will be good when the aspect is 90° and poor at virtually all other angles.

3.3.2 Surface texture

The extent to which reflection is specular is dependent upon the surface texture of the target, i.e. whether the surface is 'rough' or 'smooth'. Whether a surface is rough or smooth has to be related to the wavelength of the waves which are striking it. A surface which reflects light poorly because the indentations or facets in the surface are of the same order as the wavelength of the light (approximately 0.001 mm) will appear smooth to radar waves whose wavelength (some 3 to 10 cm) is very much longer, and specular reflection will result. It should be noted that objects which appear rough to radar waves, and therefore scatter a large proportion of the waves, can occasionally improve the response from a target which has an intrinsically poor aspect (see Figure 3.2).

3.3.3 Material

In general, materials which are good conductors of electricity also return good radar responses. This occurs as a result of absorption and re-radiation of the waves at the same wavelength as those received, rather than from simple specular-type reflection.

Some bodies absorb radiation but, when they re-radiate, the wavelength is different from that at which it was received; still other bodies absorb radiation and re-radiate very little of the energy (this results in the temperature of the body rising, i.e. the received radiation is converted to heat). Some materials are simply transparent to radar energy. GRP behaves to a large extent in this way, steel will return good responses, while wooden boats generally produce poor responses.

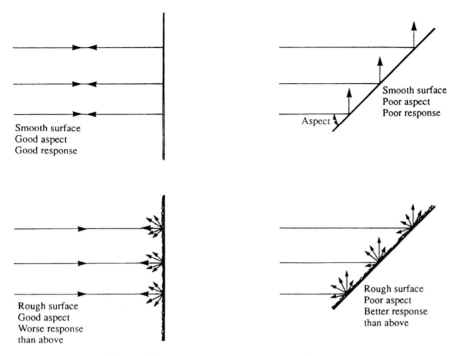

Figure 3.2 The effects on target response of aspect and surface texture

Figure 3.3 Some effects of material on target response

3.3.4 Shape

It is frequently suggested that shape might be considered as the variable aspect of an object. This is true, but when attempting to assess the degree of response which one might expect from a particular target it is often convenient to consider the target as of fixed shape but able to change its aspect (e.g. a conical buoy rolling in a seaway).

3.3.5 Size

In general, the more energy intercepted by the target, the better the response is likely to be, i.e. the response is related to the area of the target irradiated by the beam (at any instant). This is not necessarily the same as the intrinsic size of the target. Since the radar beam is angularly wider in the vertical plane than in the horizontal, tall targets will in general produce stronger responses (all other factors being equal).

Consider two targets presenting the same area to the radar; if the linear width of the horizontal beam at the range of the targets is equal to the linear width of target A then, in the case of B, only the small irradiated portion of the target will contribute to echo strength, while, in the case of A, virtually the total area will be irradiated.

It is essential to understand clearly that what is being considered here is target response as opposed to actual target size (and therefore its potential *brightness* on the

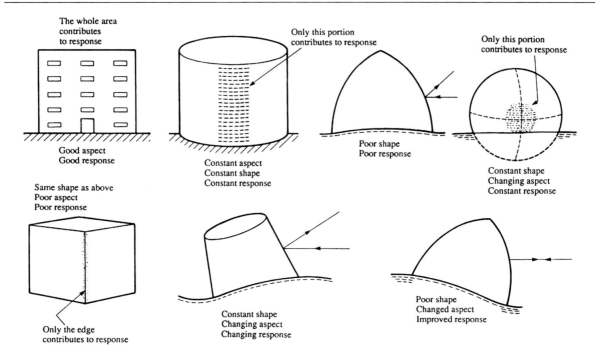

Figure 3.4 The effect of target shape on target response

Figure 3.5 The effect of irradiated area on echo strength
Area A = Area B = cross-section of the radar beam

screen) and not its displayed size (i.e. the *area* of the screen which it occupies).

It is also necessary here to consider the 'resolution cell' in relation to the three-dimensional size of the target. The cell is defined by the transmitted pulse length, the horizontal beamwidth and the vertical beamwidth.

Only that portion of the target which falls within the resolution cell at any instant can contribute to the response. In general, as the beam sweeps over small

targets, they will fall completely within the resolution cell. With larger targets, all the energy may be intercepted when the target is at short range, whereas at longer ranges, as the cell 'expands', the target may still exceed the horizontal beamwidth but is unlikely to fill the vertical beam.

Where, within the cell, the target is sloping, e.g. a coastline, two consequences of the slope need to be considered.

3.3.5.1 *Sloping surfaces – the effect of coherence on response amplitude*

Consider the face of the slope to be made up of small steps. The radial length of the step will determine the phase relationship of the elements of the returning composite wave. If the elements are out of phase on their return to the antenna then the echo strength will be poor, while if they are in phase the response will be good.

Figure 3.6 The resolution cell

Note The radial length of the steps being considered here is of the order of a fraction of a wavelength (and will take the form of an odd number of quarter wavelengths).

3.3.5.2 *Sloping surfaces – the effect of signal integration on echo strength*

In this case, the steps which are to be considered are of the order of one-half pulse length, i.e. half of 0.1 to 1 μs, which equates to a radial distance of some 15 to 150 m.

Consider a stepped sloping surface (Figure 3.9) where each step is 10 m in length and the radar pulse length is 0.2 μs, i.e. the spatial length of the pulse is $0.2 \times 300 = 60$ m.

It can be seen from Figure 3.9 that the responses from the individual steps on the target can integrate (i.e. add up) to a maximum from that portion of the target which lies within any one-half pulse length, but cannot increase indefinitely as the target increases in height. In the above example the one-half pulse length is 30 m.

If, with the same overall size of target, the step height and length are varied so that each step height is halved and the step length is halved, the same aggregate response will be obtained, which is the integration of a larger number of smaller responses. It is evident that the land still rises to the same height over half the pulse length. This suggests an alternative approach, which is to consider only the vertical height over the one-half pulse length i.e. *projected height* (or, in three dimensions, the *projected area* – Figure 3.10).

Portion irradiated

Figure 3.7 The portion of the vessel irradiated

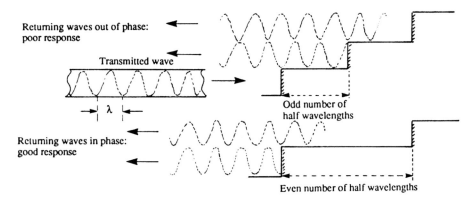

Returning waves out of phase: poor response

Transmitted wave

λ

Odd number of half wavelengths

Returning waves in phase: good response

Even number of half wavelengths

Figure 3.8 The effect of coherence on echo strength

Figure 3.9 Integration of signals from sloping surfaces

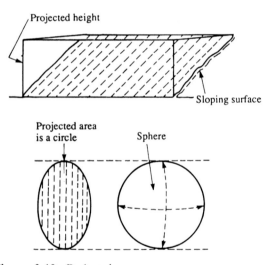

Figure 3.10 Projected area

Note (a) If the step lengths are not precisely the same and if the difference is of the order of one-half the wavelength, then the effects of coherence will also have to be considered when deciding on whether or

not the elements of the response will integrate.

(b) If the facets are not true steps, random scattering will also have to be considered.

(c) As a result of the most favourable integration of the elements of the response, the maximum echo *strength* would be the same as if a flat plate were placed in the path of the pulse. The plate would have a vertical height equivalent to the projected vertical height of the target which lies within half the radial length of the transmitted pulse.

Where a target is small in relation to the resolution cell, it is convenient to consider the projected area of the target (see also Section 3.3.5.4), but its surface texture, material, aspect and shape must not be ignored.

3.3.5.3 *The equivalent flat plate area (A_t) of a target*

This is the area of a flat plate orientated at right angles to the incident radiation which would return the same energy as the object. The equivalent flat plate areas for some common shapes are given in Figure 3.11.

Note (a) The values given in Figure 3.11 are maximum values, having been simplified by the removal of terms relating to aspect. If the aspect in either or both planes is changed, the response may decrease. For example, if the flat plate were tilted there would be a marked drop in response, whereas, with the cylinder, a change about a vertical axis would result in no change in response while a change about a horizontal axis would result in a marked drop in response.

(b) In deriving the formulae, there is an assumption that the size of the object is very large in comparison with the wavelength. (The formulae should not be applied, for instance, to spherical rain drops.)

3.3.5.4   *The radar cross-section of a target* (σ)

The radar cross-section (or equivalent echoing area) of an object is the area intercepting that amount of power which, *when scattered isotropically*, produces an echo equal to that received from the object.

Since a sphere is generally accepted as a typical isotropic radiator (i.e. it radiates in all directions), this definition is indicating the cross-section of a sphere which, if it replaced the target, would produce the same response.

It can be seen that if there is some directivity in the target's response, its radar cross-section will be much greater than its actual physical cross-section or projected area.

Example 3.2   Compare the radar cross-section of a flat plate with that of a sphere if the plate is at right angles to the radiation; both plate and sphere have projected areas of $1\,\mathrm{m}^2$ and the wavelength in use is $3.2\,\mathrm{cm}$.

$$\frac{\text{Radar cross-section of a flat plate}}{\text{Radar cross-section of a sphere}} = \frac{4\pi a^2 b^2/\lambda^2}{\pi c^2}$$

but $a \times b = 1 = \pi c^2$

$$= \frac{4\pi ab}{\lambda^2}$$

$$= \frac{4\pi A}{\lambda^2}$$

$$= \frac{4 \times 3.142 \times 10^4}{3.2^2}$$

$$= 12\,273 \text{ times}$$

This means that the flat plate would produce a response some 12 000 times greater than the sphere or, alternatively, a sphere having some 12 000 times the projected area of the plate would have to be placed at the same range as the plate to produce the same response. It is interesting to note that any slight change in the aspect of the plate will result in a massive drop in the response, whereas no change will occur if the sphere is reorientated.

One of the surface objects referred to in the IMO Performance Standards, in specifying range performance (see Sections 11.2.1), is a navigational buoy having an effective echoing area of approximately $10\,\mathrm{m}^2$. This means one that produces the same strength of echo as a sphere having a projected area of $10\,\mathrm{m}^2$, i.e. a spherical buoy having a diameter of some $4\,\mathrm{m}$.

The relationship between radar cross-section and equivalent flat plate area is given by the formula

$$\sigma = \frac{4\pi A_t^2}{\lambda^2}$$

3.3.5.5   *The Rayleigh roughness criterion*

It can be shown that the roughness of a surface depends on the size of the discontinuities in relation to the incident wavelength and the angle at which the radiation strikes the surface (the grazing angle). Application of the Rayleigh criterion indicates that the surfaces for all practical purposes are smooth if $(8 \times \delta h \times \sin\theta) < \lambda$, where λ is the wavelength and θ is the grazing angle (Figure 3.12).

Example 3.3   If the antenna is at a height of $15\,\mathrm{m}$, at what distance, d, from the ship, will the sea surface appear smooth if wave height is $1\,\mathrm{m}$ (the radar

Target	Dimensions	Max. equivalent flat plate area A_t	Max. radar cross-section σ
Sphere		$\dfrac{a\lambda}{2}$	πa^2
Cylinder		$b\sqrt{\dfrac{a\lambda}{2}}$	$\dfrac{2\pi ab^2}{\lambda}$
Flat plate		ab	$\dfrac{4\pi a^2 b^2}{\lambda^2}$
Dihedral corner		$ab\sqrt{2}$	$\dfrac{8\pi a^2 b^2}{\lambda^2}$
Triangular trihedral		$\dfrac{a^2}{\sqrt{3}}$	$\dfrac{4\pi a^4}{3\lambda^2}$
Rectangular trihedral		$a^2\sqrt{3}$	$\dfrac{12\pi a^4}{\lambda^2}$
Cone		$\dfrac{\lambda^2 \tan^2\theta}{8\pi}$	$\dfrac{\lambda^2 \tan^4\theta}{16\pi}$
Lunenburg lens		πa^2	$\dfrac{4\pi^3 a^4}{\lambda^2}$

Figure 3.11 Radar cross-sections and equivalent flat plate areas for some common targets

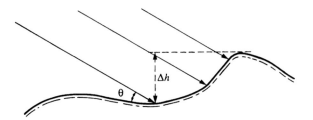

Figure 3.12 Grazing angle and roughness

is working in the X-band)? (At the limit of clutter, $8 \times \delta h \times \sin \theta = \lambda$.)

$$\frac{8 \times 1 \times 15}{\sqrt{(225 + d^2)}} = 0.03$$

$$d^2 = 4000^2 - 225$$

The sea surface will appear smooth at a distance.

$$d \geqslant 4\,\text{km}(2.16\,\text{n mile})$$

3.3.6 Responses from specific targets

3.3.6.1 Ice

Large icebergs, such as those which are formed on the east coast of Greenland and drift down toward the North Atlantic shipping routes, have been found to give greatly varying radar responses. Detection ranges as great as 11 n miles have been experienced while, on the other hand, quite large

icebergs have approached to within 2 n miles without being detected. Even the same iceberg may give greatly differing responses when viewed from different directions.

Particular concern has been expressed because of radar's apparent difficulty in 'detecting ice'. The point should be made that the ice which causes most concern is that form which comprises what are known as growlers. Many theories have been put forward and there have been many practical experiments carried out to determine the best way to use the radar in areas where growlers are expected: two major points emerge.

1   Growlers are intrinsically poor targets because, as melting ice, the surface tends to be smooth and this does nothing to improve their essentially poor shape and aspect. They present a small projected area above the water and the signal returned is frequently of strength comparable to or weaker than that returned from the sea waves which are prevalent in the area in which the growlers are commonly found.

    Theories relating to the effects of high temperature gradients in the immediate vicinity of the growler and also to the re-radiation characteristic of the ice have not proved conclusive.

2   In areas where growlers are to be expected, radar should not be relied upon to give adequate or even any warning of their presence, especially at night or in poor visibility. Speed and the visual lookout should be set with this in mind.

Figure 3.13 The theoretical extent of sea clutter

The best use of radar under these circumstances is:

(a) a dedicated radar watch by one observer;
(b) regular searching with the anti-clutter control on the short ranges (see Section 6.10.1), remembering to check at frequent intervals on the longer ranges for larger targets;
(c) use of the long pulse in weak clutter;
(d) use of the longer wavelength of the S-band radar.

3.3.6.2 *Radar-conspicuous targets*

Targets which are designated *radar-conspicuous* should be those which are known to provide good radar responses and are readily identifiable (see Section 8.2.5). In the past, particular land features which satisfied those criteria were highlighted on charts by the addition of the legend 'Radar Conspic'. This practice has been discontinued but there is no reason why observers should not mark their own charts in this way and also make notes in the radar log for the benefit of their successors.

3.3.6.3 *Ships*

The structure of ships is such that there are many natural 'corner reflectors' (see Section 3.4.1) and hence, when a target vessel is rolling and pitching in a seaway, its echo strength does not vary quite as much as might be expected. Some rather peculiar effects can be observed, although they are usually quite easily explained by reverting to first principles. For example, long vessels may appear as two or three individual echoes (each of which when tracked by ARPA might appear to be going in a slightly different direction). They may also be confused for a tug-and-tow or vice versa. Supertankers, because of their low freeboard, may not be detected at inordinately great ranges, when loaded.

3.4 Target enhancement – passive

It is essential that some targets which would normally provide poor radar responses, e.g. buoys, glass fibre

and wooden boats etc., are detected at an adequate range by radar. It was recognized at a very early stage in the development of radar that some form of echo enhancement was needed. IMO have Performance Standards for radar reflectors (see Section 11.2.6).

3.4.1 Corner reflectors

A corner reflector was seen as a simple device which would return virtually all of the energy which entered it, i.e., the energy would be returned in the direction from which it had come almost irrespective of the angle at which it had entered the corner (see Figure 3.14). In its simplest form, such a corner consists of two metal plates placed at an angle of 90° to each other, attached to a navigation mark which then

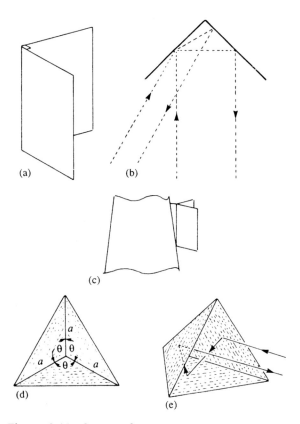

Figure 3.14 Corner reflectors

returns an improved radar response and consequently is detectable at a greater range.

An essential principle of all echo enhancement is that it provides *reserve gain*, which means that, in adverse conditions of sea or weather clutter, the target's improved response can be expected to be greater than the clutter responses and therefore be detectable (see Sections 6.10.1 and 6.10.2), despite the reduced gain necessary for the suppression of the clutter.

While a simple corner is adequate on non-floating objects, if the attitude of the target is likely to change as it moves in a seaway it is necessary to use the now familiar *closed corner* or triangular trihedral (see Figure 3.14(d)) rather than the dihedral corner. The closed corner will ensure that the energy is returned even though the corner is moving through quite a large angle in both the horizontal and vertical planes.

3.4.1.1 *The accuracy of construction*

The angle between each pair of planes must be 90° and very little error can be tolerated without affecting the efficient operation of the corner. Where, as a result of damage or careless construction,

the angle is other than 90°, even by a very small amount, the response from the corner can be seriously impaired.

Figure 3.15 shows that, with a wavelength of 3 cm and a side length of 1.05 m (i.e. side length to wavelength ratio of 35); if the angle between the planes is 88° the gain is only 10 dB instead of the 30 dB that might be expected − this difference of 20 dB represents a reduction in response by a factor of 100. Note that with smaller sides but still working at the same wavelength, the loss would not be so severe.

Over the years, many designs for the 'home' construction of the corner reflectors and in particular 'collapsible' octahedral arrays (see Section 3.4.2.2) have been published, but it is never made clear how important is the precision required in the construction and assembly of the corners, in order for the full potential of the reflector to be achieved.

The suggestion that 'crumpled' aluminium foil (in a plastic container!) will provide adequate radar responses is a serious over-simplification. The physical principles of adequate enhancement require precise corners and that the size of each facet is at least greater than and preferably a function of wavelength.

Figure 3.15 The effect of an error in all three corner angles of a corner reflector

3.4.1.2 The response from a corner reflector

The three forms of the corner reflector may be compared by referring to Figure 3.11. The following points should be noted.

1 Values shown are maximum values. Where aspect in either plane is changed, additional terms will need to be included in the equations.
2 A_f indicates the area of a flat plate, orientated so as to be perpendicular to the direction of the incident radiation. For example, a triangular trihedral reflector which has a side length a of 50 cm reflects as if it were a flat plate having an area of 1443.4 cm^2 and a 90° aspect.

This would appear to indicate that a corner reflector is not as good at returning a response as a flat plate. While this is true, the very important proviso is that a flat plate will only respond at optimum level when it is perpendicular to the incident radiation. If there is only a very slight change in aspect of the flat plate, the response, however, will drop theoretically to zero; with the corner, the level will suffer very little reduction over some ±50° of change in attitude.

A second point which is worthy of note is that the dihedral and rectangular trihedral corners both have better response figures than the triangular trihedral but the former's response is markedly susceptible to change of attitude while the latter does not have such a wide coverage angle since the square plates tend to intercept the incident radiation at an earlier stage as aspect is varied.

3.4.2 Arrays of reflectors

A single triangular trihedral corner does not provide 360° of azimuth coverage. By use of a group or array, irrespective of the direction from which it is viewed and of its attitude in the vertical plane, the response will remain virtually unchanged. The array may be incorporated in the basic structure of the navigation mark (Figure 3.16).

The following points should be noted with regard to arrays:

1 Reflectors which have surfaces of wire mesh, especially if a is greater than 20 times the wavelength, tend to warp and so produce poor results.
2 Deterioration of response is likely to result from (a) imprecise construction or damage (b) poor intrinsic orientation and (c) changes in coherence.

3.4.2.1 Types of array

The *didhedral array* has been found to be most appropriate for shore-based navigation marks because the rapid fall off in response associated with change of attitude in the vertical plane was not a factor.

The *octahedral array* (Figure 3.17) was until recently regarded as the standard for most situations.

In the *pentagonal array* (Figure 3.18), the polar diagram in the horizontal plane shows quite serious arcs of reduced response where the beam passes between the elements.

In the vertical plane, as the navigation mark heels, the response falls off rapidly with angle of heel.

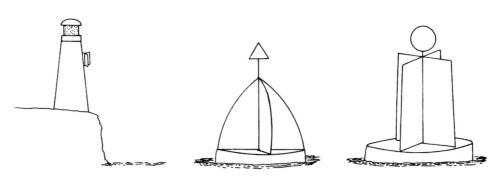

Figure 3.16 Arrays of reflectors incorporated into the structures of navigation marks

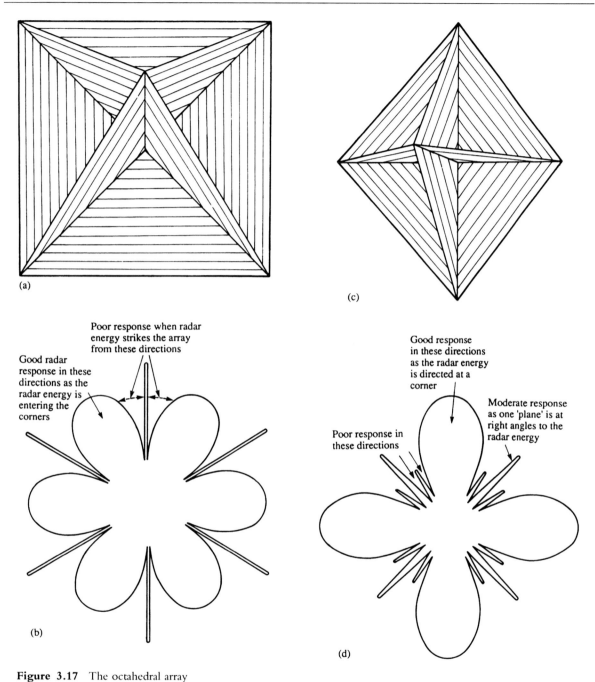

Figure 3.17 The octahedral array
   (a) Correct orientation
   (b) Polar diagram corresponding to (a)
   (c) Incorrect orientation

(d) Polar diagram corresponding to (c) – the 'point-up' orientation gives reduced coverage

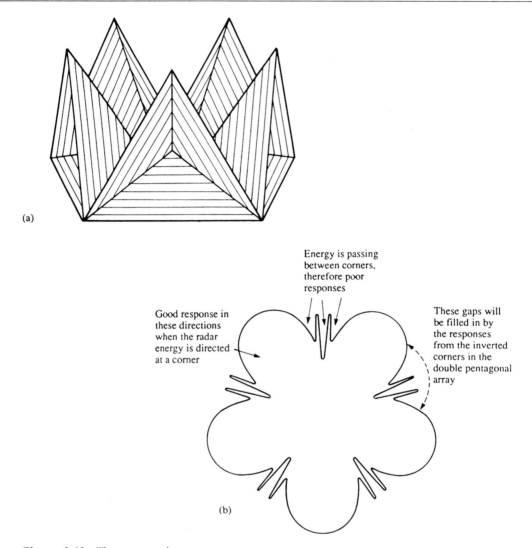

Energy is passing
between corners,
therefore poor
responses

Good response in
these directions
when the radar
energy is directed
at a corner

These gaps will
be filled in by
the responses
from the inverted
corners in the
double pentagonal
array

(a)

(b)

Figure 3.18 The pentagonal array
(a) The array   (b) Polar diagram

In the *double pentagonal array*, as can be seen from Figures 3.18(b) and 3.19 the interspaced corners fill out the polar diagram in the horizontal plane, thus improving the 360° coverage pattern.

3.4.2.2 Stacked arrays (Figure 3.20)

In order to overcome the effect of the gaps in the polar diagrams for the arrays described above, the individual triangular trihedral corners can be arranged in such a way that, as the response from one corner decreases, the response from the next corner starts to increase and so compensates for that drop. In this way, uniformity of response is maintained over 360° of azimuth.

An advantage of the many commercial forms of stacked arrays is that they are enclosed in a glass fibre housing which protects the metallic element from damage.

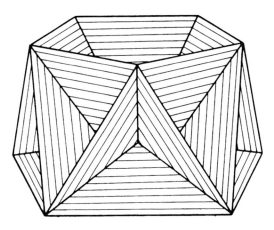

Figure 3.19   The double pentagonal array

3.4.3   The Lunenburg lens

The Lunenburg lens has been in use for quite a number of years, both on navigation marks and on small craft, but frequently goes unrecognized. It comprises a series of concentric shells of differing refractive index.

3.4.3.1   *Principle of operation (Figure 3.21)*

Paraxial rays, impinging on the outer spherical surface, are refracted by different amounts at each shell interface so that they are focused at a point on the opposite surface of the sphere. Here the energy is reflected by a metal band in such a way that the exit path of the returning energy is in a direction reciprocal to that of the incident energy.

3.4.3.2   *The polar diagram*

Figure 3.22 gives the theoretical polar diagram, and Figure 3.23 shows its practical effect when applied to a buoy. It should be noted that in the horizontal plane there are no significant 'dropout' sectors. In the vertical plane the coverage is also good, allowing the

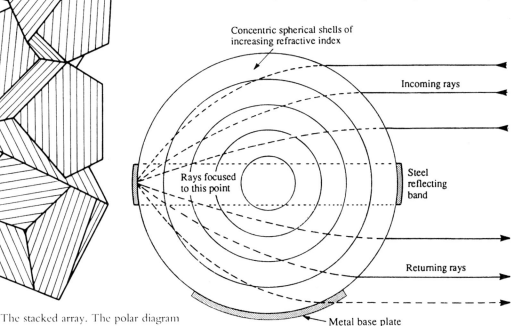

Figure 3.20   The stacked array. The polar diagram varies according to how the stack is constructed: in general, there are few blind spots even with 20°–30° of heeling

Figure 3.21   The Lunenburg lens – the principle

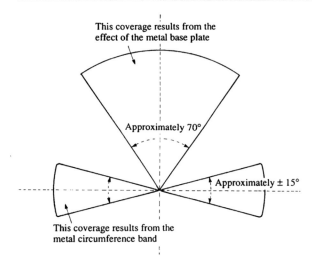

Figure 3.22   Theoretical vertical polar diagram of the Lunenburg lens. The horizontal polar diagram is virtually a circle, i.e. there are no 'preferential' directions

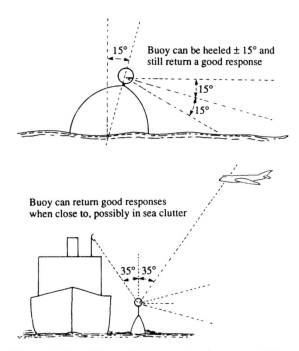

Figure 3.23   The vertical plane polar diagram applied to a buoy

buoy an angle of heel of some 35° or, conversely, the response will be enhanced even when the buoy is close to a vessel with quite a large antenna height.

3.4.4   Buoy patterns

Although the addition of a radar reflector array improves the overall radar response of a target, it does not assist in the identification of the target. Some experiments were carried out where targets (such as spar bouys) were fitted with arrays and placed in patterns. Although these patterns were readily recognizable on the radar display, the use of patterns as an aid to recognition has not received widespread acceptance. Patterns which exist naturally can prove most helpful.

3.5   Target enhancement – active

In about 1958 it became possible to apply what had been primarily military identification techniques to civil marine targets. These result in improved responses and facilitate identification. There were two major thrusts in the development of a solution – the *racon* and the *ramark*. The ramark is now obsolete but it is covered for historical reference in Section 3.5.4.

3.5.1   The racon principle (Figure 3.24)

A simple explanation of the operation is that the ship's radar pulse triggers the racon transmitter on the navigation mark, which then responds by transmitting a pulse

Figure 3.24   The racon principle

(virtually instantaneously). This pulse is both longer and more powerful than the ship's transmitted pulse.

3.5.2 The racon appearance on the display

The racon signal appears on the radar screen as depicted in Figure 3.25 i.e. as a radial 'flash' some 1° to 2° in angular width. Its radial length depends on the duration of the racon pulse, which is specified by IMO (see Section 11.2.5) as being approximately 20 per cent of maximum range but not more than 5 miles. Values are likely to lie in the range 20 μs to 40 μs, which represents a length on the radar screen of some 1.5 to 3 n miles.

3.5.2.1 Coding

The racon transmitter may be interrupted by on/off keying in such a way as to give a displayed racon signal of a specific appearance. This normally takes the form of an appropriate morse coding; for instance, a harbour authority might mark a shoal called 'King's Bank' by the morse letter K, as in Figure 3.25(b). This is of particular importance in aiding identification where there are several racons in the same area. The spacing between dots and dashes should be one dot. A dash should be equivalent in length to three dots.

3.5.2.2 Racons at close range

When radar is being used in close proximity to a racon-equipped light vessel, it frequently occurs that energy transmitted in the side lobes triggers the racon at times other than when the radar's main beam is scanning the light-vessel. In such cases, the 'racon clutter' (Figure 3.26) can cover a large arc of the radar screen close to the observing vessel (see also 'side echoes', Section 3.9.4).

Some racons are equipped with means to reduce the possibility of sidelobes triggering the racon. This is achieved by frequency-agile racons (see Section 3.5.3.3) storing the received signal strength at particular frequencies and then only responding when the signal strength at a particular frequency is close to the stored maximum value.

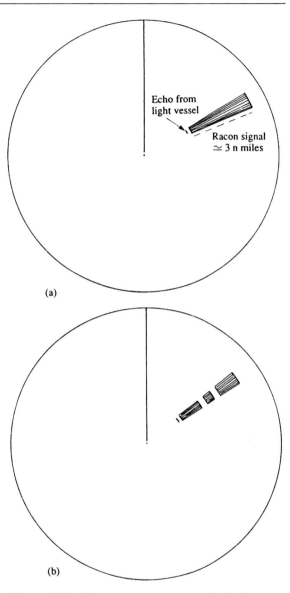

Figure 3.25 The racon appearance on the display
(a)   Standard response
(b)   Coded response

Cheaper versions of the racon may use adaptive regulation of the racon receiver's sensitivity but this can result in weaker signals from more distant vessels being denied a racon response.

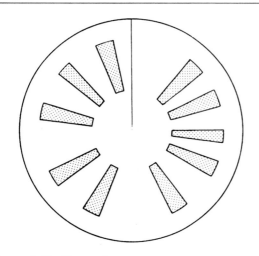

Figure 3.26 Racon clutter

3.5.2.3   Racons at long range

Since one of the reasons for fitting a racon is to improve the detection range of what might otherwise be a poor response target, at longer ranges the response from the actual target may not be detected/displayed although the racon flash appears quite clearly. In this case, measuring the range to the nearest edge or the racon flash is acceptable as it will result in an error of only a hundred metres (the maximum racon receive/transmit delay time) and at long range such an error should not be significant. However, additional care must be exercised when navigating in close proximity to off-lying hazards while using a distant racon to fix position.

3.5.2.4   The danger in using racons to assess correct tuning of the radar receiver

It is advocated (see Sections 6.2.4.2, 6.3.4.3 and 6.4.4) that the radar receiver be accurately tuned by observing the change in display brightness of certain received signals while adjusting the tuning control. Racon signals *must not* be used in this way since:

(a)   The racon signal is frequently above saturation level and will not therefore show any marked change as the tuning control is varied.

(b)   The racon response will be displayed irrespective of the frequency to which the receiver is tuned (see Section 3.5.1), i.e. the racon will be displayed even when the receiver is off tune.

3.5.3   Frequency and polarization

It is evident that if the racon signal is to appear on the ship's radar, then the beacon response must be transmitted at the transmission frequency of the ship's radar. During periods of restricted visibility in areas of high-density traffic, the demand on the racon can be extremely heavy, both in the number of interrogations and also the range of frequencies at which a response is required.

For example, at X-band the marine radar transmissions will fall within the approximate band 9320 to 9500 MHz. The radar receiver bandwidth, i.e. the band of frequencies within which an individual receiver can detect signals, is in the approximate range 2 to 20 MHz (see Section 2.5.2.4) and so it can be seen that some form of tunable oscillator is required within the racon transmitter if its responses to all interrogations are to be detectable.

One concession in the demand for a response is that it is not normal for the racon to be 'observed' on every radar scan, i.e. every 3 seconds or so. This can also be beneficial in that there will be less likelihood of an observer failing to detect a real target which might be obscured by the racon flash.

Racons traditionally operated on X-band, but S-band racons and combined S/X-band racons were encouraged. The latest standards (see Section 11.2.1) only require that X-band radars produce a pulse of sufficient power to trigger a marine racon. This is to allow low power radars to be operated on S-band. The use of racons on S-band is therefore predicted to decline (see Section 3.10).

X-band racon signals have to be horizontally polarized, but S-band racons should respond to both horizontal and vertically polarized radar signals.

3.5.3.1   Slow sweep racons

Rather than attempt to respond to each ship's radar pulse every time it is received, the racon oscillator

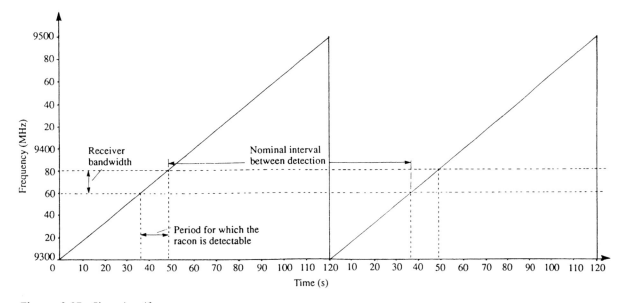

Figure 3.27 Slow time/frequency racon sweep

is swept comparatively slowly across the marine radar band. Racon sweep periods of some 60 to 120 seconds are typical (Figure 3.27).

By careful consideration of radar receiver bandwidths, scanner rotation rates, and also the racon sweep time, some estimate can be made of duration and interval between racon appearances on an individual observer's radar display. This will in general be for sufficient time to allow the identification of the racon-fitted navigation mark (or to obtain a range and bearing of the racon itself). Typically, the racon flash will appear on some two to four consecutive scans of the ship's radar in each sweep period of the racon.

Although the frequency is shown as being continuously swept, an alternative technique which had similar results was to increase the frequency in discrete steps which were held for a short period of time, with the overall 'sweep' period being as before.

Example 3.4 A racon with a sweep period of 100 s is triggered by a ship's radar which has an antenna rotation rate of 20 rpm and a receiver bandwidth of 10 MHz. Determine the theoretical maximum and

minimum number of responses which can be expected during a single racon frequency sweep if the sweep band was 9300 to 9500 MHz. Find also the nominal interval between responses from consecutive racon

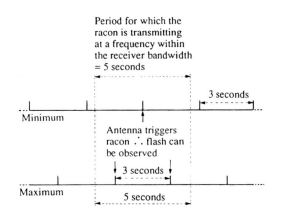

Figure 3.28 Calculation for Example 3.4
200 MHz in 100 s
therefore 10 MHz in 5 s
Time for 1 antenna rotation = 3 s
maximum 2 flashes
minimum 1 flash
Nominal interval between pulses = 100 s

sweeps. Slow-sweep racons are no longer recommended by IMO.

3.5.3.2 Fast-sweep racons (Figure 3.29)

In this type, when triggered, the racon transmitter will rapidly (1 μs to 10 μs) sweep the particular radar frequency band, producing a series of brief flashes beyond the target. Each transmitteed pulse will trigger the racon so that if it is triggered say, 10 times as it is

swept by the radar beam on each scan, the paints will integrate on the radar screen to give a typical but distinctive displayed flash. The racon will display on virtually every scan but, because of low power, can be masked by noise, rain or sea clutter. There is no easy way of encoding the response.

Fast-sweep racons are obsolete and no longer used.

3.5.3.3 Frequency-agile racons

In such a system, the frequency of the interrogating radar is measured, the racon transmitter is then tuned to that frequency and a (coded) response is transmitted. The time taken for this operation is some 0.4 μs, which corresponds to a ranging error of some 60 metres.

The block diagram of a frequency-agile racon is shown in Figure 3.30.

The following points should be noted:

(a) Racons which appear on each scan could mask other targets and so the racon is made to be 'silent' for a short period in each minute.

(b) The application of FTC (see Section 3.7.4) and some video processing techniques including 'interference suppression' (de-fruiting, see Section 3.9.5.1) can mutilate racon signals and should be switched off.

(c) The claimed 'mean time between failures' (MTBF) is some 10 years.

(d) With frequency-agile racons it is essential that the receiver is on tune, especially if the receiver bandwidth is narrow (i.e. on longer range scales).

(e) The ON periods of the racon should be not less than 15 seconds and there should be an ON period at least once every 60 seconds.

The reduced ON period conserves battery power (important for offshore navigational aids) as well as reducing clutter. The US coast guard recommends that racons are on 50 per cent of the time (20 seconds ON, 20 seconds OFF) for buoys and a maximum of 75 per cent of the time for onshore installations where power supplies are not a problem.

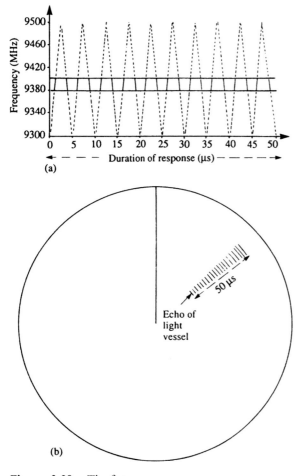

Figure 3.29 The fast-sweep racon
(a) Racon response
(b) Displayed response

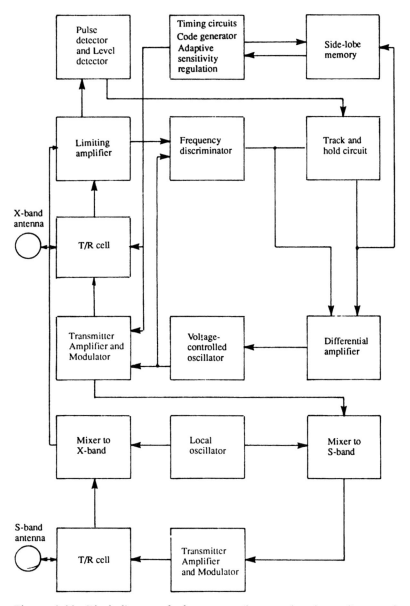

Figure 3.30 Block diagram of a frequency-agile racon (based on a diagram of AGA-Ericsson Radio Systems of Sweden)

3.5.3.4 Racon 'clutter'

It has always been feared that with the proliferation of radar beacons, racon clutter could become a problem and mask targets. Alternatively, beacon responses can be masked by strong land and rain/sea clutter echoes.

Three solutions have evolved.

1 *Beacon band operation.* This requires all radar beacons to transmit at a particular fixed frequency within a band at the edge of the marine radar frequency band, e.g. 9300 to 9320 MHz. A switch

on the radar console sets the radar receiver to this 'fixed' frequency and only the radar beacons, but no targets, are displayed. The extra circuitry for all potential users could be expensive.

2 *Interrogated time-offset frequency-agile racons* (ITO-FAR). The ITOFAR system requires specially modified beacons and radar sets to operate. When this frequency-agile racon is triggered at a very precise PRF (1343.1 pulses per second), it recognizes it as an ITOFAR interrogation and delays its response by a very precise amount (374 μs). If the trigger to the display is delayed by the same amount, the racon signal will be displayed in what was previously the 'clear' outer portion of the radar screen on long range but is now at the correct range on the displayed range scale on a modified set (see Figure 3.31). The circuitry required for this solution is less costly than for beacon band operation. On unmodified sets the ITOFAR appear as normal frequency beacons.

3 *Side lobe suppression.* Circuitry is included in the racon to recognize the side lobes of a radar. Basically the main beam is assumed to be the most powerful signal received and the racon will ignore all lesser signals.

3.5.3.5 *The application of racons*

The IMO Performance Standards, (see Section 11.2.4) make it very clear that racons are to be used for improving the detection of fixed objects and not moving ones. However, the interpretation of this standard is up to individual administrations. For instance some administrations use racons to mark turning points (way points) and leading lines, but the USC does not.

3.5.3.6 *Leading lines using racons*

Figure 3.32 shows a leading line using two racons. Figure 3.33 shows a leading line using one racon and a buoy with a radar reflector.

3.5.4 The ramark

This is an older radar beacon in which the frequency is swept continuously at such high speed that the trans-mission at each frequency is in effect continuous (not triggered).

Figure 3.34 illustrates the principle of ramark operation and Figure 3.35 shows the appearance of the ramark on the radar display. Ramarks are now obsolete and their function replaced by racons.

3.5.5 Sources of radar beacon information

The *Admiralty List of Radio Signals* volume 2 contains information relating to racons working in both the S-band and the X-band as well as ramarks. Figure 3.36(a) gives typical extracts. Figure 3.36(b) shows chart symbols used on UK charts.

3.5.6 The Radaflare

This is a rocket which is fired from a pistol. At some 300 to 400 metres altitude, the rocket ejects a quantity of dipoles which respond strongly to 3 cm radar waves and at the same time the rocket gives out a very bright white light. The radar response has a maximum detection range of 12 n miles and will last for some 15 minutes, depending upon weather conditions. It is intended for use as a distress signal for small craft.

3.5.7 Search and rescue transponders (SARTs)

The detection of survival craft has been a matter of concern for sometime. Traditionally this function was carried out on radio frequencies by the RDF (Radio Direction Finder), but this responsibility has now been transferred to the radar display and the RDF is obsolete and no longer a current IMO requirement. Instead, all vessels that come under the Global Maritime Distress and Safety Service (GMDSS) regulations are required to carry a SART to use in survival craft, so that there is an active indication of its presence on a radar screen. The SART is normally mounted on a short pole on the survival craft. It is a transponder and only transmits when interrogated by a radar signal.

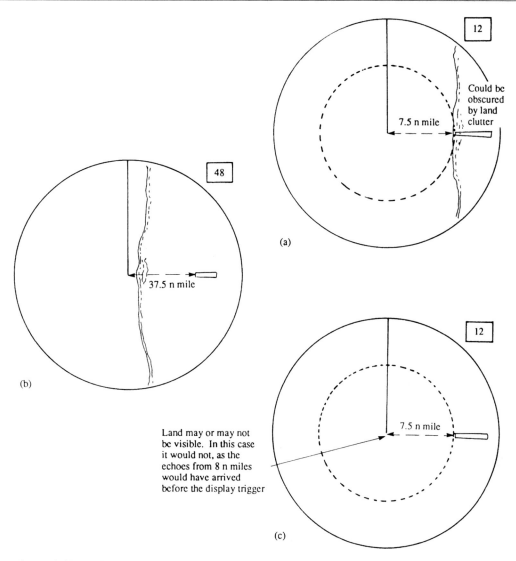

Figure 3.31 ITOFAR response

(a) ITOFAR beacon response on all radars

(b) Appearance of the ITOFAR beacon response
     when display trigger has not been delayed but
     beacon response has

(c) Display of ITOFAR beacon response if ITOFAR
     operation is selected at the radar display

The SART works at X-band frequencies only and the IMO Performance Standards (see Section 11.2.5) state that the SART should operate when interrogated by a vessel's radar at 5 n miles with an aerial height of 15 metres and 30 n miles by an aircraft radar at 3000 ft. SARTs can typically be detected at 8 n miles by marine craft.

The SART is activated by a radar pulse from a vessel and transmits a series of 12 short radar pulses on the same frequency. The SART appears on the

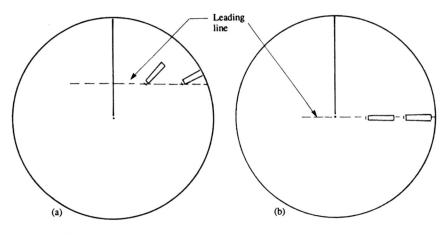

Figure 3.32 Leading line using two racons
(a)   Approaching the line
(b)   On the leading line

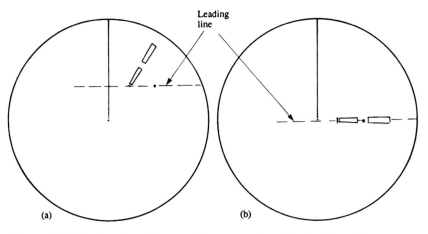

Figure 3.33 Leading line using a coded racon and buoy fitted with a reflector
(a)   Approaching the line
(b)   On the leading line

screen as a series of 12 dots (see Figure 3.37(a)). Even if the target (survival craft) is not radar conspicuous, the target will be slightly closer than the first dot. However, unlike beacons, side lobe suppression is not included in a SART, so the dots become arcs (see Figure 3.37(b)), as the target gets closer. At very close

range, the arcs can extend to be complete circles (see Figure 3.37(c)).

The SART has a battery life on standby (listening for radar signals) of at least 96 hours and an operational life transmitting of at least 8 hours. The case should be brightly coloured (yellow or orange) and should

Figure 3.34 The principle of ramark operation

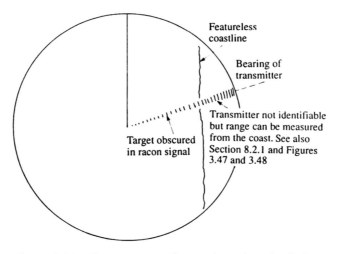

Figure 3.35 The appearance of a ramark on the radar display

be capable of floating, unless it is built into a craft. Its construction is very rugged (see Section 11.2.5). It should also survive immersion to a depth of 10 metres for 5 minutes as well as being dropped into the water from a height of 20 metres.

The SART indicates by audible or visual means (or both) that radar has triggered it into operation, which should be a valuable stimulus for those about to be rescued. The operation of the SART is simple and it should be operable by unskilled personnel. There is also an audible or visual means that it is operating correctly.

Testing of SARTs at sea is allowed, but the transmission should be limited to a few seconds to avoid attracting the unnecessary attention of other radar users.

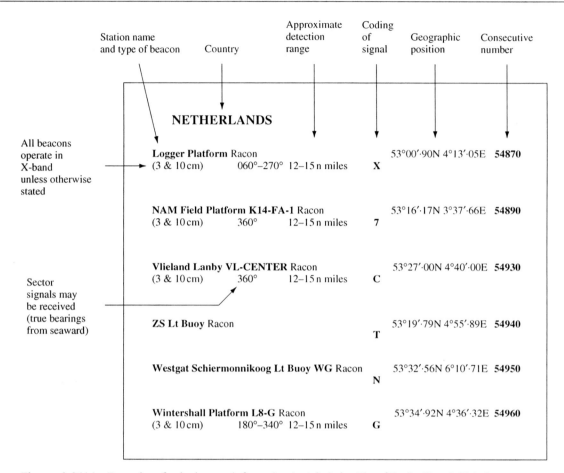

Figure 3.36(a)   Examples of radar beacon information in Admiralty List of Radio Signals Vol. 2

3.6   The detection of targets in sea clutter

In general, the term 'clutter' is used to describe the accumulation on the screen of unwanted echoes. Sea clutter describes the particular case of echoes which arise as a result of the radar energy being scattered back from the surface of the sea. The presence of sea clutter echoes may make it difficult or even impossible to detect wanted targets and this represents an important limitation of even the most modern civil marine radar systems. It is essential that the

radar observer understands not only the nature of this phenomenon but also the principle of the various arrangements available to assist in combating the effect. Since the mid-1970s, with the advent of digital storage (see Section 2.6.6.1), the complexity of anti-clutter arrangements has increased progressively and the limitations of these must be appreciated.

The ever-changing surface of the sea represents an immensely complex population of varying radar targets. The radar cross-section (see Section 3.3.5.4) of any element of the sea surface fluctuates in a largely random fashion and can thus only be evaluated in terms of averages or probabilities. In an effort to

1	⊙ Ra	Coast radar station providing range and bearing from station on request		485.1 *M11*
2	⊙ Ramark	Ramark, radar beacon transmitting continuously		486.1 *M14a*
3.1	⊙ Racon(Z) (3 cm)	Radar transponder beacon, with morse identification, responding within the 3 cm (X) band	† ⊙ Racon(Z)	486.2 486.3 *M12*
3.2	⊙ Racon(Z) (10 cm)	Radar transponder beacon, with morse identification, responding within the 10 cm (S) band		486.3
3.3	⊙ Racon(Z)	Radar transponder beacon, with morse identification, responding within the 3 cm (X) and the 10 cm (S) bands	† ⊙ Racon(Z) (3 & 10 cm)	
3.4	⊙ Racon(P) *Racon Obscd* Racon(Z) ⊙ *Racon(Z)*	Radar transponder beacon with sector of obscured reception Radar transponder beacon with sector of reception		486.4
3.5	Racon ⊙---⊙ Racon Racons ≠ 270° Racon ☆---☆ Racon Lts ≠ 270° / Racons ≠ 270°	Leading radar transponder beacons Leading radar transponder beacons coincident with leading lights		486.5
3.6	🔺 Racon ⊖ Racon	Floating marks with radar transponder beacons		486.2 *M12*
4	⋏⋏	Radar reflector (not usually charted on IALA System buoys)	† Ra.Refl.	460.3 465 *M13*
5	⋏⋏	Radar-conspicuous feature	† Ra conspic	485.2 *M14*

Figure 3.36(b)   UK chart symbols

identify the radar and sea surface characteristics which determine the magnitude of the sea clutter response, eminent radar engineers have spent much time and effort in using statistical techniques to obtain a mathematical model of the sea clutter mechanism. Because of the complexity of the problem, and in particular the

difficulty of carrying out controlled experiments with the sea, it is not possible to reconcile completely the detailed mathematical predictions with the observed phenomena and to this extent it is true to say that the mechanism is not yet fully understood. However, a discussion of such quantitative considerations

(a)

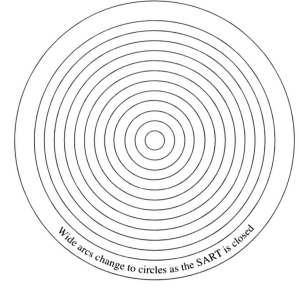

(c)

(b)

Figure 3.37(a–c) The appearance of a SART on a rescuing ship display

is beyond the scope of this manual and the reader who wishes to pursue the mathematical approach is referred to any good radar enginering text. To the extent of understanding required for effective radar observation, the mechanism can be explained in the fairly simple qualitative terms used in the following section.

From the point of view of the radar observer, the essence of the clutter problem is that targets weaker than the clutter returns cannot be detected and even targets which return responses which are very much stronger than the clutter may be masked if the clutter returns saturate the receiver or the display (see Section 2.5.2.1).

3.6.1 The nature of sea clutter response

In absolutely flat calm sea conditions, the sea surface will behave like a mirror and specular reflection will take place (see Section 3.3.1). All radar energy which strikes the surface of the sea will be reflected away and none will be scattered back toward the antenna (some of the energy which strikes targets will travel via the sea surface, as described in Section 2.4.3).

If there is any wind at all it will tend to ruffle the surface of the sea producing small wavelets and as the wind strength increases so too will the height of the waves which are generated. In deep water the height and period of the waves depends on the wind speed, the fetch and the length of time for which the wind has been blowing. In shallow water the waves tend to steepen and the distance between successive wave crests decreases. When the wind is blowing against the tide, wave height and steepness will be greater than the observed wind would perhaps suggest. Where two wave patterns are present, as for example may occur in an area where a large wind shift has taken place with the passage of a frontal system, constructive interference between the patterns will produce, from time to time, wave heights larger than the individual component heights. As wave height increases for whatever reason, a point will be reached at which the waves break, producing confused tumbling water and wind-blown spray. A more complex and less predictable target is difficult to conceive.

Despite the complexity of the problem, one can consider there to be three elements which contribute to the aggregate response:

1 *Specular reflection from those sloping parts of the wavefront which present a good aspect to the incident radar energy.* This would be the sole contribution if the wind could produce a completely smooth sloping wavefront. It is well represented by the situation which arises when swell is present in calm conditions. (*Swell* is the term used to describe waves which have been generated by wind in some distant area and have travelled across the ocean.) Swell may be present in isolation or it may have locally generated *sea* waves superimposed upon it.

2 *Scattering of energy from the surface of the wavefront.* Except when swell is present in flat calm conditions the sloping surface of the wavefront will be disturbed by the wind and will thus produce a surface texture which is *rough* in terms of the wavelengths used in civil marine radar (see Section 3.3.5.5). The face of the wave can be thought of as being com-

posed of a large number of facets whose aspects change at random with the ruffling and tumbling of the surface water. The resulting backscatter of radar energy will yield responses whenever a favourably placed facet lies within the resolution cell (see Section 3.3.5). It is essential to appreciate that although these facets may be quite small, possibly a few square centimetres, they will produce echoes whose displayed size is determined by the resolution cell. Thus if a facet remains favourable for the time taken by the radar beam to sweep across it (say 10 to 20 milliseconds) it will produce an echo which is one half-pulse long, one beamwidth wide and subject to spot size effect.

3 *Reflection from water droplets close to the surface of the wave.* In higher wind conditions water from the crests tends to be blown off the wave and the droplets so formed will reflect radar energy if sufficiently large (see also Raindrops in Section 3.7.3.1).

Opinions differ as to the relative significance of each contribution, but it is nonetheless evident that a large number of independent targets capable of producing backscatter exist on and around the sloping surfaces of sea waves. The observed response from this backscatter depends on characteristics of both the waves and the radar installation and these will be considered in turn.

3.6.1.1 The effect of wave height

Although, as indicated in the previous section, various factors can affect wave height, in general as the wind force rises so too does the wave height. In attempting to translate the growth in wave height into an increase in clutter response one must consider not only the increase in the strength of signals received from nearby waves but also the increases in the range from which detectable signals are received.

The response from an individual wave increases with wave height up to a certain level and then tends to flatten off. The precise nature of the law is a matter for the scientist rather than the radar observer who is more concerned with the effects which can be observed on the display. As wave height increases, the clutter returns close to the observing vessel will in due course saturate the receiver or display; a further increase in wave height will be observed to extend the radius to which this saturation is manifest. Beyond the radius of saturation the amplitude of the displayed clutter signals will decay progressively with range (see Section 3.6.1.2) toward the maximum radial extent of visible clutter, at which the grazing angle has reduced to that at which the radar sees the surface as smooth (see Section 3.3.5.5). In conclusion, the range within which the observer must combat the masking effects of saturation will increase with wave height, as will the range within which targets are undetectable if their response is less than that of the ambient clutter.

3.6.1.2   The variation of sea clutter response with range

In the introduction to this chapter it was shown that, in general, received echo strength varies inversely as the fourth power of range. Sea clutter response does not obey this law and it can be shown that it varies inversely as $(range)^3$ except that at very short ranges this becomes $(range)^2$. This arises because the radar cross-section of sea clutter (which is a statistical quantity) is a function of range. A proof of this is beyond the scope of this work but if desired will be found in any good radar engineering text having a mathematical treatment of the sea clutter mechanism. The relationship between the two decay rates favours the detection of clutter except at very short ranges.

In the absence of saturation, the variation of sea clutter with range will be as illustrated in Figure 3.38(a). For the reasons set out in Section 2.5.2.5, saturation usually takes place in the case of the linear amplifier, resulting in the waveform being modified as illustrated in Figure 3.38(b). Comparison of sections of the figure shows the masking effect of the presence of sea clutter. The difficulties which arise from the masking and the benefit of employing a logarithmic receiver (see Section 2.5.2.6) will be discussed further in Sections 3.6.3.2.

3.6.1.3   The effect of wind direction

Even casual observation of the waves generated on the sea surface will reveal that the upwind wavefronts

are steeper than their more gently sloping downwind counterparts. The steeper wavefronts present a more effective echoing surface and thus the radial extent of sea clutter echoes will be found to be greater to windward than it is to leeward, as illustrated by Figure 3.39.

The outer limit of the pattern represents the minimum detectable signal (see Section 3.2.3) and hence the radial extent of the pattern offers a suitable criterion by which to judge the setting of the tuning control (see Sections 6.2.4.2 and 6.3.4.3).

In coastal and estuarial areas the pattern may be modified by seas breaking on banks or in areas of shallow water and the waves may be steepened where the wind blows against the tide.

3.6.1.4   The effect of antenna height

Increased antenna height extends the radial limit of the overall sea clutter pattern which appears on the screen and also the range within which the clutter echoes saturate the receiver or the display (see Sections 2.5.2.1 and 2.5.2.5). This is illustrated by Figure 3.40.

Sloping wavefronts close to the observing vessel present a more favourable aspect for the reflection of the radar energy than those at a distance. This arises because at large angles of depression the beam *looks down* at nearby wavefronts and there is as a consequence a high probability that some energy will be normal to the general surface of the wavefront. If the surface is smooth, specular reflection will take place but in most cases the surface will be sufficiently rough to ensure scattering and thus a response from surfaces which are not exactly normal to the beam (see Section 3.3.1). In theory, with the ship upright, one might expect the maximum depression angle to be 10°, i.e. half the vertical beamwidth (see Section 2.4.3), but in practice the energy in the lower vertical side lobes will increase this effective angle considerably. As range from the observing vessel increases, the aspect of the wavefront will become progressively less favourable for reflection as the direction of the incident energy approaches that which is tangential to the top of the wave. At about this distance, most of the energy will just graze the crest of the wave and clutter echoes will not be detected beyond this limit.

(a)

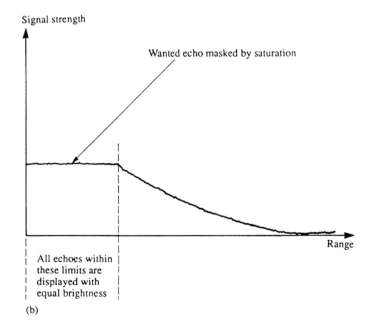

(b)

Figure 3.38 The variation of clutter response with range
(a)   Unsaturated response
(b)   Saturated response

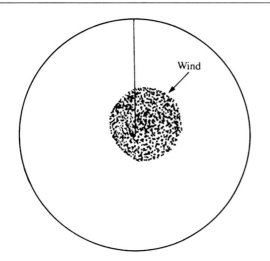

Figure 3.39 Sea clutter pattern in the open sea

3.6.1.5 The effect of radar wavelength

Like most aspects of the sea clutter phenomenon, experimental determination of the exact relationship between the wavelength being transmitted by the radar and the clutter response is difficult to achieve, as is an explanation of the results in terms of the necessarily complex theoretical mathematical model of the mechanism. There is general agreement that the response decreases with increase in wavelength, though there is some debate as to the significant power – (wavelength)^2 or (wavelength)^3. At best, the civil marine radar observer will have the choice between the selection of 3 cm or 10 cm wavelength (see

Section 2.3.3.1) and for practical purposes can consider the clutter response to be inversely proportional to wavelength. This is consistent with the concept of surface texture as set out in Section 3.3.5.5 which suggests that the *roughness* of the surface of the sloping wave-front will be greater for 3 cm than it will be for 10 cm radiation. It is similarly consistent with the theory that reflection from water droplets forms one component of the aggregate response (see Section 3.6.1).

Thus, in general, the sea clutter response will be less troublesome at S-band than it will be at X-band and where dual antenna/transceiver units are fitted the observer may well be able to exploit the potential of S-band transmissions in adverse sea clutter conditions. It is also a factor which should be considered when planning the radar installation for a new vessel or updating an existing installation.

3.6.1.6 The effect of pulse length

In general, subject to any saturation, selection of long pulse rather than short pulse will improve the displayed response of any given target (see Section 2.5.2.4) and sea clutter is no exception to this rule. Thus if wanted targets are masked as a result of saturation (see Sections 2.5.2.1 and 2.5.2.5) it may be possible to combat the effect by judicious choice of pulse length. Selection of short pulse will reduce the response of both clutter and wanted targets and may bring the clutter response below saturation level or at least to a level which will allow the observer to apply smaller amounts of clutter suppression (see Section 3.6.3).

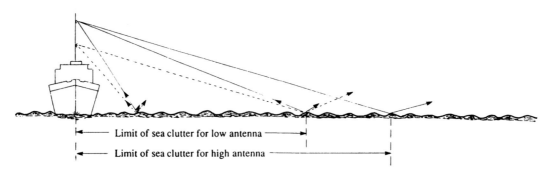

Figure 3.40 The effect of antenna height on sea clutter response

Selection of short pulse will also reduce the radial extent of the resolution cell (see Section 2.6.5.2). This effect can only begin to show if the distance between the farthest scattering element of a wavefront and the nearest scattering element (including any associated spray) of the next wave beyond exceeds half the transmitted pulse length. In certain sea conditions it is possible to recognize the line of approaching wavefronts, especially in ocean conditions where a long swell is present.

3.6.1.7 The effect of polarization (see Section 2.4.1.8)

In clutter conditions there is little if any difference between the response from horizontally polarized radiation and that which is vertically polarized. In almost all cases any difference is in any event academic since to comply with the traditional IMO Performance Standards relating to the ability to detect radar beacons (see Section 3.5), all systems operating in the 3 cm band must be capable of operating in a horizontally polarized mode. There was thus no stimulus for designers to produce an X-band system with vertical polarization. Although vertical polarization offers some improvement in target response in calm conditions, particularly at S-band, vertically polarized S-band systems are very much the exception rather than the rule. Thus, in general, polarization is not a system characteristic which is under the control of the observer.

In the past, a system offering circular polarization was offered in an attempt to reduce the response from droplets of precipitation. This is discussed under that heading in Section 3.7.4.6; at this stage it is relevant to observe that any reduction so gained would have an effect on that element of sea clutter response originating in reflection from spray. It must, however, be borne in mind that there is some debate as to the significance of the contribution of the droplet component to the aggregate sea clutter response.

3.6.2 The clutter problem summarized

Sea clutter echoes may make it impossible to detect some targets, while the presence of others may only be revealed by skilful adjustment of the controls or with the assistance of some form of signal processing. Before discussing the techniques available for the suppression of sea clutter it is appropriate to summarize the clutter problem in terms of three distinct cases of target amplitude which are set out below and illustrated by Figure 3.41.

1 *Targets weaker than the ambient clutter.* A target which returns a signal that is weaker than the clutter surrounding it cannot be detected, because any technique used to suppress the clutter will also suppress the echo of the wanted target. Marginal targets may be recognized by the regularity of their paint.

2 *Targets stronger than ambient clutter that does not saturate the receiver or display.* Such a target is capable of detection but it may not be obvious because of the poor contrast when viewed against the background of the clutter echoes. This is likely to be a particular problem if the targets are only marginally stronger than the ambient clutter. The target may be made more obvious by suppression of the clutter returns.

3 *Targets stronger than ambient clutter that saturates the receiver or display.* Such a target will be masked because its echo will have exactly the same brightness on the display as all the sea clutter echoes surrounding it. It is capable of detection subject to suppression of the clutter signal. Skill is required to reveal targets which are only marginally stronger than the ambient clutter.

3.6.3 The suppression of displayed sea clutter signals

In Sections 3.6.1.4, 3.6.1.5 and 3.6.1.6 it was indicated that a judicious choice of antenna height, wavelength and pulse length would reduce sea clutter responses. Except in very light sea conditions it is unlikely that such reduction will alone be sufficient to combat the sea clutter problem and it will normally have to be supplemented by some form of active suppression applied in the receiver or the display.

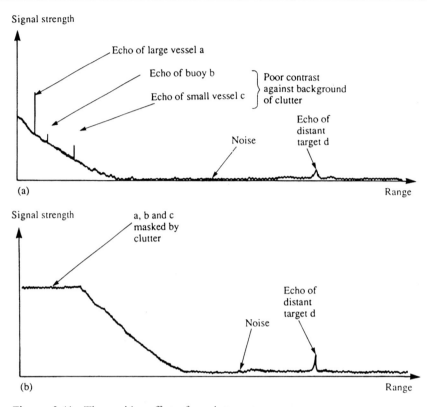

Figure 3.41 The masking effect of sea clutter returns
(a)   Clutter does not saturate receiver or display
(b)   Clutter saturates receiver or display

3.6.3.1   The sea clutter control

The probability of detecting targets in clutter will be maximized by adjusting the controls so that the echoes of the targets paint against a background of light residual clutter speckle similar to the noise speckle used as the criterion for setting the gain control. This can be achieved for a target at any given range by reducing the setting of the gain control. However, it can be seen from Figure 3.42 that this may only be achieved at the expense of losing more *distant targets* and without achieving the desired degree of suppression for nearer targets.

Essentially, the problem is that the gain reduces the amplification uniformly across the radius of the timebase, whereas the clutter signals are strongest near the origin and decay with range (see Section 3.6.1.2).

The sea clutter control is a specialized type of gain control which reduces the gain at the origin of each radial line and restores it with time as each radial line is written. The control thus allows a varying amount of suppression to be applied. The amount of initial suppression is variable and can be adjusted by the observer by the setting of the front panel control, whereas the rate at which the suppression decays is preset by the manufacturer (see Figure 3.43). The joint effect determines the radius to which suppression is effected.

The control is sometimes referred to as *swept gain* or *sensitivity time control* (STC) because of the time-related variation of the gain. Ideally the decay of the suppression curve should obey the same law as that governing the decay of the sea clutter response with range (see Section 3.6.1.2). Normally, it will be found

Figure 3.42 Suppression of clutter by use of the gain control
(a)   Normal gain setting
(b)   Gain suppressed

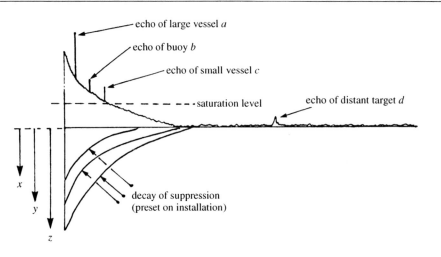

echo of large vessel a

echo of buoy b

echo of small vessel c

echo of distant target d

saturation level

decay of suppression
(preset on installation)

x

y

z

x, y, z represent varying degrees of initial suppression set by sea clutter control

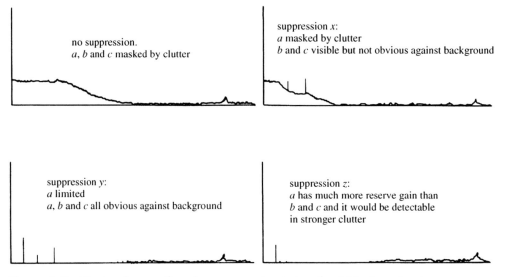

no suppression.
a, b and c masked by clutter

suppression x:
a masked by clutter
b and c visible but not obvious against background

suppression y:
a limited
a, b and c all obvious against background

suppression z:
a has much more reserve gain than
b and c and it would be detectable
in stronger clutter

Figure 3.43 Varying degrees of sea clutter suppression (echo of a visible throughout)

that the suppression decays exponentially with time. This law was adopted in the very early days of marine radar for the very practical reason that it is the waveform generated by discharging a capacitor through a resistor and hence has the merit of simplicity, reliability and cheapness. It has stood the test of time because although the exponential decay ($e^{-\text{range}}$) is not exactly the same as that of $(\text{range})^{-2}$, it is a reasonable fit

except at very short range. In any event, in practice the sea conditions may not exactly follow the theoretical predictions and hence the complications of producing a $(\text{range})^{-2}$ law would not be justified.

Ideally, the observer wishes to optimize the suppression to match the clutter response, thus leaving wanted targets painting against a light residual clutter speckle. This is illustrated in Figure 3.43 which shows three (excluding the zero setting) particular levels of suppression which have been chosen in such a way that while one level is optimum, the other two levels are representative of the cases of insufficient and excessive suppression *for that particular line* of responses on the display. However, the clutter response varies from line to line (see Section 3.6.1.3) and thus it follows that if the control is set correctly for one radial line, it is likely to be set incorrectly for most, if not all, other radial lines. Thus there is no single *correct* manual setting for the sea clutter control; to maximize the probability of detecting targets in clutter, the observer must, at regular intervals, systematically adjust the control in small steps through the extent of its travel from full clutter suppression to zero effect. This operation is known as *searching* and considerable skill and practice are required to perform it successfully. It is one of the most important skills associated with marine radar operation; the appropriate practical procedure is described in detail in Section 6.10.1.1.

3.6.3.2   The effect of receiver characteristic

In older systems which employ a linear IF amplifier (see Section 2.5.2.5), saturation is likely to take effect early in the amplifier chain. In such cases the sea clutter control will normally be designed to effect the suppression prior to such a point in the receiver. In heavy clutter conditions, extensive suppression may be required at an early stage in the receiver and particular care and skill will be required in carrying out the searching operation with the sea clutter control.

In more modern systems the use of a logarithmic amplifier (see Section 2.5.2.6) will ensure that in almost all cases an unsaturated output is available for input to the video section of the receiver (see Section 2.5.3). Thus saturation due to sea clutter returns will not normally take effect until some stage in the video amplifier (see Section 2.5.3) or possibly not even until the CRT, in which case, the sea clutter control will operate in the video section of the receiver. With a logarithmic amplifier, the masking effect of sea responses is likely to be less troublesome and the operation of the sea clutter control will in

most situations be found to be less critical than in the case of a linear receiver.

From the treatment presented in Section 2.5.2.6 it is fairly evident that the use of a logarithmic amplifier reduces the risk of targets being masked by sea clutter because it extends the range of signals that will not saturate the IF amplifier. It can also be shown that the logarithmic relationship between receiver output and input also produces a swept gain effect on the clutter signals, thus further improving the potential performance of the system in heavy clutter conditions. Proof of this requires a mathematical treatment beyond the scope of this text. The reader who wishes to pursue this further is referred to a good radar engineering text or to the various technical papers published on the subject of logarithmic receivers.

3.6.3.3   Adaptive gain

This is a more recent approach to automatic clutter suppression. In discussing the manual sea clutter control, the point was made that ideally the clutter suppression should be set correctly for each radial line. Clearly no human operator possesses the speed or dexterity to perform such a task but it can be achieved with a considerable degree of success by electronic means. The general name for the technique is *adaptive gain* and it is so called because the associated circuitry is designed to adjust continually the receiver gain so as to *adapt it* to the level of clutter present at any point on each radial line. For practical engineering reasons it is necessary to perform the adaptive gain process in the video stage of the receiver and, because it is necessary to deduce an analogue of the clutter response (see below), it must operate on an unsaturated signal. It follows that the technique cannot be used successfully in systems which have a linear receiver (see Section 2.5.2.5). As a result, the advent of adaptive gain in civil marine radar systems dates from the mid-1970s when solid-state logarithmic receivers became available for civil applications at sea. Since then it has become progressively more common because of the need for effective automatic clutter suppression in systems that use digital storage for picture generation and automatic tracking (see Section 2.6.6). If the clutter responses are not suppressed before digitization the masking problem is likely to be exacerbated, particularly if the clutter echoes are stored at high level (see Section 2.6.6.7). The principle of adaptive gain is illustrated by Figure 3.44.

The theory of adaptive gain is that if an analogue of the clutter signal is used to produce the suppression signal, only signals stronger than the clutter will be displayed. Examination of the combined target and clutter signal shown in Figure 3.44 reveals

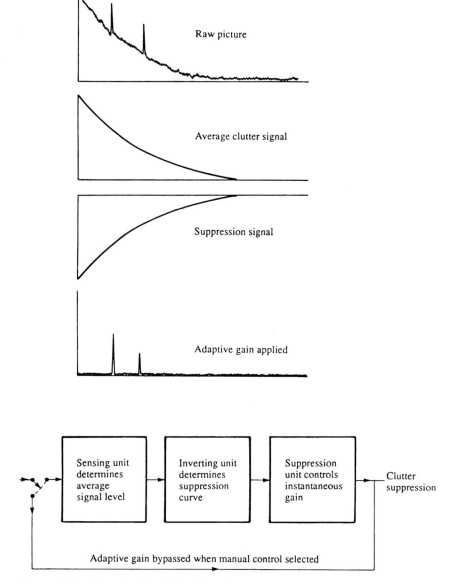

Figure 3.44 The principle of adaptive gain

that its characteristic has two main components, one being the relatively slow general decay with range (see Section 3.6.1.2) from maximum at the origin to zero at the radial limit of the sea clutter response. Superimposed on this is the second component which has the form of relatively rapid spikes which represent the presence of targets and clutter peaks. The total signal can be thought of as a slowly changing average signal about which rapid excursions occur. The reaction time of the sensing section (sometimes referred to as the integrator) of the adaptive gain circuitry (see Figure 3.44) is designed to be too slow to respond to the rapid excursions but sufficiently fast to react to the slowly changing average signal level. The sensing section thus effectively filters out the high frequency fluctuations and generates a slowly changing average signal level which is inverted and used as a suppression signal to modify, continuously and instantaneously, the overall gain level set by the observer.

Clearly the slow reaction time of the sensing section will not allow it to respond immediately to a change from zero clutter at the end of one line to maximum clutter at the commencement of the next. This difficulty is overcome by using the initial clutter signal from the previous line to produce the suppression for the first part of the current line. The adaptive gain effect is normally enhanced by the limited use of a further technique known as *differentiation* which tends to emphasize the leading edge of echoes. This is described in detail in section 3.7.4.4.

If the suppression signal is a faithful analogue of the average signal level, the resultant video signal made available for display (see Figure 3.44) should comprise those signals which are rapid excursions from that level and which represent the presence of targets that are stronger than the clutter and also the clutter peaks. Targets which are much stronger than the clutter should be easy to detect as they will be displayed (on an analogue display) against the background of the light residual speckle of clutter peaks. Targets very close to clutter level will be difficult to detect and the observer may have to rely on an ability to recognize their regular paint against the background of random clutter echoes.

The setting up of the adaptive gain circuitry must be carried out by qualified service personnel but it should be done in consultation with experienced radar observers who, on the basis of systematic use, are in a postion to comment on the performance of the system in a wide variety of sea conditions. It has to be recognized that it is virtually impossible to adjust the adaptive gain circuitry so that it will give optimum response over the full range of wind and sea conditions between calm and gale force winds. For this reason, exclusive reliance *should not* be placed on the ability of such circuitry to remove clutter and to display only targets. The practical procedure for the use of the facility is set out in Sections 6.10.1.2 and 6.10.2.3.

Because of the averaging effect and the differentiation (see Section 3.7.4.4), adaptive gain circuitry will suppress radar beacon signals (see Section 3.5) and it is for this reason, among others, that the IMO Performance Standards (see Section 11.2.1) require that it should be possible to switch off those signal processing facilities which might prevent a radar beacon from being shown on the radar display. Adaptive gain will have a similar effect on radial performance monitor signals (see Section 6.5.5) and clearly must be switched off when a performance check is carried out. The effect of adaptive gain on land echoes will vary depending on whether the beam is parallel with or normal to the coastline; in general, it will tend to display the leading edge and suppress what lies behind. For this reason, identification of coastal features (see Section 8.2) is best performed with the adaptive gain facility switched off.

The adaptive gain facility may be effective in suppressing rain clutter responses (see Section 3.7.4.5). In some systems a single adaptive gain facility is offered, whereas in others separate sea and rain adaptive gain facilities may be provided. The adaptive gain principle described above is valid in both cases, the essential difference being that the sea clutter facility applies the adaptive gain to a limited preset range whereas the rain clutter facility is effective for the full timebase. The principal reason for separating the functions is that a sea clutter adaptive gain facility will allow suppression of proximate clutter while permitting the detection of more distant radar beacons. 'Adaptive gain' is a general engineering term: the display control which effects this function may be labelled in a variety of ways by different radar manufacturers (see Section 6.10.1.2). Normally, when the adaptive gain facility is selected the manual sea and rain clutter controls (see Sections 6.10.1.1 and 6.10.2.2) are disabled.

3.6.3.4 *Rotation-to-rotation correlation*

This is a further approach to automatic clutter suppression and is only available in systems which can store the range and bearing data for a full aerial rotation (see Section 2.6.6.4). The other methods of clutter suppression so far described use difference of amplitude (i.e. signal strength) in their attempt to distinguish between clutter and targets, though it has been mentioned that an observer may identify a weak target in clutter by virtue of the regularity of its paint when compared with random sea clutter responses. Rotation-to-rotation correlation sets out to perform this latter operation automatically.

The principle is similar to line-to-line correlation which is described in Section 3.9.5.1, but differs in that, instead of comparing the contents of two *different* range cells at the same range on successive lines, the comparison is made between the content of the *same* range cell on two (or more) successive aerial rotations. The theory of operation can be understood by asking the question: 'If a wave with a favourable aspect is present in a given range cell, what is the probability that a favourable wave will be present in the same range cell after one aerial rotation, i.e. after approximately 3 seconds?' Evaluation of this probability is clearly an exercise in statistics but it is fairly obvious that the probability of a wave being present in the same cell for two successive rotations is considerably less than that of a target. The difference between the probabilities will increase if the comparison is made for three or more rotations, provided of course that the target does not move out of the cell in question. Thus it is possible, to an extent which depends on the number of rotations over which the comparison is made, to distinguish between regular target returns and random clutter returns.

The way in which the probability theory is exploited and the name given to the facility (see Section 6.10.1.3) vary considerably with manufacurer. In a simple application of the principle, echoes which are present on successive rotations may be displayed at a higher level or in a different colour to those which appear at random from rotation to rotation. In a more complex approach, the comparison may be made over several successive rotations, and multi-levels of synthetic video (see Section 2.6.6.7) may be used to indicate the consistency of echo return by promoting them to higher levels of echo brightness as the number of successive rotations on which they appear increases. Demotion to a lower brightness level will occur if a target ceases to be consistent, though probably on the basis of a more tolerant law. The general effect of the correlation will be to favour consistent targets at the expense of clutter but it must be borne in mind that targets which return an intermittent response, such as a buoy or a small boat in a seaway, will be penalized.

It is essential for radar observers using such a facility on any particular system to be aware of the logical rules on which that version operates. It is also important to appreciate that echo brightness modified in this way is in no way a measure of echo strength.

Normally in radial-scan synthetic displays only one, or possibly two, radial lines are stored and it is for this reason that rotation-to-rotation correlation first became available only with the development of raster-scan displays suitable for use on large merchant vessels.

Rotation-to-rotation correlation tends to eliminate some receiver noise and it is thus important to switch the facility off when setting the gain control (see Section 6.4.4).

3.7   The detection of targets in precipitation clutter

Precipitation is the general term used to describe collectively various states in which water can manifest itself in the atmosphere, of which rain, snow and hail are examples. Reflections from precipitation can produce unwanted echoes on the screen and these are in practice (perhaps somewhat loosely) referred to as *rain clutter* though it is recognized that they may originate from other forms of precipitation. The effect of rain clutter in some ways resembles that of sea clutter but it has other characteristics which are quite different. Like the responses from the sea, those from rain can mask even strong target echoes by causing saturation within the receiver. They can also make it difficult to detect unsaturated responses against the background of clutter due to poor contrast, and impossible to detect targets whose response is weaker than that of the rain. However, precipitation echoes can occur anywhere on the screen and may well change their position quite rapidly. Additionally the transmitted pulse and the returning echo suffer scattering and attenuation (see Section 3.7.2) on their journey through the precipitation, thus reducing the received echo strength below what it would be in the absence of the precipitation. This has the effect of exacerbating the masking effect of the clutter and reducing the probability of detecting targets located beyond the area of precipitation. It is important to recognize that the solutions to the problems of detecting targets in and beyond rain are distinctly different (see Sections 3.7.5.1 and 3.7.5.2).

3.7.1 The nature of precipitation response

The area of precipitation can be considered to be an aggregation of a large number of randomly distributed individual particles which may take the form of water droplets, snowflakes or ice. Energy from the radar beam may strike these particles and will as a consequence be scattered in a multitude of directions. The aspect of some of the particles will favour backscatter, i.e. reflection in the direction of the antenna, and energy so reflected may produce detectable responses on the radar screen of the observing vessel. Like the backscatter from the multiple facets of sea waves (see Section 3.6.1), the mechanism is extremely complicated and quantitative analysis of the response involves complex statistical theory beyond the scope of this text. However, it is not altogether surprising that it can

be shown that the amplitude of the response depends on the size and material of the particles, the number present per unit volume of space illuminated by the radar beam at any time and the range of the precipitation (also the energy in the pulse and the transmission frequency, although, for a particular radar at a particular time, these may be considered fixed: see Sections on pulse length, transmitted power/PRF and wavelength for the effects of deliberately varying each one).

3.7.1.1 The effect of particle size

As is evident from the treatment presented in Section 3.3, particle size is only significant when considered in relation to transmitted wavelength. Theoretical calculations show that, provided the particle diameter is small when compared to wavelength, for a given wavelength the scattering response increases in direct proportion to the square of particle diameter. Thus a doubling of particle size will produce a fourfold increase in response.

Conversely, for a given particle size, the response is inversely proportional to the square of transmitted wavelength. Thus in given precipitation conditions selection of an S-band (see Section 2.3.3.1) system will reduce the rain clutter responses to approximately one tenth of that on an X-band radar.

3.7.1.2 The effect of particle intensity

Particle intensity is the number of particles present per unit volume of space illuminated by the radar beam at any time. Clearly, for any given particle size the response will increase with the particle intensity.

3.7.1.3 Precipitation rate

It is evident from the two preceding sections that the response from precipitation increases with both the intensity of the particle population and the size of the individual members. Both of these factors determine the precipitation rate which is a measurement meteorologists use to quantify precipitation in units of the volume falling per unit time. The term *precipitation* or *rainfall rate* is quite commonly used in discussing precipitation response. In general, the rain clutter response increases in proportion to the rainfall rate.

3.7.1.4   *The effect of range*

It was shown in the introduction to this chapter that in general, target response decays in proportion to the fourth power of range. By contrast, the response from precipitation falls off in proportion to the square of range. This arises because the radar cross-section of precipitation, a complex statistical quantity, is range dependent. A proof of this is beyond the scope of this manual but will be found in any good mathematical text on radar engineering. The relationship between the two decay rates favours the detection of clutter except at very short ranges.

The remote limits of the rain clutter pattern represent the minimum detectable signal (see Section 3.2.3) and hence the extent of the pattern offers a suitable criterion by which to judge the setting of the tuning control (see Sections 6.2.4.2 and 6.3.4.3).

3.7.2   Attenuation in precipitation

Even when the radar waves travel through clear atmosphere, some attenuation takes place. It occurs because some of the energy is absorbed by the gaseous constituents of the atmosphere, in particular oxygen and water vapour. The effect starts to become of practical significance only at wavelengths shorter than that of X-band. However, the presence of precipitation considerably increases the amount of attenuation that takes place. The extent to which the energy is absorbed depends on particle size, particle form (e.g. water or ice) and rainfall rate. It also increases exponentially with the distance travelled by the energy through the attenuating medium. In any given set of precipitation conditions, S-band transmissions will suffer less attenuation than those at X-band.

3.7.3   The effect of precipitation type

In the preceding sections, the strength of the response, the extent of scattering and the amount of attenua-

tion to be expected from precipitation in general have been considered in terms of the physical characteristics that affect them. Such characteristics will vary with precipitation type and it is therefore appropriate to discuss the effects in terms of various forms in which the precipitation may be manifest.

3.7.3.1   *Rain*

In the case of rain the particles which effect the scattering and attenuation take the form of water droplets. The droplet size cannot exceed a diameter of about 5.5 mm because at this limit the surface tension which holds the water in droplet form is overcome and the droplet subdivides.

Large droplets tend to be found in tropical rainstorms and in general in the rain associated with vigorous convection such as occurs for example at and after the passage of a cold front. In such cases the droplet size is an appreciable proportion of the X-band wavelength, very strong clutter echoes will be produced and there will be serious loss of energy due to scattering and absorption. The detection ranges of strongly responding targets within the rain area will be reduced and their echoes may be severely masked by saturation within the receiver. Weaker target responses, for example those from small vessels and buoys, will be rendered undetectable if their echoes are not stronger than that of the rain. While targets in clear areas beyond the rain will not be subject to masking, scattering and absorption will significantly reduce the energy reaching them and therefore reduce their detection ranges. As the droplet size is a much smaller proportion of the 10 cm wavelength, and bearing in mind the square law relationship (see Section 3.7.1.1), it is evident that the problems will be significantly reduced by the selection of S-band under such circumstances.

The droplet size of rain associated with stratiform clouds, such as those which might be expected at a warm front, tends to be smaller than those so far described. It must be remembered that the response and attenuation depend not only on the size of the droplets but also on the number falling, i.e. on the rainfall rate.

Drizzle is a form of light rain characterized by low rainfall rate and small droplet size of less than about 0.25 mm and as a consequence is unlikely to cause serious problems other than in the case of very weak targets. However, the higher relative humidity normally associated with drizzle can result in greater absorption.

3.7.3.2   Clouds

The water droplets which form clouds are too small (less than 0.1 mm) to produce detectable responses even at X-band. However, if there is rain or other precipitation within the cloud it may well be detected.

3.7.3.3   Fog

Because of the very small particle size and density it is most unlikely that fog and mist will return detectable echoes. In most circumstances attenuation results in only a slight reduction in maximum radar detection range. However, in the special case of the intense fogs which arise in polar regions a significant reduction in detection range may occur.

Smog is an acronym of smoke and fog and describes the effect of the condensation of water droplets on the dirt particles in areas of industrial smoke. It is likely to produce a somewhat higher degree of attentuation than a clean sea fog.

3.7.3.4   Snow

Where no melting is taking place, snowflakes are single ice crystals or a conglomeration of such crystals. When precipitation rates are compared, snowfall rates are in general less than rainfall rates. If this is considered in parallel with the lesser response of ice, it is evident that the echoes from snow are likely to be less troublesome than those from rain. *Sleet* describes the condition in which the snow is partially melted and the response will tend toward that of water. The attenuation produced by snow is similarly less than in the case of rain.

The fact that snow reflects radar energy less effectively than rain may be considered to be fortunate but it must be borne in mind that where snow lies on the surface of wanted targets its relatively poorer reflecting property and its albeit limited absorption characteristic may reduce the detection range of good targets such as land and also render undetectable poor targets such as growlers (see Section 3.3.6.1).

3.7.3.5   Hail

Hail is essentially composed of frozen raindrops. Ice reflects radar energy less effectively than water and hence, size for size, hailstones will produce a lesser response than raindrops. Melting on the surface of the stone will improve its response toward that of water. In general, the precipitation rates associated with hail are lower than those experienced with rain and so clutter and attenuation from hail are likely to prove less troublesome than those from rain.

3.7.3.6   Dry sand and dust haze

Clearly such phenomena cannot be described as precipitation but, as the effects are similar, it is appropriate to consider them under this general heading. On the basis of particle size and distribution, theory suggests that the effects should be similar to those of fog; practical experience substantiates this. Detectable responses, though not impossible, are extremely unlikely, and a fairly low level of attenuation is to be expected. These characteristics may prove very useful in conditions where visual sighting is severely hampered.

3.7.4   The suppression of rain clutter

As suggested in Section 3.6, in some ways the rain clutter problem resembles that of sea clutter and it is thus not surprising that some suppression techniques may be effective in both cases.

3.7.4.1   The choice of pulse length

As in the case of sea clutter, selection of a shorter pulse length will reduce the amplitude of all received echoes and hence may well assist in the detection of targets within an area of rain by bringing rain clutter echoes below saturation and in general improving the contrast between clutter echoes and those of wanted targets. It will of course not assist in combating the attenuation caused by the presence of the precipitation (see Section 3.7.5).

3.7.4.2   The choice of wavelength

Selection of S-band as opposed to X-band transmission will increase the probability of detection of targets within an area of precipitation clutter by reducing the response from the precipitation and the associated attenuation.

3.7.4.3   Searching techniques

The probability of detection of targets within areas of precipitation may be improved by using the gain control or the sea clutter control to systematically suppress and restore the clutter signals in a searching fashion similar to that described in Section 3.6.3.1. Where the clutter surrounds the observing vessel, the sea clutter control is likely to prove helpful but it will not be effective for more distant precipitation. The practical procedures for carrying out such searches are described in Section 6.10.1.

3.7.4.4   The rain clutter circuit

This is an alternative approach to the problem of saturation and employs a technique known as differentiation which is performed in the video section of the receiver. The signal is conditioned by circuitry which responds only to increases in signal strength. The term 'differentiation' is mathematical in origin and essentially means to measure the rate of change of some quantity. The theoretical principle of operation is illustrated by Figure 3.45. Figure 3.45(a) and (b) show the effect of varying degrees of differentiation on a single idealized rectangular pulse, while Figure 3.45 (c) shows three idealized rectangular echoes which overlap one another, saturate the receiver and hence are representative of the masking effect of rain clutter. The first pulse represents the rain echo which returns immediately ahead of the target response and the third

pulse represents the rain return immediately following that of the target.

Because the circuitry responds only to those sections of the waveform where the signal strength is increasing, its effect is to remove the trailing edges of the echoes, thus making it possible to display the leading edge of the rain and that of the target as separate returns. Clearly the displayed echoes must not be made so short that they become difficult to discern. The finite radial length of the differentiated echo depends on the *time constant* of the circuit which is a measure of the time taken by the circuitry to respond to a levelling off or decrease in signal strength (see Figure 3.45(a) and (b)). For this reason the rain clutter control may sometimes be referred to as the *fast time constant* (FTC). In some systems this is preset by the manufacturer in which case the rain clutter control is an on/off FTC switch; in other systems it can be set by the observer over a continuous range of values. The effect of the rain clutter control on a practical set of echoes is illustrated by Figure 3.46.

Reference to Figure 3.46 shows that the two principal features of the differentiated output are the leading edges of the rain and the target which is stronger than the rain. It should also be noted that the raw rain signal shows a slow decrease with range, on which is superimposed a small high frequency fluctuation of the instantaneous signal level. Depending on the setting of the rain clutter control, the differentiated output will also tend to show to a greater or lesser extent the rising edges of the fluctuating peaks: targets close to rain level will have to compete with these for attention. Targets weaker than the rain response cannot be detected. It is emphasized that differentiation will be carried out before any digitization (see Section 2.6.6.1) and the output illustrated in Figure 3.46 is analogue.

It is important to appreciate that although the rain clutter control is so called, it is not necessarily the most effective way of dealing with rain echoes. Many users find the use of the gain control in a searching action much more effective. This is discussed further in Section 6.10.2, which sets out the practical procedures for detecting targets in rain. It is worth mentioning

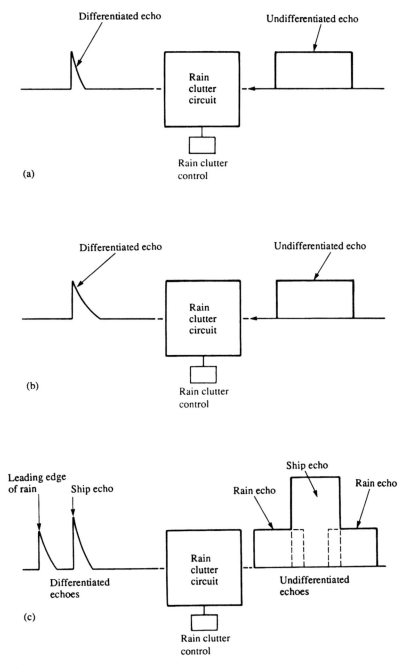

Figure 3.45 The principle of differentiation

(a) High degree of differentiation
(b) Low degree of differentiation
(c) Separation of echoes by differentiation

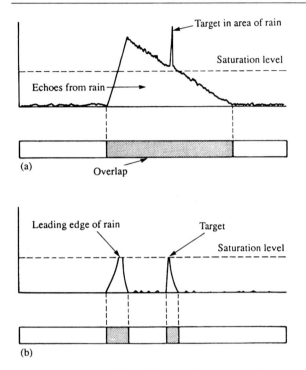

Figure 3.46 The effect of the rain clutter control

(a)   No rain clutter control applied: displayed echoes of rain and target overlap radially

(b)   Rain clutter control applied: there is radial (not necessarily amplitude) discrimination between leading edges of rain and target

that the differentiating effect may be found particularly useful for improving discrimination on short range pictures.

Targets within the rain clutter area can sometimes be detected by observing their shadowing effect in the rain clutter beyond them.

3.7.4.5   Adaptive gain

This technique was described in detail in Section 3.6.3.3 and represents an automatic approach which may be found effective in the suppression of rain clutter echoes. In most systems, when adaptive gain is selected, a fixed amount of differentiation is also applied.

3.7.4.6   Circular polarization

For the reasons set out in Section 3.6.1.7 there is no stimulus for designers to produce X-band equipment other than with horizontal polarization. Hence, in civil marine applications, vertical polarization is very much the exception rather than the rule. In Section 2.4.1.8 it was explained that the terms 'vertical' and 'horizontal' refer to the plane of the fluctuating electric field associated with the electromagnetic wave.

The visualization of a circularly polarized wave may require some mental effort. Its effect is best explained by considering it to be produced by generating a horizontally polarized wave, and adding to it a vertically polarized wave which has the same amplitude and frequency but is a quarter-cycle out of phase with it. The polarization of the resultant wave thus rotates and hence the use of the term 'circular polarization'. On the return of echoes, the two components of the wave are separated and a further quarter cycle phaseshift is applied to the vertically polarized wave. If the two components of the wave have suffered identical reflection, they will be equal in amplitude, out of phase by one half-cycle and thus will cancel one another. Such symmetrical reflection will be experienced if the target is a small smooth sphere (radar cross-section is a function of polarization). In many circumstances a raindrop comes close to this ideal. Thus the response from raindrops will tend to be cancelled or at least considerably reduced. If the reflection of both components is not symmetrical then the degree of the cancelling will be reduced to a greater or lesser extent, depending on the lack of symmetry. The cancelling achieved in the case of other types of precipitation will not be as effective if the particle is not spherical, as in wet snowflakes. When compared with linear polarization, the response of wanted targets will also be reduced by the use of circular polarization. In general, cancellation can be expected, where the energy has suffered an odd number of reflections, but not with an even number. A ship target is a complex arrangement of many reflecting surfaces. It thus behaves as a large scatterer and the energy returned to the observing vessel will contain components which have suffered an even number of reflections.

The effectiveness of circular polarization for the suppression of precipitation thus depends on the reduction in response of wanted targets being less than that suffered by the precipitation. This hope may well not be realized in the case of small targets and this limitation must be firmly borne in mind should such a facility be available. In the past some civil marine radar systems offering this facility were produced but few, if any, are still at sea and there is no sign at present that they will be produced again. One might speculate that the additional cost and complication was not justified by the benefit gained. However, other radar applications can benefit from the use of circular polarization.

3.7.5 Combating the attenuation caused by precipitation

The nature of the problem differs depending on whether the target lies within or beyond the area of the precipitation.

3.7.5.1 The attenuation of the signal from a target beyond precipitation

The response from a target beyond an area of precipitation will be reduced as a result of scattering and attenuation of the radar signal on its two-way journey through the precipitation (see Section 3.7.2). This attenuation can be combated by the selection of the S-band and the use of a longer pulse length. While searching for specific targets it may be useful temporarily to turn the gain above the normal setting or to use an echo-stretching facility (see Section 6.11.1) if the latter is available.

3.7.5.2 The attenuation of the signal from a target within precipitation

This is a more difficult problem: the only way in which this attenuation can be effectively reduced is by the use of S-band in preference to X-band transmission (see Section 3.6.1.5). The other techniques suggested in Section 3.7.5.1 will certainly increase the target response but they will also increase the response from

the precipitation, thus exacerbating the already serious problem of saturation.

3.7.6 Exploiting the ability of radar to detect precipitation

The ability of radar to detect precipitation at long range has been found useful in a number of meteorological applications. Shore-based radars having a range of several hundred miles have been used to track the movement of the large areas of precipitation present in hurricanes and other similar storms in order to provide warning of possible danger and damage from the associated weather conditions. The detection range offered by shipboard radar cannot provide sufficient warning to permit avoiding action. The presence of precipitation in other less dramatic weather systems has led to the use of long range surveillance radars in day-to-day general weather forecasting. Again, shipboard equipment does not offer the range necessary for weather forecasting but the ability to track the movement of precipitation in the short term can prove useful.

Early warning of the approach of precipitation should make it possible to ensure that the vessel is adequately prepared to deal with the additional problems this may pose in the use of radar for collision avoidance. The Master can be called in adequate time, the engine room staff can be prepared for manoeuvres and arrangements can be made for such additional bridge and lookout personnel as may be required. It may be possible to commence the plotting of targets before they enter areas of precipitation. This may well assist in the detection of targets even in the presence of masking as it is always easier to find an echo if its approximate location is known. The data extracted should also prove useful in planning collision avoidance strategy, although the observer must always be alert to the possibility of a target manoeuvring while masked.

In port, the ability to track approaching rain showers may make it possible to close cargo hatches in sufficient time to prevent cargo damage. At sea, the ability to avoid isolated showers might benefit a freshly painted deck or perhaps an outdoor event on a passenger vessel.

3.8   The radar horizon

At marine radar transmission frequencies (nominally 10 000 and 3000 MHz), the paths followed by the signals may be considered as 'line of sight'. This means that even though the radar is delivering a powerful pulse and the target is capable, if irradiated, of returning a detectable response, the target will not be detected if it is below the *radar horizon*. This is analogous to the visual observation of objects in the vicinity of the horizon.

The effect of the atmosphere on the horizon is a further factor which must be taken into account when assessing the likelihood of detecting a particular target and especially when considering the expected appearance of coastlines.

3.8.1   The effect of standard atmospheric conditions

Under standard atmospheric conditions, the radar beam tends to bend slightly downward, the distance to the radar horizon being given by the formula

$$d_{\text{n mile}} = 1.22 \sqrt{h_{\text{ft}}} \quad \text{or} \quad d_{\text{n mile}} = 2.21 \sqrt{h_{\text{m}}}$$

where h is the height of the antenna in feet or metres.

It can be seen from Figure 3.47 that the possibility of detecting targets beyond the radar horizon will, in addition to all the other factors discussed in this chapter, depend upon the height of the target (i.e. whether or not a responsive part of it extends above the horizon). Thus the theoretical detection range based purely on the antenna and target heights is given by the formula

$$R_{\text{d}} = d + D$$
$$R_{\text{d}} = 1.22 \sqrt{h_{\text{ft}}} + 1.22 \sqrt{H_{\text{ft}}} \quad \text{or}$$
$$R_{\text{d}} = 2.21 \sqrt{h_{\text{m}}} + 2.21 \sqrt{H_{\text{m}}}$$

where h and H are heights of the antenna and the target respectively in feet or metres. In both cases, R_{d} is the theoretical detection range in nautical miles.

This relationship is of course theoretical since it assumes that:

(a)   Standard atmospheric conditions prevail.
(b)   The radar pulses are sufficiently powerful.
(c)   The target response characteristics are such as to return detectable responses.
(d)   The weather conditions, such as precipitation etc., through which the pulses have to travel, will not unduly attenuate the signals.

3.8.1.1   *The increase in detection range with increased antenna height*

While in theory it is correct to say that detection ranges can be increased by increasing the antenna height, in practice there is a limit to the extent to which it is worth pursuing this increase. Above moderate height, the increase in detection range is minimal and not worth the effort (or the consequent additional expense of waveguide etc.). The reason for this can be appreciated by considering the theoretical relationship set out above: to double the distance to the radar horizon, the antenna will have to be four times as high. If the antenna is at a height of 16 m, the distance to the radar horizon is 8.84 n mile. To double this to

Figure 3.47   The radar horizon under standard atmospheric conditions

some 17.7 n mile would require an antenna height of some $(17.68/2.21)^2$ n mile $= 64$ m. This point should be borne in mind when considering the extent to which radars offering 96 n mile range scales can be effective.

It can be seen from Figure 3.47 that if targets are observed beyond the horizon, it must *not* be assumed that nearer targets will necessarily also be detected. Note that, although the cliff may be detected, there is no chance of receiving an echo from the buoy at this stage.

Consider a vessel having its radar antenna at a height of 16 m above the water. The distance to the radar horizon will be $2.21 \times 4 = 8.84$ n mile. This means that when assessing the possibility of detecting a target at a range greater than some 8.5 n mile, one must first consider whether or not the target has sufficient height.

The theoretical range at which a sheer cliff face rising to a height of 64 m should be detected on a vessel whose antenna is at a height of 16 m is

$$2.21\sqrt{(64)} + 2.21\sqrt{(16)}$$
$$= 2.21 \times 8 + 2.21 \times 4$$
$$= 26.5 \text{ n miles.}$$

Note   Although sheer cliffs immediately suggest a good response target, aspect must be borne in mind, i.e. whether the cliffs are 'square on' or at an angle to the radar rays.

Consider the case where a vessel has its antenna at a height of 16 m above the water and first detects land at a range of 23 n mile:

$$23 = 2.21\sqrt{(16)} \times 2.21\sqrt{H}$$
$$\text{therefore } H = \left(\frac{23 - (2.21 \times 4)}{2.21}\right)^2$$
$$= 41.05 \text{ metres}$$

The indication here is that, if standard atmospheric conditions prevail, the land which is being detected must be at least 41 m high. When attempting to relate what is being observed on the radar to the chart, only land having a height of at least 41 m should be being considered. As can be seen in Figure 3.48, it would be completely incorrect to assume that the vessel is 23 n mile from the coastline.

Great care must be exercised when attempting to identify targets which are beyond the radar horizon. Using the example above (and Figure 3.48) it is evident that the land detected is unlikely to be the coastline but is probably higher ground lying inland. It is important to appreciate this principle as failure to do so gives the impression that the vessel is farther offshore than is in fact the case.

It should be noted that, when making in toward a sloping coastline such as that in Figure 3.49, the coastline as displayed on the radar screen can have a disconcerting effect of 'appearing' to come toward the vessel as more of the low-lying land comes above the horizon. This is especially so if it has been assumed that it was the coastline that was being observed in the first instance and positions have been laid off as if this were the case.

Considering a vessel with an antenna at a height of 16 m and assuming standard atmospheric conditions, if echoes from land are observed at a range of 26 n mile then whatever is being observed must be at least some 60 m high (see Table 3.2).

Table 3.2 gives the least theoretical height (in metres) of a target detected beyond the radar horizon for various antenna heights. Since the distance to the radar horizon in the above example is some 8.8 n mile, any target observed at a greater range than 8.8 n mile should be checked against the table to ensure that it has adequate height for detection.

Figure 3.48   The effects of target and antenna height

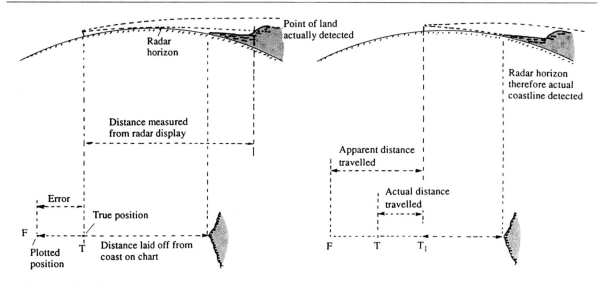

Figure 3.49 The apparent movement of the coastline as it comes above the horizon

3.8.1.2 Standard atmospheric conditions

'Standard' conditions are precisely defined as:

Pressure = 1013 mb decreasing at 36 mb/1000 ft of height

Temperature = 15°C decreasing at 2°C/1000 ft of height

Relative humidity = 60 per cent and constant with height.

These conditions give a refractive index of 1.003 25 which decreases at 0.000 13 units/1000 ft of height.

The term 'standard' should not be confused with the term 'normal', which is extremely subjective and imprecise. Standard conditions are rarely likely to equate to what might be considered normal at any particular location on the earth.

It can be seen that the definition of 'standard' conditions relates to the vertical composition of the atmosphere. The mariner is unlikely to be able to obtain a precise knowledge of this and so must rely on a more general appreciation of the weather conditions, the area of the world, and the time of the year, as well as on past experience for guidance as to the likelihood of the existence of standard or non-standard atmospheric conditions and of the effects that they can have on the detection ranges of targets in the area.

In general, 'normal' conditions in the more highly frequented sea areas of the world tend to be super-refractive.

Note The attenuating and clutter effects of the atmosphere are considered in Section 3.7.2.

3.8.2   Sub-refraction

3.8.2.1   The effects of sub-refraction on detection ranges (Figure 3.50)

Sub-refraction occurs when the refractive index of the atmosphere decreases less rapidly with height than under standard conditions. As a result, the radar beam is bent downward slightly less than under standard conditions. This means that, with all other factors constant, the same target will be detected at a slightly reduced range. In practice, this is likely to mean something of the order of 80 per cent of the detection range under standard conditions but will obviously depend on the severity of the conditions prevailing at the time.

Table 3.2 Least height of a target detected beyond the radar horizon (metres)

Antenna height (m)

	8	10	12	14	16	18	20	22	24	26	28	30
12	6.8	5.1	3.9	2.9	2.0	1.4	0.9	0.5	0.3	0.1	0.0	
14	12.3	10.1	8.2	6.7	5.5	4.4	3.5	2.7	2.1	1.5	1.1	0.7
16	19.5	16.6	14.3	12.2	10.5	9.0	7.7	6.5	5.5	4.6	3.8	3.1
18	28.3	24.8	21.9	19.4	17.2	15.2	13.5	11.9	10.5	9.3	8.1	7.1
20	38.7	34.7	31.2	28.2	25.5	23.1	21.0	19.0	17.2	15.6	14.1	12.8
22	50.8	46.1	42.1	38.6	35.5	32.6	30.1	27.7	25.6	23.6	21.7	20.0
24	64.5	59.3	54.7	50.7	47.1	43.8	40.8	38.1	35.5	33.2	31.0	29.0
26	79.9	74.0	68.9	64.4	**60.3**	56.6	53.2	50.0	47.1	44.4	41.9	39.5
28	96.9	90.4	84.7	79.7	75.2	71.0	67.2	63.7	60.4	57.3	54.4	51.7
30	115.5	108.4	102.2	96.7	91.7	87.1	82.9	78.9	75.3	71.8	68.6	65.6
32	135.8	128.1	121.3	115.3	109.8	104.8	100.2	95.8	91.8	88.0	84.4	81.0
34	157.7	149.4	142.1	135.6	129.6	124.1	119.1	114.4	109.9	105.8	101.9	98.2
36	181.2	172.3	164.5	157.5	151.0	145.1	139.7	134.5	129.7	125.2	121.0	116.9
38	206.4	196.9	188.5	181.0	174.1	167.8	161.9	156.4	151.2	146.3	141.7	137.3
40	233.2	223.1	214.2	206.1	198.8	192.0	185.7	179.8	174.3	169.0	164.0	159.3

Detection range of target (n mile)

Figure 3.50 The effect of sub-refraction on detection ranges

3.8.2.2 *Atmospheric conditions that give rise to sub-refraction (Figure 3.51)*

These can be specified precisely but since the mariner is unlikely to have access to data relating to the vertical composition of the atmosphere it is perhaps more appropriate to consider the conditions which, from experience, are likely to accompany this phenomenon. These are:

(a) An increase in relative humidity with height.
(b) A rapid fall in temperature with height.

Both of these conditions do not have to be satisfied at any one time but, obviously, the greater the changes in temperature and relative humidity with

height, the greater will be the effect that they will have on the radar beam. This does not mean that, under extreme conditions, the whole beam will rise above the sea surface or that no targets will be detected at all.

These conditions, to a greater or lesser extent, may be encountered virtually anywhere but are most likely in the polar regions, the Grand Banks (especially in the Gulf Stream with northerly winds), east of Japan in winter, and in the Mediterranean in winter.

Sub-refraction is generally associated with bad weather conditions, i.e. with low pressure systems, which is typically the time when radar is most likely to be needed.

3.8.3 Super-refraction

3.8.3.1 *The effects of super-refraction on detection ranges (Figure 3.52)*

Super-refraction occurs when the rate of decrease in refractive index with height is greater than under standard conditions. When super-refraction occurs, the radar beam tends to be bent down slightly more and so targets may be detected at ranges which are slightly greater than standard. Increases of some 40 per cent are not uncommon.

Again, the mariner has no means of knowing exactly what sort of atmospheric conditions are being experienced and so has to rely on some form of subjective assessment; it is always best to err on the cautious side.

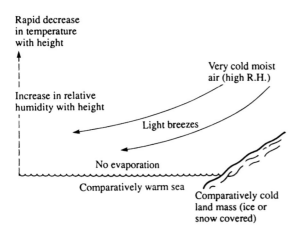

Figure 3.51 Atmospheric conditions associated with sub-refraction. The critical factor is land/sea (or sea/sea) temperature difference. When the sea is cold, sub-refraction can occur provided that the air is even colder

Figure 3.52 The effects of super-refraction on detection ranges

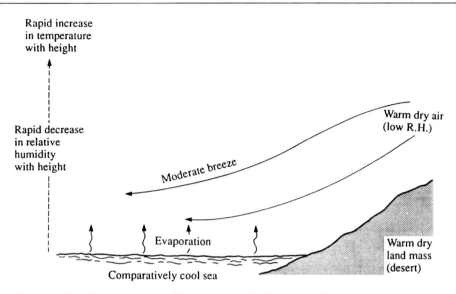

Rapid increase
in temperature
with height

Rapid decrease
in relative
humidity
with height

Warm dry air
(low R.H.)

Moderate breeze

Evaporation

Comparatively cool sea

Warm dry
land mass
(desert)

Figure 3.53 Atmospheric conditions associated with super-refraction

*3.8.3.2 Atmospheric conditions associated with
super-refraction (Figure 3.53)*

These are:

(a) A decrease in relative humidity with height.
(b) Temperature falling more slowly than standard,
or even increasing with height.

These conditions tend to be more frequently encountered in the maritime trading areas of the world, in particular, the tropics; other areas include the Red Sea, the Arabian Gulf, and the Mediterranean in summer.

Super-refraction is generally associated with fine settled weather, i.e. with high pressure weather systems.

3.8.4 Extra super-refraction or ducting

*3.8.4.1 The effects of extra super-refraction
(Figure 3.54)*

Under these conditions, the radar energy is, in effect, trapped in a 'duct' formed by the Earth's surface and a highly refractive layer which may be as little as a 100 ft (30 m) above the ground. The effect is to concentrate

energy which would otherwise have been lost into space together with the energy which would normally travel in the direction of the targets. This increased energy now follows the Earth's surface, thus reducing the constraint of the radar horizon and considerably extending the detection ranges of targets. This can result in the detection of unwanted 'second-trace echoes' (see Section 3.9.6).

*3.8.4.2 Atmospheric conditions which give rise to extra
super-refraction*

If the rate of change of refractive index is of the order of 4 times the 'standard' rate, initially horizontal rays will follow the curvature of the Earth. It is more effective, though, for the energy to be trapped between the Earth and a highly refractive layer (such as a temperature inversion), thus forming a duct in which the energy will travel in a similar manner to propagation within a waveguide with a 'leaky' upper wall.

Note (a) A temperature inversion by itself must be very pronounced to produce a duct.
(b) Relative humidity gradients are more effective than temperature gradients alone.

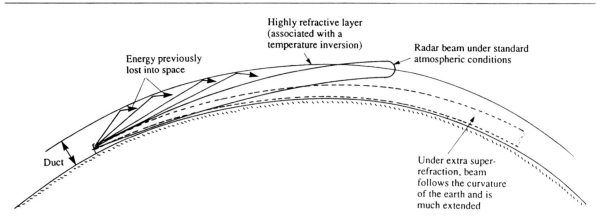

Figure 3.54 The effect of extra super-refraction

The areas which are normally associated with extra super-refraction are the Red Sea, the Arabian Gulf, the Mediterranean in the summer with the wind from the south, and the area off the west coast of Africa in the vicinity of the Canary Islands. However, extra super-refraction can occur anywhere if the conditions are right. The usual indication that these conditions exist is the appearance of second trace echoes (see Section 3.9.6).

3.9 False and unwanted radar responses

3.9.1 Introduction

These responses may also be referred to as spurious echoes and are the result of a number of specific causes. In all cases, echoes are displayed on the screen in positions where no genuine targets exist. In general, these are likely when genuine targets are close but this is not always the case (see Section 3.9.6).

3.9.2 Indirect echoes (reflected echoes)

These can occur when radar energy is deflected in the direction of an object by some obstruction in the path of the radiated energy, either on board the ship or ashore.

The returning energy follows a reciprocal path and so causes an echo to be displayed in the direction of the obstruction. This form of false echo can be particularly misleading when the obstruction is on board the ship.

3.9.2.1 The effect of on-board obstructions

Consider the situation, depicted in Figure 3.55, where energy strikes the foremast and some of it is deflected in the direction of the target on the starboard quarter. Energy reflected by the target follows a reciprocal path and so returns to the antenna from a direction fine on the starboard bow (i.e. the reflection point on the foremast). As a result, a false echo will be displayed at a range which is similar to that of the genuine target (this assumes that the distance to the on-board obstruction is small by comparison with the range of the target), but on the bearing of the obstruction (i.e. the foremast).

Typical of on-board obstructions which can give rise to this form of false echo are a mast, a funnel and cross-trees. In fact, any structure which intercepts energy in the beam can produce the effect. There is a tendency to associate indirect echoes with blind arcs and shadow sectors (see Section 2.7.1.1); while this is frequently the case, in recent times other less obvious causes have been identified. Most notable have been the indirect echoes resulting from reflections from the

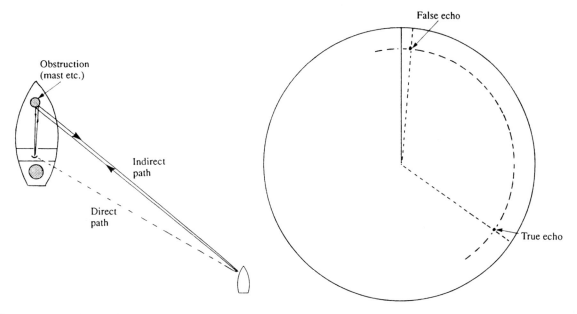

Figure 3.55 Indirect echoes

aft-facing surface of containers (Figure 3.56). Here, three points should be noted:

(a) The traditional blind/shadow sector theory need not apply.
(b) There is a likelihood of other true echoes appearing on the radar display on the same bearing as the false echoes.

(c) The cause of the problem may change each time the stowage of the containers on deck is changed.

It is advisable, when containers are stowed in isolated stacks, that a warning of the possibility of indirect echoes is displayed alongside the radar.

Figure 3.56 Reflections from aft-facing surfaces of containers

3.9.2.2   *The recognition of indirect echoes*

The more obvious causes (blind and shadow sectors) should be studied in clear weather when there are a number of other vessels in the vicinity of the observing ship. Blind and shadow sectors should have been logged (see Section 2.7.1.1) and any echo which appears in these sectors should be regarded as suspect. Visual comparison with the radar should confirm whether the echo is genuine or indirect. Where it is decided that the displayed echo is indirect, it is reasonable to expect to find a genuine target at about the same range, although even this search may be inconclusive.

Many unusual causes of indirect echoes have been reported but, without a careful study of the conditions obtaining at the time, it is very difficult to come to reliable conclusions and to take steps to prevent their recurrence. Deck cargo, deck cranes, break waters, ventilators and a host of other on-board structures have aroused suspicion at one time or another.

Indirect echoes can give rise to serious concern when they appear ahead of the vessel, particularly at night or in restricted visibility. At night, it may be suspected that the 'vessel' ahead is not showing the necessary navigation lights or that the onset of restricted visibility is imminent.

If this phenomenon occurs in restricted visibility and it is considered necessary to manoeuvre to avoid what one must assume is a real target, the resulting apparent behaviour of the echo (if false) is quite unpredictable. For example, the 'target' may appear to make a simultaneous countermanoeuvre or may even disappear (Figure 3.57).

Figure 3.57   The effect of a manoeuvre by own ship on an indirect echo

The following safety precautions should be observed:

1 Where echoes are suspected of being false, they should be assumed to be real until proved false beyond all reasonable doubt.
2 Potential causes of indirect echoes such as blind and shadow sectors should be constantly borne in mind and any suspect arc investigated, preferably before arrival in areas of known restricted visibility.
3 Unexplained 'target' behaviour should be logged.
4 Where the cause of indirect echoes has been identified, steps to prevent their recurrence should be taken immediately.

3.9.2.3 The prevention of indirect echoes

Where shipboard structures have been identified as the cause of indirect echoes, steps should be taken to prevent their future recurrence. In principle, this means that the energy striking the deflecting obstruction must be dissipated by re-direction, scattering or absorption.

Each cause has to be treated individually; typical solutions in the past have included attaching plates angled upwards to the crosstrees, welding angle iron

to the after surfaces of the cross-trees and surfacing the obstruction with radar absorbent material (RAM).

Note Where attempts are made to scatter the energy by 'roughening' the surface, it must be remembered that facets must be of the order of wavelength (see Section 3.3.2).

3.9.2.4 Indirect echoes from objects external to the ship (Figure 3.58)

These can frequently be seen when vessels are in built-up areas and other vessels are moving in the vicinity. Because of the conditions under which they occur, they are frequently not recognized.

In general, the obstructions which cause the deflection of energy tend to be large and the false echoes will display on the farther side of them. In many cases they will appear to move over the land, making it easy to recognize them and dismiss them as false. In the open sea, this recognition might not be quite so positive but there is always the consolation that the nearer of the targets on the same bearing is invariably genuine.

One special form of false echo arising from this cause can be extremely misleading. This is where the

Figure 3.58 Indirect echoes which occur as a result of objects external to the ship indirect echoes occur as a result of a bridge structure spanning the waterway. Consider a vessel approaching a bridge as in Figure 3.59. Energy reflected back and forth between the bridge and the vessel (in a similar manner to that described in 3.9.3) will result in a false echo appearing about as far beyond the bridge as the observer's vessel is from it. As the vessel approaches the bridge, so the false echo will appear to approach the bridge from the opposite direction. In most cases, the bridge will cross the waterway at right angles which will mean that, however the vessel manoeuvres in an attempt to avoid the 'other ship', the observed echo will appear to have undertaken a complementary countermanoeuvre, i.e. the false echo's position will be on the perpendicular from the observing vessel to the bridge and its distance from the bridge will be about the same as that of the observing vessel.

Indirect echoes from objects ashore which result from reflections at the bridge can result in a considerable amount of 'clutter' appearing in the water area beyond the bridge. It should be noted that this clutter will be moving as the observing vessel moves and so changes its position in relation to the objects ashore. This clutter can also mask the real responses from other vessels using the waterway.

3.9.3   Multiple echoes

Multiple echoes are likely when a target is close and energy bounces back and forth between the hulls of the target and the observing ship, with some of the energy entering the antenna at each return (Figure 3.60). The features of this form of response are that the echoes:

(a)   Lie along a single direction.
(b)   Are consistently spaced.
(c)   Tend to move in accord.
(d)   Tend to diminish in strength with the increase of range.

It should be noted that, while it would seem logical from Figure 3.60 for this form of response to occur when vessels are abeam, it has been observed to occur on virtually all relative bearings.

Since it is most likely to occur when vessels are close (maybe as much as 4 n mile but usually less), if the vessels are constrained within channels or rivers etc., the false echoes will be seen to be navigating outside the channel or even on the shore.

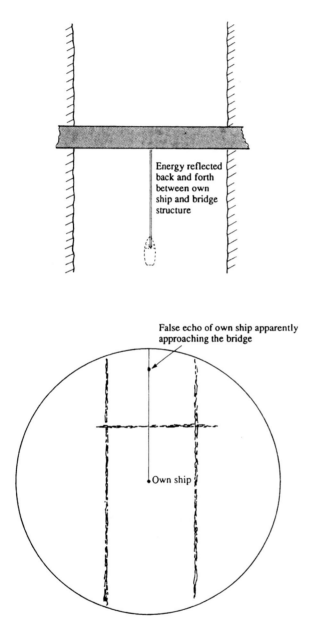

Figure 3.59   False echoes from bridges

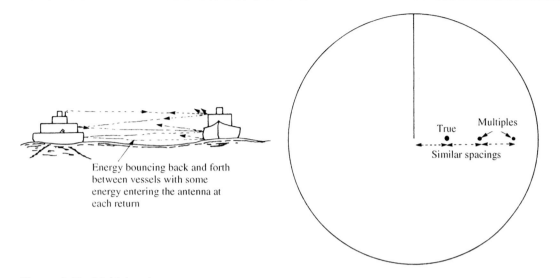

Figure 3.60 Multiple echoes

Note Because the outer echoes must keep on the same bearing line as the nearer ones, if plotted, their movement can be found to be higher than or contrary to that which might be anticipated.

The chances of multiple echoes can be reduced by ensuring that shorter pulse lengths are selected when using the lower range scales. It may be possible to produce this phenomenon deliberately in order to observe it, by selecting the longer pulse when on a lower range scale and with a close target.

In general, this form of false echo should not give real cause for concern since the genuine target producing the effect is always the nearest. Nonetheless, it is worth while to watch out for it in clear weather, when the absence of real targets beyond the nearest one can be confirmed.

Multiple echoes can also be produced by targets ashore, but the multiples will generally be lost amidst the confusion of other land echoes.

3.9.4 Side echoes

Side echoes are again associated with targets that are at close range, and result from the radar beam being surrounded by smaller beams or lobes (see Section 2.4.2).

In the case of the farther target in Figure 3.61, the radar beam sweeping over it will result in the display of an echo of angular width which is approximately equal to the horizontal beamwidth (see Section 2.6.5.3).

In the case of the nearer target, if energy is returned as each lobe sweeps over it, the angular width of the displayed echo will be of the order of 100°. Some of the echoes will appear to be separate but all will be at the same range, i.e. as if all were lying on the same range circle.

This phenomenon is generally associated with smaller antennae and those which are dirty or damaged. While it is normal for the side echoes to be symmetrical about the genuine response, this may not be so in all cases; it is reasonable to expect the true response to be the strongest (see Section 2.4.2.1). If it is essential to identify the genuine echo, this can be achieved by the use of the gain or anti-clutter controls to suppress the weaker side echoes, as when dealing with sea clutter (see Section 6.10.1.1).

The effect of side echoes on sea clutter is to intensify the displayed clutter by integration of the echoes and this can be a definite disadvantage.

When side echoes are observed where they have not been seen before, their cause should be determined

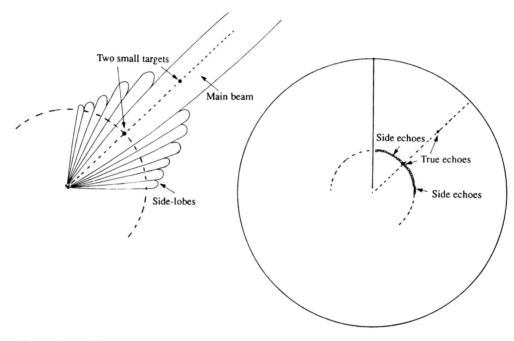

Figure 3.61 Side echoes

(a damaged or dirty antenna should be the first suspect) and rectified at the first possible opportunity.

3.9.5 Radar-to-radar interference

All civil marine radar systems are required to operate within a fairly narrow slot of approximately 200 MHz allocated in the X-band or S-band (see Section 2.3.3.1). When it is considered that the receiver bandwidth (see Section 2.5.2.4) of a marine radar system may be as much as 20 MHz, and given the high power and antenna height of a shipboard system, it is obvious that, except in mid-ocean, there is a very high probability of receiving interfering radiation from other vessels in the vicinity which are operating radar equipment.

If the radiation received is within the limits of the receiver bandwidth the signals will be amplified in the same way as those reflected from targets and will produce a visible response on the display. In the case of returned echoes there is a strict time sequence relationship between transmission and timebase cycles and both have the same repetition rate (see Section 2.3.1). By contrast, there is no synchronism in the relationship between the transmission sequence of the interfering radar and the timebase of the receiving system, nor are their repetition rates necessarily similar. As a result, the interfering signals produce a pattern on the screen which is totally random. It can take any form but frequently has a spiral character, as illustrated by Figure 3.62.

At best, the presence of interference may be a source of slight irritation which the practised observer may be able to cope with by mental filtering. In severe cases it may seriously impair the ability of the observer to detect targets.

If observers make prudent use of the stand-by condition (see Section 6.7), the general level of radar-to-radar interference present in the atmosphere can be reduced at source. Despite this, there is still a need

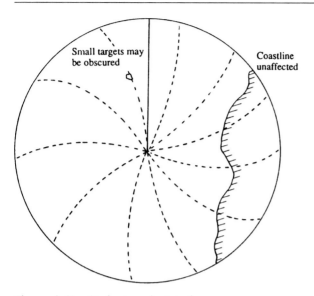

Figure 3.62 Radar-to-radar interference – appearance on the display

to provide the observer with a means of suppressing displayed interference.

3.9.5.1 Interference rejection

Where picture data is stored, interference can be filtered out by comparing the signals present in successive range words (see Section 2.6.6.3) and rejecting those which do not appear on successive lines. The principle of operation is known as *line-to-line correlation* and is illustrated by Figure 3.63.

The underlying logic is that, because of the random nature of interference, the probability of two signals appearing in the same range cell on successive range words is negligible. By contrast, as a point target is swept by the radar beam, it will be struck by a number of successive pulses (see Section 2.4.4) all of which will register in the same range cell in successive lines. Thus interference will be removed by the correlation process, whereas the echoes of targets will be unaffected other than the rejection of the first strike. This loss is acceptable since even a point target should experience some 10 to 20 strikes. The output from

the interference rejection circuit is known as *correlated video*.

In Figure 3.63 successive lines of digital radar information are shown 'line by line'. The previous line of information is stored (S). This is compared with the current line (C) and only if the target appears on both lines is it displayed. The current line (C) then becomes the new stored (S) line in preparation for comparison with the next new current line.

Such a facility will also reduce the amount of displayed receiver noise and should therefore be switched off when setting the gain control (see Sections 6.2.4.1, 6.3.4.2 and 6.4.4). Correlation may also result in the rejection of the signals from some radar beacons (see Section 3.5). The IMO Performance Standards (see Section 11.2.1 and 11.2.4) state that it should be possible to switch off *any* signal processing facility that might prevent a radar beacon from being shown on the display (see also Adaptive gain in Section 3.6.3.3).

Some modern radar systems offer a more sophisticated facility described as *beam processing* by which all hits within the antenna beamwidth are compared with criteria for probability of detection. The information so derived is used to eliminate interference and reduce noise and, additionally, to reduce the angular width of the echo in an attempt to reduce the distorting effect of the horizontal beamwidth (see Section 2.6.5.3).

Mutual interference may be particularly troublesome where two X-band or two S-band systems are fitted on the same vessel. Where the two systems are interswitched (see Section 2.7.8), a pulse synchronization unit may be incorporated. This unit will synchronize the PRFs of both units and time-shift the transmissions in an attempt to ensure that neither system will transmit during the timebase of the other. This will not necessarily eliminate all interference from the adjacent system. However, the strongest interfering signals are likely to be those reflected from the ship's structure and nearby targets and these will be not be displayed. A pulse synchronization circuit will make no contribution to the reduction of interference generated by other vessels.

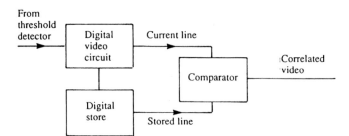

		Input line								Displayed line							
	S	0	0	1	0	1	0	0	0								
S	C	1	0	1	0	1	0	0	1	0	0	1	0	1	0	0	0
C	S	0	0	1	0	1	0	0	0	0	0	1	0	1	0	0	0
S	C	0	1	1	0	0	0	0	0	0	0	1	0	0	0	0	0
C	S	0	0	1	0	0	0	1	0	0	0	1	0	0	0	0	0
S	C	0	0	1	0	0	0	1	0	0	0	1	0	0	0	1	0
C	S	0	0	1	1	0	0	1	0	0	0	1	0	0	0	1	0
S	C	0	0	1	0	0	0	1	0	0	0	1	0	0	0	1	0
C	S	0	0	1	0	0	0	1	1	0	0	1	0	0	0	1	0
S	C	0	0	1	0	0	0	1	0	0	0	1	0	0	0	1	0
C	S	0	1	0	0	0	0	1	0	0	0	0	0	0	0	1	0
S	C	0	0	0	0	0	0	1	0	0	0	0	0	0	0	1	0
C	S	1	0	0	1	0	0	1	0	0	0	0	0	0	0	1	0
S	C	0	0	1	0	0	0	1	0	0	0	0	0	0	0	1	0

Figure 3.63 Line-to-line correlation. S = Stored line, C = Current line

3.9.6   Second-trace echoes

The conditions which must exist before this form of false echo will appear are fairly exceptional:

(a) Extra super-refractive atmospheric conditions must exist.

(b) Targets must be in the vicinity of the ship and in areas which are precisely defined by the PRF selected by the observer at the time.

Nonetheless, false echoes of this type are regularly reported in the meteorological journals, while on many more occasions observations go unreported as they are not recognized for what they are.

Under conditions of extra super-refraction (see Section 3.8.4), the radar energy follows closely the surface of the Earth and travels to greater distances than under standard conditions. This means that echoes from distant targets can arrive back at the receiver one trace late (i.e. on the 'second trace') or even later, be accepted by the receiver and so be displayed but obviously at an incorrect range.

Consider a radar system operating with the following parameters:

PRF = 1250 pulses/second (pps) and therefore the PRP = 800 μs (an echo which returns after an interval of 800 μs from transmission will be from a target which is at a range of 64 n miles).

Long pulse is being used on the 12 n mile range scale (timebase = 150 μs) and there are objects at 6 n miles and 72 n miles which will respond well to radar pulses if struck.

Note Under standard atmospheric conditions, the object at 72 n miles would be well below the radar horizon; also, the energy in the transmitted pulse would be insufficient to travel to and from targets at that range.

Figure 3.64 shows the time sequence graph for the above data. Consider how this can be translated to the area around the vessel. Figure 3.65 gives the standing area coverage pattern.

By allowing a fairly long resting period for the spot, radar designers are generally able to ensure that the energy in the pulse is sufficient to detect most targets out to the range of the scale in use (12 n miles in this case) but insufficient to return echoes from targets in the 64 to 76 n mile band, which would otherwise arrive while the receiver was again receptive and the spot on its way from the centre of screen to the edge. If this were not the case, an echo arriving back during this period would display together with those coming from within the range of the scale in use at the time.

Under extra super-refraction conditions, the situation changes in that the energy trapped in the duct is capable of returning echoes from much greater ranges and so second (or even third and fourth) trace echoes become a real possibility.

As can be seen from Figures 3.64 and 3.65, the positioning of the bands from which reception is possible

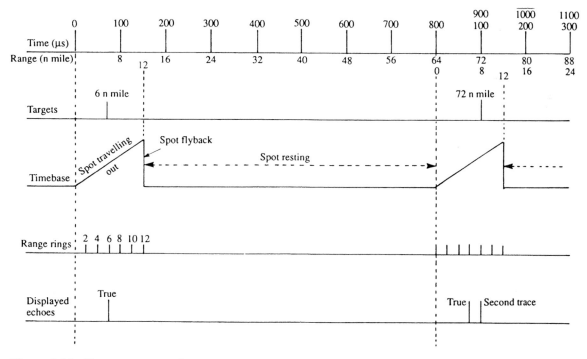

Figure 3.64 Time sequence graph

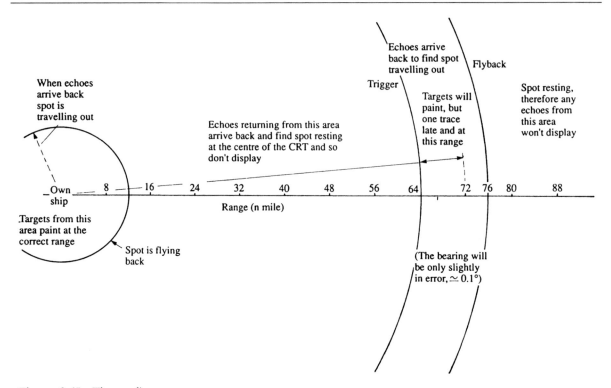

Figure 3.65 The standing area coverage pattern

is fixed by the PRF in use at the time, while the width of the band is equal to the range of the scale in use.

3.9.6.1 The recognition of second-trace echoes

It should be remembered that second-trace echoes are generally associated with fine weather conditions and so in most cases it will be possible to compare the radar picture with the visual scene. In some areas, notably the Red Sea and Arabian Gulf, some parts of the Mediterranean and off the west coast of Africa, extra super-refraction conditions are accompanied by a dry sand haze which can severely restrict visibility, thus rendering visual comparison with the radar picture impossible.

Where conditions are unfavourable for visual comparison, some indications as to the second-trace nature of the echoes may be recognizable. The radar picture

should be compared with echoes from the coastline which might be expected from the vessel's present position. Where the DR position is sufficiently far in doubt, other effects should be sought.

Consider a long straight coastline which is returned as a second-trace echo. The coastline would be as depicted in Figure 3.66, with the distortion toward the origin of the display. Also, as the vessel steamed parallel to the coast, the 'point' of land would appear to remain abeam to starboard.

Alternatively, the relative track which the island would follow when plotted should be parallel to the heading marker but, as a second-trace echo, would produce a plotted apparent-motion line akin to the curve of the straight coastline. It might also move out of the band, either at long range or short range, and so disappear. The latter experience can be somewhat

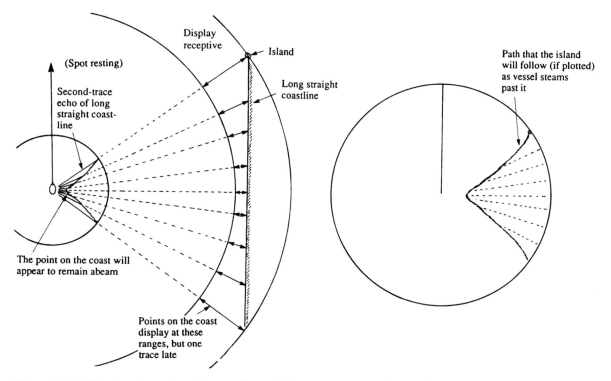

Figure 3.66 The distortion of a straight coastline which returns as a second-trace echo

disconcerting, especially as the 'target' would appear to be on a collision course for much of the time.

To assess (assuming atmospheric conditions are appropriate) whether it is possible for echoes to be second-trace or multi-trace, it is necessary to study the charted coastline and the accuracy with which the vessel's position is known. This must then be related to the radar's PRF and range scale in use at the time.

Example 3.5 An echo is observed at a range of 4 n miles but visual observation shows nothing in the vicinity of the vessel. If the PRF is 1000 pps and the 12 n mile range scale is in use at the time, what could be the range of the true target? (atmospheric conditions suggest extra super-refraction).

PRF = 1000 pps therefore PRP = 1000 μs, which relates to 80 n miles.

The bands from which echoes could return are

80–92 n miles   160–172 n miles
240–252 n miles . . .

therefore the target's range could be

84 n miles   164 n miles   244 n miles . . .

In general terms, it can be shown that

R_{nt} = PRP in n miles + target's displayed range

$$= \frac{8 \times 10^4 \times (n - 1)}{\text{PRF}} + R_d$$

where R_{nt} is the range (n miles) of an nth-trace echo
R_d is the displayed range of the target
n is the number of the trace on which the echo appears (the trace associated with transmission is counted as 1).

In the example above, if the false echo were third-trace then its range would be

$$R_{nt} = \left(\frac{80\,000 \times 2}{1000}\right) + 4\,n \text{ miles}$$

$$= 164\,n \text{ miles (as above)}$$

3.9.6.2 The elimination of second-trace echoes

By using a knowledge of the PRFs selected by the observer on the various range scales, it is possible to vary the areas from which second-trace echoes are possible.

If, in the example above, it had been possible to change from a PRF of 1000 to one of 500 pps then the bands at 80 and 240 n miles would have been eliminated. By observing what happened to the echo when this change was made, some deduction as to the true range of the target could have been made. If, after the change of PRF, the echo still remained, the true target must have been at a range of 164 n miles; if it had disappeared, then its true range could have been either 84 or 244 n miles with the former being more likely. The principle here is to change to a lower PRF by selecting a longer range scale. If this is to be done, a knowledge of the parameters of the particular radar is essential.

Some designers have appreciated this principle. By means of the false target elimination (FTE) control, one radar system allows the observer to deliberately change the PRF to one which is not a submultiple of the PRF in use at the time, and so move the bands to totally different areas which eliminate second-trace echoes arising from the original areas.

For a time, some radar systems incorporated an automatic elimination circuit which continually varied the PRF at a frequency of 50 Hz on the nominal value. This had the effect of moving the second-trace echo areas 50 times per second, which in turn had the effect of making the individual strikes of any second-trace echoes move in and out. Thus successive strikes would paint at different ranges and so would not line up side by side on the display and therefore

no recognizable paint would result (see Figure 3.67). These circuits have been fitted in some radars; because they require no action on the part of the observer and appear to have no side effects which give cause for concern, their presence has gone largely unnoticed.

3.9.7 False echoes from power cables

It has for some time been recognized that electromagnetic waves can react with the electromagnetic field surrounding a cable carrying a current in such a way that a false echo appears on the radar display. The false echo so produced will appear in the direction of the perpendicular from the vessel to the power cable and at the range of the cable (Figure 3.68).

Unfortunately, the actual power cable itself does not produce a response and so it can be very difficult to associate the observed echo with the cable and thereby have some indication that the echo may be false. Where the cable is at right angles to the channel, the false echo will appear in the channel so that, however the vessel manoeuvres in the channel to avoid it, the false echo will always move into the vessel's path.

Where the cable is angled across the waterway, the false echo may initially appear among the shore echoes and so go unnoticed, but as the vessel approaches the cable, the false echo will appear on the water as if from a vessel on a converging course.

Consider the situations illustrated in Figures 3.68(b) and 3.68(c). As the vessel approaches the cable, a 'vessel' would appear to put out from the starboard bank and proceed on a collision course. Any attempt by the observing vessel to pass under the 'stern' of the false echo would cause the false echo to return toward the bank, i.e. again into the vessel's path. If the observing vessel stopped, the 'target' would also appear to stop.

In Figure 3.68(c), the false echo would put out from the port bank, again on a collision course. Here the logical manoeuvre would be for the observing vessel to move farther over to the starboard side of the channel. The false echo would continue to crowd the observing vessel into the starboard bank. The result of

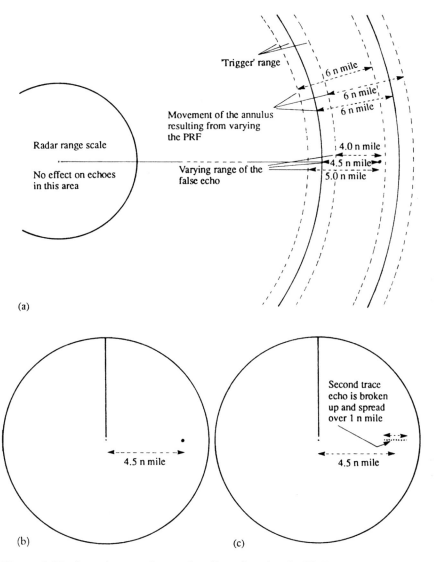

Figure 3.67 Second-trace echoes – the effect of varying the PRF
(a)   Effect on the standing pattern
(b)   The target as a second-trace echo with a fixed PRF
(c)   The effect of varying the PRF

stopping or a port manoeuvre would be as described above.

On some waterways, power cables have had radar reflectors fitted to them in order that their line will appear on the radar display. The unusual behaviour of echoes in the vicinity of the cable may thus be associated with the cable and should be treated with due caution.

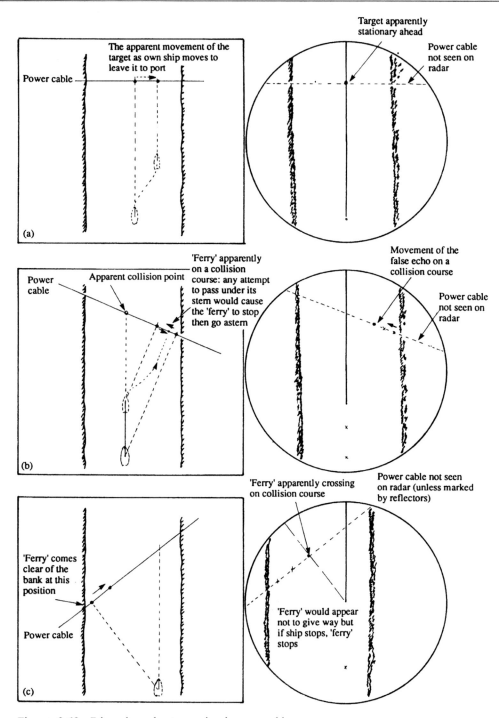

Figure 3.68 False echoes due to overhead power cables

3.10 Future advances in target detection

The ability to detect weak targets reliably in any type of clutter (background, sea or precipitation) is the fundamental function of a marine radar set. The relative merits of different display presentations, automatic or manual plotting, integrating with different equipment, etc., are secondary as without the reliable detection of targets the other radar features are meaningless. The principle of target detection in marine radar has traditionally been to detect targets with an amplitude level above that of clutter. The technology has become better and better at detecting smaller and irregular differences in amplitude between clutter. There is a body of expert opinion that suggests there will be very little ability to further improve detection of weak targets within clutter solely by the amplitude approach, in fact we may have already reached the peak.

However, existing technology already in use in other areas allows radio signals to be detected below the level of clutter. A classic navigation example is the use of coded radio signals in GPS (see Section 10.1). The receiver receives low power signals simultaneously from several satellites and background noise. They may all be at a higher level of amplitude than the specific satellite signal that the receiver would like to use. The receiver monitors and analyses the phase of signals received and detects the sequence (the code) of phase reversals to identify the satellite signal required and hence calculate the length of time the signal has travelled.

When a target reflects a radar signal it changes its properties of amplitude, phase, polarization and frequency. Different targets will cause different changes in these properties and hence by analysis of all the properties, a solid target can be identified from surrounding clutter caused by, for example, sea or rain. It is therefore likely that future improvements in target detection for marine radar are going to be achieved by controlling and monitoring more properties of the radar signal than just amplitude. One method currently already in use is the coherent radar system.

3.10.1 Coherent radar systems

A coherent radar system transmits a 'coded' radar signal carefully controlled and defined by amplitude, phase and frequency. The receiver monitors these three properties on any reflected signals received. Even if a solid target produces an amplitude of return less than the surrounding clutter, it will have minor differences in phase and frequency from the clutter that are detectable by the receiver. By this means the detection of weak radar targets would be greatly enhanced in any type of clutter, even if of lesser amplitude than the clutter.

The pulses are much longer than traditional (incoherent) radar pulses because there is no longer a theoretical minimum range problem (see Section 3.2.4). The receiver does not have to stop transmitting before reception because firstly, the power output is much lower and secondly, the receiver can separate the reflected signals from the transmitting signal, by using the same principles as it uses to differentiate between clutter and targets. The longer (sometimes continuous) signal improves the chance of detection because an area is effectively searched for a much longer period of time.

Coherent radar systems are currently in use for certain mapping, meteorological and military systems. The attraction to the military is that the power output is significantly lower (watts instead of kilowatts) so it is much more difficult for a potential enemy to detect when radar is being operated. The maximum range of marine coherent radar will be less than traditional incoherent radar, but coherent radar should be able to reach the IMO Performance Standards that require a maximum range scale of 24 nautical miles and a maximum target detection range of 20 nautical miles (see Section 11.2.1). It is questionable if mariners need radar range scales in excess of 24 nautical miles.

The power reduction has two other significant advantages that may affect the use of the two major components of marine radar for many years past, the magnetron and the mechanical rotating scanner.

3.10.1.1   Transmission device

The magnetron is presently the only practical device capable of producing a radar pulse of sufficient power at the X-band and S-band frequencies. However, the power levels required for coherent radar at these frequencies can be produced by solid-state circuitry. The advantage is that the high voltages will no longer be required in a radar set (see Section 2.7.7) and more importantly the frequencies (including harmonics) transmitted can be more carefully controlled.

The cavity magnetron is often criticized because it produces significant out-of-band transmissions, which is an increasingly important issue as more use is made of this part of the radio frequency spectrum by other users, particularly communications users. One advantage of producing out-of-band transmissions in incoherent traditional radar is that it improves the 'squareness' of the short pulses (see Section 2.5.2.4) and increases range measurement accuracy. This is less important in coherent radar as any part of the radar signal can be identified for accurate measurement not just the front edge of the pulse. The use of solid-state devices with filters will significantly reduce the interference to other spectrum users outside the radar bands. Indeed, if marine radar were a new product introduced today, it would be unlikely to get approval from radio regulatory authorities.

Furthermore, the bandwidth of the radar signal used can be much narrower and tightly filtered on in-band frequencies, reducing the range of transmission frequencies used by any one radar within the permitted X- or S-band. This will reduce the interference caused to other radar users on the same band, as well as encourage the use of more sensitive narrow bandwidth receivers (see Section 2.5.2.4).

The transmission device would also be more flexible, as it would control its frequency more precisely. Therefore, if the receiver on one set detects transmission from another set it could intelligently adjust its own transmission frequency slightly (perhaps only for that bearing sector) resulting in less interference for both sets.

3.10.1.2   Aerial system

The low transmission power permitted by using coherent radar also means that a radar phased array aerial system could replace the mechanical rotating aerial. The phased array system is a fixed structure and apart from eliminating the mechanical parts, it enables a more varied and intelligent use of the aerial beam to search for targets. This is covered in more detail in Section 2.4.7.

3.10.1.3   The future

In summary, there are outside pressures to make more efficient use of the radio spectrum and stop out-of-band transmissions. Coherent radar offers an alternative and more efficient use of the radar spectrum, with the added benefits of better target detection in clutter, better reliability, and smaller and lighter equipment. Recent changes in regulations have been made to allow coherent radar techniques for civil radar. The main change was because such devices would not meet the then current IMO specifications, particularly in regard to SARTs and racons (see Section 3.5) as only high power short pulses activate them. A rethink in future radar and other equipment provision was therefore required.

In the new regulations (see Section 11.2.1) allow only X-band radars are required to trigger and detect SARTS and racons. S-band can therefore now be developed for coherent radar. In future, there will probably be a decline in dual frequency and S-band racons. SARTs already work only on X-band, so this change does not affect it. All ships are required to have X-band equipment (see Section 4.1.3), but not S-band so the racons and SARTS system would work on just X-band.

Other potential ideas for the future are that SARTs and racons may be replaced with AIS devices so that the information will display on AIS displays. During the period of changeover there could be dual devices (i.e. SART and AIS or racon and AIS). Another alternative is that there is a redesign of SARTs and racons to be compatible with coherent radar.

4 Automatic target tracking, specified facilities

4.1   Introduction

With computers developing at an ever-increasing pace, it was only a matter of time before their capabilities were harnessed to assist the mariner in resolving the continuing problem of tracking targets and analysing movements when faced with heavy traffic.

In the past, many semi-automatic devices were developed to assist in this task. The first device recognized by IMO and other regulatory bodies was called Automatic Radar Plotting Aid (ARPA). Performance Standards were provided for the ARPA and it was a requirement for there to be a navigator trained on ARPA on the bridge, if one was fitted. It gradually became a requirement that larger ships were fitted with ARPA, although they were often found on other ships.

In the IMO Performance Standards of 1997, a slightly reduced specification was defined for smaller ships or for a second plotting device on larger ships. This was termed an Auto-Tracking Aid (ATA) which has many (but not quite all) of the features of an ARPA. These differences are explored in Section 4.1.3. At the same time the IMO specified the standards for an Electronic Plotting Aid (EPA) that aids manual plotting for installation on very small ships and which is covered in Section 7.11.4.

The latest standards (see Section 11.2.1), which will apply to new vessels from 2008, have removed the previous separate terminology of ARPA and ATA and instead refer to both as 'Automatic Target Tracking' (ATT). The EPA device mentioned in the 1997 regulations has also disappeared from the new regulations, as all SOLAS vessels are now required to have an ATT. The main difference is that ATT for larger vessels is required to have a trial manoeuvre facility and automatic acquisition (see Table 4.2).

One suspects that the industry will continue to refer to the ATT and ATA devices as an ARPA for a significant time period. ATA has not entered into the standard seafarer vocabulary even after many years. It is therefore predicted that ARPA will remain the generic name for all ATT devices even if not strictly correct according to the performance standards (see Section 11.2.1).

The original IMO Performance Standards for ATA and ARPA both state that they should:

'...reduce the workload of observers by enabling them to automatically obtain information about plotted targets, so that they can perform as well with several separate targets as they can by manually plotting a single target'.

Although this statement is not in the latest IMO Performance Standards, it still remains a good description of the function of automatic radar plotting aids.

4.1.1 Integral and stand-alone displays

When ARPA was first introduced, many of the installations were 'add-ons' to the existing conventional radars. They provided all of the ARPA facilities, but they derived their data from a host radar. The attraction was that the installation expense was reduced and the existing radar retained. Such displays became known as stand-alone ARPAs. It was never an ideal solution and very few, if any, such stand-alone equipment exists today.

In modern integral equipment all radar, tracked targets and data from other sources are processed in one unit and shown on one display. This has considerable operational and processing advantages.

4.1.2 Current plotting carriage requirements, standards and operator training (1997 and 2001 standards)

In this section the current requirements for a new vessel are covered. Section 4.1.3 will cover the performance standards for vessels built after 1 July 2008.

IMO Performance Standards define the standards for an ATA. These are almost identical to the IMO Performance Standards for an ARPA. The ATA is intended for smaller ships or as a second plotting device on larger ships. Table 4.1 summarizes the carriage requirements for radar and plotting devices on new vessels as stated by the IMO-SOLAS Chapter V as amended 2001 (see Section 11.1). The fullblown ARPA is only a requirement for vessels above 10 000 grt and even then the second radar can be fitted with an ATA. Ships between 500 grt and 10 000 grt are not required to carry an ARPA, but

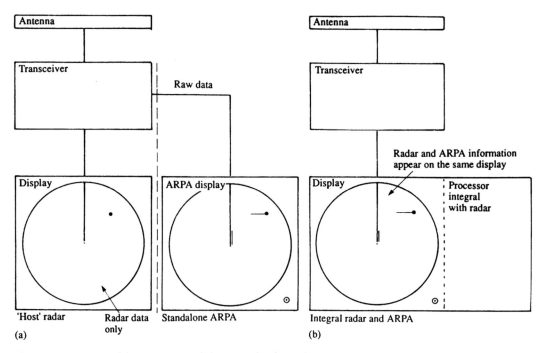

Figure 4.1 (a) Standalone ARPA and (b) integral radar and ARPA

Table 4.1 Minimum IMO radar and plotting provision for new ships

Ship size	Radar	Plotting	Display diameter
300–499 grt (and all passenger vessels below 300 grt)	1 X-band radar	EPA or equivalent	180 mm
500–2999 grt	1 X-band radar	ATA	<1000 grt: 180 mm ≥ 1000 grt: 250 mm
3000–9999 grt	1 X-band 1 S-band (or second X-band)	2 ATA	250 mm
10 000+ grt	1 X-band 1 S-band (or second X-band)	1 ARPA 1 ATA	340 mm

only one or two ATAs depending on their size. Vessels under 500 grt are not required to have auto-tracking devices of any kind, but are required to have an electronic aid to manual plotting (see EPA, Section 7.11.4).

New ships carrying ARPA and ATA also require an integrated input from a gyro and a water track speed log.

The differences between the IMO Performance Standards of an ATA and ARPA are summarized in Table 4.2. Essentially, the regulations for ATA are identical apart from a few omissions in the case of the ATA standard.

As noted in Section 4.2.6, automatic acquisition has not been found as useful as first predicted (for a vessel underway) when ARPA standards were first introduced. This omission from ATA standards reflects this low usage and usefulness. The logic for the lower minimum number of tracked targets follows mainly by removing this automatic acquisition option. There is also a school of thought that too many tracked targets simply clutter up the screen. Therefore, it would follow that ten tracked targets are more than adequate, provided the navigator selects the ten targets having the most potential threat. Many ATA models offer more than ten targets anyway. Similarly, the history dot option (see Section 4.3.7) is one not often used in practice, especially as manufacturers provide a traditional smear 'snail' trail (true or relative track) to show

Table 4.2 Differences between minimum ARPA and ATA standards for new ships

	ATA	ARPA
Acquisition (see Section 4.2)	Manual	Manual and (optionally) automatic
Minimum tracked target capability (see Section 4.2)	10	20
History dots (see Section 4.3.7)	None required	4 equally spaced past positions over time period suitable for range scale
Trial manoeuvre (see Section 4.4.3)	None	Yes, including with or without a time delay

target progress. The biggest loss of function between the ATA and the ARPA is probably the lack of a trial manoeuvre facility (see Section 4.4.3).

All told, the differences between ARPA and ATA are actually quite small and one would speculate that the difference in costs of production between a minimum specification ARPA and a minimum specification ATA is actually quite small (mainly software and computer memory). The most significant cost

at the time of writing the regulations would probably have been the smaller minimum screen size (see
Table 4.1), but all display screens have since come
down in price (see Section 2.6.7.13). In practice,
many ARPAs have additional facilities (see Chapter 5)
and the differences between an ATA model and an
ARPA model may be that the ATA has significantly
less (or none) of the optional features, in order to
make a significant difference in cost between the
two sets.

Ever since ARPA was introduced, most maritime
administrations have insisted that the operator should
be specifically trained to use the ARPA and not just
in radar observer manual plotting techniques. For
instance UK regulations state that:

'When a UK ship which is required to be fitted with
ARPA is at sea and a radar watch is being kept on the
ARPA, the installation shall be under the control of a
person qualified in the operational use of ARPA, who
may be assisted by unqualified personnel'. (Edited extract
from UK SI 1993 No. 69, part IX, see Section 11.4.2.)

The ATA has no such provision and would come
under the regulation for radar, not ARPA. For instance
in UK ships, it would come under the requirement:

'While a UK ship which is required to be fitted with a
radar installation is at sea and a radar watch is being kept,
the radar installation shall be under the control of a qualified radar observer who may be assisted by unqualified
personnel'. (Extract from UK SI 1993 No. 69, part IV,
see Section 11.4.1.)

It is hard to justify the difference in minimum training
between an ATA and an ARPA on the basis of the
difference in features. The only basis for the difference in training is that personnel who are not ARPA
trained are effectively restricted to smaller vessels, and
traditionally smaller vessels have always had lesser qualifications. However, it is a tradition that does not stand
up to close scrutiny as smaller vessels often spend more
time in high-density traffic and navigate in waters with
little sea room.

4.1.3 Future carriage requirements, standards and operator training

The carriage requirements for the IMO Performance
Standards applicable to new installations from 2008
(see Section 11.2.1) are listed in Table 4.3.

One difference (already noted) is in the terminology, in that ATA and ARPA have been replaced

Table 4.3 Differences in the performance requirements for various sizes of ship/craft to which SOLAS applies

Size of ship/craft	<500 grt	500 grt to <10 000 grt and HSC <10 000 grt	All ships/craft ≥ 10 000 grt
Minimum operational display area diameter	180 mm	250 mm	320 mm
Minimum display area	195×195 mm	270×270 mm	340×340 mm
Auto acquisition of targets	—	—	Yes
Minimum *acquired* radar target capacity	20	30	40
Minimum *activated* AIS target capacity	20	30	40
Minimum *sleeping* AIS target capacity	100	150	200
Trial manoeuvre	—	—	Yes

by automatic target tracking (ATT). However, functionally the differences for small and large ships are very similar to the standards covered in the previous section.

The two main functional differences from the previous standards are the requirement for an automatic target tracker on vessels less than 500 grt instead of the EPA device and the specific requirement to include information from AIS targets (see Section 11.4 for a full discussion of AIS).

Other differences are that the minimum number of radar tracked targets has been increased for all ship sizes and that the standards have split ship sizes into three categories not four. Effectively, the 500 to 3000 grt category has now been merged with the 3000 to 10 000 grt.

The new regulations also make a separate distinction between the operational radar display diameter and the dimensions of the display screen of which the operational radar is a part. There is an implicit assumption that the display is rectangular and therefore that raster display technology is used.

At the time of publication it is not clear how training standards will be applied for the new equipment standards and if the current distinction which requires specific training on large vessel equipment (the old ARPA) and basic radar training on smaller vessels (the old ATA) will continue.

4.1.4 Compliance with the IMO Performance Standards

Irrespective of which type of equipment is installed, it is still necessary for it to comply with the IMO Performance Standards as well as with the various requirements of national legislation. Only the facilities which are specified by the IMO Performance Standards will be considered in this chapter. Where appropriate, at the beginning of each relevant section, extracts from the current IMO Performance Standards for ARPAs and ATAs will be quoted (in the form of indented paragraphs) to the extent necessary to support the section. Generally, the differences between ARPA

and ATA are the same as the distinction between vessels of more than and less than 10 000 grt in the future standards for 2008.

4.2 The acquisition of targets

Acquisition is the term used to describe the process whereby target tracking is initiated. This may be 'manual', in which case the operator, using the screen marker (see below) indicates to the computer which targets are to be tracked, or may be 'automatic', when the computer is programmed to acquire targets which enter specified boundaries. When a target is 'acquired', the computer starts collecting data relating to that target.

A graphic symbol known as the *screen marker*, controlled by a joystick or tracker ball, is positioned over the target. When the 'acquire' button is pressed, an area centred on the screen marker is defined within the computer memory. This area is termed the 'tracking gate' or 'tracking window'. The gate is made to appear automatically on some ARPA displays; on others, the operator may display it if desired. Within the gate, the computer will expect to find evidence of a target, i.e. a binary 1 in the appropriate memory location (see Sections 2.6.6.1 and 4.3.6).

4.2.1 The acquisition specification

Target acquisition may be manual or automatic for relative speeds up to 100 knots. However, there should always be a facility to provide for manual acquisition and cancellation. ARPAs with automatic acquisition should have a facility to suppress acquisition in certain areas. On any range scale where acquisition is suppressed over a certain area, the area of acquisition should be indicated on the display.

Automatic or manual acquisition should have a performance not inferior to that which could be obtained by the user of the radar display.

If automatic acquisition is provided, a description of the criteria of selection of targets for tracking should be provided to the user.

Although it would seem that anything is possible in today's technological climate, some practical problems still exist and fully automatic acquisition systems do not give quite the results which one might have been led to expect. The main problem with automatic acquisition is that the 'sensitivity' of the detection circuitry, if set too high, will acquire thermal noise and clutter, leading to false alarms, while if its sensitivity is reduced, poor-response targets can evade the plotter.

The ATA acquisition is simpler as it only covers manual acquisitions.

4.2.2   Manual acquisition (Figure 4.2)

In this case, the operator specifies the target to be acquired and subsequently tracked. To do this, a joystick and screen marker or tracker ball and screen marker are used. The target is entered into (acquired) or removed from (cancelled) the computer memory when the *acquire* or *cancel* button is pressed.

In some ARPAs, tracking can be initiated by touching the position of the target on a special touch-sensitive screen (see Section 2.6.7.3).

This is the only acquisition type in an ATA (vessels <10 000 grt). Sections 4.2.3 to 4.2.6 are not relevant to the ATA.

4.2.3   Fully automatic acquisition

Every echo (up to some 200 maximum) which is detected in the receiver is tested against a set of published criteria. Large (land-sized) targets are rejected and the remainder prioritized according to the set criteria. (*Note* This may only be on the basis of range, e.g. the nearest 20, or, at the other extreme, it may involve tests of CPA, TCPA, range, bearing and other criteria). Tracking is then initiated on the first 20 in the priority order. Targets at the bottom of the list are deleted or acquired as their ranking changes, e.g. a target moving away may be dropped when there are 20 nearer than it. Some ARPAs have more complicated priority criteria where parameters can be varied by the operator.

4.2.4   Automatic acquisition by area (Figure 4.3)

In this type, an area around the ship is specified by the operator and any target that is detected within this

Figure 4.2 Manual acquisition

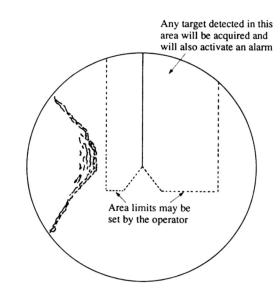

Figure 4.3 Automatic acquisition by area

area is acquired. Some prioritizing system must operate when the number of targets exceeds the number of tracking channels.

4.2.5 Guard zones (Figure 4.4)

In this system, zones (usually up to two) may be specified by arc and depth. Targets entering the zone will be acquired and an alarm activated. A 'tracks full' warning will be given when all tracking channels are in use and it will then be up to the operator to decide which of the acquired targets can be cancelled.

Note Target 'A' may only be acquired at a late stage in the encounter and target 'B', which appears for the first time inside the inner zone, may not be acquired at all. Careful thought must be given when setting up guard zones and the display must be regularly observed.

4.2.6 Guard rings and area rejection boundaries (ARBs)

With this method of acquisition, the usual provision is for up to two 'rings' (of predetermined depth) plus

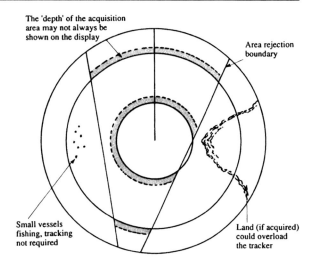

Figure 4.5   Guard rings and ARBs

up to two area rejection boundaries (ARBs). The rings and ARBs may be positioned by the operator (Figure 4.5).

When a target is automatically acquired in a guard zone/guard area, it is usual for an alarm to be activated to attract the operator's attention (see Section 4.7.1). The target activating the alarm will be indicated on the screen by, for example, a flashing symbol.

In general, automatic acquisition has not been as successful as was at first predicted. There is a tendency to acquire sea clutter, rain clutter, noise and interference, while disassociated elements of land echoes will very quickly fill up the available tracking channels. Land echoes can be excluded by careful setting of the zones/areas and ARBs, but spurious targets (e.g. clutter), after having been acquired, are quickly lost and the 'lost target' alarm can sound continually.

While it is argued that automatic aquisition will reduce the operator's workload, in practice there is a tendency for it to acquire spurious targets, also to 'over-acquire' and so clutter the screen with unnecessary and unwanted vectors. This has led to auto-acquisition falling out of favour. Enquiries have indicated that it is rarely used in areas of high-density traffic, but can be useful on long ocean passages where

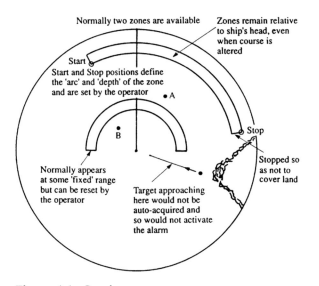

Figure 4.4   Guard zones

the number of targets is small and there is the danger of loss of concentration by the officer of the watch due to boredom.

Manual acquisition can be very quick and also selective and hence the perceived need for automatic acquisition has not really materialized.

Guard zones/areas should be regarded as an additional, rather than an alternative means of keeping a proper lookout.

4.3   The tracking of targets

4.3.1   The tracking specification

If the ARPA does not track all targets visible on the display, targets which are being tracked should be clearly indicated with the relevant symbol on the display. The reliability of tracking should not be less than that obtainable using manual recordings of successive target positions obtained from the radar display.

In many cases it may be obvious that a target is being tracked by virtue of the fact that its predicted movement will be indicated by a graphic line known as a vector (see Section 4.4). The line originates on the target and its remote end indicates the predicted position of the target after an elapsed time selected by the observer. However, the need for tracked targets to be clearly indicated on the display is important because in the early stages (up to about one minute) of tracking a fresh target, in most systems the vector is suppressed because the available data is unlikely to be sufficiently accurate or stable. Furthermore, in certain cases, even when the vector is present it may have zero length (e.g. the true vector of a stationary target or the relative vector of a target on the same course and speed as the observing vessel).

Once tracking is initiated, by whatever method, the tracker will continue to follow the target until tracking is cancelled (manually, or automatically because some

other criterion has been met, e.g. 'more than 16 miles away and range increasing') or the target is 'lost'.

The precise nature of the algorithms used to ensure that the tracking window will faithfully follow the target varies with manufacturer. The fine detail of such methods are beyond the scope of this text but the general principle can be illustrated by the following description of the technique known as *rate aiding*.

4.3.2   Rate aiding

When the target is first acquired, a large gate is necessary since there is uncertainty as to the direction in which the target will move. Figure 4.6 shows how successive positions can be used to improve the forecast of the next position in which the target is expected to appear. The radius of the gate is really a measure of confidence in the tracking and the smaller this value becomes, the more precise the prediction will be. In this way it is possible to establish a feedback loop in the computer which will progressively reduce the size of the tracking gate.

The advantages of a reduced tracking gate are:

(a)   A lower likelihood of target swap (see Section 4.3.5).
(b)   An improved ability to track targets through rain and sea clutter.
(c)   An ability to continue tracking, even when target response is intermittent.

One problem which can arise with reduced gate size is that if a target manoeuvres and, as a result, is not found by the computer in the predicted position, the computer may continue to track and look in the predicted direction and end up by losing the target altogether. To avoid this possibility, as soon as the target is missed, i.e. not found in the predicted position, the gate size is increased (and the tracking duration reduced – see Section 4.3.6). If the target is still detectable and subsequently found, the tracking will resume and a new track will gradually stabilize.

If, after six fruitless scans, the target is still not found then an alarm is activated and a flashing marker

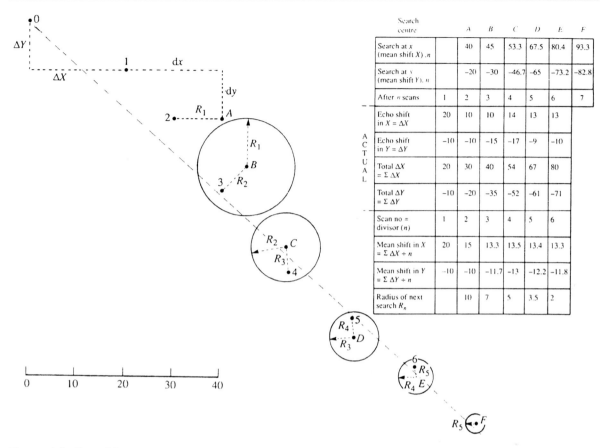

	Search centre	A	B	C	D	E	F
Search at x (mean shift X) .n			40	45	53.3	67.5	80.4	93.3
Search at y (mean shift Y). n			-20	-30	-46.7	-65	-73.2	-82.8
After n scans	1	2	3	4	5	6	7
Echo shift in X = ΔX		20	10	10	14	13	13
Echo shift in Y = ΔY		-10	-10	-15	-17	-9	-10
Total ΔX = ΣΔX		20	30	40	54	67	80
Total ΔY = ΣΔY		-10	-20	-35	-52	-61	-71
Scan no = divisor (n)		1	2	3	4	5	6
Mean shift in X = ΣΔX ÷ n		20	15	13.3	13.5	13.4	13.3
Mean shift in Y = ΣΔY ÷ n		-10	-10	-11.7	-13	-12.2	-11.8
Radius of next search R_n			10	7	5	3.5	2

(Column block below "Echo shift" rows is labelled vertically: ACTUAL)

Figure 4.6 Rate aiding

is displayed at the target's last observed position (see Section 4.7.3).

4.3.3 The number of targets to be tracked

The ARPA should be able to automatically track, process, simultaneously display and continuously update the information on at least 20 targets, whether manually or automatically acquired.

The ATA Performance Standard is the same except 10 tracking channels are required and not 20. However,

from 2008, the minimum requirement is 20 to 40 (see Table 4.3).

It has been suggested that even 20 tracking channels might be insufficient in heavy traffic but from practical experience it has been found that ship's officers can quickly identify the targets which need to be tracked and acquire them. (Although at times there will be some 40 plus targets on the screen, not all of them will need to be tracked.) In fact, it has been found that an excess of vectors can produce 'ARPA clutter' and be counter-productive.

It should be noted that a higher tracking capability is required by the Performance Standard where the manufacturer has the option to provide automatic acquisition. This recognizes the tendency of the latter facility to over-acquire (see Section 4.2.6) and compensates for it to some extent.

4.3.4   Target loss

The ARPA (or auto-tracking) should continue to track an acquired target which is clearly distinguishable on the display for 5 out of 10 consecutive scans, provided the target is not subject to target swap (see Section 4.3.5).

(The term *scan* tends to be used rather loosely in radar terminology. Sometimes it is used to describe one line, as in the term 'interscan period', while on other occasions it refers to one aerial rotation. In the above context it refers to the latter.)

It should be noted here that if, for some reason, a response from a tracked target is not received on a particular scan, the ARPA must not immediately declare the target lost. Also it is implied that some form of 'search' for it must take place, e.g. by opening the tracking gate rather than merely looking in the limited area in which it was expected but failed to be detected.

4.3.5   Target swap (Figure 4.7)

The possibility of tracking errors, including target swap, should be minimized by ARPA (and auto-tracking) design. A qualitative description of the effects of error sources on the automatic tracking and corresponding errors should be provided to the user, including the effects of low signal-to-noise and low signal-to-clutter ratios caused by sea returns, rain, snow, low clouds and non-synchronous emissions.

Target swap is likely when two targets respond within the tracking gate at the same time. When this happens, the tracker can become confused and the vector(s) may transfer to the wrong target. To minimize this problem, the gate should be made as small as possible, the movement of the target should be predicted and the gate moved on at each scan as described under 'rate aiding' (see Section 4.3.2).

Figure 4.7 Target swap

The two requirements that target swap be minimized by the ARPA (and auto-tracking) design and that tracking be continued even if no response is received for a period of time are thus to some extent achieved by the common solution of rate aiding.

4.3.6   The analysis of tracks and the display of data

When a target appears on the radar and, in the case of automatic acquisition, enters within the acquisition area chosen by the observer or, in the case of manual acquisition, has been acquired by the observer, the ARPA should present, in a period of not more than 1 minute, an indication of the target's motion trend and display, within 3 minutes, the target's predicted motion in accordance with the Performance Standard described in Sections 9.2 and 9.3 of this textbook.

The paragraphs to which this section of the Performance Standards refer specify the format in which the data must be displayed and also set out accuracy levels which must be achieved. It would have been preferable for the contents of these paragraphs to be reproduced within the above extract. This is not practical since they are necessarily detailed because a number of formats such as vector, alphanumeric and graphic areas can be used and moreover the potential accuracy is a function of the geometry of the OAW triangle and must be stated in terms of specified scenarios (see Figures 9.1 to 9.4). In each case two levels of accuracy are specified:

1   A lower level relating to the target's motion trend, which is an early indication of the target's relative motion.
2   A higher level relating to the target's predicted motion; this means the best possible estimate of the target's relative and true motion data.

The contents of the various paragraphs are examined in detail in Sections 9.1 to 9.4. However, for the general discussion of tracking philosophy which follows, it is adequate to appreciate that essentially the Performance Standard requires the computer to deduce and display relative motion data to a specified level of accuracy after one minute of steady state tracking, and both relative and true motion data to a higher specified accuracy after 3 minutes of steady state tracking. Steady state tracking means that neither the target nor the observing vessel has manoeuvred and no significant change has taken place in the errors of the input sensors.

There is no difference between the ATA and ARPA standards with respect to these issues.

4.3.6.1   General tracker philosophy

In order to calculate the data required by the Performance Standard, the computer must store sequential positions of each tracked target and then analyse the movement represented by such successive positions so as to evaluate the relative motion and the true motion of each target. The computer is thus required to automate the operation which has traditionally been carried out manually by the recording of successive target positions (either by the plotting of ranges and bearings on a paper sheet or by the use of a reflection plotter) and the subsequent resolution of the OAW triangle (see Chapter 7). Automation of any process normally carried out by an intelligent being is always complex. The injection of pseudo-intelligence and the difficulty of satisfying conflicting requirements gives considerable scope to the inventiveness of the designer and it is not surprising that various solutions to the problem exist, all of which differ in mathematical detail to a greater or lesser extent. A detailed consideration of the options open to the designer in carrying out the data processing is beyond the scope of this text, but it is important for the observer to have some general knowledge of how the operation relates to the way in which the same task would be tackled by manual plotting. This understanding is relevant not only to the above extract from the Performance Standard but to that of Section 4.3.1, which requires the results to be at least as good as would be obtained by using manual recordings, and to the introduction to the Performance Standards (see Section 4.1), which requires that the ARPA (or auto-tracking) should enable observers to perform as well with multiple targets as they can by manually plotting a single target. It should thus be appreciated that the ARPA (or auto-tracking) is carrying out a task which could be undertaken manually by an observer, given the time and the inclination, and that there is no reason to believe that the results obtained by an ARPA (or auto-tracking) are any better, or any worse, than those that can be achieved by such an observer.

For acceptance by the ARPA (or auto-tracking) data must be in digital form, since the necessary calculations must be performed by a digital computer. Thus, in the first instance, the analogue radar data must be stored, radial line by radial line, in a digital memory. The presence of a response will be registered as a binary 1 in the appropriate range cell(s) and will be associated with the appropriate bearing word, as was described for the general radar memory in Section 2.6.6.3. Filtering techniques are used to establish the likelihood of any particular response being a target and hence whether or not it should be stored for tracking purposes. During each timebase the detected responses are read into what is known as the *prime register*, which is a group of memory elements of the form shown by one line of the memory matrix illustrated in Figure 2.39. During the rest (or interscan) period, the contents of the prime register are transferred into the number one register which is the first of a group of N identical registers. At the same time the contents of number one are transferred into number two, and so on down the group. The contents of the Nth register (i.e. the oldest data) are discarded. During the transfer period a comparison is made of the contents of the N cells in each column and if more than M out of N cells in the column contain a binary 1, a hit is registered in the correct location in a further section of the tracker memory which holds only filtered responses. The filtering technique helps to reduce the probability of false echoes reaching the tracker and also improves the chances of a real but weak or intermittent response being tracked.

Targets within the filtered area of the memory are selected for tracking when, either manually or automatically, a gate is placed over their responses. As the aerial beam sweeps past a ship-target, it will register a number of strikes (see Section 2.4.4) on successive timebases and it may be that such a target activates more than one successive radial range cell. In the case of picture storage (see Section 2.6.6.5) these digitized responses will aggregate in the memory to generate on the display an echo having the outline of the distinctive echo paint (see Section 2.6.5). Clearly it is neither necessary nor desirable for the computer to track each individual element present in the resolution cell. For this reason the input responses to the tracker are processed to produce a single registration which represents the location of the target to be tracked and

about which the gate will in due course attempt to centre itself. The area of memory which is used to store the assembly of such registrations is known as the *hit matrix*.

If the target has been acquired, and is being successfully tracked, a tracking window will be centred on that particular memory location within the hit matrix which corresponds with the target's range and bearing. The co-ordinates of the window can be extracted and stored in a further area of the tracker memory. This area is sometimes referred to as the *track file* and there will have to be a separate track file for each tracked target. Thus, rotation by rotation, as the gate moves in steps following the target's position through the hit matrix, sequential positions of each tracked target can be stored in the appropriate track file.

The processor (which is that part of the computer which manipulates the data and carries out the mathematical operations) must operate on the recorded positions to calculate the most probable track of the target. It is difficult to carry out calculations based on positions which are expressed in terms of range and bearing because the rates at which the bearing and range change are not constant for a target on a straight track. Further, the spatial resolution varies with range (i.e. it is geometrical). For these reasons it is usual to convert the target positions into cartesian co-ordinates of northings and eastings, the mathematical operation being the same as that described for scan conversion in Section 2.6.7.2.

When laying off observed ranges and bearings on a plotting sheet (see Section 7.8) the effect of inherent errors is that, even for a target on a steady track, the plotted positions do not form a perfectly straight line but are scattered about the correct track; the observer has to attempt to draw the line that is the best fit. Exactly the same effect occurs with automatic plotting and it is further exacerbated by quantizing errors introduced by the digital storage (see Sections 2.6.6.1 and 9.5). Since the data must eventually be displayed as a stable straight line vector, the processor must calculate a length and direction which represents the best fit to the scattered observations. This operation is known as smoothing and involves the application of quite complex mathematical techniques such as Kalman filtering, the mechanics of which are beyond the scope of this text. However, it is important for the observer to appreciate that such smoothing does take place and to understand the implications.

If the smoothing is carried out over too long a period, the tracker will be insensitive to changes in tracks as a result of which small manoeuvres may go undetected and there will be a long delay before large manoeuvres become apparent. On the other hand, if smoothing is carried out over a short period, the output data will fluctuate, rendering decision-making difficult. Clearly the amount and duration of smoothing is a compromise and the difficulty of reconciling the twin requirements of sensitivity to target manoeuvres and data stability provides the designer with a considerable challenge. As a result, the particular algorithms used for smoothing vary in detail with manufacturer.

When a target is first acquired, the computer will commence storing positions, obtaining updated co-ordinates each time the aerial sweeps across the target (i.e. about once every 3–5 seconds). These positions will have an inherent scatter and initially the mean line will be very sensitive to plots which fall some distance from it. However, as the plotting duration increases and more plots are obtained, the mean line will stabilize and accuracy will improve. During the first minute of tracking the target will normally display only a symbol to indicate that it is being tracked. In most systems the vector (or other graphical indication of target movement) will be suppressed until sufficient observations have been obtained to produce the indication of the target's motion trend to the level of accuracy required by the Performance Standard. Some systems were designed to display vectors within a few seconds of acquisition. This should not be seen as a sign of instant accuracy. Accuracy demands a number of successive observations and until the one minute interval has elapsed there is no requirement to meet the Performance Standard accuracy. Any data derived directly or indirectly from these very early indications could be highly misleading. In general, where such early display takes place, a study of the instability of the vector (or other indication of movement) should convince the user that it is based on insufficient observations. After one minute the tracker will have smoothed about 12–20 observations and must then produce data to the lower of the two accuracy levels set out in the Performance Standard. In some systems a graphic symbol on the target is used to indicate that the data is based on more than one but less than 3 minutes of observation. As long as the target continues to be detected at the location predicted by the rate aiding (see Section 4.3.2), the tracking period is allowed to build up to three minutes, at which stage the processor will be able to smooth some 36–60 observations and must then reach the higher accuracy level. Thereafter as each new plot is added the *oldest* is discarded.

If a target response is not detected in the location forecast by the rate aiding, one possible explanation is that the target has manoeuvred. The tracking gate will be opened out and if the target is detected, tracking will continue. If the departure from the three-minute track is not significant, the processor will conclude that the departure was due to scatter and will continue to smooth the track over a period of 3 minutes. On the other hand, if the departure is significant, the processor will treat the situation as a target manoeuvre and will reduce the smoothing period to one minute. This reduction in smoothing period is analogous to the situation in which an observer decides that a target has manoeuvred and therefore discards a previous *OAW* triangle and starts a new plot. If steady state conditions resume, low level accuracy must be obtained within one minute and then the tracking period can again be allowed to build up to 3 minutes, allowing high level accuracy to be regained.

Most systems have two smoothing periods, a short period of about one minute and a long period of about three minutes. For compliance with the Performance Standard the periods must not be more than 1 minute or 3 minutes respectively but in practice manufacturers quite often use slightly shorter periods and hence reach the required accuracy a little more quickly than the standard requires.

While the mathematical detail of the smoothing is beyond the scope of this work, what is of importance to the observer is the question of whether the smoothing is performed on the relative tracks or on the true tracks. This is a fundamental decision which must be taken by the designer and there are merits in both choices.

In general trackers will *either*

(a) smooth and store the relative track of a target to produce directly the output relative-motion data and hence calculate the true-motion data from the smoothed relative-track data and the instantaneous input course and speed data, which is normally unsmoothed to avoid any loss of sensitivity to manoeuvres by the observing vessel; *or*

(b) smooth and store the true track of a target to produce directly the smoothed true-motion data and reconstitute the relative-motion data from the smoothed true-track data and the (normally unsmoothed) input course and speed data.

Note In order to smooth and store true tracks, the normally unsmoothed course and speed data are applied to the raw relative-motion data (see Section 4.3.6.3).

In the steady state situation, i.e. where neither tracked target nor the observing vessel manoeuvres and no changes take place in any errors in the input data, both approaches will produce the same result. If a change takes place, the two different approaches will produce differing results over the succeeding smoothing period. To understand the differences it is necessary to consider in general terms how the calculations are performed.

4.3.6.2 *The storage of relative data*

In this approach the ranges and bearings of the tracked target are scan-converted, smoothed and stored to produce the direction and rate of the target's relative motion. The displayed relative vector (see Section 4.4.1) and the CPA/TCPA (see Section 4.6) data are derived directly from this, as illustrated by Figure 4.8. The merit of this approach is that, just as when an observer constructs a relative plot, the CPA data is totally independent of the course and speed inputs to the system. This is a feature which many users believe to be of paramount importance

because they take the view that the miss distance ranks in importance above all other data.

If the true-motion data relating to the target is requested, the computer will calculate that information by vector addition of the instantaneous course and speed data to the smoothed relative track. Thus, as might be expected, the accuracy of the true-motion data depends on the accuracy of the input course and speed data (see Section 9.6.3). Where trial manoeuvre data (see Section 4.4.3) is requested, the vector addition will involve the smoothed relative track and the proposed course and speed.

An inherent difficulty which besets relative track storage is that if the observing vessel manoeuvres, the direction and rate of the relative track of all targets will change. There will thus be a tendency for the relative vectors to become unstable, because the tracker is vainly attempting to smooth a curve to produce a straight line. It follows that, during the time of the manoeuvre and for a short period thereafter, relative and true track data will be suspect. The effect is likely to be particularly dramatic on board vessels such as ferries which can change their heading and speed by a large amount in a fairly short time; the tracking data may give the mistaken impression that all tracked targets are manoeuvring. This is not intended as a criticism of the systems which elect to store relative data but merely a recognition of the basic laws of relative motion which demand steady state conditions for a stable and reliable assessment of relative motion, however it is deduced. In general, the system will attempt to recover stability by smoothing the relative motion over the shorter period (approximately one minute) once the computer has decided that a significant track change has taken place.

4.3.6.3 *The storage of true data*

In this approach the ranges and bearings are scan-converted to produce cartesian co-ordinates. Before each position is stored, its co-ordinates are modified by the direction and distance moved by the observing vessel since the first observation (see Figure 4.9). The effect of this is to produce within the track file a

Range and bearing
observations extracted
at approximately 3
second intervals,
smoothed over long or
short period, and
stored as smoothed
relative track

Relative vector
deduced from
smoothed
relative track

Smoothed relative
track used in
calculation of
true vector

CPA and TCPA
deduced from
smoothed relative
track

True vector deduced
from resolution of
OA and WO

Input of
unsmoothed
course and
speed of
observing
vessel

True course and speed
of target calculated
from resolution of OA
and WO

Figure 4.8 The storage of relative data

succession of positions whose co-ordinates represent the unsmoothed true track of the selected target. These positions are smoothed to produce the best estimate of the target's true course and speed. The operation

is analogous to the construction of a true plot, as described in Section 7.3.

If the relative-motion data relating to the target is requested, the computer will calculate that information

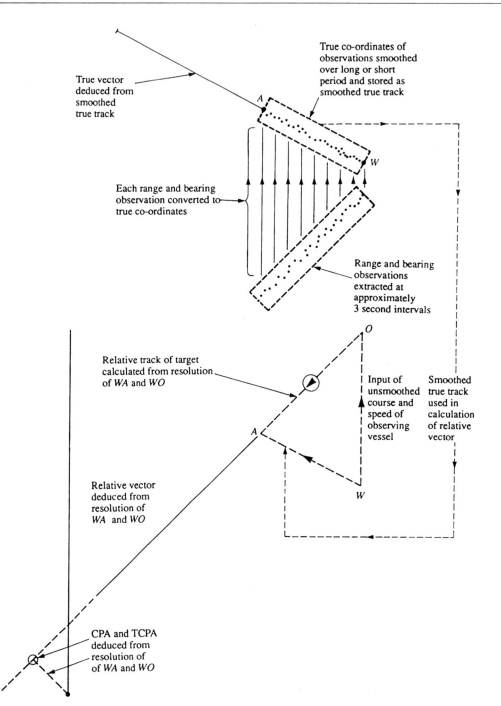

True vector
deduced from
smoothed
true track

True co-ordinates of
observations smoothed
over long or short
period and stored as
smoothed true track

Each range and bearing
observation converted to
true co-ordinates

Range and bearing
observations
extracted at
approximately
3 second intervals

Relative track of target
calculated from resolution
of WA and WO

Input of
unsmoothed
course and
speed of
observing
vessel

Smoothed
true track
used in
calculation
of relative
vector

Relative vector
deduced from
resolution of
WA and WO

CPA and TCPA
deduced from
resolution of
of WA and WO

Figure 4.9 The storage of true data

by vector addition of the instantaneous input course and speed data to the smoothed true track of the target. Where trial manoeuvre data (see Section 4.4.3) is requested, the vector addition will involve the smoothed true track and the proposed course and speed.

The merit of this approach is that if the observing vessel manoeuvres, the relative vector will remain stable (though changing) because it is updated, rotation by rotation, being calculated from the smoothed true course of the target and the instantaneous course and speed of the observing vessel. On the debit side it would appear at first sight that the calculated relative motion of the target is dependent on the accuracy of the input course and speed data. This is not the case provided that the input course and speed data are consistent over a full smoothing period. If the input data error is constant for the full smoothing period, the smoothed true track will of course similarly be in error. The computer will then use the wrong input data and the consistently wrong true track and as a result will arrive at the correct relative motion (see Figures 4.9 and 9.11(b)).

It is thus evident that, provided any error in the input course and speed data is consistent for the full smoothing period, it will not affect the accuracy of the CPA/TCPA data. However, if there is a fluctuating error, for example due to an erratic log input, the relative vector will be inaccurate and unstable. While recognizing the advantage of this approach in ensuring relative data stability during manoeuvres by the observing vessel, many users are concerned about the ability of random input errors to influence the CPA. Most users are prepared to tolerate some degree of instability or inaccuracy of true vectors when the observing vessel is performing a manoeuvre, but most, if not all, believe that the CPA is inviolate.

4.3.6.4 Storage philosophies compared

The two forms of storage which in general terms are described above represent two different approaches to dealing with the difficulty of maintaining stable tracking data when the observing vessel manoeuvres.

This is an inherent difficulty which is experienced whether the plotting is carried out manually or automatically and arises from the fact that the basic information, i.e. range and bearing, is being measured from a moving vessel. The implications for tracking accuracy are discussed further in Section 9.6.3. However, at this stage it has to be emphasized that the observer must be alert to the likelihood of the data being inaccurate during non-steady state conditions and to the way in which the method of track storage will influence the nature of these inaccuracies.

4.3.7 Tracking history

The ARPA should be able to display on request with relevant symbols at least four equally time-spaced past positions of any targets being tracked over a period appropriate to the range scale in use. The time scale of the past position plot should be indicated. The operating manual should contain an explanation of what the past position plots represent.

This enables an observer to check whether a particular target has manoeuvred in the recent past, possibly while the observer was temporarily away from the display on other bridge duties. This is a feature not required by ATA standards.

Not only is this knowledge useful in showing the observer what has happened but it may well help him to form an opinion of what the target is likely to do in the future. Manoeuvres by targets may be for navigational purposes and it may be possible to gain an indication from the general overview that this is the case. Alternatively, there may be an indication from the nature of the manoeuvre, when considered in relation to the general traffic pattern, that it has been undertaken for collision avoidance and hence the observer can be alert for a resumption of previous conditions.

'True history' is without doubt the only meaningful way in which this data can be displayed since the nature of the manoeuvre is readily apparent. A curve in the trail indicates an alteration of course by the target, whereas a change in the spacing of the dots will occur when there has been a change in speed. Since changes in speed are much slower to take effect, they are consequently more difficult to detect.

'Relative history' is not always provided but where it is, it is important to remember that any change in the direction or spacing of the dots can result from a change of course, a change of speed, or a combination of the two. It is therefore essential that the true manoeuvre is identified. Relative history should be used with great caution (see Section 7.4.2). Relative history will not be considered further.

The history dots can be likened to a vessel dropping buoys (with radar reflectors) at *equal intervals of time*, thus a change in the spacing is indicative of a change in the target's speed but it is important to appreciate the significance of the distance between the echo and the last dot. For example, in Figure 4.10, target *A* has not just executed a crash stop but has just dropped a buoy and is now steaming away from it.

When history is requested, only that of tracked targets can be displayed and even then the number of dots which are displayed will depend upon the period for which a particular target has been tracked. A target which has been tracked for two minutes can only display a maximum of two minutes' worth of history and so probably only one dot will be displayed, others being added as the tracking period increases.

Some manufacturers cause the plots to flash sequentially, e.g. 2 minutes ago, 4 minutes ago etc., while others cause the dots to decrease in brightness with time. The fourth plot is always removed as the latest plot is added to the display.

Although 'four equally time-spaced past positions over (at least) eight minutes' would suggest two-minute intervals, this is not necessarily the case. For a variety of philosophical as well as practical reasons, manufacturers have used intervals other than two minutes and so it is essential to establish just which intervals are being used on the display. On some equipment there is also an automatic change in time interval when range scale is changed. The argument for this option is that on the shorter range scales, the range spacing of two-minute dots could be so large as to place some or all of the dots 'off the screen' and hence not observable. As a result, an important target manoeuvre could be missed. On some equipment, 'fixed' or 'variable with

range scale' spacings can be selected by an 'internal' switch, while another manufacturer has the switch as a front panel operator control.

Uneven tracks of targets or apparent instability of motion may be taken to indicate that tracking of that target is less precise than it might be and the displayed data should be treated with caution.

Because of the variations in the way this facility can operate, great care should be taken when observing history to ensure that one is certain of exactly what is being displayed. In particular, one must establish whether true or relative history is being displayed and also which time spacings are in use.

The new 2008 standards do not necessarily require the history dots as described above (see Section 11.2.1). Instead the display is required to show scaled trails of past positions. Such information should be available within the equivalent of two scans after a change of range or picture reset or picture presentation. This reflects the fact that since the introduction of raster displays, all trails are artificial and therefore can be displayed on demand.

4.4 Vectors

The course and speed information generated by both ATA and ARPA for acquired targets should be displayed in a vector or graphic form (e.g. predicted areas of danger, see Section 5.6) which clearly indicates the target's predicted motion. In this regard:

1 ARPA (or auto-tracking) presenting predicted (extrapolated) information in vector form only should have the option of true and relative vectors. There should be an indication of the vector mode selected and, if true vector mode is selected, the display should show whether it is sea or ground stabilized.

2 An ARPA (or auto-tracking) which is capable of presenting target course and speed information in graphic form should also, on request, provide the target's true and/or relative vector.

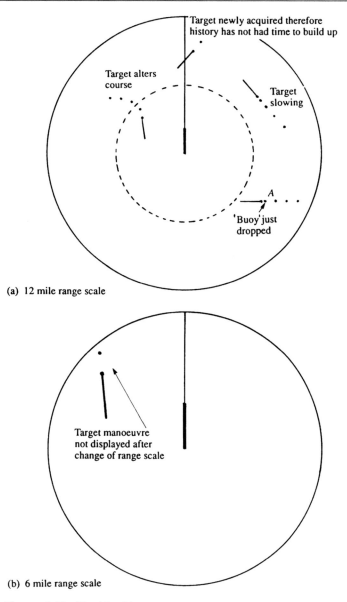

Figure 4.10 Tracking history

(*Note* This means that vectors of some kind must be provided, irrespective of the availability of any other method such as PADs, used to display collision-avoidance information.)

3 Vectors displayed should be time adjustable.

4 A positive indication of the time-scale of the vector in use should be given.

Vectors must be capable of indicating the rate and direction of the target's relative motion (relative vectors), or indicating the rate and direction of the target's proper motion (true vectors). The direction and rate forecast by a true vector will only be fulfilled if the tracked target maintains its course and speed. In the case of a relative vector, the fulfilment depends additionally on the observing vessel similarly maintaining course and speed.

In all cases, the displayed vector length is time related and normally can be adjusted by using a 'vector length' control. An alternative approach is to have a fixed physical length which remains the same irrespective of the range scale, e.g. 3 minutes on the 6 n mile range scale, 6 minutes on the 12 n mile range scale, etc.

Note Vectors of either of the two types can be displayed on a true- or relative-motion radar picture presentation, i.e. *true vectors* can be selected to appear on a *relative-motion* presentation and vice versa. It was originally considered in some quarters that this might result in confusion and at least one manufacturer provides a default condition where relative vectors are displayed when relative motion is selected and, likewise, true vectors on the true-motion presentation, with the alternative vector mode being temporarily selectable in each case by the user holding down a 'spring-loaded' control (see also Section 9.7,1, incorrect interpretation).

4.4.1 Relative vectors

As described in Section 4.3.6, the ARPA or ATA must track the target(s) for a period of time, after which a vector can be displayed as in Figure 4.11(a). Using the vector length control, the vectors can be extended to determine the CPA by observation against the background of the range rings and the TCPA can be read off from the vector length control.

4.4.2 True vectors

As an alternative, the observer may request that the true vector(s) be displayed (Figure 4.11(b)). In this case, own ship will also have a vector which will increase in length as the time control is increased. The likelihood of a close-quarters situation developing can be ascertained by running out the true vectors

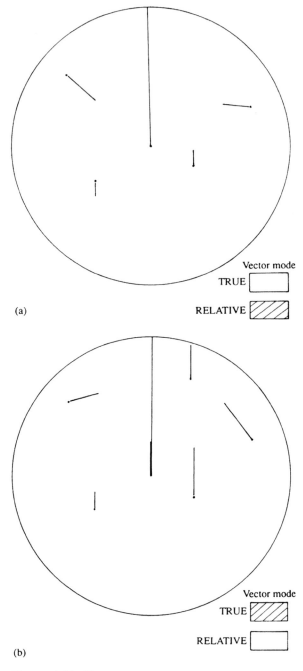

(a)

Vector mode

TRUE

RELATIVE

(b)

Figure 4.11 Vectors

(a) Relative vectors

(b) True vectors for the situation displayed in (a)

progressively to show the predicted development of the encounter. The dynamic nature of this technique appeals to many users but it must be borne in mind that any evaluation of CPA/TCPA is a matter of trial and error and thus better avoided. It is essential to appreciate that the CPA is *not* represented by the point at which the target's true vector intersects own ship's true vector, except in the case of zero CPA.

4.4.3   Trial manoeuvre

The ARPA should be capable of simulating the effect on all tracked targets of an own ship manoeuvre with or without time delay before manoeuvre without interrupting the updating of target tracking and display of actual target alphanumeric data. The simulation should be indicated with the relevant symbol on the display.

The feature is not included in the standards for an ATA and nor is it a requirement for vessels below 10 000 grt in the new 2008 standards.

With the availability of computer assistance, the problem of predicting the effect of a manoeuvre prior to its implementation by own ship is much simplified. While it is relatively easy to visualize mentally the outcome of a manoeuvre where two ships are involved, in dense traffic this becomes very difficult. In particular, with large ships and limited sea room, it is necessary to plan and update the whole collision avoidance strategy as quickly as possible in light of the continually changing radar scene.

While planning, it is important to bear in mind the following points.

(a)   Own ship may temporarily need to be on a 'collision course' with more distant vessels, i.e. collisions may require sequential avoidance since it is unlikely that a single manoeuvre will resolve all the problems.

(b)   Extrapolation of the present situation using the trial manoeuvre facility with current course and speed as inputs can provide valuable information on which of the 'other' vessels in the vicinity may have to manoeuvre in order to avoid collisions between each other. Obvious avoiding

manoeuvres may present themselves and should be watched for.

(c)   Constraints imposed by navigation may dictate the manoeuvre of 'other' vessels. This should be taken into account when planning strategy and watched for when carrying out the plan and assessing its effectiveness.

(d)   The ease with which this facility allows the navigator to establish the course to steer for a given passing distance may encourage the choice of a small alteration. This temptation must be avoided at all costs as it loses sight of the need to make a substantial alteration. The rules require the latter in recognition of the fact that other vessels may be using much more rudimentary methods of data extraction and may not be able to detect a small manoeuvre.

Unfortunately, although there is a single requirement for all approved ARPAs to possess a facility for simulating a trial manoeuvre, different methods of providing this have been devised by the various manufacturers.

When information relating to the proposed manoeuvre is fed in, the true or relative vectors which would result from such a manoeuvre are displayed on request. This, combined with the ability to adjust the vector length, can give a clear presentation of potential close-quarters situations between other vessels as well as with the observer's vessel.

It is important to select *relative vectors* when assessing the effect of a manoeuvre as this will give an indication of how far the target will pass clear (Figure 4.12). It is also possible to vary the inputs while observing this display and note the effect on the CPA.

The ARPA has to produce a plot similar to that discussed in Section 7.5.6. There is a range of facilities available, with an increasing number of factors being taken into account when presenting the trial data. In the simplest form, it is possible to feed in only the intended course, speed and alteration time and observe their effect on the display.

In some ARPAs it is possible for the vessel's handling characteristics to be included in the evaluation, but

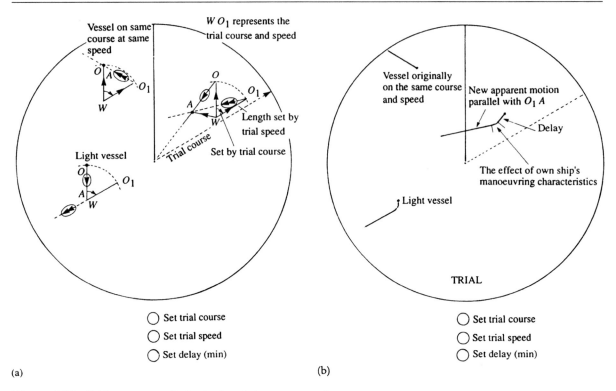

Figure 4.12 Trial manoeuvre display in the relative vector mode

(a)   Construction of relative vectors
(b)   The trial manoeuvre display

this will of necessity be restricted to one (or possibly two) conditions of loading.

On some equipment, provision is made for two successive manoeuvres to be displayed. This can be extremely helpful when endeavouring to assess the time for which an alteration must be held.

In order that there should be no confusion between the 'trial' data and the current situation, when trial is in operation the screen will display some distinctive indication such as the word SIM or TRIAL. The use of a 'T' to indicate trial is frequently mistaken for an indication that true vectors are being displayed. The letter 'T' as it stands is meaningless and has not been particularly helpful. There is the danger that one officer sets up the display and another officer (or the master) observes it without realizing the special nature of the display.

Some systems require the observer to hold down a button, which means that the observer has to make a positive decision to operate the switch and hold it over while he observes the display. Few systems offer such a failsafe control.

Note (i)   While trial manoeuvres are being presented on the display, the computer continues its normal task of tracking all acquired targets.

(ii) Where 'predicted areas of danger' (see Section 5.6) are provided, all the possible alterations of course should be simultaneouly apparent.

(iii) A 'trial speed' facility is also provided since any given family of PADs is drawn for a specific speed of the observing vessel.

4.5   The ARPA and ATA display

4.5.1   The continued availability of radar data in the event of an ATA or ARPA malfunction

The design should be such that any malfunction of ARPA (or auto-tracking) parts producing data additional to information to be produced by the radar as required by the performance standards for navigational equipment, should not affect the integrity of the basic radar presentation.

In general, this means that when a malfunction is detected (see Section 4.7.4) an alarm is activated and those ARPA (or auto-tracking) facilities affected are disabled, the radar presentation must continue 'normally'. For example, a fault in the own ship tracking circuitry may cause the ARPA as well as the true-motion facilities to be discontinued, but the relative-motion radar display will still be available.

4.5.2   The size of the display

The sizes of display for different vessel sizes are summarized in Tables 4.1 and 4.3. The ATA should have an effective diameter of at least 250 mm (180 mm if below 1000 grt). The ARPA for a vessel above 10 000 grt should be at least 340 mm, but may be 250 mm if fitted to a smaller vessel.

4.5.3   The range scales on which ARPA and ATA facilities should be available

The ARPA and ATA facilities should be available on at least the following range scales:
  3 miles
  6 miles
  12 miles

There should be a positive indication of the range scale in use.

In actual practice, the provision is normally far in excess of this requirement: ARPA and auto-tracking facilities are usually provided on all range scales from 1.5 n miles to 24 n miles inclusive.

4.5.4   The modes of display

The ARPA and auto-tracking should be capable of operating with a relative-motion display with 'north up' and 'course up' azimuth stabilization. In addition, the ARPA and auto-tracking may also provide for a true-motion display. If true motion is provided, the operator should be able to select for his display either true or relative motion. There should be a positive indication of the display mode and orientation in use.

The term 'mode' is used here to describe the 'radar' features of picture orientation and picture presentation which are discussed in detail in Sections 1.4 and 1.5.

4.5.5   ARPA or ATA data should not obscure radar data

The ARPA (and auto-tracking) information should not obscure the visibility of radar targets. The display of ARPA (and auto-tracking) data should be under the control of the radar observer. It should be possible to cancel the display of unwanted ARPA (and auto-tracking) data within 3 seconds.

There was a tendency in the past for alphanumeric data relating to the current operation, and also warnings, to appear on the radar screen temporarily (see Section 4.6 and Figure 4.13). This practice has been discontinued in current ARPAs.

4.5.6   The ARPA and ATA data brilliance control

Means should be provided to adjust independently the brilliance of the ARPA (or auto-tracking) data, including complete elimination of the ARPA (or auto-tracking) data.

This control allows the observer to remove all ARPA data from the screen in order to see just which is radar and which is ARPA data. It can be particularly

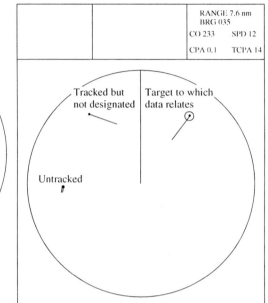

Figure 4.13 The display of alphanumeric data

useful when searching for a poor-response target (e.g. in clutter) while still wishing to continue tracking the other vessels in the vicinity.

Unfortunately, many a mariner has been caught out by this control and has spent some frustrating minutes trying to find the screen marker, only to realize that the ARPA data brilliance control was turned down.

4.5.7 The ability to view the display

The method of presentation should ensure that the ARPA (or auto-tracking) data is clearly visible in general to more than one observer in the conditions of light normally experienced on the bridge of a ship by day and by night. Screening may be provided to shade the display from sunlight but not to the extent that it will impair the observer's ability to keep a proper lookout. Facilities to adjust the brightness should be provided.

The reasons for this requirement are fairly evident but the way in which it has been complied with in practice has been somewhat uncertain. The provision

of a tinted 'glass' cubicle has been the most effective as it has still allowed the watchkeeper to maintain a lookout while not requiring the traditional radar hood.

The introduction of radial-scan synthetic displays helped to a limited extent and, more recently, raster-scan radar displays have gone a long way to comply with this requirement without the need to resort to special radar cubicles.

4.5.8 The use of the marker for range and bearing measurement

Provisions should be made to obtain quickly the range and bearing of any object which appears on the ARPA (or auto-tracking) display.

To comply with this requirement, most manufacturers have enabled the range and bearing of the screen-controlled marker to be displayed. In this way, the range and bearing of an object can be obtained by placing the marker over it. Like all range and bearing measuring devices, they should be regularly checked against the range rings and heading marker respectively (see also Sections 6.9.8 and 6.9.9).

4.5.9 The effect of changing range scales

After changing range scales on which the ARPA (or auto-tracking) facilities are available or re-setting the display, full plotting information should be displayed within a period of time not exceeding one scan.

It should be appreciated that, in order to fulfil this requirement, the ARPA needs to track and plot the acquired targets continually out to some 16 miles, irrespective of the range scale selected by the operator. Because of this, if the shorter range scales are selected and accompanied by a short pulse, targets at a longer range returning a poor response may be lost.

4.6 The display of alphanumeric data

At the request of the observer the following information should be immediately available from the ARPA in alphanumeric form in regard to any tracked target.

(1) Present range to the target.
(2) Present bearing of the target.
(3) Predicted target range at the closest point of approach (CPA).
(4) Predicted time to CPA (TCPA).
(5) Calculated true course of target.
(6) Calculated true speed of target.

When a target is 'marked' or 'designated', i.e. the joystick and gate are used to indicate to the computer the target about which data are required, data relating to that target can then be read out in alphanumeric form, i.e. range, bearing, CPA, TCPA, course and speed (Figure 4.13). In some systems the data available also includes the distance at which it is predicted that the target will cross ahead (BCR) and the interval which will elapse until this event occurs (BCT).

The readout may be on a separate tote displaying all quantities, or, in some cases, displaying the data in sequential groups of two items or on the radar screen itself.

Although vectors are suppressed during the first minute of tracking (for the reasons described in Section 4.3.6), the observer can normally select a target during that period and read out the alphanumeric data. This is acceptable as a means of quickly obtaining the range and bearing of the target, but it must be appreciated that other alphanumeric values will at that stage be based on only a few observations and hence can be dangerously misleading.

When *trial manoeuvre* is selected, modern systems continue to provide the real alphanumeric data while some older ARPA systems produce the trial values. In the case of any given ARPA, it is essential to establish exactly which data are being made available.

4.7 Alarms and warnings

It should be possible to activate or de-activate the operational warnings.

4.7.1 Guard zone violation

The ARPA (and auto-tracking) should have the capability to warn the observer with a visual and/or audible signal of any distinguishable target which closes to a range or transits a zone chosen by the observer. The target causing the warning should be clearly indicated with relevant symbols on the display.

It is possible to specify an area in the vicinity of own ship, e.g. at 10 miles, a zone 5 cables in depth (see Figure 4.14) which, if entered by a target, would activate an alarm. It is usual to have two zones, one which may be at some pre-set range and the other at a range which may be varied according to circumstances.

The target which has activated the alarm may be made to 'flash' or alternatively be marked in some

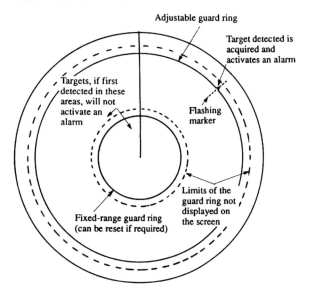

Figure 4.14 Guard rings

other way, such as having a short bearing marker through it. In some equipments, the range and bearing of the target entering the zone is displayed in numerical form. It is important to remember that a target which is detected for the first time *at a lesser range than* the guard ring will not activate the alarm: this warning system should not be regarded as an alternative to keeping a proper look-out, but rather as an additional means of ensuring the safety of the vessel. Each guard zone may be set for 360° coverage or for a specific sector of threat. See also Figures 4.3 to 4.5.

Note This provision is normally coupled with the 'automatic acquisition' facilities, in which case, in addition to activating the alarm, the target will also be acquired if there is an available tracking channel. Even where automatic acquisition is not provided (as in auto-tracking), the guard zone facility is still required.

4.7.2 Predicted CPA/TCPA violation

The ARPA (or auto-tracking) should have the capability to warn the observer with a visual and/or audible signal of any tracked target which is predicted to close to within a minimum range and time chosen by the observer. The target causing the warning should be clearly indicated with the relevant symbols on the display.

It is possible to specify a CPA and TCPA (sometimes referred to as *safe limits*) which will activate an alarm if *both* are violated. For example, if the CPA and TCPA controls are set to 0.5 n miles and 30 min respectively and a target which is being tracked will come to a CPA of less than 0.5 n miles in less than 30 min, then the alarm will be activated (see Figure 4.15). This will occur, even if the 'relative vector' has not been extended into the specified area. The displayed echo and vector of the target activating the alarm may be made to flash or, alternatively, marked in some other way.

Where own ship's heading marker intersects a predicted area of danger (PAD) (see Section 5.6), a warning will be activated and will continue until such time as own ship's course is altered to clear the PAD.

4.7.3 Lost target

The ARPA (or auto-tracking) should clearly indicate if a tracked target is lost other than out of range and the target's last tracked position should be clearly indicated on the display.

Consider a target which is being tracked but, for one of a number of reasons does not return a detectable response on one scan: the tracker will open up the gate and, if it finds a response, will continue to track as described in Section 4.3.6.1. If it fails to find a response, it is required that the tracker should continue to search for the echo in an area, where it might be expected until it has failed to appear for five out of 10 consecutive scans. If, after this searching, the target is still not detected, the 'target lost' warning is activated and the last observed position of the echo is marked on the screen. It is also normal to activate an audible alarm.

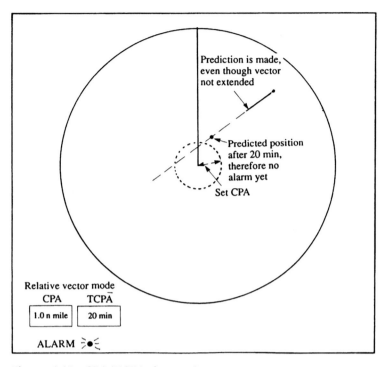

Figure 4.15 CPA/TCPA alarm settings

4.7.4 Performance tests and warnings

The ARPA (or auto-tracking) should provide suitable warnings of ARPA (or auto-tracking) malfunction to enable the observer to monitor the proper operation of the system. Additionally, test programmes should be available so that the overall performance of the ARPA (or auto-tracking) can be assessed periodically against a known solution. When a test programme is being executed the relevant test symbols should be displayed.

In the case of conventional radar, there was always a basic requirement to ensure that the radar controls were properly adjusted and that correct operation of the radar had been established by means of a performance check (see Section 6.5).

All ARPA and ATA equipments incorporate some form of self-diagnostic routine which monitors the correct operation of the various circuits. This check is repeated at regular intervals (which may range from once per hour to many times per second) or on request from the operator. In the event of a fault, a warning is given to the operator and, in some cases, an indication of the cause or location (e.g. printed circuit board No. 6) of the fault is also given.

However, it must be appreciated that some faults cannot be detected internally, e.g. a failure of certain elements in a numeric read-out can cause an 8 to appear as a 6 or a 9 to appear as a 3 etc. In such cases, a typical test may provide for the operator to switch all of the elements on so that each indicator should display an 8.

To ensure that the processor which deals with data has sufficient overall accuracy, four test scenarios are specified (see Sections 9.1 and 9.2) together with the tolerances within which the output must fall. All ARPAs and ATAs should be able to conform to this level of accuracy.

Where the effect of a fault is confined to certain facilities, those facilities may be 'shut down' (e.g. true motion not available), while allowing the remainder of the system to continue to be used.

4.8   Connections with other equipment

The ARPA (or auto-tracking) should not degrade the performance of any equipment providing sensor inputs. The connection of the ARPA (or auto-tracking) to any other equipment should not degrade the performance of that equipment.

The 1997 ARPA Performance Standards also state that there should be an indication when an input from an external sensor is absent.

This requirement was not in the previous regulations although it was commonly provided by ARPA manufacturers. Interestingly, the ATA Performance Standards of 1999 do not incorporate this as a requirement.

However, the 2008 standards have a much larger section on data (see Section 11.2.1). This includes statements that data indicated as invalid should not be used and that if the data is known to be of poor quality then this should be clearly indicated. Data should also be checked prior to use to see if it is within plausible limits.

5 ARPA and ATA – additional facilities

5.1 Introduction

With increased processing capability, manufacturers have been able to provide facilities additional to those specified in the IMO Performance Standards, some of which, in particular alerts, mariners had indicated would be of value.

Further design potential was realized by providing a facility whereby the ARPA would automatically deduce reliable values for the vessel's course and speed over the ground by tracking a designated stationary target. Such a facility, known as *automatic ground-stabilization*, can provide a reliable input to the ARPA but it is not the correct input for collision avoidance. The implications of this are discussed in Section 5.3. This feature is usually available on ATA.

With memory becoming less expensive, the means for the storage and display of navigation lines and simple 'maps' became a possibility, and the availability of automatic ground-stabilization made it possible to maintain such maps in a fixed position on the screen.

Also, some designers saw the potential for development in other areas, primarily in the provision of assistance in determining a collision avoidance strategy – notably predicted points of collision (PPCs) and predicted areas of danger (PADs).

Theoretically there is no reason why any of these additional features could not be applied to an ATA, but as this is sold as a minimum specification device, it is not likely. In this chapter we will therefore refer to ARPA only.

5.2 Additional alarms and warnings

In addition to the alarms and warnings specified, manufacturers have seen fit to provide alarms and warnings which they consider to be of benefit to the mariner.

5.2.1 Time to manoeuvre

Where a 'delay' facility is provided with trial manoeuvre (see Section 4.4.3), an alarm may be provided to warn the officer of the watch that it is, say, one minute until 'time to manoeuvre'. Depending on the size of ship and its manoeuvrability, this warning can be used as an indication to apply helm and/or ring the telegraph, in order that a pre-planned manoeuvre is executed on time.

5.2.2 Track change

This alarm is associated with an algorithm which quantifies departures from the predicted tracks of targets. The target(s) activating the alarm will be indicated by some graphic symbol. Its operation is likely to be associated with the change from a long to a short smoothing period (see Section 4.3.6.1).

It can be useful, but it does depend on the application of some arbitrary decision as to when the change in track is 'significant'. There is the possibility on some equipment to reduce the sensitivity of this alarm where it is found that the incidence of false alarms is too high. In some systems, the track change alarm will be activated by large or rapid manoeuvres performed by the observing vessel. This is likely to arise where relative track storage is used (see Section 4.3.6.2). In general, this condition can be recognized as all targets will exhibit the track change symbol.

5.2.3   Anchor watch

This facility attempts to offer automatic warning of the observing vessel or other vessels dragging in an anchorage. If a known stationary target (for example, a small isolated navigation mark) is acquired and designated as such then an alarm will be activated if the designated target moves more than a preset distance from the marked position. If the stationary target appears to move, then it must be due to the observing vessel dragging her anchor. Alternatively, it will give a warning if another 'tracked' vessel in the anchorage drags her anchor; it will, of course, be activated if such a vessel heaves up her anchor and gets under way.

5.2.4   Tracks full

There is a limit to the number of targets which an ARPA is capable of tracking. In areas of high traffic density, there may well come a time when all the tracking channels are in use. This is particularly likely when automatic acquisition (see Sections 4.2.4, 4.2.5 and 4.2.6) is in operation. An alarm will warn the operator to inspect the untracked targets for potential dangers and to transfer tracking from less important targets which are being tracked. This is a compulsory alarm in the future IMO Performance Standards (See Section 11.2.1).

5.2.5   Wrong or invalid request

Where an operator feeds in incorrect data or data in an unacceptable form, e.g. course 370°, an alarm and

indicator will be activated and will continue until the invalid data is deleted or overwritten.

5.2.6   Safe limit vector suppression

This facility, if selected, suppresses the vectors of targets whose predicted motion does not violate the safe limits (see Section 4.7.2) and is an attempt to reduce ARPA 'clutter'. The computer continues to track the targets whose vectors are suppressed. If any of them should manoeuvre in such a way as to violate the set safe limits, the vector of that target will reappear and the safe limit alarm will be activated. If a decision is taken to use this facility, considerable thought must be given to the implications of the selected values of safe limits. In general, it is advisable to switch the facility off before contemplating a manoeuvre.

5.2.7   Trial alarm

This facility is analogous to the safe limit alarm but operates only when the trial manoeuvre is selected. It is not available on all systems.

5.3   Automatic ground-stabilization

The difficulties of achieving ground-stabilization on a raw radar display are outlined in Section 6.8.3. With computer assistance, ground-stabilization can be achieved easily and automatically. In general this stabilization is also applied to all true target vectors. It is particularly important to appreciate the implications of this, which are discussed later.

An isolated land target with good response is selected as reference. It is acquired and tracked by one of the ARPA tracking channels and then designated as a fixed target. This makes it possible for the tracker to calculate the ground track of the observing vessel and hence to maintain the movement of the electronic origin of the display in sympathy with it. When using this facility the observer should be particularly watchful for other targets which approach the reference target and, in particular, for those which pass between the observing vessel and the reference target. If the intervening target shadows the reference target the chances of target swap (see Section 4.3.5) may be greatly increased. If target swap does involve the reference target, it may have quite dramatic effects on the presentation of all vectors, particularly if the reference attaches to a fast moving target. If such an eventuality seems likely, it may be expedient to move the reference to another fixed target.

The facility has been developed in such a way that the same stabilization is applied to the radar picture presentation and to the true vectors, i.e. either both are sea-stabilized or both are ground-stabilized. Thus in general, where automatic ground-stabilization is selected, true vectors will indicate the ground tracks of targets and *not* their headings. Failure to appreciate this can render the presentation dangerously misleading if it is mistakenly used in the planning of collision avoidance strategy. This is illustrated in the right-hand display of Figure 5.1. One might expect the danger of

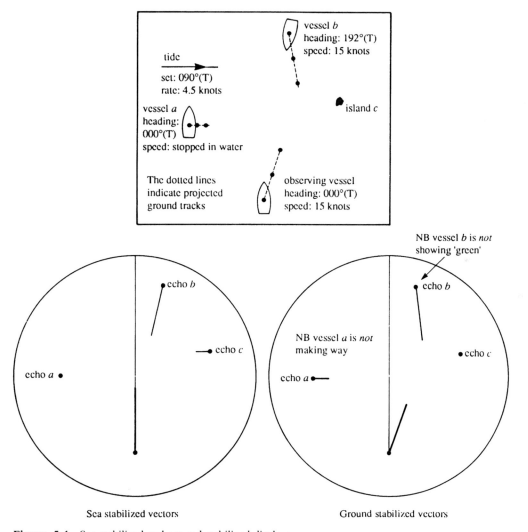

Figure 5.1 Sea-stabilized and ground-stabilized displays

observers being misled in this respect to be less than in the case of a raw radar display (see Section 1.5.2.2) because, except in case of an along-track tide, there will be angular displacement of the observing vessel's vector from the heading marker. Experience has indicated that this expectation cannot be justified in all cases.

The useful feature is that it makes true-motion parallel indexing a practical proposition, which is scarcely if at all the case with manual ground-stabilization (see Section 8.4.5). It also makes it possible to maintain electronic navigation lines and maps (see Sections 5.4, 8.4.6.2 and 8.4.6.3) in a fixed position on the screen. Some users find the availability of a fixed map particularly attractive in coastal navigation. However, it must be stressed that the penalty paid is that the presentation may not afford traffic heading information and may therefore in principle be unsuitable for collision avoidance.

Automatic ground-stabilization can also be achieved by using the output from a twin axis doppler log which is locked to the ground (see Section 6.8.1.3) and by integration with GNSS (see Section 10.2).

The ease of integration with GNSS and the accuracy make this a very popular display for modern navigators. However, it is important to remember the potential for misleading anticollision information in a cross track tide.

5.4   Navigational lines and maps (see also Section 8.4.6.3)

Most radar sets (even without ARPA or ATA) offer a graphics facility whereby electronic lines can be drawn on the screen. The position, length and orientation of the lines can be adjusted, thus making it possible to produce parallel indexing lines (see Section 8.4) and to delineate navigational limits in channels, traffic separation schemes, poor-response coastlines etc. It may also be possible to indicate points of interest such as isolated rocks and floating marks with a specific symbol.

The range of facilities available under the general heading of a navigation lines package is consider-

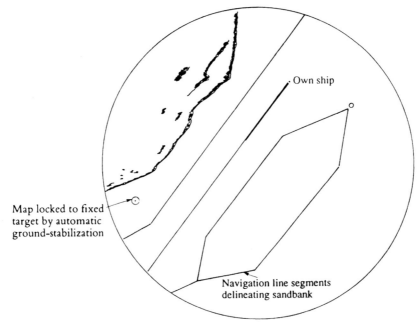

Figure 5.2   Map presentation

able. In simple facilities only some ten to fifteen lines may be available, thus merely allowing the construction of fairly crude patterns or maps (see Figure 5.2). The pattern may be lost if the equipment is switched off and it may or may not be possible to edit or move the pattern around the screen, once drawn. More advanced packages will allow the observer to prepare and store the pattern at a convenient time when planning the passage and subsequently to recall it when required. It will then be possible to move the pattern around the screen in order to align or realign it with displayed radar echoes and there will be provision for easy editing. A non-volatile memory allows the storage of several maps even when the equipment is switched off. The most comprehensive mapping facilities will provide for the permanent storage of maps containing as many as a thousand or more elements. While there is no rigid distinction in names between the two extremes, the simpler packages tend to be referred to as navigation lines while the more comprehensive are usually described as mapping facilities. The facility will frequently be used in association with automatic ground-stabilization (see Section 5.3).

The concept of adding maps to the radar display has now extended to the integration of electronic charts (ECDIS) with the radar/ARPA. The advantages are that:

(a) the data is not prepared by the navigator which improves the reliability and accuracy as well as being more convenient,

(b) it allows a more sophisticated selection of features to be added.

This topic is covered in more detail in Section 10.2.

5.5 The predicted point of collision (PPC)

The predicted point of collision (PPC) is that point towards which the observing ship should steer at her present speed (assuming that the target does not manoeuvre) in order for a collision to occur.

Some designers have recognized that the positions of these points can be quickly calculated and displayed for all tracked targets. The argument made for displaying the PPCs is that they assist in developing a collision avoidance strategy by showing the navigator, at a glance, the courses which are completely unacceptable because they intersect a collision point. This is the only contribution which can be claimed for PPCs. They do not give any indication of *miss distance* (other than in the zero CPA case) and any attempt to extrapolate the clearing distance either side of the point will be fraught with danger. A safe course is one which, among other things, results in passing at a safe distance, which implies a knowledge of clearing distance. Safe and effective use of PPCs depends upon a thorough understanding of the factors which affect their location and movement. As is evident from the following treatment this is, in many cases, not a simple matter. Some systems make it possible to display these points as small circles when, but only when, true vectors are selected.

5.5.1 The concept of collision points

When two ships are in the same area of sea, it is always possible for them to collide. The point(s) at which collision can occur may be defined and depends upon:

(a) the speed ratio of the two ships,
(b) the position of the two ships.

Considering any two ships, usually one is moving faster than the other; the possibility that one is at exactly the same speed as the other and will maintain that ratio for any period of time is remote enough to be disregarded for the moment.

The ship which is the faster of the two will always see displayed one and only one collision point, since it can pursue the target if necessary. This collision point is always on the track of the target as shown in Figure 5.3.

The ship which is the slower of the two may see displayed two collision points, both of which must be on the target track. One exists where the slow ship heads toward the target and intercepts it,

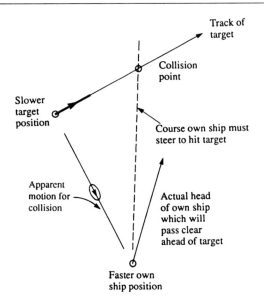

Figure 5.3 Single point of collision

while another exists where the slow ship heads away from the target but is struck by it. The two cases appear in Figure 5.4. Alternatively there may be no way for the slower ship to collide with the faster (even though the faster may collide with the slower) because it is just not fast enough to reach the target (see Figure 5.5).

Note   A critical in-between case of one collision point exists where the slow ship can just reach the track of the fast ship.

5.5.2   The behaviour of collision points if the observing ship maintains speed

5.5.2.1   *The initial collision case*

It is important to realize that collision points exist, whether an actual collision threat exists or not. The only significance is that in the event of an actual collision threat, the collision points are the same for both ships. Figure 5.6 shows how the collision points move in a collision situation and how they will appear to the two ships involved. On the faster ship, the single collision point appears on the heading marker and moves down, decreasing in range as the collision approaches. On the slower ship, one of the two collision points will move down the heading marker, while the other moves down a steady bearing.

5.5.2.2   *The non-collision case*

In a non-collision case, the collision point moves according to well defined rules but it will never cross the heading marker. In the case of the faster ship, the movement depends on whether the fast ship will cross

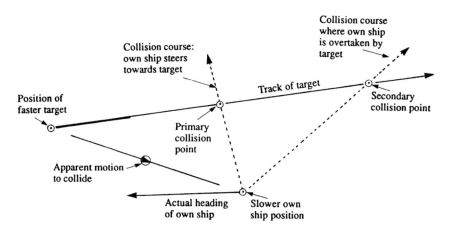

Figure 5.4 Dual points of collision

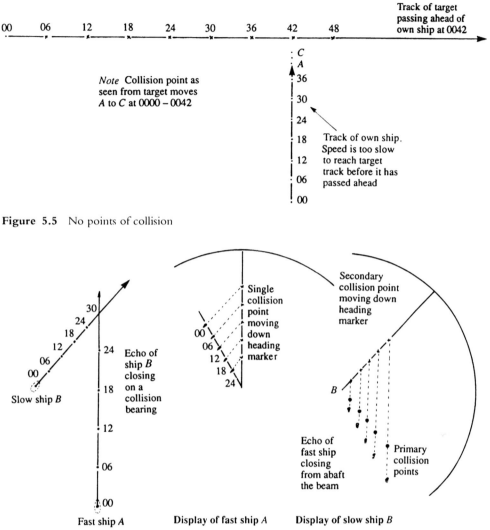

Figure 5.5 No points of collision

Figure 5.6 The movement of the PPC in the collision situation

ahead of, or behind the target ship. Figure 5.7 shows the two possible cases and typical track lines.

The case of the slower ship is more complicated because of the two collision points and the possibility of no collision point existing. If the observing ship's course is to pass between the two collision points, they will pass down either side of the observing ship, generally shortening in range, and then draw together

under the stern of the observing ship. As they meet they become one collision point before they finally disappear, as in Figure 5.8.

If the observing ship is steering to pass astern of the fast ship, the collision points will draw together, form one point and then disappear. It is noticeable that the collision point more distant from the target ship, usually termed the secondary point, moves much

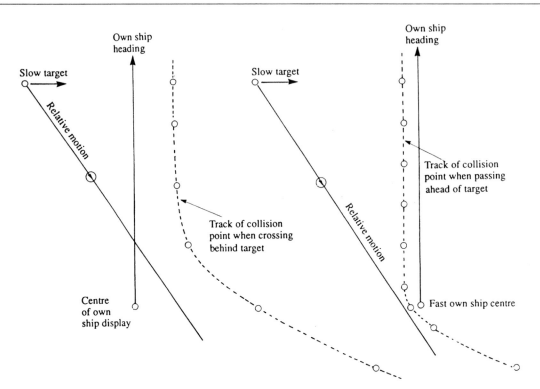

Figure 5.7 The track of the collision point

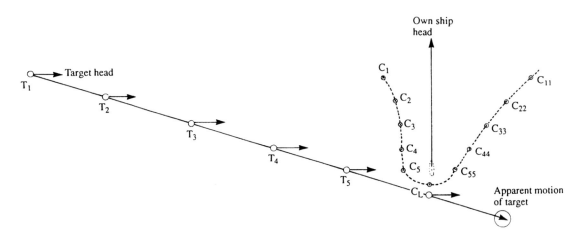

Figure 5.8 The movement of dual collision points. Own ship is steering to pass between the collision points at speed 7 kn. Target speed = 24 kn

  C_n = primary collision point

  C_{nn} = secondary collision point when target is at T_n

  C_L = limiting condition where the hazard disappears

faster than the point nearer to the target, which is termed the primary collision point.

5.5.3 The behaviour of the collision point when the target ship's speed changes

If the speed ratio is infinitely large, e.g. when the target is stationary, then obviously the collision point is at the position of the target. If the observing ship maintains speed while the target begins to increase speed, the collision point will begin to move along the target track. When the target speed has increased to that of the observing ship, the secondary collision point will appear at infinity. Further increase of the target speed will move the primary and secondary collision points toward each other (not necessarily by equal amounts); eventually, own speed in comparison to target speed may be so slow that the two points will merge and then disappear. This behaviour is shown in Figure 5.9.

5.5.4 The behaviour of the collision point when the target changes course

If the two ships have the same speed, the collision point moves on a locus which is the perpendicular bisector of the line joining the two ships. The greater the aspect, the farther away the collision point will be (Figure 5.10). Theoretically, the limiting aspect in this case is 90°, but then the collision point would be at infinity and hence an aspect of some 85° plus is considered the practical limit.

5.5.4.1 For a slower observing ship

When the observing ship is slower than the target, two collision points exist and they are seen to be on the circumference of a circle whose centre and radius are dependent on the speed ratio; the circle is always on the 'observing ship' side of the unity speed ratio locus. A limiting aspect can be defined which is also dependent on the speed ratio. A slower observing ship will mean that a target will have a smaller limiting aspect angle.

Aspects greater than the limit pose no hazard since the observing ship can never catch up with the target.

5.5.4.2 For a faster observing ship

When the observing ship is the faster, the circle of collision points lies on the target side of the equal-speed locus. As the aspect increases, the collision point moves farther away from the observing ship. There is no limiting aspect and collision is always possible.

An interesting point to note in Figure 5.10 is that the inverse of the idea of a limiting aspect to the slow observing ship appears when the observing ship is faster; this is effectively a limiting course for the observing ship. If the actual heading is to the remote

Figure 5.9   The behaviour of the collision point with the change of speed ratio (i.e. own speed: target speed)

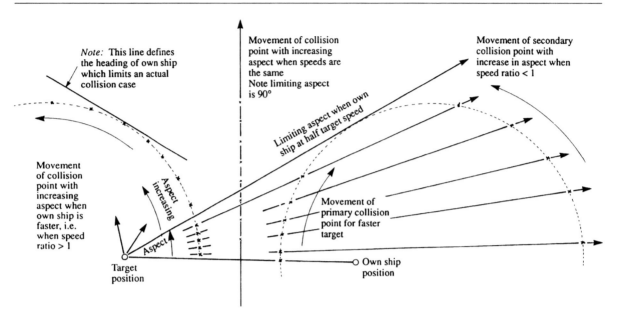

Figure 5.10 The movement of the collision point(s) as target aspect changes, drawn for speed ratios of 2:1 and 1:2

side of this line, all collision points appear on the one bow. If own heading is inside this limiting direction, the collision point will move across the heading marker as the target changes aspect.

5.6 The predicted area of danger (PAD)

The shortcomings of collision points can be listed as follows:

(a) Inaccuracies in data acquisition are likely to displace the points.
(b) No account is taken of the dimensions of the ships involved.
(c) They offer no quantitative indication of miss distance which is the essential data required for collision avoidance.

The logical development is to construct, around the PPC, a plane figure which is associated with a chosen

passing distance and in the calculation of which due margin of safety can be allowed for the effects of data inaccuracies and the physical dimensions of the vessels involved. The area within the figure is to be avoided to achieve at least the chosen passing distance and is referred to as a predicted area of danger or PAD. The technique was patented by Sperry Marine Systems and is exclusive to the ARPAs produced by that company. The PAD approach is an extremely elegant solution to the problem of how best to present collision avoidance data. It is essential that the user has a thorough understanding of the principles underlying the presentation with particular reference to the location, movement, shape and change of shape of the PAD. As will be seen from the following explanation, this is not a simple subject.

In the case of the collision point there is a course which intercepts the target's track at the given speed ratio, whereas in the predicted area of danger there are generally two intersection points. One of these is where the observing ship will pass ahead of the target and the other where the observing ship will pass astern of the target. The angle subtended by these two limiting courses will depend upon:

(a) The speed ratio.
(b) The position of the target.
(c) The aspect of the target.

As shown in the case of the collision point, a faster observing ship must always generate a single cross-ahead and cross-astern position. A slower observing ship produces much more complex possibilities and, depending on the three variables noted above, these may include:

(a) Two cross-ahead and two cross-astern points.
(b) One cross-ahead and two cross-astern points.
(c) Two cross-astern points.
(d) No hazard.

In the case of the single or primary collision point, the position at which the observing ship will cross ahead of the target is always farther from the target than the collision point, while the cross-astern point is always nearer to the target.

In the case of a slower observing ship, where there is a secondary collision point, the second cross-ahead position is nearer to the target and the associated cross-astern position more remote from it (see Figure 5.11).

To indicate limits within the 'cross-ahead/cross-astern' arc, it is necessary to draw a bar parallel to the target's track and at the intended miss-distance closer to the observing ship's position.

The limits defined by the arc and the bar are such that, if the observing ship were to cross those limits, then it would be at a less distance than the desired miss-distance from the target. Figure 5.12 shows the generation of the two boundaries in the case of a slower observing ship.

5.6.1 The PAD in practice

In order to produce an acceptable system for practical operation, these limits are normally encapsulated by a symmetrical figure such as an ellipse or a hexagon.

In the case of the ellipse, the major axis is equal to the difference between the cross-ahead and cross-astern distances as measured from the target, while the minor axis is equal to twice the intended miss-distance. In the case of the hexagon, it is drawn from a rectangle and two isosceles triangles. The base of the triangle is always twice the miss-distance and the vertical height is one quarter of the distance E_1E_2 as shown in Figure 5.13. It should be noted that the collision point is not necessarily at the centre of either of the traditional figures.

In many cases the stylized figures do not follow the limits exactly, but any bias is on the safe side.

Figure 5.11 The sequence of cross-ahead/cross-astern points

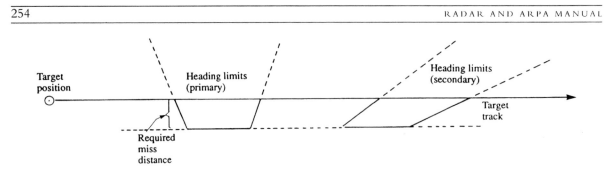

Figure 5.12   The development of areas to keep clear: heavy lines indicate boundaries of danger areas

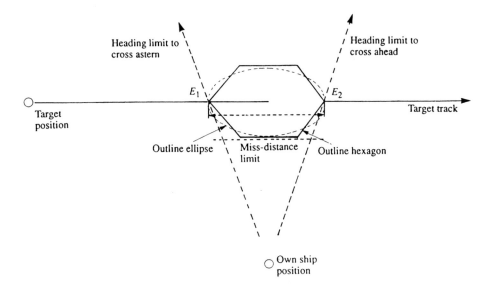

Figure 5.13   Acceptable symmetrical figures

5.6.2   Changes in the shape of the PAD

Due to the lack of symmetry in the geometry which generates the area, the cross-ahead and cross-astern positions do not move symmetrically about the collision point when the miss-distance is changed. The cross-ahead position usually moves more markedly than the cross-astern position (see Figure 5.9, showing the movement of the two collision points, where the primary movement is much slower than the

secondary). The overall result is an asymmetrical growth of the area with the cross-ahead position moving rapidly away from the collision point.

5.6.3   The movement of the PAD

5.6.3.1   The collision case

As in the case of the collision point, when a danger area is violated by the heading marker the danger area will continue to move down the heading marker with the cross-ahead and cross-astern points on opposite bows. The shape of the danger area may change but it will never move off the heading marker. In the case of a slower ship, where either of the two predicted areas is violated, the other will move in towards the target and eventually merge with the one on the heading marker.

In the limiting case where the observing ship's heading marker just touches the limit of either of the predicted areas of danger, the limit will remain in contact with the heading marker, although the shape of the area may change considerably.

5.6.3.2 The 'passing clear' case

In the non-collision case where the heading marker does not violate one of the danger areas, the areas themselves will move across the screen, changing in shape and position. The movement will be very similar to that described for the collision point in Figure 5.7, depending on whether the observing ship is heading farther ahead than the cross-ahead position or farther astern than the cross-astern position. In the case of the dual areas of danger, although the movement will generally be the same as that shown for the dual collision points, a special case can arise when two danger areas may merge. This special case indicates the possibility of two cross-astern positions existing but no cross-ahead position. It is also possible that cross-astern positions may exist and an area of danger be drawn, which does not embrace an actual collision point.

5.6.3.3 Special cases

In some cases, for example, an end-on encounter, a cross-ahead and cross-astern position is not valid. In this context it is necessary to consider a pass-to-port and pass-to-starboard as defining the limits of the miss-distance. In the practical case, this results in the generation of a circle about the target's position.

5.6.4 The future of PADs

PADs are additional to the display of standard relative and true vectors. They have never become recognized by the regulatory authorities and do not have to be part of an ARPA training course. PADs are no longer provided on the present radar models manufactured by the company to which Sperry now belongs, although this does not necessarily mean that PADs will not be introduced on a new model.

PADs require some understanding of the principles and misunderstanding of the data that can occur. There has been some suggestion that PADs take no account of the Collision Avoidance Regulations and encourage less well-trained navigators to alter course for the biggest gap rather than in accordance with the rules. Thus there has been some reluctance to accept PADs at sea, not helped by the fact that availability has been restricted to Sperry models.

They remain an elegant solution to the collision avoidance problem and a study of PADs becomes an interesting test of encounter geometry for the academic. Perhaps PADs will again be provided on ARPAs and ATAs in the future.

6 The radar system – operational controls

6.1 Optimum performance

A major aim of the radar observer should be to ensure that all the targets which can be detected *are detected*. This is sometimes described as achieving the maximum probability of detection of targets. For any given radar system, the performance is limited in all circumstances by certain design parameters such as transmitter power, aerial gain and receiver sensitivity (see Section 3.2). On any particular occasion the performance of the system may be further limited by weather and atmospheric conditions (see Sections 3.6, 3.7 and 3.8). Although design features and environmental conditions place limits on the potential performance of the system, the ability of the observer to set and maintain the operational controls in correct adjustment determines whether or not such potential performance is realized. Maladjustment of the controls may result in a failure to detect targets at a sufficiently early stage or may allow them to escape detection completely. It is therefore of crucial importance that the radar observer knows, understands and implements the correct practical procedures for the setting up of the operational controls and for maintaining them in optimum adjustment according to changing requirements and circumstances.

Further, when basic data is extracted by making measurements from the display, the observer must ensure that the full potential accuracy is realized. Maladjustment of certain controls may impair the accuracy of such measurements and this must be avoided by the use of the proper procedures.

This chapter presents detailed practical procedures which, if followed, will ensure the correct initial setting of the controls at switch-on and the appropriate subsequent adjustments necessary to maintain optimum performance. The procedures also deal with the use of the controls in routine tasks, including the combating of the adverse effects of weather conditions and the extraction of basic radar and ARPA data from the display.

There exist long established criteria by which the setting of the radar controls can be judged. These criteria derive historically from the characteristics of the traditional analogue picture (see Section 2.6.2) and cannot necessarily be applied directly to a synthetic display. Some controls found on modern synthetic displays (see Sections 2.6.6 and 2.6.7) have no counterpart on their analogue ancestors. For these reasons this chapter, in dealing with setting-up procedure, will treat real and synthetic displays separately (see Sections 6.2, 6.3 and 6.4). The setting up of an ARPA display requires the optimization of the radar controls and the correct adjustment of the ARPA controls to achieve effective and accurate tracking and this is also treated separately (see Section 6.12). Where the procedure deals with routine tasks such as clutter suppression, the differences between traditional and digital techniques will be highlighted.

6.2 Setting-up procedure for an analogue display

The operational controls are all located on the display unit and for this reason the procedure is commonly referred to as *setting up the display*. However, it should be borne in mind that some of the controls do not perform display functions. The tuning control operates within the radio frequency section of the transceiver (see Sections 2.5.1 and 2.7.2). The gain and sea clutter controls also perform receiver functions (see Sections 2.5.2 and 2.5.3), although the section of the receiver in which they operate may well be located within the display unit. The pulse length selector (which may also be affected by the range selector) operates in the transmitter (to control the pulse length and PRF – see Section 2.3.4) and in the receiver (to control the bandwidth – see Section 2.5.2.4).

6.2.1 Preliminary procedure

Before switching the equipment on, the following preliminary checks should be carried out:

1 Ensure that the antenna is clear. In particular it is important to check that no personnel are working on or close to the antenna and that there are no loose halyards or other such rigging which may foul it.
2 Check that the power switch that makes the ship's mains available to the installation is on. This switch may not necessarily be located in the wheelhouse.
3 Set the following front panel controls to zero effect:

   (a) Brilliance: This precludes the possibility of the screen being flooded with light when the set becomes operational and hence the danger of the phosphor being damaged (see Section 2.6.1.2). In any event this is the first control to be adjusted when setting up and it is convenient to start from zero effect.
   (b) Gain, range rings brilliance, variable range marker brilliance, sea clutter and rain clutter (any automatic clutter controls should be

switched off): All of the controls mentioned here have some effect on the overall brightness of the picture and, if they are not set to zero effect, they make it very difficult to judge correctly the setting of the brilliance control.

6.2.2 Switching on

It is convenient to consider that this operation carries out three distinct functions:

1 The supply of power to the antenna.
2 The supply of power to the transceiver and display.
3 The switching of the system from the *stand-by* condition to the *operational* condition (see below).

In some systems an individual switch may be associated with each function. It is perhaps more common to find that a single switch combines functions 1 and 2. In a further variation, a single multi-position switch may service all three functions.

The application of power to the system initiates a warming-up period. Very high voltages (EHT) and working temperatures are associated with certain elements of the system, in particular the transmitter (see Section 2.3) and the CRT (see Section 2.6.1). Good engineering practice dictates that such elements should be raised gradually to working temperature before the high voltages are applied. Some form of thermal or other delay timer will normally be used to isolate the EHT during the warming-up period, which is likely to exceed one and a half minutes. The maximum duration is set by the IMO Performance Standards (see Section 11.2.1) which require that, after switching on from cold, the equipment should become fully operational within 4 minutes. For situations other than that of a cold start the same section of the standard requires the provision of a stand-by condition from which the equipment can be brought to an operational condition within 5 seconds.

The precise status of the equipment in the stand-by condition may vary with manufacturer but in all cases the transmitter will be in the quiescent state, i.e. it will be maintained at or close to working temperature but no pulses will be transmitted. The use of the stand-by condition is discussed in detail in Section 6.7. If the operational condition is selected at initial switch-on (see function 3 above), the system will automatically switch from the stand-by condition to the operational condition when the warming-up period has elapsed. While the system is warming up the observer may make the following selections:

Orientation and presentation. This selection is a matter of personal choice and navigational circumstances. Features which might influence such a selection are considered in Sections 1.4.4, 1.5.3, Chapter 7 and Chapter 8.

Range scale. It is usually best to set up on a medium range scale such as 12 miles. The likelihood of echoes and sea clutter which have not been affected by saturation (see Section 2.5.2.1) make such a scale best suited for judging the quality of the picture when it is subsequently obtained.

Pulse length. This should be appropriate to the range scale selected, e.g. medium range scale would suggest medium pulse length (see Section 2.3.4).

6.2.3 Preparing the display

This involves the setting of the controls directly associated with the CRT (see Section 2.6.1) so as to prepare the tube to display a marine radar picture; they should be adjusted in the sequential order set out below. In modern systems some of these controls may be preset. Nevertheless it is important to check that the preset control is having the desired effect, since they have no automatic correcting action. If they go wrong, they will stay wrong.

6.2.3.1   Setting the brilliance

The brilliance control sets the *no signal* level of the spot brightness (see Section 2.6.1.1). Since the presence of an echo is indicated by a temporary increase in that brightness, the setting of this control is fundamental to successful echo detection.

The brilliance control should be set so that the rotating trace is barely visible. If the brilliance is set lower than this, weak echoes may be missed because a small increase in electron beam strength may be insufficient to make the spot visible. Conversely, if the setting is too high, echoes may be missed, not because they are not displayed, but because a small increase in spot brightness may be difficult to see against an already bright background. The latter effect is sometimes described as lack of contrast (this use of the word contrast should not be confused with its use to name one of the controls associated with synthetic displays – see Sections 2.6.6.5, 6.3.4.1 and 6.4.3.1).

Excessive brilliance will tend to de-focus the spot, resulting in a reduction in discrimination and the accuracy with which ranges and bearings can be measured (see Sections 2.6.1.1, 6.2.3.2, 6.3.3 and 6.4.3.2).

6.2.3.2   Setting the focus

This control, by adjusting the position to which the electron beam is converged (see Section 2.6.1.1), determines the spot size. As the latter is one of the factors which affects the area of echo paint (see Section 2.6.5.1) the control must be set to produce the smallest possible spot diameter.

To set the focus control, switch on the range rings and adjust the control until the range rings appear as sharp as possible. Choose a ring half-way between the centre and the edge of the screen, as it is difficult to achieve perfect focus over the whole screen. Poor focus is evidenced by the ring appearing thick and *woolly*. In modern marine equipment the focus is invariably preset and no user control is provided. When the check has been completed the rings should be switched off.

Where focus adjustment is necessary, it is important that it is carried out after the brilliance has been correctly set because an excessive brilliance setting will tend to defocus the spot.

6.2.3.3   Centring the origin

A pair of centring or shift controls (see Section 2.6.1.3) allow the observer to make small adjustments to the position of the origin of the rotating trace. As its name suggests, the *horizontal shift* (or centring) control produces horizontal movement of the origin, i.e. movement parallel to the 090/270° axis of the graduated circular bearing scale which surrounds the tube (see Section 1.3.5), while the *vertical shift* produces movement at right angles to this direction.

Although the picture may subsequently be used in an offset position, when first setting up the display, the position of the origin should be adjusted to coincide with the centre of the fixed bearing scale and the centre of the Perspex cursor (see Sections 1.3.5 and 6.9.3). This is necessary to facilitate the subsequent alignment of the displayed heading marker with the bearing scale (see Section 6.2.3.4). Further, it should be noted that failure to centre the origin of the trace will result in errors in bearings which are obtained by the use of the Perspex cursor (see Section 6.9.3).

The centre of the Perspex cursor disk is normally marked by a cross formed by the intersection of the main cursor line, which is engraved along a diameter, and a short line which bisects it at right angles. To centre the origin, the cursor should be aligned to the 000°/180° direction on the bearing scale and the horizontal shift control should be adjusted to place the origin below the engraved diameter. The vertical shift control should then be adjusted to place the origin below the cross at the centre of the Perspex cursor disk and thus (assuming that there has been no mechanical damage to the mounting of the disk), at the geometrical centre of the bearing scale.

Because the cursor disk is located some distance above the tube face, care must be taken to avoid parallax by ensuring that the eye is directly above the centre of the screen when judging the position of the origin. In many display units the cursor markings are engraved on the top and bottom surfaces of the Perspex disk. By adjusting the eye position so that the top and bottom sets of lines are in transit, i.e. such that only a single cross can be seen, the observer can ensure that the effect of parallax has been eliminated. Alternatively, use may be made of the visor or viewing hood. Most displays have some such arrangement which can be removed at night but which, when fitted, allows the display to be viewed in daylight. This will be designed to ensure that the eye is placed in such a position as to avoid parallax.

6.2.3.4 Orientating the picture

The picture must be correctly orientated by rotating it so that the heading marker intersects the correct graduation on the circular bearing scale surrounding the tube. In many older systems it was necessary to rotate the picture manually, whereas in more modern systems auto-alignment takes place provided that the compass repeater has been correctly set to the vessel's heading. The procedure will thus depend on the preferred orientation and can be set out as follows:

Ship's-head-up (unstabilized) – see also Section 1.4.1. The ship's-head-up orientation should be selected. Where a manual alignment control is provided, the heading marker should be rotated to align it with the 000° graduation on the bearing scale. In the case of an auto-aligned system, the display should be observed to ensure that the heading marker has aligned correctly.

True-north-up (stabilized) – see also Section 1.4.2. It is expedient to start by selecting the ship's-head-up (unstabilized) orientation as this ensures that the heading marker will not yaw in sympathy with the azimuth stabilizing signal until the observer is ready to switch in the latter (see Section 2.6.3).

The display compass repeater should be correctly aligned to the vessel's instantaneous true heading. The alignment control which adjusts the repeater normally operates in association with a clutch mechanism. When the control is pressed in against a spring, the gyro repeater card is disconnected from the gyro follow-up system and it can be freely rotated to the desired reading by turning the alignment control. On release of the control, the clutch re-engages the repeater card to the gyro follow-up system and the alignment control can be rotated freely. The repeater should be aligned to the true course and, at an instant when the vessel is right on course, the alignment control should be released. A check should then be made to ensure that the repeater does follow variations in the ship's heading.

Where a manual alignment control is provided, the heading marker should be rotated to align it with that graduation on the bearing scale which corresponds with the vessel's true course. At an instant when the vessel is *right on course*, the true-north-up orientation should be selected (see also Section 1.4.2).

In the case of an auto-aligned system, true-north-up should be selected and the display should then be observed to ensure that the heading marker has aligned correctly.

In both cases, after the heading marker has been aligned, the display should be observed for a short period to ensure that the heading marker is following variations in the ship's heading.

Course-up (stabilized) – see also Section 1.4.3. It is expedient to start by selecting the ship's-head-up (unstabilized) orientation as this ensures that the heading marker will not yaw in sympathy with the azimuth stabilizing signal until the observer is ready to switch in the latter (see Section 2.6.3).

The display compass repeater should be correctly aligned to the vessel's instantaneous true heading in the same way as described for the north-up orientation.

Where a manual alignment control is provided, the heading marker should be rotated to align it with the 000° graduation on the bearing scale. At an instant when the vessel is *right on course*, the course-up orientation should be selected.

In the case of an auto-aligned system, course-up should be selected and the display should then be observed to ensure that the heading marker has aligned correctly.

In both cases, after the heading marker has been aligned, the display should be observed for a short period to ensure that the heading marker is following variations in the ship's heading.

In the particular case of course-up orientation, it will be necessary to reset the reference course each time the vessel makes a sustained alteration of course. In older systems this will have to be done manually, while in more modern systems it is merely necessary to press some form of reset control when the vessel is steady on the new course.

It is essential to appreciate that, irrespective of the orientation which is selected, all bearings are measured from the reference of the heading marker (see Section 6.9); if the picture is not correctly orientated, all bearings read from the graduated scale around the

CRT will be in error. The operation of aligning the heading marker on the bearing scale should not be confused with that of the alignment of the heading marker with the ship's fore-and-aft line. The latter operation is concerned with ensuring that the heading marker contacts (see Section 2.4.6) close and produce the heading marker signal at the instant the radar beam crosses the ship's fore-and-aft line in the forward direction. This alignment cannot be checked without reference to both visual and radar observations (see Section 6.9.9).

6.2.4 Obtaining the optimum picture

Optimum picture is obtained by setting the receiver controls to maximize the detection of weak echoes. This involves the adjustment of, firstly, the gain control and, secondly, the tuning control.

6.2.4.1 Setting the gain control

The gain control, which is sometimes referred to as the sensitivity control, adjusts the amounts by which all received echoes and receiver noise are amplified (see Section 2.5.2). It should be advanced until a low level, close-grained speckling can be seen all over the screen. The speckling is the visual indication of the phenomenon known as thermal or receiver noise. This important feature is described in detail in Section 2.5.2.3 which explains that signals weaker than the noise cannot be detected and that those signals close to noise level will only be detected with difficulty. The problem is analogous to attempting to listen for the fog signal of another vessel against the background of audible noise from the engine and other sources on board the observing vessel.

Because it determines the minimum level of detectable signal, the amplitude of displayed noise, and thus the setting of the gain, is of critical importance. Noise is a fluctuating signal and if the gain is set too low the peaks will not be displayed and genuine echoes close to noise level may well escape detection (see Figure 6.1.) If the gain is set too high, again weak

level at which signal amplitudes
limit owing to receiver saturation

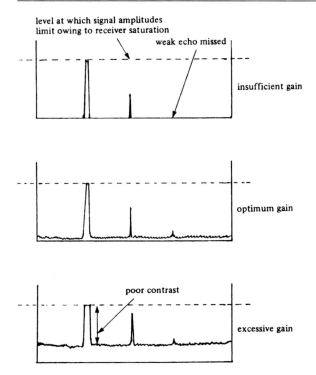

Figure 6.1 Setting the gain control

echoes may be lost, not because they are not displayed but because, as a result of poor contrast, they may not be obvious against the background of the noise (see Figure 6.1). Further, excessive noise may also make it difficult to detect even strong echoes. If strong signals saturate the receiver (see Sections 2.5.2.1 and 2.5.2.5) additional gain will not increase their brightness but will increase the amplitude of the noise echoes and hence reduce the contrast which is related to the signal-to-noise ratio.

Excessive gain may cause defocusing of the spot, resulting in loss of discrimination and measurement accuracy (see Sections 2.6.5, 6.3.4 and 6.4.4).

In the presence of extensive and strong echoes, e.g. in harbour, it may be difficult to assess reliably the level of speckles present. In such circumstances it may be found helpful temporarily to set the tuning control well away from the optimum position while the gain is adjusted.

6.2.4.2 Setting the tuning control

The function of the tuning control is to adjust the frequency of the receiver (see Section 2.5.1) so that it coincides with that of the transmitter, rather in the same way as one might tune a broadcast receiver to listen for a distant station.

If the receiver is only slightly mistuned, the extent of the bandwidth (see Section 2.5.2.4) may still allow stronger echoes to be displayed even to the level of saturation. It is important not to be misled by this because weak echoes will most certainly be lost. It is thus important to establish criteria against which it is possible to make a sensitive assessment of the setting of the tuning control.

One of the most sensitive criteria is the response of a weak echo from land (see Figure 6.2). The tuning control should be adjusted while carefully watching such a response. As the correct frequency is approached, the brightness of the displayed echo response will increase. It will peak at the correct setting and decay after that setting has been passed. By adjusting the control to achieve the maximum displayed brightness of such a target, the correct setting may be easily and reliably found. As the correct setting is approached it will be necessary to adjust the control in progressively smaller steps. It is important to appreciate that after each small adjustment is made, it is necessary to wait until the echo is re-painted in order to judge what effect an adjustment has had. If the coarse tuning has been set correctly by service personnel (see Section 2.5.1.2), the correct setting for the display tuning control should lie close to the centre of its range of travel. If the correct position is found to approach either end of the range of travel, the coarse tuning control (which will be located inside the transceiver) should be readjusted by qualified service personnel.

Strong echoes should not be used because they may saturate the receiver even when it is mistuned and if this is the case their displayed response will not be sensitive to the position of the fine tuning control. A land echo is chosen because it will give a constant response against which to judge the setting. If, for example, the echo of a buoy were chosen, the observer would be unable to tell the difference between fluctuations due

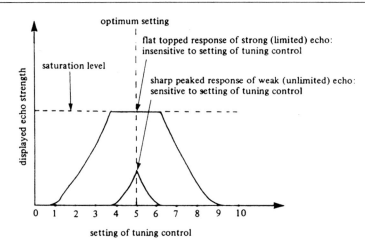

Figure 6.2 Setting the tuning control

to movement of the buoy in a seaway and those due to adjustment of the control.

Alternative acceptable criteria involve adjusting the control to achieve:

1   The maximum radial extent of sea clutter echoes. These are described in Section 3.6.
2   The maximum area of precipitation echoes. These are described in Section 3.7.
3   The maximum extent of the receiver monitor signal. This is discussed in Section 6.5.

Some displays offer features such as *magic eyes*, tuning meters and tuning indicators. They should not be used in preference to the above criteria. Such devices are not required by the IMO Performance Standards and the danger of the observer being misled by such indicators is discussed in Section 2.5.1.5.

The tuning may drift as the equipment warms up and to a lesser extent with the passage of time (see Section 2.3.3.2). The setting of the control should therefore be checked frequently during the first 30 minutes after switching on and periodically thereafter.

Where full automatic tuning is provided (see Section 2.5.1.4), a performance check should be carried out to ensure that optimum tuning is being achieved. The procedure for carrying this out is described in Section 6.5.6.

6.3   Setting-up procedure for a radial-scan synthetic display

In many respects the setting-up procedure for a radial-scan synthetic display is identical to that for an analogue display. Differences do however exist and these will be highlighted in Sections 6.3.1 to 6.3.4.3. The differences arise largely because, as a result of the digitization of the radar signals (see Section 2.6.6), it is not always possible to judge the settings of the gain and tuning controls by the criteria traditionally used in the case of analogue displays. Further, the contrast control which is almost invariably a feature of the synthetic display has no counterpart on the traditional analogue display. While it is true to say that some analogue displays did offer interference suppression, in general signal processing (see Section 2.6.6.6) is only available with synthetic displays.

6.3.1   Preliminary procedure

The procedure is the same as described for an analogue display in Section 6.2.1, with the exception that the contrast control should be set to zero effect and any signal processing facilities (such as interference suppression or echo stretching) should be switched off.

In some systems it will be found that the contrast is preset.

6.3.2 Switching on

The procedure is essentially the same as described for an analogue display in Section 6.2.2. However, in the more modern systems it may well be found that orientation, presentation, range scale and pulse length are selected automatically on switch-on. The conditions automatically selected are known as the *default conditions*.

The use of default conditions has been made possible by the availability of modern controls designed particularly for computer applications. Traditionally, marine radar controls have been analogue in their action, normally taking the form of rotary knobs and multi-position mechanical switches, but there is a tendency for more and more of these controls to be replaced by electronic switches which send a digital signal to the display computer when operated by touch or pressure. They may take the form of push buttons, touch-sensitive switches or a tracker ball. The touch-sensitive screen described in Section 2.6.7.3 is an extension of this technique.

On receipt of the signal, the display computer will carry out some programmed checks on the status of the equipment. The controls can be configured and programmed to operate in a variety of ways. They may operate on the *alternative action* or *toggle* principle, i.e. one push or touch selects a function and a further push deselects that function. Alternatively they may be used to control more than one function, e.g. the first push selects function 1, the second push selects function 2 and the third push de-selects both functions. They can be used in pairs to perform an incremental action. For example, each push of one control may select the next higher range scale while its partner will reduce, in steps, the range scale selected. The list of variations is almost endless but the common feature of all actions is that, other than the actual push or touch, the action is not mechanical.

The display computer can be programmed to select the default conditions when the power is first applied at switch-on. For example, it might default to true-north-up orientation, relative-motion presentation, 12 mile range scale and long pulse. If the observer wishes conditions other than those to which the system defaults, the necessary selection can be made by pushing the appropriate switches immediately after switch-on.

In older systems all of the controls are likely to be of the mechanical type. Default conditions are not possible because these controls will remain in their last selected positions and the observer will need to make positive selection of the initial conditions required. Some systems may have a mix of analogue and computer controls.

6.3.3 Preparing the display

The procedure is identical to that described for an analogue display in Section 6.2.3.

6.3.4 Obtaining the optimum picture

It is in this area that the setting up procedure for a synthetic display diverges from that of the traditional analogue display.

6.3.4.1 Setting the contrast control

Traditionally the term contrast has been used to describe, in general, the difference between two levels of brightness and, in particular, the difference in brightness between the echoes and the background noise on an analogue display. In a synthetic display, contrast is the name given to the control which adjusts the brightness of all synthetic echoes (see Section 2.6.6.5). If the control is set to zero no synthetic echoes will be displayed. Conversely if the control is set to high, individual echoes will *bloom*, i.e. become large and defocused. Between these two extremes is a wide range of settings intended to allow the observer to adapt the overall brightness of the display to suit the ambient light conditions. (Compare this with the analogue case, in which the brightness of the weaker echoes is limited by the extent to which the noise restricts the amount of gain that can be applied.) In some systems the contrast is preset by the manufacturer.

There is a 'chicken and egg' relationship between the contrast and gain/tuning. Some measure of contrast must be applied initially or there will be no visible signal on which to judge the setting of the gain and tuning. Conversely, it may not be possible to make a final decision as to the setting of the contrast until after the gain and tuning have been adjusted, because the overall picture brightness is to some extent dependent on picture content. The correct strategy is to find an initial contrast setting which gives sufficient brightness to allow the subsequent setting of the gain and tuning controls. The operator's manual will normally give guidance but, if not, the setting can be found easily by experiment. If there is not enough time to experiment, set the contrast control to the middle of its travel. The setting is not crucial at this stage as the control may well be readjusted after the setting of the gain and tuning controls. Furthermore it is important to appreciate that the control affects only the brightness of the picture; it does *not* affect the content, which depends upon the setting of the gain and the tuning.

The procedure is thus iterative and can be summarized as follows:

1 Select the initial setting of contrast.
2 Set the gain correctly (see Section 6.3.4.2).
3 Readjust the contrast if necessary to suit the ambient light conditions.
4 Set the tuning correctly (see Section 6.3.4.3).
5 Readjust the contrast if necessary.

6.3.4.2 Setting the gain control

The gain must be set to achieve the optimum relationship between the threshold level and the noise amplitude (see Section 2.6.6.2). In some systems, by operating the gain, the observer controls the threshold level while in others the receiver gain is affected. The difference is academic as, in both cases, advancing the setting of the gain control brings the threshold closer to the noise.

Ideally one would wish the gain to be set so that the threshold level is sufficiently low to display all detectable echoes yet sufficiently high to miss the noise. Because noise is a very rapidly fluctuating signal, such an ideal cannot be achieved. If the setting of the gain is sufficiently high for all detectable targets to cross the threshold, many noise peaks will also cross the threshold. Conversely, if the gain is set so that no noise peaks cross the threshold, detectable targets may well be missed. For the case of a single-level digitized picture, the dilemma is illustrated by Figure 6.3. Clearly a compromise setting must be found. The ease with which this setting can be made depends on the number of discrete video levels offered by the system (see Section 2.6.6.7).

In the single-level video case any noise which crosses the threshold will be displayed with the same brightness amplitude as a detectable echo. This makes it much more difficult to assess the background noise than in the analogue case, where there is a very obvious amplitude difference between most echoes and the noise background. In some older synthetic displays it is possible to revert to an analogue picture, albeit in some cases on only one range scale (see Section 2.6.6.5); the difficulty can then be avoided by setting the gain while viewing the analogue picture. Later synthetic displays do not offer the analogue option and in such cases it is necessary to live with the difficulty of single-level noise and targets. With practice the observer should be able to identify the noise by its random nature and the radial length of individual noise pulses. The peaks of real noise are sharply spiked and thus the number of successive elements of a range word (see Section 2.6.6.3) occupied by a single noise pulse is likely to be noticeably less than that occupied by most genuine targets. This does not mean that every very short digital response is necessarily noise. A weak, but genuine, received echo which barely crosses the threshold may well activate only one range cell.

The difficulty of achieving a suitable noise setting is reduced where more than one video level is offered. The extent to which the additional levels are beneficial in this regard depends not just on how many levels are provided but also on how they are

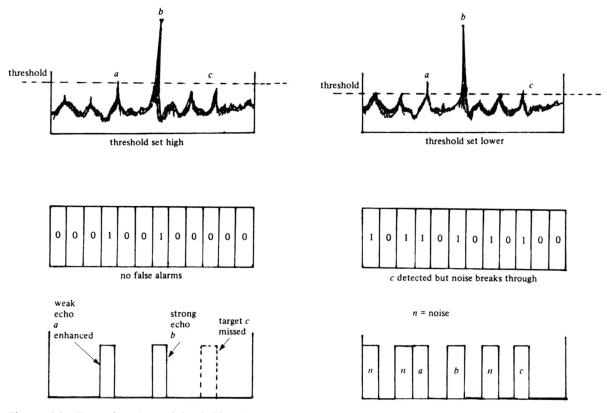

Figure 6.3 Target detection and threshold setting

disposed (see Figures 2.45, 2.46 in Section 2.6.6.7). The arrangement shown in Figure 2.45 is clearly an improvement on the single-level case, but only those systems which provide a *grey level*, as illustrated by Figure 2.46, assist the observer in identifying the noise as easily as with real signals. The grey-level approach makes it comparatively easy to judge the setting of the gain control because it can be set so that the noise produces an even speckled background at *low threshold*. Although a fair number of noise pulses will cross the grey-level threshold, because they are displayed at a fraction of high-level amplitude, the practised observer will not confuse them with strong echoes. Further, although low-level echoes will have the same amplitude as the noise, their coherence, persistence and radial length will favour detection when compared with the random noise pattern.

6.3.4.3   Setting the tuning control

The use of a weak land echo as the sensitive criterion by which to judge the setting of the tuning control (see Section 6.2.4.2) cannot be applied in the case of a synthetic display due to the quantizing effect of digital storage (see Section 2.6.6.7). This is illustrated for a single video level system by Figure 6.4.

Reference to Figure 6.4 shows that there may be little or no relation between the amplitude of the synthetic echo and the analogue response which produced it. The setting of the tuning control must not be judged with respect to the amplitude of the synthetic echoes because their brightness is not sufficiently sensitive to the position of the control. Even if several video levels are offered, the displayed echo strength will change only when the real echo moves into a new

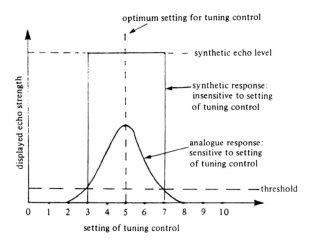

Figure 6.4 Setting the tuning control – the effect of quantizing

inter-threshold band, and even then in steps which may be quite large. Only if the synthetic display provided as many digital levels as there are phosphor brightness levels (see Section 2.6.1.2) would this limitation be removed. The vast majority of systems do not attempt to attain this goal.

In some older synthetic displays it is possible to revert to an analogue picture, albeit in some cases on only one range scale (see Section 2.6.6.5). The difficulty can then be avoided by adjusting the tuning control while observing the analogue picture. With later synthetic displays that do not offer the analogue option it is necessary to adjust the control to achieve one of the following results:

1 The maximum radial extent of sea clutter echoes: these are described in Section 3.6.
2 The maximum area of precipitation echoes: these are described in Section 3.7.
3 The maximum radial extent of the receiver monitor signal: this is discussed in Section 6.5.

It should be noted that all the above criteria are suitable because they are based on the area of response rather than on its brightness.

In the case of systems which have a grey level it may be possible with practice to choose an isolated

land target and tune for the maximum area displayed at grey level.

The tuning may drift as the system warms up and to a lesser extent with the passage of time. The setting of the control should therefore be checked frequently during the first thirty minutes after switching on and periodically thereafter.

Where fully automatic tuning is provided (see Section 2.5.1.4), a performance check should be carried out to ensure that optimum tuning is being achieved. The procedure for carrying this out is described in Section 6.5.6.

The warning on the limitations of tuning indicators set out in Section 6.2.4.2 is equally valid for synthetic displays.

6.4 Setting-up procedure for a raster-scan synthetic display

The raster-scan display is based on digital storage and as a result the setting-up procedure relates in many ways to that described for the radial-scan synthetic display. However, significant differences do exist due to the 'television' nature of the display and the availability of signal processing made possible by the greater inherent memory capacity of the raster-scan system. Such differences are highlighted in the succeeding Sections 6.4.1 to 6.4.4.

6.4.1 Preliminary procedure

The procedure is essentially the same as that described for a radial synthetic display in Section 6.3.1. However, although the antenna safety checks are of vital importance regardless of the type of display, it may not be necessary to set certain of the raster-scan system controls to zero before switching on.

In general, the low burn characteristic of the phosphor used in television CRTs (see Section 2.6.7.1) renders it unnecessary to turn the screen brilliance to zero before switching on. By comparison, the radial-scan display is more susceptible to burn damage, not only because of the phosphor characteristic, but because of the slowly rotating trace. The light from a 20 ms burst of excessive brilliance would be dissipated over an entire television frame, whereas it would be concentrated within a sector of about 2° on a radial-scan display.

In Section 6.4.3.1 it will be seen that the adjustment of raster-scan screen brilliance is more subjective and much less critical than in the radial-scan case. For this reason the presence of range rings or a variable range marker (VRM) is not likely to cause the observer to set the control incorrectly: it is not necessary to switch these two functions off before the power is applied to the display. In some systems it will be found that the range rings and VRM actually default to the *on* condition. The contrast between the background and the range rings/VRM is determined by the setting of the screen contrast and as a result separate range ring/VRM brilliance controls are not normally provided.

In the radial-scan case the contrast must be set initially to zero (see Section 6.3.1) to ensure that there is no possibility of the observer's assessment of the *no signal* brilliance setting being influenced by the presence of any very strong echoes which might display even with the gain set to minimum. The subjective nature of the screen brilliance setting mentioned in the previous paragraph (and described in Section 6.4.3.1) renders it unnecessary to set the contrast to zero.

The gain, sea clutter and rain clutter controls should be set to zero. In addition, particular attention should be paid to ensuring that signal-processing facilities, such as interference suppression, echo stretch, adaptive gain and rotation-to-rotation correlation, are inoperative (see Sections 3.9.5.1, 6.11.1, 3.6.3.3 and 3.6.3.4 respectively). In some raster-scan systems these facilities default to the *off* condition at switch-on. The setting of the gain is fundamental to achieving the correct relationship between threshold and noise levels (see Sections 2.6.6.2 and 2.6.6.7). All of the other foregoing controls and facilities also affect the echo content of the picture and may result in the gain being set incorrectly if not switched to zero effect when the gain level is assessed.

6.4.2   Switching on

The procedure is similar to that for the radial-scan synthetic display described in Section 6.3.2, but in the case of a raster-scan display it may be found that the system defaults to the stand-by condition at switch-on. Generally the number of functions which have default conditions is likely to be more extensive than with a radial-scan display. In addition to orientation, presentation, range scale, pulse length and signal processing, this may include the status of the range rings, the variable range marker and the electronic bearing line. If the observer does not wish any given default setting, appropriate selection can be made after switch-on.

If the raster-scan display uses a colour CRT the steel shadow mask (see Section 2.6.7.7) may become magnetized with the passage of time. The effect of such magnetism is to degrade the purity of the colours displayed on the face of the tube. When the system is switched on, a degaussing circuit automatically demagnetizes the shadow mask. In a domestic television display, if the colour purity is degraded during normal use the mask can be demagnetized by switching the set off and switching it on again. Clearly it may not be convenient or practical to do this in the case of a marine radar, which may have to run continuously for a long period. Some form of spring-loaded switch or similar arrangement will be provided to operate the degaussing circuit when required.

Most modern raster-scan displays warm up very quickly and the synthetic PPI circle, bearing scale, range rings and other graphics may well be visible within as little as 30 seconds (assuming that the brilliance and contrast have not been set to zero). It may be possible to select the operational condition at switch-on, but the system will remain in the stand-by condition until the transmitter delay expires. The latter is a transmitter function. As in all systems, it must not exceed 4 minutes (see Section 6.2.2) but is unlikely to be less than 1.5 minutes.

6.4.3   Preparing the display

The procedure involves preparing a television screen to display a marine radar picture; here there are major differences when compared with that appropriate to a radial-scan display.

6.4.3.1 *Setting the screen brilliance*

The setting of the brilliance is judged by a criterion which differs fundamentally from that traditionally used in radial-scan displays, where the control adjusts the brilliance of the slowly rotating trace and the criterion for optimum setting can be rigidly specified in terms of the principle on which echoes are displayed (see Section 6.2.3.1). In a high-refresh-rate television display, the screen brilliance controls the brightness of the entire picture frame. The perceived brightness of the picture is largely a function of the ambient light conditions. It is also affected by the screen contrast control which defines the difference between dark and light for both graphics and echoes. In some systems the contrast is preset. The relationship between the brilliance and contrast settings for a green monochrome display is illustrated by Figure 6.5.

Reference to Figure 6.5 shows that the screen contrast adjusts the difference in brilliance level between the darker/darkest areas of the screen and the brighter/brightest areas. In general, the graphics will be single-level, i.e. bright on dark, and this will also be the case for target echoes in a simple single-threshold system. Where multi-level video is offered, the number of levels of echo brightness is the same as the number of thresholds used for the storage of range (see Section 2.6.6.7). (If rotation-to-rotation correlation is not switched off, the number of levels may be related to the number of rotations used – see Section 3.6.3.4.) The perceived effect of the screen contrast will depend to some extent on the screen brilliance setting. At higher brilliance settings, a greater absolute difference between light and dark will be necessary for an observer to perceive a difference between the two levels. Similarly, at very low levels of brilliance both light and dark levels may be so dark as to be indistinguishable.

Clearly there is an interrelationship between screen brilliance and screen contrast. Both contribute to the overall brightness of the picture as perceived by the observer and must be adjusted alternately until the best joint setting is found. The assessment of 'best' is a matter of subjective judgement for which a simple specific criterion, such as that prescribed for the radial case, cannot be given. However, consideration of the following factors will assist in making the judgement.

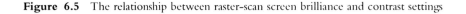

Figure 6.5 The relationship between raster-scan screen brilliance and contrast settings

Excessive brilliance. If the overall brightness is too high the picture will be uncomfortable to view in the same way as any source of bright light. Tiredness, stress and headaches may result. At night the high level of illumination associated with the display may impair night vision and distract the watchkeeper by producing reflections on the inside of the wheelhouse windows and other such surfaces. Even at maximum screen contrast setting it will be difficult to achieve an adequate difference between background and picture content, because both will already be very bright.

Insufficient brilliance. If the overall brightness is too low it will be difficult to view the display and distinguish picture detail in full daylight, particularly at a distance. Even at maximum screen contrast setting, it will be difficult to achieve an adequate difference between background and picture content, because both will be very dark.

Excessive contrast. If the screen brilliance is set at a level which is comfortable to the eye, excessive screen contrast will make the picture stark and harsh.

Inadequate contrast. Insufficient contrast will result in a picture which is flat and featureless.

In most cases it will be found that if at switch-on the screen brilliance and contrast controls are left in the position in which they were last used, the settings will be sufficiently close to the optimum as to require only a small amount of adjustment to suit the new ambient light conditions. If the controls have been set to zero or have been badly maladjusted, the following procedure should be used:

1   If the system offers alternative daytime and night-time monochrome or colour combinations, select the option appropriate to the ambient light conditions.

2   Set the screen brilliance and screen contrast controls to the middle of their travel. The PPI circle, synthetic bearing scale and other graphics should be visible. (If they are not, advance each control in turn by small amounts until the graphics are visible.)

3   Adjust the screen brilliance to a level consistent with comfortable viewing in the ambient light

conditions and such that the light issuing from the display does not interfere with the keeping of a proper lookout.

4   Adjust the screen contrast to achieve an obvious but comfortable difference in tone between the graphics and the background.

5   It may be necessary to make further repeated small alternate adjustments to the screen brilliance and screen contrast controls to obtain optimum overall level of brightness.

6.4.3.2   Checking the focus

It would be most unusual to find a raster-scan display in which the focus was not preset. Nevertheless, when preparing the display the focus should be checked. The graphics, in particular alphanumeric characters, are a good indicator of focus. If they are blurred and indistinct, focus adjustment is necessary and this should be carried out by qualified service personnel.

6.4.3.3   Centring the origin

The use of shift controls to centre the origin is not applicable to raster-scan displays because, in a centred display, the limit of the PPI is a graphics circle drawn about the origin as centre and the bearing scale is written in graphics and is concentric with it. Despite a visual impression which might suggest the contrary, there is no rotating trace corresponding to the radial-scan display. The appearance of rotation arises because, in the approximately 20 ms period required to refresh one frame of the cartesian raster, the radial memory is updated in an angular sector of about 2°. Thus the observer may see the moving pattern of updated data which gives the impression of a trace rotating in sympathy with the aerial.

All facilities for measuring bearings are generated graphically and in the default condition emanate from the electronic origin. In some systems the origin can be off-centred within the PPI circle.

6.4.3.4   Orientating the picture

In principle the procedure is the same as that described for a traditional radial-scan display in Section 6.2.3.4.

In general, raster-scan displays default to one of the preferred orientations when the system is switched on. Although the heading marker normally automatically aligns itself to the input provided by the display compass repeater, the latter must be aligned to the master compass by the observer.

6.4.4   Obtaining the optimum picture

In a raster-scan display the synthetic echoes are generated by threshold detection followed by digital storage (see Sections 2.6.6.1 and 2.6.6.2) and it is not always possible to judge the settings of the gain and tuning controls by the criteria traditionally used in setting up analogue displays. As a result, the procedure for setting the gain and tuning controls on a raster-scan display is the same as that described for a radial-scan synthetic display in Sections 6.3.4.2 and 6.3.4.3 respectively. Additionally, it should be borne in mind that rotation-to-rotation correlation (see Section 3.6.3.4) tends to eliminate some receiver noise: this facility should be switched off when setting up. It should be remembered that in the raster-scan case the screen contrast (which has a different function from that of the contrast control in a radial-scan display – see Section 2.6.6.5) will have been set at the same time as the screen brilliance. The presence of the digital noise background and a large number of digital echoes may have some slight effect on the overall brightness of the display and may necessitate minor readjustment of screen brilliance and/or screen contrast.

The warning on the limitations of tuning indicators set out in Section 6.2.4.2 is equally valid for raster-scan systems.

6.5   Performance monitoring

As soon as practical after the initial setting up of the display, the system performance should be monitored. In the case of a shore-based radar system it may be possible to assess the level of performance from a knowledge of the identity of those targets which were at the limit of detection when the system was installed and the performance was tested and optimized by the manufacturer. However, at sea it is usually not possible to discern whether or not the system is giving optimum performance merely by viewing the displayed picture, because the observer does not have exact knowledge of which targets should be seen. Although the picture may look good, the observer cannot be sure that the equipment is operating at the level of performance that was intended by the manufacturer. In the open sea in calm, foggy weather, the absence of echoes, despite the presence of receiver noise, may be due to a loss in performance rather than an empty ocean. Failure to appreciate this fundamental principle could lead to a very dangerous situation. The absence of echoes deprives the observer of the normal criteria by which to judge the setting of the tuning control.

The IMO Performance Standard (see Section 11.2.1) requires that means be available, while the equipment is in use operationally, to determine readily a significant drop in performance relative to a calibration standard established at the time of installation, and that the equipment is correctly tuned in the absence of targets. This facility is commonly referred to as a *performance monitor*. The sensitive element which makes monitoring possible is usually a unit known as an echo box and is described in the next section. Some systems use a device known as a transponder (see Section 6.5.4).

6.5.1   The principle of the echo box

Any normal target which was mounted on the ship to reflect signals for test purposes would be unsatisfactory because, apart from the fact that it would probably be inside the minimum detection range (see Section 3.2.4), the strength of the echo would probably be so great as to saturate the receiver even if the performance was well below optimum. The problem is commonly overcome by using what is known as an echo box.

The echo box is essentially a hollow metal container of precisely machined dimensions. In theory a variety of shapes can be used but, in practice, modern systems normally use a cylinder about the size of a small food can. The theory of the operation of the echo box is quite complex but its behaviour can be described in fairly simple terms. When a pulse of radar energy is transmitted into the box, the energy reverberates within the cavity and if, but only if, the cavity is the correct size in relationship to the wavelength of the radar signal, intense oscillations build up over the duration of the pulse length. At the end of the transmitted pulse the oscillations continue but their amplitude gradually decays over a period which is much longer than the duration of the transmitted pulse. As long as the oscillations persist, radar energy is re-radiated from the box. The energy re-radiated from the echo box can be treated in the same way as other returning radar signals and thus produces a visible, radial response on the display which is known as the *performance monitor signal*. This general principle is illustrated by Figure 6.6 but it should be noted that the angular extent of the monitor signal depends on other factors which are discussed in Section 6.5.2. The echo box and its associated circuitry is referred to as a performance monitor.

It may be found helpful to liken the action of the echo box to that of a bell which rings for a long time after being struck by a comparatively swift blow. In fact, engineers often refer to the re-radiation from the box as 'ringing'. (A full explanation of the action of the echo box is beyond the scope of this work, requiring an understanding of the theory of the resonant cavity: the reader who wishes to pursue this is referred to any good radar engineering text.)

Pursuing the analogy of the bell further, the length of time for which a nearby listener hears the bell ringing depends on the vigour with which it has been struck, and the sensitivity of the listener's ear at the frequency emitted by the bell. Applying this reasoning to the echo box, it should be evident that the radial extent of the monitor signal on the display is a measure of the performance of the radar system since it depends on:

1   *The transmitter performance.* The energy entering the echo box is a function of transmitted power and

(a) Transmitted pulse

Echo box

Minimum detectable signal

(b) Received signal

Maximum extent of monitor signal

(c) Displayed response

Figure 6.6   The echo box response

pulse length (see Sections 2.3.2.1 and 2.3.2.2). Thus the greater the amount of transmitted energy, the longer the echo box will ring.

2   *The receiver sensitivity.* The re-radiated signal is capable of detection until its amplitude has decayed to less than that of the receiver noise (see Section 2.5.2.3). Thus the more sensitive the receiver, the greater is the visible extent of the monitor signal (see Figure 6.6).

3   *The receiver tuning.* The frequency re-radiated by the echo box is the same as that of the transmitter. The maximum monitor signal depends on the

receiver being tuned to the same frequency (see Section 2.5.1.2).

4 *The display control settings.* Maladjustment of the display controls may prevent the observer detecting the full potential extent of the signal emitted by the echo box.

It is evident that if the system is adjusted by the manufacturer to optimum performance on installation (or after a service visit), and the radial extent of the monitor signal is measured at that time, the observer can be supplied with an objective calibration, in terms of miles and cables, against which to judge the performance of the system in the future. In particular this facilitates an assessment of the setting of the tuning control in the absence of echoes. It should be noted that if the echo box is sited external to the radar system, e.g. on some part of the ship's structure, it additionally monitors the aerial and waveguide performance. However, if the echo box is located within the radar system, as is quite common, it only monitors the transmitter and receiver functions. The implications of echo box siting are discussed further in the next section.

6.5.2 Echo box siting

In older systems it was common for the echo box to be mounted in a blind sector on a mast, Samson post or other part of the ship's structure. Such boxes were large and rectangular in shape with a parabolic reflector to focus the received energy at the entrance to the cavity. They are now really only of historical interest. One of a number of subsequent variations which developed from this was the incorporation of the echo box within the aerial drive unit and the fitting of a horn (see Section 2.4.2.1) with a short length of connecting waveguide below the level of the scanner, as illustrated by Figure 6.7(b).

As the beam sweeps the horn once per revolution, some 10–20 pulses (see Section 2.4.4) will energize the horn and be conveyed down the waveguide to the echo box. This approach, like all external sitings, has the virtue that the length of the monitor signal is a measure of aerial and waveguide performance in

addition to that of the transmitter and receiver. Such an echo box and its associated circuitry can justifiably be referred to as an *overall performance monitor* because it monitors the performance of all units of the system. The principal draw-back of an external echo box is the general expense of producing such a unit (in particular the cost of making it suitable for above-deck fitting) and the problems which result if water does penetrate the system. The monitor can be switched on and off by means of an attenuator which effectively blocks the short length of waveguide when the signal is not required. Because external echo boxes are only energized as the radar beam sweeps across them, they produce a monitor signal which has a limited angular width the form of which is illustrated in Figure 6.7(c). This form is commonly described as a *plume*.

Many systems site the echo box on the waveguide just on the aerial side of the T/R cell (see Section 2.2.3) as illustrated in Figure 6.7(a). This dispenses with the need to make the unit suitable for above-deck mounting and allows the unit to be more compact and less expensive. However, it does have the serious shortcoming that it does not monitor aerial or waveguide performance. If the echo box is sited in this position it forms, with the associated circuitry, a *transceiver monitor* and to comply with the IMO Performance Standards this must be supplemented by some arrangement which monitors the radiation from the antenna. Such an arrangement is normally referred to as a *power* or *output monitor* (see Section 6.5.3).

In the transceiver monitor the cavity is cylindrical and its size can be varied by adjusting a plunger. This allows service personnel to tune the cavity (i.e. make the cavity the correct size) so that it will ring at the magnetron frequency. The monitor can be switched on or off from the display position by means of some form of electromechanical control which de-tunes the cavity when the monitor signal is not required. Because the echo box is located on the waveguide, the response is not sensitive to aerial direction and hence the monitor signal extends for the full 360° of azimuth. The resulting pattern is sometimes referred to as a *sun* and is illustrated in Figure 6.7(d). Some observers might have a natural reluctance to switch

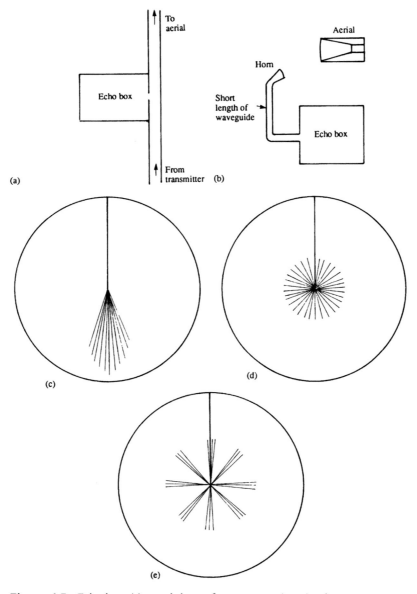

Figure 6.7 Echo box siting and the performance monitor signals
(a)   Echo box located on waveguide between transmitter and aerial
(b)   Echo box located below aerial
(c)   'Plume' from external echo box
(d)   'Sun pattern' from internal fixed-tune echo box
(e)   'Multi-plume' from internal echo box with oscillating plunger

on a monitor which produces such an extensive pattern. It is also sometimes argued that it is more difficult to discern the extent of a sun pattern than that of a plume, in which the contrast on either side assists in identifying the pattern. Some manufacturers break up the sun pattern as shown in Figure 6.7(e) by driving the tuning plunger in and out of the cavity. The echo box rings each time the plunger passes the tuned position, producing a 'family' of plumes which rotate at a speed governed by the relationship between the periods of the plunger oscillation and that of the aerial rotation. A plunger which makes a single sweep of the cavity and is triggered once per scan by the antenna as it rotates will produce a plume.

6.5.3 Power monitors

Where a transceiver monitor is fitted, the performance of the system is only monitored as far as the location of the echo box. Thus the presence on the display of a monitor signal of the specified length is no guarantee of optimum radiation from the aerial, which may be reduced by a variety of causes. These may include puncture or distortion damage to the waveguide, the presence of moisture or dirt in the waveguide space, damage to the antenna or the accretion of dirt or ice on the GRP envelope which protects the antenna.

The sensitive element commonly used in power monitors is a neon tube – a glass envelope which is filled with the inert gas neon and contains two separate metal electrodes. Neon gas has the particular property that it normally behaves as an insulator but, if it is subjected to an adequate level of radio frequency radiation, the gas is ionized and behaves as a conductor. Thus, within the tube, in the quiescent condition the electrodes are insulated from one another, whereas, when the gas ionizes in the irradiated state, the electrodes are effectively connected by a conducting medium. The neon tube is mounted close to the scanner so that radiated energy from the beam falls on it at each revolution. The tube is connected in series with some circuitry which produces a visual indication at the display position. In the absence of adequate

radiation the de-ionized neon will interrupt the circuitry and give a visual indication of an absence of power. If the output power from the aerial is adequate, the ionized neon will complete the circuitry with a low-resistance path, giving a visual indication of the presence of radiation at the aerial output. (The particular feature of the neon tube is that the ionization level can be fixed very precisely.)

The form of visual indication employed can vary considerably with manufacturer. It may take the form of a simple light which is illuminated when adequate power is present, or the signal from the neon may be used to indicate the output power by the deflection of a meter. The meter scale may well have a red arc or some other feature to give an indication of an unacceptably low output power level. In both cases it is likely that the indication will be smoothed over a period of one aerial revolution, otherwise the light or meter reading would fluctuate as the beam swept across the neon sensor. Some systems have used the signal detected by the neon to produce on the display a plume whose radial length represents the level of output power.

6.5.4 Transponder performance monitors

The sensitive unit of this modern type of performance monitor is an active (as opposed to passive) element known as a transponder, which is located on the aerial drive unit in such a way that it is irradiated by the beam as it sweeps past. The transponder reacts to reception of the radio frequency pulses by transmitting, after a short delay, a low-level coded response at the same frequency. A threshold set within the active element ensures that the response will only be given if the received signal is above a power level determined by the manufacturer.

The power level within the limits of the horizontal beam of the radar system falls off on either side of the axis. Thus, as the beam sweeps past the transponder, the latter responds over an arc bounded by the limits at which the radiated power is above the preset level. The transponder is thus a monitor of transmitted power.

The response returned to the aerial is treated as any other received signal and thus the ability to receive the response is a measure of receiver response. The response is displayed in the form of a series of arcs (see Figure 6.8), the angular limits of which are a measure of performance.

The angular limits are measured by the manufacturer when the performance is known to be optimum and supplied as a calibration level against which performance can be judged.

6.5.5 Calibration levels

Given the wide variety of purely arbitrary ways in which the monitor information may be displayed, and considering, in particular that, for example, one manufacturer may use a plume as an indicator of output power whereas another may use it as a transceiver monitor signal, it should be evident that it is essential to study the operator's manual to establish which signal or indicator to observe and to appreciate precisely what it measures.

The calibration levels should be measured by the manufacturer when the performance of the system is known to be optimum. In the case of a sun or plume pattern, such measurement will be made in miles and cables. The following information should be shown on a tally close to the display:

1 The length of the signal (or status of indicator) consistent with optimum performance.
2 The length of the signal (or status of indicator) corresponding to a significant drop in performance.

If the overall performance is not monitored by a single signal or indicator, the values for both transceiver and power monitors should be shown separately and unambiguously.

6.5.6 Performance check procedure

It must be remembered that the length of the monitor signals (or the status of other indicators) is influenced by the position in which the operational controls have been set. When carrying out a performance check it is vital that controls are set as instructed in the maker's manual – otherwise comparison with the calibration level is meaningless.

It cannot be stressed too strongly that the way in which the performance signals are displayed, and the extent to which they monitor the performance, vary considerably from manufacturer to manufacturer and even with different types made by the same company. Thus the important basic rule for carrying out a performance check is: *Consult the maker's manual and follow exactly the instructions given therein.*

A performance check should be carried out as soon as practicable after setting up and thereafter at regular intervals. In the United Kingdom, it is a requirement (see Section 11.4.1) that a check should be carried out before sailing and at least every four hours when a radar watch is kept. This should be regarded as a minimum.

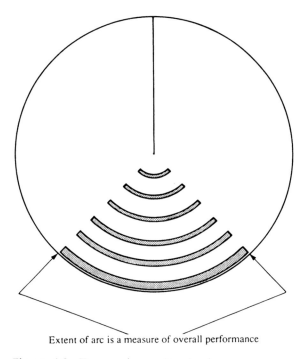

Extent of arc is a measure of overall performance

Figure 6.8 Transponder monitor signal

6.6   Change of range scale and/or pulse length

During normal operation of the radar system it will be necessary for a variety of reasons to change range scale from time to time. For example, having considered factors such as traffic density, speed of the observing vessel and the frequency of observation, a suitable range scale may have been selected on which to carry out radar plotting (see Section 7.2.4) but it may be necessary to change to a longer range scale at intervals in order to fix the vessel's position or to obtain early warning of approaching vessels. When using the radar for position-fixing or progress-monitoring it may be necessary to change scale in order to maximize the available accuracy of range and bearing measurement (see Sections 6.9.8 and 6.9.9). From time to time during general observation it may be necessary to select a suitable scale on which to search for targets among sea clutter returns. Many other circumstances will arise in which the range scale selected for some aspects of watchkeeping is not suitable for others. Intelligent use must thus be made of the range scale selector.

A change of range scale may be associated with a change in pulse length and some pulse lengths may not be available on all range scales (see Section 2.3.4). Change of pulse length may be necessary for a variety of reasons such as the need to improve range discrimination, minimum range, detection in sea clutter, long-range detection and detection in and beyond areas of rain (see Sections 2.6.5.5, 3.2.4, 3.6, 2.5.2.4, and 3.7 respectively).

In analogue displays, particularly in older systems, it may be found that the *no signal* brilliance level alters with change of range scale and also with change of pulse length. In the case of change of range scale this occurs because in a real-time display the spot speed alters (see Section 2.6.1.3). For example, when changing to a shorter range scale, the spot will travel faster, the time for which it dwells on each element of the phosphor will become shorter and the perceived brightness of the trace will decrease. Because the setting of the gain also contributes to the overall *brightness*

of the picture, it is difficult to detect and compensate for this change. The correct procedure for ensuring that optimum picture is maintained is as follows:

1   Turn down the gain. This reduces the problems of the afterglow generated by the previous picture but, more importantly, allows the brilliance level to be observed.
2   Change the range scale and/or pulse length.
3   Reset the brilliance control if necessary.
4   Restore the gain.

In a modern radial-scan display with a fixed time-base (see Sections 1.2.5 and 2.6.6.5) the problem should not arise in theory, but it is prudent to check that this is in fact the case.

In a raster-scan display the screen brilliance is independent of range scale selection. It may however be found that, if a change of range scale produces a large change in the distribution of the picture content, slight adjustment of the screen brilliance may make viewing more comfortable. For example, if a change is made from a very long range scale, where the clutter pattern (see Section 3.6.1.2) is a tiny bright area around the origin, to a very short range scale, where the bright clutter pattern covers most of the screen area, the overall brightness of the picture may appear to increase and comfort may dictate a slight decrease in the screen brilliance setting accompanied possibly by a small contrast adjustment.

6.7   The stand-by condition

As indicated in Section 6.2.2, the IMO Performance Standards require that such a condition be available. This requires the radar to be brought into full operational condition in 5 seconds (see Section 11.2.1)

The detailed nature of the stand-by condition will vary with manufacturer, but in all cases transmission is inhibited. Thus, although the radar is virtually ready for immediate use, limited-life components in the transmitter are not operational. A further, more general benefit is that the amount of radar-to-radar interference (see Section 3.9.5) experienced by other vessels (which may need to operate their radar systems) will be reduced over a potentially large geographical area. The life of components and hence the reliability of the radar system will be far less affected by continuous running than by frequent switching on and off, so that in periods of uncertain visibility it is better to leave the radar in full operation or in the stand-by condition.

Rule 7(b) of the Collision Regulations requires that 'proper use shall be made of radar equipment if fitted and operational'. There are many occasions on which *proper use* means continuous running. However, there are other occasions, for example in the open sea on a clear day with fog forecast, when the stand-by condition constitutes proper use. Thus, compliance with the letter and spirit of the rule is ensured as there is no excessive delay should the equipment be required quickly yet there is no unnecessary transmission in the meantime.

If the equipment is to be left on stand-by, the controls may be left in the optimum position, but the settings, particularly that of the tuning control, should be checked immediately on returning to the operational condition.

If the equipment is likely to be on stand-by for a long period, it is probably better in the case of a radial-scan display to set the controls listed in the setting-up procedure (see Section 6.2.1 and 6.3.1) to minimum effect and reset immediately on returning to the operational condition. Under the same circumstances in the case of a raster-scan display the gain, sea clutter and rain clutter controls should be set to minimum effect and all signal-processing facilities should be switched off, all being subsequently reset on returning to the operational condition.

6.8 Setting up the display for a true-motion picture presentation

The basic quantities measured by a marine radar system are range and bearing and, as a consequence, the system inherently produces a relative-motion presentation (see Section 1.5.1). To generate a true-motion presentation additional circuitry and controls must be fitted to the display (see Section 2.6.4). In many systems the additional circuitry and controls form a discrete module which can be added directly to an existing relative-motion display. A fundamental principle of the true-motion presentation is that the displayed information is only as true as the input data from which it is generated. It is of critical importance that the correct procedure should be followed both for the setting up of the true-motion presentation and for the monitoring of its accuracy.

6.8.1 The controls

The format of the true-motion control panel and the precise nature of the individual controls vary somewhat with manufacturer but the underlying principles are the same for all systems. In the following sections the controls are described in general terms, with some indication of the variations in detail that may be encountered in practice. Subsequent sections set out the practical procedures for setting up sea-stabilized and ground-stabilized true-motion presentations.

6.8.1.1 The presentation selector

This may take the simple form of a two-position switch offering the choice between relative-motion and true-motion. In most systems it will be found that it is not possible to select true-motion on very long or very short range scales. On very long range scales echo movement is so slow as to be barely perceptible, whereas on very short scales the movement of the origin will be so rapid as to require resetting (see Section 6.8.1.4) at unacceptably short intervals.

In some systems the presentation selector may be combined with the orientation selector and might, for example, offer the observer the choice of some or all of the following options:

- Ship's-head-up relative-motion.
- True-north-up relative-motion.
- Course-up relative-motion.
- True-north-up true-motion.
- Course-up true-motion.

6.8.1.2 The compass repeater

The compass repeater determines the direction in which the origin will track (see Section 2.6.4.2). In some systems the repeater merely reproduces *changes* in the heading detected by the master gyro and has no inherent sense of absolute direction. It is vital that the repeater is correctly aligned to the vessel's true course because, if it is not, the origin will track in the wrong direction, causing all the displayed tracks to be in error, and may dangerously mislead the observer (see Section 7.10.2).

The compass repeater normally takes the form of a conventional circular compass card or a three-digit read-out, though in some older systems no card was provided and the repeater was aligned by rotating the heading marker to the appropriate graduation on the circular bearing scale around the PPI.

6.8.1.3 The speed input

Normally two controls are provided. One control, the input speed selector, enables the observer to choose the input either of a signal from the ship's log or of an artificial log signal generated within the radar display (see Section 2.6.4.3). The artificial log position is sometimes referred to as *manual speed*. The second control is used to set the speed generated by the artificial log.

The input speed selector is commonly a two-position switch, though in some cases it has a third position labelled *zero speed*. The use of this third position is described in Section 6.8.1.5. Alternatively, all three functions can be combined in a single rotary control similar to that used to combine the on/off and volume functions on a domestic radio. In the *off* position ship's log is selected, the *on* position at zero gives the zero speed function, and advancing the control gives a continuously variable manual speed setting.

As in the case of the course input, it is vital that the correct value of speed is fed in, otherwise all the displayed tracks will be in error and may dangerously mislead the observer (see Section 7.10.3).

Most shipboard logs measure speed through the water and will thus, if selected, produce a sea-stabilized presentation. The doppler log is an exception to this rule. Where a doppler log is used to provide the speed input, particular care must be taken to establish the answers to the following questions:

1 Is the log measuring speed through the water or speed over the ground?
2 Is the log a single-axis or a dual-axis type?

Most doppler logs can be set to operate either on signals returned from the water mass or on signals returned from the ground. These two options are commonly referred to as *water lock* and *ground lock*, respectively. In very shallow water it will only be possible to obtain ground lock, while in very deep water only water lock will be possible.

A single-axis doppler log uses one transducer which measures fore-and-aft movement only. If the log is ground locked and the vessel is experiencing a tide having an athwartships component, the reading will be neither the speed through the water nor the speed over the ground (see paragraph 3 below).

A dual-axis doppler log has a second transducer which additionally measures athwartships movement. The output from the dual-axis doppler log can be in the form of the individual velocity components or their resultant. Some radar displays are designed to accept both a fore-and-aft input and an athwartships input and to cause the origin to track in sympathy with the resultant of both, whereas others will only accept a single input. The possible effects on the true-motion tracking of these various options are illustrated by Figure 6.9 (see also Section 7.9.3) and can be analysed by considering the following three possible cases:

1 If the doppler log is correctly water locked the input speed to the true-motion computer will represent the speed through the water whether it is a single-axis or a dual-axis log and irrespective of whether the radar display is designed to accept single-axis or dual-axis inputs (assuming that leeway can be neglected). The effect of this input will be to produce a sea-stabilized presentation.
2 If the doppler log is correctly ground locked, and the radar display is designed to accept a dual-axis input, the resultant input to the true-motion unit will represent the vessel's speed over the ground.

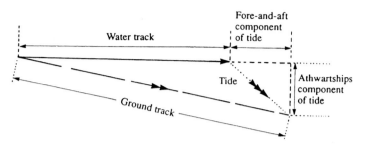

Figure 6.9 The use of a doppler log as speed input for true motion

The effect of this will be to produce a ground-stabilized presentation. Attention is drawn to the danger of using this presentation when planning collision avoidance strategy (see Section 1.5.2.2).

3 If the doppler log is ground locked, and it is of the single-axis type and/or the radar display is designed to accept a single-axis input only, the speed fed to the true-motion computer will be neither the vessel's speed over the ground nor the vessel's speed through the water: it will be the vessel's speed through the water plus that component of the tide which lies in the direction of the vessel's course (see Figure 6.9). The effect will be to produce an erroneous presentation which is neither sea-stabilized nor ground-stabilized. Such a presentation will be highly misleading and could lead to the development of a dangerous situation. The effect of errors on the true-motion presentation is discussed in Section 7.10.

It is evident that, where a doppler log is used, great care must be taken to establish the nature of the input to the true-motion computer. Failure to do so may result in inadvertent use of the ground-stabilized presentation or the use of a presentation with an inherent error in the speed input.

In some older systems a provision was made for using the propeller revolutions as a speed input. Errors can arise when using this source as, particularly in large vessels, there will be a finite time delay between a change in revolutions and the consequent change in the ship's speed through the water. Additionally, an allowance must be made for propeller slip, of which

the value may vary significantly with weather and condition of loading. Particular problems will arise where controllable-pitch propellers and/or twin screws are fitted.

6.8.1.4 The reset controls

As the origin tracks across the screen, the view ahead decreases and from time to time it will be necessary to reset the position of the origin.

In some systems the reset controls function in the same manner as shift controls (see Sections 2.6.1.3 and 2.6.4), producing N/S and E/W movement of the origin. Analogue reset controls normally operate in association with a clutch mechanism similar to that used when aligning a gyro repeater (see Section 6.2.3.4). When the origin is tracking they have no effect and turn freely, but when the control is pushed in against the action of a spring, a clutch disengages the drive from the true-motion computer and allows the observer to move the origin anywhere within a fairly large circular limit which must not exceed 75 per cent of the radius from the centre of the screen (see IMO Performance Standard in Section 11.2.1). In more modern synthetic displays, where the display functions are computer controlled under the direction of the observer, the equivalent action is achieved by holding in a push-button type control and *steering* the origin to the desired reset position by means of a joystick or tracker ball (see Figure 6.15).

An alternative approach is to offer the resetting facility in terms of direction and radius from the centre of the PPI. Where analogue controls are provided they will normally take the form of a rotary control with which to choose the direction and a second similar control for the radius. A third control of a push-button type will, when pressed, reset the origin in the chosen direction and at the chosen radius from the centre of the PPI. In modern synthetic displays a joystick or roller ball is used to place a graphics marker at the position within the circular resetting area to which it is desired to reset the origin. On pressing a reset button, the origin is reset to the screen co-ordinates of the joystick (or tracker ball) marker. A variation on this approach is to have two push-button controls, one of which performs the function already described. The second button, when pressed, resets the origin on the reciprocal of the observing vessel's course at the maximum permitted radius, thus seeking to make the best possible use of the screen area ahead (see Section 6.8.2).

If the observer fails to reset the origin and allows it to approach the outer extent of the tracking limit, the display will produce some form of automatic response. One approach is to illuminate a *reset warning* indicator supplemented by an audible warning. If this warning is ignored the origin will be stopped at the outer limit and the reset warning replaced by a *relative-motion warning*. There may be some provision to allow the observer to override this action manually in order to maintain observation of a developing situation but it has to be said that good practice dictates that an early and suitable occasion should be found to reset the origin to avoid being trapped in this dilemma. An alternative approach is that the display resets the origin automatically if the tracking limit is exceeded. This facility is usually associated with resetting that is based on direction and radius and in a computer-based system the reset position is likely to lie on the reciprocal of the vessel's course at the tracking limit. In similar displays with analogue controls it is more likely to be determined by the direction and radius to which the reset controls were last set.

In some systems automatic resetting takes place when a new range scale is selected. This function is not necessarily beneficial: it will disrupt manual tracking of echoes on a reflection plotter and may inhibit the observer from reducing range scale at the proper time (see Section 6.6).

6.8.1.5   The zero-speed control

Some radial scan systems had provision for setting the origin speed to zero while true-motion is selected. Commonly it takes the form of a two-position switch. In one position (the ship's-speed position) it has no effect but in the other (the zero-speed position) it isolates the speed input to the true-motion computer. Alternatively it may be combined with the manual/log speed selector in the form of a three-position switch. This may seem a rather odd provision, since the whole point of the traditional true-motion display is to produce a moving origin. However, the reason for making this facility available can be understood by considering the complementary nature of the true-motion and relative-motion presentations (see Sections 1.5.1 and 1.5.2).

The sea-stabilized true-motion presentation gives direct indication of target heading but does not give a similar indication of CPA, whereas the relative-motion presentation gives that quantity directly. The operation of the zero speed control allows the observer to stop the origin temporarily and hence produce relative-motion tracks for a period of sufficient length to make it possible to assess the CPA of chosen targets. Having established this information, the observer can then restore the speed input on the basis that the assessed CPAs will be fulfilled provided that the targets do not manoeuvre. The true-motion presentation will give immediate indication should such manoeuvres occur and thus warn the observer of the need to re-assess the situation.

The zero-speed control must be used with extreme caution as there is always an inherent danger of mistakes being made when true and relative tracks are displayed on the same screen. For example, members of the bridge team, other than the observer who has operated the control, might mistake the consequent change in tracks for manoeuvres by target vessels. Conversely, the change in tracks may mask a change produced by the real manoeuvre of a target. If the facility is to be used, bridge organization must ensure that all team members understand an agreed procedure for the use of the control and that an appropriate convention is adopted in marking the reflection plot (e.g. by using a different colour or symbol) in order to ensure obvious differentiation between relative tracks and true tracks. The symbols used to indicate true-motion (plane arrow) and relative-motion (arrow in a circle) in the description of radar plotting in Section 7.2.3 would serve this purpose.

Ideally, the complementary nature of the true-motion and relative-motion presentations is best exploited by the use of two separate displays. The zero-speed function undoubtedly makes it possible to obtain true-motion and relative-motion from a *single* radar display but it has to be said that appraisal aids which use threat assessment markers (see Section 7.11.2) perform this function more effectively and with less possibility of confusion between relative and true tracks.

The zero-speed control may be labelled as such but other names used include *hold* and *check*. Even if a specific control is not fitted the technique can always be used by selecting manual speed and setting the speed to zero. A convenient method of achieving this involves using the true-motion presentation with a log speed input while leaving the manual speed setting permanently at zero. When the zero-speed facility is required it is merely necessary to select manual speed.

An alternative use of the zero-speed control is to achieve an *off-centred* relative-motion display. In many systems, when relative-motion is selected the origin can only be off-centred by the small scope allowed by the shift controls (see Section 2.6.1.3). However, by selecting the true-motion presentation it is possible to use the resetting arrangements to off-centre the display by a large amount and hence to extend the view ahead, albeit at the expense of the view astern. A possible extension of the off-centre presentation is to use the zero-speed technique for collision avoidance in the reverse sense to that already described in this section. In this way a relative-motion display is maintained but, from time to time, the zero-speed switch is set to the ship's-speed position, allowing the observer temporarily to view the true tracks of the targets.

In some systems such an off-centre presentation is actually available directly as one of the options offered by the orientation/presentation

selector (see Section 6.8.1.1.) without the need to achieve it by selecting true motion.

6.8.1.6 Tidal controls

Where the option to ground-stabilize the true-motion presentation is offered (see Section 1.5.2.2), additional controls are necessary to allow input of the observer's estimate of the set and rate of the tide (see also Section 2.6.4.4).

In many systems the tidal inputs simply take the form of two rotary controls. One control is adjusted on a 0°/360° scale to feed in the observer's estimate of the tidal set being experienced, while the other is set on a scale of knots, facilitating input of the estimated rate of the tidal stream. The origin of the display tracks along the resultant of the vector which represents the observing vessel's course and speed through the water and the vector which represents the set and rate of the tidal stream. On some systems an additional three-position switch is provided to allow the observer to choose to have the selected rate of tide applied in the direction of the set control (as described above) or always ahead (contrary tide) or always astern (following tide). The two additional positions might be found useful in successive straight reaches of a winding river or channel where the true direction of the tide will vary from reach to reach but will always be in the direction of the reach. It must be appreciated that this assumes that the vessel maintains its heading parallel to the stream and takes no account of the inevitable cross component of tide on the bends.

In an alternative approach, the tidal set and drift are applied indirectly in terms of the difference between the observing vessel's course and speed through the water and that over the ground. The underlying principle is described in Section 2.6.4.4. The relevant controls are the *course-made-good* correction and the *manual speed* (see Section 6.8.1.3). The course-made-good correction control adjusts the angle by which the direction in which the origin track differs (to port or starboard) from the observing vessel's heading. The manual speed control is set to the ground speed rather than water speed. As a result, the origin tracks in a direction and at a rate which corresponds with the vessel's track over the ground.

In certain systems ground-stabilization can also be provided by the input of course and speed data from a dual-axis doppler log (see Section 6.8.1.3). Where the radar display forms an integral part of an automatic radar plotting aid, the tracking computer can be used to produce automatic ground-stabilization of the picture (see Section 5.3). More commonly now, the ground stabilization is achieved by integration with the GNSS (see Sections 10.1 and 8.4.6).

Irrespective of the source of the method used to obtain ground-stabilization, it must be remembered that ground-stabilized tracks do not indicate the headings of other moving vessels (see Section 1.5.2.2). Failure to appreciate this may result in the observer being dangerously misled in the planning of collision avoidance strategy.

6.8.2   Setting up a sea-stabilized presentation

1 Ensure that the optimum picture has been obtained as described in Section 6.2, 6.3 or 6.4 as appropriate to the type of display.
2 Check that the display is correctly orientated and azimuth-stabilized (see Section 6.2.3.4).
3 Select true-motion presentation.
4 Select log or manual speed input. Check that the log is reading the correct water speed (see Section 6.8.1.3) or that the manual speed control has been set to that value.
5 Adjust the reset controls so that the origin is placed to avoid the necessity of frequent resetting by making the best possible use of the screen area, bearing in mind possible forthcoming manoeuvres.
6 Commence systematic plotting of the origin to ensure that it tracks in the correct direction and at the correct rate. Such plotting will not be possible where the display is of the raster-scan type. In such cases the synthetic afterglow trails (see Section 2.6.7.5) should be selected. Check that the trail left by the observing vessel is consistent

with the vessel's course and that the length of the trail, which is generated for a fixed time, is consistent with the vessel's water speed. The length of the trail can be measured with the variable range marker (see Section 6.9.2).

Remember that the true-motion presentation is only as true as the course and speed information being supplied to it — in this case the course and speed through the water.

7 Be vigilant for loss of *view ahead* as the origin moves across the screen. Anticipate a suitable opportunity to reset the origin.
8 Reset the origin at an appropriate time and resume monitoring the tracking of the origin by reference to the reflection plot or synthetic afterglow.
9 It should be borne in mind that an underlying assumption of the true-motion presentation is that the target vessel is heading in the same direction as she is moving through the water. A vessel making leeway would not fulfil this condition. In many cases this does not present a serious problem since frequently the poor visibility associated with fog arises in calm conditions or with light winds. However, this is not always the case. Further, visibility may be severely restricted by precipitation accompanied by strong winds. In such circumstances due account must be taken of the possible disparity which may exist between the heading and water track of the target vessel.

It is important to appreciate that the problem is not peculiar to the true-motion presentation. Headings, whether calculated by manual resolution from the traditional relative plot (see Section 7.2) or derived by the most modern automatic tracking techniques (see Section 4.3.6), may be subject to the same disparity.

6.8.3   Setting up a ground-stabilized presentation

The modern method of setting up a ground-stabilized display is to select the ground stabilization from a GNSS or perhaps a dual axis ground locked doppler log (see Section 6.8.1.3).

The following instructions are for setting up a ground-stabilized display with a manual plotting system and using the tidal controls. They have been retained for historical reference and to demonstrate the difficulties of using such a technique.

1 Correctly sea-stabilize the display.

2 Plot an isolated ground-stationary target on the reflection plotter (see Section 7.8.4) and deduce the set and rate of the tide. The ground-stationary target will move at a rate equal to that of the tide but in the reciprocal direction (see Section 1.5.2.2). In the case of a raster-scan display, the length and direction of the synthetic afterglow of the ground-stationary target should be measured using the *free* electronic bearing line and variable range marker (see Section 6.9.6).

3 Where set and drift controls are provided (see Section 6.8.1.6), adjust them to the values deduced in step 2.

4 Where direct tidal inputs are not supplied (see Sections 2.6.4.4 and 6.8.1.6), use the known values of the observing vessel's course and speed together with the set and drift established in step 2 to construct a vector triangle, the third side of which is the observing vessel's track over the ground. Figure 6.9 includes an example of such a triangle. The construction can be carried out on the reflection plotter by transferring the plot of the set and drift through the end of the plot used to monitor the tracking of the origin, assuming that the latter is correct. Alternatively, the construction may be carried out on a chart, plain paper or squared paper as convenient.

   From the vector triangle establish the course-made-good correction and the ground speed. Set the course-made-good correction to the appropriate value, remembering the convention that a *starboard correction is applied if the ground track lies to starboard of the water track*. Select manual speed input and set the manual speed to the ground speed value.

5 Continue systematic monitoring of the ground-stationary target to ensure that it maintains its position as plotted on the reflection plotter. Re-adjust the tidal inputs if necessary to remove any residual movement.

   In the case of direct tidal inputs the residual movement represents the reciprocal of the difference between the input and actual tide values and the observer must visualize this when deciding how to modify the tidal controls. In the case of a course-made-good input it is somewhat easier to decide how to modify the setting, as any athwartships movement of the echo of the ground-stationary target can be substantially removed with the course-made-good correction and any fore-and-aft movement substantially removed by adjustment of the manual speed control. The use of indirect inputs suffers from the disadvantage that the values change when the observing vessel alters course. In all cases it must be borne in mind that the tide, and thus the appropriate settings for the controls, will vary with the passage of time and with the position of the vessel. In estuarial conditions it is possible that the vessels observed may be experiencing a set and drift which are different from those experienced by the observing vessel.

6 Continue systematic plotting of the origin or observation of the artificial afterglow of the origin, as this is the only really obvious indication that the display is ground-stabilized. In observing any true-motion display, be wary of the case in which the tide is fore-and-aft as there will be no indication from the direction of the trail of the observing vessel.

6.9 Controls for range and bearing measurement

A wide range of facilities are provided to enable the observer to measure the range and bearing of targets. Some arrangements measure range and bearing while others measure one quantity or the other. In older systems the facilities are associated with rotary controls and mechanical scales, whereas more modern equipments employ a joystick/tracker ball and graphic read-out. There is considerable variation in the precise detail of facilities provided by different manufacturers but the principle is essentially the same in each case.

The new IMO Performance Standards (see Section 11.2.1) also require that all radar displays are fitted with compensation for an offset antenna so that all positional data is relative to a consistent common reference point (normally the conning position). This could be very useful for multiple antenna installations.

6.9.1 Fixed range rings

The IMO Performance Standard requires that fixed rings should be provided. The number of rings required depends on the range scale selected; six rings are typical for range scales above 1 n mile, but this can be reduced to two rings for range scales below 1 n mile. There is also a requirement that the range scale displayed and the interval between the range rings should be clearly indicated at all times.

The fixed range rings take the form of a pattern of equally spaced circles concentric with the electronic origin of the picture. The pattern is generated by sub-dividing the timebase into equal intervals of time and rotating the trace through 360° as described in Sections 1.2.4 and 1.3.3. In a radial-scan display the rings should appear as perfect circles because all elements of a ring will be displayed at the same distance from the origin.

In a raster-scan display, a slight 'staircase' effect may be noticed due to the quantizing effect of scan conversion (see Sections 2.6.7.2 and 2.6.7.3). The effect will be most noticeable close to bearings of 0° and 180°, because in that area the circumference of the circle runs parallel or nearly parallel to the raster lines and will be exacerbated at lower line standards. The effect may offend the eye of the observer who is accustomed to the perfect circles of a radial-scan display, but it should be appreciated that it does not in itself represent a ranging error. This can be understood from consideration of the fact that a circular stretch of coastline at the range represented by the ring would have the same steps due to quantizing.

In a radial-scan display a facility will be provided to switch the rings on/off and to adjust their brilliance.

This may take the form of a single control or two separate controls. The brilliance of the rings should be adjusted to obtain the finest possible line. Excessive brilliance will make the rings thick and fuzzy, thus making accurate range measurement more difficult. There also exists the risk that a weak target will be obscured.

The IMO Performance Standards require that the fixed range rings should enable the range of an object to be measured with an error not exceeding 1 per cent of the maximum range of the scale in use or 30 metres, whichever is greater. Thus, when using the range rings to measure the range of a target, the most open range scale appropriate should be selected so as to maximize the inherent accuracy of the measurement.

The measurement of range should be taken to the nearer edge of the echo, as this represents the leading edge of the returned echo. Time measurement commences at the leading edge of the transmitted pulse and thus elapsed time must be measured to the same reference on the received pulse (see Figure 2.4). It must be appreciated that the leading edge of the echo represents the range of the nearest *detectable* facet of the target and not necessarily the nearest part of the target (for example, possibly the bridge rather than the bow of a ship approaching head-on).

The circuitry which produces the range rings is simple, reliable and can be set up by service personnel with suitable test equipment to a high degree of accuracy.

The only situation in which an observer can conveniently fix the vessel's position with a sufficient degree of precision to be able to check the accuracy of the rings is when the vessel is alongside a berth. It is possible for an observer to check the accuracy of the rings by observing the echo of an known small, isolated and steep-sided target when secure in a known charted position.

The range rings are highly suited to the measurement of the range of a target which lies on a ring and there may well be situations in which it is convenient to measure the range of a target as it crosses a ring. In general it will be necessary to interpolate between the rings and this is best done with the aid of the variable range marker (see Section 6.9.2).

If the decision is taken to interpolate by eye, a visual check should be made to ensure that the rings are equally spaced. A fault condition known as a *non-linear timebase* can develop in old radial-scan displays. In this condition the spot does not travel at constant speed and as a result the ring spacing is cramped toward the origin (if the spot is accelerating) or toward the edge of the display (if the spot is slowing down). The ranges of targets whose echoes fall on a ring will not be affected (because both ring and displayed echo are affected by the same amount). However, a target which lies midway between two rings will have a range which does *not* lie midway between the ranges represented by the two rings. Thus linear interpolation between the rings is not possible. This is illustrated by Figure 6.10 for the case of the spot accelerating.

If this fault is noticed the set is still usable, as the variable range marker will give the necessary non-linear interpolation between the rings (see Figure 6.10). However, steps should be taken to have the fault corrected by qualified service personnel as soon as possible because the picture and the movement of echoes will be distorted.

There is inevitably a small amount of non-linearity at the beginning of each trace as the spot accelerates from the rest position (see Section 1.2.3), though in some systems arrangements have been made to start the spot a little early and a little before the origin to avoid this.

Non-linearity should seldom, if ever, occur on a good quality, well set up raster-scan display. If it does, the direction of the distortion will depend on whether it occurs in the horizontal or vertical timebase. In either case visual interpolation should be avoided and the fault attended to as soon as possible.

The factors affecting the inherent accuracy of range measurement and the procedure for ensuring that this accuracy is realized are summarized in Section 6.9.8.

6.9.2 Variable range marker (VRM)

The new IMO Performance Standards (see Section 11.2.1) require that two electronic range markers with a numerical read-out of range be provided. It also requires that arrangements are made so that it is possible to vary the brilliance of each marker and to remove it completely from the screen. Such arrangements will in general be similar to those described for the fixed rings in Section 6.9.1. The accuracy requirement, i.e. 1 per cent of the maximum range of the scale in use or 30 metres (whichever is greater) is also the same as that required for the fixed range rings.

The VRM is a variable-radius ring generated at a selected elapsed time after the instant of trigger as described in Section 1.2.4 for radial scan displays. The elapsed time, and hence the radius of the ring, can be varied by the observer over a continuous set of values from zero to the limit of the maximum range of the scale in use. The radius of the VRM was traditionally set by a rotary control which also drove a mechanical three or four digit scale. In modern systems *increase* and *decrease* push-button controls (see Section 6.3.2) or a joy stick/tracker ball will be employed (see Section 6.9.7) and the read-out may form part of the graphics on a raster-scan display.

In the raster-scan case, the VRM will be similarly liable to exhibit the staircase effect described for the fixed range rings in Section 6.9.1.

Although the electronic circuitry which generated the traditional VRM was simple and reliable, errors

Figure 6.10 Timebase non-linearity
VRM set to 7 miles: on a non-linear timebase it appears closer to the 6 mile ring than the 8 mile ring
Echo *A* has a correct range 11 miles: on a non-linear timebase it appears closer to the 10 mile ring than the 12 mile ring

frequently arose due to its association with controls, scales and read-outs which were of a mechanical nature. For this reason it was essential to check the accuracy of the VRM regularly by placing it over a ring and comparing the read-out value with that of the ring. To maximize the inherent accuracy of any range measurement made with the VRM, the most open range scale appropriate should be selected. The VRM brilliance should be adjusted to obtain the finest possible line and the range should be taken to the nearer edge of the echo (see also Section 6.9.1). More modern systems are less likely to suffer this kind of error, but it is prudent to check the VRM anyway.

The factors affecting the inherent accuracy of range measurement and the practical procedure for ensuring that this accuracy is realized are summarized in Section 6.9.8.

6.9.3   The Perspex cursor

The IMO Performance Standards (see Section 11.2.1) require that provision be made to obtain quickly the bearing of any object whose echo appears on the display. On radial-scan displays, the Perspex cursor offers a simple mechanical means of satisfying this requirement. This has been made obsolete by the introduction of raster-scan displays, but it is included here for historical reference.

It consists essentially of a Perspex disk mounted so as to be free to rotate about the centre of the circular bearing scale which surrounds the CRT. The disk is rotated either by hand through direct access to a part of the circumference or by a rotary control acting through gearing or some other form of drive. A line is inscribed across the diameter, usually on the upper and lower sides of the disk so that it is possible to tell when the eye is directly above the line and thus avoid parallax (see Section 6.2.3.3). Additional lines, known as parallel index lines, may also be engraved on the disk. These are described separately in Section 6.9.4.

A bearing is taken by rotating the cursor until the diametric line intersects the target (see Figure 6.11),

avoiding parallax by use of the double engraved markings. The value is read off on the circular scale around the edge of the CRT. Bearings are quickly and easily obtained by this method.

Before using the cursor it is essential to check that the origin of the trace has been correctly centred (see Section 6.2.3.3). Failure to centre the origin will result in errors in the measured bearing. The magnitude of such errors will depend not only on the direction and distance by which the origin is off-centre but also on the range and bearing of the target, as illustrated in Figure 6.11.

The orientation selected will determine the type of bearing which is obtained as follows:

Ship's-head-up orientation.   A bearing relative to the instantaneous direction of the ship's head will be obtained. To obtain a true bearing it is necessary to observe the ship's heading at the instant of taking the bearing and to add this to the relative bearing obtained, subtracting 360° from the total if necessary.

True-north-up orientation.   A true bearing will be obtained directly.

Course-up orientation.   A bearing relative to the reference course (see Section 1.4.3) will be obtained. To obtain a true bearing it is necessary to add the reference course to the relative bearing obtained, subtracting 360° from the total if necessary.

Some systems do provide arrangements to make it possible to read off true bearings when the ship's-head-up orientation is selected. One approach is to fit a gyro-stabilized bearing scale outside the fixed bearing scale which surrounds the tube. When the ship is right on course the scale is aligned so that the graduation representing the course coincides with the 000° graduation of the fixed bearing scale and, subsequent to alignment, the gyro repeater signal rotates the outer scale in sympathy with the vessel's instantaneous heading. True bearings can thus be read off directly from the outer scale.

In general, the bearing should be taken through the centre of the echo because of the effect of horizontal beamwidth on echo paint (see Section 2.6.5.3). This is fairly straightforward where the echo is comparatively

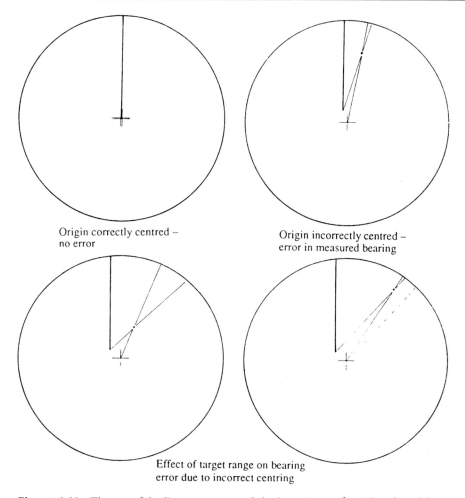

Origin correctly centred –
no error

Origin incorrectly centred –
error in measured bearing

Effect of target range on bearing
error due to incorrect centring

Figure 6.11 The use of the Perspex cursor and the importance of centring the origin

small and isolated as, for example, when measuring the bearing of a ship echo when carrying out radar plotting or the bearing of a small island when using the radar for navigation. Where bearings have to be taken of more complex coastal features it may be more difficult to decide on the location of the centre of the echo. This will be discussed under the use of radar for navigation in Section 8.3.

When taking a bearing, the most open range scale appropriate should be selected so as to place the echo as near to the edge of the screen as possible and hence to maximize the inherent accuracy of the measurement.

This follows from the IMO Performance Standards (see Section 11.2.1) which require that the means provided for obtaining a bearing should enable the bearing of a target whose echo appears *at the edge* of the display to be measured with an accuracy of ±1° or better. It is essential to appreciate that the permitted error of ±1° refers only to the measurement of the angle and does not take into account other sources of bearing errors. The inherent accuracy of radar bearings is discussed, and the procedures for ensuring that the potential accuracy is realized are summarized in Section 6.9.9.

6.9.4   Parallel index lines

An additional feature of the Perspex cursor was that parallel index lines were also engraved into the Perspex.

This comprises a pattern of equally spaced lines (probably double engraved) inscribed parallel to and on one or both sides of the diametric cursor line. In some displays the pattern is inscribed in such a way as to be coincident with the fixed range rings when the display is centred. As illustrated by Figure 6.12, the facility offers a quick method of taking bearings when the picture is off-centred as, for example, when the true-motion presentation is in use.

To obtain a reasonable degree of accuracy, skill and practice are required. Care must be taken to avoid parallax, by using the double engraved lines or the visor where appropriate (see Section 6.2.3.3). In radar navigation this facility is of considerable use in

association with a progress monitoring technique generally referred to as *parallel indexing*. This technique is described in detail in Section 8.4.

On a raster-scan display these lines are only available electronically (see Chapter 8).

6.9.5   The electronic bearing line (EBL)

This may also be referred to as the electronic bearing indicator (EBI) or electronic bearing marker (EBM). It takes the form of a continuous or dashed line which is generated electronically (see Figure 6.13(a)). Because it emanates from the electronic origin it can be used even if the origin is not centred. In radial-scan displays the brilliance of the line will normally be continuously variable, from 'off' to 'maximum', under the control of the observer. In raster-scan displays the levels may be restricted to on/off or possibly to off/low/high,

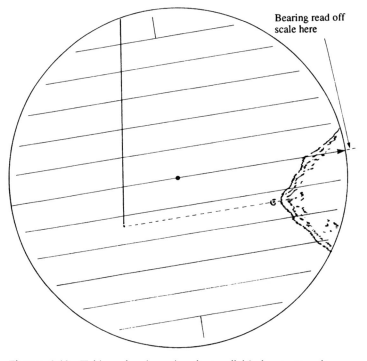

Figure 6.12 Taking a bearing using the parallel index cursor when off-centre

(a) **EBL and VRM**

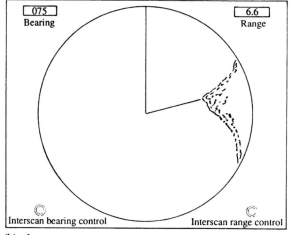

(b) **Interscan cursor**

Figure 6.13   Electronic bearing line, VRM and interscan cursor

though the EBL brilliance will be indirectly affected by the setting of the screen brilliance control.

In older radial-scan systems it is produced by the closing of a mechanical contact once per rotation of the scan coils (see Section 2.6.1.3). The angular position of the contact with respect to the scan coils is adjusted by a rotary control which also drives some form of circular or three–digit remote mechanical read-out. When adjusting the position of this type of EBL, the observer may have to wait for a period

of up to one aerial revolution to see whether or not the desired target has been intersected and hence it is somewhat slower than other methods of bearing measurement.

In radial synthetic systems the EBL can be made visible continuously by brightening it once per trace rather than once per revolution. This is achieved by using the spot to write the EBL in the rest period between timebases (see Section 2.6.2). For this reason, such an EBL is sometimes referred to as an *interscan cursor*. The cursor position is adjusted by a rotary mechanical control which also drives a mechanical or electronic read-out. The bearing measurement function may be combined with that of range measurement by making it possible to vary the length of the inter-scan cursor, in which case it may be referred to as an electronic range and bearing line (ERBL) (see Figure 6.13(b)). Alternatively, the continuous line may be retained and a variable range indication given by generating a mark of some sort at an adjustable point somewhere along the line.

In raster-scan systems the EBL is generated continuously along with other graphics.

In the synthetic radial and raster-scan displays the EBL or ERBL may be controlled by incremental touch controls (see Section 6.3.2), a joystick, or a tracker ball (see Section 6.9.7).

While the electronic circuitry which generates the EBL and ERBL has a high degree of inherent accuracy it must be remembered that in older radial sets the associated mechanical drives, scales and controls are a potential source of errors. For example, if the drive from the rotary control to the scale slips, the read-out can be seriously in error. For this reason it is prudent to check the EBL by superimposing it on the heading marker and checking that the bearing read-out is in agreement. Similarly, the ERBL should be checked for range measurement against the rings.

In general, the type of bearing (i.e. relative or true) which is read off using the EBL will depend on the orientation selected as described in Section 6.9.3. In some systems arrangements are made for the EBL to read off true bearings even when a ship's-head-up orientation is selected. This is only possible where there is a gyro repeater input, as the ship's instantaneous heading must be added automatically to the relative bearing to produce a true read-out. For any given system, care must be taken to establish the type of bearings available with each orientation.

As indicated in Section 6.9.3, when taking a bearing the most open range scale appropriate should be selected and the bearing should be taken through the centre of the echo. The inherent accuracy of radar bearings and the procedures for ensuring that the potential accuracy is realized are discussed in detail in Section 6.9.9.

6.9.6 Free electronic range and bearing line

This facility takes the form of an ERBL, the origin of which can be positioned at any point on the screen. It allows the observer to measure the range and bearing between two displayed targets, as illustrated by Figure 6.14.

The following three examples serve to indicate that there is a range of circumstances in which this facility might be found useful.

1   Approaching port it may be useful to ascertain the distance of other approaching vessels from the pilot station.

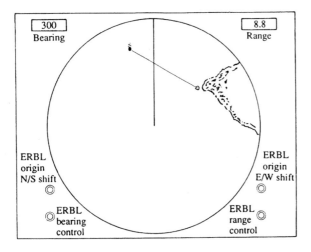

Figure 6.14 Free electronic range and bearing line

2   Having heard another vessel broadcast its position in terms of bearing from a well defined charted object, it may be possible to identify positively the radar echo of that vessel. (The incorrect use of VHF in collision avoidance can contribute to the development of a dangerous situation, see also AIS, Section 10.3.)

3   Having positively identified one land echo, it may be possible to positively identify others by measuring their range and bearing from the known echo.

Other applications which are particularly appropriate to a given trade will no doubt suggest themselves to readers. The facility is often used to draw *navigational lines* in systems which offer automatic tracking (see Section 8.4.6.3).

6.9.7 Joystick/tracker ball and screen marker

This facility makes use of the fact that in modern synthetic displays range and bearing data are stored in digital form (see also Section 2.6.6 and Section 4.5.8).

A joystick is a short spindle which is mounted on the display adjacent and normally to the right of the screen (see Figure 6.15). In its neutral position it lies perpendicular to the plane of the screen. A small sphere or other suitable hand-grip is fitted on the outer end of the spindle, while the inner end is pivoted in such a way that it can be moved fore-and-aft, athwartships or in any direction which lies between these two. The movement of the joystick controls two independent voltages which are analogues of the displacement of the joystick from its neutral position. If these analogue signals are converted into digital numbers they can be used to control the X and Y screen co-ordinates of a graphics marker and to generate the corresponding digital angle and range in the form of a read-out of bearing and range. The engineering details of the technique by which the displacement of the joystick is translated into marker position (or bearing and range) may vary in detail with manufacturer.

The graphics marker is commonly a small circle or cross which is located at the origin of the picture

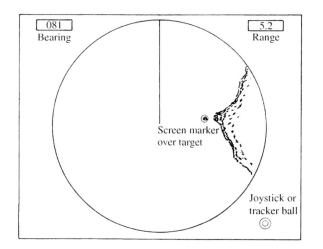

Figure 6.15 Joystick and screen marker

when the joystick is in its neutral position. By steering the marker with the joystick, it is placed over the chosen target and the bearing and range are read out on a computer-controlled digital scale. This facility offers a simple and rapid method of range and bearing measurement. As with any form of range and bearing measurement, it should be monitored for errors by checking it against the rings and heading marker.

In some systems a tracker ball is used as an alternative to a joystick. This comprises a sphere, half of which projects above the top panel of the display. It is pivoted in such a way that it can be rotated in any direction, thus allowing control of the graphics marker in a similar fashion to that of the joystick (see Section 2.6.7.13).

6.9.8 Range accuracy

The IMO Performance Standards (see Section 11.2.1) require that the fixed range rings and the variable range marker enable the range of a target to be measured with an error not exceeding 1 per cent of the maximum range of the scale in use or 30 metres, whichever is greater. Where appropriate in the preceding descriptions of the various facilities available for range measurement, mention was made of procedures for ensuring that the potential accuracy is realized. For

ease of reference it is appropriate to summarize these procedures in this section.

1 Adjust the brilliance of the VRM, or ERBL to obtain the finest possible line.
2 Measure the range to the nearer edge of the displayed echo.
3 Use the rings when the target is on or close to a ring.
4 Use the VRM, ERBL or joystick marker to interpolate between the rings.
5 Regularly check the VRM, ERBL or joystick marker against the rings.
6 Use the most open scale appropriate.
7 When it is not necessary to display the rings, good practice dictates that they should be switched off in order to prolong the life of the phosphor area on which they paint (see Section 2.6.1.2).

6.9.9 Bearing accuracy

As stated in Section 6.9.3, the IMO Performance Standards require that the means provided for measuring bearings should enable the bearing of a target whose echo appears at the edge of the display to be measured with an accuracy of $\pm 1°$ or better.

It is essential to appreciate that the permitted error of $\pm 1°$ refers only to the measurement of the angle (whose accuracy will depend on the correctness of the alignment of scanner and trace/digital bearing word and the graduation accuracy of the measuring device). It does not take into account the accuracy of the heading marker (see Section 2.4.6) from which the angle is measured or of the accuracy of the gyro signal (see Section 2.6.3) used where azimuth stabilization is provided. The Performance Standards specify an accuracy of $\pm 1°$ for the heading marker and $\pm 0.5°$ for the gyro input. If these error sources are aggregated, a bearing measured from the display could be in error by 2.5° without the provisions of the Standards being contravened. However, it must be said that each error will have a component which is substantially constant throughout the period of taking a series of bearings. For example, only in the case of mechanical fault would one expect the error from the heading marker source to change from $+1°$ to $-1°$ during the taking of a series of bearings. The significance of the aggregate error will depend on whether the bearings are being used for radar plotting or for position-fixing. The implications of bearing errors are discussed separately in terms of their significance in the accuracy of radar plotting in Section 7.9 and of the accuracy of position-fixing in Section 8.3.

Where appropriate in the preceding descriptions of the various facilities available for bearing measurement, mention was made of procedures for ensuring that the potential accuracy is realized. For ease of reference it is appropriate to summarize these procedures in this section.

1 It is important to check regularly that the heading marker accurately represents the ship's fore-and-aft line. The procedure for carrying out this check is as follows:

   (a) On radial displays adjust accurately the centre of the trace. On all displays switch off azimuth stabilization and ensure heading marker is aligned with $0°$ on bearing scale.

   (b) Select an object which is conspicuous but small visually and whose echo is small and lies as near as possible to the maximum range scale in use. Measure simultaneously the relative visual bearing of this object and the bearing on the PPI relative to the bearing scale. It is important that the visual bearing is taken from a position near the radar antenna in plan. Repeat at least twice and calculate the mean difference between bearings obtained visually and by radar.

   (c) If an error exists, adjust the heading marker contacts to remove the error. Traditionally, the adjustment was in the antenna unit, but modern systems allow adjustment to be done in the processing unit.

   (d) Repeat (b) above to check accuracy of the adjustment.

2 Ensure that centring has been carried out before using the Perspex cursor on radial sets.

3 Ensure that the picture is correctly orientated.

4 Use an appropriate range scale with the target as near to the edge of the screen as possible.

5 Take care to avoid parallax when using the Perspex cursor or parallel index lines on radial sets.

6 If using a ship's-head-up unstabilized orientation, the ship's head must be read at the instant of taking the bearing.

7 Check the EBL, ERBL or joystick marker by superimposing them on the heading marker, at which time the bearing and heading should agree. Any error should be noted, applied to bearings and the cause investigated.

8 For a small isolated target align the cursor, EBL, ERBL or marker with the centre of the target.

9 Temporarily reduce the gain if it will give a more clearly defined echo.

In general it should be borne in mind that radar range position circles have a much higher inherent accuracy than is obtainable from position lines derived from radar bearings. Further, radar bearings are not as accurate as visual bearings.

6.10 Controls for the suppression of unwanted responses

Controls for the suppression of unwanted responses naturally group themselves under the headings of sea clutter, rain clutter and interference. Each of these controls will be dealt with in turn but it should be borne in mind that the usefulness of their effects is not necessarily limited to the heading under which they are considered. For example, the sea clutter control may assist in the detection of a target masked by proximate rain clutter or strong side-lobe response (see Sections 3.7.4 and 3.9.4) and the rain clutter control may be efficacious in improving range discrimination (see Section 3.7.4.4).

6.10.1 Sea clutter suppression

The theory of the sea clutter response and of the various techniques available for its suppression is treated in detail in Section 3.6 and it is intended in this chapter merely to deal with the appropriate practical procedures.

It should be appreciated that many targets will be visible *before* they enter the clutter area and the probability of detecting them within the clutter will be improved if their position is regularly monitored as they approach. As the range of any target decreases its response will improve (see Section 3.1), but once within the clutter it must compete for attention with clutter signals which will be weak at the point of entry but the response of which improves with decreasing range. If the clutter response overtakes that of the target the latter will be undetectable. Thus, where weak targets are approaching, it is important to attempt to detect them before this occurs. Very weak targets may of course be within the clutter area before they return a detectable response.

The above principle is well illustrated by the situation in which a vessel engaged in a Search and Rescue mission is attempting to locate the echoes of survival craft close to her in clutter conditions. Under such circumstances it may be that the rescue vessel cannot detect the echoes of the survival craft because of the clutter. Another vessel stationed sufficiently far away that the first vessel and the survival craft responses are clear of the clutter response may well be able to locate all the craft involved, because it does not have to view them against a clutter background.

6.10.1.1 The manual sea clutter control

It is evident from the theory (see Section 3.6) that there is no single correct setting for the sea clutter control and that the correct use of the control is to perform regular *searching* operations. The practical procedure for carrying out searches can be set out as follows:

1   Turn the manual sea clutter control to maximum effect. This will immediately suppress the responses within the receiver but the afterglow of previously displayed echoes will persist on the screen for a short period. To maximize the possibility of detecting targets it is necessary to pause and allow the afterglow to fade.

2   Reduce the suppression by a small step and study the screen for the appearance of echoes.

3   Continue to reduce the suppression in small steps, pausing at each step to examine the screen for the appearance of echoes. In due course the clutter peaks will begin to appear and, as the suppression continues to be removed, it will become progressively difficult to detect targets against the clutter background. In this connection it should be remembered that sea clutter paints will tend to be random while those of targets will tend to be steady.

4   Repeat the search procedure at frequent intervals. The frequency with which this is done must be matched to the prevailing conditions. In particular, consideration should be given to the speed of the observing vessel, the visibility and the type of floating object which is likely to be encountered.

5   Between searches it is prudent to set the control so that just a few echoes are painting, thus extending the life of that important area of the phosphor (see Section 2.6.1.2).

6   The effectiveness of the searching operation may be assisted by the overall reduction in response which can be achieved by the use of a short pulse length, a logarithmic receiver and the selection of S-band transmission. In very heavy clutter, it may be found that even the full suppression offered by the sea clutter control is inadequate, in which case its effect will have to be supplemented by that of the gain control.

Where two transmitters of different powers are available, it may be helpful to select the one having the lower power.

Effective sea clutter searching requires considerable skill which can only be developed by practice. It is recommended that, wherever possible in clear weather, the observer should make use of opportunities to carry out such practice. It must always be remembered that targets weaker than the clutter cannot be detected.

6.10.1.2 Adaptive gain

When adaptive gain is selected, the manual sea clutter and rain clutter controls are rendered inoperative, a fixed amount of differentiation is applied, and the gain is varied instantaneously and automatically according to the dictates of a suppression waveform derived from the signals present on the current or previous radial timebase (see Section 3.6.3.3).

The name 'adaptive gain' is a general engineering term but the control which selects the facility may be variously named by different manufacturers. Examples include video processor, automatic clutter, auto sea clutter and CFAR (*constant false alarm rate* – a statistical term used in the theory of threshold detection). In this, unwanted targets, such as noise and clutter, which cross the threshold are referred to as *false alarms*. In the case of noise, which is a random phenomenon as described in Section 2.5.2.3, the false alarm rate, i.e. the number of false alarms per unit time, should be the same whatever the screen location. This makes it comparatively easy to make a judgement on threshold setting. In the case of sea clutter, the false alarm rate is likely to have a high value at the centre of the screen falling to a lower value where only noise is present, making the choice of threshold setting a problem. Adaptive gain seeks to simplify the problem of threshold setting by producing a *constant false alarm rate*, i.e. reducing the clutter to a noiselike response (see Section 3.6.3.3).

The particular virtue of adaptive gain is that, if correctly set up, it will provide near optimum instantaneous clutter suppression, line by radial line, hour after hour, without tiring, losing concentration or becoming distracted. In general, it is not possible to set up the circuitry so as to guarantee optimum performance over the entire range of sea conditions that may be experienced and exclusive reliance must not be placed on its ability to remove *all* clutter responses and display *all* targets. In some conditions, particularly heavy clutter, it may well be found that skilled use of the manual sea clutter control will provide a higher probability of detection. The adaptive gain facility should be regarded as having the ability to display *most* of the targets masked by clutter for *most* of the time. However, the observer must from time to time switch off the adaptive gain and use the manual clutter control to check for targets close to clutter level. Commonly,

the control for the selection of adaptive gain is integral with the manual clutter control.

The manual gain control remains operative and thus the observer maintains control of the gain level which obtains in the absence of automatic suppression. At initial setting up (see Sections 6.2.1, 6.3.1 and 6.4.1) the manual gain control should be set with the manual and adaptive clutter controls at zero effect. If the adaptive gain circuitry is functioning correctly, further adjustment of the gain should not be necessary. However, at any time that the observer suspects that excessive suppression is being applied, the gain may be adjusted to produce a higher level of residual speckle in order to ensure maximum probability of detection of targets.

For the reasons set out in Section 3.6.3.3, it may be necessary to switch off the adaptive gain facility in the following circumstances:

1   When attempting to detect radar beacons. In some systems separate automatic sea and rain adaptive gain controls are provided and it may be possible to detect a distant radar beacon while maintaining the ability to use the limited range of the automatic sea clutter adaptive gain facility.
2   When carrying out a performance check.
3   When attempting to identify coastlines.
4   In rivers, narrow channels and enclosed dock areas.

6.10.1.3   *Rotation-to-rotation correlation*

This facility is only available on raster-scan displays and seeks to remove clutter responses by identifying their random character (see Section 3.6.3.4). The signal produced as a result of the processing is sometimes referred to as *integrated video* and the control may be similarly labelled.

Only two states, *on* and *off*, are associated with the facility. In some systems the facility defaults to *off* at switch-on and the observer is required to make a positive selection if the correlation is required. In other systems the facility defaults to the *on* condition and the observer must switch it off if not desired. In some cases the switch is spring-loaded. In cases where the facility does default to the *on* state, it is important to switch it off when setting the gain control because it will produce some reduction in the displayed noise.

The use of the facility in combination with adaptive gain will greatly reduce the displayed clutter response. It will also make manual searching a simpler operation. However, it must be borne in mind that echoes close to clutter level, such as those from small boats, buoys and small icebergs, may also be random in their character. Small fast-moving targets may also be displayed at low level if the facility is selected.

6.10.2 Rain clutter suppression

The theory of the rain clutter response and of the various techniques available for its suppression is treated in detail in Section 3.7 and it is intended in this chapter merely to deal with the appropriate practical procedures.

As in the case of sea clutter, targets may well be visible before they enter areas of precipitation and it is self-evident that the task of detecting any target is made easier by knowing roughly where to look. Thus every effort should be made to track such targets so as to improve the probability of detecting them once they are within the clutter area. One must of course always be alert to the danger of a target manoeuvring within the clutter region. Rain clutter differs from sea clutter in that the echoes may appear in any part of the screen and may move quite rapidly. The probability of problems arising with targets being lost in precipitation can be anticipated if efforts are made to track the direction in which particular areas of precipitation are moving.

6.10.2.1 The rain clutter control

As described in Section 3.7.4.4, this control seeks to deal with the saturation problem by displaying only the leading edges of echoes. Because it is so called, there is a tendency for observers to assume that it is the most effective way of dealing with rain echoes. On the basis of practical experience many users hold the view that the use of the gain control in a searching fashion is much more effective. It can of course be argued that this view is to some extent subjective. The

important point to appreciate is that suppression and differentiation are two quite different attempts to solve the same problem. Given the subjective element that exists, an observer should take every opportunity to establish which particular technique he or she finds most helpful, and whether the preference applies to particular circumstances.

6.10.2.2 Manual searching for targets within rain

The masking effect of rain can be dealt with as follows:

1 If the rain is close to the ship, searching with the sea clutter control may be effective.
2 In general the most effective technique is to use the gain control in a searching fashion.
3 If preferred, the rain clutter control may be used in a searching fashion, either alone or in combination with some suppression of the gain.
4 The effectiveness of the searching operation may be assisted by the overall reduction in response which can be achieved by the use of a short pulse length, a logarithmic receiver, the selection of S-band transmission, the selection of a low power transmitter or the selection of circular polarization.

6.10.2.3 Adaptive gain

This is an effective way of providing automatic rain clutter suppression. Attention however is drawn to the practical limitations of the technique set out in Section 6.10.1.2.

6.10.2.4 Searching for targets beyond precipitation

Because of the attenuating effect of precipitation (see Section 3.7.2), it may be difficult to detect weak targets which lie beyond areas of precipitation. It may be possible to overcome this difficulty by using S-band transmission, a higher power transmitter (if fitted) or selecting a longer pulse length. While searching for specific targets it may be useful temporarily to turn the gain above the normal setting, or use an echo-stretching facility if available (see Section 6.11.1).

6.10.3   Interference suppression

This is normally a two-position control which allows a line-to-line correlation facility to be switched off or on. Such a facility will tend to reduce the noise content of the picture and should be switched off when initially setting the gain control. Certain types of step sweep racons can also be removed by this facility (see Section 3.5.3).

6.11   Miscellaneous controls

This section deals with some specialized controls which will not be found on all civil marine radars.

6.11.1   Echo stretch

In a synthetic display, the radial length of the displayed echo is normally fixed by the number of elements of memory activated by the detected response (see Section 2.6.6.3). Some systems offer an additional facility whereby the number of radial elements representing the target can be increased, as a result of which the observer can cause the displayed echoes to be stretched radially away from the origin in order to make them more obvious, while preserving the leading edge at the correct range. The rules which govern the stretching vary somewhat with manufacturer, but in general the availability of the facility is limited to:

1   The longer range scales.
2   Targets beyond a preset minimum range.
3   Targets whose received echoes exceed a preset duration.

Such a facility may be particularly useful when trying to detect distant land echoes. Once detection has been achieved and identification becomes a priority, the stretching effect will become counter-productive (see Section 8.2.1).

6.11.2   Second-trace echo elimination

Some systems provide a facility whereby second-trace echoes can be eliminated. The facility can normally be switched on or off. The theory of the techniques used to eliminate the second-trace echoes is described in Section 3.9.6.

6.12   Setting-up procedure for an Automatic Radar Plotting display

Most automatic radar plotting aids offer a host of facilities, some of which are required by the IMO Performance Standards and others which are not (see Chapters 4 and 5). The precise way in which even the specified facilities are controlled varies considerably with manufacturer. This general treatment seeks to deal with the setting up of the display for basic tracking in terms of the important guiding principles which are common to all systems.

6.12.1   The input of radar data

Irrespective of whether the ARPA or ATA is of the integral or stand-alone type (see Section 4.1.1), it is essential to ensure that the radar system supplying the raw data to the ARPA/ATA tracker is correctly set up (see Sections 6.2, 6.3, and 6.4). Particular attention must be paid to pulse length selection, tuning and *any* control that affects receiver gain (for example, the sea clutter control – see Sections 3.6.3.1 and 6.10.1). Failure to use the correct pulse length or to tune the receiver will reduce the probability of targets being detected and tracked by ARPA or ATA. The effect of the setting of the receiver gain controls on the video fed to the tracker varies from one manufacturer to another. In some systems the signal level fed to the tracker (see Section 4.3.6) is independent of the operator's gain controls, being continuously set by some form of adaptive gain or other form of automatic signal processing. In other systems, the manual gain control determines the signal level fed to both the tracker and the CRT. When first using an ARPA or ATA with which the observer is not familiar it is prudent to establish which gain control settings affect the input to the tracker. This can be done quite simply by acquiring a target, adjusting each relevant control in turn, and observing any consequent loss of tracking (see Section 4.7.3).

6.12.2   Switching on the computer

In some systems the ARPA or ATA computer is switched on when the radar is switched to the 'operate' condition while in others a separate switch is provided. After the computer is switched on, it may be necessary to wait for a short time, not normally more than a minute, for the computer to carry out a self-checking programme.

When the computer becomes active, many ARPAs or ATAs have default conditions by which all but the basic facilities are switched off. This ensures that the user obtains the additional facilities only if they are positively requested and is thus not confused by uncertainty as to the status of the controls nor plagued by the need to find the control necessary to switch off unwanted facilities. Care must be exercised where analogue controls are used as they are likely to remain as set by the last user.

6.12.3   Heading and speed input data

The observer should check that the correct heading and *water speed* information is being fed to the computer; if not, the necessary adjustments should be made. The procedure is essentially similar to that carried out when setting up a true-motion sea-stabilized presentation (see Section 6.8.2). It is vital that this check is made, otherwise no reliance can be placed on the tracking. The importance of heading and speed inputs cannot be overstressed and the navigator must always be watchful for errors in these fundamental data sources.

6.12.4   Setting the ARPA or ATA brilliance

This control adjusts the brilliance level of the vectors and other graphics used to display the ARPA data (see Section 4.5.6). It is not usually possible to adjust this control correctly until after some targets have been acquired, since it is only at that stage that one can judge what level of brightness allows comfortable viewing of the vectors and other graphics in the ambient light conditions. When setting up it is usually best to set the control about mid-travel and to optimize it later when tracking has commenced.

6.12.5   Setting the vector time control

In many systems the vector time control will default to some non-zero setting, probably in the range of 6–12 minutes. This ensures that, when vectors are initially displayed after acquisition has commenced, they will in general have a length which is sufficient to be obvious but not excessive. In due course the length can be set to suit the traffic conditions and will of course have to be adjusted from time to time as the vectors are used to extract data from the display. Where there is no default condition the observer should, when setting up, adjust the vector time control to a suitable non-zero value, preferably in the range 6–12 minutes.

6.12.6   Setting the vector mode

Most systems will have a default condition which will select a particular vector mode (see Section 4.4) at switch-on. Some systems default to relative vector mode, some to true vector mode, while in others the default condition depends on the radar picture presentation that has been selected. A further variation is for the system to default to neither mode, requiring the observer to make positive selection of one mode or the other. The observer clearly must be able to select the alternate mode to the default condition but in some systems the vector mode is biased to the default condition, i.e., to select the other mode the observer must activate a control which returns to the default condition on release. Such are the variations found in practice that it is essential to consult the operating manual and discover what options are available.

6.12.7 Safe limits

The observer should set in suitable safe limits in terms of CPA and TCPA (see Section 4.7.2). The judgement of what is suitable is to some extent subjective. Excessive alerts can be distracting and counter-productive whereas, by contrast, if very small limits are used the dangerous target alarm will not be activated by a vessel which is standing into a close-quarters situation.

6.12.8 Preparation for tracking

If the observer is unfamiliar with the system some time should be spent in locating the joystick (or tracker ball), the *acquire* button and the *cancel* button and practising their use. This can be done using live targets if available or, failing that, use can be made of the synthetic targets provided by the training programme supplied with many ARPAs and ATAs.

6.13 Switching off

When finally switching the radar off, if the system has analogue controls it is prudent to set the controls as you would wish to find them when initially switching on, e.g. as set out in Section 6.2.1. In many modern systems having computer controls and default conditions, this will not be necessary.

7 Radar plotting including collision avoidance

7.1 Introduction

It may be argued that the prime function of the radar system is avoidance of collision, either with other vessels or with navigation marks in restricted visibility. After the initial euphoria of being able to detect other vessels in fog, the plethora of accidents involving vessels equipped with radar left no doubt as to the need for systematic observation of the radar display and for proper techniques for the extraction of data relating to other vessels. The method by which this information has been displayed to the navigator has seen a steady progression from paper plotting sheets via true-motion displays to the present day ARPAs. All have sought to provide the mariner with the most meaningful portrayal of the situation in the proximity of his ship with the least amount of distraction to the other bridge routines. In order to understand the more complex operations performed by ARPAs and for the benefit of those who are not so fortunate as to have that aid or where it has broken down, it is still necessary to have a fair degree of skill and dexterity in practical plotting. In order to maintain this dexterity, it is essential to engage in regular practice, preferably in clear weather where visual confirmation of results will build confidence in the information obtained when using the radar in restricted visibility.

This chapter covers the basics of plotting from a manual plotting perspective. It also covers electronic aids to plotting (including the EPA standards). The chapter concludes with a section on the use of radar and ARPA/ATA for collision avoidance.

7.2 The relative plot

Since the radar is carried along by the vessel as it proceeds, the direct measurements obtainable are always *relative to the observing vessel* (see Section 1.5.1). Thus, in order to determine the true courses and speeds of other vessels, it is necessary to resolve this observed relative or apparent motion into its components by using a knowledge of own ship's true course and speed. The means by which this may be achieved ranges from pencil-on-paper plotting sheets via reflection plotters and true-motion displays to computer-based collision avoidance systems. Irrespective of the mechanism used, if a complete appreciation of the dynamic situation in the vicinity of own ship is to be obtained, the relative motion of targets must be systematically recorded and the true motion derived by means of a plot. The techniques employed to extract the relevant data and the use to which it is put will

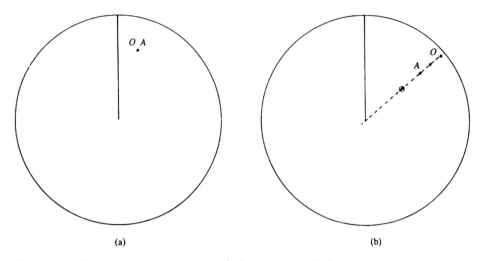

(a)   (b)

Figure 7.1 Common misinterpretations of relative-motion displays

(a)   The target, believed to be stopped, is in fact on the same course and at the same speed as own ship

(b)   A vessel which might be expected, if observed visually at night, to be showing both sidelights, i.e. to be head-on and to present no threat, is in fact crossing broad starboard-to-port and on a collision course

form the major part of this chapter. Failure to carry out such systematic observation has resulted in many dangerous misconceptions (see Figure 7.1).

If systematic observations are made of the bearing and range of a displayed echo and the positions are plotted on a traditional plotting sheet or reflection plotter (see Section 7.8), the line joining the plotted positions will depict the target's apparent motion *OA* (Figure 7.2), which if extended will enable a measure of the target's closest point of approach, CPA, to be obtained. The time to closest point of approach, TCPA, can be obtained by stepping off the rate from *O* to *A* along *OA* extended to CPA. This does of course assume that both vessels maintain their present courses and speeds. If this condition is not met, the apparent motion will not be uniform, i.e. the echo will not move across the screen in a constant direction at a constant rate.

It is important to realize that the measurements obtained thus far are only subject to those errors inherent in the radar system itself, the azimuth stabilization (see Sections 7.9.1 and 7.9.2) and in the observations.

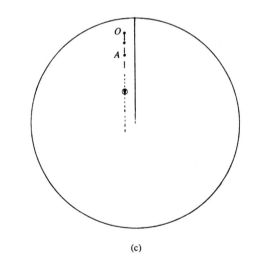

(c)

(c)   The target appears to be proceeding slowly on a reciprocal course, showing a red light: it is actually being overtaken and showing a stern light

They are therefore uncontaminated by errors (or blunders) to which other inputs – notably own ship's speed – might be subjected. For this reason, relative

Distance (n mile)

Figure 7.2 The relative-motion plot

motion (or the relative plot) is probably the most reliable, although not the only data on which to base decisions.

While CPA and TCPA are two important pieces of information, it is essential that, prior to manoeuvring own ship, the true course and speed of the target(s) are derived and this can only be done by resolving the vector triangle.

7.2.1   The vector triangle

By plotting the apparent motion of a target and with a knowledge of own ship's true course and speed, it is possible to determine the true course and speed of the target (see Figure 7.3).

7.2.2   The plotting triangle

Example 7.1   While steering 090°(T) at 12 knots, the echo of a vessel is observed as follows:

0923 echo bearing 127°(T) at 9.5 n mile
0929 echo bearing 126°(T) at 8.0 n mile
0935 echo bearing 124°(T) at 6.5 n mile

At 0935, determine the target's true course and speed; CPA and TCPA; and aspect.

The data relating to the target in Figure 7.4 as extracted from the plot at 0935 is as follows:

Course: 008°(T)   CPA: 1.0 n mile   Aspect: Red 65°
Speed: 11 kn   TCPA: in 26 min

7.2.3   The construction of the plot

(a)   Draw in own ship's heading line on the plotting sheet.
(b)   Plot the first position of the target. Label it O. Insert the time.

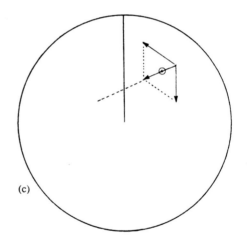

(c)

Figure 7.3   The vector triangle
(a)   With own ship stopped, target moves with true course and speed
(b)   With target stopped, own ship movement causes the target to appear to move
(c)   The resultant motion of the echo when both vessels are moving

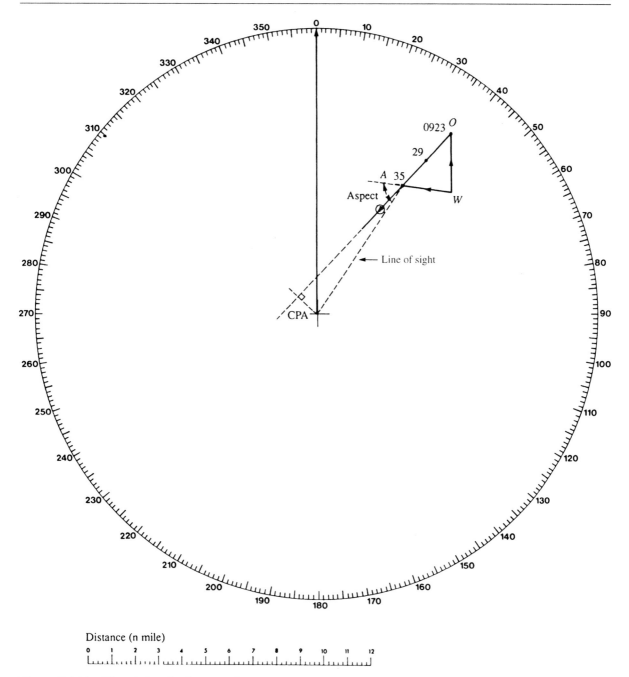

Figure 7.4(a) The relative plot for Example 7.1 Ship's head up

Distance (n mile)

Figure 7.4 (b)   True north up

(c) Lay off a line to represent the apparent motion of a stationary target, from *O*, opposite to the direction of the heading line.

(d) Plot at least one intermediate position of the target to ascertain that its apparent motion is not changing. Insert the time.

(e) Plot the final position, with the time, and label it *A*. Ensure that the apparent motion is consistent in direction and rate. Join *OA* and label it thus: ⊖

(f) Produce the apparent motion line *OA* to find the closest point of approach (CPA) and the time to closest point of approach (TCPA).

(g) The 'plotting interval' is the time between the readings of range and bearing for *O* and *A*. Calculate the distance that own ship has steamed in this time and plot the position in which you would expect to find the stationary target *W* at the end of the plotting interval. (*OW* is derived from own ship's speed and course reversed.)

(h) If *A* and *W* coincide, the target is stationary. If they do not, the line *W* to *A* represents the proper motion of the target in the plotting interval.

(i) 'Aspect' is measured between the 'line of sight' and the *WA* direction as in Figure 7.4.

It can be seen that, whichever orientation is used for the plot, the answers obtained will be the same, but some consideration must be given to the actual practicalities of plotting and the way in which the results are to be used. Where it is not possible to compass-stabilize the radar display (see Section 2.6.3), the ship's-head-up display will be the obvious choice. Where the radar display is capable of being compass-stabilized, it makes good sense to orientate the plot in the same way as the radar display, i.e. true-north-up when the radar display is true-north-up etc., especially when the vessel is on a southerly heading. There can be considerable confusion and even potential danger in trying to relate a ship's-head-up plot to a displayed radar picture which is 'upside down' e.g. when heading south. On the other hand, when conning the vessel and therefore relating the plot to the visual scene ahead of the vessel, it is sensible to orientate the display and to plot ship's-head-up or course-up accordingly.

7.2.4 The practicalities of plotting

The way in which the plot is constructed in practice is very different from the way in which one theoretically tackles a plot, such as the example in Section 7.2.2 above. In the first place, ranges and bearings are obtained only at intervals of some 3 to 6 minutes (not all at the same time), and it is unlikely that the plotter will be able to enjoy the luxury of radar plotting as a dedicated task, having rather to dovetail this activity into the many other bridge duties. If plotting is not to become all-consuming or if it results in peaks and troughs of activity, some wrinkles will have to be adopted to assist in spreading the load:

(a) Always draw in the heading line before starting to plot.

(b) When a target is first plotted, draw in *OW* and graduate it in 3-minute steps up to about 12 minutes. This is not to suggest that one should plot slavishly at 3-minute intervals but, rather, that one should plot when the opportunity arises and interpolate visually between the 3-minute graduations on the *OW* line.

The frequency with which the target should be plotted is dependent on a number of factors, namely, the range, the approach rate and the CPA. A target which is closing fast will require more frequent plots than, say, one which the observing vessel is slowly overhauling.

(c) Make a quick, early plot after, say, 3 minutes. Although the triangle will be small and not particularly accurate, it will give early warning of the potential of the encounter which is arising and allow time for some pre-planning. *Do not wait 12 minutes* before drawing the first triangle.

(d)   Obtain at least three consistently spaced positions in a reasonably straight line before being prepared to make a decision based on the plot.

(e)   Plotted positions should be in a reasonably straight line and spaced at distance intervals which are related to the time intervals between the plots. Where a plotted position appears significantly different from what is anticipated, it should be investigated immediately for an error either in reading the range and bearing from the radar or in plotting the position. Where a change in apparent motion is found to have occurred, a new triangle should be started (see Section 7.4).

(f)   Only essential lines should be put on the plot and then kept to a minimum in length. Extending WA beyond A should be avoided as it can be dangerously misleading and mistaken for an indication of CPA. On the other hand, *OA* should *not* be stopped short but extended at least beyond CPA.

(g)   It can be extremely helpful, especially when other officers are likely to observe the plot, to adopt some standard form of labelling (the labelling used in all figures in this text conforms with the United Kingdom Department of Transport's recommendations).

(h)   Times should be placed alongside each plotted position. This is essential when the plotting interval varies as it can justify the unequal spacing of the positions. 'Minutes' are quite sufficient, with the occasional indication of the hour.

(i)   TCPA should be given as the 'time to elapse', i.e. 'CPA in 16 minutes' rather than 'CPA at 1743' which is far less meaningful to someone who has then to check the time and subtract mentally. Also, time to elapse will in itself convey the degree of urgency in the situation.

(j)   After some 12 minutes there should be no real need to continue plotting bigger and bigger triangles, but it is essential to continue to plot positions and ensure that the target's apparent motion is being maintained. As soon as the apparent motion is observed to change, a new plot should be commenced (see Section 7.4).

(k)   Neatness is essential at all times. An untidy plot – lines everywhere, no labels, with times not related closely to plots, crossings out etc. – is likely to be more of a hindrance than a help. There is no merit in a plot which even the plotter has difficulty in understanding.

(l)   The range scale on which to plot requires some consideration. As a general rule, plots should be initiated on the 12 n mile range scale, but two differing requirements can arise. Where targets are likely to be closing fast, the earlier the plot is commenced the better, in which case the 12 n mile range scale should be adequate; when targets are close, a shorter (3 or 6 n mile) scale should be in use, possibly off-centred. The advantages of the shorter range scale are that there is better intrinsic accuracy and that changes in the target's movement are quickly and easily identifiable. As a target closes, a shorter range scale should be selected, but the plotter should, at intervals, temporarily return to the longer range scale(s) to search for newly arrived targets which could be a potential threat.

7.2.5   The need to extract numerical data

Plotting theory provides for the extraction of data in numerical form but this takes time and is needed only rarely. Also, the precision with which it is displayed often belies its accuracy and therefore the reliance which can be placed upon it.

Of the information normally available on a clearly constructed plot, CPA and the target's aspect/course should be directly observable with sufficient accuracy and without precise measurement. The target's speed should be mentally assessable by visual comparison with own ship's speed vector, i.e. by comparing WA with WO, which is known. By this means, the target's aspect/course, speed and CPA should be obtainable with sufficient accuracy for the practical assessment of the situation and only TCPA will require some form of measurement.

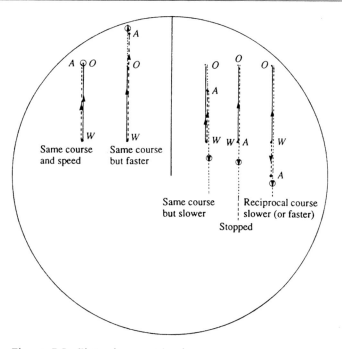

Figure 7.5 Plots where no triangle appears

7.2.6 The plot in special cases where no triangle 'appears'

As can be seen in the cases shown in Figure 7.5, all of the vector values are represented but in some of the cases their value is zero while, in others, the vectors are superimposed, all of which requires a little more care in the drawing of the plot and its subsequent analysis.

7.3 The true plot

The data given in Example 7.1 in Section 7.2.2 can be plotted on graph paper or on the chart as a 'true plot' (Figure 7.6).

In this case, own ship's course line is laid off on the plotting sheet and own position marked. From this position the bearing and range of the target are laid off. Own ship's position at, say, 3 minute intervals is

then marked off along the course line. What will be obtained directly is the target's course and the distance travelled in the plotting interval but, as already stated, perhaps the most important single piece of information available from a plot is the target's CPA, which is not immediately available and must be determined by the following geometrical construction:

(a) Lay off a line WO, parallel with the course line and of a length equal to the distance that own ship has travelled in the plotting interval.

(b) Join O to the current position of the target A and extend OA to pass O_2 i.e. own ship's current position, thus giving CPA. The static situation is identical with that depicted in Figure 7.4 and the required information is extracted in the same way. To this extent, relative and true plots are equally valid, but some practical points are worth noting:

(i) The convenience of a bearing scale and range circles on a relative plotting sheet are not

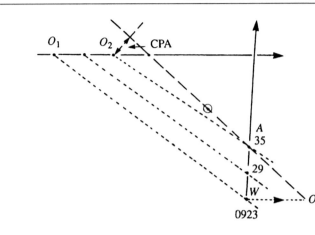

(a) Ships head up   (b) True north up

Figure 7.6 The true plot for Example 7.1

possible with a true plot where own position is continually moving. In plotting the target's position, protractor (or equivalent) and dividers will have to be used and the operation will be somewhat slower.

(ii) Each target position will have to be laid off from own ship's current position, which can be very time-consuming if a number of targets are being plotted.

(iii) Any error in plotting own ship's position (i.e. an error in the course and/or speed input) will result in an error in the directly obtained answer, i.e. the course and speed of the target. *Note.* If this error is repeated when laying off *WO* the CPA of the target will in fact be correct.

(iv) Perhaps the most disconcerting product of this plotting technique is the temporary nature of the apparent-motion line. (Figure 7.7). It is essential to appreciate that the 'displayed' CPA relates to *only one* own ship position, after which the appar-

ent motion line can be at worst misleading. Where a number of targets are being plotted on the same sheet, apparent-motion lines can relate to *different* own ship positions.

In general, where manual plotting has to be carried out, time is of the essence and in this respect the relative plot is better. For this reason the subsequent treatment will assume the use of the relative plot except in the case of reflection plotting on a true-motion display. In the latter case, a true plot can be easily and quickly produced.

7.4 The plot when only the target manoeuvres

Example 7.2 Your own ship is steering 310°(T) at a speed of 12 knots. Echoes are observed as follows:

Time	Echo A	Echo B
0923	brg 270°(T) at 9.0 n mile	brg 347°(T) at 9.5 n mile
0929	brg 270°(T) at 7.5 n mile	brg 346°(T) at 8.0 n mile
0935	brg 270°(T) at 6.0 n mile	brg 344°(T) at 6.5 n mile

(a) Determine the CPA, TCPA, course and speed of each target.

Plotting is continued as follows:

0941	brg 270°(T) at 4.5 n mile	brg 341°(T) at 5.0 n mile
0947	brg 253°(T) at 2.8 n mile	brg 350°(T) at 4.0 n mile
0953	brg 206°(T) at 1.7 n mile	brg 004°(T) at 3.1 n mile

(b) Say what action each target has taken. (Your vessel maintains course and speed throughout.)

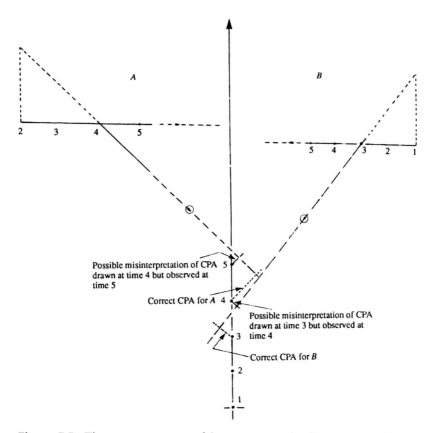

Figure 7.7 The temporary nature of the apparent-motion line on a true plot

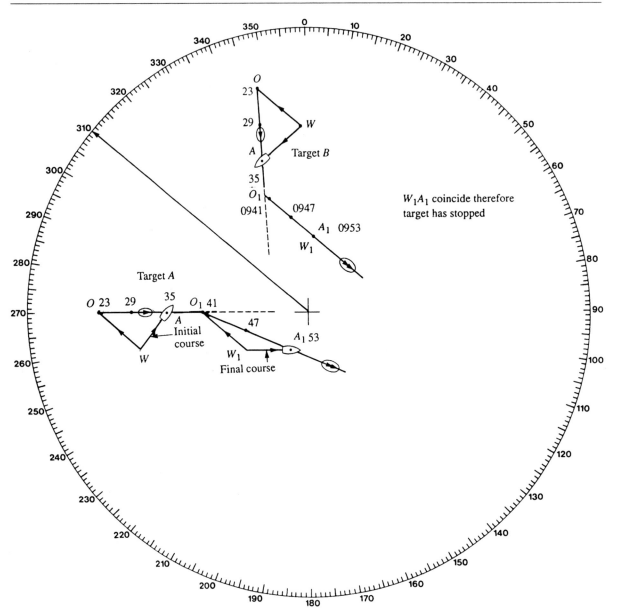

Figure 7.8 The plot when only the target manoeuvres (Example 7.2)

The apparent-motion line *OA* which is produced when determining CPA and TCPA depends upon four factors: Own ship's course and speed and the target's course and speed. If any of these factors change then the apparent-motion line will also change. Changes in own ship's proper motion are known (but in this example remain unchanged) and the resulting apparent motion can be predicted (see Section 7.5), but where a change in the apparent motion of the target is observed, the procedure set out in Section 7.4.1 should be followed to determine the change in the target's proper motion.

Answer

		Target A	Target B
(a)	CPA :	collision	1.0 n mile
	TCPA :	24 min	25 min
	Course :	040°(T)	226°(T)
	Speed :	10 kn	10.5 kn
(b)	Target has altered course only: 50° to starboard		Target has stopped.

Note that target *B* is similar to that used in the previous example and although, in this case, the bearings are re-orientated, the plots CPA and TCPA are identical.

7.4.1   The construction of the plot (Figure 7.8)

(a)   Own ship's heading line should have been drawn in.

(b)   The *OAW* triangle should have been constructed and the basic information extracted.

(c)   Continue to plot the apparent motion of the target, making sure the direction and rate are as predicted in the initial plot.

(d)   *As soon as a change in the target's apparent motion is noticed*, plot more frequently and, when a new steady apparent motion is established, choose a position, label it O_1, and insert the time.

(e)   Plot the new apparent motion as if it were a new target. Predict the new CPA and TCPA, also course and speed, from which any changes from the previous proper motion may be noted.

7.4.2   The danger in attempting to guess the action taken by a target

Since the change in the target's apparent motion can result from virtually any combination of changes in its course and speed, one should always construct a new plotting triangle and never attempt to assume a particular manoeuvre has taken place even though it fits in with what is both logical and desirable under the collision avoidance rules. In the typical crossing situation shown in Figure 7.9, one might expect the target to give way by altering her course to starboard. While the change in apparent motion would seem to indicate that this is what has happened, when the plot is completed it is clearly indicated that the target has in fact reduced her speed. If the observing vessel is subsequently presented with the development of a close-quarters situation with another vessel, the assessment of the appropriate manoeuvre will be dangerously flawed if it assumes the wrong heading for the pre-existing target.

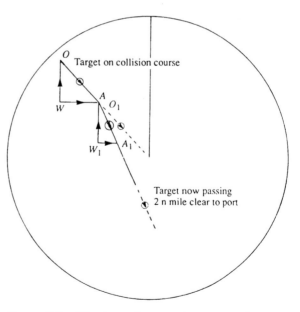

Figure 7.9   The danger in attempting to guess the action taken by a target

7.5 The plot when own ship manoeuvres

When it is decided (after assessment of the initial plot) that it is necessary for own ship to manoeuvre, it is essential to determine the effect of that manoeuvre *prior to* its execution and to ensure that it will result in a safe passing distance. After the manoeuvre has been completed, plotting must be continued to ensure that the manoeuvre is having the desired effect.

7.5.1 The plot when own ship alters course only

Because of the time taken for a change in speed to have any effect on the apparent motion line, the mariner will frequently select a change in course if it will achieve a satisfactory passing distance. This has some distinct advantages:

(a) It is quick to take effect.
(b) The vessel retains steerage way.
(c) The encounter may be more quickly cleared.
(d) It is more likely to be detected if the other vessel is plotting.
(e) It complies with the spirit of rule 8c (see Section 7.12.6).

Example 7.3 With own ship steering $000°(T)$ at a speed of 12 knots, an echo is observed as follows:

0923	echo bears	$037°(T)$	at	9.5 n mile
0929	echo bears	$036°(T)$	at	8.0 n mile
0935	echo bears	$034°(T)$	at	6.5 n mile

At 0935 it is intended to alter course 60° to starboard (assume this to be instantaneous).

(a) Predict the new CPA and TCPA.
(b) Predict the new CPA and TCPA if the manoeuvre is delayed until 0941.
(c) Predict the range and bearing of the echo at 0953, if the (instantaneous) manoeuvre is made at 0941.

Answer

(a) CPA is 4.4 n mile, 13 min after the alteration, i.e. at 0948.
(b) CPA is 3.6 n mile, 10 min after the alteration, i.e. at 0951.
(c) Predicted range is 3.8 n mile on a bearing of $334°(T)$.

7.5.2 The construction of the plot (Figure 7.10)

(a) The original OAW triangle should have been drawn.
(b) With compasses at W and radius WO, draw an arc.
(c) Draw from W a line at an angle to port or starboard of WO, equal to the proposed alteration of course.
(d) Label as O_1 the point at which this line cuts the arc.
(e) Join O_1 to A – this now represents the new apparent motion in direction and rate.
(f) Draw in the ship's *new heading line* and expunge the old heading line.
(g) Until the manoeuvre takes place, the target will continue to move down the original apparent-motion line. Predict the position of the target at the time at which it is proposed to alter own ship's course and label it O_2.
(h) Draw O_2A_2 parallel with and equal to O_1A and produce if necessary to find the new CPA.

Note (a) The prediction is based on the assumption that the target will maintain its course and speed. If the target also manoeuvres then the target will not follow the predicted apparent motion in both direction and rate and a new plot will have to be started.

(b) It is assumed that the alteration of course is instantaneous. For a more practical prediction:

(c) When manoeuvring at sea, to obtain a more realistic indication of the new CPA, one could predict the effect of the manoeuvre and check that it is acceptable. If so, bring the ship round to the new course and, when steadied on the new course, plot the

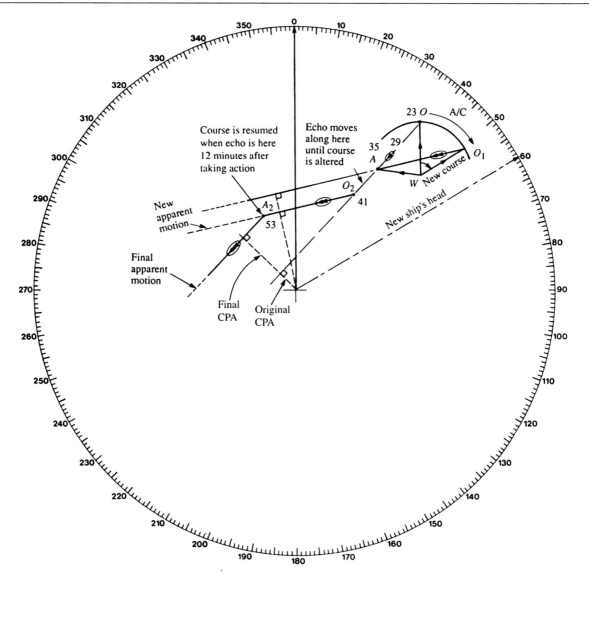

Figure 7.10 The plot when own ship alters course only (Example 7.3)

position of the target and transfer the new apparent motion, O_2A_2, through this position.

7.5.3 The plot when own ship alters speed only

Example 7.4 With own ship steering 000°(T) at a speed of 12 knots, an echo is observed as follows:

0923	echo bears	037°(T)	at	9.5 n mile
0929	echo bears	036°(T)	at	8.0 n mile
0935	echo bears	034°(T)	at	6.5 n mile

At 0935 it is intended to reduce speed to 3 knots (assume this to be instantaneous).

(a) Predict the new CPA and TCPA.
(b) Predict the new CPA and TCPA if the manoeuvre is delayed until 0941 (assume an instantaneous reduction of speed).
(c) Predict the bearing and range of the echo at 0953, if the manoeuvre is made at 0941.

Answer
(a) New CPA is 4.8 n mile, 24.5 min after the alteration of speed, i.e. at 0959.5.
(b) New CPA is 3.9 n mile, 19 min after the alteration of speed, i.e. at 1000.
(c) At 0953 the bearing should be 007°(T), range 4.0 n mile.

7.5.4 The construction of the plot (see Figure 7.11)

(a) The original *OAW* triangle should have been drawn.
(b) From *W*, measure off in the direction *WO*, the distance at the new speed that own ship will steam in the plotting interval and label the point O_1. Join O_1 to *A*. This represents, in direction and rate, the new apparent motion.
(c) Until the proposed alteration takes place, the target should continue to move along the old apparent-motion line. Predict the position of the

target at the time it is proposed to alter own ship's speed and label it O_2.
(d) Lay off O_2A_2 parallel with and equal to O_1A and extend it if necessary to find the new CPA.

Note (a) This prediction is based on the assumption that the target will maintain its course and speed and that own change in speed is instantaneous.

(b) It should be appreciated that when changing speed, especially in large vessels, it can take a considerable time to achieve the required new speed. Because of this, the new apparent motion line, O_2A_2, will be much nearer own ship than predicted in the example above.

This is demonstrated in Figure 7.12 where a ship's engines are stopped after a 12 minute plotting triangle has been constructed. The own ship's head reach (stopping distance) is 2.3 n miles. The limit line constructed on Figure 7.12 will represent a line the target will not cross, but will eventually meet as own ship comes to a complete stop.

7.5.5 The use of 'stopping distance' tables, graphs and formulae

7.5.5.1 *Stopping distance tables*

In the radar period before the arrival of ARPA, several organizations produced stopping distance tables to enable the manual plotter to estimate the stopping distances. The most notable of these was produced by the Honourable Company of Master Mariners in London, which included tables of stopping distances for a variety of ship types and tonnages.

7.5.5.2 *Manoeuvring data which should be available on board*

The International Maritime Organization (IMO) recommends in Resolution A160 (ES IV) that booklets containing manoeuvring information should be on board and available to the masters of large ships and also on board smaller ships, especially those carrying dangerous chemicals.

Part 1 of the booklet should contain manoeuvring data and/or diagrams (preferably the latter), typical

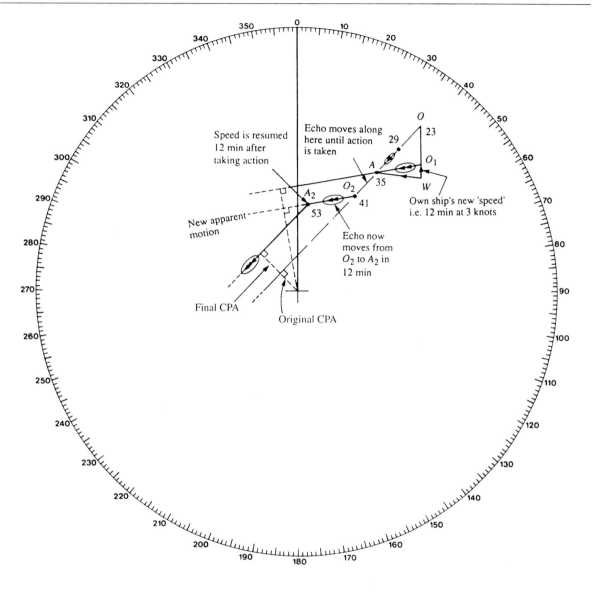

Figure 7.11 The plot when own ship alters speed only (Example 7.4)

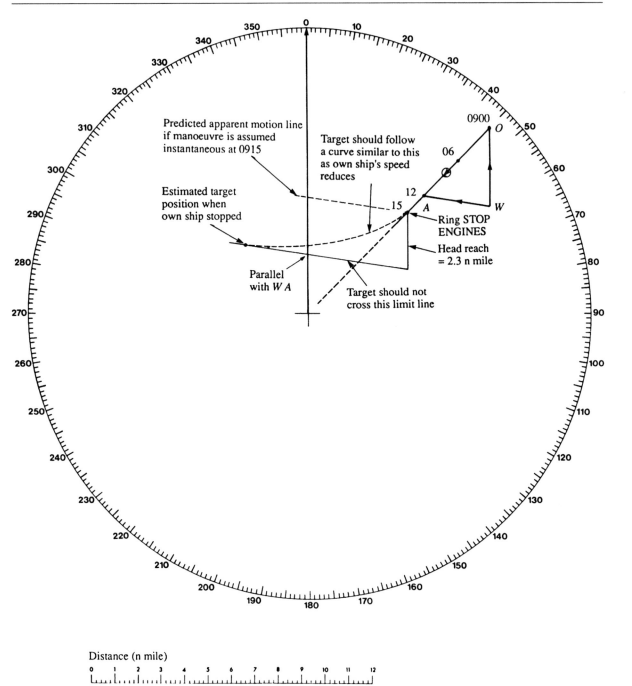

Figure 7.12   The plot when own ship stops: the effect of head reach and construction of a limit line

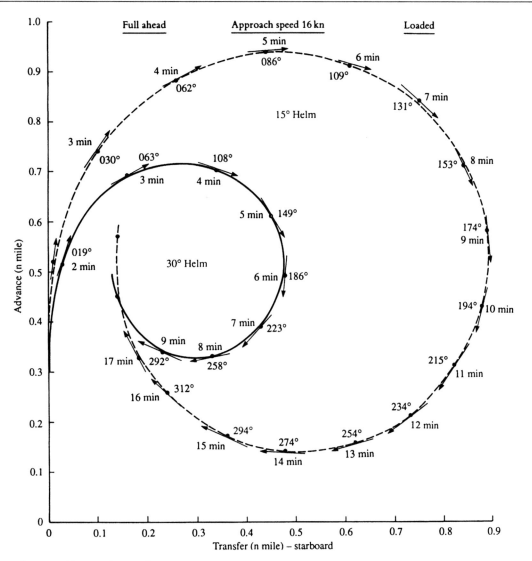

Figure 7.13 Turning circles

The response actually experienced may differ from that shown if any of the following conditions is not met:

Calm weather	Displacement 97 440 tonnes
No current or tidal stream	Draught forward 9.14 m
Water depth at least 2 × vessel's draught	Draught aft 9.14 m
Clean hull	

Figure 7.14 Stopping curves

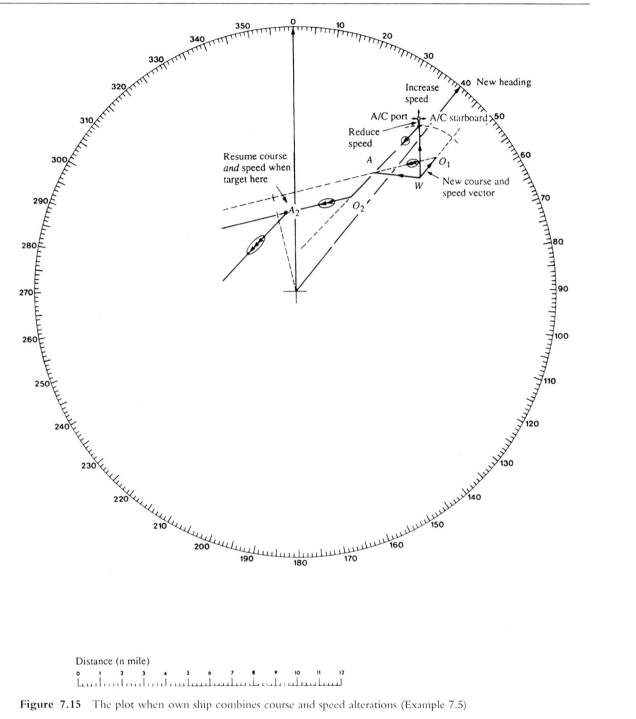

Figure 7.15 The plot when own ship combines course and speed alterations (Example 7.5)

of which are the turning circle and stopping curve diagrams (see Figures 7.13 and 7.14).

The form of the booklet should be such that additional information can be added from 'trials' and during the normal course of the voyage. Shipmasters are encouraged to add to this basic information as they gain experience in the handling of the vessel in conditions not covered by the original data.

Copies of the appropriate diagrams should be posted on the bridge.

7.5.5.3 *The use of stopping curves drawn up from data recorded during trials*

Consider a vessel proceeding at 16 knots. If the engines are put to *stop*, it will take some 3.2 n mile to run off the way, i.e. the readings associated with *A*, Figure 7.14.

If the engines are put to *half astern*, the vessel will be stopped in the water in some 17 minutes having covered some 1.7 n mile in running the way off, i.e. the readings associated with *B*.

If proceeding at 10 knots and full astern is demanded, the vessel will be stopped in the water in 10 minutes having covered some 7 cables while running the way off, i.e. the readings associated with *C*.

The stopping curves are intended primarily for use when the engines are to be put astern in order to stop the vessel in the water, e.g. when picking up a pilot, anchoring or in an emergency.

Note The curves assume that the environmental and loaded conditions etc. are the same as when the trials data was obtained. They should only be used as a rough guide as to what might be expected. It should also be borne in mind that as speed reduces, a critical speed will be reached when the vessel will no longer answer to the helm. When it is necessary to reduce speed even more quickly, other techniques such as rudder cycling may have to be employed. The prediction of how the speed may change or the vessel may turn under any conditions of loading, weather etc. can be very difficult. While the tables give some indication as to what may be expected, one should always work with a margin of safety and not leave manoeuvres until the last possible moment which theory suggests.

7.5.6 The plot when own ship combines course and speed alterations

Example 7.5 With own ship steering 000°(T) at a speed of 12 knots, an echo is observed as follows:

0923	echo bears 037°(T) at 9.5 n mile
0929	echo bears 036°(T) at 8.0 n mile
0935	echo bears 034°(T) at 6.5 n mile

At 0935 it is intended to alter course 40° to starboard and reduce speed to 6 knots (assume this to be instantaneous).

(a) Predict the new CPA and TCPA.
(b) Predict the new CPA and TCPA if the manoeuvre is delayed until 0941.
(c) Predict the range and bearing of the echo at 0953 if the manoeuvre was made at 0941.

Answer (Figure 7.15)
(a) CPA is 4.4 n mile, 20 min after the manoeuvre.
    Note The new apparent motion direction is the same as that when course only was altered (see Figure 7.10) but the new rate, O_1A, is much slower.
(b) CPA is 3.6 n mile, 14.5 min after the manoeuvre at 0941, i.e. at 0955.5.
(c) Predicted range is 3.6 n mile on a bearing of 355°(T).

7.5.7 The plot when own ship resumes course and/or speed

When taking action to avoid a close-quarters situation, the action should be *substantial enough* and *held for long enough* to show up in the plotting of radar observers on other vessels.

In order to determine the effect of resuming own ship's course and/or speed:

(a) The original *OAW* triangle should have been drawn.
(b) The apparent motion after manoeuvring should have been predicted and, provided that the target has maintained its course and speed, the target will follow the new apparent motion line, O_2A_2.

(c) If the target still maintains its course and speed and own ship resumes her original course and/or speed, the direction and rate of the final apparent motion will be the same as in the original OAW triangle. Thus, from the target's predicted position at the time of resumption, draw O_3A_3 parallel and equal to OA and produce if necessary to find the new CPA after resumption.

(d) If it is required to find the time to resume course/speed so that the CPA will not be less than, for example, 4 n miles, lay off a line parallel to OA and tangential to the 4 n mile range circle. The point at which this final apparent-motion line crosses the second apparent-motion line should be labelled O_3. Predict the time at which the target will reach O_3. This will be the earliest time to resume course/speed if the target is not to come within the required CPA.

Note   When predicting the movement of a target along an apparent-motion line, be sure to use the appropriate rate of apparent motion.

Example 7.6   Using Examples 7.3 and 7.4, predict in each case the CPA if the original course and speed respectively are resumed at 0953 (see Figures 7.10 and 7.11).

Answer
(a) If course is resumed at 0953, CPA = 3.5 n mile.
(b) If speed is resumed instantaneously at 0953, CPA = 2.4 n mile.

Note   If the order for an increase in speed is given at 0953, then by the time the vessel has worked up to the required speed the target will have passed in excess of the 2.4 n mile CPA.

7.5.8   The plot when both vessels manoeuvre simultaneously

It has been assumed until now that only one of the two vessels in the encounter manoeuvres. In such cases, the resulting apparent motion can be predicted when own ship manoeuvres, or resolved when only the target manoeuvres. When ships of about the same size meet, it is not uncommon for them to commence plotting

at about the same time and subsequently manoeuvre simultaneously or nearly so. If each vessel has plotted initially and completed the construction showing the effect of an own ship manoeuvre, then the target in each case will not follow the predicted apparent motion. In some cases this will result in each 'target' clearing by a greater distance than predicted but this will not always be the case. Thus it is essential when own ship manoeuvres:

(a) To predict the target's new apparent motion, assuming that it maintains course and speed.
(b) To ensure that the manoeuvre is having the (desired) predicted effect. It is not sufficient merely to assume that, because the target 'appears' to be going clear, it is moving in the direction *and rate* predicted. Where the predicted direction and rate are not as expected, a new plot must be started and the action taken by the target must be determined.

The latter can have important consequences in deciding when it is safe to resume course/speed. No longer can it be assumed that the 'final' apparent motion will be parallel and equal to the original apparent motion, as was assumed in Section 7.5.7.

Consider the situation in fog, as set out in Figure 7.16. If both vessels manoeuvre simultaneously or at nearly the same time, B as observed from A will move along the new apparent-motion line (but at the wrong rate, which is now much slower) and so appear to be going clear. No longer will B move along O_2O_3 when A resumes: it will move down parallel to the heading marker, since B is now stopped in the water.

If the apparent motion of B had not been predicted, monitored and re-appraised after the manoeuvre was detected, A might well have resumed course when B was at O_2, only to find a vessel stopped directly in its path. This would have manifested itself by B coming down A's heading marker and thus requiring sudden emergency action, possibly by both vessels at a very late stage in the encounter.

If systematic observation and interpretation is not carried out on B, as the way is run off, the relative motion plot would start to relate to the true situation, in which case B would have observed a vessel steering

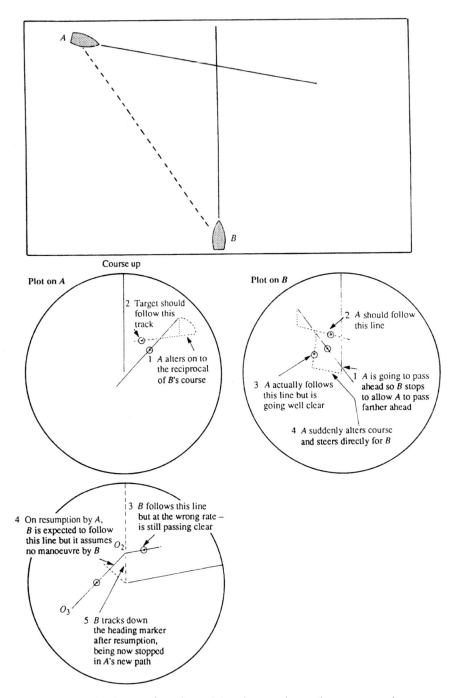

Figure 7.16 The danger of not determining the target's actual manoeuvre when apparently passing clear

to pass clear down the port side but then appearing to turn to port and steer directly toward it. Having very little way on at this stage, there is very little that B can do to avoid the close-quarters situation.

The encounter considered above is frequently carried out with the best of intentions but it is clear that, where manoeuvres are executed without proper prediction, monitoring and re-appraisal, the consequences can be dire.

7.6 The theory and construction of PPCs, PADs, SODs and SOPs

The harnessing of computers and ARPAs to assist in the resolution of the plotting triangle led to the question of whether some assistance could be given which would be of a higher order than that provided by the *trial manoeuvre* facility on the ARPA (see Section 4.4.3). Without going to the extreme of an *expert system* (see Section 7.13), some attempts were made to give a graphical representation of the encounter geometry which would assist the mariner in selecting an acceptable manoeuvre. The major problem was to devise a way in which this 'advice' should be presented to the mariner so that it was most meaningful. What follows is the theory and construction of the graphic representations that were devised; the philosophy and shortcomings are discussed in Sections 5.5 and 5.6. It is stressed that it is not envisaged that an observer would construct these points or areas manually. Where available, they will be generated by computer graphics. However, it is essential that any observer who elects to use such facilities understands the principles upon which their construction is based.

7.6.1 The predicted point of collision (PPC)

This is the point or points toward which own ship should steer at her present speed (assuming that the target does not manoeuvre) in order for a collision to occur (Figure 7.17(a) and Section 5.5). The logic

of this is that if one knows the course(s) which will result in collision then, by not steering those courses, collisions will be avoided. Also, by picking one's way between the PPCs, a more far-reaching collision avoidance strategy can be evolved.

Example 7.7 With own ship steering 000°(T) at a speed of 10 knots, an echo is observed as follows:

0923	echo bears 037°(T) at 10.3 n mile
0929	echo bears 036°(T) at 8.5 n mile
0935	echo bears 034°(T) at 6.7 n mile

Determine the bearing and range of the PPC(s).

Answer (Figure 7.17(b))
(a) P_1 bearing 337° at a range of 4.4 n mile.
(b) P_2 bearing 270° at a range of 18.0 n mile.

7.6.2 The construction to find the PPC

For a full explanation of PPCs, refer to Section 5.6. The plot is constructed as follows:

(a) Plot the target and produce the basic triangle.
(b) Join the own ship position 'C' to the target's position 'A' and extend beyond 'A'.
(c) With compasses at W and radius WO, scribe an arc to cut CA produced at O_1 or, if own ship is the slower (i.e. $WO < WA$), at O_1 and O_2.
(d) Join WO_1 (and WO_2).
(e) Draw CP_1 parallel to WO_1 to cut WA produced at P_1 (and CP_2 parallel to WO_2 to cut WA produced at P_2).
(f) P_1 (and P_2) is the PPC.

For a clearer appreciation of the determination of the PPC, Example 7.7 should be drawn out full size and to scale on a plotting sheet.

7.6.3 The predicted area of danger (PAD)

The PPC gives no indication of the course which needs to be steered to clear the PPC by some specific distance: to this end, the PAD was devised (Figure 7.18(a)). A further improvement is that the

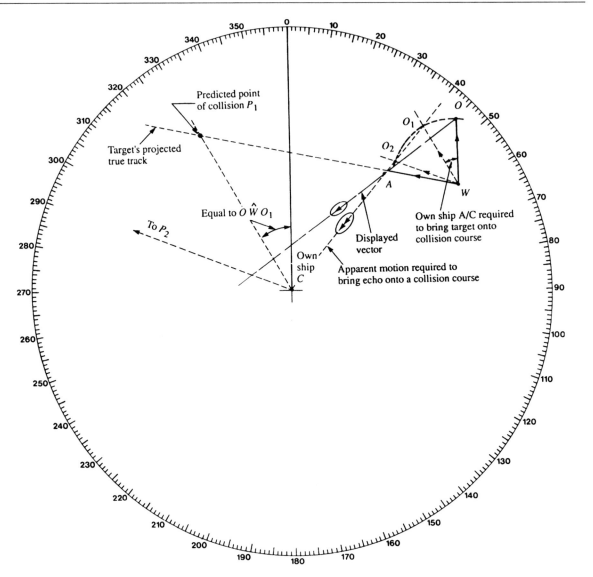

Figure 7.17(a) The predicted point of collision (PPC)

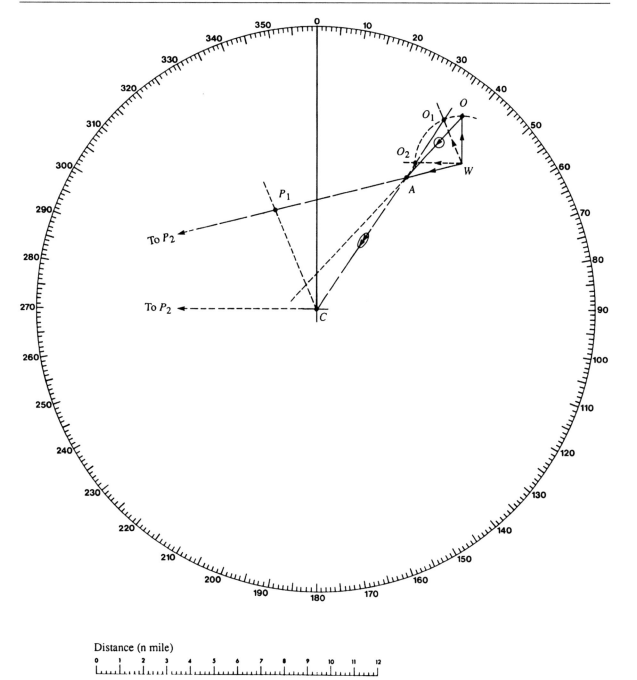

Figure 7.17(b) Answer to Example 7.7

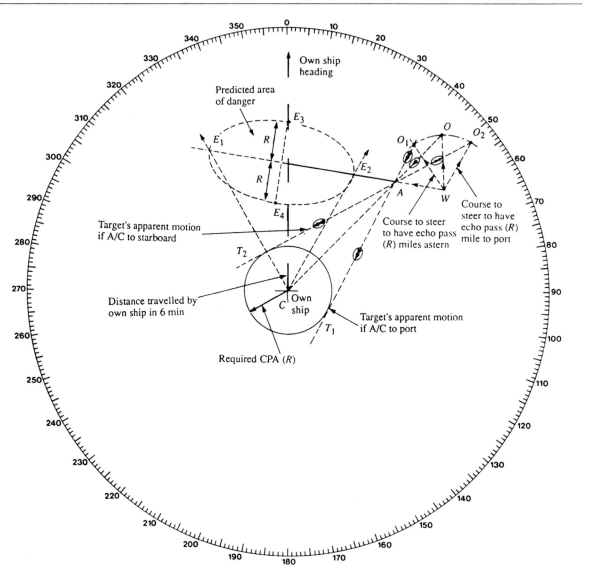

Figure 7.18(a)   The predicted area of danger (PAD)

target is connected to its PAD on the display, which was not the case with the PPC.

Example 7.8 With own ship steering 000°(T) at a speed of 12 knots, an echo is observed as follows:

1000	echo bears 045° (T) at 10.0 n mile
1006	echo bears 045°(T) at 8.5 n mile
1012	echo bears 045°(T) at 7.0 n mile

Plot the target and draw in the PAD for a 2.0 n mile clearing.

Answer See Figure 7.18(b).

7.6.4   The construction of the PAD

(a) Plot the target and produce the basic triangle.
(b) Draw lines AT_1 and AT_2 from the target's position, *A*, tangential to a circle of radius equal to the required CPA. Extend beyond *A*.
(c) With compasses at *W* and radius *WO*, scribe an arc to cut T_1A and T_2A at O_1 and O_2 respectively.
(d) Join WO_1 and WO_2. These represent the limiting courses to steer to clear the target by the required CPA.
(e) Draw CE_1 and CE_2 parallel to WO_1 and WO_2 respectively, to cut *WA* produced at E_1 and E_2 respectively.
(f) At the mid-point of E_1E_2, draw the perpendicular to E_1E_2 and extend it in both directions. In each direction, mark off the 'required CPA' and label the points E_3 and E_4.
(g) Draw in the ellipse passing through the points E_1, E_2, E_3, and E_4 (or the hexagon as indicated in Figure 7.18(b)). In the interest of simplicity, the ellipse was replaced by the hexagonal PAD in later equipment.

For a clearer appreciation of the PAD, Example 7.8 should be drawn out full size and to scale on a plotting sheet.

7.6.5   The sector of danger (SOD)

In this approach, a line *CH*, equal in length and direction to *OW* is drawn from the centre of the plotting sheet. This line is referred to as the *own ship vector*.

The sector of danger is an area constructed to provide a chosen passing distance. If the remote end of the own ship vector lies outside the SOD, a passing distance greater than the chosen value will be achieved, provided that the target does not manoeuvre.

Example 7.9 With own ship steering 000°(T) at a speed of 12 knots, an echo is observed as follows:

1000	echo bears 045°(T) at 11.0 n mile
1010	echo bears 045°(T) at 9.0 n mile
1020	echo bears 045°(T) at 7.0 n mile

Plot the SOD and suggest the minimum alteration of course to starboard at 1020 (instantaneous) which will achieve a 2 n mile CPA if own ship's speed is maintained throughout.

Answer. If own ship alters course to 027°(T) at 1020 then the target's new apparent motion will be along AT_1 (see Figure 7.19).

7.6.6   The construction of a sector of danger

(a) Plot the target for a set period.
(b) Draw own ship's vector for the same period – *CH*, equal to the distance that own ship will travel in the plotting interval, i.e. equal to *OW*.
(c) Draw *HS* parallel and equal to *OA*.
(d) Draw AT_1 and AT_2 tangential to the 'required CPA' range circle. (*Note.* If it were intended to delay the manoeuvre, then the tangents would be drawn from the predicted position of the target at the manoeuvre time.)
(e) Draw parallel lines to T_1A and T_2A through *S*.
(f) Any manoeuvre which takes *H* outside the shaded sector will achieve a CPA in excess of the required CPA.
(g) Swing *CH* until it just touches the sector boundary at H_1. This is the minimum alteration of course to starboard which own ship can make at the present speed to keep the target to a 2 n mile CPA.

Alternatively, 'speed' could have been reduced to CH_2 which would also have taken own ship's vector just outside the sector.

Distance (n mile)

Figure 7.18(b) Answer to Example 7.8

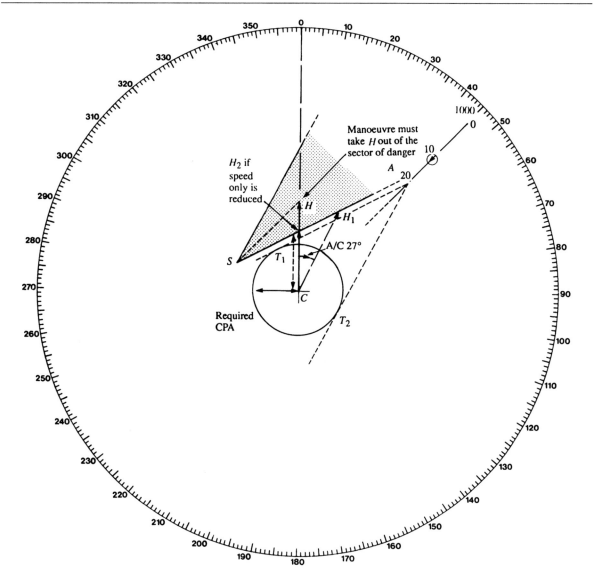

Figure 7.19 The sector of danger (SOD) – Example 7.9

While this will take care of the geometry, it is essential to ensure that the manoeuvre selected is still in accordance with the collision avoidance rules and the practice of good seamanship (see Section 7.12).

7.6.7 The sector of preference (SOP)

This relates to a stationary target or navigation mark and is a sector into which one must steer to achieve a passing distance within prescribed limits (Figure 7.20).

Example 7.10 With own ship steering 310°(T) at a speed of 15 knots, a light vessel, identified by its racon, is observed as follows:

0900   echo bears 296°(T) at 10.0 n mile
0906   echo bears 290°(T) at 8.6 n mile
0912   echo bears 282°(T) at 7.4 n mile

It is intended to manoeuvre at 0924.

(a) Construct the SOP if the light vessel is required to pass at not less than 2 n mile nor more than 4 n mile to port.
(b) Determine the course alteration which would be needed to achieve a CPA of 2 n mile to port (assume the alteration to be instantaneous).

Answer. (a) See Figure 7.20. (b) Alter course to 258°(T), i.e. 52° to port.

7.6.8 The construction of a sector of preference

(a) Plot the stationary target for a set period of time.
(b) Draw own ship's vector for the same period, *CH*, equal to the distance that own ship will travel in the plotting interval, i.e. equal to *OW*.
(c) Draw *HS* parallel and equal to *OA*.
(d) Plot the position of the target at the time at which it is intended to manoeuvre, A_1.
(e) From A_1, draw tangents to range limits for clearing the target, $A_1 T_1$ and $A_1 T_2$.
(f) Draw parallel lines to $T_1 A_1$ and $T_2 A_1$ through *S*.
(g) Any manoeuvre which takes *H* into the shaded sector will result in the target clearing within the limits for which the sector was drawn (provided

that any tidal effect remains constant). This could be achieved by an alteration of course or speed or both. If *CH* is swung until it intersects either of the limits of the shaded sector then that will be the course required to achieve the specific CPA.

7.7 The plot in tide

Example 7.11 With own ship steering 310°(T) at a speed of 15 knots, the echo from a light vessel fitted with a racon is observed as follows:

0900   echo bears 346°(rel) at 10.0 n mile
0906   echo bears 340°(rel) at 8.6 n mile
0912   echo bears 332°(rel) at 7.4 n mile

(a) Find the set and rate of the tide.
(b) It is required that your ship should pass 2 n mile off, leaving the light vessel to port.

  (i) If action is taken instantaneously at 0912, find the alteration of course which would be necessary.
  (ii) If instead, the action is to be taken at 0924 instead of 0912, find the alteration of course which would then be necessary.

Answer. See Figure 7.21

(a) Set = 032°(T) at 5 knots
(b) (i) course to steer at 0912 is 278°(T)
     (ii) course to steer at 0924 is 260°(T)

7.7.1 The construction of the plot

(a) Establish the identity of the target beyond all doubt (see Section 8.2). Plot the target and construct the basic triangle.
(b) *W* and *A* should coincide if there is no tide. If they do not, then *A* to *W* is the direction in which the tide is setting. Note that this is the reverse of what is normally deduced from a plot but since the target cannot be moving, it is the ship which must be experiencing set. The distance *WA* is the drift of the tide in the plotting

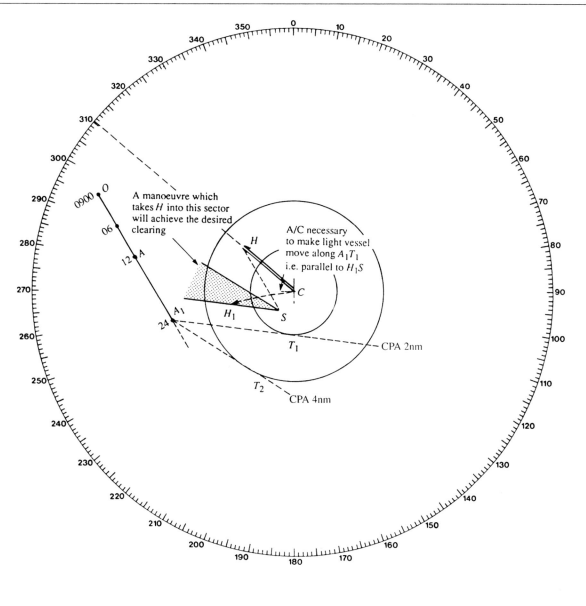

Figure 7.20 The sector of preference (SPO) – Example 7.10

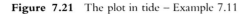

Figure 7.21 The plot in tide – Example 7.11

interval and it is from this that the tidal rate can be calculated.

Note When plotting other (moving) targets while experiencing tide, it is their movement through the water which is evaluated. It is precisely this which needs to be known when applying the collision avoidance rules and so it is essential that *no* attempt should be made to apply the effect of tide or current to their courses as determined from the plot.

7.7.2 The course to steer to counteract the tide

(a) Plot the target and determine the tide or current.
(b) Predict the position of the target at the time at which it is intended to manoeuvre.
(c) Draw in the apparent motion which is required, e.g. $A_1 T$.
(d) Draw in a line in the reverse direction through A, i.e. AO_2 (and AO_3 for the manoeuvre at 0924).
(e) Swing WO to cut the line through A at AO_2 (and AO_3).
(f) WO_2 is the new course to steer (and WO_3 if the manoeuvre is delayed).

Note All of the above assume instantaneous manoeuvres. When handling large ships in tide, due allowance will need to be made for their handling characteristics, especially when a speed change is demanded.

7.7.3 The change of course needed to maintain track when changing speed in tide

When proceeding while experiencing tide, any change in own ship's course and/or speed and/or tidal set and/or rate will affect the vessel's ground track.

Example 7.12 While steering 090°(T) at a speed of 16 knots, a beacon marking the anchorage is observed as follows:

0900   echo bears 076°(T) at 10.0 n mile
0906   echo bears 070°(T) at 8.6 n mile
0912   echo bears 062°(T) at 7.4 n mile

It is intended to anchor 2 n mile due South of the beacon.

(a) Determine the set and rate of the tide.
(b) Determine the course to steer at 0912 to counteract the tide.
(c) If the speeds which are represented by the engine room telegraph settings of Half Ahead, Slow Ahead and Dead Slow Ahead are 9, 6 and 3 knots respectively, determine the courses to be steered as the speed is progressively reduced when approaching the anchorage.

Answer. See Figure 7.22

(a) The tide is setting 184°(T) at 5 knots.
(b) At 0912, alter course to 060°(T).
(c) Half Ahead – steer 052°(T)
    Slow Ahead – steer 035°(T)
    Dead Slow Ahead: it is necessary to steer 004°(T) and stem the tide but note that the tide is 1 knot greater than the ahead speed.

7.8 The theory and practice of reflection plotters

The work involved in the transferring of data from the radar display to a plotting sheet is both time-consuming and a potential source of errors and so is a discouragement to practical plotting. The advantage of being able to plot directly on the screen surface was recognized at a very early stage in the development of radar. As a result, the anti-parallax reflection plotter was developed.

It has rapidly disappeared from general use due to the introduction of the raster-scan display. The UK regulations (see Section 11.4.1) still require that plotting facilities shall be at least as effective as a reflection plotter.

7.8.1 The construction of the reflection plotter

As can be seen from Figure 7.23, the plotting surface has the same curvature as the cathode ray tube (see Section 2.6.1). By inverting it and placing a flat

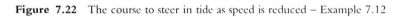

Figure 7.22 The course to steer in tide as speed is reduced – Example 7.12

Figure 7.23 The reflection plotter

partial reflecting surface midway between the two curved surfaces, it is possible to put a mark on the concave plotting surface such that its *reflection* will be aligned with the target's response on the CRT surface irrespective of where the observer's eye is positioned. This overcomes the problems of parallax which would arise if one were to try to plot on the plastic cursor placed some inches above the CRT surface.

7.8.2 Testing and adjustment

The relative positioning of all three surfaces is critical if parallactic errors are to be avoided. In many plotters, means are provided for adjusting the position of the partial reflecting surface as well as its 'tilt'. This is usually done by means of four adjusting screws. In order to test and adjust for freedom from parallax it is necessary to have four targets, one in each quadrant. These are marked on the plotting surface and then viewed from various directions and positions. If the plotted positions do not remain co-incident with all four targets, adjustment is necessary. This may take more than one 'round', as the adjustment of one screw can mean that all the others will require further trimming.

In order to overcome this need for adjustment, most modern plotters are now sealed units, but the plotter should still be regularly checked for misalignment.

7.8.3 Care and maintenance

The exposed surfaces and, in particular, the plotting surface should be wiped regularly with a dry cloth, taking care not to disturb the positioning of the surfaces.

On occasions, the plotting surface may require additional cleaning, when Perspex polish, supplied by the manufacturer, can be used. This should *never* be used on the partial reflecting surface.

It should be possible for the reflection plotter to remain in place but when it becomes necessary to remove it temporarily and store it, care should be taken to avoid it being bumped or scratched.

7.8.4 The practical use of reflection plotters, including the use of the Perspex cursor and parallel index

Plotting should be carried out on the plotting surface as if working on a plotting sheet but it is the 'reflections' which must be continually

observed. Two techniques are peculiar to reflection plotting:

(a) It will be necessary to make a 'scale' rule for measuring distance on the plotting surface. This is done by brightening the range rings, placing a mark on each ring and then, using stiff card, marking the position of each ring on the card. Sub-divisions may be put in by eye or more precisely, using the variable range marker. See Figure 7.24.

(b) It will be necessary to draw parallel lines on the plotter surface, e.g. *OW* parallel to the heading marker. This is done by lining up the Perspex cursor (see Section 6.9.3) with the heading marker. The parallel index lines on the cursor will now be parallel with the heading marker. Align the edge of the scale rule with the nearest parallel index line below it – this may mean

Figure 7.24 Constructing and using a scale rule

that one has to move the position of one's head slightly, or slide the card a short distance.

Note When drawing a line from a point, tangential to a range ring, e.g. when determining the time to resume, it is best first to mark the position of the range ring on the plotter surface.

7.8.5 Changing range scale

The reflection plotter had two distinct advantages: namely, it eliminated the need for reading and transferring of ranges and bearings to a plotting sheet and it maintained the immediate contact between display and plot. However, there is a certain reluctance on the part of the observer to change range scale because of the perceived potential loss of the plot. Nonetheless, it is important that when targets are close, the most appropriate range scale is used. This will mean adapting the plot to the new range scale. As can be seen in Figure 7.25, once the target is within the inner portion of the screen, the range scale should

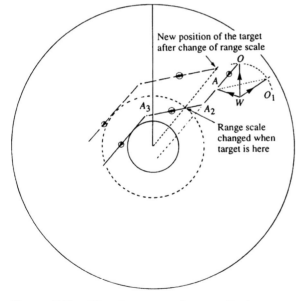

Figure 7.25 Changing range scale on a reflection plotter

be changed and the predicted apparent motion line A_2A_3 drawn parallel through the new position of the target.

It can often prove useful to retain the original plot and, provided that the lines do not become confusing, they can be left on.

7.8.6 The use of the 'free' EBL to draw parallel lines (see Section 6.9.6)

The 'free' EBL can prove extremely useful for transferring parallel lines in conjunction with a reflection plotter in preference to the use of the parallel lines on the Perspex cursor.

The EBL origin is positioned on the reflection of the line to be transferred and is rotated so that it is aligned with the line to be transferred. The EBL will maintain its orientation as it is moved about the screen using the joystick (see Figure 7.26).

7.8.7 Fixed and rotatable surfaces – use with a ship's-head-up unstabilized display

While using a plotter on a ship's-head-up unstabilized display, if it becomes necessary to alter own ship's course, the target and plot will come out of alignment as own ship changes course. For example, in Figure 7.27, after an initial plot, own ship alters course 55° to starboard; at the completion of the manoeuvre, the plot and target will be as depicted. To re-align the plot to the target, rotate the plotter surface anticlockwise (i.e. in the opposite direction to the alteration of course) by the amount which own ship has altered course.

When a rotatable surface has not been provided, there are means by which the plot can be continued. However, they can be complicated and consequently confusing, and are best avoided.

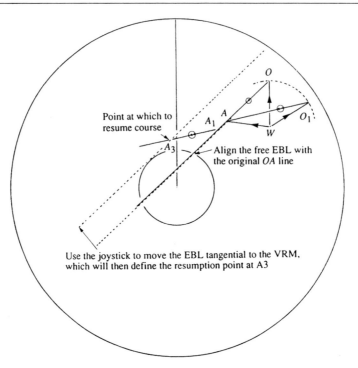

Figure 7.26 The use of the 'free' EBL to draw parallel lines
Note Transfer the line to the plotting surface if the EBL is required for another use; if not, leave it in place

When a fixed-surface plotter is provided, it is virtually essential that the true-north-up stabilized presentation is selected (see Section 1.4.2).

7.8.8 Flat and concave surfaces

The concave surface can be rather awkward to work on and so more complex plotters were provided with flat plotting surfaces. This was made possible by using a curved partial reflecting surface. However, apart from that, its use is exactly the same as for a plotter with a concave plotting surface.

7.8.9 Use in conjunction with parallel indexing

The provision of a reflection plotter made it possible for a prepared navigation plan to be marked out on the plotter and the movement of particular navigation marks to be observed in relation to their predicted movement. Any deviation from the pre-planned track will be readily apparent and compensation can be made (see Section 8.4).

7.8.10 Reflection plotters and raster-scan displays

No manufacturer has produced an optical reflection plotter which can be used with a television-type CRT or LCD. Where there was a requirement to carry radar equipment includes a reflection plotter or equivalent means of plotting and especially where only one radar display is to be fitted, a raster-scan display is in effect precluded unless it has some form of electronic plotting facility known as the EPA (electronic plotting aid, see Section 7.11.4).

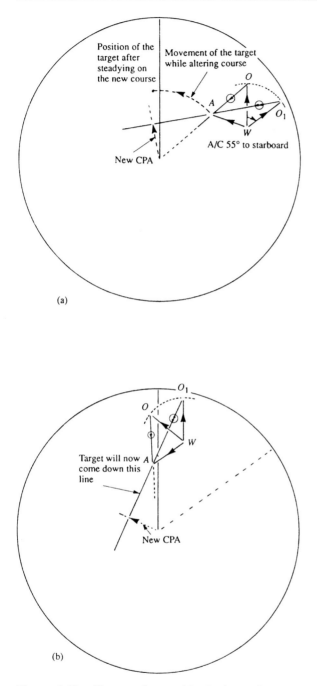

Figure 7.27 The use of a rotatable plotting surface
(a) Before or during alteration of course
(b) After rotation of the plotting surface

7.9 Manual plotting – accuracy and errors

The error in the result from any computation depends upon the accuracy of the data used. The intrinsic sources of error in the radar system relate to the measurement of ranges and bearings. Other data needed to complete the radar plot and subject to error are own ship's course and speed, and the plotting interval. Also, there are of course personal errors and blunders. While a *constant* (or systematic) error in input will result in a constant error in the answer obtained, it is the errors which are of a random nature which govern the size of the 'circle of uncertainty' around the plotted position which, if not actually drawn, should be borne in mind when plotting a position.

Note *Precision of measurement and accuracy of measurement* should not be confused. For example, it is no good being able to measure bearings to 0.1° if the 'free play' in the mechanical gearing is ±2°.

7.9.1 Accuracy of bearings as plotted

Errors in bearings may arise from any of the following causes:

1 The existence of inherent errors which fall within the limits allowed by the IMO Performance Standard (see Section 11.2.1). The individual error sources are discussed in detail in Section 6.9.9 where it is shown that they may aggregate to as much as ±2.5°. It is also indicated that some components of the total error can be expected to remain constant over a series of bearings and these will have the effect of slewing all plotted positions by a fixed amount. There will, of course, be a random component which is most likely to arise from an instantaneous misalignment of the antenna and trace and should not exceed ±1°. This error will have the effect of scattering the observed positions about the correct apparent motion.

2 Parallax when bearings are taken with a Perspex cursor (see Section 6.9.3).

3   Failure to centre the origin correctly when use is to be made of a Perspex cursor. The magnitude of this error will depend upon several factors which are described in Section 6.2.3.3.
4   Errors of alignment of the electronic bearing line. This error is likely to be constant over a series of bearings (sec Section 6.9.5).
5   Failure to check the heading at the time a bearing is taken when a ship's-head-up unstabilized orientation is selected. This error is likely to be random.
6   Personal errors and blunders.

7.9.2   Accuracy of ranges as plotted

Sources of error in the measurement of range may include any or all of the following:

1   Range errors inherent in radar systems which comply with the IMO Performance Standards. These are described in Section 6.9. They should not exceed 1 per cent of the maximum range of the scale in use or 30 metres, whichever is the greater. On the 12 n mile range scale this gives 1.2 cables or 222 metres. These errors should be constant over a series of ranges.
2   Inaccurate interpolation. This will give rise to random errors.
3   Mechanical errors in the variable range marker of old radial CRT displays. Such errors should normally be constant over a series of ranges unless a serious mechanical fault exists.
4   Personal errors or blunders.

7.9.3   Accuracy of own ship's speed

In general, the means of obtaining the ship's speed can be flawed in the extreme and is the quantity most susceptible to error. Speed (or rather, distance travelled in the plotting interval) can be derived from a variety of sources, for example:

1   *Distance (towed) log.* In this case, it is not possible to know one's speed quickly, particularly when altering speed (e.g. in poor visibility). Also, it is common practice to hand the log when the engines are put on stand-by, so as to avoid fouling the propeller when the engines are put astern (some towed logs do have an additional unit which provide a read-out of speed.
2   *Speed (pitot, impeller, electromagnetic) log.* Although the speed may be read at any instant, the sensor is frequently withdrawn when the vessel is in shallow water, e.g. in port approaches.
3   *Engine revolutions.* This is only accurate in so far as 'slip' is accurately known and this is rarely the case when changing speed such as when manoeuvring in fog.
4   *Doppler log.* It should be borne in mind that if ground locked, this indicates speed over the ground which in tide can lead to misinterpretation of the aspects of other ships (see Ground-stabilization, Section 6.8.1.3). Also, there is some uncertainty as to just what 'speed' is being measured if using a single-axis sensor which is 'ground locked'.
5   *Speed derived from positions plotted on the chart or GNSS (see Section 10.1).* There is a common misconception that this is the ship's 'correct' speed and on this basis it is used for plotting and as the manual input to the true-motion unit and ARPA (see Sections 6.8.1.3 and 6.12.3). It must be remembered that the speed derived is measured over the ground, whereas it is the speed through the water which is required for plotting. Thus, if there is any tide involved, its effect *must* be allowed for in order to deduce the water speed.

Note   The slower own ship's speed, the greater will be the proportionate effects of errors in the knowledge of own ship's speed. Unfortunately, the plot can be at its most inaccurate when both vessels are moving slowly as they might be when proceeding in fog.

7.9.4   Accuracy of own ship's course

Compass error should be small and relatively constant so, although it will produce errors in target course and speed, they too should be small and constant. Where the ship is off course for minutes at a time and this

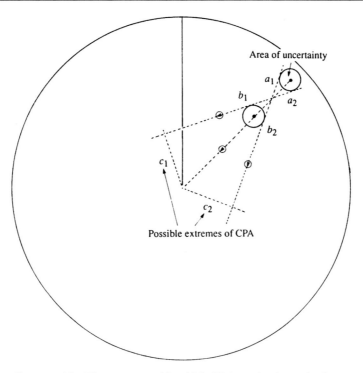

Figure 7.28 The accuracy with which CPA can be determined

is not taken into account in the plot, errors in the target's course and speed will result (see Figure 7.29).

7.9.5 Accuracy of the plotting interval

The times of each plot are normally recorded to the nearest minute and so an error of up to half a minute can be quite common when plotting a position. This can mean an error of up to 1 minute in a plotting interval of, say, 5 minutes, i.e. 20 per cent. As the plotting interval is used to calculate the distance run (OW), an error here will have the same effect as an error in speed.

7.9.6 The accuracy with which CPA can be determined

Random errors in obtaining the range and bearing of a target will mean that when a position is plotted, it should be surrounded by an *area of uncertainty* based on the errors referred to in Sections 7.9.1 and 7.9.2. In Figure 7.28, the apparent-motion line through the plotted positions indicates a vessel on a collision course. However, if 'worst accuracy' is considered, i.e. that the target's position is at a_1 and some time later at b_2 or, alternatively, is at a_2 and later at b_1, then the CPA of the target will lie in the range between c_1, to port and c_2 to starboard.

The means by which accuracy can be improved are:

(a) Improve the inherent accuracy of the system, i.e. decrease the size of the circles of uncertainty.

(b) Plot frequently. This has the advantage of being a quick check for blunders while also allowing for a better 'mean' line to be drawn through the plotted positions. It has been suggested that the ideal time period for which plotting should be continued before accepting that the result is of sufficient accuracy should be calculated by allowing the

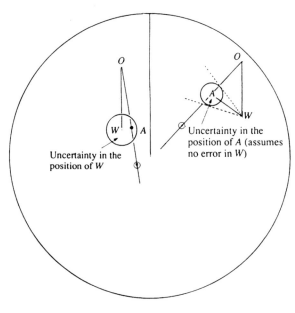

target to traverse some $0.2 \times$ radius of screen, e.g. *OA* should be some 2.4 n miles when using the 12 n miles range scale.

7.9.7 The consequences of random errors in own ship's course and speed

We assume in the following that positions *O* and *A* are without error.

In the *OAW* triangle (Figure 7.29), the position of *W* is determined from a knowledge of own ship's course and speed. It is important to note here, that, when dealing with a slow-moving target, if *A* falls within the error circle around *W* then it is impossible to determine the course and/or speed of the target (see Figure 7.30).

7.9.8 Summary

1 It has been estimated that the full maximum error occurs only in some 1 per cent of encounters.

Figure 7.29 Errors resulting from inaccuracy
(a) in own ship's speed
(b) in own ship's course
Note Assume no error in *O* or *A*

Figure 7.30 Slow-moving targets

2 In deciding what is an acceptable CPA, the consequences of inaccuracies should be borne in mind
   and one should err on the safe side.
3 Small alterations of course and speed by plotted
   targets can be completely swamped by errors, especially when speeds are low.

In an attempt to evaluate the errors, the following
have been suggested:

$$\text{Error in CPA} = \frac{\pm 0.03 \times \text{mean range}}{\text{range change}}$$

$$\begin{array}{l} \text{Error in} \\ \text{vessel's} \\ \text{estimated} \\ \text{course} \\ \text{(degrees)} \end{array} = \frac{103 \times \text{mean range}}{\left(\begin{array}{c}\text{estimated speed} \\ \text{of target}\end{array}\right) \times \left(\begin{array}{c}\text{plot interval} \\ \text{in minutes}\end{array}\right)}$$

$$\begin{array}{l} \text{Error in} \\ \text{target's} \\ \text{speed (\%)} \end{array} = \frac{180 \times \text{mean range}}{\left(\begin{array}{c}\text{estimated speed} \\ \text{of target}\end{array}\right) \times \left(\begin{array}{c}\text{plot interval} \\ \text{in minutes}\end{array}\right)}$$

7.10 Errors associated with the true-motion presentation

The true-motion display (see Section 2.6.4) is, in fact,
a contrived mode of display in that the 'received data'
is processed by applying the ship's course and speed in
order to achieve the desired method of presentation.
Because of this, the accuracy of this form of presentation is subject, in addition to the errors discussed in
Sections 7.9.7 and 7.9.8, to errors which may arise in
the accuracy with which the origin tracks across the
screen.

7.10.1 Incorrect setting of the true-motion controls

When setting up the true-motion presentation for
manual plotting, the method of course and speed input
will have to be selected by the operator. The course

input will invariably be from a repeating compass and
will be automatic, but the repeater in the radar will
have to be aligned with the master compass. Provided
that this has been done correctly, errors from this
source should be minimal (see Section 6.8.2).

The source of speed input can be provided by
log, by manual input or with ARPA, by means of
automatic ground-stabilization (see Section 5.3). The
points discussed in Section 7.9.7 apply here and will
affect the displayed movement of the target(s) (see
Figures 7.32 and 7.33), but it is the setting of the
'manual' input of speed that warrants special attention.

While steaming at a steady speed it is possible to set
the manual speed input and virtually forget about it, but
in fog, heavy traffic and in port approaches it may be
necessary to change speed frequently. Amid all the other
bridge activity, it must be remembered that the manual
speed control on the radar will also need to be re-set
each time there is a change in the demanded speed. It
is logical at times like these to use the 'log' input to the
true-motion unit but on some vessels these are also the
times when the log is least likely to be deployed.

It is very easy to order a change in speed and forget
to change the manual speed input to the radar and
so have it portray a most misleading presentation of
the situation. Such forgetfulness will be less likely if
the observer maintains a plot of the origin, as recommended in Section 6.8.2.

Consider own ship steaming at 16 knots, using manual speed input to the radar which is correct during
the initial plotting period. Having passed ahead of vessel A, own ship now reduces speed (the other vessels
maintain course and speed throughout) but forgets to
alter the manual speed input to the radar. The target A
would *appear* to alter course to starboard as indicated
in Figure 7.31, but on 'visual' observation would still
be showing a green light (her starboard side) instead
of the expected red light. Careful observation of the
land would show that it too is now 'moving' – but at
times like this, one rarely has time to analyse the more
subtle discrepancies on the display.

One must also be conscious of the fact that an error
in the log input will produce a similar effect.

Other inputs which can inadvertently cause problems are the tide input controls (see Sections 2.6.4.4

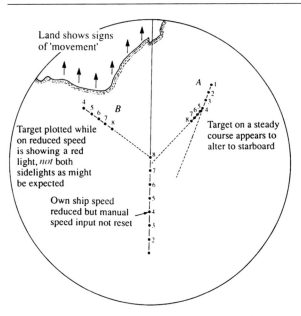

Land shows signs of 'movement'

A

B

Target plotted while on reduced speed is showing a red light, *not* both sidelights as might be expected

Target on a steady course appears to alter to starboard

Own ship speed reduced but manual speed input not reset

Figure 7.31 The misleading effect caused by failing to reset the manual speed input to the true-motion unit after a manoeuvre – a reduction of speed in this case

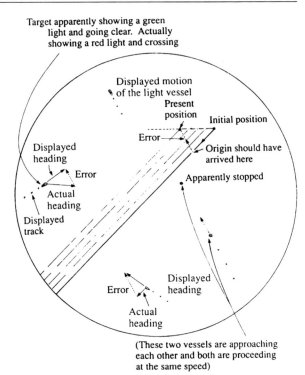

Target apparently showing a green light and going clear. Actually showing a red light and crossing

Displayed motion of the light vessel

Present position

Initial position

Error

Origin should have arrived here

Displayed heading

Error

Apparently stopped

Actual heading

Displayed track

Error

Displayed heading

Actual heading

(These two vessels are approaching each other and both are proceeding at the same speed)

Figure 7.32 Tracking course errors on a true-motion presentation
True course 225° Speed 10 kn
Origin tracking 270° Speed 10 kn

and 6.8.1.6). When setting up the true-motion display, it is essential to check that these controls are set as required (see Section 6.8.3) or are completely inoperative. If allowed to remain as when previously in use, they can cause the origin to track in completely the incorrect direction and thus give a totally wrong impression of the direction in which the targets are tracking. Again, the importance of plotting the origin (see Section 6.8.2) must be stressed.

7.10.2   Tracking course errors

In achieving true motion, the origin must track in the direction in which the vessel is travelling. If it does not, then the target's courses and/or speeds will be in error. The magnitude and direction of these errors will vary from target to target and will be dependent upon the encounter geometry and the magnitude and direction of the tracking error.

Causes of tracking course error can include a fault in the true-motion unit, incorrect alignment of the com-

pass repeater (heading marker), and incorrect setting of the tidal correctors (see Sections 6.8.2 and 6.8.3).

7.10.3   Tracking speed errors

As with tracking course errors, these will result from errors in the movement of the origin across the display (see Figure 7.33). Causes may include a fault in the true-motion unit, an error in the transmitting log, an error in the estimated speed, failure to re-set the manual speed control after ordering a change in speed and failure to reset the tidal correctors.

It is essential not only to plot the origin of the display when using the true-motion presentation but also to ensure that the movement is correct in both direction and scale speed. This may mean that a future position of the origin must be predicted and marked on

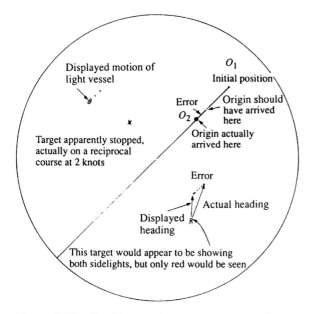

Figure 7.33 Tracking speed errors on a true-motion presentation
True course 225° Speed 5 kn
Origin tracking 225° Speed 7 kn

the reflection plotter. If the prediction is not achieved then the cause should be investigated.

7.11   Radar plotting aids

Many pieces of equipment have been developed over the years which were intended to assist the mariner in plotting and thereby interpreting the display. Most are now only of historical interest, having been superseded by ARPAs/ATAs but one or two are worthy of individual mention.

7.11.1   The radar plotting board

This took a number of forms as various manufacturers attempted to provide something more permanent and durable than the paper plotting sheet. Effectively, this was little more than a plotting sheet, overlaid with Perspex or heavy transparent film, which was free

to rotate and so assist in predicting the effect of an alteration of course by own ship.

It is not intended here to discuss its construction and use since it has been superseded, but this was a fruitful area for personal innovation and some boards are still in use in the pleasure boat market.

7.11.2   Threat assessment markers ('matchsticks' or 'pins')

It has long been the practice of mariners to observe the compass bearing of an approaching vessel and, where there is no appreciable change, to assume that risk of collision exists. Unwary mariners have been seriously misled when using an unstabilized display as the source of bearing measurement.

With the increased use of compass-stabilized displays, the principle of observing the compass bearing of a target again manifested itself by mariners adopting the practice of placing the cursor on the target and observing how its bearing changed in relation to this datum.

Where it is necessary to monitor more than one target, the technique is difficult to implement. Recognizing this problem, Decca Radar in 1966 made provision for the observer to use up to five 'threat assessment markers'. These are, in effect, sections of electronic cursor which can be positioned in range and azimuth so that, when placed on a target as shown in Figure 7.34, they will quickly show whether the bearing of the target is changing. The remote end of the marker, which represents a constant range and bearing from the observing vessel, is brightened and thus the marker resembles a match or pin.

Correct use of the markers provides much more information than merely an indication of change of bearing. It enabled the observer to deduce the relative- and true-motion data for each marked target. To exploit this facility, the true-motion sea-stabilized presentation must be selected. Used in this way, the true plot of the target will indicate its true motion, but the position of the target in relation to the bright end of the marker will indicate its potential threat. By joining the 'head' of the marker to the current position of the

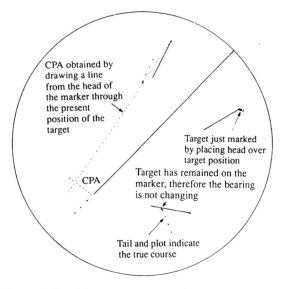

Figure 7.34 Threat assessment markers on a true-motion presentation

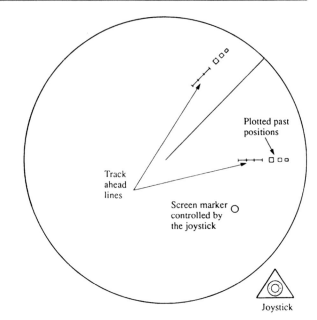

Figure 7.35 The 'E' plot

target and extending the line, the CPA of the target can be assessed.

Note When used with a true-motion display, the markers track across the screen in the same manner as the origin but with their orientation and position in relation to the origin remaining unchanged.

Other manufacturers have produced variations on this basic idea. In one system, the markers are bright spots (i.e. only the head of the 'match' is shown) and a free electronic bearing line, having time divisions on it, is used to lay off the relative motion of the chosen target. In this particular system, if relative motion is selected, the marker traces out the track of a water-stationary target and there is a provision temporarily to move the marker to the O_1 plotting position (see Section 7.5) in order to assess the effect of a proposed manoeuvre by the observing vessel.

7.11.3   The 'E' plot

This system used a joystick and marker to record 'electronically' the position of a target (Figure 7.35). The operator recorded the positions of targets at regular intervals, after which the data was processed and

extrapolated to provide the information which would be available from a normal plot, i.e. course, speed, CPA and TCPA. Up to 10 targets can be manually tracked.

Manual recording as practised here should not be confused with manual acquisition followed by automatic tracking which takes place in the simplest of ARPAs.

The system was unique to Kelvin Hughes. However, other types of plotting aids using graphics were common. Development of such facilities is a natural result of the need to provide plotting facilities on a raster-scan display which are at least equivalent to a reflection plotter (see Section 7.8.10), and has been assisted by the ease with which lines and points can be drawn electronically on such a display.

The 'E' plot has now been superseded by the EPA (see Section 7.11.4).

7.11.4   Electronic Plotting Aid (EPA)

The IMO has produced performance standards for an electronic aid to manual plotting. It is a refinement of earlier graphical devices such as the E plot covered in the previous section. The IMO have called the device an Electronic Plotting Aid (EPA) and it is the minimum requirement for the smallest vessels (under 500 grt) that come under SOLAS (see Section 4.1.3), although not for high-speed craft.

It should be noted that future standards (see Section 11.2.1) will require all new vessels to carry an automatic target tracker and the EPA will disappear with time.

The performance standards require that the radar/EPA has azimuth-stabilization, which can be provided by either a gyro or transmitting magnetic compass. There is no requirement for an electronic speed input, thus the speed may have to be input manually.

The observer simply plots a target initially by using the joystick or tracker ball controls to position a marker symbol over the target to be plotted. A second plot is added any time between 30 seconds or 15 minutes later. A target symbol and vector then appears on the display. The symbol will move in an extrapolation of the two plots across the screen. The observer should enter more plots in time, particularly if the symbol's relative motion does not match the underlying relative motion of the target across the screen. Individual plots can be corrected if not plotted accurately.

As soon as a second position has been plotted the observer can obtain the traditional alphanumeric target information associated with ARPA and ATA equipment. That is: present range and bearing, CPA, TCPA, true course and speed. The observer is also able to switch between true and relative vectors, as well as adjust the time length of vectors. As the observer adds more plots to the target, the information and vectors are updated based on *calculations from the last two plots only*. It obviously follows that best results will be obtained by plotting at reasonably regular intervals. Plotting at too small an interval will cause minor plotting errors to have a large effect on the accuracy of the result. On the other hand, if the time interval is stretched too much then any target manoeuvres are less accurately detected and followed. The best interval to use will vary according to the target relative speed and direction and the range scale in use at the time (see also Section 7.9).

The standard calls for a minimum capability of 10 targets to be tracked in this way, so each target symbol must be assigned a target number, which (when appropriate) is included on the alphanumeric display as well as on the radar picture. The observer selects an appropriate target first, before reading the alphanumeric display or adjusting its plot.

7.11.4.1 Alarms

The traditional target violation of preset CPA and TCPA limits found on both ARPA and ATA (see Section 4.7.2) are provided on an EPA.

In addition there is a warning if a target plot has not been updated by the observer for more than 10 minutes. The plot is dropped completely if this update time exceeds 15 minutes.

7.11.4.2 Comparison between EPA and the reflection plotter

The EPA has effectively superseded the requirement for a reflection plotter on non-ARPA/ATA radars. The modern raster CRT and LCD displays do not lend themselves to a reflection plotter and the EPA eliminates the need for calculations by the observer that are associated with hand plotting.

The plotting errors due to working with a thick grease pencil are reduced and a major advantage is that it is no longer a requirement for the navigator to record the precise time of the plot as it is done by the EPA. Indeed while it may improve accuracy of EPA to plot at a suitable regular interval (as discussed above), the EPA is more likely to obtain accurate results than a reflection plotter if the plotting periods are a little irregular.

The EPA also maintains plots at the correct range and predicted speed when the range scale is changed, unlike the reflection plotter (see Section 7.8.5).

The main disadvantage of the EPA over the reflection plotter is that only two plots are used for the calculations and it is up to the observer to monitor the target motion to ensure that the target achieved the second plot in a straight line and at constant speed. The results would not be valid if (unbeknown to the observer) the target adjusted its course or speed and ran a dogleg to the second plot.

It is of course possible for an observer using a reflection plotter to make this error, but in this case it is less likely as the observer is encouraged to take three or more plots and the change in relative motion would be more obvious. The human observer may also obtain a more accurate indication of target relative motion by averaging it over three or more target plots. This is likely to be particularly true if, for example, the azimuth input is from a transmitting magnetic compass and the vessel is yawing badly.

As in all manual plotting, the results are still only as good as the diligence of the observer.

7.12 The regulations for preventing collisions at sea as applied to radar and ARPA/ATA

7.12.1 Introduction

The specific function of radar plotting (whether carried out on a paper plotting sheet, with the aid of an ARPA or with any of the intermediate facilities or techniques) is to provide the data on which a collision-avoidance strategy can be based. It is not intended that this section should represent a treatise on collision-avoidance strategy in restricted visibility. This section aims to provide the radar observer with an appreciation of the need to carry out radar plotting (or equivalent systematic observation) in order to comply with the rules for preventing collisions at sea and with an understanding of the relationship between the data extracted and the provision of the Regulations to the extent necessary to provide informed support for the master or other officer responsible for the collision-avoidance strategy.

A notable feature of the 1972 Collision Regulations was that many specific references to the use of radar were made in the body of the rules. Subsequent amendments have not changed the role of radar as an anti-collision aid.

When considering the application of radar and ARPA to collision avoidance, it is particularly pertinent that the term *radar plotting or equivalent systematic observation of detected objects* (rule 7b) appears for the first time. Although the rules do not define this term, consideration of the various instructions and cautions given in the specific references to radar make it possible to deduce a procedure which would enable competent personnel to comply with both the letter and spirit of the rules. In this respect, ARPA should merely be seen as readily providing data which would otherwise have to be obtained from the radar by lengthy and tedious manual extraction.

7.12.2 Lookout – rule 5

Every vessel shall at all times maintain a *proper lookout* by sight and hearing as well as by *all available means appropriate* in the prevailing circumstances and conditions so as to make a full appraisal of the situation and of the risk of collision.

Although this rule does not specifically mention radar, there seems little doubt that radar is embraced by the term 'all available means'; for its ability to detect targets and in its role as a source of information allow an observer to make a more complete appraisal of the situation. It would also appear that there is an implied requirement to use the equipment in clear weather where it can augment or clarify the visual scene, e.g. in dense traffic, especially at night.

7.12.3 Safe speed – rule 6

Every vessel shall at all times proceed at a safe speed so that she can take proper and effective action to avoid collision and be stopped within a distance appropriate to the prevailing circumstances and conditions.

In determining a *safe speed* the following factors shall be among those taken into account:

(a) By all vessels;
    (i) the state of visibility;
    (ii) the traffic density including concentrations of fishing vessels or any other vessels;
    (iii) the manoeuvrability of the vessel with special reference to stopping distance and

turning ability in the prevailing conditions;

(iv) at night the presence of background light such as from shore lights or from backscatter of her own lights;

(v) the state of wind, sea and current, and the proximity of navigational hazards;

(vi) the draught in relation to the available depth of water.

(b) Additionally, by vessels *with operational radar*:

(i) the characteristics, efficiency and limitations of the radar equipment;

(ii) any constraints imposed by the radar range scale in use;

(iii) the effect on radar detection of the sea state, weather and other sources of interference;

(iv) the possibility that small vessels, ice and other floating objects may not be detected by radar at an adequate range;

(v) the number, location and movement of vessels detected by radar;

(vi) the more *exact assessment of the visibility* that may be possible when radar is used to determine the range of vessels or other objects in the vicinity.

In listing the factors to be considered when determining a safe speed, this rule devotes a complete section to those factors which can be determined by the use of radar. It is important to realize that the factors listed extend beyond the context of basic radar into that of collision-avoidance systems such as ARPA.

7.12.4 Risk of collision – rule 7

(a) Every vessel shall *use all available means* appropriate to the prevailing circumstances and conditions to determine if risk of collision exists. If there is any doubt, such risk shall be deemed to exist.

(b) *Proper use shall be made of radar equipment* if fitted and operational, including long range scanning to obtain early warning of risk of collision and

radar plotting or equivalent systematic observation of detected objects.

(c) Assumptions shall not be made on the basis of scanty information, especially *scanty radar information.*

(d) In determining if risk of collision exists the following considerations shall be among those taken into account:

(i) such risk shall be deemed to exist if the compass bearing of an approaching vessel does not appreciably change;

(ii) such risk may sometimes exist even when an appreciable bearing change is evident, particularly when approaching a very large vessel or a tow or when approaching a vessel at close range.

Any discretion as to whether to make use of radar if fitted and operational, which may have existed under the previous rules, appears to have been removed by rule 7b. This section specifies that proper use shall be made of such equipment and the well established warning about 'scanty information' is now embodied in this rule.

7.12.5 Conduct of vessels in restricted visibility – rule 19

(a) This rule applies to vessels not in sight of one another when navigating in or near an area of restricted visibility.

(b) Every vessel shall proceed at a safe speed adapted to the prevailing circumstances and conditions of restricted visibility. A power-driven vessel shall have her engines ready for immediate manoeuvre.

(c) Every vessel shall have due regard to the prevailing circumstances and conditions of restricted visibility when complying with the rules of section I of this part.

(d) A vessel which *detects by radar alone* the presence of another vessel *shall determine* if a close-quarters situation is developing and/or *risk of collision exists.* If so, *she shall take avoiding action* in ample time, provided that when such action consists of an alteration of course, so far as possible *the following shall be avoided*:

(i) an alteration of course to port for a vessel forward of the beam, other than for a vessel being overtaken;

(ii) an alteration of course towards a vessel abeam or abaft the beam.

(e) *Except where* it has been determined that a *risk of collision does not exist, every vessel* which hears apparently *forward of her beam the fog signal* of another vessel, or which cannot avoid a close-quarters situation with another vessel forward of her beam, *shall reduce her speed to the minimum* at which she can be kept on her course. She shall if necessary take all her way off and in any event navigate with extreme caution until danger of collision is over.

7.12.5.1 *The development of a close-quarters situation*

In cases where a target is detected by radar alone, rule 19d places a specific obligation on the observer to determine whether a close-quarters situation is developing. To comply with this requirement, the target should be plotted and its CPA and TCPA determined. With ARPA or ATA, this information can be made available in alphanumeric form if the target is designated. (The TCPA will assume particular importance if a close-quarters situation is developing.)

At this juncture, it is the duty of the officer of the watch to decide if the CPA constitutes a close-quarters situation; the CPA which would suggest that the encounter be deemed 'close quarters' will depend upon:

(a) The geographical position of the vessels.
(b) The handling capability of the ship.
(c) The density of the traffic.

7.12.5.2 *Manoeuvres to avoid collision*

If it is decided that a close-quarters situation is developing, the observer must take action to resolve the situation in ample time, subject to the recommendations laid down in rule 19d(i) and (ii). Any avoiding

manoeuvre not based on a knowledge of the true vector of all relevant targets would be unseamanlike and could certainly attract criticism as an assumption based on scanty radar information.

When ARPA is being used, the true vector data may be obtained in alphanumeric form and cross-checked by interpretation of the graphical presentation but, since these are often generated from the same database, a good comparison should not be taken as an assumption of accuracy of the information. It is important to remember that the success of the action by own ship may be influenced by recent changes in the target's true vector. It is thus useful to check, by using the *history* presentation on the ARPA, whether such changes have occurred, although there is *no* requirement to have this facility on an ATA.

7.12.6 Action to avoid collision – rule 8

(a) Any action taken to avoid collision shall be taken in accordance with the rules of this part and shall, if the circumstances of the case admit, *be positive*, made *in ample time* and with due regard to the observance of *good seamanship*.

(b) Any alteration of course and/or speed to avoid collision shall, if the circumstances of the case admit, *be large enough* to be readily apparent to another vessel *observing* visually or *by radar*; a *succession of small alterations* of course and/or speed should be avoided.

(c) If there is sufficient sea room, alteration of course alone may be the most effective action to avoid a close-quarters situation provided that it is made in good time, is substantial and does not result in another close-quarters situation.

(d) Action taken to avoid collision with another vessel shall be such as to result in passing at a safe distance. *The effectiveness of the action shall be carefully checked* until the other vessel is finally past and clear.

(e) If necessary to avoid collision or *allow more time to assess* the situation, a vessel shall *slacken her speed* or take all way off by stopping or reversing her means of propulsion.

7.12.6.1 The forecast

Rule 8d requires that action taken to avoid collision with another vessel shall be such as to result in a safe passing distance. This rule applies to all states of visibility but, in restricted visibility, the safe passing distance may have to be greater than that which would be tolerated in clear weather.

When employing radar and ARPA, passing distances may and should be determined by the construction of a 'predicted OA line' on the plot or the use of the 'trial manoeuvre' facility which all ARPAs are required to have. Such a forecast will also enable the observer to check that the manoeuvre will not result in a close-quarters situation with other vessels (rule 8c) and can often indicate where targets may manoeuvre to avoid each other.

It is essential to remember that a further criterion for an acceptable manoeuvre is that it must be readily apparent to another vessel observing by radar (rule 8b). In making this judgement one must consider own ship's speed and the speeds of target vessels. Further, it must be appreciated that, even if the target vessel is equipped with radar, the plotting facilities may be very basic. Hence the rate at which the other observer can extract data, and thus become aware of changes, may be slow and the ability to identify small changes may be particularly limited (for this reason, rule 8b gives a warning about a succession of small alterations).

Finally, the possibility that a target vessel may not be plotting, or may not even have an operational radar, must be continually kept in mind.

7.12.6.2 The effectiveness of a manoeuvre

Rule 8d requires that the effectiveness of the avoiding action be checked until the other vessel is finally past and clear. This requirement can be satisfied by monitoring:

(a) *The true motion* of all relevant targets (to ensure early detection and identification of target manoeuvres).

(b) *The relative motion* of all relevant targets to check for the fulfilment of the forecast nearest approach.

7.12.6.3 Resumption

When the target is finally past and clear, the decision must be made to resume course and/or speed.

As in the case of the avoiding manoeuvre, prior to resuming, the apparent motion of the target after resumption (see Section 7.5.7) or the trial manoeuvre on the ARPA should be employed to verify that a safe passing distance will be achieved with respect to all relevant targets. It should be remembered that the resumption will be most obvious to other observing vessels if it is performed as a single manoeuvre as opposed to a series of small alterations. The common practice of resuming course in steps by 'following the target round' will make it difficult for other observing ships to identify the manoeuvre positively and could be considered to be in contravention of the spirit, if not the letter, of rule 8b.

7.12.7 The cumulative turn

This set of related manoeuvres based on wrongly interpreted radar information (in restricted visibility) has probably done more than anything else to give radar a bad name and to indicate the need for a proper appreciation and use of the data displayed on the screen.

A number of elements have been identified which are common in the majority of the cases which have come before the courts and which are of interest when endeavouring to understand just how, in spite of repeated warnings, the same fatal scenario has been played out on so many occasions.

The common elements are:

(a) The encounter is end-on or nearly end-on.

(b) In most cases, only the two ships are involved, i.e. no constraints by other vessels or by the land etc.

(c) There was no proper assessment of the situation based on acceptable plotting techniques, but rather a subjective judgement based on casual observation of the display. Because of the small change in bearing, each assumes (on scanty information) that the other vessel is on a reciprocal course.

(d) With only one *other ship* on the screen, each considers that there is no need to go to the trouble of a formal plot.

(e) Speeds have invariably been excessive.

(f) Small alterations of course have been seen as adequate and usually the justification has been that it was done 'only to give the other vessel a wider berth'.

(g) Each vessel alters into the apparently 'clear water', i.e. *A* alters to starboard while *B* alters to port (Figure 7.36). In other words, each vessel alters course away from the target.

(h) The misunderstanding of the true situation can be aggravated by the use of a ship's-head-up unstabilized relative-motion display where, after the completion of the manoeuvre, the impression obtained from the casual observation of the display is that the target will now pass farther off (Figure 7.37).

(i) In the agony of the final moments any manoeuvre might be ordered but, in general, the wheel will be put hard over and the engines put astern. The outcome or the intention of the manoeuvre is extremely difficult to predict and rarely has time to take effect.

With the aid of ARPA or ATA, the true situation can be more readily understood at an early stage in the encounter so that if early and substantial action is taken to avoid the collision followed by rigorous subsequent monitoring, the irretrievable situation should not be allowed to develop. Where there is no ARPA or ATA assistance, it is essential that both the letter and spirit of the collision avoidance rules are adhered to in terms of plotting, predicting ahead, monitoring target manoeuvres, while at the same time making an early and substantial avoiding manoeuvre. The importance of 'making time to plot' by reducing speed at an early stage in the encounter cannot be too strongly stressed.

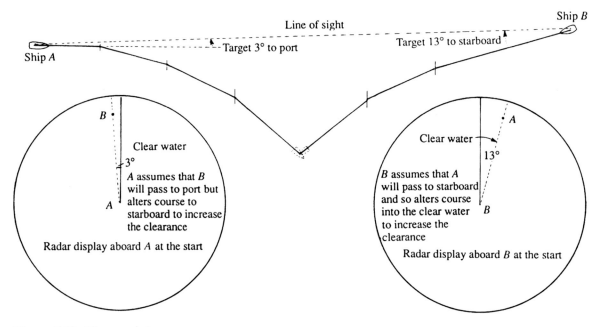

Figure 7.36 The cumulative turn

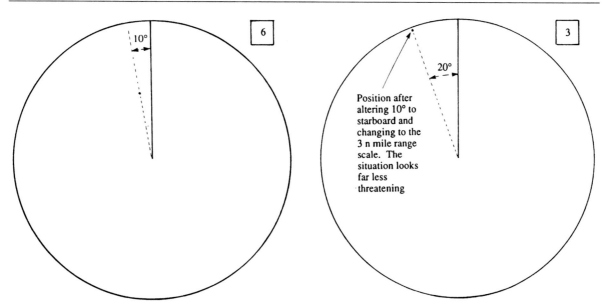

Figure 7.37 The effect of altering course and changing range scale on a ship's-head-up unstabilized radar presentation

Classical cases which have followed the above scenario with fatal consequences are: the *Stockholm–Andrea Dona; Crystal Jewel–British Aviator; Dalhanna–Staxton Wyke*, as well as the *Canopic–Hudson Firth* and many more which followed the same basic pattern but in which no lives were lost.

7.12.8   Conclusion

In any potential collision situation, particularly in restricted visibility, the interpretation of displayed radar information facilitates the determination and execution of action to avoid close-quarters situations. Traditionally this is achieved by a decision based on data extracted by manual plotting. ARPA and ATA should be seen as a device that extracts and presents such data. It thus reduces the workload on the observer by carrying out routine tasks and allows him more time to carry out decision making on the basis of the data supplied.

The ability of the ARPA and ATA equipment to carry out routine tracking and computation in no way relieves the observer of the need to understand fully the principles of radar plotting, or of being capable of applying such principles to a practical encounter, such as might be the case in the event of an equipment failure.

It is imperative that the observer is capable of interpreting and evaluating the data presented by the ARPA or ATA system. Equally essential is the ability to detect any circumstances in which the equipment is producing data which is inconsistent with the manner in which a situation is developing as observed, say, from the raw radar.

In general, it is vital that the observer understands the limitations of the system in use and hence is aware of the dangers of exclusive reliance on the data produced by an ARPA or ATA. In particular, the implicit reliance on the validity of the prediction of small non-zero passing distances should be avoided. The CPA errors tabulated in sections of the Performance Standards for ARPA (see Section 9.3) clearly indicate that predicted passing distances of less than one mile should be treated with the utmost caution.

The importance of regular comparison of the visual situation with that presented by the radar/ARPA/ATA cannot be stressed too strongly.

7.13 Intelligent knowledge-based systems as applied to collision avoidance

Systems have been developed to supply the navigator with advice as to the manoeuvre (or manoeuvres) that will be most effective in the existing circumstances.

The International Regulations for Preventing Collisions at Sea provide a framework within which all manoeuvres must conform. Unfortunately, the regulations only work well for two-ship encounters in open water. The presence of other vessels and restrictions in navigable water may cause apparent conflicts with the rules. Furthermore, terms such as 'early', 'substantial' and 'close-quarters' are quantitatively imprecise and so application and encoding of the rules is far from simple.

Computational techniques can facilitate the encoding of experience. If experienced mariners are presented with complex encounters that are known to cause difficulty, their solutions can be analysed. The principles behind the solutions are learned by the computer which then applies them to a future similar (but not necessarily identical) encounter.

These systems at present are mainly experimental and do not have any validation from international

Table 7.1 Summary of the Regulations for Preventing Collision at Sea as applied to radar, ARPA and ATA

1 Use ARPA and radar if they can be of the slightest assistance	(a) Clear weather with heavy traffic (b) Proper lookout (especially at night)
2 Does risk of collision exist, and/or is a close-quarters situation developing?	(a) Analyse displayed information • Relative tracks, CPA and TCPA • True tracks – course and speed • History of past position
3 Determine best manoeuvre	(a) Trial facility (ARPA only) • Will targets pass safely? • Will targets have to manoeuvre? (b) Avoid A/C to port, or turning toward converging overtaking ships
4 Manoeuvre	(a) Bold – avoid succession of small A/C (b) Large – obvious to others (c) In good time – time to correct (d) Good seamanship
5 Ensure its effectiveness	(a) Continuous check of relative motion and history (b) Watch for changes in true motion of targets
6 Resume	(a) Are targets clear? (b) Trial – check other vessels for likely manoeuvres (ARPA only) (c) Make one manoeuvre

agencies. Systems based solely on ARPA information have the following features:

1   The navigator must select whether the restricted visibility or unrestricted visibility rules apply.
2   The user must designate manually the targets believed to have extra rights under the rules (e.g. vessels engaged in fishing, restricted in ability to manoeuvre, NUC etc.).
3   The navigator must designate manually if there are areas not navigable by own ship.
4   The systems also should present the navigator with the rationale behind the recommended manoeuvre strategy.
5   The system can also predict the likely manoeuvres of other vessels based on the rules, which also aids the decision-making process, although it should be remembered that the other vessel might be constrained by vessels not seen on own ship radar.

These systems will also benefit from the increased use of other navigation technologies. The integration with ECDIS and GNSS (see Sections 10.1 and 10.2) means that geographic information can be input into the computer and overcomes point 3 above. The universal adoption of AIS (see Section 10.3), if it happens, will overcome many of the above limitations. Targets will automatically be transmitting their status under the rules (e.g. engaged in fishing, NUC, etc.). They also can transmit their intended route so that changes in course for navigational reasons can be included in the analysis. The detection range of AIS is potentially further than radar and is less affected by blind areas (see Section 10.3.4) overcoming the problem identified in point 5.

The recommendation of a particular set of manoeuvres is not intended to take over the navigational function of the navigator, but rather to support, in quantitative terms, the overall strategy that should be followed.

8 Navigation techniques using radar and ARPA

8.1 Introduction

The availability of information from radar and ARPA forms the basis of a number of techniques which may assist in the safe navigation of vessels. Successful and safe use of these require an ability to relate the echoes displayed by the radar to the information shown on the chart and an understanding of the levels of performance and accuracy which can be achieved under given circumstances. Where radar information alone is used in making a landfall, the ship's position may be in considerable doubt and it may be difficult positively to identify specific echoes, particularly if the observer is unfamiliar with the locality. In routine coastal navigation there may be more general certainty as to the vessel's position, but effective use of these techniques will require organization, skill, practice and a thorough awareness of the capability of the radar system. They will also be found to be of assistance in certain pilotage situations but it has to be said that current civil marine radar equipment has a very limited ability to contribute to the docking of vessels.

This chapter discusses the difficulties of making comparison between the radar picture and charted features before passing on to describe the navigation techniques in terms of the underlying theory covered elsewhere in this text.

It is often stressed that radar is *only an aid* to navigation. This does not mean that radar information is necessarily of any less value than that obtained from other sources. What it does mean is that radar data should not be used in isolation and to the exclusion of that available from other sources. The radar system should be seen as one element in a variety of data sources which must be taken into account in arriving at decisions related to directing the safe navigation of the vessel. The exercise of command decision-making based on an evaluation of navigation information derived from all sources is referred to as *navigation control*.

8.2 Identification of targets and chart comparison

It is sometimes suggested that the radar picture offers a *bird's-eye view* of the area surrounding the observing vessel. This analogy is imperfect on a number of counts but two are particularly evident in the use of radar for navigation. The radar aerial does not look down on the terrain from a great height and thus its *view* can be obstructed. Further, it does not offer the optical resolution (see Section 2.6.5) which the use of the word 'eye' may imply. As a consequence, the radar picture may be an incomplete and fairly coarse version of the chart's finely detailed plan view of the terrain. This may limit the observer's ability to identify positively elements of the terrain echoes and relate them to the charted representation.

Interpretation of the displayed picture involves consideration of a number of factors each of which will be discussed in turn.

8.2.1 Long range target identification

When making a landfall, the radar must be carefully observed in order to obtain an early indication of the presence of the terrain. In the absence of clutter (see Sections 3.6 and 3.7) the first echoes will have to be found against the background of receiver noise (see Section 2.5.2.3). If the observer knows the approximate bearing and range at which to expect the first echoes, early detection may be assisted by, from time to time, temporarily setting the gain control a little higher than the normal optimum level (see Section 6.2.4.1). A slight loss of contrast is traded for an increase in received signal strength and this may be beneficial when looking in a specific area as opposed to scanning the entire screen area. Where an echo stretch facility (see Section 6.11.1) is provided, it may be found similarly helpful. A knowledge of where to look for the expected echoes on the screen pre-supposes other sources of information concerning the vessel's likely position and the probable detection range of specific terrain features. Such information may stem from dead reckoning techniques, knowledge of leeway and tidal streams, other position-fixing systems (GNSS or LORAN C), and an assessment of specific target detection ranges in the light of radar, target and environmental characteristics (see Chapter 3). This emphasizes the complementary nature of the various data sources available for the safe navigation of the vessel.

Initially the presence of the land may be indicated by only a few responses and these will be considerably distorted by the angular width of the resolution cell (see Sections 2.6.5 and 8.2.2) which will be large at long range. Under these circumstances it will be extremely difficult, if not impossible, to identify positively specific terrain features from the few distorted echoes which are being observed. It must be appreciated that the use of the echo stretch technique is likely to exacerbate the problem by adding radial distortion and it should be switched off after it has fulfilled its

role of assisting initial detection. Identification may be assisted if the observer knows which parts of the terrain are likely to show first and also the approximate range and bearing at which they should appear. As indicated in the previous paragraph this pre-supposes other sources of information related to probable position and target detection considerations.

To exploit fully the use of radar in making a landfall, adequate preparation should be made in terms of collating the information from other sources. An up to date and best available estimate of the ship's position should be maintained using information from all available sources. Prior to making the landfall, the chart and the Admiralty Sailing Directions should be consulted in order to assess the ranges at which the radar should detect specific terrain features which are likely to be easy to identify. This assessment should take into account the characteristics of the radar system, the characteristics of the target, the atmospheric conditions and any limits to detection which may be imposed by clutter or attenuation, all of which are dealt with in detail in Chapter 3. In particular it should be remembered that frequently coastlines are backed by higher terrain and at long ranges it must be borne in mind that the first land to show is not necessarily the *coastline* (see Section 3.8.1). Failure to appreciate this can be dangerously misleading because the measured range will suggest that the vessel is farther to seaward than is in fact the case. Also, as the land is closed, responses will be obtained from land which is lower and closer than that originally detected and as it comes above the horizon it may give an exaggerated impression of the speed at which the vessel is approaching the land. When a particular landfall has been made on more than one occasion, it may be possible to establish a list of good landfall targets which may supplement those tabulated in the Sailing Directions.

It has to be recognized that, while civil marine radar offers early warning of the presence of most land formations, long range target identification is not a function at which it excels. A coded racon (see Section 3.5.2.1) is probably the only sure source of early positive target identification and its range may well be limited by the height of its aerial. Positive identification of just one target is a major step forward because it may then be possible to identify other terrain echoes by virtue of their known range and bearing from the identified target. A *free EBL* (see Sections 6.9.6 and 8.4.6.1) is ideally suited to making the necessary measurements.

Care must be taken not to jump to conclusions when a radar echo appears in the general area in which a particular point of land is expected by DR. There appears to be a great temptation to ascribe immediately and unquestioningly the hoped-for identity to the target. This temptation must be resisted until cross-checks have established that any fix so obtained is consistent with all other available sources of information.

8.2.2   The effect of discrimination

In the previous section attention was drawn to the difficulty of identifying targets in the landfall situation because of the effect of the size of the resolution cell

on the few echoes which may be detected at extreme ranges. Even at the more moderate ranges likely to be employed when using the radar for routine coastal navigation, the effect of resolution (see Section 2.6.5) may still make it difficult to identify specific coastal features, despite the fact that there will be a larger aggregation of land responses forming some sort of *chart-like* coastline on the PPI.

The angular width of the resolution cell produces an angular distortion on both sides of all targets by an amount equal to half the horizontal beamwidth plus the spot size effect. Neglecting for the moment the spot size effect, it is evident that if two headlands forming the entrance to a bay are separated by less than the horizontal beamwidth, their echoes will overlap. Thus the effect of the limited bearing discrimination may be to mask coastal features such as bays, river entrances, sea lochs and other similar inlets. The echoes of an island close to the mainland may appear as a peninsula and small islands close together may

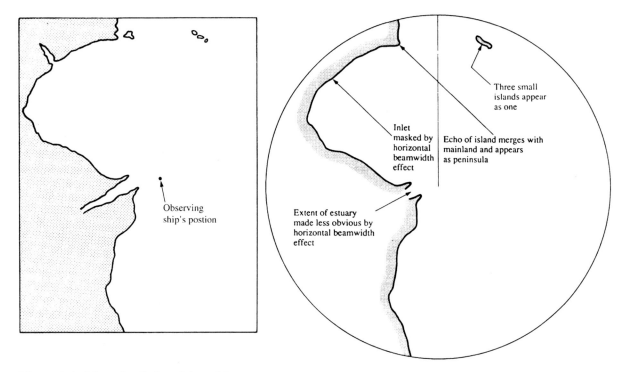

Figure 8.1   The radar display of charted features

appear as one large island. Thus a charted coastline having many indentations may translate to a featureless coastline on the PPI. It must be borne in mind that, while the width of the beam is a fixed angle, the linear measurement of the arc it cuts off increases in direct proportion to the range at which it is considered. Thus features which are masked at a distance may become identifiable as their range decreases.

The pulse length/spot size dimension of the resolution cell will produce radial distortion of all responses. Except at very short ranges this will have an effect which is much less significant than that of the angular distortion. However, where two features lie one behind the other, for example an island or a buoy located close to the shore, they may appear as one feature due to the limited range discrimination.

The observer's ability to minimize the effects of the angular and radial distortion are fairly limited. In both cases the spot size effect will be reduced by using the shortest appropriate range scale. Where a dual or interswitched system (see Section 2.7.8) is available, selection of the aerial having the narrower beamwidth will assist, as would a modern raster-scan display offering beam processing (see Section 3.9.5.1). A temporary reduction in the setting of the gain control may help to locate features which have been masked by angular distortion but this requires some practice and is not invariably successful. Use of differentiation (see Section 3.7.4.4) may improve the picture by combating the radial distortion. However, this technique must be used with care as if two echoes overlap and the farther is the weaker of the two, the effect of differentiation may be to remove the remote echo.

Thus, due to the inherent difficulty of relating the radar picture to the chart, care must be taken to ensure positive identification of any target before selecting it for use in position fixing (see also Section 8.3).

8.2.3 Shadow areas

Because the line of sight of the radar system is substantially horizontal, some features of the terrain may be shadowed by others. These shadows are a further factor which may make it difficult to relate the radar picture to that of the chart, the problem being compounded by the fact that the shadow pattern will vary with the position of the observing vessel.

8.2.3.1 Vertical shadowing

Figure 8.2 shows an example of vertical shadowing. To a vessel which is close inshore, the lower range of coastal hills may shadow higher mountains lying inland, whereas from another vessel farther offshore, the radar may be able to 'see' the mountains over the top of the coastal range.

Bearing in mind that, as described in Section 8.2.1, a vessel making landfall on such a coastline may well detect the higher inland mountains first, it is evident that if a ship closes the coastline from seaward the character of the radar picture will change through three distinct phases. Initially the vessel will observe the higher mountains only, then both coastal and inland mountains and finally only the coastal range. If there are gaps in the coastal range, horizontal shadowing (see Section 8.2.3.2) will also take place, further complicating the pattern.

8.2.3.2 Horizontal shadowing

Figure 8.3 shows an example of horizontal shadowing from which it is clear that the radar picture obtained by a vessel at location *A* looks quite different from that which would be obtained at location *B*. It follows that a ship whose course takes it from *A* to *B* will notice a progressive change in the character of the radar picture.

8.2.3.3 Composite shadowing

In many cases both vertical and horizontal shadowing occur and the interaction between the two as a ship steams past the terrain may produce a complex and changing pattern of responses. In the early days of radar some experimental attempts were made to produce radar *maps* by producing a collage of radar photographs. Such attempts proved to be of little practical value, because the character of the radar picture portrayed by each element in the collage was heavily dependent on the location at which the photograph

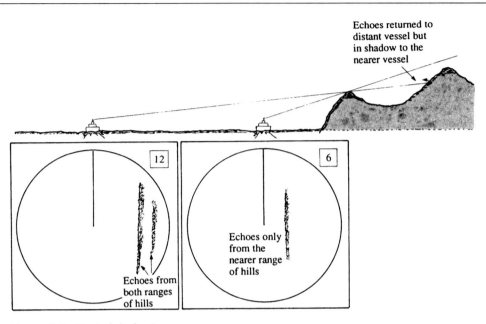

Figure 8.2 Vertical shadowing

was taken and the characteristics of the radar installation used.

If a ship is uncertain of its position, the complex shadow pattern may make it difficult to recognize the particular stretch of coastline or to identify specific targets on the terrain.

8.2.4 Rise and fall of tide

The radar picture may appear quite different at various states of the tide. The changes will depend very much on the character of the area. For example, at low water an area with off-lying, drying sandbanks may produce large areas of no response (where the smooth sloping surfaces reflect the radar energy away from the aerial) surrounded by fringes of clutter (where the waves break on the shore) which depend on the strength and direction of the wind. By contrast, at high water, in calm conditions there may be no response at all whereas in strong winds there may be extensive clutter in the shallow water over the banks. The ability to understand and recognize such effects may be of value to the radar observer in identifying specific targets.

8.2.5 Radar-conspicuous targets

A radar-conspicuous target is one which produces a good response that can be positively identified. While the ability of radar waves to penetrate fog is of great assistance to vessels navigating in restricted visibility, all targets obscured visually by the fog are not necessarily conspicuous when viewed by the radar.

A particularly important example is a lighthouse, which traditionally represents a key navigational mark whose charted position is known. It is visually conspicuous and can be identified beyond doubt. Unless other adequate sources of position lines are available, it is a serious loss to the navigator if the lighthouse is obscured by poor visibility and that loss may not be made good by the radar. In general, the shape of a lighthouse makes it an inherently poor target (see Section 3.3.4) and, unless it is situated on an isolated rock, whatever response there is tends to be lost in the land echoes from the terrain surrounding it. Thus, unless the lighthouse is fitted with a radar beacon (see Section 3.5), in many cases it may be difficult or impossible to identify on the radar. Buoys represent

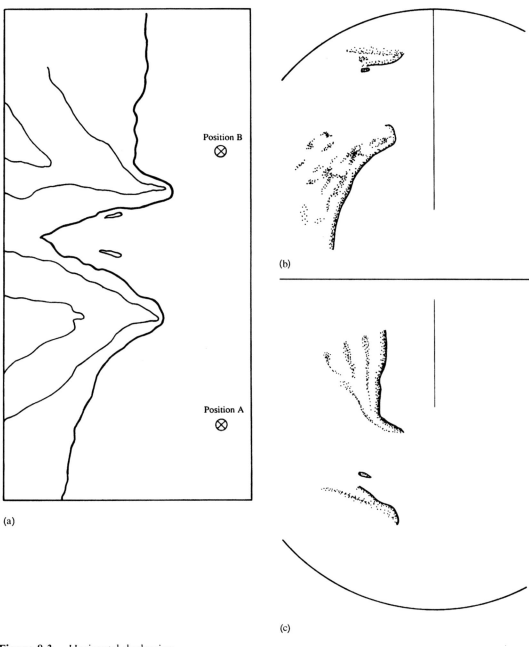

(a)

(b)

(c)

Figure 8.3   Horizontal shadowing
(a)   The chart
(b)   The radar picture from position
A: shadowing takes effect particularly in
the south, west and northwest areas of the bay

(c)   The radar picture from position
B: shadowing takes effect particularly in
the north, west and southwest areas of the bay

another example of navigation marks which, because of their inherently poor reflecting characteristics, may be difficult to detect and hence identify unless fitted with a reflector or a racon (see Sections 3.4 and 3.5). This may be particularly so in cases where vessels anchor in the vicinity of a floating navigation mark such as a fairway buoy.

However, some man-made features are particularly conspicuous when observed on radar. Tank farms and small built-up areas are particularly good examples. Their response is among the strongest likely to be encountered and, if isolated from other areas of response, they may be very conspicuous. Naturally occuring features such as small isolated islands offer a further example of radar-conspicuous and potentially identifiable targets.

Sloping sandy coastlines may be quite conspicuous to the eye even when fairly low-lying, but their radar response is likely to be poor because most of the energy is not reflected back toward the aerial. The response may be improved if waves are breaking on the beach, but this will only be experienced at fairly short range.

8.2.6   Pilotage situations

In most pilotage situations targets are so close that detection scarcely presents a problem. However, identification may be a problem, and an urgent one given the proximity of hazards and the speed with which manoeuvres must be effected.

In estuary and port approach situations, the need for continuous position monitoring may well be met by using parallel indexing techniques (see Section 8.4), provided that suitable preparation has been carried out beforehand and the necessary indexing targets can be easily and positively identified. Some high-definition radars are designed with very short range scales, low minimum range and good discrimination that suit them for use in pilotage. In the absence of such equipment the observer must attempt to make the best use of the available system. In an interswitched system, aerial siting, beamwidth, pulse length, and the setting of gain and clutter controls should receive attention.

Where a single system is fitted, fine detail can be improved by use of the shortest pulse length and differentiation.

In the docking phase of pilotage, the presence at very close range of targets which produce strong and spurious responses (see Section 3.9) will conspire with the limited discrimination of the radar system (see Sections 2.6.5.5 and 2.6.5.6) to obscure the fine detail of the picture. On the short range scales in use under such circumstances, only relative-motion presentation will be available and the consequent movement of the land echoes on the screen, together with the changes in shadow areas and indirectly reflected echoes, will greatly exacerbate this effect and make it very difficult to identify the extent of berths, lock entrances and other essential features.

While the problem can be to some extent reduced by judicious use of differentiation, it has to be said that the docking phase of pilotage is one for which current civil marine radar equipment is not particularly suited. In the past the docking of very large vessels has been assisted by the siting of doppler equipment ashore to measure the rate of approach of the vessels. There is considerable debate at the present time as to how the problem might be solved for the frequent and regular berthing of ferries in fog. The more traditional suggestion is to use radar having a wavelength of a few millimetres while more recent applications use DGPS in conjunction with an electronic chart (see Sections 10.1.6 and 10.2).

8.3   Position fixing

Essentially two types of position lines are available directly from the radar, namely radar range circles and radar bearings. These can of course be used in association with position lines from other sources. In making a decision as to which particular position lines should be used to obtain a fix in any given circumstances, consideration must be given to the accuracy that can be obtained. This will depend on the targets chosen and the type of position lines selected.

8.3.1 Selection of targets

In selecting targets for position fixing, attention must be given to the certainty with which they can be identified and the suitability of their angular disposition.

8.3.1.1 Target identification

The importance of positive target identification and the difficulties of achieving this have been discussed at length in the proceeding sections of this chapter. Mistaken identification can seriously mislead the observer as to the vessel's most probable position. Even where the feature has been correctly identified, unless it is small, it is essential to identify which part of the feature has reflected the radar energy; otherwise, accuracy may suffer. For example, when measuring a range from a sloping surface, the high level of ranging accuracy can be lost if the range is not laid off from the correct contour on the chart.

Similarly, if taking a bearing from the edge of the radar echo of a point, considerable thought must be given to the effect of any slope of the terrain and the beamwidth effect of the radar before deciding from which charted position to lay off the observed bearing. In general, if radar bearings are used it is better to attempt to avoid the effect of the half beamwidth distortion by using the centre of small isolated targets or, if it is necessary to use a point of land, to take a bearing which runs along the axis of the headland rather than one which is tangential to it.

8.3.1.2 Angle of cut

In selecting targets for position fixing, the considerations given to angles of cut are not confined to radar but are based on the general principles of position lines. Where two position lines are involved, the angle of cut should be as close to 90° as possible as this minimizes the displacement of the fix due to any errors in the position lines used. To provide cross-checking, good practice dictates that where possible at least three position lines should be used. Under these circumstances, angles of cut less than 30° or greater than 150° should be avoided as small errors in the position lines can produce relatively large errors in the fix.

8.3.2 Types of position line

The position lines available from radar and other sources can be used in a variety of combinations. The considerations of radar accuracy affecting these combinations are discussed in turn.

8.3.2.1 The use of radar range circles

The inherent accuracy of radar range circles is very high, the IMO Performance Standards (see Section 11.2.1) requiring that the fixed range rings and the variable range marker should enable the range of a target to be measured with an error not exceeding 1.0 per cent of the range scale in use or 30 metres, whichever is greater. On the 12 mile range scale the error should not exceed 222 metres and is adequate for most navigation at this range from the coast. Care must be taken in using the facilities provided for range measurement to ensure that the full potential accuracy is realized. The practical procedures for doing this are summarized in Section 6.9.8. Additionally, as indicated in Section 8.3.1.1, it is essential to establish with certainty the charted location of the reflecting surface. There is little point in measuring with a high degree of accuracy the range of a target which has been incorrectly identified. Assuming that the foregoing procedures are followed, radar range circles have the potential to produce a highly accurate fix.

8.3.2.2 The use of radar bearings

When compared with that of radar ranges, the inherent accuracy of radar bearings is very much lower. In Section 6.9 the various error sources set out in the IMO Performance Standards are discussed and it is shown that the inherent accuracy of radar bearings is such that a bearing measured from the display can be in error by as much as 2.5° without the system being in breach of the Standard. The arc subtended by an angle of 2.5° at 12 miles is approximately 870 metres, which does not compare favourably with the inherent accuracy offered by radar range circles. Suitable practical procedures must be followed to ensure that the potential accuracy is realized; these are summarized in

Section 6.9.9. Additionally, care must be exercised to ensure that the target has been correctly identified (see Section 8.3.1.1).

In general, given the relative inherent accuracy levels, wherever possible radar ranges should be used in preference to radar bearings.

8.3.2.3   *The combination of radar ranges and bearings*

Inevitably, circumstances will arise in which a combination of ranges and bearings will have to be used. Where only one feature is available for fixing, a single range and bearing fix does have the virtue that the angle of cut is 90°. However, in such circumstances the respective accuracies of the two position lines must be borne in mind.

8.3.2.4   *The use of single position lines*

A single radar range or bearing can be used in the same way as any other single position line to exploit the various general navigation techniques, such as the running fix, which maximizes the use of such observations.

8.3.2.5   *The combination of radar position lines with those from other sources*

Radar ranges and bearings should be seen as one of several sources of position lines all of which may be combined to arrive at a decision as to the vessel's most probable position.

A particular example is the situation which arises in clear weather when only one feature can be positively identified. Under such conditions the accuracy of a visual bearing (which is higher than that of a radar bearing) can be combined with that of a radar range circle to produce a fix having a potentially high degree of accuracy. In conditions of poor visibility of course the lower accuracy of a radar bearing would have to be substituted for the visual.

In general, the radar should be seen as one source of position-fixing information which should be compared and combined with the others that are available. Any disparity between the information available from different sources such as is manifest by a 'cocked hat' should alert the observer to consider carefully why the disparity exists. Serious thought should precede any decision to discount a particular data source. In particular, a large 'cocked hat' should be a warning to check all position lines and not an excuse for discarding the one which is most embarrassing.

8.4   Parallel indexing

8.4.1   Introduction

While navigating from one port to another, it is inevitable that for part of the time the ship will be in confined waters, be it the approaches to the port and berth, or in a busy waterway such as the Dover Strait or Malacca Strait. Leaving aside for the moment any consideration of avoiding collision with other vessels, restrictions on the available sea room require the navigator to monitor the vessel's position, not just with an increased accuracy commensurate with the reduced safety margins and clearing distances imposed upon him, but also with an increased frequency to ensure that environmental and other forces that take the vessel off her desired track are recognized in sufficient time for corrective action to be taken and the vessel to be maintained on a safe track.

Traditionally the navigator would identify the vessel's proximity to the track or danger by putting a fix on the chart, the data for this fix having been obtained from one of a variety of navigation instruments. Depending upon which navigation system is being used, the time needed to establish the fix will probably be, at best, about two minutes. However, a single fix does not reveal the whole story, merely the ship's position some two minutes ago. Before the navigator can take corrective action, it is necessary to know the trend of the movement, i.e. a series of fixes is required – probably three or more, bearing in mind the inherent imprecision of most fixing systems. Consequently, there may be a time delay of the order of six to ten minutes between the vessel beginning to deviate from its desired track to the time when proper considered action is taken to return the vessel to safety.

If the reason for the deviation is a five knot cross-current and the shoal water is only a few cables away, a reaction time in excess of six minutes is too great.

One might expect that, under conditions such as these, where the shoal water is so close, there ought to be sufficient visual navigation marks nearby to enable the person conning the vessel, be it the master, pilot or officer of the watch, to react almost instantly to any deviation from the planned track. This will probably be the situation in a port approach with moderate to good visibility. In poor visibility, however, when all the visual marks disappear, conning becomes extremely difficult even with the radar giving the relative positions of some of these marks. Consider also the very large vessel fully laden. Its deep draft means that it may be 'confined' to waters well away from port approaches in an area where the navigation marks necessary for the visual conning are sparse.

The usefulness of parallel indexing in the above circumstances is indisputable. There have been numerous incidents of grounding which have resulted from the navigator using a position-monitoring method that had too long a reaction time for the conditions in which the vessel was operating (for instance, the *Metaxa*, and also the *Sundancer* casualties) or where the navigator failed to recognize that the data he was appraising was insufficient on which to base remedial action.

It is in situations like these that parallel indexing shows its true worth by enabling the navigator to monitor the vessel's progress moment by moment and by providing enough data to allow corrective manoeuvres to be made in a time scale which is very similar to that of visual conning, i.e. about two to three minutes.

8.4.1.1 *Parallel index facilities*

The facilities for parallel indexing have evolved from the reflection plotter (see Section 7.8) to electronic lines or maps drawn by the user (see Section 5.4). Effectively parallel indexing has further evolved into the integration of ARPA or ATA with ECDIS and GNSS where all fixed radar features can be compared with the chart for accuracy, simultaneously checking the GNSS system against the radar. This is covered fully in Sections 10.1 and 10.2.

The simplest parallel index facilities possible are an azimuth-stabilized radar with a reflection plotter. With this simple system it is usual to use a relative parallel index plot on a relative-motion display. It is difficult to use a true parallel index plot on a ground-stabilized true-motion display for reasons covered in Section 8.4.5. The relative-motion parallel index plot is covered in Sections 8.4.2 to 8.4.4.

The ability for the user to draw electronic lines on the display has replaced the Perspex reflection plotter. In fact the lines provided can be relative lines (which remain relative to ownship) or true lines (which are fixed to wherever the system sensors tell the radar the ground remains). The facilities associated with drawing these lines are covered in Section 8.4.6.3.

The use of electronic lines also means that it is now more straightforward for an azimuth-stabilized radar to use a true parallel index plot, where the user moves the map manually over the radar plot keeping the radar marks in line with marks on the electronic map as covered in Section 8.4.5.

The advantage of the true parallel index technique is that the index lines have the same orientation as the chart and take less skill to interpret. However, this technique becomes far more powerful when the display is additionally automatically ground-stabilized. The automatic ground-stabilization can be provided by:

1 Reference to a known fixed radar target or targets plotted by an ATA or ARPA.
2 Theoretically a ground track dual-axis doppler log, although this would be unusual.
3 Input from a position fixing system such as a GNSS.

These automatic ground-stabilized displays are covered in Section 8.4.6.

In the following sections the techniques specifically for using the reflection plotter are mentioned when appropriate, as some may still be in use. The relative-motion parallel index plot still has a useful future using electronic lines particularly for use on simple low cost radar displays without speed input but also on more complicated systems for simple parallel index plotting including the 'unplanned' techniques covered in Section 8.6.7.

8.4.2 Preparations and precautions

8.4.2.1 Pre-planning

Navigators who conduct their vessels in confined waters using blind pilotage techniques such as parallel indexing must never lose sight of the fact that safety margins are often minimal and on no account must operator errors be allowed to creep in to the parallel indexing data. By the time an error becomes apparent it can very likely be too late to recover the situation. Considerable care must be taken therefore in deriving the parallel indexing data from the navigation chart and transferring it onto the radar display, to ensure that it is as accurate as possible. All data should be cross-checked and, indeed, the whole process of acquiring the parallel indexing data is best carried out when there is a minimum of pressure and distraction. It would be inviting trouble to attempt to derive and use parallel indexing data in quantity when the vessel is already proceeding through the confined area. Most 'off the cuff' work suffers from inadequate checking and hence is susceptible to error. On occasions, parallel indexing may be employed directly from the radar screen without any pre-planning (see Section 8.4.7) but generally the need for parallel indexing should be assessed during the passage planning stage and all the necessary data to carry out the task, extracted from the chart and stored in suitable form (see Section 8.4.3.5), hours before it is intended to make use of the data. Only by doing this can one be sure of reliable data of sufficient quality to realize the full benefits of parallel indexing.

8.4.2.2 Preparing the on-board equipment

The radar set is an integral part of the parallel indexing process and must be in proper working order, able to display the *indexing* target, be operated correctly orientated and stabilized and with proper discrimination and accuracy. Particular care must be exercised with the

tuning, gyro compass error and heading marker accuracy (see practical setting-up procedures in Chapter 6).

If a mechanical cursor is to be used to lay off bearings, then it is essential to centre the origin of the timebase on the PPI. Alternatively, the electronic bearing line will be used, so the readout accuracy must be confirmed. Similarly, if the variable range marker is to be used, then any errors must be removed or known so that due allowance can be made. Distance measurement, when working on the reflection plotter, has proved to be a prolific source of inaccuracy. The observer must derive his own distance scale from the PPI and (being unable to use dividers on the reflection plotter) using a piece of paper or plastic, attempt to transfer distances from the derived scale to his drawing on the face of the reflection plotter (see Figure 8.4). An alternative to the 'home-made' distance scale is to use the off-centre electronic range and bearing line (ERBL) to position a line on the display. The pencil line can be over-drawn on the reflection plot and the ERBL moved on to the position of the next line to be drawn.

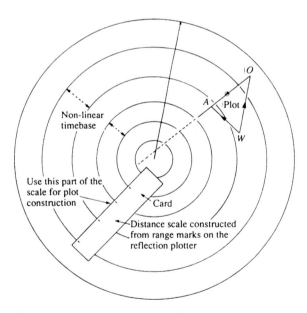

Figure 8.4 Constructing a working range scale on a reflection plotter

This process is difficult and considerable care must be taken to minimize inaccuracies in the distances laid off.

With some older radar sets, the timebase is not perfectly linear, especially near the start of the timebase (see Section 6.9.1). Hence, a distance scale derived from this timebase will also be non-linear. With this in mind, it is advisable always to use that part of the range scale which is at a similar distance from the centre of the PPI to that where the plot is being constructed.

8.4.2.3 The radar presentation

In theory, parallel indexing can be employed either on a relative-motion north-up azimuth-stabilized display or on a ground-stabilized true-motion display.

There are practical difficulties in achieving a reliable ground-stabilized display with a simple radar without ARPA or ATA or a GNSS position input (see also Sections 6.8.3 and 8.4.5). For instance:

1 Obtaining the present tidal rate and set can be time-consuming and not necessarily very accurate. Even if good values are obtained, changing conditions may mean that the values need to be frequently re-assessed.
2 An accurate knowledge of our own ship's course and speed through the water is not always easily available, especially when using unreliable speed logs.
3 Given good information regarding the vessel's movement over the ground, it still remains for the radar equipment to track accurately in response to this information. On some older radar sets, this cannot be taken for granted.

Bearing in mind that parallel indexing is intended to improve navigational safety, the operational difficulties mentioned above that could influence the reliability of this work means that true-motion parallel indexing must be considered second best to relative-motion parallel indexing for a simple radar with azimuth stabilization.

A further disadvantage of reflection plotter work on a true-motion display is that all the constructions must be done as they are needed, since most true-motion presentations do not have the ability to determine precisely where the origin will be situated at any given instant. Because of this, the parallel indexing construction on the reflection plotter cannot be pre-worked.

Modern radar equipments have the ability to draw electronic lines (see Sections 5.4 and 8.4.6.3) for navigational purposes on the PPI. Once drawn, these may be moved around at will on the screen using the tracker ball or joystick. This feature overcomes the disadvantage mentioned above as experienced with reflection plotters and at the same time introduces a distinct advantage in that the construction can be transferred between range scales with no effort on the part of the operator.

8.4.2.4 Selecting the indexing target and its effect on accuracy

The *indexing target* is a chosen radar target which appears on the PPI and whose movements relative to the observing vessel as it transits a particular confined area will be closely monitored. If everything goes according to plan, the ship will be manoeuvred to make this target track along the lines that have been drawn on the reflection plotter, or at least within certain limits from these index lines, and in so doing the navigator can ensure that the vessel follows the chosen track line.

For a target to be suitable, there are certain conditions which must apply to the indexing target:

1 It must be a good radar target, i.e. clearly visible on the PPI at the ranges at which it is intended to use it.
2 It must be identifiable among all the other land targets in the area and also there must be some recognizable feature on the target to which all the measurements can be related. This latter requirement can be difficult to resolve in the case of non-point targets, since most change their radar aspect and therefore their appearance as the relative position of the ship changes (see Section 8.2).

The navigator, in preparing for parallel indexing, must study the chart of the area with particular care to find the most suitable indexing targets, such as the end of a breakwater, the tip of a headland, small islands, isolated rocks, isolated lighthouses etc. Lighted navigation marks are of no consequence in this context of course and it is advisable never to rely on a float-ing navigation mark as an indexing target (except as provided in Section 8.4.7), not so much because of their slight variations in position but because of the possibility of their not being there at all when the vessel arrives. It is impossible to change all the pre-worked parallel indexing data to another target at short notice.

Note   Whenever a vessel is operating in a confined area where parallel indexing can be useful, the naviga-tor is advised to watch the radar picture carefully with a view to identifying suitable indexing targets for use on a future occasion. This method is far more certain than studying the chart. This information should be stored for future use, e.g. by marking the chart.

Another important consideration is the choice of the working range scale for the radar. Inevitably, the longer the range scale, the lower the accuracy with which one can monitor the position. The navigational requirements will determine the accuracy required and also the safety margins which will apply. The navigator must therefore be sure that the working range scale of the radar meets this accuracy requirement and that the selected indexing target will be 'in range'. This should not be taken to imply that a complete parallel index transit should be completed on one range scale. As accuracy requirements change, so should the working range scale. Similarly, as the vessel progresses through the confined area, so the indexing target will also need to be changed.

8.4.2.5   *Preparing the navigation data*

Parallel indexing is part of the navigation of the ship and therefore any guidance lines that appear on the display should be directly related to actual data of navigational significance on the chart, e.g. the safety margins and course lines (Figure 8.5).

Figure 8.5   Adjacent dangers, margin lines and course lines

In planning a passage through a confined area, the adjacent dangers need to be assessed in detail. Adjacent dangers in addition to shoal water can include areas of strong tidal sets and the boundaries of traffic separation schemes. The navigator should also assess the state of preparedness of the vessel for the passage, i.e. for the time of the intended transit, speed and engine readiness, method of steering and turning circles, preparedness for anchoring and manning levels etc. and, with these factors in mind, decide on a safe distance at which to clear the adjacent dangers.

This data is put onto the chart as a safety or 'margin' line spaced away from the danger by the estimated safe distance.

Common sense and experience must be relied upon here when estimating where to position the margin lines, as it is impracticable to draw a 'contour' line around every adjacent danger. Furthermore, it is extremely difficult to reproduce curved lines from the chart on a reflection plotter with any degree of accuracy and impossible on modern radars equipped with electronic lines. The purpose of this part of the passage planning process is to identify clearly all the clear water that can safely be used by the vessel during a transit of the area. Naturally the intention is to maintain the course line but unfortunately the seaways have to be shared with many other vessels and therefore one must be prepared to leave the course line should an anti-collision manoeuvre be required at any time.

The final stage of this navigation process is to draw in the course lines on the chart, taking care at all times to keep within the defined safe/clear water areas.

8.4.3   Relative parallel indexing, the technique

8.4.3.1   The relative parallel indexing principle

On a relative-motion compass-stabilized radar display, a land target will always move across the screen in a direction which is the reciprocal of the observing vessel's course made good over the ground and at a rate directly related to the vessel's speed over the ground.

In the example shown in Figure 8.6(a), as the vessel steams from position A to position B (3.6 miles off island C), the radar echo of the island on the PPI will move from a position on the starboard bow until it is 3.6 miles off on the starboard side bearing 100°(T), having moved in a direction 190°(T), i.e. reciprocal to the ship's course made good over the ground.

With an understanding of this principle, it is possible for the navigator to predict the movements of an echo on the PPI, of a 'fixed' object while the ship follows a series of course lines near this object and to draw lines (index lines) on the display to represent these movements prior to arriving in the area.

8.4.3.2   Positioning the index line on the radar display

In the example illustrated in Figure 8.7(a) it is intended to make good a course of 010°(T) and to pass 3.6 miles off the island C (the indexing target). The index line can usually be positioned on the display in one of three ways: either

(a) Set 3.6 miles on the variable range marker and then turn the mechanical cursor to 010°/190°(T). Now, lay off the index line at a tangent to the variable range marker and parallel to the cursor as shown in Figure 8.7(b); or

(b) Measure the range and bearing of the indexing target from a chosen position on the course line (any position will do, but preferably a beam position, an alter-course position or another position where the highest accuracy is needed). Plot the range and bearing on the reflection plotter, turn the cursor to 010°/190°(T) and lay off the index line, parallel to the cursor and passing through the plotted position; or

(c) Electronic index lines (when provided) can usually be set up by entering the desired angle and offset required. The latest standards require four of these lines (see Section 11.2.1).

Figure 8.6 A simple index line

(a)   A charted plan

As a variation on method (b), if two points on the course line are fixed and plotted on the reflection plotter then they can be simply joined by a straight line. This method is useful in that it allows a simple cross-check, i.e. fix the start and end of a particular index line and then confirm from the chart, the actual direction and distance between the two (see Figure 8.7(c)).

Figure 8.8(a) shows a more complex series of intended tracks within a parallel indexing area and Figure 8.8(b) illustrates how this data translates onto the reflection plotter.

Example 8.1   Figure 8.8(a) has been drawn to scale. Extract the appropriate data and then, using either (a) the beam distance method or (b) the range and bearing method, construct the parallel indexing lines as they would be drawn out on the display. The accuracy

of the construction should be verified by measuring the directions and distances A to B and B to C or the distances W, X, Y and Z, as appropriate. The plot should appear as in Figure 8.8(b).

8.4.3.3   Transferring the margin lines to the radar display

(a)   *Normal lines.* Adding the margin line data to the parallel indexing plot is simply an extension of what has already been done, i.e. draw another series of lines on the display representing the acceptable limits for deviation of the indexing target. These are usually drawn in such a way as to distinguish them from the normal cross-index lines. see Figures 8.9(a) and (b).

(b)   *The danger circle.* Figures 8.9(a) and (b) also illustrate the special case of an isolated danger with a

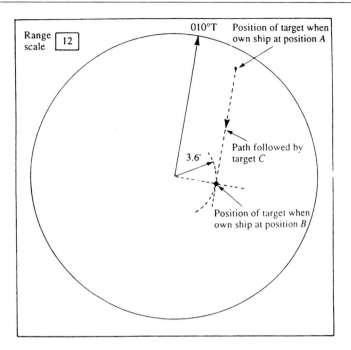

Figure 8.6(b) The relative movement of a fixed target on the
PPI as prepared in (a)

circular margin of safety or 'danger circle'. In this case, its position on the display is determined by first measuring the position of the indexing target from the isolated danger and then transferring that to the display. Then the margin of safety is drawn as a circle of appropriate radius centred on the plotted point X.

A position circle can only be constructed on a reflection plotter. It is not usual to find this option to plot a circle electronically on modern raster display equipment. However, many radar sets allow the addition of symbols, which could indicate the centre of such a circle.

Note   Although position X has been plotted on the display, this should not be misinterpreted as the actual position of the isolated danger relative to the observing vessel. As the ship transits the area, the indexing target moves along the index line. When the index target reaches position Z (the alter-course position),

the vessel is 2.8 n mile away from the danger, i.e. by the distance XZ.

(c) *An alternative method of defining margin lines.* In confined waters where the margin lines are relatively close to the course line, it may be found more convenient to fix the margin lines on the plotter using the index lines as the datum rather than the indexing target. This technique is depicted in Figure 8.10(a) and (b).

Note that the distances being measured from the chart are the beam distances between the alter-course positions 1 and 2 and the adjacent margin line for both headings. The margin lines on the final 310° course are additionally referenced by the directions and distances.

As confirmation that the resultant margin lines on the plotter are in the correct position, check that their individual directions and lengths agree with those laid off on the chart. Provided that the distances

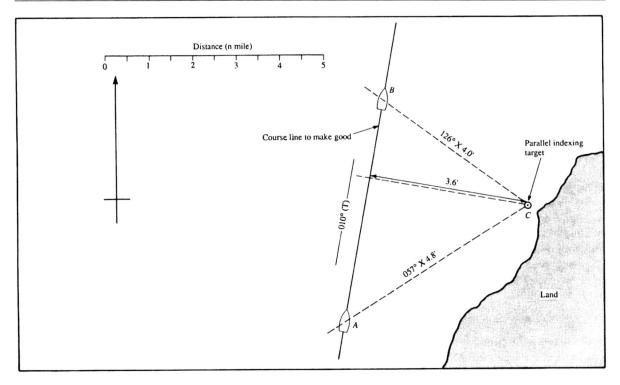

Figure 8.7 Positioning the relative index lines

(a)   A charted navigation plan

A, B, C etc., are relatively small, it will not be found necessary to measure the beam angle but to lay off the direction by eye and measure the appropriate distance.

8.4.3.4   The 'wheel-over' position

When transiting a very confined channel and/or conning a large vessel, it is advisable to plan the wheel-over positions using a knowledge of the ship's turning characteristics including any interaction effects. Use of this data should make it possible to keep on the track line required. This information will appear on the chart as a point on the course line spaced a calculated distance prior to the alter-course position. This distance can be used on the display to indicate the point on the index line where the ship should begin to turn. see Figures 8.11(a) and (b).

Note   It is advisable to make these turning predictions for a moderate value of helm (10° to 15°) on the understanding that, if the conditions are other than calm (and assuming deep water), the actual turn as executed may not correspond with the predictions. Consequently the person conning the ship should be prepared to increase or reduce the amount of helm applied in order to meet the precise requirements of the turn.

The track line may be regained using the wheel-over position. When the vessel is not exactly on the course line and is approaching an alteration point, provided circumstances allow, it is common practice to take the new course either early or late, as necessary, in order to recover the course line (see Figure 8.12(a)).

To identify the position at which to begin the alteration of course, a construction line is drawn through the wheel-over position and parallel to the new course

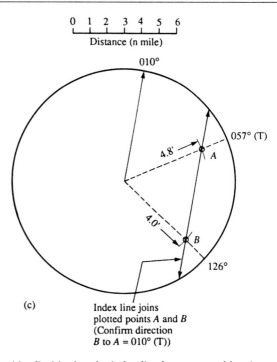

Figure 8.7(b)   Positioning the index line by beam distance using a mechanical cursor

(c)   Positioning the index line by ranges and bearings

line. On the parallel index plot (see Figure 8.12(b)), when the indexing target reaches the construction line through the wheel-over position, the turn begins.

8.4.3.5   Recording the parallel indexing data

Having spent the necessary time and effort in planning a coastal passage or port approach and having defined the areas where parallel indexing will be used, the data needed for the plot must be extracted and recorded in a suitable form, i.e. either in a notebook or in a diagrammatic form so that, when the time comes to use the data, it can be used with an absolute minimum of delay. It is essential to remember that no mistakes can be tolerated at this stage.

The diagrammatic method of data storage gives the operator the additional advantage of being able to cross-check by direct comparison of the indexing lines drawn on the plot with the previously prepared data.

An extension of the diagrammatic method involves drawing the parallel indexing data accurately on one or more acetate sheets which have been cut to fit the face of the display. Apart from the normal parallel indexing data, these sheets would need careful marking with reference points for centre and north.

The recording of this navigational data is part of the normal passage-planning process and the operator should not look on the data as permanent and able to be used repeatedly on future occasions without amendment. It should be remembered that, in deciding on the margin of safety lines, the tide and present vessel status, for example, are important factors. Hence the parallel indexing data contained on the acetate overlays should not be used subsequently without first checking that the data is still valid.

Included with the parallel-indexing lines will be the operational instructions, such as the point at which to begin using the data, the range scale to use, the appropriate point/time to change range scale or to change the indexing target.

Where a radar's 'mapping' facility is used to construct the indexing lines, the map may be stored for

Figure 8.8 More complex indexing

(a)   A complex charted plan

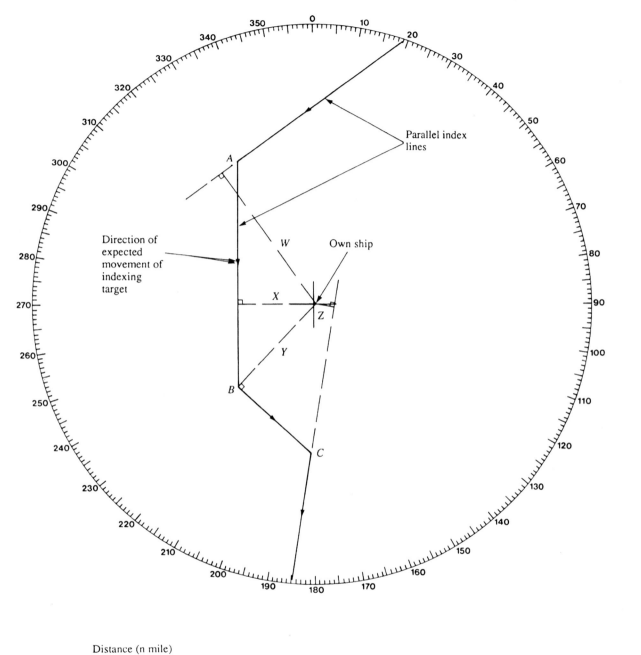

Figure 8.8(b)   A series of parallel index lines

Figure 8.9 Margin lines and danger circles
(a)   A navigation plan including margin lines and a danger circle

future use. The fact that an index map has been used and tested is useful as the possibility of an error in its construction has been removed. However, the map should always be rechecked before use in case of changes in the navigational regime which may have occurred in the interim.

8.4.4   Progress monitoring

As described in Section 8.4.2.4, the intention while navigating using parallel indexing is to keep the indexing target on the relative indexing line that has been drawn for it, or at least within the margin lines that may apply. To do this the navigator must continuously monitor the movement of the indexing target and take particular note of (a) the actual position of the indexing target relative to the index line and safety

margin lines and (b) the present trend of movement relative to the desired direction of movement.

Simple observation of the echo and its afterglow can provide this information but on the traditional reflection plotter it was possible to plot the indexing target with grease pencil to make the data more obvious. The actual position of the indexing target relative to the margin lines confirms that the vessel is in safe water and how much sea room is presently available. The trend of movement as provided by the plotting confirms whether or not the vessel is at that time making good the required track. The navigator can now decide, on the basis of these two pieces of information, whether corrective action is needed, either to regain the planned course line or to make good the required track direction.

For example, in Figure 8.13, monitoring the indexing target as the vessel transits the narrow channel shows that over the past few minutes the indexing

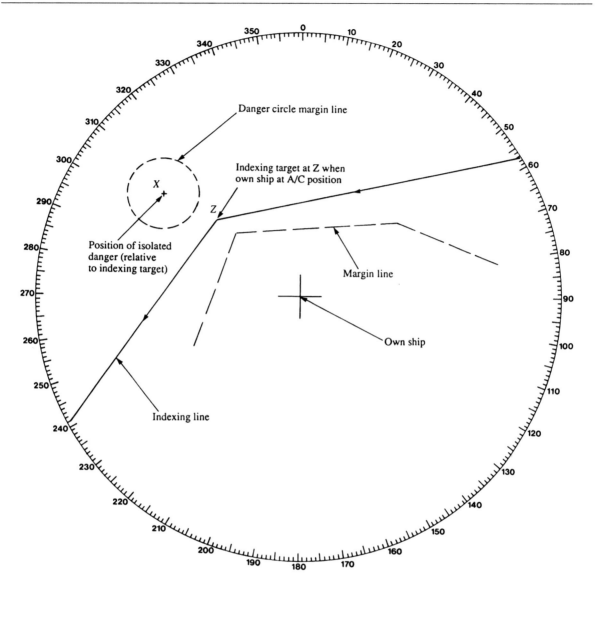

Danger circle margin line

Indexing target at Z when
own ship at A/C position

X
+

Position of isolated
danger (relative
to indexing target)

Z

Margin line

Own ship

Indexing line

Distance (n mile)

Figure 8.9(b) A parallel indexing plot of margin lines and a danger circle

Figure 8.10 Narrow margins
(a)   A navigation plan with narrow margins

target has left the indexing line and is approaching the margin line. This indicates that the ship is being set to the west and that the required corrective action is to turn to starboard by a few degrees so that the indexing target moves back onto the index line, or at least does not move any farther away from it.

Notice that no reference is made to the ship's head in this process because what in fact is relevant here is the course which is being made good rather than the direction in which the ship is pointing. The difference between the two can be large in a tideway when the ship's speed is low. When visibility is restricted, these differences can be very disorientating. It is not being suggested here that the ship's head should be totally disregarded; obviously there should be some logical relationship between the two directions provided by a knowledge of the tidal set and rate.

As the indexing target moves along the indexing line there is no need to keep the earlier information and plots behind it and these may be progressively cleared from the plotter. While the vessel is being navigated using parallel indexing it is very important to fix the ship's position on the chart by normal methods at frequent intervals as confirmation that the ship *is* in fact in safe water and *is* in fact moving in agreement with the parallel indexing information.

8.4.5   Parallel indexing on a true-motion display

As explained in Section 8.4.2.3, the use of a true-motion radar presentation for parallel indexing requires an ability to ground-stabilize the display reliably. Assuming that this condition can be met, the

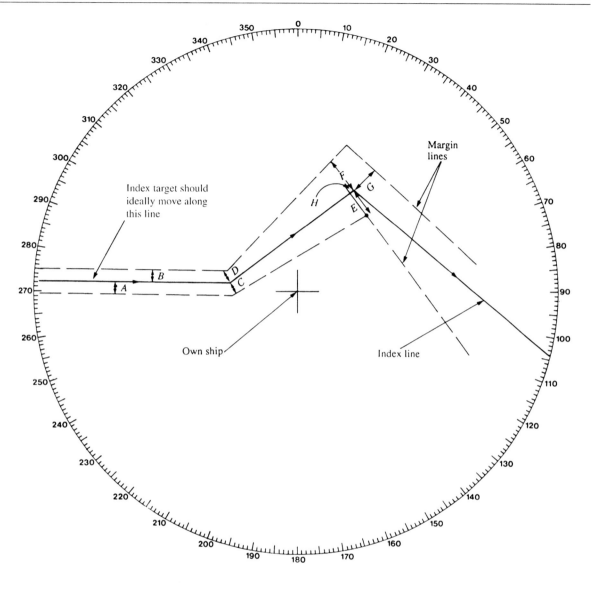

Figure 8.10(b)   A parallel indexing plot with margin lines fixed relative to index lines

Figure 8.11   Incorporating the wheel-over position

(a)   A navigation plan with alter-course and wheel-over positions

PPI may be used as an extension of the chart. The navigational data additional to the radar targets already on the PPI, such as course lines and margin-of-safety lines, can be marked on the display.

The data needed to be transferred to the plotter is identified during passage planning in exactly the same way as when working with relative indexing, except that the lines will be located relative to any fixed recognizable target on the PPI rather than to a single indexing target. This implies that, if the data is to be maintained at a high level of accuracy, careful consideration must be given to the identification of these fixed targets. In addition, the overall accuracy of this process will be enhanced by using the shortest range scale which is capable of showing the required data and by using reference navigation marks that are the nearest available. Each individual line should also be cross-checked by confirming from the chart the

direction and length of each leg. Figure 8.14(a) shows the navigational situation with own ship approaching an alter-course position north of island Y, to be followed by the transit of a narrow passage. Suitable radar navigation marks are identified at point X, island Y and point Z. The alter-course position and margin lines are referenced relative to these points. As our vessel approaches the area (see Figure 8.14(b)), the radar echoes of the selected navigation marks are identified and the navigation lines are drawn on the display using the previously recorded ranges and bearings. Each individual line should also be cross-checked by confirming, from the chart, its length and direction.

As the ship transits the area in question, the navigator must be prepared to reset the origin and/or change the range scale at the appropriate time. Where the navigation data is on a reflection plotter, this necessitates redrawing, therefore the point at which to do this

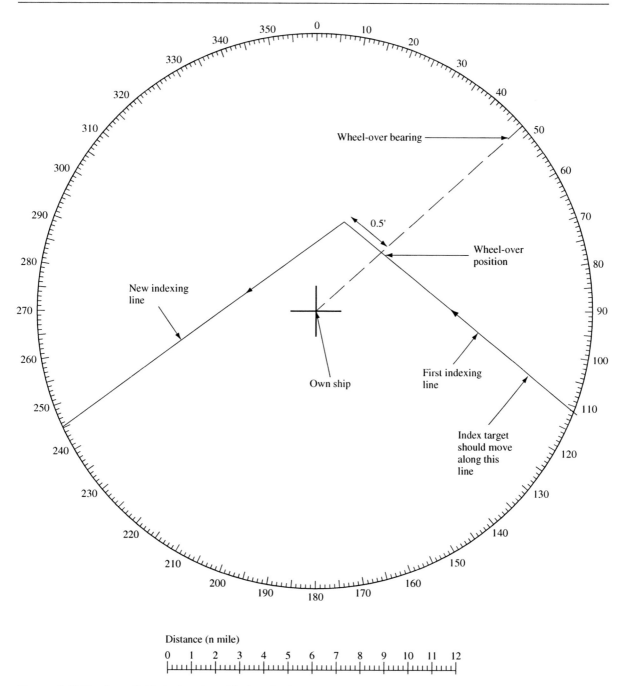

Figure 8.11(b)   A parallel indexing plot with the wheel-over position marked

Figure 8.12 Recovering the track

(a)   A navigation plan to recover the track line using the wheel-over line

needs to be pre-planned and the data stored in a form suitable for rapid application to the plotter. It has to be recognized that if ground-stabilization is not perfectly maintained, the fixed targets will drift away from their marks on the reflection plotter. The picture reset controls are normally fairly coarse and it may be difficult or even impossible to recover from this situation without redrawing the lines. Many users believe that this limitation of true parallel indexing renders the technique unsuitable for practical use on radars equipped with azimuth stabilization and reflection plotter.

However, if electronic lines or maps are employed it becomes more feasible for the observer to move the map as it drifts due to tide and other effects.

The process is further improved by the use of automatic ground-stabilization. This technique requires the use of more advanced facilities of either ARPA,

dual-axis ground track speed log, GNSS or other positioning system.

8.4.6   Modern radar navigation facilities

8.4.6.1   Ground-stabilization using ARPA and ATA (see also Section 5.3)

The target-tracking capability of the ARPA or ATA can provide the navigator with an important and potentially very useful piece of data to help with the navigation problem, namely a continuously updated rate and set of the current being experienced. This is a significant improvement on the previous situation where relatively long periods of plotting or position fixing were needed to be able to deduce the rate

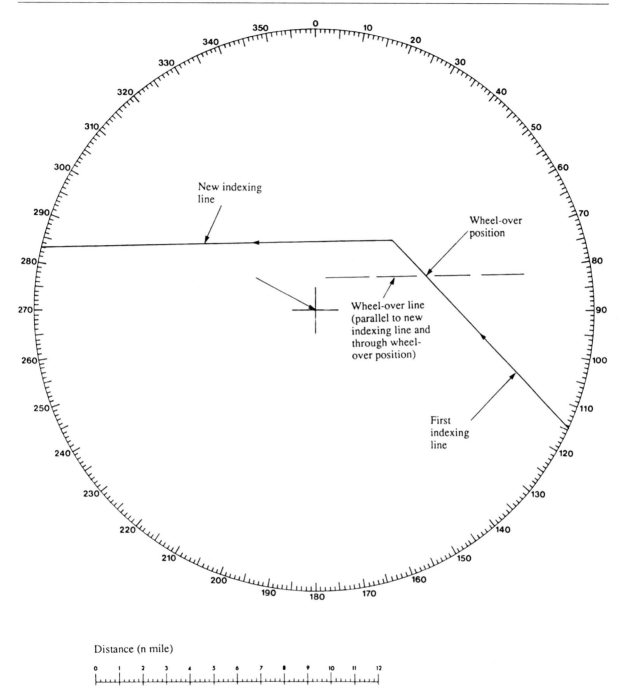

Distance (n mile)

Figure 8.12(b) A parallel indexing plot with wheel-over line to assist in the recovery of the track line

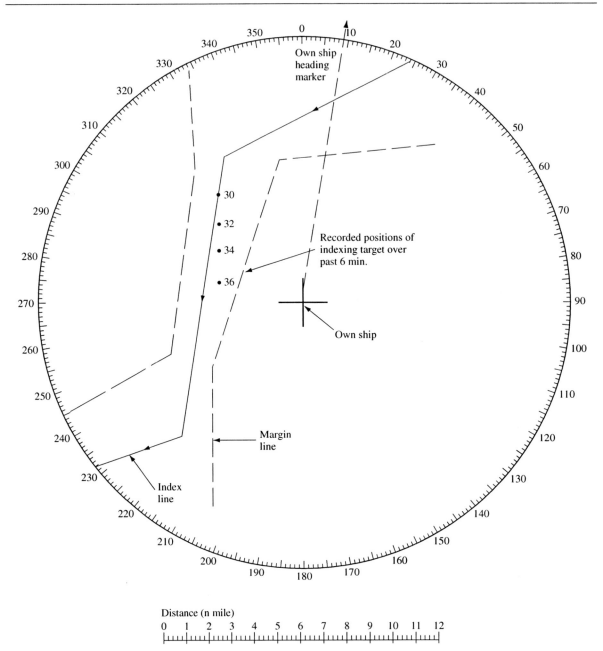

Figure 8.13 A parallel indexing plot with the target movement recorded

Figure 8.14 Parallel indexing on a true-motion ground-stabilized presentation
(a)   A navigation plan to transit a narrow passage

and set experienced over that period. The navigator then had to assume that this data was constant and use it to plan future action, naturally with varying degrees of success as this data can be very time-variable.

There are two pre-requisites for the ARPA or ATA to provide the navigator with accurate tidal data:

1   The computer must be provided with accurate values of own ship's motion *through the water*, i.e. true heading and speed (see Sections 6.8.1.2 and 6.8.1.3).
2   There must be a radar echo from a known fixed reference target showing on the PPI and capable of being tracked by the ARPA or ATA. In most cases this means that it must be small and isolated, otherwise the point being tracked will tend to wander randomly within the echo area and so provide random spurious data. In some geographical areas, this

type of fixed target can be hard to find. However, the rigorous selection requirements associated with parallel indexing targets (see Section 8.4.2.4) do not apply in this case and, provided that the target is small and isolated and does not move its geographical location during the period of time that it is being used for this purpose, it will suffice. Hence floating marks are acceptable with due caution in this regard.

The accuracy of the tidal data calculated is dependent not only on the accuracy with which the reference target is tracked (yielding the ground track) but also on the accuracy of the input of the observing vessel's water track since the tidal values are deduced from the vector difference of these two tracks. For practical purposes, the accuracy of the set and drift so obtained should be at least as good as would be obtained by using more traditional methods, i.e. better

Distance (n mile)

Figure 8.14(b)   A parallel indexing plot on a true-motion ground-stabilized presentation

than ±0.5 knot for rate and ±20° for direction. The fact that it has been obtained very rapidly and with only token effort by the navigator makes it an ideal source of information with which to ground-stabilize the radar presentation. This may be done by setting in the relevant values on separate controls, or the radar manufacturer may provide a direct internal route such that, at the touch of the appropriate control, the tidal data is automatically applied to the tracking of own ship (see Section 5.3). Since the tidal data is continually updated, the result is an almost perfect degree of ground-stabilization where own ship and all target motions are now indicated with respect to the ground.

Note   When the display is being automatically ground stabilized by a reference target, the accuracy of own ship's perceived movement through the water does not affect the indicated movements on the screen. If, however, a read-out is taken of tidal rate and set, then the computation involves own ship's input course and speed data and this factor must therefore be correct.

The reliability with which the ARPA or ATA continues as a ground-stabilized display depends on how well it continues to track the *reference* fixed target. Tracking can be lost under certain circumstances (see Section 5.3) and, remembering the purpose for which ground-stabilization is selected for the radar presentation, it is advisable to pay close attention to the performance of the ARPA or ATA in this respect. In particular, always try to keep the reference target visible on the PPI and under observation. Other fixed targets suitable for the purpose of ground-stabilizing should already be being tracked and available to take over the role of reference target at short notice. Some ARPA manufacturers allow the simultaneous tracking of several fixed targets from which the mean value of tidal data is derived and applied. This makes the system less vulnerable to the loss of tracking of a single reference target.

Once the radar presentation has been stabilized, the additional navigational data can be applied to the reflection plotter as described in Section 8.4.5. Although this automatic ground-stabilizing function is not affected by changing range scales or by repositioning the display origin, the lines drawn on a reflection plotter will be out of position and to the wrong scale and hence will have to be redrawn. Even if the navigator returns to the original range scale, it is not always possible to re-position the origin with the precision needed.

8.4.6.2   Other automatic ground-stabilization methods

The main disadvantage of the reference target method of stabilization is the availability of fixed small radar targets. Other methods of automatic ground-stabilization exist that do not require ARPA or ATA plotting facilities.

The inputs from a dual-axis ground track doppler log can be used, but this is not common because of accuracy issues with logs in general and the limited depth range in which the equipment will operate.

The most popular method of ground-stabilization tends to be the input from GNSS (see Sections 10.1 and 10.4) as they have a high degree of accuracy and availability and are easily connected. It is also possible to use other position fixing systems such as LORAN C, but the superior accuracy, reliability and availability of GNSS mean that other systems are not popular for this purpose.

When using these sources for fixing position, the observer has no need to worry about the availability of reference targets and the system will run until switched off. However, in using GNSS data the observer should remember that the operation of the GNSS depends on equipment outside the vessel over which he has no control and may not be informed of system problems. GNSS position fixing should therefore be checked regularly. This can be done externally to the radar set by comparing radar, GNSS and other data positions on the chart. However, if the facilities are available, it can be done on radar display by comparing the radar image with an electronic true map (see Section 8.4.6.3) or integration with ECDIS (see Section 10.2). If not available, conventional parallel indexing may be used.

The comments on the accuracy of derived tidal data in the previous sections also apply to GNSS automatic ground-stabilization.

*8.4.6.3 Electronic navigation lines (see also
           Section 5.4)*

Many radars provide some form of optional navigation line package. This facility allows the navigator to
use graphics to draw electronic lines directly on the
screen. A major advantage of such a facility is that
the observer has complete freedom to reset the origin of the picture and change range scale, because the
lines are automatically scaled and referenced to suit the
selected range scale and presentation.

In theory, the pattern of lines may be referenced
to the observing vessel, or to the ground. There is
considerable variety in the way manufacturers have
approached the provision of this facility, and both
modes are not necessarily available in any given
package.

Where the lines can be referenced to the observing vessel they will maintain constant position on
the screen when the relative-motion presentation (see
Section 1.5.1) is selected, thus facilitating relative-
motion parallel indexing as described previously.

The ready availability of automatic ground-
stabilization in radar and ARPA systems makes it simple to generate a line pattern which remains stationary
on the screen when the ground-stabilized true-motion
presentation (see Section 1.5.2.2) is selected. This facilitates true-motion parallel indexing as described previously in Section 8.4.5 and, additionally, allows the
navigator to arrange the lines in such a way as to form
simple maps giving a *chart-like* presentation. It is essential to appreciate that in the case of many systems this
will be accompanied by ground-stabilization of the
true vectors, as a result of which they will *not* represent
the headings of other vessels. If the radar is also being
used for collision avoidance, the observer may be dangerously misled. This important limitation of ground-
stabilization is discussed in Sections 8.4.8.2 and 5.3. In
some ARPA systems it is possible to display ground-
referenced lines when the relative-motion presentation is selected. In such a situation the map or other
pattern should maintain its registration with a ground-
stationary target.

The format in which navigation line data is read into
the computer is not standardized and many different

systems exist while yet others are being developed. In
general, the method will involve one of the following:

(a) A series of ranges and bearings.
(b) A cartesian co-ordinate system.
(c) A series of latitudes and longitudes.

In each case the navigator must have some datum
(or reference) from which to measure so as to establish
the relationship between the chart and the radar picture (e.g. if a navigation line is referenced on the chart
relative to a prominent navigation feature such as the
end of a breakwater, then, when the vessel arrives in
the area in question and the breakwater echo appears
on the radar screen, the navigation line can be positioned in the correct relationship to the radar echo
of the breakwater and will thus take up its proper
geographical location).

The navigator must be very aware of the accuracy
with which the datum can be defined and, similarly,
of the accuracy with which the lines can be positioned
on the screen. It is also a condition that the datum
used must be an identifiable radar target.

Many radar 'navigation' packages provide a storage
facility such that the map can be drawn at some convenient time prior to use and put into the computer's
memory. Depending on the sophistication of the particular package, several maps of varying sizes may be
stored simultaneously and called up when required.
When recalled to the PPI, the map needs precise positioning; to assist in this function, a *map align* control
is usually provided. It is worth remembering that it
may be impossible to turn the map in azimuth once
drawn and therefore, before constructing any map,
the navigator must check that the radar presentation
is accurately north-referenced and stabilized.

A fundamental precaution that must be taken by
all navigators designing maps which are to be used to
assist with navigation in confined waters is the inclusion of check marks within the map such that, at any
time while the maps are being used, it is possible for
the navigator to confirm by simple inspection of the
PPI screen that the lines drawn are in correct registration with geographical features. Happily, the lines
drawn on the chart do not move without warning,
but this may happen with electronic lines. For any

radar there is likely to be one or more sets of circumstances that would allow the maps to shift their position. Usually the drift is very slow but therein lies the danger, for the gradual movement easily escapes detection unless there are obvious marks within the map to highlight the discrepancy. Generally, when the radar presentation has been ground-stabilized by *fixed target* reference, the map stabilization is reliable provided that the ground-stabilization is accurately maintained. The commonest form of check is to include points or lines in the map which correspond to recognizable fixed radar targets. Only when these markers lie on the appropriate radar echoes is the map known to be properly positioned. These markers, if they include floating reference marks, have the complementary function of attracting the attention of the navigator to buoys which are out of position or missing.

8.4.7 Unplanned parallel indexing

Occasionally, the navigator may realize a need for parallel indexing data while actually conning the vessel in an area where the passage planning appraisal had not foreseen the need. In such a case it is necessary to devise a strategy which, with the minimum of measurements, will allow a simple and rapid application of data to the reflection plotter or a rapid input of data to the facility which generates the navigation lines.

For example, suppose that the vessel is experiencing difficulty, due to tide or wind, in making an altercourse position off a buoy or other radar target:

(a) With a relative-motion radar presentation, set the variable range marker (VRM) at the required passing distance (CPA) from the radar target and draw a line on the display from the radar target at a tangent to the VRM. Thereafter, steer the vessel so that the echo remains on the index line.

(b) With a true-motion ground-stabilized radar presentation, set the VRM at the required passing distance from the radar target, then draw a line on display through the radar echo at a tangent to the VRM. Thereafter, steer the vessel to maintain the tangent relationship between the VRM and the index line.

The advantage of these methods is their instant response to a particular need. Navigators should not, however, lose sight of the dangers inherent in failing to pre-plan thoroughly, such as the absence of cross-checking and the inability to detect the proximity of danger. The navigator also needs to be able to pick out, at short notice, a reliable indexing target.

8.4.8 Anti-collision manoeuvring while parallel indexing

Parallel indexing is purely a radar navigational technique which is unlikely to be employed unless navigational constraints are present and which requires the continuous attention of the navigator. However, non-navigational obstructions in the form of other vessels may appear at any time requiring anti-collision action. This action must not take the vessel into unsafe water and it is in integrating this anti-collision action with the navigational constraints that the *margin-of-safety lines* included in the parallel indexing data show their true value.

8.4.8.1 Using a relative-motion presentation

Unless ARPA or ATA data is available, the relative-motion display with parallel indexing data on the display is most unsuitable as a source of anti-collision data, mainly due to the disruption it causes to the navigation process while the plotting is taking place. To determine the motion of a target, it is preferable to use one of the following techniques:

(a) Use a second radar set solely for anti-collision data acquisition. In a confined water situation with no ARPA or ATA, true-motion would probably be of assistance as it allows the tactical situation to be more apparent and, consequently, possible action by targets to be more predictable and detectable.

(b) Plot the target's position on the navigation chart. A period of such plotting puts the anti-collision problem into its proper context and the navigator can then plan his actions to avoid the traffic while still remaining in safe water.

When working on the relative-motion plot, it can be difficult to assess rapidly the importance of any particular moving target and much time and effort can be used in plotting each one as it appears. A 'rule of thumb' method to resolve this problem is to take an approximate range and bearing of the moving target from own ship, transfer the line defined by this vector to the indexing target (the end of the line which intersected the target to be placed on the indexing target). The other end of the line now indicates the position of the moving target relative to the fairway. If it is in or close to the fairway margin lines then it should be given further consideration immediately. If, however, it falls completely away from the parallel indexing fairway then it can be discounted for the time being as it is not in or close to the intended route. Obviously it could subsequently enter the fairway so it cannot be ignored completely.

In Figure 8.15, while indexing on the present heading of 110°(T), target a has appeared on the starboard bow. By transferring line Oa so that a lies on the indexing target at A, it is established that the target is well outside the fairway at O_1 and the observing vessel expects to turn to 050°(T) before reaching the target.

Where ARPA or ATA facilities are provided, it should be possible to extract collision-avoidance data in the usual way.

8.4.8.2   Using a true-motion ground-stabilized presentation

(a)   *Without automatic ground-stabilization.* In this case stabilization is achieved by the navigator observing a known fixed mark and making adjustments based on these observations (see Section 6.8.1.6). Moving targets within the vicinity are soon recognized after a small amount of plotting. Their positions and approximate movements with respect to the navigation problem can be deduced. However, it is essential to bear in mind that all targets will exhibit their *ground* tracks.

This limitation is resolved by turning the tidal speed control to zero for long enough to assess the course and speed of the target through the water, i.e. two to three minutes, depending on the range scale. (*Note*   The parallel indexing lines on the plotter are now out of position and the origin will need to be reset to restore the parallel indexing plot.)

(b)   *With automatic ground-stabilization.* In this case the ground-stabilization is provided by a fixed target reference, dual axis log or position fixing system such as GNSS. Echoes of moving targets can be tracked in the normal manner and their true vectors displayed. The relative vectors or data will provide CPA and TCPA information as required.

However, the true vectors may well represent the movement of the targets *over the ground* and if the tidal component is significant there could be a large discrepancy between the ARPA ground tracks and the target's course and speed *through the water* (see Section 5.3). Since it is the *course through the water* which provides the aspect, the distortion of this piece of information can result in a complete misunderstanding of the situation which is facing the navigator. For example, in clear visibility at night, as a vessel approaches a port and is presented with an array of lights from moving targets against a backdrop of shore lights, unless there is a fairly close correlation between observed aspects and those illustrated on the PPI, the navigator may become disorientated or, alternatively, begin to lose faith in the equipment, all at a critical point in the passage. In reduced visibility, the fact that the data is distorted may go completely unnoticed and result in the navigator having a completely erroneous understanding of the traffic situation. This could lead to the wrong anti-collision action being taken.

The solution to this particular problem is that the navigator should not use a radar presentation that is primarily intended for navigation to deal with an anti-collision problem. The correct information on which to base collision-avoidance action comes from a sea-stabilized display and should always be made use of prior to making an anti-collision decision. The observer should remove the fixed target reference or

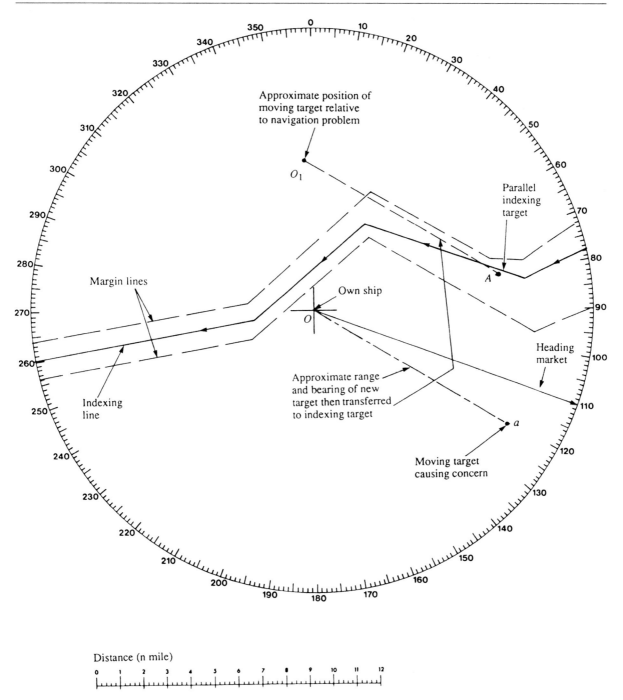

Figure 8.15 Approximate identification of the relative position of a target on a parrallel indexing plot

GNSS input and return to the display of sea-stabilized data. Most of these changes of presentation are simple and quick with modern radars and there is no excuse for attempting to guess the effect that removing the tide would have. Having assessed the relevant information, the navigator can then return to his navigation problem by re-selecting the reference and re-aligning the navigation lines which will have drifted.

9 ARPA and ATA – accuracy and errors

9.1 Introduction

Errors present in the data displayed on the ARPA or ATA screen or by the alphanumeric read-out will affect decision making. The observer must therefore have a knowledge of the level of accuracy that can be expected and the errors which will affect it. It is not a simple matter to specify the accuracy because it depends on, among other things, the geometry of the plotting triangle. For this reason, the IMO Performance Standards specify accuracy in terms of what must be achieved by the ARPA or ATA in the case of four carefully chosen test scenarios. The scenarios used for both ARPA and ATA are described and illustrated in Section 9.2 and the accuracy levels to be achieved are set out in Section 9.3.

9.2 The test scenarios used in current standards

These test scenarios are generated by a simulator and fed to the ARPA or ATA which must give the results specified in Tables 9.1 and 9.2.

In the scenarios, the target's motion is specified in terms of its *relative* course and speed, neither of which is particularly helpful to the practical ARPA operator; in fact, the use of these terms on the bridge

Table 9.1 Plotting accuracy values (95% probability) required after one minute

Scenario	Relative course (degrees)	Relative speed (knots)	CPA (nautical miles)
1	11	2.8	1.6
2	7	0.6	
3	14	2.2	1.8
4	15	1.5	2.0

Table 9.2 Plotting accuracy values (95% probability) required after three minutes

Scenario	Relative course (degrees)	Relative speed (knots)	CPA (nautical miles)	TCPA (min)	True course (degrees)	True speed (knots)
1	3.0	0.8	0.5	1.0	7.4	1.2
2	2.3	0.3			2.8	0.8
3	4.4	0.9	0.7	1.0	3.3	1.0
4	4.6	0.8	0.7	1.0	2.6	1.2

of a ship can give rise to dangerous confusion. While recognizing that specification in this way is suited to a scientific test carried out in a laboratory, it is believed that, to be of practical value to the user, it is more helpful if the target's true motion is known. To this end, the illustrations (which do not form part of the Performance Standard) show the scenarios in this way (Figures 9.1–9.4).

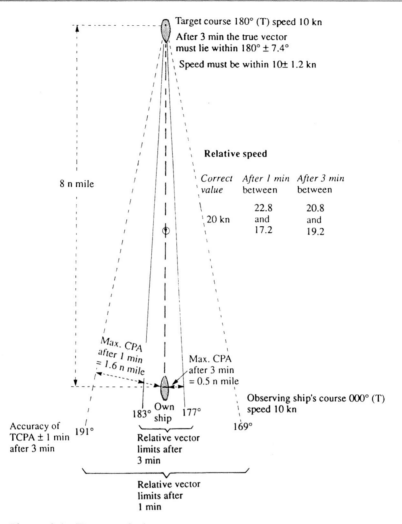

Figure 9.1 Test scenario 1

Test scenario 1 (Figure 9.1)

Own ship course 000°; own ship speed 10 kn; target range 8 n mile.
Target: bearing 000°; relative course 180°; relative speed 20 kn.

Test scenario 2 (Figure 9.2)

Own ship course 000°; own ship speed 10 kn; target range 1 n mile.
Target: bearing 000°; relative course 090°; relative speed 10 kn.

Test scenario 3 (Figure 9.3)

Own ship course 000°; own ship speed 5 kn; target range 8 n mile.
Target: bearing 045°; relative course 225°; relative speed 20 kn.

Test scenario 4 (Figure 9.4)

Own ship course 000°; own ship speed 25 kn; target range 8 n mile
Target: bearing 045°; relative course 225°; relative speed 20 kn.

Figure 9.2 Test scenario 2

9.3 The accuracy of displayed data required by the Performance Standard

9.3.1 Current standards

The ARPA should provide accuracies not less than those given in Tables 9.1 and 9.2, for the four scenarios defined in Section 9.2, with the sensor errors specified in Section 9.5.6. The values given relate to the best possible manual plotting performance under environmental conditions of ±10 degrees of roll.

An ARPA should present within one minute of steady state tracking, the relative-motion trend of a target with the accuracy values shown in Table 9.1 (95 per cent probability values).

An ARPA should present within 3 minutes of steady state tracking, the motion of a target with the accuracy values shown in Table 9.2 (95 per cent probability values).

When a tracked target, or own ship, has completed a manoeuvre, the system should present in a period of not more than one minute, an indication of the target's motion trend, and display within three minutes the target's predicted motion, in accordance with Tables 9.1 and 9.2

The ARPA should be designed in such a manner that under the most favourable conditions of own ship motion, the error contribution from the ARPA should remain insignificant compared to the errors associated with the input sensors, for the scenarios depicted in Figures 9.1–9.4.

It should be noted that the tables give 95 per cent probability values. This is necessary because any such

Figure 9.3 Test scenario 3

Figure 9.4 Test scenario 4

error treatment is essentially statistical in its nature and means that the results must be within the tolerance values on 19 out of 20 occasions.

It is important to appreciate that even though the data is analysed by a computer, this does not mean that the results are perfect. Further, the errors considered in arriving at these tabulated values *do not* include 'blunders' or errors that result from the input of incorrect data.

Data obtained from the radar, log and gyro compass will be subject to random variations which all contribute to the uncertainty of the results as predicted by the computer. It should be appreciated that, because of the very short time period over which the computer plots (usually 1 minute or 3 minutes, see Section 4.3.6), and the consequent positional precision required, a whole new appreciation of radar errors is required. Errors which were not even considered with conventional radars in the past now become significant. In any case, the tables included in the specification should be taken as a guide as to what can be expected, especially with regard to CPA. It should be noted that this only considers up to 10° of roll. Where this is exceeded in practice, poorer results might be expected.

9.3.2 Future standards

The future standards for installations on vessels built in 2008 or later are arranged slightly simpler (see Section 11.2.1). The scenarios used in all previous standards (Table 9.1) are no longer used. Instead all tracked targets should meet the standards of Table 9.3. Two different categories of equipment are specified. For craft with a speed of less than 30 knots, the standards should be met for targets moving a relative speed of 100 knots to own ship. For higher speed craft, the same Table 9.3 should be met with targets moving at a relative speed of 130 knots.

9.4 The classification of ARPA and ATA error sources

The accuracy levels discussed in the previous section are dependent on the chosen level of sensor errors but can also be affected by other errors. All errors which can affect the accuracy of displayed data can be conveniently arranged in three groups as follows:

1 Errors which are generated in the radar installation itself, the behaviour of the signals at the chosen frequency and the limitations of peripheral equipment such as logs, gyro compasses and dedicated trackers.
2 Errors which may be due to inaccuracies during processing of the radar data, inadequacies of the algorithms chosen and the limits of accuracy accepted.
3 Errors in interpretation of the displayed data.

Table 9.3 Tracked target accuracy (95% probability figures) for installations on post-2008 new vessels

Time of steady state (minutes)	Relative course (degrees)	Relative speed (knots)	CPA (NM)	TCPA (minutes)	True course (degrees)	True speed (knots)
1 min: trend	11	1.5 or 10% (whichever is greater)	1.0	—	—	—
3 min: motion	3	0.8 or 1% (whichever is greater)	0.3	0.5	5	0.5 or 1% (whichever is greater)

9.5 Errors that are generated in the radar installation

Errors in the radar, gyro compass and log which feed data to the ARPA or ATA system will result in errors in the output data. Range and bearing errors which remain constant or nearly so during the encounter, e.g. a steady gyro compass error of a few degrees, will introduce an error into the predicted vectors of other ships, but are unlikely to cause danger since all data will be similarly affected, including own ship. The effect of errors on the predicted data depends on the kind of error, the situation and the duration of the plot for which the data is stored for processing and prediction. This time is typically in the range of 1 to 3 minutes and in this respect it must be appreciated that errors which in the past could be considered to be negligible may have a significant effect on derived data. In the following examples, the situation is assumed to be a near miss or a collision.

9.5.1 Glint

As a target ship rolls, pitches and yaws, the apparent centre of its radar echo moves over the full ship's length; this is termed glint. Its distance from amidships is random with a standard deviation of one-sixth length, i.e. for a 200 m ship it is probable that the error does not exceed ±33 m. Since the beam of a ship is usually small by comparison with its length, transverse glint is negligible. If the target ship's aspect is beam-on, glint introduces random bearing errors.

9.5.2 Errors in bearing measurement

These cause false positions to be recorded on each side of the relative track of the other ship, leading to errors in the observed relative track and therefore in the predicted CPA and also in the displayed aspect of the other ship. Unfortunately, the greatest errors in displayed aspect occur in those cases where the real aspect is near end-on. Bearing errors may result from the following causes.

9.5.2.1 Backlash in gearing

Backlash can occur between the rotating antenna and its azimuth transmitter. Air resistance on the rotating antenna will tend to maintain geartooth contact, but bounce and reverse torque due to aerodynamic forces will break the contact and allow some backlash to occur. This problem has been to a large extent overcome by the use of more modern forms of bearing transmission (see Section 2.6.6.4).

9.5.2.2 Unstable platform or antenna tilt

Ship motion causes the axis of rotation of the radar antenna to tilt. When the ship is heeled to an angle of B radians, a bearing error of $-\left(\frac{1}{2}B^2 \sin\theta \cos\theta\right)$ radians is produced, where θ is the bearing of the target off own ship's bow. This error is quadrantal, i.e. zero ahead, astern and abeam, rising to alternate plus and minus maxima at 45° and 135° etc. It will not be reversed by the opposite roll since B is squared.

When the ship is rolling, the tilt has two components, a random variation between zero and a maximum, according to the value of B (i.e the actual roll angle which happens to be present when the aerial is directly on the bearing) and a rise and fall of the maximum over periods of about one or two minutes with wave height variation. For a relative bearing of 45° and a roll of 7.5° toward or away from the other ship, the error is −0.25° maximum.

9.5.2.3 Parallax due to roll of own ship (Figure 9.5)

If the radar antenna is mounted at a height H above the roll axis of the ship and the ship rolls to an angle B, the antenna moves transversely by $H \sin B$. The measured bearing of a target at a bearing of θ from the ship's head and at a range R will be in error by an angle e which is given by

$$\tan e = \frac{H \sin B}{R} \times \cos\theta$$

(*Note* H and R must be in the same units and θ is the relative bearing.)

Since c is small,

$$c = \frac{180 H \sin B \cos \theta}{\pi R} \text{ degrees}$$

This error will vary sinusoidally with time and has a period equal to the roll period.

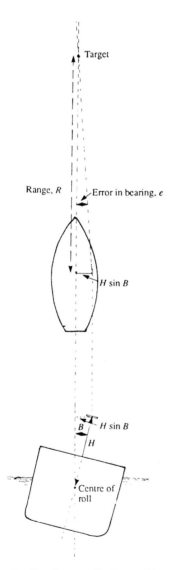

Figure 9.5 Parallax due to roll of own ship

The error is maximum when $\theta = 0°$ and $180°$ minimum when $\theta = 090°$ and $270°$ i.e. it varies with $\cos \theta$.

9.5.2.4 Asymmetrical antenna beam

The ARPA should take the bearing of the target as that of the centre of the echo. If the antenna beam is asymmetrical, the apparent position of the echo may change with the echo strength. Errors due to this cause can become very large in some systems if the echo strength is sufficient for the close-in side-lobe pattern of the antenna to become apparent. At least one system employs special techniques to eliminate this problem.

9.5.2.5 Azimuth quantization error (Figure 9.6)

The antenna position must be converted to digital form before it can be used by the computer, for example, by using a shaft encoder (see Section 2.6.6.4). A 12-bit shaft encoder has a least significant bit (LSB) equivalent to $0.09°$ (i.e. $360°/4096$) so that the restriction to 12 bits introduces a quantization error of $0.045°$. The same error will arise if the computer truncates the input azimuth information to 12 bits. Antenna azimuth is often taken to a resolution of either 12 or 13 bits.

Note Since gyro compass error is of the order $0.1°$ to $0.5°$ at best, there is no real point in making the antenna encoder bit size very much smaller.

9.5.3 Errors in range measurement

9.5.3.1 Range change due to roll of own ship

If the radar antenna is mounted at a height H above the roll axis of the ship and the ship rolls to an angle B, the antenna moves transversely by $H \sin B$. For a target bearing θ from the ship's head, the measured range will be in error by a distance d which is given by

$$d = H \sin B \sin \theta$$

Pitch error is much less significant, but if roll and pitch occur together the effects add non-linearly and must be worked out separately.

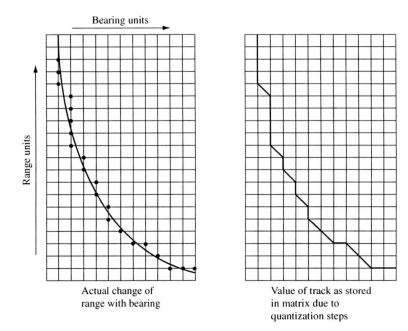

Bearing units

Range units

Actual change of
range with bearing

Value of track as stored
in matrix due to
quantization steps

Figure 9.6 Quantization errors

9.5.3.2   Range quantization error (Figure 9.6)

The range of a target must be converted into a digital number for the computer to use and it is likely
that this will be done by measuring the range using
counting techniques. A convenient clock rate is that
corresponding to 0.01 n mile steps on the 12 mile
range scale (see Section 2.6.6.3).

Typical step functions due to range and bearing
quantizing are shown in Figure 9.6.

Note   During some periods, it will appear that
the target is on a collision course, i.e. steady bearing,
although this is never the case in fact.

9.5.3.3   Pulse amplitude variation (Figure 9.7)

The equipment will typically measure the range of
an echo at the point at which the echo strength rises
above a pre-set threshold. Because of the finite bandwidth of the radar receiver, the echo pulse will have
a sloping leading edge and the measured range will

vary with the pulse amplitude (see Section 2.3.2.3).
For the pulse length commonly used on anti-collision
range scales, the receiver bandwidths are chosen for
long range performance rather than for discrimination,
so that it is likely that the leading edge slope will be
nearly as long as the transmitted pulse.

The resulting apparent range variation will depend
upon some assumptions about echo amplitude
variations but is likely to be about 40 metres as
a maximum.

9.5.4   The effect of random gyro compass errors

A gyro compass master unit, mounted at an arbitrary height above the roll axis of the ship, is subject to transverse acceleration at each extremity of the
roll. This includes a false vertical as the pendulous
unit tilts in its gimbals. This puts an error into
the gyro compass output affecting all bearings; it

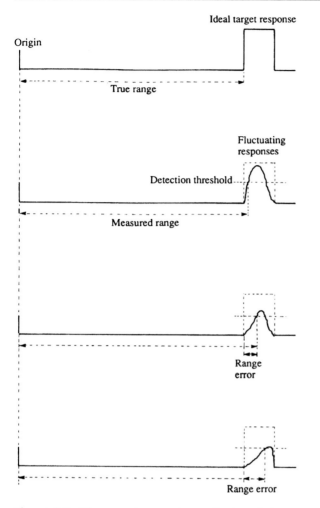

Origin

Ideal target response

True range

Fluctuating responses

Detection threshold

Measured range

Range error

Range error

Figure 9.7 The error due to pulse amplitude variation

9.5.4.1 Gyro compass deck-plane (gimballing) errors

The true heading of a vessel is the angle between the vessel's fore-and-aft line and the meridian when measured in the horizontal plane. In several gyro compass designs, the sensitive element has sufficient degrees of freedom to assume a north-south, horizontal attitude. However, the compass card may be constrained to the deck plane. In this case there can be a discrepancy between the compass card reading and the ship's heading detected by the sensitive element.

9.5.4.2 Yaw motion produced by the coupling of roll and pitch motions

When a ship is rolling and pitching, these two motions interact to produce a resultant yawing motion. The motion can be resolved into horizontal and vertical components. The horizontal component is the yaw motion and is detected by the gyro compass sensing element.

9.5.5 The effect of random log errors

An error in own ship's log will produce a vector error in every tracked ship's true speed and/or course. This will also result in an error in the displayed aspect of other ships; however this aspect error is minimum in all cases where the real aspect is end-on. A further effect will be to produce non-zero speed indications on all stationary targets being tracked. This cause may also produce large errors in the aspects of very slow-moving targets. If this error is assumed not to exceed 0.4 knots, it will give rise to a positional error of some 15.5 metres in a plot time of 75 seconds.

Where true tracks are stored by the tracker (see Section 4.3.6.2), a fluctuating log error can also affect the relative vectors. However, the errors being considered here are the small random variations in the log output and not the large fluctuations which can occur if the log's performance becomes erratic due to technical malfunction or problems caused by outside influences such as fouling or aeration. Such larger fluctuations are more appropriately considered under errors in input data (see Section 9.6.3).

has random and slowly varying components in just the same way as the radar tilt error. Observation at sea indicates that 0.25° is the error in many typical installations.

The gyro compass also has other errors. Long term errors (e.g. settling point ±0.75°) are unimportant if they remain sensibly constant, as they normally do, but short term random errors (e.g. settling point difference ±0.2°) are significant.

9.5.6 The magnitude of sensor errors specified in the Performance Standard

The accuracy figures quoted in Section 9.3 are based upon the following sensor errors and are appropriate to equipment complying with the current Performance Standards for shipborne navigational equipment. Note that σ denotes standard deviation.

Radar

Target glint (scintillation) (for 200 m length target)
Along length of target $\sigma = 30$ m (normal distribution)
Across beam of target $\sigma = 1$ m (normal distribution)

Roll-pitch bearing   The bearing error will peak in each of the four quadrants around own ship for targets on relative bearings of 045°, 135°, 225° and 315° and will be zero at relative bearings of 0°, 090°, 180° and 270°. This error has a sinusoidal variation at twice the roll frequency.

   For a 10° roll the mean error is 0.22° with 0.22° peak sine wave superimposed.

Beam shape   Assumed normal distribution giving bearing error with $\sigma = 0.05°$.

Pulse shape   Assumed normal distribution giving range error with $\sigma = 20$ m.

Antenna backlash   Assumed rectangular distribution giving bearing error $\pm0.5°$ maximum.

Quantization

Bearing   Rectangular distribution $\pm0.1°$ maximum.

Range   Rectangular distribution ±0.01 n mile maximum.
Bearing encoder assumed to be running from a remote synchro giving bearing errors with a normal distribution $\sigma = 0.03°$.

Gyro Compass
Calibration error 0.5°
Normal distribution about this with $\sigma = 0.12°$

Log
Calibration error 0.5 knots.
Normal distribution about this with $3\sigma = 0.2$ knots.

9.6 Errors in displayed data

9.6.1 Target swap

When two targets are close to each other, it is possible for the association of past and present echoes to be confused so that the processor is loaded with erroneous data.

   The result is that the historical data on one target may be transferred to another target and the indicated relative (and true) track of that ship will be composed of part of the tracks of two different target motions. Target swap can occur with any type of tracker but is least likely in those which use a diminishing gate size as confidence in the track increases and those which adopt rate aiding. It is most likely to occur when two targets are close together for a comparatively long time and one target echo is much stronger than the other, see Figure 9.8. It is particularly likely to occur if one target shadows the other (see also Section 4.3.5).

9.6.2 Track errors

The motion of a target is rarely completely steady and even steady motion will return positions which are randomly scattered about the actual track, due to basic radar limitations. Quantization errors in range and bearing which are introduced by the translation of the basic radar information to the processor database further exacerbate the effects of these system errors. The only way in which the tracker can deal with these is to use some form of smoothing over a period of time by applying more or less complicated filtering techniques (see also Section 4.3.6). The aim of the filtering is to give the best possible indication of the steady track and at the same time detect real changes quickly.

   Given the need to satisfy these two conflicting requirements it is inevitable that the tracker will be limited in its ability to predict precisely the relative and true motion of a tracked target at any instant and thus track errors will result. The effect of these errors should of course fall within the limits set out in Section 9.3 but the prudent observer will use suitable

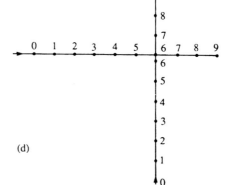

Figure 9.8   Target swap

(a)   At position 6, tracker transfers to stronger target
(b)   At position 6, and later, the profusion of echoes confounds tracker accuracy. The tracker may easily pick up random clutter instead of the target ship
(c)   Targets travel close together for a period, then separate. The tracker may not follow the diverging target ship
Note It is often difficult to acquire a target that is close to others already being tracked

(d)   Two tracked targets pass close to each other, so that both are in the tracking gate at one time
Note In this case, longer rate aiding may be an advantage

clear weather opportunities to gain some evaluation of the practical performance of the tracker which is producing the ARPA or ATA data. Such performance can be usefully judged against two important criteria. These are the stability of the track shown on the display for a vessel which is observed to be standing-on and the rapidity with which the track responds to a target which has been observed to manoeuvre. It has to be recognized that alterations of course are easy to detect by visual observation whereas speed changes are not. However, in clear weather the former are very much more common than the latter, except in very confined waters.

Accuracy is most difficult to achieve with targets whose track movement is slow. In the case of relative track storage (see Section 4.3.6.2) this will affect a target whose course and speed are close to those of the observing vessel. The length of the relative track will be small and thus the system errors are a much more significant proportion of track length than would be the case with a target having a rapid relative motion. Thus the inherent accuracy of CPA data will be low. Conversely, in the case of true track storage (see Section 4.3.6.3) a near-stationary target will suffer the same low accuracy in the prediction of its true motion.

In general the tracker is likely to offer the best indication of both the relative motion and the true motion when both the target and the observing vessel maintain their course and speed for a full smoothing period. In the changing situation the track errors will depend on the nature of the changes and the form of track storage adopted (see Section 4.3.6.2 and 4.3.6.3).

Where only the target manoeuvres there will be a finite response time in which the displayed vector will seek to follow the change and to stabilize on the new track. Under such circumstances, irrespective of whether the tracker smoothes relative or true tracks, there should in theory be no difference in the tracker performance when measured in terms of the accuracy with which it provides output of both relative and true vectors. In both cases the vectors may be erratic when the processor reverts to smoothing over the short period.

Where only the observing vessel manoeuvres, the method of storage is significant because the relative tracks of all targets will be curves for the duration of the manoeuvre. If the smoothing is applied to relative tracks, the tracker will be faced with the task of trying to produce a straight line from a curve and will hence obtain a mean track. Errors in the relative track will result and the relative vectors of all targets may be erratic in the short term. True-motion data derived from this will also be in error, just as where a manual plotter constructs an OAW triangle on the basis of an apparent motion which is not consistent (see Section 7.2). The effect may be exacerbated by the fact that, during the vessel's manoeuvre, the path traced out by the mass of the vessel, and hence the aerial, may differ significantly from that indicated by the gyro compass and log. Systems which smooth true tracks should derive a more accurate indication of the target's true track during the observing vessel's manoeuvre, as the true track is in theory rendered independent of changes in the observing vessel's course and speed. This independence will be reduced by any difference between the velocity of the ship's mass during the manoeuvre and the direction and speed fed in by the gyro and log. Again, all errors must fall within the limits of the Performance Standards but the prudent observer can assess the effect of manoeuvres on the performance of the tracker by observing a known

stationary target during a manoeuvre. In this connection it must be remembered that, even in steady-state conditions, a land-stationary target may display some component of motion due to the effect of tide, and water-stationary targets may have small non-zero vectors due to system errors.

Where both observing vessel and target manoeuvre at the same time, it is unlikely that any system will commence to provide a reliable indication of any target data until either the observing vessel or the target ceases to manoeuvre.

If targets are tracked down to very close ranges, the relative motion will give rise to very rapid bearing changes and this may make it impossible for the tracker to follow the target; thus the 'target lost' condition may arise, not because the echo is weak, but because the gate cannot be moved fast enough or opened up sufficiently to find it. It is also worth remembering that the use of true vectors as an indication of target heading is based on the assumption that the target is moving through the water in the direction in which it is heading. Leeway is the prime example of a case where this may not be correct. Unless one can see the target it is impossible even to begin to make an estimate of leeway. In poor visibility and high winds the observer must be alert to the possibility and use the displayed data with additional caution.

In summary, it must be remembered that whenever the steady-state conditions are disrupted there will be a period in which the data will be particularly liable to the track errors described above, in the same way as is the case when a target is first acquired. When the steady state is regained, accuracy and stability will improve, first over the short smoothing period and then over the long period. Any track data extracted during periods of non-steady-state conditions must be viewed with suspicion.

9.6.3   The effect on vectors of incorrect course and speed input

From the theory of manual radar plotting (see Section 7.2) it is evident that it is possible to deduce

the relative motion of a target without using a knowledge of the true motion of the observing vessel (other
than to produce stabilized bearings). Deduction of the
true motion of the target requires a knowledge of the
true motion of the observing vessel to allow resolution of the *OAW* triangle and the accuracy of the
result depends largely on the accuracy of the course
and speed data used. Extrapolation of this reasoning
suggests that the accuracy of relative vectors and the
associated CPA data are independent of the accuracy
of the course and speed input, whereas the accuracy
of true vectors and the associated data are dependent
on the accuracy of the input course and speed. In the
case of systems which smooth relative tracks, this is
invariably correct; in the case of systems which store true
tracks, it is correct subject to the qualification that the
input errors are constant. In the case of a fluctuating error
input, the two storage approaches will produce different
results. For this reason the effect of steady input errors on
relative and true vectors is discussed in Sections 9.6.3.1
and 9.6.3.2 respectively, while the case of a fluctuating
error is treated separately in Section 9.6.3.3.

Whatever approach the tracker uses, it is essential for
the observer to ensure that the correct course and speed
inputs are fed in when setting up (see Section 6.12.3)
and that regular and frequent checks are made to
ensure that the values remain correct. Failure to do this
will in general result in the erroneous display of true
data which may seriously mislead the navigator when
choosing a suitable avoiding manoeuvre strategy.

9.6.3.1   Relative vectors

The relative vectors and the associated CPA/TCPA
data should be unaffected if the observer allows a fixed
erroneous input of course and speed data to be applied.
In the case of relative storage the information is not
used in the calculation. In the case of true storage it is
used twice and one could say that this illustrates a classic case of 'two wrongs making a right', as illustrated
by Figure 4.9 in Section 4.3.6.3.

A fixed gyro compass error present at the point at
which the bearings are digitized (see Section 2.6.6.4)
would result in the picture being slewed but would
not affect the CPA/TCPA data.

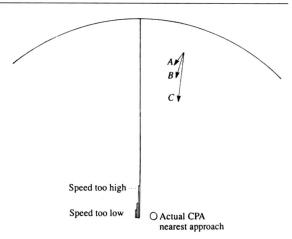

Figure 9.9   The effect of incorrect speed input on a
true-vector presentation
Vector B is correct
Speed input 'too high' shows Vector *A*, a crossing slow
ship
Speed input 'too low' shows vector *C*, a fast target on near
parallel crossing

9.6.3.2   True vectors

The true vectors will be displayed incorrectly if the
observer allows an erroneous input of course and speed
data to be applied, irrespective of the storage format. This may give the observer a seriously misleading
impression of the other vessel's heading and speed and
may prompt an unsafe manoeuvre. Such a situation is
illustrated by Figures 9.9 and 9.10.

Figure 9.9 shows a target which is moving at a
similar speed to the observing vessel, is showing a red
light and which will pass clear down the starboard side.
Incorrect speed input could make this appear to be a
slower vessel in a broad crossing situation or a faster
ship passing green to green.

The effect of an incorrect heading input will have
a similar capacity to produce misleading results, as
illustrated in Figure 9.10.

9.6.3.3   The effect of fluctuating input error

The most probable source of a fluctuating input error
is the log. There are a number of circumstances in

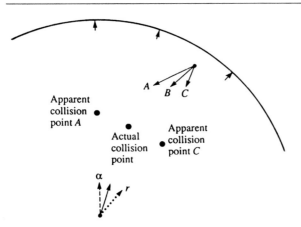

Figure 9.10   The effect of incorrect compass input on a
true-vector presentation
Vector B is correct
Incorrect compass input to the left at α shows a target
broad crossing to port and faster than own ship
Incorrect compass input to the right at r shows a target fine
crossing to starboard and slower than own ship

which this might arise. An example is the case of
some doppler logs which tend to give erratic output
in bad weather when the transducer has to operate
through an aerated layer. The fluctuating effect will
affect the display of the true vectors whatever the form
of storage but the behaviour of the relative vectors will
depend on the mode of storage used. Where relative
tracks are smoothed the fluctuating error will have
no effect on the relative vectors and the associated
CPA/TCPA data. Where true tracks are smoothed,
the relative vector will tend to change erratically in
sympathy with the input fluctuations, since the relative
vector is derived from the smoothed true track and
the instantaneous input course and speed data.

The difference in effect can be considered by an
example shown in Figure 9.11. Consider the case
where the observing vessel has been on a steady course
and speed for a full smoothing period and the correct course and speed data has been consistently fed
in. Both methods of smoothing will have settled to
produce the correct relative and true vectors.

Suppose that the log develops an instantaneous fault
and reads half the correct speed. The relative track
system, shown in Figure 9.11(a), will show no change

in the relative vector (because the relative track is
smoothed) but the true vector will immediately go
to the erroneous value because it is derived from the
smoothed relative track and the instantaneous course
and speed input.

The true track system will show no immediate
change in the true vector, because it is insulated by the
smoothing, whereas the relative vector will immediately go to an erroneous value since it is derived from
the smoothed true track and the instantaneous course
and speed input. If no further change takes place in the
error and the vectors are observed over a full smoothing period, the true vector will gradually change to the
erroneous value while the relative vector will gradually come back to the correct value as the previously
smoothed track is progressively discarded. Thus, in this
type of storage, if the speed input fluctuates the relative vector will also fluctuate. This disadvantage has
to be set against the advantage gained in being able to
maintain a stable relative vector when the observing
vessel is manoeuvring (see Section 9.6.2).

An erratic course input would have a similarly dis-
ruptive effect. However, such a condition would also
affect the digitization of bearings. This would tend to
cause targets to jump and it would be fairly obvious
to even a casual observer that something was wrong.

9.6.3.4   Comparison of relative and true vectors

Given that one or other of the vectors can be affected
by input errors in a way which may be dependent
on the tracker philosophy, it is important to stress the
need for the observer continuously to compare one
data source with another to ensure that, in all cases,
indications given from relative vectors and true vectors
sensibly agree.

9.6.4   The effect on the PPC of incorrect data input

9.6.4.1   Errors in speed input

If incorrect speed is input to a collision situation,
the collision point will still appear correctly on the

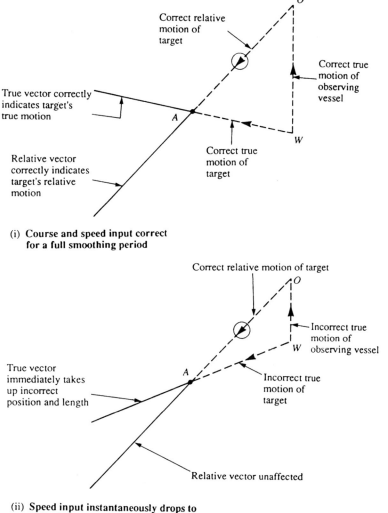

(i) **Course and speed input correct for a full smoothing period**

(ii) **Speed input instantaneously drops to half of correct value due to log error**

Figure 9.11 The effect of a step change in the error of speed input
(a) Where relative track storage is used

heading marker, but at an incorrect range, and will move down the heading marker at an incorrect speed.

In the case where there is, in fact, a miss distance, the collision point will appear in the wrong position, which may give rise to a misjudgement of the danger or urgency of the situation. Figure 9.12 shows how the collision point may be displaced due to a speed error in the two cases where the target is crossing ahead and crossing astern.

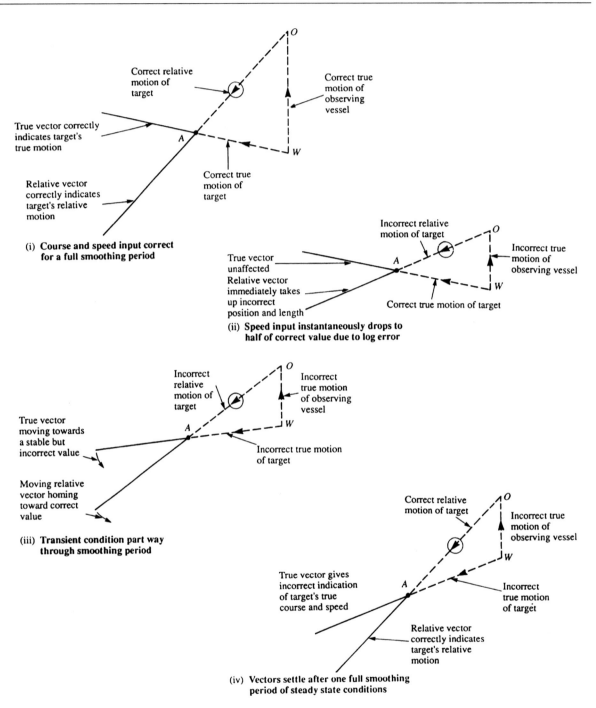

Correct relative
motion of
target

Correct true
motion of
observing
vessel

True vector correctly
indicates target's
true motion

Correct true
motion of
target

Relative vector
correctly indicates
target's relative
motion

(i) **Course and speed input correct
for a full smoothing period**

Incorrect relative
motion of target

Incorrect true
motion of
observing vessel

True vector
unaffected

Correct true motion of target

Relative vector
immediately takes
up incorrect
position and length

(ii) **Speed input instantaneously drops to
half of correct value due to log error**

Incorrect
relative
motion of
target

Incorrect
true motion
of observing
vessel

True vector
moving towards
a stable but
incorrect value

Incorrect true motion
of target

Moving relative
vector homing
toward correct
value

(iii) **Transient condition part way
through smoothing period**

Correct relative
motion of target

Incorrect true
motion of
observing vessel

True vector gives
incorrect indication
of target's true
course and speed

Incorrect
true motion
of target

Relative vector
correctly indicates
target's relative
motion

(iv) **Vectors settle after one full smoothing
period of steady state conditions**

Figure 9.11(b)   Where true track storage is used

PPCs would appear here if own ship's speed used in their calculation is greater than the correct value

B_1

B

B_2

A_1

A

A_2

PPCs would appear here if own ship's speed used in their calculation is less than the correct value

Figure 9.12 The effect on the PPC of a speed error

A, target passing astern, correct speed used

B, target passing ahead, correct speed used

A_1, B_1, PPC appears here if a speed greater than the correct value is used

A_2, B_2, PPC appears here if a speed less than the correct value is used

9.6.4.2   Errors in course input

The behaviour of the collision point when an error in the course is input is too complex to allow definition of a pattern. If the error occurs only in the calculation and does not appear in the position of the heading marker, the collision point could appear on the heading marker in a miss situation. More dangerously, a collision point could appear off the heading marker in a collision situation. When the same error appears in both heading marker and calculation, as might occur due to a gyro compass error, the collision case will always show the collision point on the heading marker.

Similarly, if a miss distance exists, the collision point will not be on the heading marker.

9.7   Errors of interpretation

These errors are not within the system but are those likely to be made by the operator through misunderstanding, inexperience or casual observation.

9.7.1   Errors with vector systems

In the case of vector systems, the most common mistakes arise because the observer, either from lack of concentration due to stress of the moment or through lack of knowledge, confuses relative and true vectors (as in the collision between *Norwegian Dream* and *Ever Decent*). Typical blunders are:

(a)   measuring the CPA as the tangential distance at which the true vector passes the origin;

(b)   mistaking the direction of the relative vector for the target's true heading.

A further source of error sometimes occurs where the observer runs out the true vector to see the dynamic development of the situation (which in itself is a useful ploy) to assist in determining collision avoidance strategy, but deduces the point of closest approach as being where the vectors cross. This is of course only correct in the collision case. Attempts to find the passing distance by trial and error using this technique also frequently mislead the observer and are not necessary when the CPA is so easily available from other sources.

Some manufacturers fit spring-loaded switches or hold down buttons to ensure that the equipment always reverts to either true or relative vector mode in an attempt to reduce the chance of misinterpretation of the data in this way.

Other common errors include the confusion of real and trial values of CPA and omitting to set in the correct trial speed where analogue controls are provided (see Section 4.4.3). Where the displayed vectors and history of a different type are simultaneously presented, the difference between the two may be mistaken for a manoeuvre by the target.

During the second and third minute of tracking, the vectors will be stabilizing and care must be taken not to be misled into assuming that this is an alteration by the target or that it is yawing.

9.7.2 Errors with PPC and PAD systems

In the case of PPCs and PADs, the commonest mistakes arise when attempting to interpolate or extrapolate data from the display. Typical errors arise because of failure to appreciate the following:

1 The line joining the target to the collision point is not a time-related vector and does not indicate speed (see Figure 9.13(a)).
2 The collision point gives no indication of miss distance.
3 Changes in collision point positions do not necessarily indicate a change in the target's true course or speed.
4 The area of danger does not change symmetrically with a change in the selected miss distance (see Figure 9.13(c)).
5 The collision point is not necessarily at the centre of the danger area (see Figure 9.13(d)).

It is always important to realize that the areas of danger generated on the screen apply only to own ship and the target, and that they do not always give warning of a mutual threat between two targets. If two areas of danger overlap, it is reasonable to suppose that the two targets involved will also pass each other within the stated miss distance (see Figure 9.13(f)), but separated danger areas do not imply safe passing between the targets. Two targets may eventually have a close passing although their danger areas, as applied to own ship, appear to be well separated (see Figure 9.13(e)).

9.7.2.1 Resumption of course

Where a 'chained' bearing cursor is available and the chain divisions are an indication of time, care must

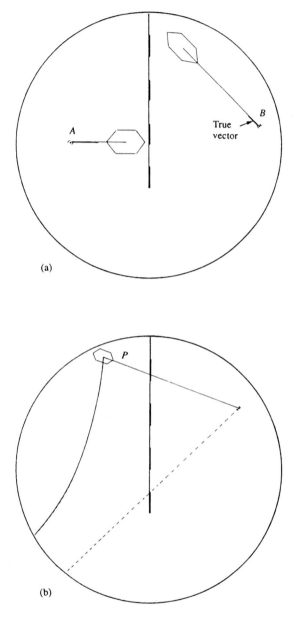

(a)

(b)

Figure 9.13 Errors of interpretation
(a) Target *A* is faster and target *B* is slower than own ship, despite appearances
    Note Vectors will show this
(b) The solid line shows the track of the PPC from *P*. The apparent track of the echo is shown by the broken line

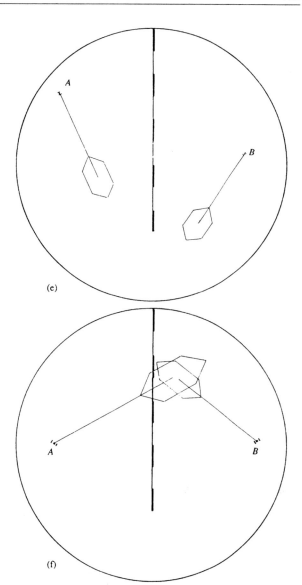

Figure 9.13 (*Continued*)

(c)   The broken line shows the PAD for 2 miles. The solid line shows the PAD for 1 mile

(d)   The PPC is not at *A*, the centre of the hexagon

(e)   Targets *A* and *B* will collide, although this is not apparent from the display

(f)   Targets *A* and *B* will not collide, although they may pass within the miss distance

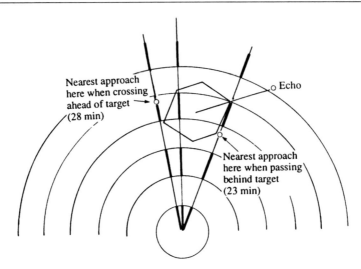

Figure 9.14 The misleading effect of using the bearing cursor to
determine the time to resume course
Note There are four intervals to the point of crossing ahead and five
intervals to the point of crossing astern, but nearest approaches occur,
as indicated, at 4.9 and 3.6 intervals, respectively

be exercised in the measurement of time to resume
course. As shown in Figure 9.14, the marker correctly indicates the time own ship will cross ahead
and astern on the target track, but the time at
which the required miss distance occurs cannot be
determined.

9.7.3 The misleading effect of afterglow

Because the vector mode (i.e. relative or true) is not
necessarily the same as the radar presentation which
has been selected, vectors and afterglow trails may not
match. When true vectors are selected on a relative-
motion presentation, the vectors and the afterglow will
not correlate. When relative vectors are selected while
using a true-motion presentation, the true afterglow
will not match the relative vector.

9.7.4 Accuracy of the presented data

Over-reliance on, and failure to appreciate inaccuracies in, presented data which has been derived

from imperfect inputs should be avoided at all costs.
It must always be borne in mind that a vec-
tor/PAD/alphanumeric read-out is not absolutely
accurate, just because it has been produced by a
computer, no matter how many microprocessors it
may boast. An indication by the ARPA or ATA that a
target will pass one cable clear of own ship should not
be regarded as justification for standing-on into such
a situation.

The errors given in Table 9.2 are quite typical and
should always be allowed for.

9.7.5 Missed targets

An automatic acquisition system may totally fail
to detect and acquire a target of vital importance,
for one of a number of reasons. Similarly, it may
also drop or cancel a fading target. In the latter
case, the target may subsequently be re-acquired and
present a course and speed which may indicate that
the target has manoeuvred when, in fact, the track
is new and has not yet established its long term
accuracy.

10 Ancillary equipment

Whereas, in the past, the radar/ARPA equipment was essentially a standalone module and could, apart from cross-checking, be considered in relative isolation, this is no longer the case. Now that virtually all data is digitized prior to display, it has become possible and to some extent desirable for the display of data to be integrated (see Section 10.4). For this reason, some insight into the way other major data sources interact with the radar/ARPA/ATA system is included here.

10.1 Global navigation satellite systems (GNSS)

With the availability of artificial earth satellites and highly accurate clocks, it was soon recognized that there was the potential for a satellite-based global navigation system. At first, the 'Transit' system was developed in the United States. This was basically a hyperbolic system, with the ship's position being derived from a series of measurements obtained from a single satellite. With the advance of technology and the US requirement for a 24-hour high precision position fixing system for military purposes, the global positioning system (GPS) was developed and the Transit system discontinued. It is not intended to discuss GNSS systems to any great depth here but rather to consider the manner in which they interact with the radar/ARPA/ATA equipment. Where a deeper understanding of a particular GNSS is required, readers should consult a more specialized text. The American GPS will be discussed here as being typical of a satellite system from which positional data is derived.

10.1.1 Global positioning system (GPS)

The first experimental GPS satellite was launched in 1978, but the full system was only declared operational with 18 satellites in 1994. The system comprises three segments, viz. the tracking and control segment; the satellite or space segment; and the user segment.

10.1.1.1 The tracking and control segment

In general, the overall control and operation of the system is in the hands of the United States Air Force who monitor the performance of the satellites via a series of ground tracking stations around the world. They also update the information transmitted by the satellites and from time to time correct the satellite positions to ensure that their orbits remain within the desired tolerances. The whole of the system is supervised from a master control station in the USA. They also launch new satellites to replace those that have come to the end of their useful life or have malfunctioned (see Figure 10.1).

10.1.1.2 The space segment

This is now based on a theoretical constellation of some 24 satellites in six near-circular orbits, each orbit being inclined at an angle of 55° to the equator and separated by some 60° in longitude. Within each orbit, the four satellites are spaced at 90°. The relationship between satellites in consecutive orbits is that as one satellite is crossing the equator heading northwards, the one in the orbit 'ahead' will have crossed the equator 60° to the east and will now be some 15° to the east along its track and north of the equator.

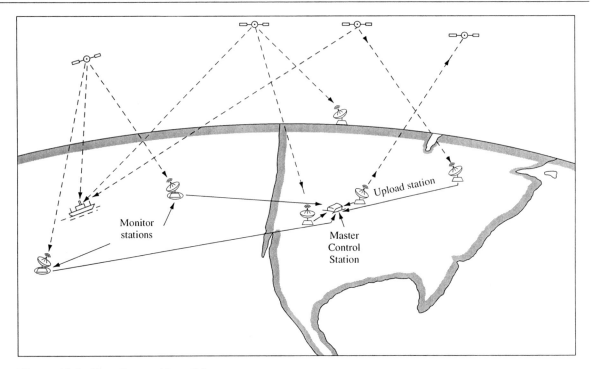

Figure 10.1 Overall supervision of the system

The maximum declination of each orbit is 55° north and south (see Figures 10.2 and 10.3). The orbits have a mean altitude of 20 200 km, which is designed to result in the satellite completing two orbits in precisely one sidereal day. While the satellites move along the orbits, the Earth will rotate within this 'bird cage'. There is a tendency for the orbits to be perturbed but this is corrected by the master control station (MCS) as necessary.

For practical reasons, the constellation has been developed over a period of years and in a climate of advancing technology. Satellites have been replaced and in most orbits, there is at least one spare satellite. Consequently, the actual constellation is not precisely as described above but the basic principle, i.e. to have at least four visible and usable satellites available worldwide at all times, is being sought.

Each satellite carries a number of high precision 'clocks' on board with all clocks in the system synchronized to a common standard. All satellites trans-

mit signals on two frequencies in the 'L'-band – L1 = 1575.42 MHz and L2 = 1227.6 MHz, derived from a basic clock frequency of 10.23 MHz, both of which are uniquely coded to provide satellite identification and orbital data and also a signal which provides the means for signal transit time to be measured. Currently only the L1 frequency is available for civilian users.

10.1.1.3 The user segment (see Performance Specifications Section 11.3.1)

As each satellite proceeds along its orbit, it transmits information regarding its identity, position and also 'timing pulses' which allow a receiver to determine the time taken for a particular pulse to travel from the satellite to the receiver. With knowledge of the speed of the pulse, the range from the satellite can be determined. Then, using the transmitted data, the satellite's position can be fixed at that instant and using the distance from the observer, a position sphere

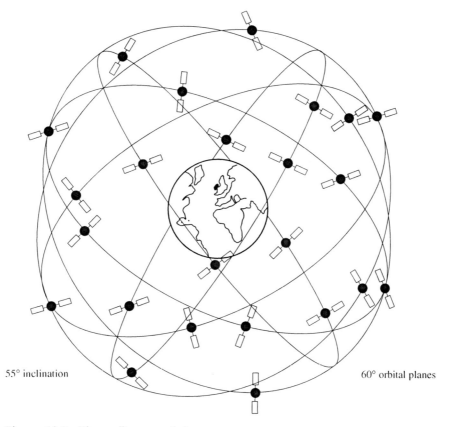

55° inclination   60° orbital planes

Figure 10.2 The satellite constellation

around the satellite can be defined. If similar measurements are made from a second satellite, the intersection of the two gives a circular ring or position circle in space. The position sphere derived from a third satellite cuts this position circle in two places. Given that one of these positions will be in the reaches of outer space and can be discarded, the receiver's position can therefore effectively be calculated in three dimensions from three satellites.

The timing signals have two levels of potential precision. The higher level, or Precision code (P code) is primarily intended for military and other specialized users and is available on both L1 and L2, while the Coarse/Acquisition Code (C/A code) is currently freely available to all users on L1 only.

10.1.2   The measurement of range and time from the satellite

The timing signal transmitted by the satellite can be thought of as a continuous train of pulses having a unique format. Within the user's receiver, having identified the satellite from its navigation message, an identical train of pulses relating to that satellite is generated which is then time adjusted until it matches the incoming signal. The amount of this time adjustment is a measure of the signal travel time and hence the range from the satellite is calculated.

All this presupposes that the clock in the user's receiver is as accurate as the atomic clocks in the satellites. This is patently not true as the majority of receivers are designed to be low cost, portable

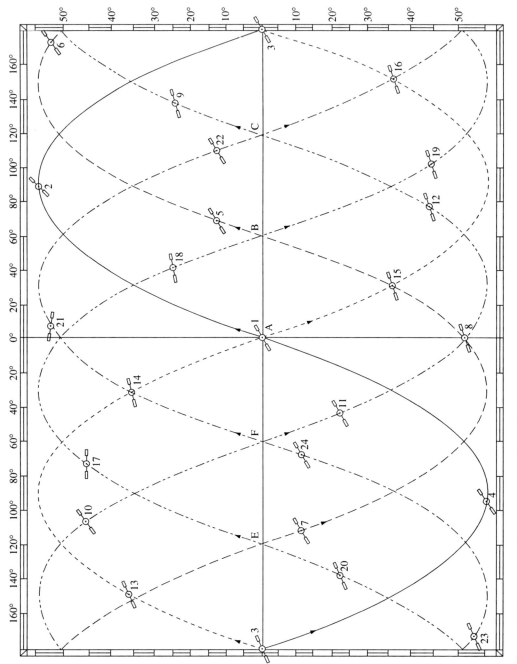

Figure 10.3 Mercator diagram of the satellite orbits

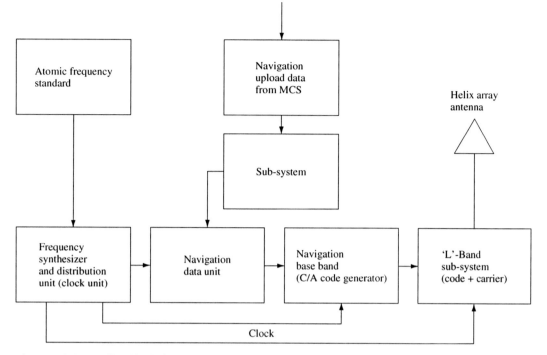

Figure 10.4 Satellite block diagram

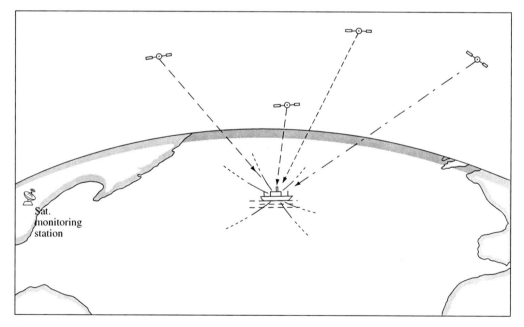

Figure 10.5 The ranging principle

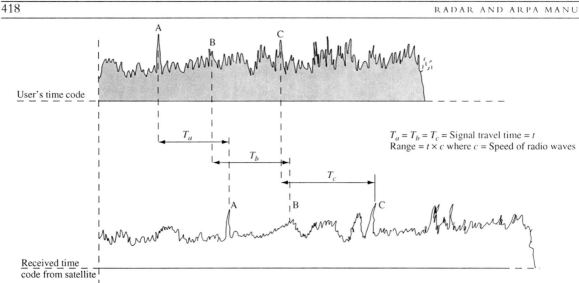

Figure 10.6 Time signal matching

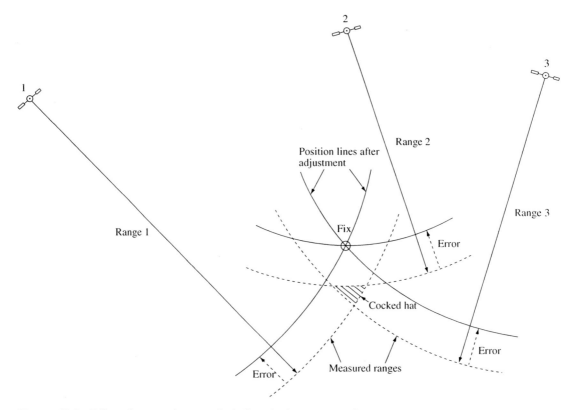

Figure 10.7 Effect of systematic errors (including time) on measured ranges

and robust. However, the error in ranges due to any receiver clock error will be the same for all observations. Also, the system is specified to be able to receive four satellites worldwide (not the theoretical three) so that the positional errors in three dimensions and time can all be resolved very accurately. This provision of the receiver clock error also means that very accurate GPS time is maintained at the receiver, which is also useful for certain users. In simplistic terms, three satellites are required for an accurate 3-D fix; the fourth is required for accurate measurement of time, although it also resolves the theoretical ambiguity in position noted in Section 10.1.1.3.

10.1.3   The position fix

The angular movement of the satellites along their orbits is comparatively slow and with a constellation of some 24 satellites, it is intended that there should be at least four usable satellites above the preferred altitude of 10° from the horizon at any one time. It is then necessary for the receiving equipment to analyse the geometry and select four satellites whose position lines are expected to give the most accurate position. Included in the navigational data portion of the satellite's transmission are details relating to the complete constellation which makes it possible to analyse

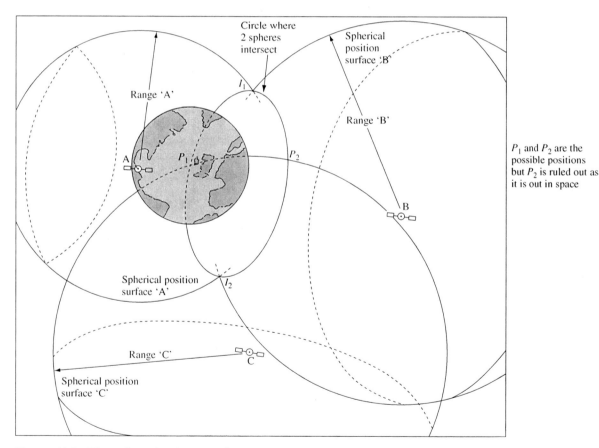

Figure 10.8   Three-dimensional position fix

the geometry of the available satellites and select the four which will give the best angle of cut for the position spheres and which give the best quality signals. In particular, the use of low altitude satellites is avoided whenever possible, due to the probability of significant atmospheric errors (see Section 10.1.5). If only three satellites are available, many receivers go into 2-D mode where the receiver's height is estimated from previous observations or entered by the user.

10.1.4   User equipment and display of data

10.1.4.1   Switching on and setting up

When first switched on, the pre-tuned receiver locks on to any satellite and its navigational message is used

to determine which satellites are available for use in that area and which are to be preferred. The preferred satellites are locked onto, their ranges determined and the position of the observing equipment fixed.

10.1.4.2   Continuity – transfer to other satellites with time

With the passing of time, the user equipment will transfer from a satellite which is being used to one whose position is navigationally more favourable either through its altitude being better, improved angle of cut of position line or higher signal quality.

10.1.4.3   Frequency of update of position

This is to all intents and purposes continuous, automatic and seamless. The whole operation after

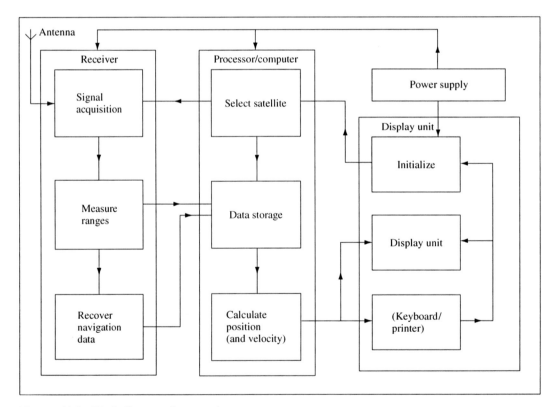

Figure 10.9 Block diagram of user equipment

switch-on, i.e. satellite acquisition, lock-on, analysis of data, timing to determine ranges and the derivation of position as well as continual assessment of the changing circumstances, continues without the operator's intervention.

10.1.4.4 *Output of position co-ordinates*

As a first choice, positions are given in latitude/longitude co-ordinates which relate to the Earth as defined by the World Geodetic System 1984 (WGS84), and for relative navigation this is sufficient. Where it is necessary to relate the output position to a navigational chart which is based on some other datum, there is usually a facility for the user to enter the name of the datum into the receiver which will then make the necessary adjustments to the output readings. Where positions are being automatically transferred to an ECDIS (see Sections 10.2.3 and 10.2.4) it is essential that the correct datum has been fed in. It is also necessary to check regularly that the correct datum is being used. It is required (see IMO Performance Specification 11.3.1) that '...the display should indicate that co-ordinate conversion is being performed,

and should identify the co-ordinate system in which the position is expressed'.

10.1.5 Accuracy and errors

The positional accuracy that is being achieved by civil marine users is exceptionally high compared with earlier position fixing methods. Nonetheless, it is important to appreciate why the quoted accuracy figures might be compromised.

10.1.5.1 *Sources of error*

Atmospheric conditions. As the signals travel through the various layers of the atmosphere, the path followed and the medium through which they pass will affect their speed and will therefore affect the calculated range from the satellite.

Signal path. The time taken to pass through the various layers and therefore the delaying effect will be different, depending on the altitude of the satellite.

It is necessary to make some estimates based on models of the atmosphere through which the satellite signal has passed. In equipment which is capable of receiving at more than one frequency, it is

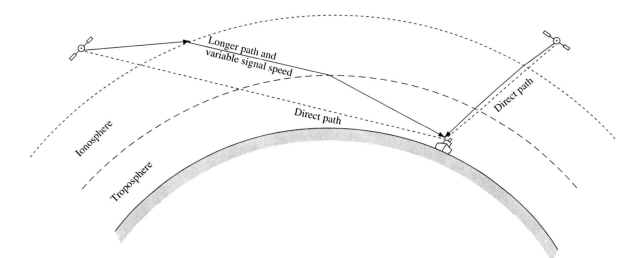

Figure 10.10 Effect of signal path

possible to determine a more accurate estimate of the value of error due to atmospheric conditions by using a more sophisticated error model. Effectively civilian users have access only to the single L1 frequency, although this situation is changing (see Section 10.1.7.3).

- *Ionosphere.* Errors due to this source are now to some extent predictable and can be modelled and applied.
- *Troposphere.* Errors arising as the signals pass through this layer of the atmosphere can vary widely and will depend on the existing weather conditions – in particular, water vapour. Very little can be done in practice to eliminate this source of error.

Multi-path. With range being measured to such a high precision, signals arriving as a result of reflections from nearby surfaces on the vessel or from the sea will have an effect on the required signals which arrive by the direct path. Multi-path signals will arrive later than those that arrive directly. In any event, all the signals are very weak and where signals arrive out of phase, the timing signal can become undetectable. Note that signals suffer phase reversal at each reflection.

Relativity. According to Einstein, as a clock travels in different gravity fields and at speeds that are a significant proportion of the speed of light, it will tend to slow down. Corrections for this effect are taken care of in each satellite's transmission.

10.1.5.2 Cross-checking with other systems

It cannot be stressed too strongly that total reliance should not be placed on a single position fixing system and GPS is no different. In spite of its reputation,

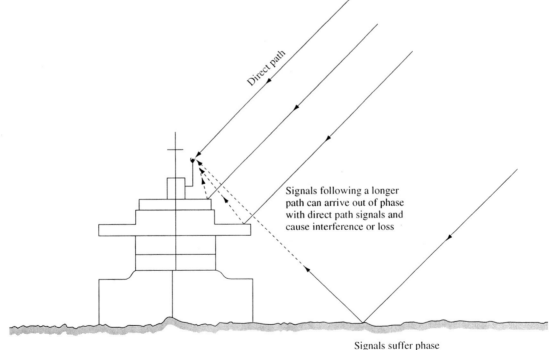

Figure 10.11 Multi-path signals

cross-checking GPS derived positions against those derived by other position fixing methods, e.g. visual or radar means, is essential. Examples have already occurred where signal loss or system malfunction has resulted in the receiver reverting to dead reckoning mode and although this was indicated on the display, its significance was missed.

10.1.5.3 Loss of signal

There are a number of possibilities why this might occur. Typical is that as time progresses or after an alteration of the ship's course, a satellite signal might be temporarily obstructed by the ship's funnel or by some other part of the ship's structure. When this occurs, the receiver will endeavour to select another satellite and use its signal to replace the one that has become unreliable. Not all receivers indicate that lock has been lost or that transfer has taken place.

10.1.5.4 System malfunction

The satellite constellation's health is being continually monitored by the ground tracking stations, and at any sign of trouble this is communicated to the master control station and action is taken to resolve and rectify the problem. However, satellites are not always in sight of the monitoring stations and they can only be corrected when they are in sight of the master control station. Both detection and correction processes may take some time (see also Section 10.1.5.7 – Warnings) and there have been documented instances when significant outages have occurred.

10.1.5.5 Expected accuracies

When first set up, the signals available to civil users (using the single L1 frequency and C/A code) were deliberately downgraded. This downgrade was referred to as selective availability (SA) and ensured that accuracies of the order of 100 metres (95 per cent accuracy) were the norm. In 2000, selective availability was discontinued and long-term average accuracies of around 35 metres (95 per cent accuracy) should therefore have been be achieved by a

24 satellite constellation. However, the system currently has more satellites (usually around 30) than the minimum constellation and accuracies of 10 to 15 metres (95 per cent accuracy) are now considered typical under standard conditions. This satellite over-population is not guaranteed to continue. It occurs now to provide redundancy for the relatively large number of satellites that are near or past their designed lifespan.

10.1.5.6 Quality of fix or dilution of precision (DOP)

This is a concept that is essentially intended to give the user a confidence figure that will indicate the reliance that he can place on the position that is being displayed. The figure is based on the geometry of the position fix (see Figure 10.12). The minimum attainable DOP which indicates a perfect fix is 1. The IMO Performance Standards require that the Horizontal Dilution of Precision HDOP ≤ 4 (see Section 11.3.1).

Note   DOP may be given for the horizontal plane – HDOP – or the vertical plane – VDOP – or in three dimensions – Position Dilution of Position (PDOP).

10.1.5.7 Warnings (see also Section 11.3.1 – Warnings and status indications)

The receiver is required to give a warning within 5 seconds if the HDOP has been exceeded, i.e. > 4 or if a new position has not been calculated for more than 1 second, in which case, the time and position of the last valid fix must be displayed, with a clear indication of what has occurred and a warning of loss of position.

When DGPS (see Section 10.1.6) is in operation, there must be an indication that DGPS signals are being received and that DGPS corrections are being applied to the displayed position. There must also be a display of DGPS integrity status and alarms (if any) plus any DGPS text messages.

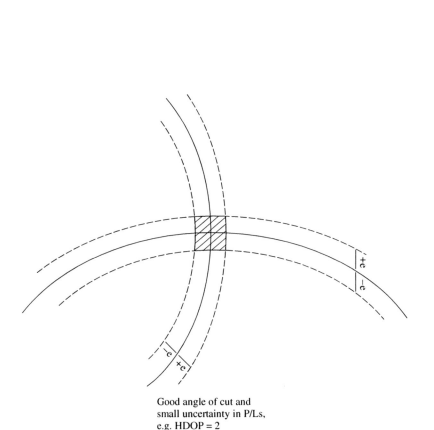

Good angle of cut and
small uncertainty in P/Ls,
e.g. HDOP = 2

Poor angle of cut and
same uncertainty in P/Ls,
e.g. HDOP = 8 – Unacceptable

Figure 10.12 Dilution of precision

10.1.5.8 Vulnerability of GPS signals

GPS signals are very low power when received on the Earth's surface and the received signal strength is about the level of background noise. The code system allows receivers to pick out an individual satellite from the transmission of other satellites and background noise all operating at the same frequency. However, if the interfering signals are powerful enough, they will swamp the GPS signals and render the receiver ineffective.

GPS jammers are widely available in military circles and there have been a number of occurrences of unintentional interferences that cause GPS 'blackspots'. Many of the causes of unintentional interference have been traced to faulty or illegal radio equipment and they usually occur in inland regions. However, there has been at least one occasion when harbours and harbour entrances were affected. There have also been a number of GPS blackspots that have not been satisfactorily explained.

It is also understood that GPS 'spoofers' exist that give false satellite signals and would enable the receiver to give a false but believable position on a user's display.

In summary, although the GPS has proved to be a very reliable and secure device, it is theoretically very vulnerable to attack and unintentional interference. The user is advised not to rely on it uniquely.

10.1.6 Differential global positioning system (DGPS)

10.1.6.1 System principle

The position of a shore-based antenna is accurately surveyed and its geo-co-ordinates calculated. The differences given by satellite fixes and the surveyed position are transmitted as corrections to be applied to positions obtained by vessels using GPS in that area. In order to receive these signals, a DGPS receiver is required. The application of these corrections is normally automatic.

The UK government has set up a public system of DGPS stations using the sites and frequencies previously used for marine RDF beacons. The US Coastguard has done much the same on the US coasts and commercial organizations can provide corrections in many areas for a fee. Wide area DGPS networks are under development to provide continuous DGPS corrections over continental areas using communication satellites.

10.1.6.2 Potential accuracies using DGPS

Using DGPS equipment, accuracies in the order of 5 metres are expected and even better results have been reported. With such high precision, it is important to appreciate that it is the position of the receiving antenna that is being displayed. Updating of the direct signal is typically within 15 seconds. The improvement in accuracy of DGPS over GPS is irrelevant for most navigators now that SA (see Section 10.1.5.5) has been removed. However, DGPS has a large advantage over GPS in that there is immediate notification of system malfunction, unlike standalone GPS (see Section 10.1.5.4). Thus many users are using DGPS because of the gain in reliability due to external monitoring and not particularly because of its increased accuracy.

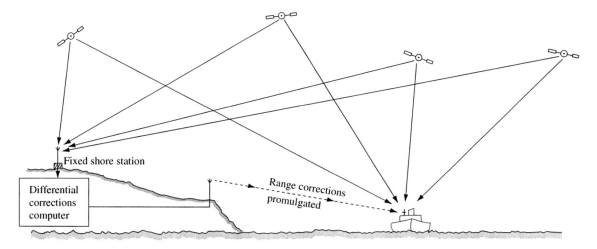

Figure 10.13 Principle of DGPS

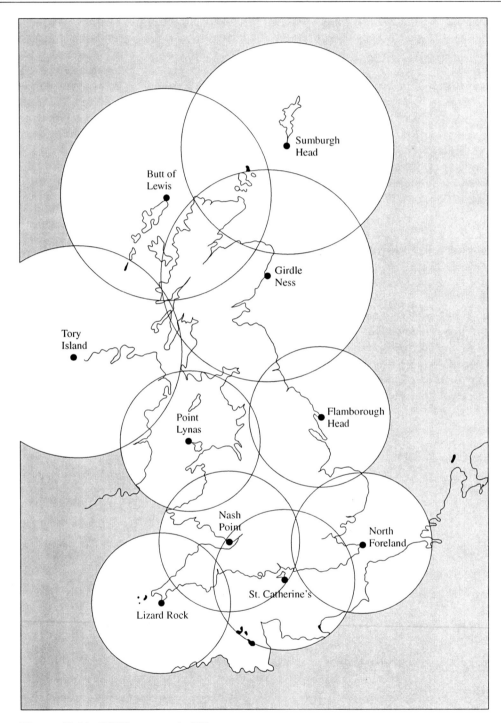

Figure 10.14 DGPS coverage in UK waters

10.1.7 Other global navigation satellite system developments

The GPS is entirely under the control of the US military. It is fully operational, is freely available and is expected to remain so for the foreseeable future. Enhancements to GPS are being implemented and other GNSS systems are available or about to be available.

10.1.7.1 GLONASS

This is a system operated by the Russian military and is similar in concept to GPS, being based on a nominal number of 24 satellites, but financial constraints have resulted in considerable delays in full implementation.

The orbit configuration is three equally spaced orbits, inclined at 64.8° to the equator. Each orbit is designed to have eight equally spaced satellites. The orbit altitude is slightly less than GPS at 19 130 km, which gives an orbit period of 11.25 hours.

The GLONASS satellites transmit on different frequencies, unlike the GPS system, which shares a single frequency with different satellite codes. Note that GLONASS satellites that are 180° apart can use the same frequency, which makes slightly more efficient use of the frequency spectrum. If fully implemented, GLONASS should achieve similar accuracies to GPS. One advantage of the system is that GLONASS satellites can communicate with each other and that satellite errors can therefore be corrected even when the satellite is not visible to the master control station.

It is possible to have a combined GPS/GLONASS receiver which means that the relatively few operational GLONASS satellites that are in operation can be used to augment the GPS satellite coverage and would mean that slightly higher DOPs and more accurate positions would generally be obtainable than without GLONASS. The receiver would of course have to deal with the fact that the GLONASS system uses different time and datum systems.

10.1.7.2 Galileo

This is a satellite system for navigation and communications, planned and led by the European Union (EU) with a projected completion date of 2008. Unlike GPS and GLONASS, it will be civilian controlled and the project has partnerships with a number of countries outside the EU. It also plans to charge some users for some of its high quality and specialist services. Although primarily a GNSS for navigation it is expected to have some communications facilities including use by emergency and distress systems.

The latest proposals have a 30-satellite system (27 satellites plus three active spares). There are three separate orbits (10 satellites in each) inclined at 56° to the equator with an altitude of 23 616 km and an orbit period of about 14 hours. Every satellite will transmit on several frequencies with E5A (1176.45 MHz), E5B (1207.14 MHz) and E2 (1575.42 MHz) being planned for public use. Another feature of the Galileo system is the large number of ground stations to control and monitor the satellites, i.e. more than provided by GLONASS and GPS.

The system plans to offer a number of services including a 'free to user' service of similar accuracy to GPS. A single frequency receiver should achieve 25 metres (95 per cent accuracy) while a dual frequency receiver should achieve 5 metres (95 per cent accuracy). Higher accuracy 'fee-paying' systems will also be available.

Galileo operates like GPS using satellite codes and is thus able to use very similar frequencies to GPS. Galileo is proposing to adopt different datum and time systems to GPS, but the differences in datum are expected to be minimal and measured in centimetres. It has been intended from the outset that Galileo and GPS will have a degree of compatibility and receivers capable of receiving both systems will be relatively easy to manufacture.

10.1.7.3 Improvements to GPS

The US military is currently implementing two main improvements in the GPS service for civilian users as well as a new military service (M code) not for civilian use. The process is a slow one because the improvements are fitted to satellites that have been either launched relatively recently or are still in reserve on the ground. Each improved service will therefore only become properly operational when a minimum of about 18 improved satellites is in orbit. It is an ironic fact that the reliability and longevity of the older satellites is actually holding up further progress.

The first civilian improvement is to open up L2 to civilian users. They are not allowed to use the P-code so the modification is to transmit the equivalent of the C/A code as well as the P-code on the L2 frequency. The addition of observations on a second frequency will enable better modelling of the atmospheric errors and hence a more accurate fix achieved (see Section 10.1.5.1). Moreover, the new L2 Civil Code (L2C) will be inherently more accurate and more reliable in weak reception conditions than the C/A code used on the L1 frequency. The L2C code has only been fitted to satellites launched since 2003 and is expected to achieve a working constellation by 2008 and a full constellation by around 2010.

The second improvement is the addition of a third frequency, 1176.45 MHz, termed L5. As well as potentially allowing more sophisticated atmospheric error modelling from using up to three frequencies simultaneously, the civilian code available on L5 will be a more sophisticated signal allowing higher accuracy and reliability than both the L2C and L1 C/A codes. Satellites with the L5 frequency are expected to be launched as replacements in 2005, with a working constellation by 2012 and a full constellation by 2015.

10.1.8   Inter-relationship of GNSS with radar

Where radar equipment is fitted with mapping facilities, it may be possible to feed co-ordinates to the radar in latitude/longitude. Where this can be done, it is usual to be able to automatically feed the GNSS derived position of the ship to the radar and thereby fix the latitude/longitude of radar derived features on the display, thus aiding identification (see also cross-checking, Section 10.1.5.2).

The availability of high quality GNSS derived positions has led to the decline in using the radar as a navigational tool. Obviously positions derived from radar are not as accurate as GNSS, but the radar remains a good source of secondary navigational information

that is independent of any external transmission and external control. The good navigator will use the radar to check the accuracy of GNSS positions, but the concern is that the less professional navigators who over-rely on the 'easiest' positional source will ignore the radar as a navigational tool and thus leave themselves exposed to increased risk in the event of a GNSS failure.

10.1.9   Inter-relationship of GNSS with ECDIS (see Sections 10.2 and 11.3.2)

GNSS equipment is able to supply position, as well as (optionally) Course Over the Ground (COG) and Speed Over the Ground (SOG) to a digital interface which can then provide an input to an ECDIS.

Radar image and ARPA information may also be added to the ECDIS but should not degrade the chart information and be clearly distinguishable from it. Where this information is added, the data should match in scale and orientation. It should be possible to remove this radar data from the ECDIS by a single operator action.

10.2   Electronic charts (ECDIS)

Electronic charts are an example of a Geographical Information System (GIS). A GIS has a database of geographical information that can be filtered and arranged in a display for the convenience of the user.

For many hundreds of years the navigator has used paper-based charts. It is only relatively recently that a computer-based alternative has become practical due to the improvements in and affordability of two computing related technologies. The first is ability to store and process large amounts of data and the second is the display technology that is able to show data to an adequate resolution and large enough view.

The standards for an approved electronic chart system were developed through IMO and IHO (International Hydrographic Organization) in the 1980s.

The new system was called ECDIS or Electronic Chart Display and Information System. The standards for ECDIS are very high. The opportunity was taken to:

- set electronic and hydrographic data storage standards to allow easy interchange of information between hydrographic services and also update ships at sea,
- set minimum hydrographic standards of accuracy and reliability, and
- set a common chart datum (basically the one used by GPS).

IMO ECDIS standards came into force in 1996 and it was then theoretically possible for a vessel coming under SOLAS regulations to replace its approved paper chart system with an ECDIS system. The reality was that although manufacturers rushed out ECDIS software display systems for ships, there was no approved ECDIS chart data. ECDIS data has been slow to emerge due firstly to the time it takes to convert existing chart data into ECDIS format, but more particularly due to the need to resurvey hydrographically many areas to the new ECDIS standards.

10.2.1 Vector charts

The data format of ECDIS is vector storage. In this system, the ECDIS data is stored in data tables of separate information. Thus there are data tables of buoys, navigation aids, digitized coastlines, sounding lines, text labels, etc. Each item is stored with details of geographic location, its characteristics and the range of chart scales at which it should be shown. When data on a specific area, at a specific scale, is requested for display, the system selects the data in the requested area, of the right type for display. Important points to note are:

- The chart data shown on the chart display can be manipulated to remove data not required by the navigator and which may be cluttering up his screen. There is no need to show all data available in a specific area. Thus information on lights could be removed from the display if the vessel is conducting a daylight transit. The IMO standards place careful limits on the information that can be removed by the navigator and also what should be displayed. For instance all information on depths need not be shown, but there must be a minimum safety contour, which shows safe/unsafe water for own ship.
- The vector chart can easily change scale or zoom. As the navigator zooms in or out, the data displayed will change according to scale parameters stored with each item of data. Thus a buoy off the Liverpool Bar will not be shown when viewing the whole Atlantic Ocean, but as the navigator zooms into the Liverpool region, the buoy will appear. All depths or soundings have minimum and maximum scale parameters so that as the navigator zooms into an area, more soundings appear so that an appropriate density of soundings is maintained. It will be appreciated that the attachment of these scale factors is a highly skilled and laborious job for a marine cartographer and this is one reason why it has taken such a long time to get approved ECDIS data published, even when the hydrographic data was up to ECDIS standard.
- The responsibility for obtaining and maintaining approved ECDIS data is divided up between different nations and all data is stored centrally by the IHO. Participating nations can then obtain approved ECDIS data from other areas through the IHO.
- Vessels that are required by SOLAS to carry an approved chart navigation system can replace their paper chart system with an approved ECDIS system which uses approved ECDIS vector data. However, it should be noted that there must be a backup system as well as regulations on installation, training and the provision of regular chart corrections.
- Vector ECDIS displays are required to show chart datum soundings in a similar way to paper and raster charts. The predicted tidal height is shown as a separate figure, when available.

10.2.2 Raster charts

An alternative method of storage is raster storage. Raster data is stored in picture format. In marine terms, the

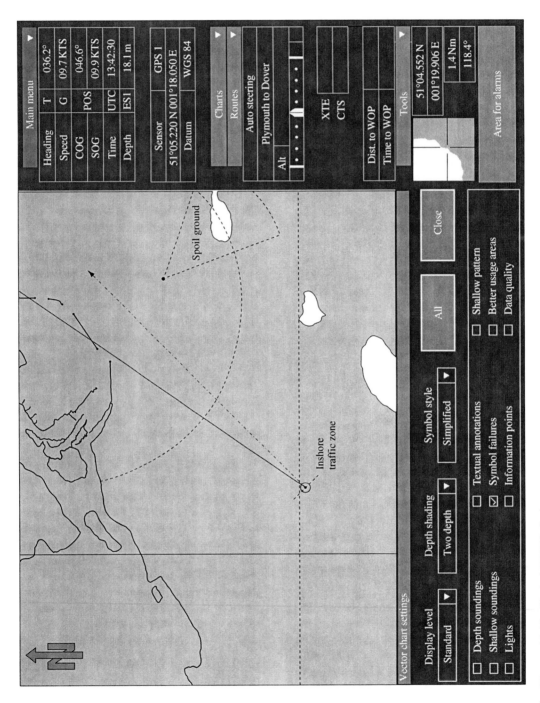

Figure 10.15 Typical ECDIS display

paper chart is scanned into a digital file using the same techniques as a photocopier or fax machine. The picture to be stored is divided into lines of very small dots or pixels. The scanner decides what the colour number of the original document was for that specific pixel, and it is the colour number that is stored for every pixel on the document. Principal points to note are:

- Raster data on display cannot be manipulated by the user. Effectively we have a photocopy of a paper chart on screen. It is not possible to suppress chart data.
- A raster chart should be displayed at the correct scale on screen as the original paper chart from which it was derived. Some chart displays do allow a limited zoom function, but the navigator should note that the system simply magnifies or shrinks the chart. At extreme zoom levels the chart becomes unreadable and/or the amount of data shown is inappropriate for the scale. Thus systems which allow zoom, display warnings that the chart is being shown underscale or overscale, as appropriate. The navigator can of course select another chart of different scale if one is available. This process is similar to using paper charts, but much faster as courses and positions will normally be transferred automatically.
- In the western world, only two organizations maintain a full worldwide paper chart system; the chart authorities of the United Kingdom and the United States. Both these countries have produced raster charts based on their existing paper charts and effectively these are also the only two raster systems that provide comprehensive and approved raster electronic chart systems. These systems were available before ECDIS received IMO approval in 1996.
- Approved raster data can be used in ECDIS systems where ECDIS vector data is not available. This is sometimes termed a 'dual-fuel' system. However, IMO has determined that raster chart data is not an acceptable replacement for paper charts. The official position is that the paper chart is the approved navigation system and the raster electronic chart is an aid to navigation. Therefore when the system switches to raster data, because of lack of vector data, the prime means of navigation switches to

the paper chart. However, some administrations are allowing a significant reduction in the number of paper charts carried, when the raster chart system is used in conjunction with the appropriate training, backup, installation and correction system.

10.2.3 Comparison between paper and electronic charts

The biggest single advantage of electronic charts over paper systems to the professional navigator is the ease of correction. Both raster and vector systems allow for automatic electronic correction of the charts onboard, with no work on the part of the navigator. This means that the corrections are inserted exactly as intended by the marine cartographer. The potential labour reductions for a ship with a worldwide portfolio of 2000–3000 charts are also significant. It is estimated that there are 10 000–15 000 manual corrections to be made by the navigator in a typical year for a worldwide paper portfolio of this size. The electronic corrections also lend themselves to electronic transmission so that corrections can be passed immediately to the ship, which is a vast improvement on a traditional paper-based system that often took months to reach a ship by post, although paper chart small corrections can now be transmitted electronically and printed out onboard. The electronic systems also allow the electronic transmission of whole new charts. This could be either because of unexpected passage changes at sea or the issue of a new chart edition when it would usually be impractical to get the chart to the ship at sea in a paper-based system.

Another significant advantage is the ability to easily add extra information, overlaid on top of the electronic chart. This can include routes, notes, links to extra material (pictures, videos, text documents), tidal currents and lines of safety. Moreover this information can be saved as both a permanent record and also brought back from storage for reusing when a vessel undertakes a second transit of the same area in the same direction. The paper chart requires much laborious preparation and rubbing out on every occasion it is used. It will wear out in time and need replacement.

Another pencil saving advantage is that the electronic chart lends itself to electronic fixing methods. GNSS systems or LORAN C systems can feed the position electronically to the chart (see Section 10.1). The improvement over the paper system means that the ship's position is continuously plotted rather than sampled at intervals convenient to the navigator and the possibility of human plotting error is eliminated. There is usually an option to stabilize the chart display on the vessel's position so the chart always shows the area around the current position, i.e. the chart moves past the ship. In these cases the ship does not have to be at the centre of the display, but can be offset to show a feature of land or to see further ahead than astern. There is also a provision to put in the vessel length and breadth so that a scaled ship shape can be displayed when the scale in use is large enough.

There can be an issue with the electronic chart datum being different to the datum of the electronic position, but provided the datum adjustments are known to the navigator, they can easily be adjusted automatically in the electronic plotting (see also Section 10.2.4).

Currently, the main disadvantage of the electronic chart is screen size, although large displays of more than 40 inches are becoming affordable. The minimum size of display for an approved ECDIS system is 21 inches, which provides about a sixth of the coverage area of the traditional paper chart. This is why zooming and panning facilities are useful, together with the ability to have different windows on the chart area open and available for easy viewing.

The other main disadvantage is the reliance on electronic equipment and the need for a power supply. Hence there is a requirement for emergency power supplies and a backup chart system that may be a duplicate system and/or a minimal number of paper charts intended to get a vessel to a pilot station.

10.2.4 Comparison between vector and raster charts

One major advantage of the ECDIS vector system is that the navigator can be assured that all the data is surveyed to an approved standard. The raster (and paper) charts traditionally represent the best available data for an area, which is not quite the same thing.

The main strength of the raster chart system is that approved worldwide portfolios are available from both the United Kingdom and the United States. It will be a long time before the approved ECDIS vector data is available for the whole world, particularly as it will take time to survey the whole world to the required hydrographic standard. However, significant portions of the world are now available in ECDIS vector data, particularly in well-frequented regions.

The ECDIS vector charts are all based on a model of the earth that is the same as the WGS 84 datum, so no corrections are needed when using the American GPS. Raster charts are copied from paper charts that traditionally tended to be based on a local chart datum developed for a particular region. As an example, the British Admiralty paper chart system uses about 300 different chart datums over its worldwide portfolio. However, in their raster electronic chart version (known as ARCS) the corrections are included electronically within approved raster chart data and applied automatically, so the navigator can still use GPS positional data directly without datum conversion. Moreover, as new paper chart editions are produced, the WGS 84 chart datum is being adopted for paper charts, so the theoretical problem is further diminished. For example, all paper and raster charts of the UK region produced by the British Admiralty are now based on WGS 84.

The raster charts have a chart edge, just like the paper chart. The navigator has to change chart or the system will itself decide to change to the next chart. Experienced mariners are already well used to dealing with chart edges and changing charts in the paper-based system. Indeed they often prefer the raster charts to vector charts as they look like the paper product with which they are familiar. ECDIS vector data can be integrated seamlessly together, although currently chart edges do effectively exist when areas without ECDIS coverage are encountered.

Both raster and vector systems are easily correctable by electronic means and while each electronic chart system may have different data storage and computer processing power requirements to cover a particular area in raster or vector format, the actual requirements of either are not significant or expensive by modern computer standards.

A major benefit of the vector system is the potential for an electronic chart to have 'intelligence'. In a vector system, the computer knows that it is a buoy, wreck or coastline ahead and the depth expected. Thus it is possible for the chart to warn the navigator if he is approaching shallow water or a danger, the times at which lights should be picked up or if he has inadvertently laid a course line over a shoal or dangerous wreck. The data stored in a raster system is simply the colours of different dots and the computer would not know if a specific black pixel was part of a buoy or coastline or text.

10.2.5 Unapproved electronic chart data

A number of commercial companies offer unapproved vector data for electronic chart systems. The data first appeared due to the long wait for approved ECDIS data. The standard of this unapproved data is very variable. The companies rarely use original hydrographic data, but usually digitize existing paper charts. They also do not provide a continuous system of chart corrections. Nevertheless there is nothing to stop them being used on small vessels not required to carry any charts or as an 'aid' on larger vessels that still have the paper system as the official navigation system. Electronic charts of this type can sometimes be associated with specialized tasks such as fishing or other underwater activities.

10.2.6 Publications associated with charts

The same regulations that require charts to be carried on ships also require that associated publications be carried. These include tide tables, tidal stream atlases, light lists, radio signal lists and sailing directions. These publications could feasibly be offered in electronic format, which would simplify usage and improve the quality of corrections. Tidal height prediction software

has been available for a while, but the provision of the other information electronically has been much slower in coming. The ideal is an integration of the combined chart and publication information into one large GIS so that the relevant textual information can be derived on a geographic basis from a visual display and be selected as required.

10.2.7 Relationship of ECDIS with radar and ARPA/ATA

The ECDIS Performance Standards (see Section 11.3.2) allow for the display of radar and ARPA information on the ECDIS display. In practice, there are two levels of integration on the display.

The first is the display of ARPA/ATA tracked targets on the ECDIS. These look similar to the symbols/vectors displayed on a standard ARPA/ATA and this can be achieved through a standard NMEA interface (see Section 10.4.4). The advantage of this transfer of data is that the traffic situation can be analysed in the context of the chart's geographical information. This is particularly useful in coastal areas as the flow of traffic around geographical features may not be obvious on the ARPA/ATA screen. These may include shoals, underwater hazards, traffic separation schemes and political boundaries. Charts can cover a larger geographical area than the radar and this can be useful for planning manoeuvres in advance.

It should be noted that AIS information (see Section 10.3) can also be integrated in a similar way to this ARPA/ATA derived information. Some level of data fusion would then be desirable to prevent both systems displaying the same target information (see Section 10.3.2.3) although it is also desirable that the data source(s) is clear.

The second level of radar integration is the superimposition of the radar image onto the ECDIS display. This will allow the easy identification of some radar targets (for example, which target is the buoy and which one is a possible fishing vessel). The radar overlay will also check that the land features or buoy patterns on the ECDIS line up with the radar overlay, which is the quickest and easiest way to check that GNSS, ECDIS, radar and compass are all working correctly.

The navigator must be able to suppress or remove all radar/ARPA/ATA derived information from the ECDIS in one operation (see Section 11.3.2).

There is also the reverse possibility of superimposing selected ECDIS data on the radar display (see Section 11.2.1). Care must be taken that the radar information has priority and is not masked by ECDIS data.

10.3   Automatic identification system (AIS)

With the advent of VHF communication systems at sea, the advantages of bridge to bridge and bridge to shore communications were widely recognized. Unfortunately, outside of pilotage waters and particu-larly in restricted visibility, there was no certainty as to who was talking to whom. While other vessels might be detected by radar, there was no means of positive identification that would allow meaningful communications or dialogue to be established. Regrettably, attempts to establish a dialogue without this positive identification resulted in the too frequently heard and dangerous practice of calling 'Ship on my starboard bow ...', with all its ramifications, especially where traffic was heavy.

The development of transponders provided the impetus to enable the identification of vessels fitted with the appropriate equipment to be established.

The ability of shore stations, particularly where a vessel traffic service (VTS) is provided, to automatically identify vessels within their surveillance area, has long been an ideal and AIS provides just such a facility.

The AIS system is based on transponders located on vessels and other locations that transmit and receive

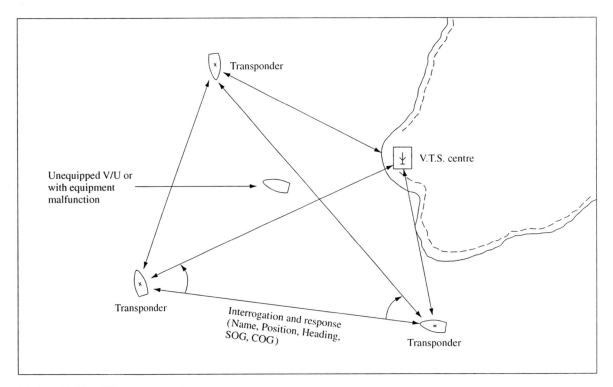

Figure 10.16   AIS system overview

Figure 10.17 Principles of SOTDMA

information on dedicated VHF frequencies. Once set up for a voyage, information is transmitted continuously from each vessel without requiring attention from the mariner. The introduction of AIS provides an alternative way of obtaining information for both collision avoidance and navigation, which has traditionally been the preserve of the radar or ARPA/ATA. Hence it is particularly important to appreciate the benefits and limitations of this new technology.

The specifications for a marine AIS system were adopted by IMO as part of the revisions in 2001 to SOLAS Chapter V. AIS became a requirement for vessels covered by SOLAS 2004, this date having been brought forward from 2007 due to international pressure.

10.3.1   Organization of AIS transmissions

Two VHF frequencies (161.975 MHz and 162.025 MHz) have been dedicated for AIS transmission, although it should be noted that there are some parts of world where only one is currently available. Conversely the system is capable of transmission on other frequencies should there be a future demand.

The potential range of AIS is therefore similar to VHF voice communications and is usually greater than radar. Thirty or 40 nautical miles is therefore typical for a VHF aerial mounted on a large vessel and 20 miles for a small craft.

In order to allow all transponders to share the limited frequencies available, each transponder transmits for very short and precisely controlled time periods. The transmission system is known as TDMA – time division multiple access. The time is regulated by the global positioning system (GPS) clocks provided by satellite and it is divided into frames, each of 1 second in length. Each frame is divided into 2250 equal slots. Thus there are normally 4500 time slots available for transmission in every second over the two frequencies. Approximately 256 bits, which can transmit the equivalent of 40–50 text characters, are sent in each slot. The allocation of the information into time slots can be made by an individual transponder under three different modes.

10.3.1.1   Autonomous and continuous mode

This is the default mode and its technical name is SOTDMA (self-organizing time division multiple access), where each transponder decides in which slot it is transmitting. The amount of information that is transmitted by each transponder varies so each transponder may use a variable number of slots on each frame. If a transponder detects that it is transmitting in the same slot as another station, it will change its slot. There is another practical interference problem in that there may be accidental interference with another vessel, as shown by vessels A and C in Figure 10.18, each out of range of the other but both within range of another vessel B. To help reduce the time over which this potential interference occurs, each transponder will periodically change the slots it uses. There is also a mechanism to reduce the range of the transmissions should the transponder detect that the system is getting saturated.

10.3.1.2   Assigned mode

The second mode of organizing the VHF time slots is the 'assigned mode' in which a suitably equipped shore station will take responsibility for all AIS transmissions within an area and will assign slots to individual AIS transponders. This may be applicable, or indeed become a necessity, in busy waters.

10.3.1.3   Polling mode

The IMO specification also allows for a third mode of AIS transmission; the 'polling mode'. In this mode the AIS transponder will give out its information whenever interrogated by another transponder. For example, this mode could be used to get static information on a vessel instead of potentially waiting 6 minutes. Another proposed use of this mode is for a long–range version of AIS using the existing AIS unit but with an interface connected to satellite communications. The INMARSAT C service would be the ideal carrier for this information.

10.3.1.4   AIS information transmitted by a vessel

The information transmitted by a vessel can be divided into four sections as shown below. Any information

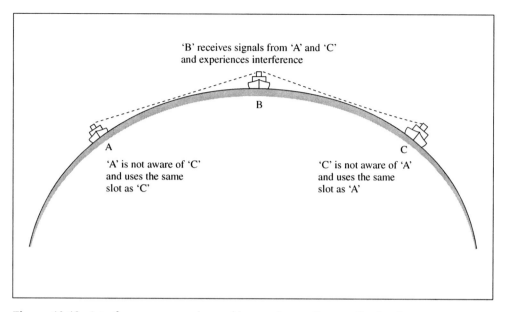

Figure 10.18 Interference to a vessel caused by vessels out of range of each other

sent by a vessel is identifiable as belonging to that vessel by the inclusion of a Maritime Mobile Service Identification (MMSI) number. This is unique to each vessel and can be used to communicate to that specific vessel using Digital Selective Calling on VHF, MF, HF or satellite communication frequencies. In addition to the MMSI number the following information is sent:

- *Static*
  IMO number
  Callsign
  Length and beam (*metres*)
  Type of ship (*container, tanker, etc.*)
  Location of position fixing antenna (*aft of bow, port or starboard of centreline*)
- *Dynamic*
  Ship position (*with accuracy indication and integrity*)
  Time in UTC
  Course over the ground
  Speed over the ground
  Heading
  Navigational status (*NUC, underway, at anchor, etc.*)
  Rate of turn (*where available*)
  Angle of heel (*optional and where available*)

  Pitch and roll (*optional and where available*)
- *Voyage related*
  Ship's draught (*metres*)
  Hazardous cargo type (*if any*)
  Destination and ETA (*at master's discretion*)
  Optional – Route plan (*waypoints*)
- *Short safety related message*
  A short text message can also be added to information transmitted

The information is updated at different time intervals, in order to keep the amount of information being transmitted to a minimum. The voyage related data and the static data block are only transmitted every 6 minutes or unless there is an outside request. The safety related message is sent as required. The dynamic data is sent according to the frequency indicated in Table 10.1.

It is claimed that the system copes with in excess of 2000 transponders in an area. It can be seen from Table 10.1 that the maximum capacity will depend on whether a large proportion of the vessels are in motion and how fast they are travelling.

Table 10.1 Data reporting rates

Vessel condition	Dynamic data reporting interval
Ship at anchor	3 minutes
Ship 0–14 knots	12 seconds
Ship 0–14 knots and changing course	4 seconds
Ship 14–23 knots	6 seconds
Ship 14–23 knots and changing course	2 seconds
Ship >23 knots	3 seconds
Ship >23 knots and changing course	2 seconds

An important point about AIS is that the system is completely dependent on an operational GPS system for its timing of radio broadcasts. Indeed many AIS units come with an internal GPS unit incorporated. The position, ground speed and ground course will also come from GPS derived data. However, it should also be noted that these should come from the GPS unit on the bridge being used by the navigators, which may not be the internal GPS fitted to the AIS. It is the position of the navigator's GPS aerial (i.e. not necessarily the aerial of the GPS internal to the AIS) which should be included in the static message.

10.3.2 AIS units and bridge displays

The AIS unit is fitted on the bridge. Much of the installation expense can be the linking of the unit to

Figure 10.19 Block diagram of AIS user equipment

other bridge equipment, especially older bridge equipment (e.g. stepper motor type gyro interfaces).

The standard of the provision of AIS data available to the navigator is very variable and can be divided into three broad types. This is because the initial (and current) standards ensure that vessels transmit AIS transmission. The integration of AIS with other bridge data is being left to a later date (see Section 10.3.2.3).

10.3.2.1 Standalone minimum keyboard display (MKD)

This is a unit with a display that provides a small data screen capable of displaying only text (not graphics) with a limited number of buttons, each performing multiple tasks (similar to mobile phones). Input and extraction of information can be tedious and prone to keying error. This is the simplest unit and popular because it meets IMO approval at the lowest cost. It is designed for the primary purpose of programming the AIS unit with the vessel's own information and the output of information on other vessels is of secondary concern. There are also reports that this philosophy has extended on some vessels to the fitting of these units away from the navigational area of the bridge or not even on the bridge at all.

However, within an MKD, it is possible to get lists of vessels that are in own ship's geographical area with range and bearing and their can be used to supplement information on other vessels derived from traditional sources such as radar/ARPA/ATA. Alarms can be set up for certain parameters, including collision threats.

10.3.2.2 Standalone graphical display

This unit is more intended for operational use by the navigators of the ship on which the AIS is fitted. Information can be displayed graphically and the display will therefore look similar in function and appearance to a radar screen. However, the graphical display only displays vessels that have AIS transponders. Additional AIS information on a displayed vessel should therefore be available at the press of a button.

10.3.2.3 Integration of AIS with ARPA/ATA and/or ECDIS

In this system, the AIS unit provides the AIS information on other vessels to an ARPA/ATA, radar, ECDIS or IBS display, possibly as part of the network of an integrated bridge system.

The advantage of overlaying the AIS information on the ARPA is that radar targets can be compared with the additional AIS information. Vessels that are poor radar targets become obvious and vessels not operating AIS can become identifiable on the radar screen. The navigator can therefore see a summary of both systems on one screen.

The advantages of overlaying the AIS on the ECDIS display is that other vessels' paths can be seen in a navigational context, which is particularly apt as the AIS gives ground track and ground speed. Additionally the projected routes of target vessels can also be displayed for consideration.

The obvious disadvantage of AIS information is the danger of information overload on the navigator. In busy situations, navigators have already demonstrated the potential (and often serious) consequences of getting the following information confused:

* ARPA/ATA derived relative and true vectors,
* ARPA/ATA derived ground and water stabilized true vectors.

The provision of additional vectors based on AIS derived information has provoked serious consideration in some quarters to reduce the problem of information overload. There are two results of this research.

1 Standard symbology
   Figure 10.20 shows the IMO approved symbols for AIS targets. These symbols have been selected for their clarity. Note that the triangle points in the direction of the ship's head and should therefore provide aspect. The vector line gives ground course and speed. The curved tail on this vector appears when a vessel is changing course and indicates the direction of the change. The triangle can be replaced by a ship outline of the correct scale dimensions when the display scale is large enough and the static information relating to that vessel is available.

AIS target	Symbols	Description of symbol
AIS target (sleeping)		An isosceles, acute-angled triangle should be used with its centroid representing the target's reference position. The most acute apex of the triangle should be aligned with the heading of the target, or with its COG, if heading information is not available. The symbol of the sleeping target may be smaller than that of the activated target.
Activated AIS target		An isosceles, acute-angled triangle should be used with its centroid representing the target's reference position. The most acute apex of the triangle should be aligned with the heading of the target, or with its COG, if heading information is not available. The COG/SOG vector should be displayed as dashed line starting at the centroid of the triangle. The heading should be displayed as solid line of fixed length starting at the apex of the triangle. A flag on the heading indicates a turn and its direction in order to detect a target manoeuvre without delay. A path predictor may also be provided
Selected target		A square indicated by its corners should be drawn around the target symbol.
Dangerous target		A bold line clearly distinguishable from the standard lines should be used to draw the symbol. The size of the symbol may be increased. The target should be displayed with: vector, heading and rate of turn indication. The symbol should flash until acknowledged. The triangle should be red on colour displays.
Lost target		A prominent solid line across the symbol, perpendicular to the last orientation of the symbol should be used. The symbol should flash until acknowledged. The target should be displayed without vector, heading and rate of turn indication.

Figure 10.20 Table of symbols

2 *Data fusion*

Algorithms have been developed to enable an integrated bridge system to compare ARPA derived data with AIS derived data. Thus where the system thinks an ARPA target and AIS source are the same vessel, it will indicate that they are the same on a combined display and will not show them as two separate vessels. The idea here is to reduce the amount of unnecessary information provided to the navigator.

It can be very computer intensive for a radar/ARPA/ATA set to track and plot a large number of AIS targets in addition to its normal workload. Radar/ARPA/ATA sets that have AIS integration include a maximum number of AIS targets that will be monitored and displayed on the screen. A typical maximum number is 50, but the navigator can usually select a lower number if required. The radar/ARPA/ATA set will plot the nearest AIS targets to own ship if the maximum number of AIS targets is exceeded.

In the new performance standards for new ships built after 2008, the radar installation must be capable of displaying a minimum number of active AIS targets. This number depends on ship size and is, in fact, the same number as the minimum number of radar tracked targets (see Section 11.2.1). The standards also allow the navigator to designate a certain number as sleeping targets, so his display is not overly cluttered with information.

10.3.2.4 Pilot plug and display

AIS units are also fitted with a 'pilot plug', which is simply a standard data connector. The pilot brings onboard a display unit which interfaces directly with the AIS. The advantage is that the pilot can then use a display device with which he is familiar while controlling and using the fixed transponder of the vessel. The pilot is also able to use the information from the ship's transponder in conjunction with other computer-based applications specific to the pilotage, such as local electronic charts.

Vessels entering US waters are additionally required to provide a convenient 120 volt power supply for the use of the pilot display.

10.3.3 Carriage and transmission of AIS

A number of SOLAS vessels can be exempted by administrations from carrying AIS. These may include warships and security vessels.

Additionally there is a far larger number of craft afloat not covered by SOLAS than covered by SOLAS. For this reason the IMO has been developing Class B AIS

performance standards for non-SOLAS vessels. Legally speaking, non-SOLAS vessels are not part of the IMO's jurisdiction, but it is obviously important that where national administrations require AIS to be fitted to non-SOLAS vessels in their waters, it is important they are compatible with the IMO AIS. The Class B standard is intended to be a simpler and lower cost version suitable for installation on small craft. There may be no requirement to interface with other ship's equipment other than GPS. This would mean loss of information regarding correct aspect from AIS.

One concern is that the compulsory provision of AIS may lead to fewer small craft fitting radar reflectors, even though the ideal will be to have both.

There will be practical limitations to implementation of AIS on some small craft due to such problems as available power supply and finding an effective aerial position. From a radar perspective, this is unfortunate as these small vessels are very often poor radar targets and AIS would give confirmation of their positions.

It is therefore not certain that every vessel encountered at sea will eventually have AIS even in those waters where the national administration have adopted the Class B AIS.

Another potential problem for AIS administrators is that there are occasions in many countries when many thousands of leisure craft congregate together in a few square miles. If all these vessels are fitted with AIS then the system will become overloaded.

Vessels fitted with AIS do not necessarily have to send all the normal information. As already indicated in Section 10.3.2, certain parameters, particularly route information, are optional. However, the AIS may be turned off completely if the master believes that it constitutes a danger to his vessel. This may be the case when transiting known piracy areas or carrying sensitive cargoes such as nuclear waste.

In summary, there is a push by some (but not all) administrations to have AIS fitted and used on all vessels in their waters whenever practical. Therefore, it is unlikely in the foreseeable future that a situation will be reached where all vessels encountered on a voyage can be depended upon to have AIS. It would appear certain that there will be a requirement for vessels to continue to carry radar.

10.3.4 Coverage by shore stations

The AIS was originally fitted for the benefit of shore-based surveillance, for security and Vessel Traffic Service (VTS) purposes. Many VTS centres operate radars, but AIS has a number of positive benefits for these centres.

AIS facilitates the positive identification of vessels on a VTS display without recourse to the VHF. Many useful details regarding the AIS equipped vessel become available and the information is passed in computer language. Thus AIS avoids the language difficulties and identification confusions often associated with VHF voice communications.

Another VTS radar plotting problem is target swap (see Section 4.3.5), when a target plotted by an ARPA/ATA loses its 'tag' to another passing vessel or static radar target. AIS does not have this problem. In fact, it can provide a warning that radar target swap has occurred.

VHF transmissions have a much longer range than radar and also have a limited ability to go round corners. This is particularly useful in fjord type regions where radar is unable to see far ahead due to blind areas, whereas AIS transmissions can be received. VHF aerials and transponders are much simpler devices than radars with less power and maintenance requirements. The net effect of all these factors is that it requires far fewer AIS transponders than radar scanners to provide shore coverage of an area and the system is a lot less expensive to operate.

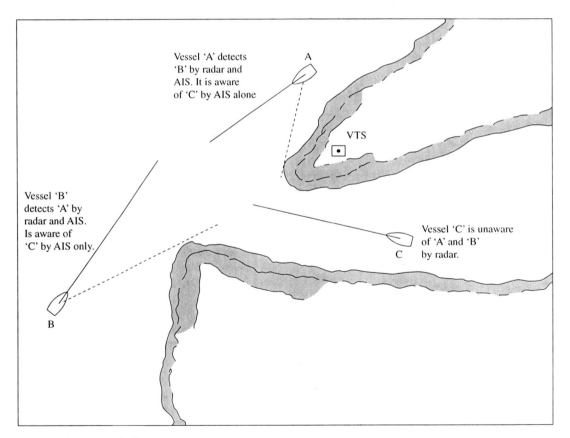

Figure 10.21 Fjord effect

10.3.5   Other applications of AIS

Experiments are ongoing as to potential further uses of AIS. These include putting AIS transponders on buoys. This has two main benefits. The buoy will be positively identified including its specific name to AIS users. Furthermore if the buoy moves out of position, the shore authorities will be alerted.

Another area being explored is the use of virtual AIS. In this scenario a shore authority could put in virtual buoys to indicate a safe channel or mark a wreck. These would appear on an AIS display to vessels even though the buoys would not physically exist. This would be of great benefit for marking safe or dangerous areas of a temporary or transient nature or in advance of real wreck-marking buoys being laid over a new wreck. A further example is in areas where, in winter, buoys are removed because of floating ice.

10.3.6   Radar and AIS comparison

The AIS information is much faster to update than ARPA/ATA. Course changes are indicated as soon as the target ship's heading starts to change instead of waiting for the ARPA/ATA to detect the change in apparent motion (at least 5 minutes later for large vessels). The AIS information is reliant totally on GPS. The positive side of this is that ground-based information does not depend on sensors such as gyro and logs for processing such information.

10.3.6.1   Shore-based radar

The benefits of AIS to a shore authority are large and will enable monitoring of vessel traffic in areas not currently feasible by radar due to geographical and/or cost considerations. Those administrations focused on security, as well as safety, will still operate radar as well as AIS, in order to check that the two sources of information match up. AIS will also allow information to be passed to vessels autonomously (Section 10.3.5).

In other areas an AIS can be used to complement the radar coverage, by providing additional information. In most port approaches, the radar/ARPA/ATA would identify vessels that did not have AIS and it would provide a check on vessels with AIS.

The addition of AIS (probably in conjunction with radar) should make remote pilotage feasible in certain areas, particularly where the pilotage demands are not intense or where severe weather might prevent a pilot from boarding a vessel. The pilot would be able to monitor course steered and ground track of a vessel very effectively in near real time and advise the master from the shore. The role of the radar in emergency pilotage would be to act both as a check that the AIS is operating correctly and as an emergency fallback should the AIS suffer malfunction.

10.3.6.2   Ship-based radar

It would also appear that AIS would have much to offer the navigator, provided that the initial teething troubles are addressed and the AIS is recognized by authorities as being an aid to navigators and not just for shore-based purposes. These initial problems include limited equipment (the standalone MKD, see Section 10.3.2.1), poor bridge installation, incorrect information being programmed, missing information and a complete lack of user training. There are some parallels here with the initial early industry experiences that led to the occurrence of 'radar assisted collisions'. In the AIS case, with current IMO standards, the equipment appears to be fitted to this minimum specification to provide a device intended for shore purposes only. In this way further costs are also not incurred, because if it is not an aid to the navigator there is no need to train the navigators in the benefits and limitations of the equipment. It is hoped that in time this attitude will change. At least new vessels from 2008 will benefit from an integrated AIS and radar display (see Section 10.3.2.3).

In Table 10.2 the comparison of radar and AIS information for anti-collision purposes is summarized. It is true that in the open ocean there is no need for the quality and depth of information that AIS provides in order to easily detect and avoid potential collisions. However, in coastal areas under pilotage type conditions, traffic can be busier, traffic movements more complex and the options to avoid collision become more restricted. In these conditions both the extra

Table 10.2   Comparison of ARPA/ATA and AIS data for anti–collision purposes

	ARPA/ATA radar derived data	*AIS/VHF derived data*
Overall accuracy (see Chapter 9)	Similar to AIS at close range but accuracy reduces linearly with range, due mainly to bearing accuracy	Positional errors 10–30 metres
Framework for calculations	Relative to ship	Ground based
Derivation of aspect	Derived by calculation and depends on accurate knowledge of own ship's course and speed through water	Obtained directly from compass of target ship (when available)
Detection of changes in target course and speed	Takes several minutes	Immediate (when compass available), as soon as gyro starts to change. Otherwise will be apparent when ground track changes
Identification of target size	Can be misleading Changes with range and aspect	Good, if static data is transmitted
Reliance on other equipment	All necessary equipment on own ship Requires compass and log	GPS system Sensors on other vessels Programming on other vessels
Reliability of detecting other vessels in the vicinity	Dependent on echo strength and weather conditions	Only if fitted with AIS Not significantly weather dependent
Target swap	Possible	No
Interference and false echoes	A possibility	Unlikely
Reduced coverage due to own-ship obstructions	Can occur depending on aerial position	Unlikely
Reduced coverage due to land mass obstructions (the 'fjord' effect)	Yes, line of sight only	Unlikely
Range	Typically 10–20 miles, depending on aerial heights and environmental factors	Typically 20–40 miles depending on aerial heights and environmental factors
Transmission and target response density causing overload	Unlikely	A possibility

information (such as vessels' destination) and the speed of reception of course/speed changes could be a useful complement to ARPA/ATA information for the navigator.

There is also the danger that AIS information could also lead to bad practices in potential collision situations with more vessels exchanging communications and agreeing to actions contrary to good seamanship and the rules of the road, but it is beyond the remit of this book to cover such issues in depth.

In summary, it is unlikely that AIS will replace radar as an anti-collision aid, because it depends on every other vessel having AIS equipment, for every other vessel to have their equipment in full working order and for every other vessels' AIS to be set up properly. However, there is no denying that when working properly and if provided in a user-friendly display to the navigator, the AIS can provide high quality and useful information. AIS should therefore be regarded as a complement to radar/ARPA and not a competitor.

10.4   Integrated systems

Traditionally bridge (and other) instruments have tended to be developed in isolation, with each having an individual (possibly mechanical) method of measuring and displaying data. Ergonomics was a discipline for the future and each instrument had to fight for its position on the bridge. As each new instrument was added to existing bridges, they were invariably placed wherever a vacant spot existed. In time, the grouping and placement of instrument displays was given some consideration in vessels under construction. It is only relatively recently, with the widespread digitization of data that the ability to integrate and display the data has become a possibility. With the development of an international standard for data format and transmission protocols (see Section 10.4.4), integration is now becoming more commonplace. Whilst initially some manufacturers did integrate instruments of their own manufacture, it is now possible to integrate instruments from different manufacturers who adhere to these common standards.

10.4.1   Integrated bridge systems (IBS)

An integrated bridge system is defined as '...a combination of systems which are interconnected in order to allow centralized access to sensor information ...'. 'The IBS should support systems performing two or more of the following operations: passage execution; communications; machinery control; and safety and security.'

While the IMO Performance Standard (see Section 11.3.4) deals with all aspects of vessel operation and safety, it is intended here to deal only with the integration of those systems which have a navigational function and are in some way related to the radar/ARPA as a sub-system of the integrated system.

10.4.2   Integrated navigation systems (INS)

An INS aims to '...enhance safe and expeditious navigation and to complement the mariner's capabilities ...'. Three levels of performance standard are specified by IMO (see Section 11.3.5).

10.4.3   Typical systems that may be integrated

Given that a sensor has the ability to export data in a universally recognized format, virtually any combination of instruments may be integrated into a single display system but the method of display and data grouping does require careful consideration.

- *Integration on smaller craft.* For some time now, sailing boats and in particular those intended for racing, have tended to concentrate on those instrument displays, crucial for strategic decision-making in a single console, readily visible (in all weathers) by the tactician.

  Although integration implies that everything is centralized in one unit, this is not necessarily the case, nor is it particularly desirable. The final navigation package may well incorporate a variety of configurations as depicted in Figure 2.56(a–c).

  While the integrated system console is intended to centralize the display of data for command and control of the craft, each of the instruments is required to be independently operable should the link to the main console or the main console itself fail or malfunction. It is usual for any 'permanent' setting-up of the sensor to be done at the sensor with data and status being transmitted to the central position. Where operating controls are in regular use (such as the radar range change control), these

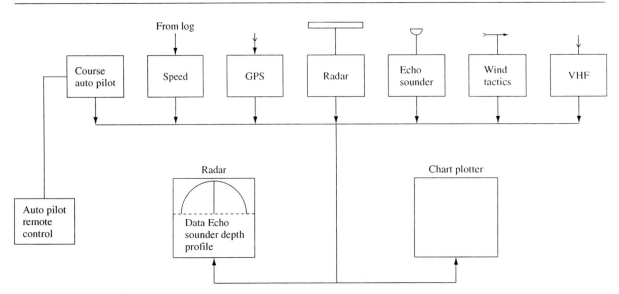

Figure 10.22 Instruments typically integrated on smaller craft

are usually duplicated at the display. There may also be remote keypads to facilitate such operations as steering and autopilot inputs which may need to be done at some distance from the console, e.g. during berthing. The system may also include facilities for data logging, recording of VHF communications and the printout of text transmissions and navigational warnings.

• Integration on larger pleasure craft and commercial vessels. This follows all the same basic principles as above with all the same sensors being integrated but expanded to embrace additional sensors and to take account of different navigational requirements. The additional sensor inputs may include radar/ARPA; rate of turn indicator; bow/stern thruster demand and status; engine and steering control demand and status, with the extra data being displayed on an additional monitor.

The three monitors would be identical and what is displayed would be interchangeable in order to provide redundancy should one display malfunction.

While virtually anything is possible, e.g. the inclusion of AIS (see Section 10.3), GMDSS, etc., the desirability of incorporating additional functions

in a single facility and the need to display data in a readily assimilated format, needs to be carefully considered. If one bears in mind the integration of other shipboard systems on the bridge (see Sections 10.4.1 and 11.3.4), especially with the additional alarms and warnings, overkill and information overload become a distinct possibility.

10.4.4 Connectivity

Initially, the interfacing between different items of navigational equipment was individual to certain manufacturers. However, more open general standards have been developed. The NMEA (National Marine Electronics Association) data standard was developed in the early 1980s and is still extensively used where the data rate required is low. Most radar devices have some NMEA connections so the NMEA 0183 standard is covered here. Other interfaces still tend to be manufacturer specific.

10.4.4.1 Binary and the ASCII standard

Computers use the binary language for all their communications and calculations. For example, in terms

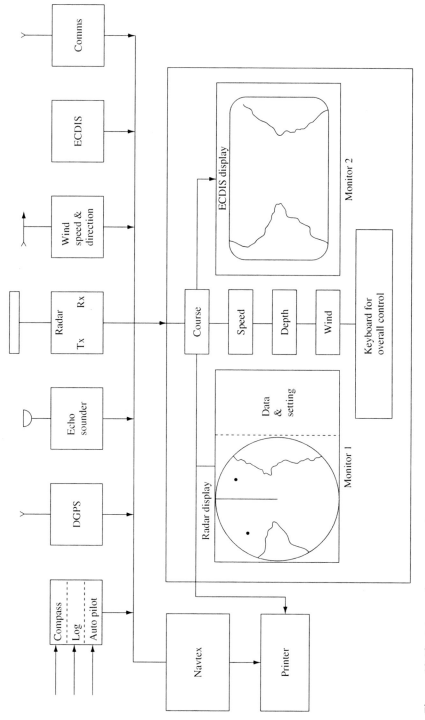

Figure 10.23 Integrated system console

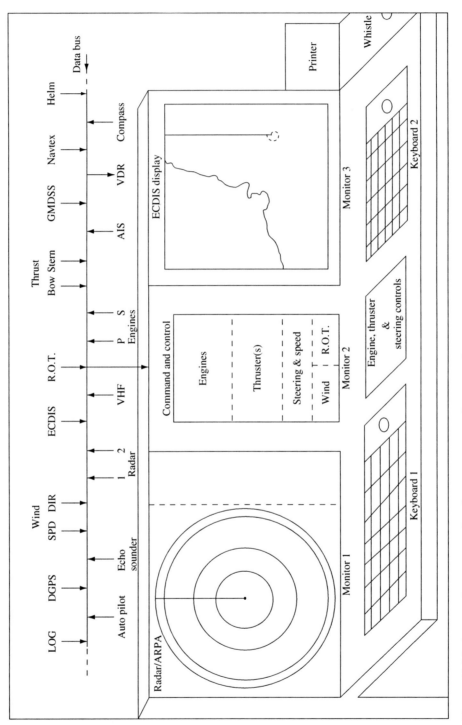

Figure 10.24 Integrated system console as it may appear on a larger vessel

of electric wires, the '0's and '1's are represented by high and low voltages, whereas in magnetic storage locations (as found on hard and floppy disks) by the polarity of the magnetic field at the location.

Standard sequences of '0's and '1's are used to store text characters and the most common one is the ASCII standard which is used by NMEA. The ASCII standards were developed before computers for telex systems and ASCII refers to the American Standard Code for Information Interchange. The code has 7-bit and 8-bit versions. The 7-bit version contains 128 characters, the additional bit in the 8-bit version allows for an additional 128 characters, 256 characters in all. The first 128 characters (numbered 0 to 127) are the same in both versions, the extra 128 bits are used for symbols for simple graphics. Some of the original ASCII characters have strange names, originally developed as a function in the telex system and do not necessarily represent printable characters. These include the code for line feed or 'LF' which is ASCII code 12 (i.e. 00001100 in 8-bit binary, see Figure 2.36) and carriage return or 'CR' ASCII code 13 (i.e. 00001101). The capital letters start at the binary for 'A' at 65 (i.e. 01000001); 'B' is 66 (i.e. 01000010), etc. The small letters start for 'a' at 97 (i.e. 01100001); 'b' is 98 (i.e. 01100010), etc. Number characters are also included: '0' is 48 (i.e. 00110000); '1' is 49 (i.e. 00110001), etc. and most symbols commonly found on keyboards are also included, for example '$' is 36 (i.e. 00100100).

10.4.4.2 NMEA message standard

The current most popular NMEA standard is NMEA 0183, which superseded versions 0182 and 0180. A version NMEA 2000 has been developed but has not yet been significantly adopted by the industry.

The adoption of new open standards can be a very time consuming and unsuccessful procedure as manufacturers have to choose between keeping something that works and is widely available and improving the technology of their products, but at the risk of not being able to connect to other manufacturers' products.

Each line (or sentence) of an NMEA 0183 message is made up of a number of ASCII characters. Each sentence starts with a '$'. Five characters immediately follow the '$'. The first two characters identify the device from which the message originated, for example 'HE' for a gyro compass, 'GP' for a GPS device and 'RA' for a radar or ARPA. The last three characters identify the NMEA standard sentence. After the identification group, the data fields follow that are associated with that sentence. Each data field is separated by a comma. Many of the sentences include the option of a checksum at the end. Sometimes it is compulsory. The checksum is the numerical binary addition (using exclusive OR logic) of all the binary code sent in a sentence between the '$' and the '*' included as the second character of the checksum (for format see example 10.1 below). The checksum is a communication error detection device. If the message received does not add up to the checksum then there has been a corruption of the sentence between transmission and reception. Each sentence is terminated with carriage return 'CR' and line feed 'LF' ASCII codes.

The range of information and instructions that can be sent via NMEA 0183 is large and ever increasing. For example, it can send information as diverse as water temperature, navigation waypoints, GPS almanac, location and type of trawler gear, autopilot and engine instructions.

Some example sentences with their potential radar related applications are given below.

Example 10.1 HDT: Heading – true.
Used to send heading information from gyro-compass to other devices including radar.

$HEHDT,035.9,T,3*56

HE	Sender ID (north seeking gyro compass)
HDT	Sentence ID (true heading)
035.9,T	Heading (035.9 true)
3*56	Checksum

Example 10.2 GLL: Geographic position.
Used to send position from GPS, LORAN C, etc. to other devices such as radar.

$GPGLL,2325.53,N,03423.67,W,143341,1

GP	Sender ID (GPS)
GLL	Sentence ID (geographic position, latitude and longitude)
2325.53,N	Latitude (23 deg, 25.53 min N)
03423.67,W	Longitude (034 deg, 23.67 min W)
143341	Fix time UTC (14:33:41 UTC)
1	Fix validity (valid), 0 if fix is doubtful

Example 10.3   TTM: Tracked target status.
Used to send tracked target information from ARPA to ECDIS. A separate sentence is sent for each target currently plotted.

$RATTM,04,5.2,034.3,T,10.5,135.7,T,0.5,15.6,N,
TAR01,T,095643.67,M,R,4*43

RA	Sender ID (radar/ARPA)
TTM	Sentence ID (tracked target status)
04	ARPA assigned target number (04), can be 00 to 99
5.2	Target distance (5.2 nautical miles)
034.3	Target bearing from own ship (034.3 deg)
T	Target bearing orientation (true), R is relative
10.5	Target speed (10.5 knots)
135.7	Target course (135.7 deg)
T	Course orientation (true), R is relative
0.5	Closest point of approach (0.5 distance units)
15.6	Time to closest point of approach (15.6 minutes), a negative number indicates the target is past its CPA
N	Distance and speed units (nautical miles and knots), K is kilometres, S is statute miles
TAR01	Target label on ARPA (TAR01)
T	Target status (tracking), L is lost target, Q is target being acquired
R	Reference target (i.e. designated fixed target), left blank if not designated
095643.67	Time of data in UTC (09 hrs 56 min 43.67 secs)
M	Type of target acquisition (manual), A is automatic
4*43	Checksum

There are a large number of standard sentences available and each manufacturer selects and incorporates the sentences that a specific piece of equipment can use, either for receiving or transmission. In many devices, it is also possible for the navigator to select from the manufacturer's list the sentences for actual transmission or reception.

NMEA is continually evolving and different versions of sentences sometimes exist. Usually later versions are longer, so some earlier equipment may only read the first part of the sentence. Another feature of NMEA is that many manufacturers add extra proprietary sentences designed to interface only with other equipment made by the same manufacturer. The format of the identifier data field is different for proprietary codes. These sentences are all prefixed by $P, the next three characters are the approved NMEA code for that manufacturer (e.g. 'GRM' is Garmin) and the last character is the sentence ID specified by the manufacturer.

10.4.4.3   RS-232 interface

The NMEA standards accept a range of electronic standards to transmit data but the interface should be compliant with EIA-422. Commonly the NMEA message data is run on a basic computer standard interface, the RS-232 interface, and it allows for easy connection to a computer. This is good for diagnostic purposes. It is very easy to connect a computer to a piece of navigation equipment to view the NMEA output or to simulate the input of another piece of navigational equipment. It should also be remembered that some navigational equipment is now often sold as part of a personal computer. It can be sold as computer hardware (e.g. a GPS card fitted inside a personal computer) or software (e.g. an ECDIS package running on a standard computer on a bridge or even away from the bridge to allow passage planning prior to the voyage).

The RS-232 interface is detailed here to show the simplicity of the connection process. Computers (and occasionally navigational equipment) are fitted with standard 9- or 25-pin D-shaped connectors commonly referred to as the serial port (or COM) on a computer. Connectors on navigational equipment come in a variety of shapes and sizes, but if the right pins are connected together, two devices (computer or dedicated navigational device) can easily be made to 'talk' to one another. Three wires are the minimum needed for full two-way communications between two devices and only two wires if one-way communication is required. Figure 10.25 shows the pin layout of the standard 9-pin D-socket. Pin 5 is the ground (or signal earth). Pin 3 is for sending data and its voltage is varied from high (above 4 volts) to low (below 0.8 volts) values to communicate 0 and 1 respectively. The voltage is measured between pins 3 and 5. Similarly outward data is transmitted on pin 3 and the voltage measured between pins 3 and 5. Obviously, if connecting to another D-socket on the second device with the same pin arrangement, the wires connecting the two devices should be 'crossed' so that pins 2 and 3 are connected to pins 3 and 2 respectively. However, manufacturers of some non-standard devices sometimes reverse pins 2 and 3 so that a 'straight through' cable (uncrossed) can be employed. One should consult the manuals of the two devices involved if unsure.

The other six pins on the 9-pin D-connector are not used for transmitting data. They are optionally used to control the data flow (also known as handshaking). Thus a voltage on pin 4 by the receiving device indicates that it is ready to receive. If not, then it is not ready to receive. Other wires are used to indicate other control information from one device or the other. Data flow control is important because if the receiver buffer is full, any additional data sent will be lost. Using these optional pins for flow control is termed hardware handshaking and obviously requires more wires in the cable and the equivalent pins on the other piece of equipment. If only using the minimum three-wire arrangement the flow control is termed software handshaking as the data flow instructions are sent as software codes on the data wires. In connecting a piece of navigational equipment (e.g. GPS or log) to a computer or another navigational equipment, it is usual to use software control as the connectors on navigational equipment (which are not often the 9-pin D-socket shown above) usually have only the minimum three pins and not the extra pins required for hardware handshaking.

The data rate for NMEA 0183 is 4800 baud (or bits per second), which is very slow in modern communication terms, as often rates are measured in Mbits/second and one Mbit is approximately 1 049 000 baud). However, 4800 baud is perfectly adequate to communicate the latitude and longitude from a GPS, or water depth from the echo sounder, etc., at intervals under 1 second, which is more than adequate for most marine navigation purposes.

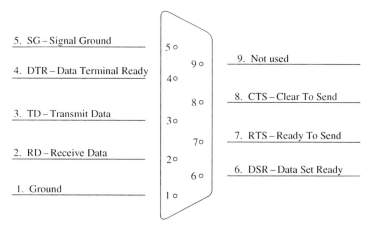

Looking at the socket

Figure 10.25 Nine-way D-socket

In addition to setting the data rate of 4800 baud for a computer serial port, it is also necessary to tell the computer how the binary data is organized. In NMEA 0183 the binary data is arranged in 8-bit groups (i.e. one ASCII character is sent at a time). These groups are called 'words' in computer jargon. Between each word there is a stop and a start bit to allow the receiver to resynchronize itself with the start of the next word. For RS-232 communications, the start bit is always 1 bit long, but the stop bit can be set to 1, 1.5 or 2 bits in length. For NMEA 0183 the stop bit is 1 bit long. Finally RS-232 also allows for the optional addition of an extra binary bit to each word for error checking purposes. This extra optional bit is termed the parity bit. It is an option not used by NMEA 0183, so the parity bit setting should therefore be 'No parity bit'. In summary, the communication settings for NMEA 0183 often appear in the short hand '4800,8,N,1'. This translates as 4800 baud, 8-bit word length, there is no parity bit and there is 1 stop bit.

It should also be noted that multiple devices can be chained using the same data wire, provided the additional devices are only readers not senders. That is, only one sender is allowed on each data wire, but it may be linked to multiple receivers as in Figure 10.26. The older 25-pin computer D-socket incorporates a second set of RS-232 connections.

10.4.4.4 Other connectivity standards

NMEA 0183 and its intended successor NMEA 2000 are not fast enough to send picture data so other faster methods are used (for example) to transfer the radar picture to ECDIS. These standards are usually proprietary and not generally open, so that such a transfer of information is only possible between equipment provided by a single manufacturer or between two manufacturers who have a working relationship.

10.4.5 Advantages of integration

There are distinct advantages to having all data upon which decisions are to be based readily available at one command and control position. However, not all of the data needs to shown all of the time. There are unique phases in a voyage – as diverse as docking and open-sea collision avoidance – where only some of the data is required and it is important during these operations that irrelevant information is not cluttering up the displays. Hence, great care is necessary when deciding on what data is to be displayed and in what format.

Having all the data outputs centrally located makes it easy for cross-checking similar data derived from different sensors and sources, for example the vessel's position may be derived from visual observations, ECDIS/GPS, and radar. A quick check of compass

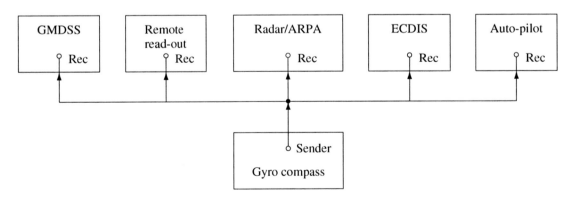

Figure 10.26 Example of a chained RS-232 connection

heading and COG as derived from the GPS will give a sense of how the vessel is being set.

While all this data is available, it is essential that great care is exercised when making decisions and that no unjustifiable weight is given to some of the data while other data is overlooked.

In earlier sections in this chapter we considered the advantages of integrating: ECDIS and GPS (Section 10.1.9); radar/ARPA with ECDIS (Section 10.2.7); ARPA, AIS and ECDIS (Section 10.3.2.3). Clearly a full integration of bridge information does not stop at integrating these suggested combinations of equipment alone.

10.4.6 Potential dangers of data overload

There is becoming an increasing awareness of the potential problem of information overload. As has already been stated, not all the data is needed all of the time, especially when one includes other data displayed on the bridge (see Section 10.4.1). It is essential, when designing the display of data, that only data essential to the operation taking place be directly displayed while additional data is available on demand.

10.4.7 System cross-checking, warnings and alarms

In order for the early detection of malfunction in a system, cross-checking between systems (either electronically or manually) is important. It is also important to check progress against a predetermined plan. Warnings and alarms can be built into the system at various levels of urgency, but the navigator can be overwhelmed and distracted by buzzers, whistles and flashing lights. Again care in design is essential.

10.4.8 Sensor errors and accuracy of integration

One would hope that similar data derived from different sources would have a high correlation factor, but this is not necessarily the case due to system and other errors, which can be random. Where there is unacceptable divergence an alarm should be activated and the navigator will need to exercise his judgement as to the possible cause of the discrepancy or if it is due to the malfunction of a specific sensor.

10.4.9 Data monitoring and loggings

In addition to voyage data recorders (see Section 10.5), data derived from a multitude of shipboard systems (see Section 10.4.1) is in digital form and may be accumulated and stored on a variety of media to facilitate record keeping (e.g. log book) and for voyage performance analysis. In many organizations, there is still a preference for hard copy of information required for permanent record and legal purposes. A printer is therefore still part of most systems.

10.5 Voyage data recorders (VDRs)

The purpose of a VDR is to record operational information of a vessel so that it can assist investigators should the vessel become involved in an incident. The idea has long been used in the aviation industry where it has often been called the 'black box'. Commercial aircraft actually record different information in two separate boxes that are coloured bright orange.

The VDR should help overcome two distinct problems in ascertaining causes of marine incidents. Firstly, there is occasionally a situation when key personnel do not survive the incident. Secondly, even when personnel survive an incident the truth is not always forthcoming. Survivors may not be aware of certain facts. They could have a mistaken impression of what happened due to the trauma of the event and they may not tell the truth in order to protect themselves or colleagues. Marine incidents are not unique in that one party has a different version of an accident to a second party.

VDR regulations were first introduced in the revisions to SOLAS Chapter V in 2001. All new vessels of more than 3000 grt and all new passenger vessels are required to have them fitted. There is also a phased requirement for fitting them to some existing ships, especially passenger ships.

10.5.1 Equipment

The VDR equipment has two main items of hardware. There is a single data storage capsule located externally on top of the vessel and a data collection unit probably located inside the bridge. Replay facilities are normally located ashore.

The data storage capsule is designed to survive a total loss of the vessel. It is a capsule designed to withstand an intense fire as well as immersion in over 4000 metres of water. Its construction is therefore very thick steel. The capsule would normally be located towards the top of the vessel in an open space. Its securing arrangements are designed to be easily released by a remotely operated vehicle (ROV) or a deep-sea diver encumbered in a heavy suit. It will not actually contain much electronic equipment, the main component being enough solid-state memory to record the last 12 hours of the vessel's operations. Solid-state memory does not actually require a battery to maintain the data recorded. The capsule is fully sealed to meet its demanding specifications with only a data wire penetrating the casing. To aid detection, it is brightly coloured, covered in retro-reflective material and an underwater locator beacon is attached.

The data collection unit is usually a standard personal computer although the usual controls and displays need not normally be provided for ships' staff. There is little for the navigator to operate except check that the system is on and functioning, indicated by some manufacturers as a simple flashing light. Connections from all the required bridge equipment are made direct to the data collection unit. The data is stored internally as well as sent to the data storage capsule. Data compression techniques are employed to enable efficient use of the storage systems.

The data storage capsule only needs to contain the last 12 hours of operation. It is also the single most expensive item in the VDR equipment and once opened cannot be easily reused (if at all). It would be an unnecessary expense to have to cut open the capsule to investigate the vast majority of marine incidents when the bridge and ship are still essentially intact. Following an incident, the stored data in the data collection unit will be maintained over a much longer duration (more than a week is typical) and standard electronic means are provided to extract the data much more cheaply than by opening up the data storage capsule. The media of extraction is at the choice of the supplier and buyer but can be via an electronic network or by standard computer storage media such as compact disk or removable hard drive.

10.5.2 Non-radar data recorded

The data recorded includes the following from bridge equipment:

> Date and time
> Position from electronic position fixing systems
> Speed
> Compass heading
> Echosounder depth
> Audio from VHF communications
> Audio from a network of microphones installed on the bridge
> Main (mandatory) alarms to be found on a bridge
> Rudder order and response
> Engine order and response
> Status of hull openings, watertight/fire doors, hull stresses (on vessels with the equipment)
> Wind speed and direction

10.5.3 Radar and ARPA/ATA data recorded

There is also a requirement to record radar and ARPA/ATA data. The system adopted makes use of the fact that all modern displays are raster. A software technique called 'frame grabbing' to store an instantaneous frame (the raster picture) is well established in the computer industry and the picture data can be compressed for efficient storage. The frame grab of the full raster display is completed at least every 15 seconds from one of the ship's radars.

The raster display on a modern raster-scan radar does not just show the picture (see Figure 2.55), it also shows the main radar settings (e.g. range scale in use, true or relative vectors in use, vector time, amount of sea clutter control applied, etc.). This trend has

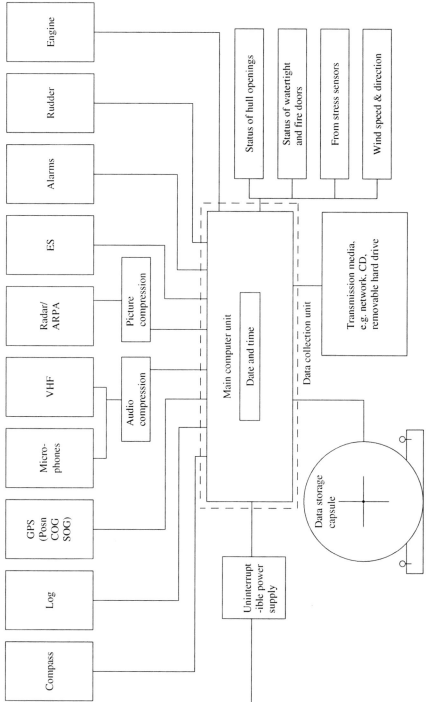

Figure 10.27 Block diagram of VDR system

increased as 'hard' analogue controls have largely disappeared and been replaced by software driven menu controls. Therefore the frame grabber will record much information of value to investigators as to the way the equipment was being used as well as the operational state of the radar equipment and the outside scenario in which the vessel was participating.

This use of the frame grabber means that there is little need to have specialized interfaces to capture this radar information. Given the number of radar models and manufacturers this would otherwise be a matter of some complexity and expense for a VDR manufacturer to handle.

The radar picture will be an important part of many marine investigations. The visual view is not recorded so the only dynamic reconstruction of physical events will be found on the radar display.

A downside to the frame grabber radar recording system is that the results are dependent on the navigator adjusting the radar to the optimum settings. If the radar is set up incorrectly the true situation (e.g. missing target echoes) will not be retrievable by the investigator. This would not necessarily be the case if the raw radar data (i.e. prior to digitization and display) was recorded by the VDR, but the potential gain in recording raw radar is small compared with the potential complexity of recording the raw radar data on a large variety of radar models.

An advantage of the frame grabber system is that it will record when navigators have not used the radar/ARPA/ATA correctly, and will probably be able to detect the occasions when human error on the part of the navigator in the use of the radar was a factor in a collision.

10.5.4   Playback equipment

It is not intended that the vessel has playback equipment. The playback software is usually installable on a standard multi-media personal computer and would normally be available in the ship manager's office. The software and the retrieved data would be made available to investigators after an accident. Most playback software allows rewinding; fast-forwarding and freeze framing of data in a similar fashion to a standard video player. A selection of different data streams (radar, helm-controls position, audio channel) can be played back simultaneously and the graphical data (radar picture, helm orders, etc.) are shown in different windows so that an overall view of the incident is obtained. The positional data can be fed to a separate electronic chart to further aid the replay analysis.

10.5.5   Future of voyage data recorders

Operational experience with VDRs is still very limited. Whilst a lot of vessels now carry them, they have had little time to be of assistance in investigations. Like the ship's lifeboat, very few of the installations will actually be used for their intended purpose. Nevertheless it is anticipated that, the few times that they are used, they will provide vital and objective information as to the causes of the incident. The IMO intends the installation of VDR to become more widespread and studies are currently being done on a low cost version (perhaps float free) for older non-passenger vessels.

The data collected by VDR also has potential for research and analysis of vessel operation when not concerned with an incident. There are already schemes where navigators report (usually anonymously) examples of a near miss that otherwise would not have been analysed. If it were possible to treat data records of these near misses in same way, future safety would be significantly improved. In fact, it would be useful for voyage data records to be examined for examples of good (and successful) navigational practice and for navigational data. For instance, this could include radar pictures of parts so that parallel index targets can be identified. This VDR information could be usefully fed back to navigators. However, it would need a large culture shift by navigators, regulators and shipowners to make this data freely available.

11 Extracts from official publications

This chapter contains extracts from official publications relating to the topics covered by this volume. They have been edited and the reader is referred to the full original text if more details are required.

Within the extracts the paragraph, table and appendix numbering of the original publications has been retained

11.1 Extracts from Regulation 19, Chapter V, Safety of Navigation, of the IMO-SOLAS Convention

Edited to show application of radar, ARPA and AIS to new vessels.

1.1 Ships constructed on or after 1 July 2002 shall be fitted with navigational systems and equipment which will fulfil the requirements prescribed in paragraphs 2.1 to 2.9.

2 Shipborne navigational equipment and systems

2.1 All ships irrespective of size shall have:

2.1.7 if less than 150 gross tonnage and if practicable, a radar reflector, or other means, to enable detection by ships navigating by radar at both 9 and 3 GHz;

2.3 All ships of 300 gross tonnage and upwards and passenger ships irrespective of size shall be fitted with:

2.3.2 a 9 GHz radar, or other means to determine and display the range and bearing of radar transponders and of other surface craft, obstructions, buoys, shorelines and navigational marks to assist in navigation and in collision avoidance;

2.3.3 an electronic plotting aid, or other means, to plot electronically the range and bearing of targets to determine collision risk;

2.3.4 speed and distance measuring device, or other means, to indicate speed and distance through the water;

2.3.5 a properly adjusted transmitting heading device, or other means to transmit heading information for input to the equipment referred to in paragraphs 2.3.2, 2.3.3 and 2.4.

2.4 All ships of 300 gross tonnage and upwards engaged on international voyages and cargo ships of 500 gross tonnage and upwards not engaged on international voyages and passenger ships irrespective of size shall be fitted with an automatic identification system (AIS), as follows:

2.4.1 ships constructed on or after 1 July 2002;

2.4.5 AIS shall:

.1 provide automatically to appropriately equipped shore stations, other ships and aircraft information, including the ship's identity, type, position, course, speed, navigational status and other safety-related information;

.2 receive automatically such information from similarly fitted ships;

.3 monitor and track ships; and

.4 exchange data with shore-based facilities;

.6 the requirements of paragraph 2.4.5 shall not be applied to cases where international agreements, rules or standards provide for the protection of navigational information; and

.7 AIS shall be operated taking into account the guidelines adopted by the Organization.

2.5 All ships of 500 gross tonnage and upwards shall, in addition to meeting the requirements of paragraph 2.3 with the exception of paragraphs 2.3.3 and 2.3.5, and the requirements of paragraph 2.4, have:

2.5.1 a gyro compass, or other means, to determine and display their heading by shipborne non-magnetic means and to transmit heading information for input to the equipment referred to in paragraphs 2.3.2, 2.4 and 2.5.5;

2.5.5 an automatic tracking aid, or other means, to plot automatically the range and bearing of other targets to determine collision risk.

2.7 All ships of 3000 gross tonnage and upwards shall, in addition to meeting the requirements of paragraph 2.5, have:

2.7.1 a 3 GHz radar or where considered appropriate by the Administration a second 9 GHz radar, or other means to determine and display the range and bearing of other surface craft, obstructions, buoys, shorelines and navigational marks to assist in navigation and in collision avoidance, which are functionally independent of those referred to in paragraph 2.3.2; and

2.7.2 a second automatic tracking aid, or other means to plot automatically the range and bearing of other targets to determine collision risk which are functionally independent of those referred to in paragraph 2.5.5.

2.8 All ships of 10 000 gross tonnage and upwards shall, in addition to meeting the requirements of paragraph 2.7 with the exception of paragraph 2.7.2, have:

2.8.1 an automatic radar plotting aid, or other means, to plot automatically the range and bearing of at least 20 other targets, connected to a device to indicate speed and distance through the water, to determine collision risks and simulate a trial manoeuvre;

11.2 IMO Performance Standards for radar and automatic plotting aids

11.2.1 Extracts from IMO Resolution MSC 192(79), Performance Standards for radar equipment for new ships constructed after 1 July 2008

INDEX

1 SCOPE OF EQUIPMENT

The radar equipment should assist in safe navigation and in avoiding collision by providing an indication, in relation to own ship, of the position of other surface craft, obstructions and hazards, navigation objects and shorelines.

For this purpose, radar should provide the integration and display of radar video, target tracking information, positional data derived from own ship's position (EPFS) and geo referenced data. The integration and display of AIS information should be provided to complement radar. The capability of displaying selected parts of Electronic Navigation Charts and other vector chart information may be provided to aid navigation and for position monitoring.

The radar, combined with other sensor or reported information (e.g. AIS), should improve the safety of navigation by assisting in the efficient navigation of ships and protection of the environment by satisfying the following functional requirements:

- in coastal navigation and harbour approaches, by giving a clear indication of land and other fixed hazards;
- as a means to provide an enhanced traffic image and improved situation awareness;
- in a ship-to-ship mode for aiding collision avoidance of both detected and reported hazards;
- in the detection of small floating and fixed hazards, for collision avoidance and the safety of own ship; and
- in the detection of floating and fixed aids to navigation (see Table 2, note 3).

2 APPLICATION OF THESE STANDARDS

These Performance Standards should apply to all shipborne radar installations, used in any configuration, mandated by the SOLAS Convention 1974, as amended, independent of the:

- type of ship;
- frequency band in use; and
- type of display,

providing that no special requirements are specified in Table 1 and that additional requirements for specific classes of ships (in accordance with SOLAS chapters V and X) are met.

The radar installation, in addition to meeting the general requirements as set out in resolution A.694(17)[*], should comply with the following performance standards.

Close interaction between different navigational equipment and systems, makes it essential to consider these standards in association with other relevant IMO standards.

3 REFERENCES

References are in Appendix 1.

---

[*]IEC Publication 60945.

TABLE 1
Differences in the performance requirements for various sizes/categories of ship/craft to which SOLAS applies

Size of ship/craft	<500 gt	500 gt to <10 000 gt and HSC<10 000 gt	All ships/craft ≥10 000 gt
Minimum operational display area diameter	180 mm	250 mm	320 mm
Minimum display area	195×195 mm	270×270 mm	340×340 mm
Auto acquisition of targets	—	—	Yes
Minimum *acquired* radar target capacity	20	30	40
Minimum *activated* AIS target capacity	20	30	40
Minimum *sleeping* AIS target capacity	100	150	200
Trial manoeuvre	—	—	Yes

4 DEFINITIONS

Definitions are in Appendix 2.

5 OPERATIONAL REQUIREMENTS FOR THE RADAR SYSTEM

The design and performance of the radar should be based on user requirements and up-to-date navigational technology. It should provide effective target detection within the safety-relevant environment surrounding own ship and should permit fast and easy situation evaluation[*].

5.1 Frequency

5.1.1 Frequency Spectrum

The radar should transmit within the confines of the ITU allocated bands for maritime radar and meet the requirements of the radio regulations and applicable ITU-recommendations.

5.1.2 Radar Sensor Requirements

Radar systems of both X and S bands are covered in these performance standards:

- X band (9.2–9.5 GHz) for high discrimination, good sensitivity and tracking performance; and
- S band (2.9–3.1 GHz) to ensure that target detection and tracking capabilities are maintained in varying and adverse conditions of fog, rain and sea clutter.

The frequency band in use should be indicated.

5.1.3 Interference Susceptibility

The radar should be capable of operating satisfactorily in typical interference conditions.

5.2 Radar Range and Bearing Accuracy

The radar system range and bearing accuracy requirements should be:

Range – within 30 m or 1 per cent of the range scale in use, whichever is greater;
Bearing – within 1°.

---

[*]Refer to MSC/Circ 878, the Human Element Analysing Process (HEAP).

5.3 Detection Performance and Anti-clutter Functions

All available means for the detection of targets should be used.

5.3.1 Detection

5.3.1.1 Detection in Clear Conditions

In the absence of clutter, for long range target and shoreline detection, the requirement for the radar system is based on normal propagation conditions, in the absence of sea clutter, precipitation and evaporation duct, with an antenna height of 15 m above sea level.

Based on:

- an indication of the target in at least 8 out of 10 scans or equivalent; and
- a probability of a radar detection false alarm of 10^{-4},

the requirement contained in Table 2 should be met as specified for X and S band equipment.

The detection performance should be achieved using the smallest antenna that is supplied with the radar system.

Recognizing the high relative speeds possible between own ship and target, the equipment should be specified and approved as being suitable for classes of ship having normal (<30 kn) or high (>30 kn) own ship speeds (100 kn and 140 kn relative speeds respectively).

5.3.1.2 Detection at Close Range

The short-range detection of the targets under the conditions specified in Table 2 should be compatible with the requirement in paragraph 5.4.

5.3.1.3 Detection in Clutter Conditions

Performance limitations caused by typical precipitation and sea clutter conditions will result in a reduction of target detection capabilities relative to those defined in 5.3.1.1 and Table. 2.

5.3.1.3.1 The radar equipment should be designed to provide the optimum and most consistent detection performance, restricted only by the physical limits of propagation.

5.3.1.3.2 The radar system should provide the means to enhance the visibility of targets in adverse clutter conditions at close range.

5.3.1.3.3 Degradation of detection performance (related to the figures in Table 2) at various ranges and target speeds under the following conditions, should be clearly stated in the user manual:

- light rain (4 mm per hour) and heavy rain (16 mm per hour);
- sea state 2 and sea state 5; and
- a combination of these.

5.3.1.3.4 The determination of performance in clutter and specifically, range of first detection, as defined in the clutter environment in 5.3.1.3.3, should be tested and assessed against a benchmark target, as specified in the Test Standard.

5.3.1.3.5 Degradation in performance due to a long transmission line, antenna height or any other factors should be clearly stated in the user manual.

5.3.2 Gain and Anti-Clutter Functions

5.3.2.1 Means should be provided, as far as is possible, for the adequate reduction of unwanted echoes, including sea clutter, rain and other forms of precipitation, clouds, sandstorms and interference from other radars.

5.3.2.2 A gain control function should be provided to set the system gain or signal threshold level.

5.3.2.3 Effective manual and automatic anti-clutter functions should be provided.

5.3.2.4 A combination of automatic and manual anti-clutter functions is permitted.

TABLE 2
Minimum detection ranges in clutter-free conditions

Target description	Target feature	Detection range in NM[6]	
Target description[5]	Height above sea level in metres	X Band NM	S Band NM
Shorelines	Rising to 60	20	20
Shorelines	Rising to 6	8	8
Shorelines	Rising to 3	6	6
SOLAS ships (>5000 gross tonnage)	10	11	11
SOLAS ships (>500 gross tonnage)	5.0	8	8
Small vessel with Radar Reflector meeting IMO Performance Standards[1]	4.0	5.0	3.7
Navigation buoy with corner reflector[2]	3.5	4.9	3.6
Typical Navigation buoy[3]	3.5	4.6	3.0
Small vessel of length 10 m with no radar reflector[4]	2.0	3.4	3.0

5.3.2.5 There should be a clear and permanent indication of the status and level for gain and all anti-clutter control functions.

5.3.3 Signal Processing

5.3.3.1 Means should be available to enhance target presentation on the display.

---

[1] IMO performance standards for radar reflectors – Radar Cross Section (RCS) 7.5 m^2 for X band, 0.5 m^2 for S band.

[2] The corner reflector (used for measurement), is taken as 10 m^2 for X band and 1.0 m^2 for S band.

[3] The typical navigation buoy is taken as 5.0 m^2 for X band and 0.5 m^2 for S band.

[4] RCS for 10 m small vessel taken as 2.5 m^2 for X band and 1.4 m^2 for S band.

[5] Reflectors are taken as point targets, vessels as complex targets and shorelines as distributed targets (typical values for a rocky shoreline, but are dependent on profile).

[6] Detection ranges experienced in practice will be affected by various factors, including atmospheric conditions (e.g. evaporation duct), target speed and aspect, target material and target structure. These and other factors may either enhance or degrade the detection ranges stated. At ranges between the first detection and own ship, the radar return may be reduced or enhanced by signal multi-path, which depend on factors such as antenna/target centroid height, target structure, sea state and radar frequency band.

5.3.3.2 The effective picture update period should be adequate, with minimum latency to ensure that the target detection requirements are met.

5.3.3.3 The picture should be updated in a smooth and continuous manner.

5.3.3.4 The equipment manual should explain the basic concept, features and limitations of any signal processing.

5.3.4 Operation with SARTs and Radar Beacons

5.3.4.1 The X band radar system should be capable of detecting radar beacons in the relevant frequency band.

5.3.4.2 The X band radar system should be capable of detecting SARTs and radar target enhancers.

5.3.4.3 It should be possible to switch off those signal processing functions, including polarization modes, which might prevent an X band radar beacon or

SARTs from being detected and displayed. The status should be indicated.

5.4 Minimum Range

5.4.1 With own ship at zero speed, an antenna height of 15 m above the sea level and in calm conditions, the navigational buoy in Table 2 should be detected at a minimum horizontal range of 40 m from the antenna position and up to a range of 1 NM, without changing the setting of control functions other than the range scale selector.

5.4.2 Compensation for any range error should be automatically applied for each selected antenna, where multiple antennas are installed.

5.5 Discrimination

Range and bearing discrimination should be measured in calm conditions, on a range scale of 1.5 NM or less and at between 50 per cent and 100 per cent of the range scale selected:

5.5.1 Range

The radar system should be capable of displaying two point targets on the same bearing, separated by 40 m in range, as two distinct objects.

5.5.2 Bearing

The radar system should be capable of displaying two point targets at the same range, separated by 2.5° in bearing, as two distinct objects.

5.6 Roll and Pitch

The target detection performance of the equipment should not be substantially impaired when own ship is rolling or pitching up to $+/-10°$.

5.7 Radar Performance Optimization and Tuning

5.7.1 Means should be available to ensure that the radar system is operating at the best performance.

Where applicable to the radar technology, manual tuning should be provided and additionally, automatic tuning may be provided.

5.7.2 An indication should be provided, in the absence of targets, to ensure that the system is operating at the optimum performance.

5.7.3 Means should be available (automatically or by manual operation) and while the equipment is operational, to determine a significant drop in system performance relative to a calibrated standard established at the time of installation.

5.8 Radar Availability

The radar equipment should be fully operational (RUN status) within 4 minutes after switch ON from cold. A STANDBY condition should be provided, in which there is no operational radar transmission. The radar should be fully operational within 5 sec from the standby condition.

5.9 Radar Measurements – Consistent Common Reference Point (CCRP)

5.9.1 Measurements from own ship (e.g. range rings, target range and bearing, cursor, tracking data) should be made with respect to the consistent common reference point (e.g. conning position). Facilities should be provided to compensate for the offset between antenna position and the consistent common reference point on installation. Where multiple antennas are installed, there should be provision for applying different position offsets for each antenna in the radar system. The offsets should be applied automatically when any radar sensor is selected.

5.9.2 Own ship's scaled outline should be available on appropriate range scales. The consistent common reference point and the position of the selected radar antenna should be indicated on this graphic.

5.9.3 When the picture is centred, the position of the Consistent Common Reference Point should be at the centre of the bearing scale. The off-centre

limits should apply to the position of the selected antenna.

5.9.4 Range measurements should be in nautical miles (NM). In addition, facilities for metric measurements may be provided on lower range scales. All indicated values for range measurement should be unambiguous.

5.9.5 Radar targets should be displayed on a linear range scale and without a range index delay.

5.10　Display Range Scales

5.10.1 Range scales of 0.25, 0.5, 0.75, 1.5, 3, 6, 12 and 24 NM should be provided. Additional range scales are permitted outside the mandatory set. Low metric range scales may be offered in addition to the mandatory set.

5.10.2 The range scale selected should be permanently indicated.

5.11　Fixed Range Rings

5.11.1 An appropriate number of equally spaced range rings should be provided for the range scale selected. When displayed, the range ring scale should be indicated.

5.11.2 The system accuracy of fixed range rings should be within 1 per cent of the maximum range of the range scale in use or 30 m, whichever is the greater distance.

5.12　Variable Range Markers (VRM)

5.12.1 At least two variable range markers (VRMs) should be provided. Each active VRM should have a numerical readout and have a resolution compatible with the range scale in use.

5.12.2 The VRMs should enable the user to measure the range of an object within the operational display area with a maximum system error of 1 per cent of the range scale in use or 30 m, whichever is the greater distance.

5.13　Bearing Scale

5.13.1 A bearing scale around the periphery of the operational display area should be provided. The bearing scale should indicate the bearing as seen from the consistent common reference point.

5.13.2 The bearing scale should be outside of the operational display area. It should be numbered at least every 30° division and have division marks of at least 5°. The 5° and 10° division marks should be clearly distinguishable from each other. 1° division marks may be presented where they are clearly distinguishable from each other.

5.14　Heading Line (HL)

5.14.1 A graphic line from the consistent common reference point to the bearing scale should indicate the heading of the ship.

5.14.2 Electronic means should be provided to align the heading line to within 0.1°. If there is more than one radar antenna (see 5.35) the heading skew (bearing offset) should be retained and automatically applied when each radar antenna is selected.

5.14.3 Provision should be made to temporarily suppress the heading line. This function may be combined with the suppression of other graphics.

5.15　Electronic Bearing Lines (EBLs)

5.15.1 At least two electronic bearing lines (EBLs) should be provided to measure the bearing of any point object within the operational display area, with a maximum system error of 1° at the periphery of the display.

5.15.2 The EBLs should be capable of measurement relative to the ship's heading and relative to true north. There should be a clear indication of the bearing reference (i.e. true or relative).

5.15.3 It should be possible to move the EBL origin from the consistent common reference point to any point within the operational display area and to reset the EBL to the consistent common reference point by a fast and simple action.

5.15.4 It should be possible to fix the EBL origin or to move the EBL origin at the velocity of own ship.

5.15.5 Means should be provided to ensure that the user is able to position the EBL smoothly in either direction, with an incremental adjustment adequate to maintain the system measurement accuracy requirements.

5.15.6 Each active EBL should have a numerical readout with a resolution adequate to maintain the system measurement accuracy requirements.

5.16 Parallel Index Lines (PI)

5.16.1 A minimum of four independent parallel index lines, with a means to truncate and switch off individual lines, should be provided.

5.16.2 Simple and quick means of setting the bearing and beam range of a parallel index line should be provided. The bearing and beam range of any selected index line should be available on demand.

5.17 Offset Measurement of Range and Bearing

There should be a means to measure the range and bearing of one position on the display relative to any other position within the operational display area.

5.18 User Cursor

5.18.1 A user cursor should be provided to enable a fast and concise means to designate any position on the operational display area.

5.18.2 The cursor position should have a continuous readout to provide the range and bearing, measured from the consistent common reference point, and/or the latitude and longitude of the cursor position presented either alternatively or simultaneously .

5.18.3 The cursor should provide the means to select and de-select targets, graphics or objects within the operational display area. In addition, the cursor may be used to select modes, functions, vary parameters and control menus outside of the operational display area.

5.18.4 Means should be provided to easily locate the cursor position on the display.

5.18.5 The accuracy of the range and bearing measurements provided by the cursor should meet the relevant requirements for VRM and EBL.

5.19 Azimuth Stabilization

5.19.1 The heading information should be provided by a gyrocompass or by an equivalent sensor with a performance not inferior to the relevant standards adopted by the Organization.

5.19.2 Excluding the limitations of the stabilizing sensor and type of transmission system, the accuracy of azimuth alignment of the radar presentation should be within 0.5° with a rate of turn likely to be experienced with the class of ship.

5.19.3 The heading information should be displayed with a numerical resolution to permit accurate alignment with the ship gyro system.

5.19.4 The heading information should be referenced to the consistent common reference point (CCRP).

5.20 Display Mode of the Radar Picture

5.20.1 A True Motion display mode should be provided. The automatic reset of own ship may be initiated by its position on the display, or time related, or both. Where the reset is selected to occur at least on every scan or equivalent, this should be equivalent to True Motion with a fixed origin (in practice equivalent to the previous relative motion mode).

5.20.2 North Up and Course Up orientation modes should be provided. Head Up may be provided when the display mode is equivalent to True Motion with a fixed origin (in practice equivalent to the previous relative motion Head Up mode).

5.20.3 An indication of the motion and orientation mode should be provided.

5.21 Off-Centring

5.21.1 Manual off-centring should be provided to locate the selected antenna position at any point within at least 50 per cent of the radius from the centre of the operational display area.

5.21.2   On selection of off-centred display, the selected antenna position should be capable of being located to any point on the display up to atleast 50 per cent, and not more than 75 per cent, of the radius from the centre of the operational display area. A facility for automatically positioning own ship for the maximum view ahead may be provided.

5.21.3   In True Motion, the selected antenna position should automatically reset up to a 50 per cent radius to a location giving the maximum view along own ship's course. Provision for an early reset of selected antenna position should be provided.

5.22   Ground and Sea Stabilization Modes

5.22.1   Ground and Sea stabilization modes should be provided.

5.22.2   The stabilization mode and stabilization source should be clearly indicated.

5.22.3   The source of own ships' speed should be indicated and provided by a sensor approved in accordance with the requirements of the Organization for the relevant stabilization mode.

5.23   Target Trails and Past Positions

5.23.1   Variable length (time) target trails should be provided, with an indication of trail time and mode. It should be possible to select true or relative trails from a reset condition for all true motion display modes.

5.23.2   The trails should be distinguishable from targets.

5.23.3   Either scaled trails or past positions or both, should be maintained and should be available for presentation within 2 scans or equivalent, following:

- the reduction or increase of one range scale;
- the offset and reset of the radar picture position; and
- a change between true and relative trails.

5.24   Presentation of Target Information

5.24.1   Targets should be presented in accordance with the performance standards for the Presentation of Navigation-related Information on Shipborne Navigational Displays adopted by the Organization and with their relevant symbols according to SN/Circ. 243.

5.24.2   The target information may be provided by the radar target tracking function and by the reported target information from the Automatic Identification System (AIS).

5.24.3   The operation of the radar tracking function and the processing of reported AIS information is defined in these standards.

5.24.4   The number of targets presented, related to display size, is defined in Table 1. An indication should be given when the target capacity of radar tracking or AIS reported target processing/display capability is about to be exceeded.

5.24.5   As far as practical, the user interface and data format for operating, displaying and indicating AIS and radar tracking information should be consistent.

5.25   Target Tracking (TT) and Acquisition

5.25.1   General

Radar targets are provided by the radar sensor (transceiver). The signals may be filtered (reduced) with the aid of the associated clutter controls. Radar targets may be manually or automatically acquired and tracked using an automatic Target Tracking (TT) facility.

5.25.1.1   The automatic target tracking calculations should be based on the measurement of radar target relative position and own ship motion.

5.25.1.2   Any other sources of information, when available, may be used to support the optimum tracking performance.

5.25.1.3   TT facilities should be available on at least the 3, 6, and 12 NM range scales. Tracking range should extend to a minimum of 12 NM.

5.25.1.4 The radar system should be capable of tracking targets having the maximum relative speed relevant to its classification for normal or high own ship speeds (see 5.3).

5.25.2 Tracked Target Capacity

5.25.2.1 In addition to the requirements for processing of targets reported by AIS, it should be possible to track and provide full presentation functionality for a minimum number of tracked radar targets according to Table 1.

5.25.2.2 There should be an indication when the target tracking capacity is about to be exceeded. Target overflow should not degrade the radar system performance.

5.25.3 Acquisition

5.25.3.1 Manual acquisition of radar targets should be provided with provision for acquiring at least the number of targets specified in Table 1.

5.25.3.2 Automatic acquisition should be provided where specified in Table 1. In this case, there should be means for the user to define the boundaries of the auto-acquisition area.

5.25.4 Tracking

5.25.4.1 When a target is acquired, the system should present the trend of the target's motion within one minute and the prediction of the target's motion within 3 minutes.

5.25.4.2 TT should be capable of tracking and updating the information of all acquired targets automatically.

5.25.4.3 The system should continue to track radar targets that are clearly distinguishable on the display for 5 out of 10 consecutive scans or equivalent.

5.25.4.4 The TT design should be such that target vector and data smoothing is effective, while target manoeuvres should be detected as early as possible.

5.25.4.5 The possibility of tracking errors, including target swap, should be minimized by design.

5.25.4.6 Separate facilities for cancelling the tracking of any one and of all target(s) should be provided.

5.25.4.7 Automatic tracking accuracy should be achieved when the tracked target has achieved a steady state, assuming the sensor errors allowed by the relevant performance standards of the Organization:

5.25.4.7.1 For ships capable of up to 30 kn true speed, the tracking facility should present, within 1 min steady state tracking, the relative motion trend and after 3 minutes, the predicted motion of a target, within the following accuracy values (95 per cent probability):

TABLE 3
Tracked target accuracy (95% probability figures)

Time of steady state (minutes)	Relative course (degrees)	Relative speed (kn)	CPA (NM)	TCPA (minutes)	True course (degrees)	True speed (kn)
1 min: Trend	11	1.5 or 10% (whichever is greater)	1.0	—	—	—
3 min: Motion	3	0.8 or 1% (whichever is greater)	0.3	0.5	5	0.5 or 1% (whichever is greater)

Accuracy may be significantly reduced during or shortly after acquisition, own ship manoeuvre, a manoeuvre of the target, or any tracking disturbance and is also dependent on own ship's motion and sensor accuracy.

Measured target range and bearing should be within 50 m (or $+/-1$ per cent of target range) and 2°.

The testing standard should have detailed target simulation tests as a means to confirm the accuracy of targets with relative speeds of up to 100 kn. Individual accuracy values shown in the table above may be adapted to account for the relative aspects of target motion with respect to that of own ship in the testing scenarios used.

5.25.4.7.2   For ships capable of speeds in excess of 30 kn (typically high-speed craft (HSC)) and with speeds of up to 70 kn, there should be additional steady state measurements made to ensure that the motion accuracy, after 3 minutes of steady state tracking, is maintained with target relative speeds of up to 140 kn.

5.25.4.8   A ground referencing function, based on a stationary tracked target, should be provided. Targets used for this function should be marked with the relevant symbol defined in SN/Circ. 243.

5.26   Automatic Identification System (AIS) Reported Targets

5.26.1   General

Reported targets provided by the AIS may be filtered according to user-defined parameters. Targets may be sleeping, or may be activated. Activated targets are treated in a similar way to radar tracked targets.

5.26.2   AIS Target Capacity

In addition to the requirements for radar tracking, it should be possible to display and provide full presentation functionality for a minimum number of sleeping and activated AIS targets according to Table 1. There should be an indication when the capacity of processing/display of AIS targets is about to be exceeded.

5.26.3   Filtering of AIS Sleeping Targets

To reduce display clutter, a means to filter the presentation of sleeping AIS targets should be provided, together with an indication of the filter status. (e.g. by target range, CPA/TCPA or AIS target class A/B, etc.). It should not be possible to remove individual AIS targets from the display.

5.26.4   Activation of AIS Targets

A means to activate a sleeping AIS target and to deactivate an activated AIS target should be provided. If zones for the automatic activation of AIS targets are provided, they should be the same as for automatic radar target acquisition. In addition, sleeping AIS targets may be automatically activated when meeting user defined parameters (e.g. target range, CPA/TCPA or AIS target class A/B).

5.26.5   AIS Presentation Status

5.27   AIS Graphical Presentation

Targets should be presented with their relevant symbols according to the performance standards for the Presentation of Navigation-related Information on Shipborne Navigational Displays adopted by the Organization and SN/Circ. 243.

5.27.1   AIS targets that are displayed should be presented as sleeping targets by default.

5.27.2   The course and speed of a tracked radar target or reported AIS target should be indicated by a predicted motion vector. The vector time should be adjustable and valid for presentation of any target regardless of its source.

5.27.3   A permanent indication of vector mode, time and stabilization should be provided.

5.27.4   The consistent common reference point should be used for the alignment of tracked radar and AIS symbols with other information on the same display.

5.27.5   On large scale/low range displays, a means to present the true scale outline of an activated AIS target

TABLE 4

The AIS presentation status should be indicated as follows:

Function	Cases to be presented		Presentation
AIS ON/OFF	AIS processing switched ON/graphical presentation switched OFF	AIS processing switched ON/graphical presentation switched ON	Alphanumeric or graphical
Filtering of sleeping AIS targets	Filter status	Filter status	Alphanumeric or graphical
Activation of targets		Activation criteria	Graphical
CPA/TCPA alarm	Function ON/OFF Sleeping targets included	Function ON/OFF Sleeping targets included	Alphanumeric and graphical
Lost target alarm	Function ON/OFF Lost target filter criteria	Function ON/OFF Lost target filter criteria	Alphanumeric and graphical
Target association	Function ON/OFF Association criteria Default target priority	Function ON/OFF Association criteria Default target priority	Alphanumeric

should be provided. It should be possible to display the past track of activated targets.

5.28 AIS and Radar Target Data

5.28.1 It should be possible to select any tracked radar or AIS target for the alphanumeric display of its data. A target selected for the display of its alphanumeric information should be identified by the relevant symbol. If more than one target is selected for data display, the relevant symbols and the corresponding data should be clearly identified. There should be a clear indication to show that the target data is derived from radar or from AIS.

5.28.2 For each selected tracked radar target, the following data should be presented in alphanumeric form: source(s) of data, actual range of target, actual bearing of target, predicted target range at the closest point of approach (CPA), predicted time to CPA (TCPA), true course of target, true speed of target.

5.28.3 For each selected AIS target the following data should be presented in alphanumeric form: Source of data, ship's identification, navigational status, position where available and its quality, range, bearing, COG, SOG, CPA, and TCPA. Target heading and reported rate of turn should also be made available. Additional target information should be provided on request.

5.28.4 If the received AIS information is incomplete, the absent information should be clearly indicated as 'missing' within the target data field.

5.28.5 The data should be displayed and continually updated, until another target is selected for data display or until the window is closed.

5.28.6 Means should be provided to present own ship AIS data on request.

5.29 Operational Alarms

A clear indication of the cause for all alarm criteria should be given.

5.29.1 If the calculated CPA and TCPA values of a tracked target or activated AIS target are less than the set limits:

- A CPA/TCPA alarm should be given.
- The target should be clearly indicated.

5.29.2 The preset CPA/TCPA limits applied to targets from different radar and AIS should be identical. As a default state, the CPA/TCPA alarm functionality should be applied to all activated AIS targets. On user request the CPA/TCPA alarm functionality may also be applied to sleeping targets.

5.29.3 If a user defined acquisition/activation zone facility is provided, a target not previously acquired/activated entering the zone, or is detected within the zone, should be clearly identified with the relevant symbol and an alarm should be given. It should be possible for the user to set ranges and outlines for the zone.

5.29.4 The system should alert the user if a tracked radar target is lost, rather than excluded by a pre-determined range or pre-set parameter. The target's last position should be clearly indicated on the display.

5.29.5 It should be possible to enable or disable the lost target alarm function for AIS targets. A clear indication should be given if the lost target alarm is disabled.

If the following conditions are met for a lost AIS target:

- The AIS lost target alarm function is enabled.
- The target is of interest, according to lost target filter criteria.
- A message is not received for a set time, depending on the nominal reporting rate of the AIS target.

Then:

- The last known position should be clearly indicated as a lost target and an alarm be given.
- The indication of the lost target should disappear if the signal is received again, or after the alarm has been acknowledged.
- A means of recovering limited historical data from previous reports should be provided.

5.30 AIS and Radar Target Association

An automatic target association function based on harmonized criteria avoids the presentation of two target symbols for the same physical target.

5.30.1 If the target data from AIS and radar tracking are both available and if the association criteria (e.g. position, motion) are fulfilled such that the AIS and radar information are considered as one physical target, then as a default condition, the activated AIS target symbol and the alphanumeric AIS target data should be automatically selected and displayed.

5.30.2 The user should have the option to change the default condition to the display of tracked radar targets and should be permitted to select either radar tracking or AIS alphanumeric data.

5.30.3 For an associated target, if the AIS and radar information become sufficiently different, the AIS and radar information should be considered as two distinct targets and one activated AIS target and one tracked radar target should be displayed. No alarm should be raised.

5.31 Trial Manoeuvre

The system should, where required by Table 1, be capable of simulating the predicted effects of own ship's manoeuvre in a potential threat situation and should include own ship's dynamic characteristics. A trial manoeuvre simulation should be clearly identified. The requirements are:

- The simulation of own ship course and speed should be variable.
- A simulated time to manoeuvre with a countdown should be provided.

- During simulation, target tracking should continue and the actual target data should be indicated.
- Trial manoeuvre should be applied to all tracked targets and at least all activated AIS targets.

5.32 The Display of Maps, Navigation Lines and Routes

5.32.1 It should be possible for the user to manually create and change, save, load and display simple maps/navigation lines/routes referenced to own ship or a geographical position. It should be possible to remove the display of this data by a simple operator action.

5.32.2 The maps/navigation lines/routes may consist of lines, symbols and reference points.

5.32.3 The appearance of lines, colours and symbols are as defined in SN/Circ. 243.

5.32.4 The maps/navigation lines/route graphics should not significantly degrade the radar information.

5.32.5 The maps/navigation lines/routes should be retained when the equipment is switched OFF.

5.32.6 The maps/navigation lines/route data should be transferable whenever a relevant equipment module is replaced.

5.33 The Display of Charts

5.33.1 The radar system may provide the means to display ENC and other vector chart information within the operational display area to provide continuous and real-time position monitoring. It should be possible to remove the display of chart data by a single operator action.

5.33.2 The ENC information should be the primary source of information and should comply with IHO relevant standards. Status of other information should be identified with a permanent indication. Source and update information should be made available.

5.33.3 As a minimum, the elements of the ECDIS Standard Display should be made available for individual selection by category or layer, but not as individual objects.

5.33.4 The chart information should use the same reference and co-ordinate criteria as the radar/AIS, including datum, scale, orientation, CCRP and stabilization mode.

5.33.5 The display of radar information should have priority. Chart information should be displayed such that radar information is not substantially masked, obscured or degraded. Chart information should be clearly perceptible as such.

5.33.6 A malfunction of the source of chart data should not affect the operation of the radar/AIS system.

5.33.7 Symbols and colours should comply with the performance standards for the Presentation of Navigation-related Information on Shipborne Navigational Displays adopted by the Organization (SN/Circ. 243.)

5.34 Alarms and Indications

Alarms and indications should comply with the performance standards for the Presentation of Navigation-related Information on Shipborne Navigational Displays adopted by the Organization.

5.34.1 A means should be provided to alert the user of 'picture freeze'.

5.34.2 Failure of any signal or sensor in use, including; gyro, log, azimuth, video, sync and heading marker, should be alarmed. System functionality should be limited to a fallback mode or in some cases, the display presentation should be inhibited (see fallback modes, section 9).

5.35 Integrating Multiple Radars

5.35.1 The system should safeguard against single point system failure. Fail-safe condition should be applied in the event of an integration failure.

5.35.2 The source and any processing or combination of radar signals should be indicated.

5.35.3 The system status for each display position should be available.

6 ERGONOMIC CRITERIA

6.1 Operational Controls

6.1.1 The design should ensure that the radar system is simple to operate. Operational controls should have a harmonized user interface and be easy to identify and simple to use.

6.1.2 The radar system should be capable of being switched ON or OFF at the main system radar display or at a control position.

6.1.3 The control functions may be dedicated hardware, screen accessed or a combination of these; however the primary control functions should be dedicated hardware controls or soft keys, with an associated status indication in a consistent and intuitive position.

6.1.4 The following are defined as primary radar control functions and should be easily and immediately accessible:

Radar Standby/RUN, Range scale selection, Gain, tuning function (if applicable), Anti-clutter rain, Anti-clutter sea, AIS function on/off, Alarm acknowledge, Cursor, a means to set EBL/VRM, display brightness and acquisition of radar targets.

6.1.5 The primary functions may also be operated from a remote operating position in addition to the main controls.

6.2 Display Presentation

6.2.1 The display presentation should comply with the performance standards for the Presentation of Navigation-related Information on Shipborne Navigational Displays adopted by the Organization.

6.2.2 The colours, symbols and graphics presented should comply with SN/Circ. 243.

6.2.3 The display sizes should conform to those defined in Table 1.

6.3 Instructions and Documentation

6.3.1 Documentation Language

The operating instructions and manufacturer's documentation should be written in a clear and comprehensible manner and should be available at least in the English language.

6.3.2 Operating Instructions

The operating instructions should contain a qualified explanation and/or description of information required by the user to operate the radar system correctly, including:

- appropriate settings for different weather conditions;
- monitoring the radar system's performance;
- operating in a failure or fallback situation;
- limitations of the display and tracking process and accuracy, including any delays;
- using heading and SOG/COG information for collision avoidance;
- limitations and conditions of target association;
- criteria of selection for automatic activation and cancellation of targets;
- methods applied to display AIS targets and any limitations;
- principles underlying the trial manoeuvre technology, including simulation of own ship's manoeuvring characteristics, if provided;
- alarms and indications;
- installation requirements as listed under section 7.5;
- radar range and bearing accuracies; and
- any special operation (e.g. tuning) for the detection of SARTs, and
- the role of the CCRP for radar measurements and its specific value.

6.3.3 Manufacturer's Documentation

6.3.3.1 The manufacturer's documentation should contain a description of the radar system and factors which may affect detection performance, including any latency in signal processing.

6.3.3.2 Documentation should describe the basis of AIS filter criteria and AIS/radar target association criteria.

6.3.3.3 The equipment documentation should include full details of installation information, including additional recommendations on unit location and factors that may degrade performance or reliability.

7 DESIGN AND INSTALLATION

7.1 Design for Servicing

7.1.1 As far as is practical, the radar system should be of a design to facilitate simple fault diagnosis and maximum availability.

7.1.2 The radar system should include a means to record the total operational hours for any components with a limited life.

7.1.3 The documentation should describe any routine servicing requirements and should include details of any restricted life components.

7.2 Display

The display device physical requirements should meet those specified in the performance standards for the Presentation of Navigation-related Information on Shipborne Navigational Displays adopted by the Organization (SN/Circ. 243) and those specified in Table 1.

7.3 Transmitter Mute

The equipment should provide a mute facility to inhibit the transmission of radar energy over a preset sector. The mute sector should be set up on installation. An indication of sector mute status should be available.

7.4 Antenna

7.4.1 The antenna should be designed to start operating and to continue to operate in relative wind speeds likely to be encountered on the class of ship on which it is installed.

7.4.2 The combined radar system should be capable of providing an appropriate information update rate for the class of ship on which it is installed.

7.4.3 The antenna side lobes should be consistent with satisfying the system performance as defined in this standard.

7.4.4 There should be a means to prevent antenna rotation and radiation during servicing, or while personnel are in the vicinity of up-mast units.

7.5 Radar System Installation

Requirements and guidelines for the radar system installation should be included in the manufacturers' documentation. The following subjects should be covered:

7.5.1 The Antenna

Blind sectors should be kept to a minimum, and should not be placed in an arc of the horizon from the right ahead direction to 22.5° abaft the beam and especially should avoid the right ahead direction (relative bearing 000°). The installation of the antenna should be in such a manner that the performance of the radar system is not substantially degraded. The antenna should be mounted clear of any structure that may cause signal reflections, including other antenna and deck structure or cargo. In addition, the height of the antenna should take account of target detection performance relating to range of first detection and target visibility in sea clutter.

7.5.2 The Display

The orientation of the display unit should be such that the user is looking ahead, the lookout view is not obscured and there is minimum ambient light on the display.

7.6 Operation and Training

7.6.1 The design should ensure that the radar system is simple to operate by trained users.

7.6.2   A target simulation facility should be provided for training purposes.

8   INTERFACING

8.1   Input Data

The radar system should be capable of receiving the required input information from:

- a gyro-compass or transmitting heading device (THD);
- a speed and distance measuring equipment (SDME);
- an electronic position fixing system (EPFS);
- an Automatic Identification System (AIS); or
- other sensors or networks providing equivalent information acceptable to the Organization.

The radar should be interfaced to relevant sensors required by these performance standards in accordance with recognized international standards*.

8.2   Input Data Integrity and Latency

8.2.1   The radar system should not use data indicated as invalid. If input data is known to be of poor quality this should be clearly indicated.

8.2.2   As far as is practical, the integrity of data should be checked, prior to its use, by comparison with other connected sensors or by testing to valid and plausible data limits.

8.2.3   The latency of processing input data should be minimized.

8.3   Output Data

8.3.1   Information provided by any radar output interface to other systems should be in accordance with international standards*.

8.3.2   The radar system should provide an output of the display data for the voyage data recorder (VDR).

---

* Refer to IEC publication 61162.

8.3.3   At least one normally closed contact (isolated) should be provided for indicating failure of the radar.

8.3.4   The radar should have a bi-directional interface to facilitate communication so that alarms from the radar can be transferred to external systems and so that audible alarms from the radar can be muted from external systems, the interface should comply with relevant international standards.

9   BACKUP AND FALLBACK ARRANGEMENTS

In the event of partial failures and to maintain minimum basic operation, the fallback arrangements listed below should be provided. There should be a permanent indication of the failed input information.

9.1   Failure of Heading Information (Azimuth Stabilization)

9.1.1   The equipment should operate satisfactorily in an unstabilized head-up mode.

9.1.2   The equipment should switch automatically to the unstabilized head up mode within 1 minute after the azimuth stabilization has become ineffective.

9.1.3   If automatic anti-clutter processing could prevent the detection of targets in the absence of appropriate stabilization, the processing should switch off automatically within 1 minute after the azimuth stabilization has become ineffective.

9.1.4   An indication should be given that only relative bearing measurements can be used.

9.2   Failure of Speed through the Water Information

A means of manual speed input should be provided and its use clearly indicated.

9.3   Failure of Course and Speed Over Ground Information

The equipment may be operated with course and speed through the water information.

9.4 Failure of Position Input Information

The overlay of chart data and geographically referenced maps should be disabled if only a single Reference Target is defined and used, or the position is manually entered.

9.5 Failure of Radar Video Input Information

In the absence of radar signals, the equipment should display target information based on AIS data. A frozen radar picture should not be displayed.

9.6 Failure of AIS Input Information

In the absence of AIS signals, the equipment should display the radar video and target database.

9.7 Failure of an Integrated or Networked System

The equipment should be capable of operating equivalent to a standalone system.

Appendix 1 – References

IMO SOLAS chapters IV, V and X	Carriage rules.
IMO resolution A.278 (VII)	Supplement to the recommendation on PS for navigational radar equipment.
IMO resolution A.424 (XI)	Performance standards for gyro-compasses.
IMO resolution A.477 (XII)	Performance standards for radar equipment.
IMO resolution A.694 (17)	General Requirements for shipborne radio equipment forming part of the global maritime distress and safety system and for electronically navigational aids.
IMO resolution A.817(19) as amended	Performance standards for ECDIS.
IMO resolution A.821 (19)	Performance standards for gyro-compasses for high-speed craft.
IMO resolution A.824 (19)	Performance standards for devices to indicate speed and distance.
IMO resolution MSC.86 (70)	Performance standards for INS.
IMO resolution MSC.64 (67)	Recommendations on new and amended performance standards (Annex 2 revised by MSC.114 (73)).
IMO resolution MSC.112 (73)	Revised performance standards for ship borne global positioning (GPS) receiver equipment.
IMO resolution MSC.114 (73)	Revised performance standards for shipborne DGPS and DGLONASS maritime radio beacon receiver equipment.
IMO resolution MSC.116 (73)	Performance standards for marine transmitting heading devices (THD).
IMO MSC Circ.982	Guidelines on ergonomic criteria for bridge equipment and layout.
IHO S-52 appendix 2	Colour and symbol specification for ECDIS.
IEC 62388	Radar Test Standard (replacing 60872 and 60936 series of test standards).
IEC 60945	Maritime navigation and radio communication equipment and systems – General requirements – Methods of testing and required test results.
IEC 61162	Maritime navigation and radio communication equipment and systems – Digital interfaces.

IEC 61174	Maritime navigation and radio communication equipment and systems – Electronic chart display and information system (ECDIS) – Operational and performance requirements, methods of testing and required test results.
IEC 62288	Presentation and display of navigation information.
ISO 9000 (all parts)	Quality management/assurance standards.

Appendix 2 – Definitions

Activated AIS target — A target representing the automatic or manual activation of a sleeping target for the display of additional graphically presented information. The target is displayed by an 'activated target' symbol including:

- a vector (COG/ SOG);
- the heading; and
- ROT or direction of turn indication (if available) to indicate initiated course changes.

Acquisition of a radar target — Process of acquiring a target and initiating its tracking.

Activation of an AIS target — Activation of a sleeping AIS target for the display of additional graphical and alphanumerical information.

Acquired radar target — Automatic or manual acquisition initiates radar tracking. Vectors and past positions are displayed when data has achieved a steady state condition.

AIS — Automatic Identification System.

AIS target — A target generated from an AIS message. See activated target, lost target, selected target and sleeping target.

Associated target — If an acquired radar target and an AIS reported target have similar parameters (e.g. position, course, speed) complying with an association algorithm, they are considered to be the same target and become an associated target.

Acquisition/ activation zone — A zone set up by the operator in which the system should automatically acquire radar targets and activate reported AIS targets when entering the zone.

CCRP — Consistent Common Reference Point: A location on own ship, to which all horizontal measurements such as target range, bearing, relative course, relative speed, closest point of approach (CPA) or time to closest point of approach (TCPA) are referenced, typically the conning position of the bridge.

CPA/TCPA — Closest Point of Approach/ Time to the Closest Point of Approach: Distance to the closest point of approach (CPA) and time to the closest point of approach (TCPA). Limits are set by the operator related to own ship.

Course Over Ground (COG) — Direction of the ship's movement relative to the earth, measured on board the ship, expressed in angular units from true north.

Course Through Water (CTW) — Direction of the ship's movement through the water, defined by the angle between the meridian through its position and the direction of the ship's movement through the water, expressed in angular units from true north.

Dangerous target — A target whose predicted CPA and TCPA are violating the values as preset by the operator. The respective target is marked by a 'dangerous target' symbol.

Display modes — **Relative motion:** means a display on which the position of own ship remains fixed, and all targets move relative to own ship.

True motion: a display across which own ship moves with its own true motion.

Display orientation — **North up display:** an azimuth stabilized presentation which uses the gyro input (or equivalent) and north is uppermost on the presentation.

Course up display: an azimuth stabilized presentation which uses the gyro input or equivalent and the ship's course is uppermost on the presentation at the time of selection.

Head up display: an unstabilized presentation in which own ship's heading is uppermost on the presentation.

ECDIS — Electronic Chart Display and Information System.

ECDIS Display Base — The level of information which cannot be removed from the ECDIS display, consisting of information which is required at all times in all geographic areas and all circumstances. It is not intended to be sufficient for safe navigation.

ECDIS Standard Display — The level of information that should be shown when a chart is first displayed on ECDIS. The level of the information it provides for route planning or route monitoring may be modified by the mariner according to the mariner's needs.

ENC — Electronic Navigational Chart. The database standardized as to content, structure and format according to relevant IHO standards and issued by, or on the authority of, a government.

EPFS — Electronic Position Fixing System.

ERBL — Electronic bearing line carrying a marker, which is combined with the range marker, used to measure range and bearing from own ship or between two objects.

Evaporation duct — A low lying duct (a change in air density) that traps the radar energy so that it propagates close to the sea surface. Ducting may enhance or reduce radar target detection ranges.

Heading — Direction in which the bow of a ship is pointing expressed as an angular displacement from north.

HSC High-speed craft (HSC) are vessels which comply with the definition in SOLAS for high speed craft.

Latency The delay between actual and presented data.

Lost AIS target A target representing the last valid position of an AIS target before the reception of its data was lost. The target is displayed by a 'lost AIS target' symbol.

Lost tracked target Target information is no longer available due to poor, lost or obscured signals. The target is displayed by a 'lost tracked radar target' symbol.

Maps/Nav lines Operator defined or created lines to indicate channels, Traffic Separation Schemes or borders of any area important for navigation.

Operational display area Area of the display used to graphically present chart and radar information, excluding the user dialogue area. On the chart display this is the area of the chart presentation. On the radar display this is the area encompassing the radar image.

Past positions Equally time-spaced past position marks of a tracked or reported target and own ship. The past positions' track may be either relative or true.

Radar (**Ra**dio **d**irection **a**nd **r**anging) A radio system that allows the determination of distance and direction of reflecting objects and of transmitting devices.

Radar beacon A navigation aid which responds to the radar transmission by generating a radar signal to identify its position and identity.

Radar detection false alarm The probability of a radar false alarm represents the probability that noise will cross the detection threshold and be called a target when only noise is present.

Radar target Any object fixed or moving whose position and motion is determined by successive radar measurements of range and bearing.

Radar target enhancer An electronic radar reflector, the output of which is an amplified version of the received radar pulse without any form of processing except limiting.

Reference target Symbol indicating that the associated tracked stationary target (e.g. a navigational mark) is used as a speed reference for the ground stabilization.

Relative bearing Direction of a target's position from own ship's reference location expressed as an angular displacement from own ship's heading.

Relative course Direction of motion of a target relative to own ship's direction. (Bearing.)

Relative motion Combination of relative course and relative speed.

Relative speed	Speed of a target relative to own ship's speed data.		monitoring may be modified by the mariner according to the mariner's needs.
Rate of turn	Change of heading per time unit.	**Standard radar reflector**	Reference reflector mounted 3.5 m above sea level with 10 m^2 effective reflecting area at X-band.
SART	Search And Rescue Transponder.		
SDME	Speed and Distance Measurement Equipment.	**Steady state tracking**	Tracking a target, proceeding at steady motion

Selected target	A manually selected target for the display of detailed alphanumeric information in a separate data display area. The target is displayed by a 'selected target' symbol.		– after completion of the acquisition process, or
			   – without a manoeuvre of target or own ship, or
			   – without target swap or any disturbance.

Sleeping AIS target	A target indicating the presence and orientation of a vessel equipped with AIS in a certain location. The target is displayed by a 'sleeping target' symbol. No additional information is presented until activated.	**Speed Over Ground (SOG)**	Speed of the ship relative to the earth, measured on board of the ship.
		Speed Through Water	Speed of the ship relative to the water surface.
Stabilization modes	**Ground stabilization:** Display mode in which speed and course information are referred to the ground, using ground track input data, or EPFS as reference.	**SOLAS**	International Convention for the Safety of Life at Sea.
		Suppressed area	An area set up by the operator within which targets are not acquired.
	Sea stabilization: Display mode in which speed and course information are referred to the sea, using gyro or equivalent and water speed log input as reference.	**Target swap**	Situation in which the incoming radar data for a tracked target becomes incorrectly associated with another tracked target or a non-tracked radar echo.
Standard display	The level of information that should be shown when a chart is first displayed on ECDIS. The level of the information it provides for route planning or route	**Target's predicted motion**	Prediction of a target's future course and speed based on linear extrapolation from its present motion as determined by past measurements of its range and bearing on the radar.

Target Tracking (TT)	Computer process of observing the sequential changes in the position of a radar target in order to establish its motion. Such a target is a Tracked Target.	**True speed**	Speed of a target relative to ground, or to sea.
Trails	Tracks displayed by the radar echoes of targets in the form of an afterglow. Trails may be true or relative.	**Vector modes**	**True vector:** Vector representing the predicted true motion of a target, showing course and speed with reference to the ground. **Relative vector:** Predicted movement of a target relative to own ship's motion.
Trial manoeuvre	Graphical simulation facility used to assist the operator to perform a proposed manoeuvre for navigation and collision avoidance purposes, by displaying the predicted future status of at least all acquired or activated targets as a result of own ship's simulated manoeuvres.	**User Configured Presentation**	A display presentation configured by the user for a specific task at hand. The presentation may include radar and/or chart information, in combination with other navigation or ship related data.
True bearing	Direction of a target from own ship's reference location or from another target's position expressed as an angular displacement from true north.	**User Dialogue Area**	Is an area of the display consisting of data fields and/or menus that is allocated to the interactive presentation and entry or selection of operational parameters, data and commands mainly in alphanumeric form.
True course	Direction of motion relative to ground or to sea, of a target expressed as an angular displacement from north.		
True motion	Combination of true course and true speed.		

11.2.2 Extracts from IMO Resolution MSC 191(79) Performance Standards for the presentation of navigation-related information on shipborne navigational displays for new ships constructed after 2008

1 PURPOSE

These performance standards harmonize the requirements for the presentation of navigation-related information on the bridge of a ship to ensure that all navigational displays adopt a consistent human machine interface philosophy and implementation.

These performance standards supplement and, in case of a conflict, take priority over, presentation requirements of the individual performance standards adopted by the Organization for relevant navigational systems and equipment, and cover the presentation of navigation-related information by equipment for which performance standards have not been adopted.

2 SCOPE

These performance standards specify the presentation of navigational information on the bridge of a ship, including the consistent use of navigational terms, abbreviations, colours and symbols, as well as other presentation characteristics.

These performance standards also address the presentation of navigation information related to specific navigational tasks by recognizing the use of user selected presentations in addition to presentations required by the individual performance standards adopted by the Organization.

3 APPLICATION

The general principles of these standards are applicable for all displays on the bridge of a ship*.

These performance standards are applicable to any display equipment associated with the navigation systems and equipment for which individual performance standards have been adopted by the Organization. They also address display equipment associated with navigation systems and equipment for which individual performance standards have not been adopted.

In addition to the general requirements set out in resolution A.694(17)** display equipment should meet the requirements of these performance standards, as applicable.

4 DEFINITIONS

Definitions are given in the Appendix.

5 GENERAL REQUIREMENTS FOR THE PRESENTATION OF INFORMATION

5.1 Arrangement of information

5.1.1 The presentation of information should be consistent with respect to screen layout and arrangement of information. Data and control functions should be logically grouped. Priority of information should be identified for each application, permanently displayed and presented to the user in a prominent manner by, for example, use of position, size and colour.

5.1.2 The presentation of information should be consistent with respect to values, units, meaning, sources, validity, and if available, integrity.

5.1.3 The presentation of information should be clearly separated into an operational display area (e.g. radar, chart) and one or more user dialogue areas (e.g. menus, data, control functions).

5.2 Readability

5.2.1 The presentation of alphanumeric data, text, symbols and other graphical information (e.g. radar

---

* The general principles are addressed in paragraphs 5 and 8.

** IEC Publication 60945 (see Appendix 1)

image) should support readability from typical user positions under all ambient light conditions likely to be experienced on the bridge of a ship, and with due consideration to the night vision of the officer of the watch.

5.2.2 Alphanumeric data and text should be presented using a clearly legible non-italic, sans-serif font. The font size should be appropriate for the viewing distance from user positions likely to be experienced on the bridge of a ship.

5.2.3 Text should be presented using simple unambiguous language that is easy to understand. Navigation terms and abbreviations should be presented using the nomenclature defined in SN/Circ. 243.

5.2.4 When icons are used, their purpose should be intuitively recognized by appearance, placement and grouping.

5.3 Colours and intensity

5.3.1 The colours used for the presentation of alphanumeric data, text, symbols and other graphical information should provide sufficient contrast against the background under all lighting conditions likely to be experienced on the bridge of a ship.

5.3.2 The colours and brightness should take into account the light conditions of daylight, dusk and night. The presentation should support night viewing by showing light foreground information on a dark non-reflecting background at night.

5.3.3 The background colour and contrast should be chosen to allow presented information to be easily discriminated without degrading the colour coding aspects of the presentation.

5.4 Symbols

5.4.1 Symbols used for the presentation of operational information are defined in SN/Circ. 243.

5.4.2 Symbols used for the display of charted information should comply with relevant IHO standards.

5.5 Coding of information

5.5.1 When colour coding is used for discrimination or conspicuousness of alphanumeric text, symbols and other graphical information, all colours in the set should clearly differ from one another.

5.5.2 When colour coding is used, the colour red should be used for coding of alarm related information.

5.5.3 When colour coding is used, it should be used in combination with other symbol attributes, such as size, shape, and orientation.

5.5.4 Flashing of information should be reserved for unacknowledged alarms.

5.6 Integrity marking

5.6.1 The source, validity, and where possible, the integrity of information should be indicated. Invalid information or information with low integrity should be clearly marked, qualitatively and/or quantitatively. Invalid information or information with low integrity may be quantitatively indicated by displaying absolute or percentage values.

5.6.2 When colour coding is used, information with low integrity should be qualitatively marked by using yellow, and invalid information should be qualitatively marked by using red.

5.6.3 In order to show that the screen is being refreshed, means should be provided to immediately make the user aware of a presentation failure on an operational display (e.g. 'picture freeze').

5.7 Alarms and indications

5.7.1 The operational status of information should be indicated as follows:

Status	Visual indication	Audible signal
Alarm, not acknowledged	Red, flashing	Accompanied by an audible signal
Alarm, acknowledged Invalid Information	Red	Suppression of audible signal
Important Indications (Warnings) (e.g. low integrity)	Yellow	Silence unless otherwise specified by the Organization
Normal state	None required, optionally green	Silence

5.7.2 A list of alarms should be provided based on the sequence of occurrence. Additional indication of priority, as set by the user, should be provided on displays showing alarms from multiple sources. Alarms that have been acknowledged and are no longer relevant should be deleted from the list of alarms, but may be retained in an alarm history list.

5.7.3 When a single display is used to present information from multiple navigation systems and equipment, the presentation of alarms and indications should be consistent for the display of the time of alarm occurrence, the cause of the alarm, the source of the alarm and the status of the alarm (e.g. acknowledged, not acknowledged).

5.8 Presentation modes

If displays are capable of presenting information in different mode(s), there should be a clear indication of the mode in use, for example orientation, stabilization, motion, and chart projection.

5.9 User manuals

The user manual and operator instructions should be available in the English language at least. The user manual or reference guide should include a list of all terms, abbreviations, and symbols and their explanations presented by the equipment.

6 PRESENTATION OF OPERATIONAL INFORMATION

6.1 Presentation of own ship information

6.1.1 When a graphical representation of own ship is provided, it should be possible for the user to select either a scaled ship's outline or a simplified symbol as specified in SN/Circ. 243. The size of the ship's outline or the simplified symbol in the graphical presentation should be the true scale size of the ship or 6 mm, whichever is greater.

6.1.2 A heading line, and where appropriate a velocity vector, should be associated with own ship symbol and should originate at the position of the consistent common reference point (CCRP).

6.2 Presentation of charted information

6.2.1 The presentation of charted information that is issued by, or on the authority of a government authorized hydrographic office, or other relevant government institution should comply with the relevant IHO standards.

6.2.2 The presentation of proprietary charted information should comply with relevant IHO standards, as far as practical. There should be a clear indication when the presentation is not in accordance with IHO standards.

6.2.3 The presentation of user-added charted information should comply with the relevant IHO standards, as far as practical.

6.2.4 If chart data derived from different scales appear on the display, the scale boundary should be clearly indicated.

6.3 Presentation of radar information

6.3.1 Radar images should be displayed by using a basic colour that provides optimum contrast. Radar echoes should be clearly visible when presented on top of a chart background. The relative strength of echoes may be differentiated by tones of the same basic colour. The basic colour may be different for operation under different ambient light conditions.

6.3.2   Target trails should be distinguishable from targets and clearly visible under all ambient light conditions.

6.4   Presentation of target information

6.4.1   General

6.4.1.1   Target information may be provided by radar target tracking and/or by reported target information from the Automatic Identification System (AIS).

6.4.1.2   The operation of the radar target tracking function and the processing of reported AIS information, including the number of targets presented, related to screen size, is defined within the Performance Standards for Radar Equipment as adopted by the Organization. The presentation of radar target tracking and AIS information is defined within these performance standards.

6.4.1.3   As far as practical, the user interface and data format for operating, displaying and indicating radar tracking and AIS information should be consistent.

6.4.2   Target capacity

6.4.2.1   There should be an indication when the target tracking and/or reported target processing/display capacity is about to be exceeded.

6.4.2.2   There should be an indication when the target tracking and/or reported target processing/display capacity has been exceeded.

6.4.3   Filtering of AIS sleeping targets

6.4.3.1   To ensure that the clarity of the total presentation is not substantially impaired, it should be possible to filter the presentation of sleeping AIS targets (e.g. by target range, CPA/TCPA or AIS target class A/B, etc.).

6.4.3.2   If a filter is applied, there should be a clear and permanent indication. The filter criteria in use should be readily available.

6.4.3.3   It should not be possible to remove individual AIS targets from the display.

6.4.4   Activation of AIS targets

6.4.4.1   If zones for the automatic activation of AIS targets are provided, they should be the same as for automatic radar target acquisition, if available. Any user defined zones (e.g. acquisition/activation zones) in use should be presented in graphical form.

6.4.4.2   In addition, sleeping AIS targets should be automatically activated when meeting user defined parameters (e.g. target range, CPA/TCPA or AIS target class A/B).

6.4.5   Graphical presentation

6.4.5.1   Targets should be presented with their relevant symbols according to SN/Circ. 243.

6.4.5.2   AIS information should be graphically presented either as sleeping or activated targets.

6.4.5.3   The course and speed of a tracked radar target or reported AIS target should be indicated by a vector that clearly shows the predicted motion. The vector time (length) should be consistent for presentation of any target regardless of its source.

6.4.5.4   The presentation of vector symbols should be consistent irrespective of the source of information. The presentation mode should be clearly and permanently indicated, including for example: True/Relative vector, vector time and vector stabilization.

6.4.5.5   The orientation of the AIS target symbol should indicate its heading. If the heading information is not received, the orientation of the AIS symbol should be aligned to the COG. When available, the turn or rate of turn (ROT) indicator and/or the path prediction should indicate the manoeuvre of an activated AIS target.

6.4.5.6 A consistent common reference point should be used for the alignment of tracked target symbols and AIS target symbols with other information on the same display.

6.4.5.7 On large scale/low range displays, a means to present a true scale outline of an activated AIS target should be provided.

6.4.5.8 It should be possible to display the past positions of activated targets.

6.4.6   Target data

6.4.6.1 A target selected for the display of its alphanumeric information should be identified by the relevant symbol. If more than one target is selected for data display, the symbols and the corresponding data should be clearly identified.

6.4.6.2 There should be a clear indication to show that the target data is derived from radar or AIS or from a combination of these.

6.4.6.3 For each selected tracked radar target the following data should be presented in alphanumeric form: Source(s) of data, measured range of target, measured bearing of target, predicted target range at the closest point of approach (CPA), predicted time to CPA (TCPA), true course of target, true speed of target. Additional target information should be provided on request.

6.4.6.4 For each selected AIS target the following data should be presented in alphanumeric form: Source of data, ship's identification, position and its quality, calculated range of target, calculated bearing of target, CPA, TCPA, COG, SOG, navigational status. Ship's heading and rate of turn should also be made available. Additional target information should be provided on request.

6.4.6.5 If the received AIS information is incomplete, the absent information should be clearly indicated in the target data field as missing.

6.4.6.6 The data should be displayed and continually updated, until another target is selected for data display or until the window is closed.

6.4.6.7 Means should be provided to present own ship AIS data on request.

6.4.6.8 The alphanumeric displayed data should not obscure graphically presented operational information.

6.4.7   Operational alarms

6.4.7.1 A clear indication of the status of the alarms and of the alarm criteria should be given.

6.4.7.2 A CPA/TCPA alarm of a tracked radar or activated AIS target should be clearly indicated and the target should be clearly marked by a dangerous target symbol.

6.4.7.3 If a user defined acquisition/activation zone facility is provided, a target entering the zone should be clearly identified with the relevant symbol and for tracked radar targets an alarm should be given. The zone should be identified with the relevant symbology, and should be applicable to tracked radar and AIS targets.

6.4.7.4 The last position of a lost target should be clearly marked by a lost target symbol on the display, and the lost target alarm should be given. The lost target symbol should disappear if the signal is received again, or after the alarm has been acknowledged. There should be a clear indication whether the lost target alarm function for AIS targets is enabled or disabled.

6.4.8   AIS and radar target association

6.4.8.1 An automatic target association function serves to avoid the presentation of two target symbols for the same physical target. If target data from AIS and radar tracking are both available and if the AIS and radar information are considered as one target, then as a default condition, the activated AIS target symbol and the alphanumeric AIS target data should be automatically selected and displayed. The user should have the option to change the default condition to the display of tracked radar targets and should be permitted to select either radar tracking or AIS alphanumeric data.

6.4.8.2 If the AIS and radar information are considered as two distinct targets, one activated AIS target and one tracked radar target should be displayed. No alarm should be raised.

6.4.9 AIS presentation status

The AIS presentation status should be indicated as follows:

Function	Cases to be presented		Presentation
AIS ON/OFF	AIS processing switched ON/graphical presentation switched OFF	AIS processing switched ON/graphical presentation switched ON	Alphanumeric or graphical
Filtering of sleeping AIS targets (6.4.3)	Filter status	Filter status	Alphanumeric or graphical
Activation of targets (6.4.4)		Activation criteria	Graphical
CPA/TCPA alarm (6.4.7)	Function ON/OFF CPA/TCPA criteria Sleeping targets included	Function ON/OFF CPA/TCPA criteria Sleeping targets included	Alphanumeric and graphical
Lost target alarm (6.4.7)	Function ON/OFF Lost target filter criteria	Function ON/OFF Lost target filter criteria	Alphanumeric and graphical
Target association (6.4.8)	Function ON/OFF Association criteria Default target priority	Function ON/OFF Association criteria Default target priority	Alphanumeric

6.4.10 Trial manoeuvre

A trial manoeuvre simulation should be clearly identified by the relevant symbol positioned astern of

own ship within the operational display area of the screen.

7 OPERATIONAL DISPLAYS

7.1 General

7.1.1 If the display equipment is capable of supporting the presentation of multiple functions then there should be a clear indication of the primary function supported by the presentation (e.g. Radar, ECDIS). It should be possible to select the Radar presentation (see 7.2) or the ECDIS presentation (see 7.3) by a single operator action.

7.1.2 If a radar image and an electronic chart are displayed together, the chart and the radar image should use a consistent common reference point and match in scale, projection and orientation. Any offset should be indicated.

7.1.3 Range scales of 0.25, 0.5, 0.75, 1.5, 3, 6, 12 and 24 NM should be provided. Additional range scales are permitted. These range scales do not apply when presenting raster chart data. The range scale should be permanently indicated.

7.1.4 When range rings are displayed, the range ring scale should be indicated.

7.1.5 No part of the operational display area should be permanently used for presentation of information that is not part of the navigation presentation (e.g. pop up displays, drop down menus and information windows). Temporary, limited and relevant alphanumeric data may be displayed adjacent to a selected symbol, graphic or target within the operational display area.

7.2 Radar display

7.2.1 General

7.2.1.1 Radar video, tracked radar targets and AIS targets should not be substantially degraded, masked or obscured by other presented information.

7.2.1.2 It should be possible to temporarily suppress all graphical information from the display, retaining only radar video and trails.

7.2.1.3 The brightness of radar echoes and associated graphic symbols for tracked radar targets should be variable. It should be possible to control the brightness of all displayed information. There should be independent means to adjust the brightness of groups of displayed graphics and alphanumeric data. The brilliance of the heading line should not be variable to extinction.

7.2.2 Display of chart information on radar

7.2.2.1 Vector chart information may be displayed on a radar presentation. This should be accomplished using layers selected from the chart database. As a minimum, the elements of the ECDIS Standard Display should be available for individual selection by category or layer, but not as individual objects. As far as practical, chart information should be presented in accordance with the ECDIS performance standards and with these presentation standards.

7.2.2.2 If chart information is displayed within the operational display area, the display of radar information should have priority. The chart information should be clearly perceptible as such. The chart information should not substantially degrade, mask or obscure the radar video, tracked radar targets and AIS targets.

7.2.2.3 When chart information is displayed, there should be a permanent indication of its status. Source and update information should also be made available.

7.2.3 Display of maps on radar

Map graphics may be displayed, but should not substantially degrade, mask or obscure the radar video, tracked radar targets and AIS targets.

7.3 ECDIS display

7.3.1 General

7.3.1.1 The ENC and all updates to it should be displayed without any degradation of their information content.

7.3.1.2 Chart information should not be substantially degraded, masked or obscured by other presented information.

7.3.1.3 It should be possible to temporarily suppress all supplemental information from the display, retaining only chart related information contained in the Display Base.

7.3.1.4 It should be possible to add or remove information from the ECDIS display. It should not be possible to remove information contained in the Display Base from the ECDIS display.

7.3.1.5 It should be possible to select a safety contour from the depth contours provided by the ENC. The safety contour should be emphasized over other contours on the display.

7.3.1.6 It should be possible to select a safety depth. Soundings equal to or less than the safety depth should be emphasized whenever spot soundings are selected for display.

7.3.1.7 An indication should be provided if the information is displayed at a larger scale than that contained in the ENC, or if own ship's position is covered by an ENC at a larger scale than that provided by the display.

7.3.1.8 Overscaled areas shown on the ECDIS display should be identified.

7.3.2 Display of radar information on ECDIS

7.3.2.1 Radar and target information may be displayed on ECDIS but should not substantially degrade, mask or obscure the chart information. As far as practical, radar and target information should be presented in accordance with the radar performance standard and with these presentation standards.

7.3.2.2 Radar and target information should be clearly distinguishable from the chart information. It should be possible to remove this information by a single operator action.

7.3.3 Display of additional information on ECDIS

7.3.3.1 Information from additional sources may be displayed on ECDIS but should not substantially degrade, mask or obscure the chart information.

7.3.3.2 Additional information should be clearly distinguishable from the chart information. It should be possible to remove this information by a single operator action.

7.4 User selected (task orientated) presentation

7.4.1 The user may configure a presentation for a specific task at hand. The presentation may include radar and/or chart information, in combination with other navigation or ship related data. When not fully compliant with the Radar or ECDIS performance standards, such a presentation should be identified as an auxiliary presentation.

7.4.2 As far as practical, the presentation of any radar and/or ECDIS related functions should be compliant with the requirements of the relevant performance standards and of these presentation standards, with the exception of size requirements for the operational area. Chartlets or windows of radar information may be presented along with other information associated with the task at hand.

8 PHYSICAL REQUIREMENTS

8.1 Display adjustment

8.1.1 It should be possible to adjust the contrast and brightness of the display provided, as applicable to the display technology. It should be possible to dim the display. The range of control should permit the display to be legible under all ambient light conditions.

8.1.2 It should be possible for the navigator to reset the values of contrast and/or brightness to a preset or default condition.

8.1.3 Where magnetic fields degrade the presentation of navigation information, a means to neutralize the effect of magnetic fields should be provided.

8.2 Screen size

8.2.1 Display equipment should be of sufficient size to support the requirements of the relevant performance standards adopted by the Organization.

8.2.2 The operational display area of the chart presentation for route monitoring should be at least 270 × 270 mm.

8.2.3 The operational display area of the radar presentation should be at least a circle of diameter of:
- 180 mm for ships smaller than 500 gross tonnage;
- 250 mm for ships larger than 500 gross tonnage and high-speed craft (HSC) less than 10 000 gross tonnage;
- 320 mm for ships larger than 10 000 gross tonnage.

8.3 Colours

8.3.1 Multicoloured display equipment should be used except where monochrome displays are permitted within individual performance standards adopted by the Organization.

8.3.2 Multicoloured operational displays including multifunction displays (e.g. conning displays) should provide a minimum of 64 colours except where permitted or not required by the Organization, or when used for a single specific purpose (e.g. speed log, echosounder).

8.4 Screen resolution

Operational display equipment including multifunction displays (e.g. conning displays) should provide a minimum screen resolution of 1280 × 1024, or equivalent for a different aspect ratio, except where permitted or not required by the Organization, or when used for a single specific purpose (e.g. speed log, echosounder).

8.5 Screen viewing angle

The display should support the reading of information under all ambient light conditions, simultaneously, by at least two users, from standing and sitting operator positions likely to be found on the bridge of a ship.

Appendix – Definitions

Activated AIS target
A target representing the automatic or manual activation of a sleeping target for the display of additional graphically presented information.

AIS target
A target generated from an AIS message.

Associated target
A target simultaneously representing a tracked radar target and AIS target having similar parameters (e.g. position, course, speed) and which comply with an association algorithm

CCRP
The Consistent Common Reference Point is a location on own ship, to which all horizontal measurements such as target range, bearing, relative course, relative speed, closest point of approach (CPA) or time to closest point of approach (TCPA) are referenced, typically the conning position of the bridge.

Dangerous target
A target with a predicted CPA and TCPA that violates values preset by the operator. The respective target is marked by a 'dangerous target' symbol.

Display base
The level of information which cannot be removed from the ECDIS display, consisting of information which is required at all times in all geographic areas and all circumstances. It is not intended to be sufficient for safe navigation.

ENC
Electronic Navigational Chart. The database standardized as to content structure and format according to relevant IHO standards and issued by, or on the authority of, a government.

Heading
Direction in which the bow of a ship is pointing expressed as an angular displacement from north.

Important indication
A marking of an operational status of displayed information which needs special attention, e.g. information with low integrity or invalid information.

Lost target
A target representing the last valid position of a target before its data was lost. The target is displayed by a 'lost target' symbol.

Operational display area
Area of the display used to graphically present chart and radar information, excluding the user dialogue area. On the chart display this is the area of the chart presentation. On the radar display this is the area encompassing the radar image.

Past positions
Equally time-spaced past position marks of a tracked or reported target and own ship. The co-ordinates used to display past positions may be either relative or true.

Sleeping AIS target
A target indicating the presence and orientation of a vessel equipped with AIS in a certain location. The target is displayed by a 'sleeping target'

symbol. No additional information is presented until activated.

Selected target A target selected manually for the display of detailed alphanumeric information in a separate data display area. The target is displayed by a 'selected target' symbol.

Standard display The level of information that should be shown when a chart is first displayed on ECDIS. The level of the information it provides for route planning or route monitoring may be modified by the mariner according to the mariner's needs.

Trial manoeuvre Facility used to assist the operator to perform a proposed manoeuvre for navigation and collision avoidance purposes,

by displaying the predicted future status of all tracked and AIS targets as a result of own ship's simulated manoeuvres.

User dialogue area An area of the display consisting of data fields and/or menus that is allocated to the interactive presentation and entry or selection of operational parameters, data and commands mainly in alphanumeric form.

User selected presentation An auxiliary presentation configured by the user for a specific task at hand. The presentation may include radar and/or chart information, in combination with other navigation or ship related data.

11.2.3 Extracts from IMO SN/Circ. 243 guidelines for the presentation of navigation-related symbols, terms and abbreviations

ANNEX 1

Guidelines for the Presentation of Navigation-related Symbols

1 PURPOSE

The purpose of these annexed guidelines is to provide guidance on the appropriate use of navigation-related symbols to achieve a harmonized and consistent presentation.

2 SCOPE

The use of these guidelines will insure that the symbols used for the display of navigation-related information on all shipborne navigational systems and equipment are presented in a consistent and uniform manner.

3 APPLICATION

These guidelines apply to all shipborne navigational systems and equipment. The symbols listed in the Appendix should be used for the display of navigation-related information to promote consistency in the symbol presentation on navigational equipment.

The symbols listed in the Appendix should replace symbols which are currently contained in existing performance standards. Where a standard symbol is not available, another symbol may be used, but this symbol should not conflict with the symbols listed in the Appendix.

Appendix – Navigation-related symbols

Table 1   Own ship symbols

Topic	Symbol	Description
Own ship		Double circle, located at own ship's reference position. Use of this symbol is optional, if own ship position is shown by the combination of Heading Line and Beam Line.
Own ship true scale outline		True scale outline located relative to own ship's reference position, oriented along own ship's heading. Used on small ranges/large scales.
Own ship radar antenna position		Cross, located on a true scale outline of the ship at the physical location of the radar antenna that is the current source of displayed radar video.
Own ship heading line		Solid line thinner than the speed vector line style, drawn to the bearing ring or of fixed length, if the bearing ring is not displayed. Origin is at own ship's reference point.
Own ship beam line		Solid line of fixed length; optionally length variable by operator. Midpoint at own ship's reference point.
Own ship speed vector		Dashed line – short dashes with spaces approximately twice the line width of heading line. Time increments between the origin and endpoint may optionally be marked along the vector using short intersecting lines. To indicate Water/Ground stabilization optionally one arrowhead for water stabilization and two arrowheads for ground stabilization may be added.

Table 1 (*Continued*)

Topic	Symbol	Description
Own ship path prediction		A curved vector may be provided as a path predictor.
Own ship past track		Thick line for primary source. Thin line for secondary source. Optional time marks are allowed.

Table 2   Tracked radar target symbols

Topic	Symbol	Description
Tracked target including dangerous target		Solid filled or unfilled circle located at target position.
		The course and speed vector should be displayed as dashed line, with short dashes with spaces approximately twice the line width.
		Optionally, time increments, may be marked along the vector.
		For a **'Dangerous Target'**, bold, red (on colour display) solid circle with course and speed vector, flashing until acknowledged.
Target in acquisition state		Circle segments in the acquired target state. For automatic acquisition, bold circle segments, flashing and red (on colour display) until acknowledged.
Lost target		Bold lines across the circle, flashing until acknowledged.
Selected target		A square indicated by its corners centred around the target symbol.
Target past positions		Dots, equally spaced by time.
Tracked reference target	R	Large R adjacent to designated tracked target. Multiple reference targets should be marked as R1, R2, R3, etc.

Table 3 AIS target symbols

Topic	Symbol	Description
AIS target (sleeping)		An isosceles, acute-angled triangle should be used. The triangle should be oriented by heading, or COG if heading missing. The reported position should be located at centre and half the height of the triangle. The symbol of the sleeping target should be smaller than that of the activated target.
Activated AIS target including dangerous target		An isosceles, acute-angled triangle should be used. The triangle should be oriented by heading, or COG if heading missing. The reported position should be located at centre and half the height of the triangle.
		The COG/SOG vector should be displayed as a dashed line with short dashes with spaces approximately twice the line width. Optionally, time increments may be marked along the vector.
		The heading should be displayed as a solid line thinner than speed vector line style, length twice of the length of the triangle symbol. Origin of the heading line is the apex of the triangle.
		The turn should be indicated by a flag of fixed length added to the heading line.
		A path predictor may be provided as curved vector.
		For a **'Dangerous AIS Target'**, bold, red (on colour display) solid triangle with course and speed vector, flashing until acknowledged.
AIS target – true scale outline		A true scale outline may be added to the triangle symbol. It should be: Located relative to reported position and according to reported position offsets, beam and length. Oriented along target's heading. Used on low ranges/large scales.
Selected target		A square indicated by its corners should be drawn around the activated target symbol.

Table 3 (*Continued*)

Topic	Symbol	Description
Lost target		Triangle with bold solid cross. The triangle should be oriented per last known value. The cross should have a fixed orientation. The symbol should flash until acknowledged. The target should be displayed without vector, heading and rate of turn indication.
Target past positions		Dots, equally spaced by time.

Table 4 Other symbols

Topic	Symbol	Description
AIS based AtoN Real position of charted object		Diamond with crosshair centred at reported position. (Shown with chart symbol. Chart symbol not required for radar.)
AIS based AtoN Virtual position		Diamond with crosshair centred at reported position.
Monitored route		Dashed bold line, waypoints (WPT) as circles.
Planned or alternate route		Dotted line, WPT as circles.
Trial manoeuvre	T	Large T on screen.
Simulation mode	S	Large S on screen.
Cursor		Crosshair (two alternatives, one with open centre).
Range rings		Solid circles.
Variable Range Markers (VRM)		Circle. Additional VRM should be distinguishable from the primary VRM.

Table 4 (*Continued*)

Topic	Symbol	Description
Electronic Bearing Lines (EBL)		Dashed line. Additional EBL should be distinguishable from the primary EBL.
Acquisition/activation area		Solid line boundary for an area.
Event mark	▱	Rectangle with diagonal line, clarified by added text (e.g. 'MOB' for man overboard cases).

ANNEX 2

Guidelines for the presentation of navigation-related terms and abbreviations

1 PURPOSE

The purpose of these guidelines is to provide guidance on the use of appropriate navigation-related terminology and abbreviations intended for presentation on shipborne navigational displays. These are based on terms and abbreviations used in existing navigation references.

2 SCOPE

These guidelines are issued to ensure that the terms and abbreviations used for the display of navigation-related information on all shipborne navigation equipment and systems are consistent and uniform.

3 APPLICATION

These guidelines apply to all shipborne navigational systems and equipment including, radar, ECDIS, AIS, INS and IBS. When navigation-related information is displayed as text, the standard terms or abbreviations listed in the Appendix should be used, instead of using terms and abbreviations which are currently contained in existing performance standards.

Where a standard term and abbreviation is not available, another term or abbreviation may be used. This term or abbreviation should not conflict with the standard terms or abbreviations listed in the Appendix and provide a clear meaning. Standard marine terminology should be used for this purpose. When the meaning is not clear from its context, the term should not be abbreviated.

Unless otherwise specified, standard terms should be shown in lower case while abbreviations should be presented using upper case.

Appendix – List of standard terms and abbreviations

Term	Abbreviation	Abbreviation	Term
Acknowledge	ACK	ACK	Acknowledge
Acquire, Acquisition	ACQ	ACQ	Acquire, Acquisition
Acquisition Zone	AZ	ADJ	Adjust, Adjustment
Adjust, Adjustment	ADJ	AFC	Automatic Frequency Control
Aft	AFT	AFT	Aft
Alarm	ALARM	AGC	Automatic Gain Control
Altitude	ALT	AIS	Automatic Identification System
Amplitude Modulation	AM	ALARM	Alarm
Anchor Watch	ANCH	ALT	Altitude
Antenna	ANT	AM	Amplitude Modulation
Anti Clutter Rain	RAIN	ANCH	Anchor Watch
Anti Clutter Sea	SEA	ANCH	Vessel at Anchor (applies to AIS)
April	APR	ANT	Antenna
Audible	AUD	APR	April
August	AUG	AUD	Audible
Automatic	AUTO	AUG	August

Term	Abbreviation	Abbreviation	Term
Automatic Frequency Control	AFC	AUTO	Automatic
Automatic Gain Control	AGC	AUX	Auxiliary System/Function
Automatic Identification System	AIS	AVAIL	Available
Auxiliary System/Function	AUX	AZ	Acquisition Zone
Available	AVAIL	BITE	Built in Test Equipment
Background	BKGND	BKGND	Background
Bearing	BRG	BRG	Bearing
Bearing Waypoint To Waypoint	BWW	BRILL	Brilliance
Brilliance	BRILL	BWW	Bearing Waypoint To Waypoint
Built in Test Equipment	BITE	C	Carried (e.g. carried EBL origin)
Calibrate	CAL	C UP(See note 2)	Course Up
Cancel	CNCL	CAL	Calibrate
Carried (e.g. carried EBL origin)	C	CCRP	Consistent Common Reference Point
Centre	CENT	CCRS	Consistent Common Reference System
Change	CHG		
Circular Polarized	CP	CENT	Centre
Clear	CLR	CHG	Change
Closest Point of Approach	CPA	CLR	Clear
Consistent Common Reference Point	CCRP	CNCL	Cancel
		COG	Course Over the Ground
Consistent Common Reference System	CCRS	CONT	Contrast
		CORR	Correction
Contrast	CONT	CP	Circular Polarized
Correction	CORR	CPA	Closest Point of Approach
Course	CRS	CRS	Course
Course Over the Ground	COG	CTS	Course To Steer
Course Through the Water	CTW	CTW	Course Through the Water
Course To Steer	CTS	CURS	Cursor
Course Up	C UP(See note 2)	D	Dropped (e.g. dropped EBL origin)
Cross Track Distance	XTD		
Cursor	CURS	DATE	Date
Dangerous Goods	DG	DAY/NT	Day/Night
Date	DATE	DEC	December
Day/Night	DAY/NT	DECR	Decrease
Dead Reckoning, Dead Reckoned Position	DR	DEL	Delete
		DELAY	Delay
December	DEC	DEP	Departure
Decrease	DECR	DEST	Destination
Delay	DELAY	DEV	Deviation
Delete	DEL	DG	Dangerous Goods
Departure	DEP	DGAL(See note 2)	Differential Galilleo
Depth	DPTH	DGLONASS (See note 2)	Differential GLONASS
Destination	DEST		
Deviation	DEV	DGNSS(See note 2)	Differential GNSS
Differential Galilleo	DGAL(See note 2)		

Term	Abbreviation	Abbreviation	Term
Differential GLONASS	DGLONASS (See note 2)	DGPS(See note 2)	Differential GPS
		DISP	Display
Differential GNSS	DGNSS(See note 2)	DIST	Distance
Differential GPS	DGPS(See note 2)	DIVE	Vessel Engaged in Diving
Digital Selective Calling	DSC		Operations (applies to AIS)
Display	DISP	DPTH	Depth
Distance	DIST	DR	Dead Reckoning, Dead
Distance Root Mean Square	DRMS(See note 2)		Reckoned Position
Distance To Go	DTG	DRG	Vessel Engaged in Dredging or
Drift	DRIFT		Underwater Operations (applies
Dropped (e.g. dropped EBL	D		to AIS)
origin)		DRIFT	Drift
East	E	DRMS(See note 2)	Distance Root Mean Square
Electronic Bearing Line	EBL	DSC	Digital Selective Calling
Electronic Chart Display and	ECDIS	DTG	Distance To Go
Information System		E	East
Electronic Navigational Chart	ENC	EBL	Electronic Bearing Line
Electronic Position Fixing System	EPFS	ECDIS	Electronic Chart Display and
Electronic Range and Bearing	ERBL		Information System
Line		ENC	Electronic Navigational Chart
Enhance	ENH	ENH	Enhance
Enter	ENT	ENT	Enter
Equipment	EQUIP	EP	Estimated Position
Error	ERR	EPFS	Electronic Position Fixing System
Estimated Position	EP	EQUIP	Equipment
Estimated Time of Arrival	ETA	ERBL	Electronic Range and Bearing Line
Estimated Time of Departure	ETD	ERR	Error
Event	EVENT	ETA	Estimated Time of Arrival
Exclusion Zone	EZ	ETD	Estimated Time of Departure
External	EXT	EVENT	Event
February	FEB	EXT	External
Fishing Vessel	FISH	EZ	Exclusion Zone
Fix	FIX	FEB	February
Forward	FWD	FISH	Fishing Vessel
Frequency	FREQ	FIX	Fix
Frequency Modulation	FM	FM	Frequency Modulation
Full	FULL	FREQ	Frequency
Gain	GAIN	FULL	Full
Galilleo	GAL	FWD	Forward
Geometric Dilution Of Precision	GDOP	GAIN	Gain
Global Maritime Distress and	GMDSS	GAL	Galilleo
Safety System		GC	Great Circle
Global Navigation Satellite System	GNSS	GDOP	Geometric Dilution Of Precision
Global Orbiting Navigation	GLONASS	GLONASS	Global Orbiting Navigation
Satellite System			Satellite System

Term	Abbreviation	Abbreviation	Term
Global Positioning System	GPS	GMDSS	Global Maritime Distress and Safety System
Great Circle	GC		
Grid	GRID	GND	Ground
Ground	GND	GNSS	Global Navigation Satellite System
Group Repetition Interval	GRI		
Guard Zone	GZ	GPS	Global Positioning System
Gyro	GYRO	GRI	Group Repetition Interval
Harmful Substances	HS	GRID	Grid
(applies to AIS)		GRND	Vessel Aground (applies to AIS)
Head Up	H UP(See note 2)	GYRO	Gyro
Heading	HDG	GZ	Guard Zone
Heading Control System	HCS	H UP (See note 2)	Head Up
Heading Line	HL	HCS	Heading Control System
High Frequency	HF	HDG	Heading
High Speed Craft (applies to AIS)	HSC	HDOP	Horizontal Dilution Of Precision
Horizontal Dilution Of Precision	HDOP	HF	High Frequency
Identification	ID	HL	Heading Line
In	IN	HS	Harmful Substances
Increase	INCR		(applies to AIS)
Indication	IND	HSC	High Speed Craft (applies to AIS)
Information	INFO	I/O	Input/Output
Infrared	INF RED	ID	Identification
Initialization	INIT	IN	In
Input	INP	INCR	Increase
Input/Output	I/O	IND	Indication
Integrated Radio Communication	IRCS	INF RED	Infrared
System		INFO	Information
Interference Rejection	IR	INIT	Initialization
Interswitch	ISW	INP	Input
Interval	INT	INT	Interval
January	JAN	IR	Interference Rejection
July	JUL	IRCS	Integrated Radio Communication
June	JUN		System
Latitude	LAT	ISW	Interswitch
Limit	LIM	JAN	January
Line Of Position	LOP	JUL	July
Log	LOG	JUN	June
Long Pulse	LP	LAT	Latitude
Long Range	LR	LF	Low Frequency
Longitude	LON	LIM	Limit
Loran	LORAN	LOG	Log
Lost Target	LOST TGT	LON	Longitude
Low Frequency	LF	LOP	Line Of Position
Magnetic	MAG	LORAN	Loran
Manoeuvre	MVR	LOST TGT	Lost Target
Manual	MAN		

Term	Abbreviation	Abbreviation	Term
Map(s)	MAP	LP	Long Pulse
March	MAR	LR	Long Range
Maritime Mobile Services Identity number	MMSI	MAG	Magnetic
		MAN	Manual
Maritime Pollutant (applies to AIS)	MP	MAP	Map(s)
		MAR	March
Maritime Safety Information	MSI	MAX	Maximum
Marker	MKR	MAY	May
Master	MSTR	MENU	Menu
Maximum	MAX	MF	Medium Frequency
May	MAY	MIN	Minimum
Medium Frequency	MF	MISSING	Missing
Medium Pulse	MP	MKR	Marker
Menu	MENU	MMSI	Maritime Mobile Services Identity number
Minimum	MIN		
Missing	MISSING	MON	Performance Monitor
Mute	MUTE	MP	Maritime Pollutant (applies to AIS)
Navigation	NAV		
Normal	NORM	MP	Medium Pulse
North	N	MSI	Maritime Safety Information
North Up	N UP(See note 2)	MSTR	Master
November	NOV	MUTE	Mute
October	OCT	MVR	Manoeuvre
Off	OFF	N	North
Officer Of the Watch	OOW	N UP (See note 2)	North Up
Offset	OFFSET	NAV	Navigation
On	ON	NORM	Normal
Out/Output	OUT	NOV	November
Own Ship	OS	NUC	Vessel Not Under Command (applies to AIS)
Panel Illumination	PANEL		
Parallel Index Line	PI	OCT	October
Passenger Vessel (applies to AIS)	PASSV	OFF	Off
Performance Monitor	MON	OFFSET	Offset
Permanent	PERM	ON	On
Person Overboard	POB	OOW	Officer On Watch
Personal Identification Number	PIN	OS	Own Ship
Pilot Vessel (applies to AIS)	PILOT	OUT	Out/Output
Port/Portside	PORT	PAD	Predicted Area of Danger
Position	POSN	PANEL	Panel Illumination
Positional Dilution Of Precision	PDOP	PASSV	Passenger Vessel (applies to AIS)
Power	PWR	PDOP	Positional Dilution Of Precision
Predicted	PRED	PERM	Permanent
Predicted Area of Danger	PAD	PI	Parallel Index Line
Predicted Point of Collision	PPC	PILOT	Pilot Vessel (applies to AIS)
Pulse Length	PL	PIN	Personal Identification Number
Pulse Modulation	PM	PL	Pulse Length

Term	Abbreviation	Abbreviation	Term
Pulse Repetition Frequency	PRF	PM	Pulse Modulation
Pulse Repetition Rate	PRR	POB	Person Overboard
Pulses Per Revolution	PPR	PORT	Port/Portside
Racon	RACON	POSN	Position
Radar	RADAR	PPC	Predicted Point of Collision
Radius	RAD	PPR	Pulses Per Revolution
Rain	RAIN	PRED	Predicted
Range	RNG	PRF	Pulse Repetition Frequency
Range Rings	RR	PRR	Pulse Repetition Rate
Raster Chart Display System	RCDS	PWR	Power
Raster Navigational Chart	RNC	RACON	Racon
Rate Of Turn	ROT	RAD	Radius
Real-time Kinematic	RTK	RADAR	Radar
Receiver	RX (See note 2)	RAIM	Receiver Autonomous Integrity Monitoring
Receiver Autonomous Integrity Monitoring	RAIM	RAIN	Anti Clutter Rain
Reference	REF	RAIN	Rain
Relative	REL (See note 3)	RCDS	Raster Chart Display System
Relative Motion	RM	REF	Reference
Revolutions per Minute	RPM	REL (See note3)	Relative
Roll On/Roll Off Vessel (applies to AIS)	RoRo	RIM	Vessel Restricted in Manoeuvrability (applies to AIS)
Root Mean Square	RMS	RM	Relative Motion
Route	ROUTE	RMS	Root Mean Square
Safety Contour	SF CNT	RNC	Raster Navigational Chart
Sailing Vessel (applies to AIS)	SAIL	RNG	Range
Satellite	SAT	RoRo	Roll On/Roll Off Vessel (applies to AIS)
S-Band (applies to Radar)	S-BAND		
Scan to Scan	SC/SC	ROT	Rate Of Turn
Search And Rescue Transponder	SART	ROUTE	Route
Search And Rescue Vessel (applies to AIS)	SARV	RPM	Revolutions per Minute
		RR	Range Rings
Select	SEL	RTK	Real-time Kinematic
September	SEP	RX (See note 2)	Receiver
Sequence	SEQ	S	South
Set (i.e. set and drift, or setting a value)	SET	SAIL	Sailing Vessel (applies to AIS)
Ship's Time	TIME	SART	Search And Rescue Transponder
Short Pulse	SP	SARV	Search And Rescue Vessel (applies to AIS)
Signal to Noise Ratio	SNR		
Simulation	SIM (See note 4)	SAT	Satellite
Slave	SLAVE	S-BAND	S-Band (applies to Radar)
South	S	SC/SC	Scan to Scan
Speed	SPD	SDME	Speed and Distance Measuring Equipment
Speed and Distance Measuring Equipment	SDME		
		SEA	Anti Clutter Sea

Term	Abbreviation	Abbreviation	Term
Speed Over the Ground	SOG	SEL	Select
Speed Through the Water	STW	SEP	September
Stabilized	STAB	SEQ	Sequence
Standby	STBY	SET	Set (i.e. set and drift, or setting a value)
Starboard/Starboard Side	STBD		
Station	STN	SF CNT	Safety Contour
Symbol(s)	SYM	SIM (See note 4)	Simulation
Synchronization	SYNC	SLAVE	Slave
Target	TGT	SNR	Signal to Noise Ratio
Target Tracking	TT	SOG	Speed Over the Ground
Test	TEST	SP	Short Pulse
Time	TIME	SPD	Speed
Time Difference	TD	STAB	Stabilized
Time Dilution Of Precision	TDOP	STBD	Starboard/Starboard Side
Time Of Arrival	TOA	STBY	Standby
Time Of Departure	TOD	STN	Station
Time to CPA	TCPA	STW	Speed Through the Water
Time To Go	TTG	SYM	Symbol(s)
Time to Wheel Over Line	TWOL	SYNC	Synchronization
Track	TRK	T	True
Track Control System	TCS	TCPA	Time to CPA
Track Made Good	TMG (See note 5)	TCS	Track Control System
Trail(s)	TRAIL	TD	Time Difference
Transceiver	TXRX (See note 2)	TDOP	Time Dilution Of Precision
Transferred Line Of Position	TPL	TEST	Test
Transmitter	TX (See note 2)	TGT	Target
Transmitting Heading Device	THD	THD	Transmitting Heading Device
Trial	TRIAL (See note 4)	TIME	Ship's Time
Trigger Pulse	TRIG	TIME	Time
True	T	TM	True Motion
True Motion	TM	TMG (See note5)	Track Made Good
Tune	TUNE	TOA	Time Of Arrival
Ultrahigh Frequency	UHF	TOD	Time Of Departure
Universal Time, Coordinated	UTC	TOW	Vessel Engaged in Towing Operations (applies to AIS)
Unstabilized	UNSTAB		
Variable Range Marker	VRM	TPL	Transferred Line Of Position
Variation	VAR	TRAIL	Trail(s)
Vector	VECT	TRIAL (See note 4)	Trial
Very High Frequency	VHF	TRIG	Trigger Pulse
Very Low Frequency	VLF	TRK	Track
Vessel Aground (applies to AIS)	GRND	TT	Target Tracking
Vessel at Anchor (applies to AIS)	ANCH	TTG	Time To Go
Vessel Constrained by Draught (applies to AIS)	VCD	TUNE	Tune
		TWOL	Time to Wheel Over Line

Term	Abbreviation	Abbreviation	Term
Vessel Engaged in Diving Operations (applies to AIS)	DIVE	TX (See note 2)	Transmitter
		TXRX (See note 2)	Transceiver
Vessel Engaged in Dredging or Underwater Operations (applies to AIS)	DRG	UHF	Ultrahigh Frequency
		UNSTAB	Unstabilized
		UTC	Universal Time, Coordinated
Vessel Engaged in Towing Operations (applies to AIS)	TOW	UWE	Vessel Underway Using Engine (applies to AIS)
Vessel Not Under Command (applies to AIS)	NUC	VAR	Variation
		VCD	Vessel Constrained by Draught (applies to AIS)
Vessel Restricted in Manoeuvrability (applies to AIS)	RIM	VDR	Voyage Data Recorder
		VECT	Vector
Vessel Traffic Service	VTS	VHF	Very High Frequency
Vessel Underway Using Engine (applies to AIS)	UWE	VID	Video
		VLF	Very Low Frequency
Video	VID	VOY	Voyage
Voyage	VOY	VRM	Variable Range Marker
Voyage Data Recorder	VDR	VTS	Vessel Traffic Service
Warning	WARNING	W	West
Water	WAT	WARNING	Warning
Waypoint	WPT	WAT	Water
West	W	WOL	Wheel Over Line
Wheel Over Line	WOL	WOT	Wheel Over Time
Wheel Over Time	WOT	WPT	Waypoint
X-Band (applies to Radar)	X-BAND	X-BAND	X-Band (applies to Radar)
		XTD	Cross Track Distance

List of standard units of measurement and abbreviations

Unit	Abbreviation	Abbreviation	Unit
cable length	cbl	cbl	cable length
cycles per second	cps	cps	cycles per second
degree(s)	deg	deg	degree(s)
fathom(s)	fm	fm	fathom(s)
feet/foot	ft	ft	feet/foot
gigahertz	GHz	GHz	gigahertz
hectopascal	hPa	hPa	hectopascal
hertz	Hz	Hz	hertz
hour(s)	hr(s)	hr(s)	hour(s)

Unit	Abbreviation	Abbreviation	Unit
kilohertz	kHz	kHz	kiloHertz
kilometre	km	km	kilometre
kilopascal	kPa	kPa	kilopascal
knot(s)	kn	kn	knot(s)
megahertz	MHz	MHz	megahertz
minute(s)	min	min	minute(s)
Nautical Mile(s)	NM	NM	Nautical Mile(s)

Notes:

1. Terms and abbreviations used in nautical charts are published in relevant IHO publications and are not listed here.

2. In general, terms should be presented using lower case text and abbreviations should be presented using upper case text. Those abbreviations that may be presented using lower case text are identified in the list, e.g. 'dGNSS' or 'Rx'.

3. Abbreviations may be combined, e.g. 'CPA LIM' or 'T CRS'. When the abbreviation for the standard term 'Relative' is combined with another abbreviation, the abbreviation 'R' should be used instead of 'REL', e.g. 'R CRS'.

4. The use of the abbreviations 'SIM' and 'TRIAL' are not intended to replace the appropriate symbols listed in Annex 1.

5. The term 'Course Made Good' has been used in the past to describe 'Track Made Good'. This is a misnomer in that 'courses' are directions steered or intended to be steered with respect to a reference meridian. 'Track Made Good' is preferred over the use of 'Course Made Good'.

6. Where information is presented using SI units, the respective abbreviations should be used.

11.2.4   Extract from IMO Resolution A615(15) Marine uses of Radar Beacons and Transponders

ANNEX 1

1   INTRODUCTION

1.1 The uncontrolled provision of radar beacons and transponders could cause degradation of ships' navigational radar and ARPA displays, produce incompatibilities among devices developed for different uses, or necessitate a succession of modifications to ships' radar displays to accommodate progressive developments of radar beacons and transponders.

1.2 To avoid these possibilities, the following recommendations are made concerning the appropriate applications for radar beacons and transponders, where an operational requirement for such a device exists, and concerning measures for general administration of radar beacons and transponders.

1.3 The technical criteria and operation of radar beacons and transponders are similar. However, the terms *radar beacon (racon)* and *transponder*, as used in this recommendation, are understood to have the following meanings:

.1   *Radar beacon (racon)*: A receiver-transmitter device associated with a navigational mark which, when triggered by a radar, automatically returns a distinctive signal which can appear on the display of the triggering radar, providing range, bearing and identification information. The terms *radar beacon* and *racon* should be reserved exclusively for this use and include devices mounted on fixed structures, or on floating aids anchored at fixed positions, for navigational purposes. The racon itself is considered a separate aid to navigation, whether used alone, or mounted on another aid to navigation (such as a visible mark).

.2   *Transponder*: A receiver-transmitter device in the maritime radio determination service which transmits automatically when interrogated, or when a transmission is initiated by a local command. The

transmission may include a coded identification signal and/or data. The response may be displayed on a radar PPI, or on a display separate from any radar, or both, depending upon the application and content of the signal.

2   GENERAL OPERATIONAL CHARACTERISTICS

2.1   Radar beacons

2.1.1   A radar beacon in the maritime radionavigation service is a device which will:

.1   be triggered automatically by the transmissions of any radar operating in the appropriate frequency band; and

.2   transmit a response immediately on receipt of the triggering pulse for display as part of the normal picture of the triggering radar.

2.1.2   Where a radar beacon incorporates a user-selectable mode, so that a user can control the presentation of a radar beacon response, it will also:

.1   be triggered automatically by the transmission of a suitably configured radar in the vicinity operating in the appropriate frequency band and using its own user-selectable facility; and

.2   transmit a response so that it can:

.2.1   be shown on the radar display in a manner distinct from that used for radar information,

.2.2   be shown on the radar display or other display without other information, or

.2.3   not be shown on the radar display.

2.1.3   In special circumstances, a radar beacon not being used for general navigational purposes may operate exclusively in the user-selectable mode.

2.2   Transponders

A transponder is a device which can provide for:

.1   ship radar target identification and echo enhancement with the proviso that such enhancement should not significantly exceed that which could be achieved by passive means on the radar display of an interrogating ship or shore station;

.2 radar target correlation with voice or other radio transmission for identification on the radar display of an interrogating ship or shore station;

.3 user-selectable presentation of transponder responses either superimposed on the normal radar display, or free of clutter and other targets; and

.4 transfer of information pertinent to avoidance of collision or other hazards, manoeuvre, manoeuvring characteristics, etc.

3 OPERATIONAL USE

3.1 Radar beacons should be used only for radionavigational purposes (not for detection of marine craft), for example:

.1 ranging on and identification of positions on inconspicuous coastlines;

.2 identification of positions on coastlines which permit good ranging but are featureless;

.3 identification of selected navigational marks both seaborne and land-based;

.4 landfall identification;

.5 as a warning device to identify temporary navigational hazards and to mark new and uncharted dangers;

.6 bridge marking;

.7 leading lines;

.8 identification of offshore structures;

.9 marking important features in channels.

3.2 Radar beacons used at locations where clutter from land, sea, ice or weather could mask their response may, at the discretion of the Administration concerned, incorporate a user-selectable mode.

3.3 Where an operational requirement exists for a responding device, other than for radionavigational purposes, a transponder should be used. Examples of requirements suitable for transponders are:

.1 identification of certain classes of ships (ship-to-ship) and towed devices;

.2 identification of ships for VTS and other shore surveillance purposes;

.3 search and rescue operations;

.4 identification of individual ships and data transfer; and

.5 establishing positions for hydrographical purposes.

4 GENERAL ADMINISTRATION OF RADAR BEACONS AND TRANSPONDERS

4.1 All radar beacons should be authorized by an Administration or by a competent navigation authority. Before authorizing or approving the setting up of a radar beacon, account should be taken of the density of such devices in the particular area and the need to prevent degradation of ships' radar displays.

4.2 Except in the case of SAR transponders (see resolution A.530(13)), transponder systems designed to respond in a frequency band used by marine radars should be authorized by an Administration. Before giving such authorization, account should be taken of the effect such transmissions would have on ships' radars.

ANNEX 2

RECOMMENDATION ON OPERATIONAL STANDARDS FOR RADAR BEACONS

1 INTRODUCTION

1.1 Radar beacons should conform to the following minimum operational standards.

1.2 Radar beacons should be operationally compatible with navigational radar and ARPA equipment which conforms to the performance standards recommended by the Organization.

2 OPERATING FREQUENCIES

2.1 Radar beacons designed to operate on a wavelength of 3 cm should be capable of being interrogated by any navigational radar equipment operating on any frequency between 9320 MHz and 9500 MHz and respond within this frequency band.

2.2 Radar beacons designed to operate on a wavelength of 10 cm should be capable of being interrogated by any navigational radar equipment operating on any frequency between 2900 MHz and 3100 MHz and respond within this frequency band.

3 TRANSMITTER TUNING CHARACTERISTICS

The tuning characteristics of the transmitter should be such that the beacon response can appear on a radar display in a recognizable form at least once every 2 mins.

4 OPERATING RANGE

The operating range should be compatible with the navigational requirements for the radar beacon at its location.

5 RESPONSE CHARACTERISTICS

5.1 On receipt of an interrogating signal, the radar beacon should commence its response in such time that the gap on the radar display between the radar target and the beacon response does not normally exceed approximately 100 m. In certain cases, the operational use of radar beacons may be aided by increasing this delay slightly. Under such circumstances, the delay time should be as short as practicable and the details should be shown in appropriate navigational publications.

5.2 The duration of the response should be approximately 20 per cent of the maximum range requirement of the particular radar beacon, or should not exceed 5 nautical miles, whichever is the lower value. In certain cases, the duration of the response may be adjusted to suit the operational requirements for the particular radar beacon.

5.3 The leading edge of the response should be sufficiently sharp to permit satisfactory range determination.

6 IDENTIFICATION CODING

6.1 Identification coding should normally be in the form of a Morse letter. The identification coding used should be described in appropriate navigational publications.

6.2 The identification coding should comprise the full length of the radar beacon response and, where a Morse letter is used, the response should be divided with a ratio of 1 dash equal to 3 dots and 1 dot equal to 1 space.

6.3 The coding should normally commence with a dash.

7 USER-SELECTABLE MODE

7.1 Radar beacons may be provided with a user-selectable mode. In this mode the radar beacon, in addition to satisfying the response characteristics set out in section 5, should be capable of transmitting a response after receipt of an interrogating signal from a suitably configured radar using its own user-selectable facility.

7.2 The characteristics of the interrogating signal and the response should conform to the appropriate CCIR Recommendations.

7.3 Radar beacons provided with a user-selectable mode should, unless operating exceptionally only in the user-selectable mode, be capable of responding to interrogations from both normal radar signals and special interrogating signals with a minimum of interruption in response to any user.

8 CONSTRUCTION

Radar beacons should be designed to provide high availability when installed permanently in a marine environment.

ANNEX 3

RECOMMENDATION ON TRANSPONDERS

1   The design of transponder systems should ensure that there is no significant degradation in the use of radar beacons, and the response of a transponder

should not be capable of being interpreted as being from a radar beacon of any type.

2 Where a transponder is to be used with a marine navigational radar or ARPA, any modifications necessary to the radar or ARPA should not degrade its performance; they should be kept to a minimum, be simple and be compatible with a user-selectable beacon facility.

3 Transponders should not be used to enhance the detection of marine craft, except for search and rescue or when specially authorized by Administrations for safety purposes. Transponders used for search and rescue purposes should be capable of transmitting signals which will appear on a radar or ARPA display as a series of equally spaced dots (resolution A.530(13)).

11.2.5 Extract from IMO Resolution A802(19) Performance Standards for Survival Craft Radar Transponders for use in Search and Rescue Operations

1 INTRODUCTION

The 9 GHz SAR transponder (SART), in addition to meeting the requirements of the relevant ITU-R Recommendation and the general requirements set out in resolution A.694(17), should comply with the following performance standards.

2 GENERAL

The SART should be capable of indicating the location of a unit in distress on the assisting unit's radars by means of a series of equally spaced dots (see resolution A.530(13)).

2.1 The SART should:

.1 be capable of being easily activated by unskilled personnel;

.2 be fitted with means to prevent inadvertent activation;

.3 be equipped with a means which is either visual or audible, or both visual and audible, to indicate correct operation and to alert survivors to the fact that a radar has triggered the SART;

.4 be capable of manual activation and deactivation; provision for automatic activation may be included;

> *Note*: If an on-board test is performed using a shipborne 9 GHz radar, activation of the SART should be limited to a few seconds to avoid harmful interference with other shipborne radars and excessive consumption of battery energy.

.5 be provided with an indication of the stand-by condition;

.6 be capable of withstanding without damage drops from a height of 20 m into water;

.7 be watertight at a depth of 10 m for at least 5 min;

.8 maintain watertightness when subjected to a thermal shock of 45°C under specified conditions of immersion;

.9 be capable of floating if it is not an integral part of the survival craft;

.10 be equipped with buoyant lanyard, suitable for use as a tether, if it is capable of floating;

.11 not be unduly affected by seawater or oil;

.12 be resistant to deterioration in prolonged exposure to sunlight;

.13 be of a highly visible yellow/orange colour on all surfaces where this will assist detection;

.14 have a smooth external construction to avoid damaging the survival craft; and

.15 be provided with a pole or other arrangement compatible with the antenna pocket in a survival craft in order to comply with requirements referred to in paragraph 2.4, together with illustrated instructions.

2.2 The SART should have sufficient battery capacity to operate in the stand-by condition for 96 h and, in addition, following the stand-by period, to provide transponder transmissions for 8 h when being continuously interrogated with a pulse repetition frequency of 1 kHz.

2.3 The SART should be so designed as to be able to operate under ambient temperatures of −20°C to +55°C. It should not be damaged in stowage throughout the temperature range of −30°C to +65°C.

2.4 The height of the installed SART antenna should be at least 1 m above sea-level.

2.5 The vertical polar diagram of the antenna and hydrodynamic characteristics of the device should permit the SART to respond to search radars under heavy swell conditions. The polar diagram of the antenna should be substantially omnidirectional in the horizontal plane. Horizontal polarization should be used for transmission and reception.

2.6 The SART should operate correctly when interrogated at a distance of up to at least 5 nautical miles by a navigational radar complying with resolutions A.477(XII) and A.222(V11), with an antenna height of 15 m. It should also operate correctly when inter-rogated at a distance of up to 30 nautical miles by an airborne radar with at least 10 kW peak output power at a height of 3,000 ft.

3 TECHNICAL CHARACTERISTICS

Technical characteristics of the SART should be in accordance with Recommendation ITU-R M.628–2.

4 LABELLING

In addition to the items specified in resolution A.694(17) on general requirements, the following should be clearly indicated on the exterior of the equipment:

.1 brief operating instructions; and

.2 expiry date for the primary battery used.

11.2.6 Extract from IMO Resolution A384(X) Performance Standards for Radar Reflectors

1 INTRODUCTION

1.1 Small craft referred to in paragraph 2 of this Recommendation should be fitted with radar reflectors to improve the range and probability of their radar detection.

1.2 Radar reflectors should comply with the minimum performance requirements as specified in this Recommendation.

1.3 In the following paragraphs the echoing areas specified are those for the frequency of 9.3 GHz (corresponding to a wavelength of 3.2 cm).

2 APPLICATION

2.1 All ships of less than 100 tons gross tonnage operating in international waters and adjacent coastal areas should, if practicable, be fitted with a radar reflector.

2.2 The radar reflector should be of an approved type with an adequate polar diagram in azimuth, and an echoing area:

- .1 preferably, of at least $10\,m^2$, mounted at a minimum height of 4 m above water level; or
- .2 if this is not practicable, of at least $40\,m^2$, mounted at a minimum height of 2 m above water level.

3 PERFORMANCE

3.1 Reflectors should be capable of performance around 360° in azimuth using a typical marine navigational radar.

3.2 The echoing areas referred to in paragraph 2 correspond to the maximum values of the main lobes of the polar diagram.

3.3 The azimuthal polar diagram should be such that the response over a total angle of 240° is not less than −6 dB with reference to the maxima of the main lobes and that the response should not remain below −6 dB over any single angle of more than 10°.

4 CONSTRUCTION

The reflector should be capable of maintaining its reflection performance under the conditions of sea states, vibration, humidity and change of temperature likely to be experienced in the marine environment.

5 INSTALLATION

5.1 Fixing arrangements should be provided so that the reflector can be fitted either on a rigid mount or suspended in the rigging.

5.2 If there is a preferred orientation of mounting this should be clearly marked on the reflector. In the case of an octahedral reflector, the correct method of mounting is one corner cavity at the top and one at the bottom. Any other method might reduce its performance below that in paragraph 3.3.

11.3   IMO Performance Standards for other related equipment

11.3.1   Extract from IMO Resolution MSC 112(73) Performance Standards for Shipborne Global Positioning System (GPS) Receiver Equipment Valid for Equipment Installed on or after 1st July 2003

1   INTRODUCTION

1.1 The Global Positioning System (GPS) is a space-based positioning, velocity and time system that has three major segments: space, control and user. The GPS space segment will normally be composed of 24 satellites in six orbits. The satellites operate in circular 20,200 km orbits at an inclination angle of 55° with a 12-hour period. The spacing of satellites in orbit will be arranged so that a minimum of four satellites will be in view to users world-wide, with a position dilution of precision (PDOP) of $\leqslant 6$. Each satellite transmits on two 'L' band frequencies, L1 (1575.42 MHz) and L2 (1227.6 MHz). L1 carries a precise (P) code and coarse/acquisition (C/A) code. L2 carries the P code. A navigation data message is superimposed on these codes. The same navigation data message is carried on both frequencies.

1.2 Receiver equipment for the GPS intended for navigational purposes on ships with maximum speeds not exceeding 70 knots should, in addition to the general requirements contained in resolution A.694(17), comply with the following minimum performance requirements.

1.3 These standards cover the basic requirements of position-fixing for navigation purposes only and do not cover other computational facilities which may be in the equipment.

2   GPS RECEIVER EQUIPMENT

2.1 The words 'GPS receiver equipment' as used in these performance standards include all the components and units necessary for the system properly to perform its intended functions. The equipment should include the following minimum facilities:

.1   antenna capable of receiving GPS signals;

.2   GPS receiver and processor;

.3   means of accessing the computed latitude/longitude position;

.4   data control and interface; and

.5   position display and, if required, other forms of output.

2.2 The antenna design should be suitable for fitting at a position on the ship which ensures a clear view of the satellite constellation.

3   PERFORMANCE STANDARDS FOR GPS RECEIVER EQUIPMENT

The GPS receiver equipment should:

.1   be capable of receiving and processing the Standard Positioning Service (SPS) signals as modified by Selective Availability (SA) and provide position information in latitude and longitude World Geodetic System (WGS)-84 co-ordinates in degrees, minutes and thousandths of minutes and time of solution referenced to UTC (USNO). Means may be provided for transforming the computed position based upon WGS-84 into data compatible with the datum of the navigational chart in use. Where this facility exists, the display should indicate that co-ordinate conversion is being performed, and should identify the co-ordinate system in which the position is expressed;

.2   operate on the L1 signal and C/A code;

.3   be provided with at least one output from which position information can be supplied to other equipment. The output of position information based upon WGS-84 should be in accordance with international standards (see IEC 61162);

.4   have static accuracy such that the position of the antenna is determined to within 100 m

(95 per cent) with horizontal dilution of precision (HDOP) $\leqslant 4$ (or PDOP $\leqslant 6$);

.5   have dynamic accuracy such that the position of the ship is determined to within 100 m (95 per cent) with HDOP $\leqslant 4$ (or PDOP $\leqslant 6$) under the conditions of sea states and ship's motion likely to be experienced in ships (see A694(17));

.6   be capable of selecting automatically the appropriate satellite-transmitted signals for determining the ship's position with the required accuracy and update rate;

.7   be capable of acquiring satellite signals with input signals having carrier levels in the range of -130 dBm to -120 dBm. Once the satellite signals have been acquired, the equipment should continue to operate satisfactorily with satellite signals having carrier levels down to -133 dBm;

.8   be capable of acquiring position to the required accuracy, within 30 min, when there is no valid almanac data;

.9   be capable of acquiring position to the required accuracy, within 5 min, when there is valid almanac data;

.10   be capable of re-acquiring position to the required accuracy, within 5 min, when the GPS signals are interrupted for a period of at least 24 h but there is no loss of power;

.11   be capable of re-acquiring position to the required accuracy, within 2 min, when subjected to a power interruption of 60 s;

.12   generate and output to a display and digital interface (see IEC 61162) a new position solution at least once every 1 s (for high speed craft 0.5 s);

.13   have a minimum resolution of position, i.e. latitude and longitude, of 0.001 minutes;

.14   generate and output to the digital interface (see IEC 61162) course over the ground (COG), speed over the ground (SOG) and universal time co-ordinated (UTC). Such outputs should have a validity mark aligned with that on the position output. The accuracy requirement for COG and SOG should not be inferior to the relevant performance standards for heading and SDME (see A424(XI) and A824(19));

.15   have the facilities to process differential GPS (DGPS) data fed to it in accordance with the standards of Recommendation ITU-R M.823 and the appropriate RTCM standard. When a GPS receiver is equipped with a differential receiver, performance standards for static and dynamic accuracies (paragraphs 3.4 and 3.5 above) should be 10 m (95 per cent); and

.16   be capable of operating satisfactorily in typical interference conditions.

4   PROTECTION

Precautions should be taken to ensure that no permanent damage can result from an accidental short circuit or grounding of the antenna or any of its input or output connections or any of the GPS receiver equipment inputs or outputs for a duration of 5 min.

5   FAILURE WARNINGS AND STATUS INDICATIONS

5.1   The equipment should provide an indication of whether the position calculated is likely to be outside the requirements of these performance standards.

5.2   The GPS receiver equipment should provide as a minimum:

.1   an indication within 5 s if either;

.1.1   the specified HDOP has been exceeded; or

.1.2   a new position has not been calculated for more than 1 s (for high speed craft 0.5 s).
        Under such conditions, the last known position and the time of the last valid fix, with explicit indication of this state, so that no ambiguity can exist, should be output until normal operation is resumed;

.2   a warning of loss of position;

.3   differential GPS status indication of:

.3.1   the receipt of DGPS signals; and

.3.2   whether DGPS corrections are being applied to the indicated ship's position;

.4   DGPS integrity status and alarm; and

.5   DGPS text message display.

11.3.2 Extract from IMO Resolution A817(19) Performance Standards for Electronic Chart Display and Information Systems (ECDIS) Valid for Equipment Installed on or after 1st January 1999

6 DISPLAY OF OTHER NAVIGATIONAL INFORMATION

6.1 Radar information or other navigational information may be added to the ECDIS display. However, it should not degrade the SENC information, and should be clearly distinguishable from the SENC information.

6.2 ECDIS and added navigational information should use a common reference system. If this is not the case, an indication should be provided.

6.3 Radar

6.3.1 Transferred radar information may contain both the radar image and ARPA information.

6.3.2 If the radar image is added to the ECDIS display, the chart and the radar image should match in scale and in orientation.

6.3.3 The radar image and the position from the position sensor should both be adjusted automatically for antenna offset from the conning position.

6.3.4 It should be possible to adjust the displayed position of the ship manually so that the radar image matches the SENC display.

6.3.5 It should be possible to remove the radar information by single operator action.

11.3.3 Extract from IMO Resolution 74(69) Performance Standards for a Universal Shipborne Automatic Identification System (AIS)

1 SCOPE

1.1 These performance standards specify the requirements for the universal AIS.

1.2 The AIS should improve the safety of navigation by assisting in the efficient navigation of ships, protection of the enviroment, and operation of Vessel Traffic Services (VTS), by satisfying the following functional requirements:

.1 in a ship-to-ship mode for collision avoidance;

.2 as a means for littoral States to obtain information about a ship and its cargo; and

.3 as a VTS tool, i.e. ship-to-shore (traffic management).

1.3 The AIS should be capable of providing to ships and to competent authorities, information from the ship, automatically and with the required accuracy and frequency, to facilitate accurate tracking. Transmission of the data should be with the minimum involvement of ship's personnel and with a high level of availability.

1.4 The installation, in addition to meeting the requirements of the Radio Regulations, applicable ITU-R Recommendations and the general requirements as set out in resolution A.694(17), should comply with the following performance standards.

2 FUNCTIONALITY

2.1 The system should be capable of operating in a number of modes:

.1 an 'autonomous and continuous' mode for operation in all areas. This mode should be capable of being switched to/from one of the following alternate modes by a competent authority;

.2 an 'assigned' mode for operation in an area subject to a competent authority responsible for traffic monitoring such that the data transmission interval and/or time slots may be set remotely by that authority; and

.3 a 'polling' or controlled mode where the data transfer occurs in response to interrogation from a ship or competent authority.

3 CAPABILITY

3.1 The AIS should comprise:

.1 a communication processor, capable of operating over a range of maritime frequencies, with an appropriate channel selecting and switching method, in support of both short and long range applications;

.2 a means of processing data from an electronic position-fixing system which provides a resolution of one ten-thousandth of a minute of arc and uses the WGS-84 datum.

.3 a means to automatically input data from other sensors meeting the provisions as specified in paragraph 6.2;

.4 a means to input and retrieve data manually;

.5 a means of error checking the transmitted and received data; and

.6 built in test equipment (BITE).

3.2 The AIS should be capable of:

.1 providing information automatically and continuously to a competent authority and other ships, without involvement of ship's personnel;

.2 receiving and processing information from other sources, including that from a competent authority and from other ships;

.3 responding to high priority and safety related calls with a minimum of delay; and

.4 providing positional and manoeuvring information at a data rate adequate to facilitate accurate tracking by a competent authority and other ships.

4 USER INTERFACE

To enable a user to access, select and display the information on a separate system, the AIS should be provided with an interface conforming to an appropriate international marine interface standard.

5 IDENTIFICATION

For the purpose of ship and message identification, the appropriate Maritime Mobile Service Identity (MMSI) number should be used.

6 INFORMATION

6.1 The information provided by the AIS should include:

.1 Static:

- IMO number (where available)
- Call sign and name
- Length and beam
- Type of ship
- Location of position-fixing antenna on the ship (aft of bow and port or starboard of centreline)

.2 Dynamic:

- Ship's position with accuracy indication and integrity status
- Time in UTC (date to be established by receiving equipment)
- Course over ground
- Speed over ground
- Heading
- Navigational status (e.g. NUC, at anchor, etc., – manual input)
- Rate of turn (where available)
- Optional – Angle of heel (where available)
- Optional – Pitch and roll (where available)

.3 Voyage-related:

- Ship's draught
- Hazardous cargo (type) (as required by competent authority)
- Destination and ETA (at master's discretion)
- Optional - Route plan (waypoints)

.4 Short safety-related messages

6.2 Information update rates for autonomous mode

The different information types are valid for a different time period and thus need a different update rate:

- Static information: Every 6 min and on request
- Dynamic information: Dependent on speed and course alteration according to Table 1
- Voyage-related information: Every 6 min, when data has been amended and on request
- Safety-related message: As required

Table 1

Type of ship	Reporting interval
Ship at anchor	3 min
Ship 0–14 knots	12 s
Ship 0–14 knots and changing course	4 s
Ship 14–23 knots	6 s
Ship 14–23 knots and changing course	2 s
Ship > 23 knots	3 s
Ship > 23 knots and changing course	2 s

Ship Reporting Capacity – the system should be able to handle a minimum of 2000 reports per min to adequately provide for all operational scenarios envisioned.

6.3 Security

A security mechanism should be provided to detect disabling and to prevent unauthorized alteration of input or transmitted data. To protect the unauthorized dissemenation of data, the IMO guidelines (Guidelines and Criteria for Ship Reporting Systems (Resolution MSC.43(64)) should be followed.

7 PERMISSIBLE INITIALIZATION PERIOD

The installation should be operational within 2 min of switching on.

8 POWER SUPPLY

The AIS and associated sensors should be powered from the ship's main source of electrical energy. In addition, it should be possible to operate the AIS and associated sensors from an alternative source of electrical energy.

9 TECHNICAL CHARACTERISTICS

The technical characteristics of the AIS such as variable transmitter output power, operating frequencies (dedicated internationally and selected regionally), modulation, and antenna system should comply with the appropriate ITU-R Recommendations.

11.3.4 Extract from IMO Resolution MSC 64(67) Performance Standards for Integrated Bridge Systems (IBS)

1 INTRODUCTION

1.1 An integrated bridge system (IBS) is defined as a combination of systems which are interconnected in order to allow centralized access to sensor information or command/control from workstations, with the aim of increasing safe and efficient ship's management by suitably qualified personnel.

1.2 IBS, in addition to meeting the functional requirements contained in applicable IMO instruments, the general requirements in resolution A.694(17) (see also IEC Publication 945) should comply with the following performance standards.

2 SYSTEM REQUIREMENT

The IBS should support systems performing two or more of the following operations:

.1 passage execution;
.2 communications;
.3 machinery control
.4 loading, discharging and cargo control; and
.5 safety and security.

3 GENERAL REQUIREMENTS

3.1 General

3.1.1 The IBS should comply with all applicable IMO requirements and recommendations. Parts executing multiple operations should meet the requirements specified for each individual function they control, monitor or perform.

3.1.2 Each 'part' of an IBS should meet the relevant requirements of resolution A.694(17) and their associated technical testing standards. In consequence, the IBS is in compliance with these requirements without further environmental testing.

Note: 'Part' is meant to be – for example – an individual module, equipment or subsystem.

3.1.3 A failure of one part should not affect the functionality of other parts except for those functions directly dependent upon the information from the defective part.

3.2 Integration

The IBS should provide functional integration meeting the following requirements:

.1 The functionality of the IBS should ensure that its operation is at least as effective as for stand-alone equipment.
.2 Continuously displayed information should be reduced to the minimum necessary for safe operation of the ship. Supplementary information should be readily accessible.
.3 Where multifunction displays and controls are used to perform functions necessary for safe operation of the ship they should be duplicated and interchangeable.
.4 It should be possible to display the complete system configuration, the available configuration and the configuration in use.
.5 Each part to be integrated should provide details of its operational status and the latency and validity of essential information. Means should be provided within the IBS to make use of this information.
.6 An alternative means of operation should be provided for essential functions.
.7 An alternative source of essential information should be provided. The IBS should identify loss of either source.
.8 The source of information (sensor, result of calculation or manual input) should be displayed continuously or upon request.

3.3 Data exchange

3.3.1 Interfacing to an IBS should comply with the relevant international marine interface standards (refer to IEC Publication 1162).

3.3.2 Data exchange should be consistent with safe operation of the ship.

3.3.3 The integrity of data flowing on the network should be ensured.

3.3.4 A failure in the connectivity should not affect independent functionality.

3.4 Failure analysis

3.4.1 A failure analysis should be performed, documented and be acceptable.

4 OPERATIONAL REQUIREMENTS

4.1 Human factors

4.1.1 The IBS should be capable of being operated by personnel holding appropriate certificates.

4.1.2 The Man Machine Interface (MMI) should be designed to be easily understood and in a consistent style for all integrated functions.

4.1.3 Where multifunction displays are used, they should be in colour, and continuously displayed information and functional areas, e.g. menus should be presented in a consistent manner.

4.1.4 For actions which may cause unintended results, the IBS should request confirmation from the operator.

4.2 Functionality

4.2.1 It should always be clear, from where essential functions may be performed.

4.2.2 The system management should ensure, that one user only has the focus of an input or function at the same time. If so, all other users should be informed about that by the IBS.

5 TECHNICAL REQUIREMENTS

5.1 Sensors

In order to ensure an adequate system functionality the sensors employed should ensure communication compatibility in accordance with the relevant international marine interface standard (refer to IEC Publication 1162); and provide information about their operational status and about the latency and validity of essential information.

5.2 Alarm management

5.2.1 The IBS alarm management, as a minimum, should comply with the requirements of the Code on Alarms and Indicators, 1995 (resolution A.830(19)).

5.2.2 Appropriate alarm management on priority and functional groups should be provided within the IBS.

5.2.3 The number of alarm types and their release should be kept as low as possible by providing indications for information of lower importance.

5.2.4 Alarms should be displayed so that the alarm reason and the resulting functional restrictions can be easily understood. Indications should be self-explanatory.

5.3 Power interruptions and shut-down

5.3.1 If subjected to an orderly shut-down, the IBS should, upon turn-on, come to an initial default state.

5.3.2 After a power interruption full functionality of the IBS should be available after recovery of all subsystems. The IBS should not increase the recovery time of individual subsystem functions after power restoration.

5.3.3 If subjected to a power interruption the IBS should, upon restoration of power, maintain the configuration in use and continue automated operation, as far as practicable. Safety related automatic functions should only be restored upon confirmation by the operator.

5.4 Power supply

5.4.1 Power supply requirements applying to parts of the IBS as a result of other IMO requirements should remain applicable.

5.4.2   The IBS should be supplied:

.1   from the main and emergency sources of electrical power with automated changeover through a local distribution board with provision to preclude inadvertent shut-down;

.2   from a transitional source of electrical power for a duration of not less than 1 min; and

.3   where required, parts of the IBS should also be supplied from a reserve source of electrical power.

11.3.5 Extracts from IMO Resolution MSC 86(70) Performance Standards for an Integrated Navigation System (INS)

1 SCOPE

1.1 The purpose of an integrated navigation system (INS) is to provide 'added value' to the functions and information needed by the officer in charge of the navigational watch (OOW) to plan, monitor or control the progress of the ship.

1.2 The INS supports mode and situation awareness.

1.3 The INS supports safety of navigation by evaluating inputs from several independent and different sensors, combining them to provide information giving timely warnings of potential dangers and degradation of integrity of this information. Integrity monitoring is an intrinsic function of the INS.

1.4 The INS aims to ensure that, by taking human factors into consideration, the workload is kept within the capacity of the OOW in order to enhance safe and expeditious navigation and to complement the mariner's capabilities, while at the same time to compensate for their limitations.

1.5 The function of passage execution in an Integrated Bridge System (IBS), as defined by the Organization (MSC 64(67)), may be performed by an INS.

2 APPLICATION

2.1 These performance standards are applicable to any combination of navigational aids that provide functions beyond the general intent defined in the respective performance standards adopted by the Organization for individual equipment.

2.2 The purpose of these performance standards is to support the proper and safe integration of navigational equipment and information.

2.3 These performance standards define three categories of INS:

.1 INS(A) for systems that provide the minimum functional requirements of the INS including a consistent common reference system;

.2 INS(B) for systems that, in addition to the functional requirements of INS(A), provide the information needed for decision support in avoiding hazards; and

.3 INS(C) for systems that, in addition to the functional requirements of INS(B), provide the automatic control functions of heading, track or speed.

3 DEFINITIONS

For the purpose of these standards the following definitions apply.

3.1 *Automatic control system* − A control system that may include a heading, track or speed control system.

3.2 *Consistent common reference system* − A subsystem of an INS for acquisition, processing, storage and distribution of data and information providing identical and obligatory reference to subsystems within an INS.

3.3 *Integrated navigation system* − An INS is a combination of systems that are interconnected to increase safe and efficient navigation by suitably qualified personnel.

3.4 *Integrity* − Ability of the system to provide the user with information within the specified accuracy in a timely, complete and unambiguous manner, and alarms and indications within a specified time when the system should be used with caution or not at all.

3.5 *Multifunction display* − A single visual display unit that can present, either simultaneously or through a series of selectable pages, information from more than one operation of a system.

3.6 *Sensor* − A navigational aid, with or without its own display and control as appropriate, automatically providing information to the INS.

4 OPERATIONAL REQUIREMENTS

4.1 Functionality

General

4.1.1 In addition to meeting the relevant requirements of resolution A.694(17), and IEC 60945, the INS should comply with the requirements of these performance standards.

4.1.2 Each part of the INS should comply with all applicable requirements adopted by the Organization, including the requirements of these performance standards. Parts executing multiple operations should meet the requirements specified for each individual function they can control, monitor or perform.

4.1.3 When functions of equipment connected to the INS provide facilities in addition to these performance standards, the operation and, as far as is reasonably practicable, the malfunction of such additional facilities should not degrade the performance of the INS below the requirements of these standards.

4.1.4 A failure of one part should not affect other parts except for those functions directly dependent upon the information from the defective part.

Basic functions

4.1.5 An INS should combine, process and evaluate data from all sensors in use. The integrity of data from different sensors should be evaluated prior to distribution.

4.1.6 An INS should ensure that the different types of information are distributed to the relevant parts of the system, applying a 'consistent common reference system' for all types of information.

4.1.7 The INS(A) should as a minimum provide the information of position, speed, heading and time, each clearly marked with an indication of integrity.

4.1.8 The INS(B) should be able to automatically, continually and graphically indicate the ship's position, speed and heading and, where available, depth in relation to the planned route as well as to known and detected hazards.

4.1.9 The INS(C) should, in addition, provide means to automatically control heading, track or speed and monitor the performance and status of these controls.

Integrity monitoring

4.1.10 The integrity of information should be verified by comparison of the data derived independently from two or more sources if available.

4.1.11 The integrity should be verified before essential information is displayed or used. Information with doubtful integrity should be clearly marked by the INS and should not be used for automatic control systems.

Data exchange

4.1.12 Standalone equipment for which performance standards adopted by the Organization exist, when connected to the INS, should comply with the applicable international standards (IEC 61162) for data exchange and interfacing.

4.1.13 Data latency should be consistent with the data requirements of the individual parts.

4.1.14 The integrity of data exchange within the INS should be ensured.

4.1.15 A failure of data exchange should not affect any independent functionality.

Integration

4.1.16 The INS should provide functional integration meeting the following requirements:

.1 where a display or control is presented on a multifunction display unit then these should be redundantly available; and

.2 validity (A529(13) and A815(19)) of the data should be provided for each part to be integrated.

Configuration control

4.1.17 It should be possible to display the complete system configuration, the available configuration and the configuration in use.

4.2 Information and accuracy

Display of information

4.2.1 The INS should be able to display the information available in accordance with paragraphs 4.1.7, 4.1.8 and 4.1.9 as applicable.

4.2.2 The INS should be capable of displaying output data available from the sensors.

4.2.3 The information should be displayed together with the indication of its source (sensor data, result of calculation or manual input), unit of measurement and status, including mode (see sub-section *Integrity monitoring*).

Accuracy

4.2.4 As a minimum, the accuracy of information should meet the requirements of the resolutions (IEC 61162) adopted by the Organization. Additionally the INS should not degrade the accuracy of the data provided by the sensors.

4.3 Malfunctions, alarms and indications

Fail safe operation

4.3.1 The system's automatic response to malfunctions should result in the safest of any other configuration accompanied by clear indications and alarms.

Reversionary mode

4.3.2 The INS should allow simple and effective operator action to override or bypass any automated functions. The INS should resume automatic functions only after an appropriate message and intended operator action, considering all necessary starting conditions.

Alarm management

4.3.3 An alarm management system should be provided.

4.3.4 The INS alarm management system, as a minimum, should comply with the requirements of the Organization (A830(19)).

4.3.5 The number of alarms should be kept as low as possible by providing indications for information of lower importance.

4.3.6 Alarms should be displayed so that the alarm reason and the resulting functional restrictions can be easily understood. Indications should be self-explanatory.

5 ERGONOMIC CRITERIA

5.1 Cognitive ergonomics

5.1.1 Integrated display and control functions should adopt a consistent human machine interface (HMI) philosophy and implementation.

5.1.2 The HMI should be so designed that the provided information is clearly understood using a consistent presentation style.

5.1.3 The HMI should be so designed that the requested manual inputs can be easily executed.

5.1.4 For manual inputs that may cause unintended results, the INS should request confirmation before acceptance, thus providing a plausibility check.

5.2 Physical ergonomics

Controls and displays

5.2.1 Particular consideration should be given to:
– symbols;
– controls; and
– layout.

Operational controls

5.2.2 The INS should be designed and implemented so that the OOW easily operates basic functions from workstations.

Presentation of information

5.2.3 Continuously displayed information should be optimized and should include position, speed, heading and time. Supplementary information should be readily accessible.

6 DESIGN AND INSTALLATION
General

6.1 The INS should meet the relevant requirements of resolution A.694(17) and appropriate international standards (IEC 60945).

Failure analysis

6.2 A failure analysis (IEC 61508) should be performed and documented for the installed configuration of the INS which includes all parts connected to or integrated into the system, including devices for manual override of automatic functions and their locations on the bridge.

Installation requirements

6.3 The INS should be installed so that it can meet the requirements of the relevant International Standards (IEC 92-101 and 533).

Power supply requirements

6.4 Power supply requirements applying to parts of the INS as a result of other IMO requirements should remain applicable.

6.5 The INS should be supplied:

.1 from both the main and the emergency source of electrical power with automated changeover through a local distribution board with provision to preclude inadvertent shutdown; and

.2 from a transitional source of electrical power for a duration of not less than 45 s.

Power interruptions and shutdown

6.6 After a power interruption full functionality of the INS should be available after recovery of all subsystems. The INS should not increase the recovery time of individual subsystem functions after power restoration.

6.7 If subjected to a power interruption the INS should, upon restoration of power, maintain the configuration in use and continue automated operation, as far as practicable. Safety related automatic functions, should only be restored upon confirmation by the operator.

7 INTERFACING

Interfacing to, and from, the INS should comply with international standards (IEC 61162), as appropriate.

8 FALLBACK ARRANGEMENTS

8.1 The INS should, after a failure, support the availability of essential information through the use of appropriate fallback arrangements.

8.2 Normal operation, after use of a fallback arrangement, should only be restored upon confirmation by the operator.

11.3.6 Extract from IMO Resolution A861(20) Performance Standards for Shipborne Voyage Data Recorders (VDRs)

1 PURPOSE

The purpose of a voyage data recorder (VDR) is to maintain a store, in a secure and retrievable form, of information concerning the position, movement, physical status, command and control of a vessel over the period leading up to and following an incident having an impact thereon. Information contained in a VDR should be made available to both the Administration and the shipowner. This information is for use during any subsequent investigation to identify the cause(s) of the incident.

2 APPLICATION

A VDR with capabilities not inferior to those defined in these performance standards is required to be fitted to ships of classes defined in SOLAS chapter V, as amended.

3 REFERENCES

3.1 SOLAS:

– 1995 SOLAS Conference, resolution 12.

3.2 IMO resolutions:

– A.662(16)   Performance standards for float-free release and activation arrangements for emergency radio equipment
– A.694(17)   General requirements for shipborne radio equipment forming part of the GMDSS and for electronic navigational aids
– A.824(19)   Performance standards for devices to indicate speed and distance
– A.830(19)   Code on Alarms and Indicators, 1995
– MSC.64(67), annex 3   Performance standards for heading control systems

– MSC.64(67), annex 4   Performance standards for radar equipment, as amended

4 DEFINITIONS

4.1 *Voyage data recorder (VDR)* means a complete system, including any items required to interface with the sources of input data, for processing and encoding the data, the final recording medium in its capsule, the power supply and dedicated reserve power source.

4.2 *Sensor* means any unit external to the VDR, to which the VDR is connected and from which it obtains data to be recorded.

4.3 *Final recording medium* means the item of hardware on which the data is recorded such that access to it would enable the data to be recovered and played back by use of suitable equipment.

4.4 *Playback equipment* means the equipment, compatible with the recording medium and the format used during recording, employed for recovering the data. It includes also the display or presentation hardware and software that is appropriate to the original data source equipment.

Note: Playback equipment is not normally installed on a ship and is not regarded as part of a VDR for the purposes of these performance standards.

4.5 *Dedicated reserve power source* means a secondary battery, with suitable automatic charging arrangements, dedicated solely to the VDR, of sufficient capacity to operate it as required by 5.3.2.

5 OPERATIONAL REQUIREMENTS

5.1 General

5.1.1   The VDR should continuously maintain sequential records of preselected data items relating to the status and output of the ship's equipment, and command and control of the ship, referred to in 5.4.

5.1.2   To permit subsequent analysis of factors surrounding an incident, the method of recording should ensure that the various data items can be co-related in date and time during playback on suitable equipment.

5.1.3 The final recording medium should be installed in a protective capsule which should meet all of the following requirements:

.1 be capable of being accessed following an incident but secure against tampering;

.2 maximize the probability of survival and recovery of the final recorded data after any incident;

.3 be of a highly visible colour and marked with retro-reflective materials; and

.4 be fitted with an appropriate device to aid location.

5.1.4 The design and construction, which should be in accordance with the requirements of resolution A.694(17) and international standards acceptable to the Organization (IEC 945), should take special account of the requirements for data security and continuity of operation as detailed in 5.2 and 5.3.

5.2 Data selection and security

5.2.1 The minimum selections of data items to be recorded by the VDR are specified in 5.4. Optionally, additional items may be recorded provided that the requirements for the recording and storage of the specified selections are not compromised.

5.2.2 The equipment should be so designed that, as far as is practical, it is not possible to tamper with the selection of data being input to the equipment, the data itself nor that which has already been recorded. Any attempt to interfere with the integrity of the data or the recording should be recorded.

5.2.3 The recording method should be such that each item of the recorded data is checked for integrity and an alarm given if a non-correctable error is detected.

5.3 Continuity of operation

5.3.1 To ensure that the VDR continues to record events during an incident, it should be capable of operating from the ship's emergency source of electrical power.

5.3.2 If the ship's emergency source of electrical power supply fails, the VDR should continue to record Bridge audio (see 5.4.5) from a dedicated reserve source of power for a period of 2 h. At the end of this 2 h period all recording should cease automatically.

5.3.3 Recording should be continuous unless interrupted briefly in accordance with 6 or terminated in accordance with 5.3.2. The time for which all stored data items are retained should be at least 12 h. Data items which are older than this may be overwritten with new data.

5.4 Data items to be recorded

5.4.1 *Date and time*

Date and time, referenced to UTC, should be obtained from a source external to the ship or from an internal clock. The recording should indicate which source is in use. The recording method should be such that the timing of all other recorded data items can be derived on playback with a resolution sufficient to reconstruct the history of the incident in detail.

5.4.2 *Ship's position*

Latitude and longitude, and the datum used, should be derived from an electronic position-fixing system (EPFS). The recording should ensure that the identity and status of the EPFS can always be determined on playback.

5.4.3 *Speed*

Speed through the water or speed over the ground, including an indication of which it is, derived from the ship's speed and distance-measuring equipment.

5.4.4 *Heading*

As indicated by the ship's compass.

5.4.5 *Bridge audio*

One or more microphones positioned on the bridge should be placed so that conversations at or near the conning stations, radar displays, chart tables, etc., are adequately recorded. As far as practicable, the positioning of microphones should also capture intercom, public address systems and audible alarms on the bridge.

5.4.6   *Communications audio*

VHF communications relating to ship operations should be recorded.

5.4.7   *Radar data, post-display selection*

This should include electronic signal information from within one of the ship's radar installations which records all the information which was actually being presented on the master display of that radar at the time of recording. This should include any range rings or markers, bearing markers, electronic plotting symbols, radar maps, whatever parts of the SENC or other electronic chart or map that were selected, the voyage plan, navigational data, navigational alarms and the radar status data that were visible on the display. The recording method should be such that, on playback, it is possible to present a faithful replica of the entire radar display that was on view at the time of recording, albeit within the limitations of any bandwidth-compression techniques that are essential to the working of the VDR.

5.4.8   *Echo-sounder*

This should include depth under keel, the depth scale currently being displayed and other status information where available.

5.4.9   *Main alarms*

This should include the status of all mandatory alarms on the bridge.

5.4.10   *Rudder order and response*

This should include status and settings of auto-pilot if fitted.

5.4.11   *Engine order and response*

This should include the positions of any engine telegraphs or direct engine/propeller controls and

feedback indications, if fitted, including ahead/astern indicators. This should also include status of bow thrusters if fitted.

5.4.12   *Hull openings status*

This should include all mandatory status information required to be displayed on the bridge.

5.4.13   *Watertight and fire door status*

This should include all mandatory status information required to be displayed on the bridge.

5.4.14   *Accelerations and hull stresses*

Where a ship is fitted with hull stress and response monitoring equipment, all the data items that have been pre-selected within that equipment should be recorded.

5.4.15   *Wind speed and direction*

This should be applicable where a ship is fitted with a suitable sensor. Either relative or true wind speed and direction may be recorded, but an indication of which it is should be recorded.

6   OPERATION

The unit should be entirely automatic in normal operation. Means should be provided whereby recorded data may be saved by an appropriate method following an incident, with minimal interruption to the recording process.

7   INTERFACING

Interfacing to the various sensors required should be in accordance with the relevant international interface standard, where possible. Any connection to any item of the ship's equipment should be such that the operation of that equipment suffers no deterioration, even if the VDR system develops faults.

11.3.7 Extract from IMO Resolution A694(17) General Requirements for Shipborne Radio Equipment Forming Part of the Global Maritime Distress and Safety System (GMDSS) and for Electronic Navigational Aids

1 INTRODUCTION

1.1 Equipment, which:

.1 forms part of the global maritime distress and safety system; or

.2 is required by regulation V/12 of the 1974 SOLAS Convention as amended and other electronic navigational aids, where appropriate;

should comply with the following general requirements and with all applicable performance standards adopted by the Organization.

1.2 Where a unit of equipment provides a facility which is additional to the minimum requirements of this Recommendation, the operation and, as far as is reasonably practicable, the malfunction of such additional facility should not degrade the performance of the equipment specified in 1.1.

2 INSTALLATION

Equipment should be installed in such a manner that it is capable of meeting the requirements of 1.1.

3 OPERATION

3.1 The number of operational controls, their design and manner of function, location, arrangement and size should provide for simple, quick and effective operation. The controls should be arranged in a manner which minimizes the chance of inadvertent operation.

3.2 All operational controls should permit normal adjustments to be easily performed and should be easy to identify from the position at which the equipment is normally operated. Controls not required for normal operation should not be readily accessible.

3.3 Adequate illumination should be provided in the equipment or in the ship to enable identification of controls and facilitate reading of indicators at all times. Means should be provided for dimming the output of any equipment light source which is capable of interfering with navigation.

3.4 The design of the equipment should be such that misuse of the controls should not cause damage to the equipment or injury to personnel.

3.5 If a unit of equipment is connected to one or more other units of equipment the performance of each should be maintained.

3.6 Where a digital input panel with the digits 0 to 9 is provided, the digits should be arranged to conform with relevant CCITT recommendations (CCITT E161/Q11). However, where an alphanumeric keyboard layout, as used on office machinery and data processing equipment, is provided, the digits 0 to 9 may, alternatively, be arranged to conform with the relevant ISO standard (ISO 3791).

4 POWER SUPPLY

4.1 Equipment should continue to operate in accordance with the requirements of this Recommendation in the presence of variations of power supply normally to be expected in a ship.

4.2 Means should be incorporated for the protection of equipment from the effects of excessive current and voltage, transients and accidental reversal of the power supply polarity.

4.3 If provision is made for operating equipment from more than one source of electrical energy, arrangements for rapidly changing from one source to the other should be provided but not necessarily incorporated in the equipment.

5 DURABILITY AND RESISTANCE TO ENVIRONMENTAL CONDITIONS

Equipment should be capable of continuous operation under the conditions of various sea states, ship's motion, vibration, humidity and temperature likely to be experienced in ships (IEC 92–101 and 945).

6 INTERFERENCE

6.1 All reasonable and practicable steps should be taken to ensure electromagnetic compatibility between the equipment concerned and other radio-communication and navigational equipment carried on board in compliance with the relevant requirements of chapter IV and chapter V of the 1974 SOLAS Convention (IEC 533 and 945).

6.2 Mechanical noise from all units should be limited so as not to prejudice the hearing of sounds on which the safety of the ship might depend.

6.3 Each unit of equipment normally to be installed in the vicinity of a standard compass or a magnetic steering compass should be clearly marked with the minimum safe distance at which it may be mounted from such compasses.

7 SAFETY PRECAUTIONS

7.1 As far as is practicable, accidental access to dangerous voltages should be prevented. All parts and wiring in which the direct or alternating voltages or both (other than radio frequency voltages) combine to give a peak voltage greater than 55 V should be protected against accidental access and should be isolated automatically from all sources of electrical energy when the protective covers are removed. Alternatively, the equipment should be so constructed that access to such voltages may only be gained after having used a tool for this purpose, such as spanner or screwdriver, and warning labels should be prominently displayed both within the equipment and on protective covers.

7.2 Means should be provided for earthing exposed metallic parts of the equipment but this should not cause any terminal of the source of electrical energy to be earthed.

7.3 All steps should be taken to ensure that electromagnetic radio frequency energy radiated from the equipment shall not be a hazard to personnel.

7.4 Equipment containing elements such as vacuum tubes which are likely to cause X-radiation should comply with the following requirements:

.1 external X-radiation from the equipment in its normal working condition should not exceed the limits laid down by the Administration concerned;

.2 when X-radiation can be generated inside the equipment above the levels laid down by the Administration, a prominent warning should be fixed inside the equipment and the precautions to be taken when working on the equipment should be included in the equipment manual; and

.3 if malfunction of any part of the equipment can cause an increase in X-radiation, adequate advice should be included in the information about the equipment, warning of the circumstances which could cause the increase and stating the precautions which should be taken.

8 MAINTENANCE

8.1 The equipment should be so designed that the main units can be replaced readily, without elaborate recalibration or readjustment.

8.2 Equipment should be so constructed and installed that it is readily accessible for inspection and maintenance purposes.

8.3 Adequate information should be provided to enable the equipment to be properly operated and maintained. The information should:

.1 in the case of equipment so designed that fault diagnosis and repair down to component level are practicable, provide full circuit diagrams, component layouts and a component parts list; and

.2 in the case of equipment containing complex modules in which fault diagnosis and repair down to component level are not practicable, contain sufficient information to enable a defective complex module to be located, identified and replaced. Other modules and those discrete components which do not form part of modules should also meet the requirements of .1 above.

9 MARKING AND IDENTIFICATION

Each unit of the equipment should be marked externally with the following information which should be clearly visible in the normal installation position:

.1 identification of the manufacturer;

.2 equipment type number or model identification under which it was type tested; and

.3 serial number of the unit.

11.4   Extracts from UK Statutory Instrument 1993 No. 69, The Merchant Shipping (Navigational Equipment) Regulations 1993

11.4.1   Extract from Part IV, Radar Installation

Radar performance standards and interswitching facilities

19.—(1) Every radar installation required to be provided shall comply with the performance standard adopted by the Organization and shall, in the case of a United Kingdom ship, comply with the relevant performance standard.

(2)

(a) Where such a radar installation includes additional radar units and facilities for interswitching, at least one arrangement of units when used together shall comply with all the requirements of this Part of these Regulations;

(b) where two radar installations are required to be provided on a ship, they shall be so installed that each radar installation can be operated individually and both can be operated simultaneously without being dependent upon one another.

Provision of plotting facilities

20.   Facilities for plotting radar readings shall be provided on the navigating bridge of every ship required to be fitted with a radar installation. In ships of 1600 tons gross tonnage and upwards constructed on or after 1st September 1984 the plotting facilities shall be at least as effective as a reflection plotter.

Radar watch

21.   While a United Kingdom ship which is required to be fitted with a radar installation is at sea and a radar watch is being kept, the radar installation shall be under the control of a qualified radar observer who may be assisted by unqualified personnel.

Performance of radar installations

22.   The performance of the radar installation shall be checked before the ship proceeds to sea and at least once every four hours whilst the ship is at sea and radar watch is being maintained.

Qualifications of radar observers

23.   For the purposes of these Regulations, a person is a 'qualified radar observer' if he holds:

(a) a valid Radar Observer's Certificate granted by the Secretary of State; or

(b) a valid certificate of attendance granted at the conclusion of a radar simulator course which has been approved by the Secretary of State; or

(c) a valid Electronic Navigation Systems Certificate granted by the Secretary of State, or

(d) a valid Navigation Control Certificate granted by the Secretary of State, or

(e) a certificate recognized by the Secretary of State as being equivalent to any of the certificates mentioned in (a), (b), (c) or (d).

Siting of radar installation

24.—(1) The antenna unit of the radar installation shall be sited so that satisfactory overall performance is achieved in relation to:

(a) the avoidance of shadow sectors;

(b) the avoidance of false echoes caused by reflections from the ship's structure; and

(c) the effect of antenna height on the amplitude and extent of sea-clutter.

(2) The radar display shall be sited on the bridge from which the ship is normally navigated. The siting of one of the displays shall be such that:

(a) an observer, when viewing the display, faces forward and is readily able to maintain visual lookout;

(b) there is sufficient space for two observers to view the display simultaneously.

Alignment of heading marker

25.   The radar heading marker (and stern marker if fitted) shall be aligned to within 1° of the ship's fore-and-aft line as soon as practicable after the radar installation has been installed in the ship. Where inter-switching facilities are provided, the heading marker shall be aligned with all arrangements of units. The marker shall be re-aligned as soon as practicable whenever it is found to be substantially inaccurate.

Measurement of shadow sectors

26. The angular width and bearing of any shadow sectors displayed by the radar installation shall be determined and recorded. The record shall be shown on a diagram adjacent to the radar display and be kept up to date following any change likely to affect shadow sectors.

Display sizes

27. A radar installation required to be provided which is or was installed onboard a ship on or after 1st September 1984 shall provide a relative plan display having an effective diameter, without external magnification, of not less than:

(a) 180 millimetres on ships of 500 tons or over but less than 1600 tons;

(b) 250 millimetres on ships of 1600 tons or over but less than 10,000 tons;

(c) 340 millimetres in the case of one radar installation and 250 millimetres in the case of the other on ships of 10,000 tons or over.

11.4.2 Extract from part IX, Automatic Radar Plotting Aid Installation

Automatic radar plotting aid performance standards

39. Every automatic radar plotting aid installation required to be provided shall comply with the performance standard adopted by the Organization and shall, in the case of a United Kingdom ship, comply with the relevant performance standard.

Siting and other requirements of automatic radar plotting aid installations

40.—(1) Where the automatic radar plotting aid installation is provided as an additional unit to a radar installation it shall be sited as close as is practicable to the display of the radar with which it is associated.

(2) Where the automatic radar plotting aid installation forms an integral part of a complete radar system that radar system shall be regarded as one of the radar installations required by regulation 3(4)(b) and accordingly shall comply with the relevant requirements of Part IV of these Regulations.

(3) The automatic radar plotting aid installation shall be interconnected with such other installations as is necessary to provide heading and speed information to the automatic radar plotting aid.

Use of an automatic radar plotting aid to assist in the radar watch

41. When at any time on or after the coming into force of these Regulations, a United Kingdom ship required to be fitted with an automatic radar plotting aid is at sea and a radar watch is being kept on the automatic radar plotting aid, the installation shall be under the control of a person qualified in the operational use of automatic radar plotting aids, who may be assisted by unqualified personnel.

Qualifications of observers using an automatic radar plotting aid to assist in keeping a radar watch

42. For the purpose of regulation 41 of these Regulations, a person shall be qualified in the operational use of automatic radar plotting aids if he holds:

(a) a valid Electronic Navigation Systems Certificate granted by the Secretary of State, or

(b) a valid Navigation Control Certificate granted by the Secretary of State, or

(c) a valid Automatic Radar Plotting Aids Certificate granted by the Secretary of State, or

(d) a certificate recognized by the Secretary of State as being equivalent to any of the certificates mentioned in (a), (b) or (c).

Glossary of acronyms and abbreviations

AEB   area exclusion boundary
AFC   automatic frequency control
AIS   automatic identification system
ARB   area rejection boundary
ARPA   automatic radar plotting aid
ASCII   American standard code for information interchange
ATA   auto-tracking aid
BCR   bow crossing range
BCT   bow crossing time
C/A   coarse/acquisition (code)
CCITT   Comité Consultatif International Téléphonique et Télégrahique (now known as ITU)
CFAR   constant false alarm rate
COG   course over ground
CPA   closest point of approach
CRT   cathode ray tube
CSR   controlled silicon rectifier
dB   decibel
DGPS   differential global positioning system
DOP   dilution of precision
DSC   digital scan converter (conversion)
EBI   electronic bearing indicator
EBL   electronic bearing line
EBM   electronic bearing marker
ECDIS   electronic chart display and information system
EHT   very high voltages
EIA   Electronic Industry Association
ENC   electronic navigation chart

EPA   electronic plotting aid
EPFS   electronic position-fixing system
ERBL   electronic range and bearing line
ETA   estimated time of arrival
FTC   fast time constant (rain clutter control)
FTE   false target elimination
GHz   gigahertz
GIS   geographic information system
GLONASS   Russian satellite navigation system
GMDSS   global maritime distress and safety system
GNSS   global navigation satellite system
GPS   global positioning system
GRP   glass reinforced plastic (fibreglass)
HBW   horizontal beamwidth
HDOP   horizontal dilution of precision
HM   heading marker
HSC   high speed craft
Hz   hertz
IBS   integrated bridge system
IEC   International Electrotechnical Commission
IF   intermediate frequency
IHO   International Hydorpgraphic Organization
IKBS   intelligent knowledge-based system
IMO   International Maritime Organization
INS   integrated navigation system
ITOFAR   interrogated time-offset frequency-agile racon

ITU	International Telecommunication Union	RH	relative humidity
kHz	kilohertz	RS232	Recommended Standard No 232 from the EIA
kn	knot(s)		
kW	kilowatt	SA	selection availability
LCD	liquid crystal display	SART	search and rescue transponder
LSB	least significant bit	SCR	silicon controlled rectifier
LSR	least sampling rate	SDME	speed and distance measuring equipment
MHz	megahertz		
MKD	minimum keyboard display	SENC	system electronic navigation chart
MMSI	maritime mobile service identity	SI	statutory instrument
ms	millisecond	SOD	sector of danger
MSB	most significant bit	SOG	speed over ground
MSC	Maritime Safety Committee (of IMO)	SOLAS	safety of life at sea
MTBF	mean time between failures	SOP	sector of preference
n mile	nautical mile(s)	SOTDMA	self-organizing time division multiple access
NMEA	National Marine Electronics Association		
		SPS	standard positioning service
NUC	not under command	STC	sensitivity time control
OAW	plotting triangle symbols	TCPA	time to closest point of approach
OOW	officer of the watch	TDMA	time division multiple access
P	precise (code)	UHF	ultra-high frequency
PAD	predicted area of danger	μs	microsecond
PDOP	position dilution of precision	UK	United Kingdom
PFN	pulse-forming network	US	United States
PPC	possible/potential point of collision	UTC	coordinated universal time
PPI	plan position indicator	VBW	vertical beamwidth
PRF	pulse repetition frequency	VDOP	vertical dilution of precision
PRP	pulse repetition period	VDR	voyage data recorder
PRR	pulse repetition rate	VHF	very high frequency
Radar	radio detection and ranging	VRM	variable range marker
RDF	radio direction-finder	VTS	vessel traffic service
RF	radio frequency	WGS	world geodetic system

See also Annex 2 of Section 11.2.3 for IMO standard terms and abbreviations.

Index

Printed in the United States
219616BV00001BA/1/P

9 780750 664349